STUDY GUIDE FOR USE WITH

Dyckman, Dukes, and Davis's

INTERMEDIATE ACCOUNTING

Sixth Canadian Edition

Morton Nelson   **Michael Zin**   **Joan E. D. Conrod**

Prepared by

Rosita S. Chen
Sheng-Der Pan
both of California State University, Fresno

and

Henry Funk
Frank Reichardt
both of Red River Community College, Winnipeg

IRWIN
Burr Ridge, Illinois
Boston, Massachusetts
Sydney, Australia

© Richard D. Irwin, Inc., 1992

Printed in the United States of America

ISBN 0-256-12335-7

2 3 4 5 6 7 8 9 0 WCB 0 9 8 7 6 5 4 3

CONTENTS

INTRODUCTION

This **Study Guide** is designed as an aid to your study of Intermediate Accounting, Sixth Canadian Edition, published by Richard D. Irwin, Inc. However, it can also be helpful to you when used with any other intermediate textbooks.

This study guide provides and organized analysis and concise summary of each chapter presented in the text. **Chapter Objectives**, which are mainly adopted from the text, identify those topics you should know after studying the chapter. **Chapter Highlights** introduce accounting issues, discuss accounting principles, describe accounting methods, and present comprehensive worksheets, as appropriate, using extensive examples and illustrations. At the end of the Chapter Highlights, there are **key concepts** provided as a glossary for your reference. The last section of each chapter consists of **Review Questions and Exercises** intended to aid and reinforce your understanding of the topics presented in the chapter. **Solutions** to the Review Questions and Exercises are provided at the end of each chapter. The solutions provide you with immediate feedback on the accuracy of your answers. By referring to the correct solutions after you have answered the questions you can **reinforce** and **evaluate** your understanding of the chapter.

This study guide also will be helpful to you when **preparing for examinations**. By reviewing the highlights of the chapters, you can gauge your recall of the subject areas and determine the topics in need of further review.

Good luck!

R. S. C.
S. D. P.
H. F.
F. R.

CHAPTER 1

The Environment of Accounting

CHAPTER OBJECTIVES

This chapter is designed to enable students to:

A.   Explain the value of the accounting function to external users of a company's financial statements.

B.   Explain the difference between the internal and external uses of accounting information.

C.   Explain the impact that accounting can have on a firm's decisions at both the national and regional levels.

D.   Explain the rule-making framework in which various organizations and environmental factors influence the setting of accounting standards.

E.   List the major sources of the pronouncements that constitute GAAP (generally accepted accounting principles).

F.   Explain the political nature of the standard-setting process and its impact on accounting standards.

CHAPTER OVERVIEW

A.   Accounting is an information system, designed to identify, collect, measure, and communicate economic information about business entities (firms) to those who have an interest in their financial affairs.

B.   The basic role of accountants is to provide **useful** economic information to external and internal decision makers (users) as specified below:

1.   **External decision makers** include present stockholders, potential investors, creditors, suppliers, customers, legislators, trade associations and many others, who lack direct access to the information generated by the internal operations of the business and must rely on general purpose financial statements to make their investment, credit and public policy decisions. The process of developing general purpose financial statements and reporting general purpose accounting information to external decision makers is called **financial accounting**, the focus of Intermediate Accounting.

2.   Internal decision makers are managers of business entities, who are responsible for managing efficiently and effectively, and who have the power and authority to obtain whatever economic information they need at dates of their choice. The process of providing accounting information to internal decision makers is called **management accounting.**

C.   Accounting is a social science. It has developed in a world of scarce resources. It is influenced by, and interacts with, the economic, social and political environments. In Canada, the environment of accounting may be described as a highly developed free-market, private ownership and monetary exchange economy. Business activities are conducted by investor-owned enterprises managed and controlled by professional managers, who are held responsible for providing reports to absentee owners, creditors and other external interested parties. In this environment, the **financial accounting** is purported to communicate information about the economic effects of accounting transactions and other events on the business entity to these external user groups.

D.   Although there are other ways to communicate external financial information such as the prospectus, news releases, the company president's letter and other supplementary schedules, the following **general purpose financial statements** are primary:

1.   The **balance sheet**, (statement of financial position) which provides information about the nature and amounts of the resources, claims to those resources and owners' equity of a firm *on a specific date.*

2.   The **income statement**, which provides information about the revenues, gains, expenses, losses and net income of a firm for a specified period of time.

3.   The **statement of changes in financial position,** which provides information about the cash receipts and cash payments of a firm *during a specified period of time.*

E.   The accounting profession has developed a network of broad guidelines, rules, and procedures to ensure the relevancy of the general purpose financial statements to the widespread use of the information by a great variety of external users. This network is known as **generally accepted accounting principles (GAAP).** In Canada, the *CICA Handbook* identifies four principal qualitative characteristics of financial statements as understandability, relevance, reliability, and comparability.

1.   The term "generally accepted" implies that a principle has been established by a designated standard-setting agency, or through practice has achieved universal acceptance over time. **GAAP** serve as a general guide to accounting practitioners in identifying, measuring and reporting financial information of a business entity. They also provide a standard by which independent auditors judge the fairness of financial statement presentation. When a departure from GAAP has a material effect, an auditor shall not issue an unqualified opinion on the financial statements.

2.   What is GAAP? Generally accepted accounting principles refers to the broad guidelines, conventions, rules, and procedures of accounting. GAAP comes from two main sources:

i)   Pronouncements by designated authoritative bodies that must be followed in all applicable cases. The primary designated bodies are the Accounting Standards Committee in Canada, the Financial Accounting Standards Board (FASB) in the United States, and the International Accounting Standards Committee sponsored by the agreement of nearly 50 countries. In the case of the first two committees, their respective prodecessor committees articulated their opinions in *Bulletins*.

ii)   Accounting practices developed by respected bodies and industries have evolved over time. This part of **GAAP** sometimes is difficult to identify by source; the source may be "general acceptability." Therefore, considerable disagreement exists among accountants about **GAAP** from these sources.

3.   The **GAAP** currently in force have resulted primarily from the continuous efforts of the accounting profession for decades. Three eras are discernible:

A.   **Pre-Standard Era -- before 1936:**   Accounting procedures have evolved for hundreds of years. However, there had been little organized effort to develop accounting standards for external reporting until 1936. In the early years, single ownership was the predominant form of business organization and accounting procedures were mainly developed by individual accountants to meet the needs of their respective companies under specific situations. A network of generally accepted accounting procedures was virtually nonexistent. From the industrial revolution to the late 1920s, organizational forms became more complex and their ownership more diversified. A demand was created for more uniformity in accounting principles and more disclosure of financial information. In 1917 in Canada, the Federal Government imposed an income tax, which added the pressures for external accountability. In addition, the inadequacy of financial disclosure was generally blamed for the 1929 crash in the stock market leading to the Great Depression. These and other environmental changes generated the growing need for setting accounting standards and assuring the reliability of financial information.

B.   **1936 to 1968:**   Primarily as a response to this need, in 1936 in Canada, the CICA formed a Terminology Committee to take steps to encourage uniformity of accounting terms by its members. This committee was replaced by the Accounting and Research Committee to parallel the (CAP) in the United States. A major part of today's *CICA Handbook* was the result. By not attempting to develop a theoretical framework for financial accounting, the CICA was criticized for its failure to develop a cohesive conceptual framework, for its application of piecemeal approach and for its inconsistent pronouncements.

C.   1968 - Present time:

1.   In Canada, since 1968, the *CICA Handbook* has been constantly updated by inclusion of approved exposure drafts on various current topics.

2.   In 1969, the *CICA Handbook*, section 1500.06, set out a landmark decision as follows:

Where *the accounting treatment or statement presentation does not follow the recommendations in this Handbook, the practice used should be explained in notes to the* financial statements with an indication of the reason why the recommendation concerned was not followed.

3.   *In 1973 the Accounting and Auditing Research Committee* gave way to two new committees--*the Accounting Research Committee (ARC)* and *the Auditing Standards Committee (ASC)*. A deviation from prior policy was the invitation to other organizations to participate in ARC work by appointing up to six of its proposed members. The chief aim of the expanded structure is to continue the search for ways of increasing the thrust and scope of accounting and auditing research. *In 1982 ARC's name was changed to the Accounting Standards Committee* and *in 1991 to the Accounting Standards Board.*

Other activities of the Institute of Chartered Accountants as well as that of the Canadian Certified General Accountants' Association and the Society of Management Accountants that have shaped accounting thought have been: (1) education programs, (2) publication of their respective journals, and (3) sponsorship and publication of special studies and research monographs of contemporary problems. The Canadian Certified General Accountants' Research Foundation publishes the *GAAP Guide* which summarizes and compares Canadian, U.S., and international accounting standards.

F. The Current Participation in Attaining a Consensus in Setting Accounting Standards

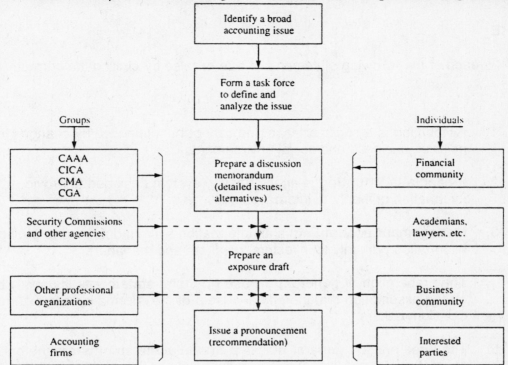

Other sources of GAAP:

    a. Canadian Income Tax Acts (with amendments).
    b. Specialized industry practices.
    c. Other professional pronouncements.
    d. Accounting textbooks and other literature.

KEY CONCEPTS

Accounting   An information system designed to identify, collect, measure and communicate economic information about business entities to those who have an interest in the financial affairs of the entities for their informed judgment and rational decision making.

Financial accounting   An information system designed to develop general purpose financial statements and to report general purpose accounting information to external decision makers.

General purpose financial statements   Primary means to communicate financial information to external decision makers, including the balance sheet, the income statement and the statement of cash flows.

Generally accepted accounting principles   A broad guidelines, conventions, rules, and procedures of accounting having substantial authoritative support and serving as financial accounting standards.

Overall objective of financial accounting   To provide financial information which is relevant to investment, credit and public policy decisions.

REVIEW QUESTIONS AND EXERCISES

TRUE-FALSE

Indicate whether each of the following statements is true or false by circling the correct response.

T   F   1.   Accounting is a social science and cannot be influenced by changes in legal, political, business and social environments.

T   F   2.   **Financial accounting** is an information system designed to provide information primarily to internal users.

T   F   3.   **Management accounting** is an information system designed to provide information primarily to investors, creditors and managers.

T   F   4.   The preparation of **general purpose financial statements** is usually based on the assumption that the primary users of the information are external decision makers.

T   F   5.   The three primary **general purpose financial statements** are the balance sheet, the statement of changes in financial position and the statement of retained earnings.

T   F   6.   Financial reporting should provide information which is relevant to investment, credit and public policy decisions.

T   F   7.   The **Canadian Institute of Chartered Accountants (CICA)** is a professional organization of accounting educators.

T   F   8.   Generally speaking, **GAAP** are those accounting principles with substantial authoritative support.

T   F   9.   The **Securities and Exchange Commission (SEC)** is a special committee of the **CICA**.

T   F   10.   Once established, **GAAP** should never be changed.

T   F   11.   **GAAP** are established to ensure the relevancy of the general purpose financial statements to the widespread use of the information by external decision makers.

T   F   12.   The **SEC** is legally empowered to prescribe accounting standards but, for the most part, has relied on the accounting profession to set and enforce financial accounting standards.

T   F   13.   The **Accounting Standards Board in Canada** was established **GAAP** in Canada.

T   **F**   14.   An independent auditor is not required to use **GAAP** as a standard to judge the fairness of financial statement presentation.

EXERCISE

Indicate in the space provided the organization or group which serves as the source for each of the following: (Some space(s) may require more than one source)

Document	Source
___ 1. Statements of Financial Accounting Standards (FASs)	A. Committee on Accounting Procedure (CAP)
___ 2. Accounting Series Releases (ASRs)	B. Accounting Principles Board (APB)
___ 3. Statements of Position	C. Financial Accounting Standards Board (FASB)
___ 4. Accounting Research Bulletins (ARBs)	D. Securities & Exchange Commission (SEC)
___ 5. Statement of Financial Accounting Concepts	E. Accounting Standards Executive Committee (AcSEC)
___ 6. Opinions	F. Canada Revenue
___ 7. Regulations S-X	G. Governmental Accounting Standards Board (GASB)
___ 8. Discussion Memoranda	H. Financial Accounting Advisory Council
___ 9. Financial Reporting Releases (FRRs)	I. Accounting Resource Committee (ARC)
___ 10. Exposure Draft	J. Auditing Standards Board
___ 11. *CICA Handbook*	

MULTIPLE CHOICE

Enter the letter corresponding to the response which **best** completes each of the following statements or questions.

___   1.   The accounting information system designed to develop general purpose financial information to **external decision makers** is referred to as:

     a.   governmental accounting.
     b.   public accounting.
     c.   financial accounting.
     d.   management accounting.

___   2.   Which of the following is not a characteristic of **management** accounting?

     a.   It is subject to management's desires.
     b.   It must be in compliance with GAAP.
     c.   It focuses on internal problems of management.
     d.   It is not audited by independent auditors.

___   3.   **General purpose financial statements** are designed primarily to meet the needs of:

    a.   potential investors.
    b.   creditors.
    c.   existing stockholders
    d.   all of the above.

___   4.   General purpose financial statements generally exclude the following:

    a.   federal income tax return.
    b.   statement of income.
    c.   statement of changes in financial position.
    d.   balance sheet.

___   5.   Which of the following **professional services** is normally provided by a Public Accountant?

    a.   Tax planning and reporting.
    b.   Auditing.
    c.   Management consulting.
    d.   All of the above.

___   6.   Generally accepted accounting principle are:

    a.   optional procedures for recording economic events.
    b.   mandatory rules applied to both financial and management accounting.
    c.   the rules of accounting, prescribed exclusively by Federal regulatory agencies.
    d.   standards of accounting, a material departure from which may result in a qualified opinion issued by a Public Accountant.

___   7.   The **sources** of generally accepted accounting standards in Canada include:

    a.   Memorandums discussion.
    b.   Pronouncements of Financial Accounting Standards.
    c.   Exposure Drafts.
    d.   all of the above.

___   8.   The development of GAAP can be traced to:

    a.   the passage of the Income Tax Act in 1917.
    b.   the stock market crash of 1929.
    c.   the diversification of business ownership.
    d.   all of the above.

9. The document that sets forth **fundamental concepts** for Canadian, American and International financial accounting and reporting standards is (are):

   a. The Technical bulletins issued by the CICA.
   b. The Interpretations of the Securities Exchange Commission.
   c. The Statement of Financial Accounting Standards (ASB).
   d. The GAAP Guide issued by CGARF.

10. Which of the following are Canadian organizations that influence accounting's evolution?

   a. The Canadian Institute of Chartered Accountants (CICA).
   b. The Certified General Accountants Association of Canada (CGA-Canada).
   c. The Society of Management Accountants (SMA).
   d. The Canadian Academic Accounting Association (CAAA).
   e. All of the above.

11. The **SEC** exerts a continuing influence on financial accounting standards mainly by:

   a. exercising its statutory authority to prescribe external financial reporting requirements.
   b. monitoring the development of GAAP within the accounting profession.
   c. providing major funding to the FASB.
   d. allying with the ARC and ASC to lobby the efforts of the CICA.

12. The Canadian Academic Accountants Association is an organization that strives to influence the development of accounting standards and its members are primarily:

   a. CAs, CGAs,CMAs and CPAs in government.
   b. accounting educators.
   c. accountants in public practice.
   d. accountants in industry.

13. Which of the following does **not** describe a characteristic of the "due process" system?

   a. Designed to attain a consensus
   b. Includes the issuance of accounting research bulletins
   c. Often includes a public hearing to provide an opportunity for interested parties to express their views
   d. Designed to carefully identify the accounting issues involved

14. Which of the following groups do **not** have any interest in the pronouncements that constitute GAAP?

   a. The preparers
   b. The auditors
   c. The politicians
   d. The users

SOLUTIONS TO REVIEW QUESTIONS AND EXERCISES

TRUE-FALSE

1.	F	5.	F	9.	F	13.	F
2.	F	6.	T	10.	F	14.	F
3.	F	7.	F	11.	T		
4.	T	8.	T	12.	T		

EXERCISE

1.	C	4.	A	7.	D	10.	C, I, J
2.	D	5.	C	8.	C, I, J	11.	I, J
3.	E	6.	B	9.	D		

MULTIPLE CHOICE

1.	c	5.	d	9.	d	13.	b
2.	b	6.	d	10.	e	14.	c
3.	d	7.	d	11.	b		
4.	a	8.	c	12.	b		

CHAPTER 2

Financial Statement Concepts and Principles

CHAPTER OBJECTIVES

This chapter is designed to enable students to:

A. Explain the need for and importance of the conceptual framework as it relates to financial reporting.

B. Identify the users of financial statements, tell why they use the statements, and list those characteristics of accounting information considered of critical importance.

C. Define the elements of financial statements.

D. Describe the recognition criteria and explain how they provide the conceptual basis of accrual accounting.

E. Explain the essential assumptions, implementation principles, and constraints underlying generally accepted accounting principles.

F. Describe the history leading to the current concepts and principles and some potential future changes in the reporting model.

CHAPTER OVERVIEW

A. Accounting concepts are based upon reasoning, economic theory, experience, pragmatism, and general acceptability. Since they cannot be derived from, nor proven by, the laws of nature as can be done in mathematics and the natural sciences, there is a need of a coherent set of hypothetical, conceptual, and pragmatic principles forming a general frame of reference, referred to as a **conceptual framework**, applied to financial accounting. The objectives of such a framework are:

1. To assure consistency across statements,

2. To provide a structure to address new issues,

3. To increase the relevance, reliability and comparability of financial reporting, and

4. To improve the ability of financial statements to communicate to users.

Attempts to formulate a conceptual framework of financial accounting have been going on for at least 50 years. The latest effort was a responsibility of the CICA as follows: under the ASAC (Accounting Standards Authority of Canada) with Conceptual framework for Financial Reporting (1987), and AcSC (Accounting Standards Committee of CICA) with Financial Statement Concepts (FSC), Section 1000 (1988). Note that these statements are not generally accepted accounting principles. Rather, they are fundamentals set forth to be used in developing standards of financial accounting and reporting.

B.   1.   Objectives of Financial Reporting - FSC

As indicated in chapter 1, the overall objective of financial accounting is to provide information that is useful to external decision makers. **FSC** makes the objective statement more specific:

The FSCs identify *decision usefulness* as the objective of financial reporting. The focus is on decision makers (financial statement users): investors, creditors, and others. The objectives state that financial reporting should provide information that assists in predicting the ability of the entity to earn income and generate cash flows in the future to meet its obligations and provide a return on investment. The statements are also used to assess how the management of an entity has performed. The statements should provide information about:

a.   an entity's economic resources, obligations and equity;
b.   changes in an entity's economic resources, obligations and equity;
c.   the economic performance of the entity.

2.   Qualitative Characteristics of Accounting Information - FSC

The FSCs the attributes of accounting information that enhance its usefulness for decision making as qualitative characteristics are understandability, relevance, reliability, and comparability.

(1)   Understandability

Information must be understandable to be useful in decision making. **Understandability** assumes investors and creditors have a reasonable understanding of business and economic activities, as well as some understanding of accounting. These users are willing to study the information with reasonable diligence. The user groups have been defined to include those who counsel investors and creditors; users who lack expertise are assumed to be properly advised.

(2)   Relevance

Relevance refers to the capacity of accounting information to make a difference to the external decision makers who use financial reports. They use accounting information with either or both of two viewpoints in mind:

*Forecasting what the economic future is likely to hold.
*Confirming the accuracy of past forecasts, to improve future forecasting techniques.

Relevant accounting information helps users make predictions about the outcomes of past, present, and future events (predictive value) and confirm or correct prior expectations (feedback value).
The degree to which accounting information is deemed to be relevant can be measured using three aspects of this quality:

1. **Timeliness.** Accounting information should be made available to external decision makers before it loses its capacity to influence decisions. Lack of timeliness reduces relevance.
2. **Predictive value.** Accounting information should be helpful to external decision makers by increasing their ability to make correct predictions about the outcome of past or present events.
3. **Feedback value.** Accounting information should also be helpful to external decision makers in confirming past predictions or in making updates, adjustments, or corrections to predictions currently outstanding.

(3) Reliability

To have **reliability**, it must be free from error and bias, and it must faithfully represent what it purports to represent:

1. **Representational faithfulness.** Sometimes called *validity*, this attribute of accounting information applies to the whole of the text and numbers contained in a financial report conveyed to the reader.

2. **Verifiability:** This quality standard is needed to ensure that a given piece of accounting information is what it purports to be. Verifiability pertains to having audit trails back to information source documents that can be checked for accuracy.

3. **Neutrality:** This standard is met if the accounting information is free from bias, slants, or the use of unfounded opinion to influence the readers of financial statements.

(4) Comparability

The FSCs define comparability as follows:
Comparability is a characteristic of the relationship between two pieces of information rather than of a particular piece of information by itself.

Comparability in the financial statements of an entity is enhanced when the same accounting policies are used consistently from period to period.

Consistency, which entails using the same accounting policies from year to year within a firm, and uniformity, which means that companies with similar circumstances use the same accounting principles.

There is a presumption that an accounting principle once used should not be changed. However, if consistency is carried too far, reliability adversely affects relevance.

A change to a preferred accounting principle is permitted, even though this would impair consistency. This apparent conflict is resolved by retroactive restatement of financial statements to reflect the new policy and supplemental note disclosure.

C.   Elements of Financial Statements - CICA, Section 1000

Elements of financial statements are the building blocks with which financial statements are constructed. These elements first specified for profit-seeking organizations, are now expanded in scope to encompass not-for-profit organizations. The following 7 elements are directly related to measuring performance and status of an enterprise (entity):

1.   Balance Sheet:

a.   **Assets** - Probable future economic benefits obtained or controlled by an entity as a result of past transactions or events.

b.   **Liabilities** - Probable future sacrifices of economic benefits arising from present obligations of an entity to transfer assets or provide services to other entities in the future as a result of past transactions or events.

c.   **Equity** (owners' equity) - The residual interest in the assets of an entity that remains after deducting its liabilities. In a business enterprise, the equity is the ownership interest.

2.   Income Statement:

d.   **Revenues** - Inflows or other enhancements of assets or settlements of liabilities (or a combination of both) of an entity during a period from activities that constitute the entity's ongoing major or central operations.

e.   **Expenses** - Outflows or other using up of assets or incurrence of liabilities (or a combination of both) of an entity during a period from activities that constitute the entity's ongoing major or central operations.

f.   **Gains** - Increases in equity (net assets) from peripheral or incidental transactions of an entity and from all other transactions and events and circumstances affecting the entity during a period except those that result from revenues or investments by owners.

g. **Losses** - Decreases in equity (net assets) from peripheral or incidental transactions of an entity and from all other transactions and events and circumstances affecting the entity during a period except those that result from expenses or distributions to owners.

3. **Transaction Characteristics**

a. To qualify as assets, the resources involved must:
1. Have future economic benefits (capable of producing profits)
2. Be under management's control (can be freely deployed or disposed of).
3. Result from past transactions (meaning they are in place now, as opposed to being under contract for manufacture, creation, or delivery)

b. To qualify as liabilities, obligations must:
1. Transfer assets having future economic benefits.
2. Specify to whom the assets must be transferred (meaning that the terms, parties, and conditions under which asset transfers will take place must be specified).
3. Result from past transactions (meaning they are in binding obligations now, as opposed to obligations that will exist once pending transactions are completed).

c. The dollar amounts reported represent the residual interest in the assets after deducting the liabilities. In addition, the equity element is used to report capital transactions as described below.

d. The two essential characteristics of a revenue transaction are:
1. It arises from the company's primary earning activity (mainstream business lines) and not from incidental or investment transactions (assuming the entity is a noninvestment company).
2. It is recurring and continuous.

e. The essential characteristic of an expense is that it must be incurred in conjunction with the company's revenue-generating process.

Expenditures that do not qualify as expenses must be treated as either assets (future economic benefit to be derived) or losses (no economic benefit) or as distributions to owners.

f. The transaction must not be one that meets the characteristics test of (1) a revenue-producing transaction (detailed above) or (2) a capital contribution transaction (detailed below).

g. The transaction must not be one that meets the characteristics test of (1) an expense transaction (detailed above) or (2) a capital distribution (investment by owner) transaction (detailed below).

D.   Financial Statements and Recognition and Measurement in Financial Statements (FSC)

1.   Recognition criteria

Recognition is the process of including an item in the financial statements. A recognized item is given a title and numerical value. Recognition applies to all financial statement elements in all companies. The conceptual basis for the accrual basis of accounting is provided by the recognition criteria: The accrual basis of accounting recognizes the effect of transactions and events in the period in which they occur, regardless of whether there has been a cash payment or receipt.

An element should be recognized in the accounts when:

1.   The element has an appropriate basis of measurement and a reasonable estimate can be made of the amount involved, and
2.   For items involving either obtaining or giving up a future economic benefit, it must be probable that the event will take place.

2.   Measurement Criteria

Measurement is the process of determining the amount at which an item is recognized in the financial statements. If there is no appropriate basis of measurement, a transaction would fail the first recognition criteria, as previously defined. There are many alternative measurement bases, including historical cost, replacement cost, current sales value, and the sum of the cash flows an item can generate over its life, discounted at an appropriate rate. The FSCs state that, *generally*, historical cost should be used as a measurement base.

Capital Maintenance

The FSCs confirmed the use of financial capital as an appropriate capital maintenance concept in financial reporting. The notion of financial capital maintenance means that if the closing amount of net financial assets exceeds the amount at the start, excluding transactions with owners such as additional investment or dividends, income results. In contrast, a return on physical capital results only when the physical assets or capacity of the organization increases over the period.

E.   Assumptions, Principles, and Constraints

1.   Environmental Assumptions

As indicated in chapter 1, financial principles have evolved from accounting environment. The present GAAP are based on the following environmental assumptions:

(a)   The **separate entity assumption:**   Accounting deals with specific and separate business entities, each of which is assumed to be an accounting unit separate and apart from its owners and other entities. Under this assumption, all accounting records and reports are developed from the viewpoint of the particular entity.

(b)   The **continuity (going concern) assumption:**   Accounting deals with business entities which are assumed to continue for a period of time sufficient to carry out contemplated operations on a regular basis.

(c)   The **unit-of-measure assumption:**   Accounting deals with the economic activities of an entity using monetary unit as the measurement unit with the assumption that the monetary unit has equal purchasing power or that the magnitude of changes in the purchasing power of the monetary unit is not material.

(d)   The **time period assumption:**   Although the business entity is assumed to have an indefinite life and the results of operations cannot be known with certainty until the business has completed its life span, the accounting process measures and reports the results of operations for a short term with the assumption that the indefinite life can be divided into a series of equal time periods, normally the calendar year.

2.   Implementation Principles

Based on these environmental assumptions, there are four implementation principles or guidelines underlying the conventional accounting system:

(a)   **The historical cost (or cost) principle:**   Historical cost is conceived as the most useful basis for accounting because the cost is not only measurable, but also verifiable. This principle specifies that cash-equivalent cost should be used for initial recognition of assets and liabilities.

(b)   **The revenue principle:**   Revenues are recognized when earned and the collection of the earned amounts is reasonably certain. A revenue is considered earned when the earning process is virtually complete and an exchange has taken place, typically at the point of sale. (CICA - all significant acts required by the seller are complete and control over the asset sold has been turned over to the buyer.)

(c)   **The matching principle:**   Expenses are recognized when incurred. An expense is incurred when it contributes to, or can be associated with a particular revenue. Therefore, expenses (efforts) incurred in the process of producing revenues (accomplishments) should be reported in the same period in which those revenues are recognized.

(d)   **The full disclosure principle:**   Financial statements should provide users with sufficient data to permit informed judgment concerning the status of the entity in question.

3.   **Implementation Constraints**

The implementation of accounting concepts and principles are subject to the following constraints, also referred to as modification principles:

(a)   **Cost-Benefit Constraint:**   The benefits to be received by users from specific information should exceed the cost of providing the information.

(b)   **Materiality Constraint:**   Materiality is defined as the magnitude of an omission or misstatement of accounting information that, in the light of surrounding circumstances, makes it probable that the judgment of a reasonable person relying on the information would have been changed or influenced by the omission or misstatement. The materiality threshold does not mean that immaterial items and amounts do not have to be accounted or reported. Rather, it means that strict adherence to the related accounting standard is not required.

(c)   **Industry peculiarities:**   Different industries may warrant selective exceptions to accounting principles and practices. (e.g., Enterprises in the extractive industries - CICA: Section 3450-1)

(d)   **Conservatism:**   Conservatism implies that when the "correct" treatment or amount is not determinable, the users of financial statements are better served by understatement rather than overstatement of net income and assets. Therefore, where two alternatives equally satisfy conceptual and implementation principles for a transaction, the alternative having the least favorable effect on net income and/or total assets would be used.

KEY CONCEPTS

Assets   Probable future economic benefits obtained or controlled by a particular entity as a result of past transactions or events.

Conservatism   When the "correct" treatment or amount is not determinable, the users of financial statements are better served by understatement rather than overstatement of net income and assets.

Continuity (going concern) assumption   Accounting deals with business entities which are assumed to continue for a period of time sufficient to carry out contemplated operations on a regular basis.

Cost-benefit constraint   The benefits to be received by users from specific information should exceed the cost of providing the information.

Equity (owners' equity)   The residual interest in the assets of an entity which remains after deducting its liabilities.

Expenses   Outflows or other using up of assets or incurrence of liabilities of an entity during a period from activities that constitute the entity's ongoing major operations.

Full disclosure principle   Financial statements should provide users with sufficient data to permit informed judgment concerning the status of the entity in question.

Historical cost principle   The exchange price is the most appropriate basis for initial recognition of financial statement elements.

Gains   Increases in equity from peripheral or incidental transactions of an entity and from all other transactions and events and circumstances affecting the entity during a period except those that result from revenues or investments by owners.

Liabilities   Probable future sacrifices of economic benefits arising from present obligations of a particular entity to transfer assets or provide services to other entities in the future as a result of past transactions or events.

Losses   Decreases in equity from peripheral or incidental transactions of an entity and from all other transactions and events and circumstances affecting the entity during a period except those that result from expenses or distributions to owners.

Materiality Constraint   The magnitude of an omission or misstatement of accounting information that makes it probable that the judgment of a reasonable person relying on the information would be influenced by the omission or misstatement.

Matching principle   Expenses incurred in the process of producing revenues are to be reported in the same period in which those revenues are recognized.

Relevant   Financial information is relevant if it allows users (a) to make predictions (predictive value), (b) to confirm or correct prior predictions (feedback value), and (c) to make decisions within the relevant time frame (timeliness).

Reliability   Financial information is reliable if it is (a) verifiable, (b) representative, and (c) neutral.

Revenues   Inflows or other enhancements of assets or settlements of liabilities of an entity during a period from activities that constitute the entity's ongoing major or central operations.

Revenue principle   A revenue is recognized when earned and the collection of sales price is reasonably certain.

Separate entity assumption   Each business entity is treated as a separate accounting unit apart from its owners and other entities.

Time period assumption   The indefinite life of an entity can be divided into a series of equal time periods, normally the calendar year.

Unit-of-Measure Assumption   Monetary unit used as the measurement unit has equal purchasing power.

REVIEW QUESTIONS AND EXERCISES

TRUE-FALSE

Indicate whether each of the following statements is true or false by circling the correct response.

T   F   1.   Statements of financial accounting concepts represent generally accepted accounting principles, and as such, are binding upon members of the accounting profession.

T   F   2.   The two primary qualitative characteristics of financial accounting information are relevance and consistency.

T   F   3.   A primary ingredient in the relevance of information is its ability to predict.

T   F   4.   Reliability of financial accounting information refers to whether the information is verifiable, neutral and faithful.

T   F   5.   Financial information should provide information to help users assess the amount, timing, and uncertainty of future cash flows.

T   F   6.   Assets are probable future economic benefits obtained or controlled by a particular entity.

T   F   7.   The separate entity assumption states that, in the absence of contrary evidence, all entities will survive indefinitely.

T   F   8.   The unit-of-measure assumption states that the elements of financial statements are to be measured at their original cost.

T   F   9.   The traditional accounting system assumes that the purchasing power of the dollar remains unchanged.

T   F   10.   The time period assumption allows accountants to divide the life of an entity into equal intervals for periodic financial reporting purposes.

T   F   11.   The historical cost principle states that exchange price is the most appropriate basis for initial recognition of financial statement elements.

T   F   12.   In general, revenue is recognized when the production process is virtually complete.

T   F   13.   The matching principle associates revenues with the accounting period in which they are earned.

T   F   14.   The materiality constraint modifies accounting and reporting requirements in that recognition of an item of accounting information should be ignored if it is not material.

SHORT EXERCISE 1

Qualitative Characteristic, basic assumptions and Implementation Constraints

      1.   Verifiability

      2.   Reliability

      3.   Neutrality

      4.   Comparability

      5.   Relevance

      6.   Materiality

      7.   Cost-benefit

      8.   Time period assumption

      9.   Separate entity assumption

   10.   Unit-of-measure assumption

Related Phrases

A.   Verifiable, neutral and faithful representation.

B.   Charging the cost of a wastebasket with 5 years of useful life to current expense.

C.   The information is capable of making a difference in user decisions.

D.   The reported information is absence of bias.

E.   Information benefits exceed the cost involved.

F.   Two or more accountants independently measure an asset at the same value.

G.   The purchasing power of Cdn. dollars remains constant.

H.   Each business unit is treated as a separate accounting unit apart from its owners.

I.   The presentation of annual financial reports.

J.   The presentation of comparative financial statements.

SHORT EXERCISE 2

| **Financial Statement Elements and Implementation Principles** | **Related Phrase** |

____   1. Assets

____   2. Liabilities

____   3. Revenues

____   4. Expenses

____   5. Historical cost

____   6. Revenue recognition

____   7. Matching

____   8. Full disclosure

A. Outflows of assets from delivering or producing goods or rendering services that constitute the entity's ongoing major operations.

B. A revenue is recognized when earned and the collection is reasonably certain.

C. The exchange price is the most useful basis for accounting.

D. Probable future sacrifices of economic benefits arising from present obligations to transfer assets to an external party.

E. Financial reporting should provide users with sufficient data including financial statements and footnotes to permit informed decisions.

F. Probable future economic benefits obtained or controlled by an entity as a result of past transactions.

G. Expenses incurred in the process of producing revenues are reported in the same period in which those revenues are recognized.

H. Inflows of assets from delivering goods or rendering services that constitute the entity's ongoing major operations.

MULTIPLE CHOICE

Enter the letter corresponding to the response which **best** completes each of the following statements or questions.

_____ 1. The underlying concept that supports the valuation of assets at cost rather than liquidation values is the:

    a. principle of substance over form.
    b. continuity assumption.
    c. unit of measure assumption.
    d. principle of conservatism.

_____ 2. One of the ingredients of the reliability of financial information is:

    a. relevance.
    b. comparability.
    c. verifiability.
    d. conservatism.

_____ 3. The two primary decision making qualities of financial reporting to enhance usefulness are:

    a. relevance and predictive value.
    b. comparability and timeliness.
    c. comparability and predictive value.
    d. relevance and reliability.

_____ 4. Which of the following is not considered a modification principle (constraint) of financial reporting?

    a. Consistency
    b. Cost-benefit principle
    c. Conservatism
    d. Materiality

_____ 5. The secondary qualitative characteristics of financial reporting are:

    a. comparability and consistency.
    b. consistency and usefulness.
    c. comparability and materiality.
    d. predictive value and feedback value.

____ 6. The elements of financial statements specified in the *CICA Handbook*, section 1000 are applicable to:

   a. business enterprises.
   b. governmental units.
   c. not-for-profit organizations.
   d. all of the above.

____ 7. In general, a revenue is considered as earned when the earning process is virtually complete and:

   a. the production is completed.
   b. an exchange has taken place.
   c. the sale price has been collected.
   d. a purchase order has been received.

____ 8. In the process of providing an allowance for bad debts based on sales, accountants are most likely concerned with:

   a. the principle of substance over form.
   b. conservatism.
   c. the historical cost principle.
   d. the matching principle.

____ 9. The primary objective of the matching principle is to:

   a. record expenses in the period that the related revenues are recognized.
   b. provide timely information to decision-makers.
   c. promote comparability between financial statements of different periods.
   d. provide full disclosure.

____ 10. Which of the following is most closely related to the consistency principle?

   a. A business entity applies the same accounting principles in the current period as in the previous periods.
   b. A business entity applies the same accounting principles as those applied by other business entities in the same industry.
   c. A business entity applied the same depreciation policies to all classes of assets.
   d. A business entity applies the same depreciation policies as those used to prepare tax returns.

____ 11. According to **SFAC 5**, comprehensive income:

   a. is the same as earnings.
   b. is the same as the net income in present practice.
   c. is the net change in owners' equity during the period.
   d. includes earnings and adjustments to earnings such as cumulative effects as well as other nonowner changes in equity.

_____ 12. Which of the following is not a financial statement element as defined in the CICA, section 1000.

    a. Net income
    b. Investments by owners
    c. Distributions to owners
    d. Comprehensive income

_____ 13. The environmental assumption that justifies quarterly financial statements is likely to be the:

    a. unit-of-measure assumption.
    b. separate entity assumption.
    c. going concern assumption.
    d. time-period assumption.

_____ 14. The principles that support cost or market, whichever is lower rule is most likely to be the:

    a. consistency principle.
    b. comparability principle.
    c. conservatism principle.
    d. full disclosure principle.

SOLUTIONS TO REVIEW QUESTIONS AND EXERCISES

TRUE-FALSE

1.	F	5.	T	9.	T	13.	F
2.	F	6.	T	10.	T	14.	F
3.	T	7.	F	11.	T		
4.	T	8.	F	12.	F		

SHORT EXERCISE 1

1.	F	4.	J	7.	E	10.	G
2.	A	5.	C	8.	I		
3.	D	6.	B	9.	H		

SHORT EXERCISE 2

1.	F	4.	A	7.	G
2.	D	5.	C	8.	E
3.	H	6.	B		

MULTIPLE CHOICE

1.	b	5.	a	9.	a	13.	d
2.	c	6.	d	10.	a	14.	c
3.	d	7.	b	11.	d		
4.	a	8.	d	12.	a		

CHAPTER 3

Review: The Accounting Information Processing System

CHAPTER OBJECTIVES

This chapter is designed to enable students to:

A. Explain the purpose of an accounting information system.

B. Explain the double-entry accounting system and the relationships among financial statements.

C. Define the relationships among accounting information system components: accounts, journals, ledgers, and financial statements.

D. Perform the accouting cycle steps leading to the financial statements.

E. State the difference between two methods of recording common operating transactions, and explain the effects of each on adjusting and reversing entries.

F. Explain the role of the worksheet in the accounting cycle.

G. Describe special journals and ledgers.

CHAPTER OVERVIEW

A. Chapter 1 indicates that financial accounting is an information system designed to identify, collect, measure, and communicate economic information to external decision makers. In this chapter, a summary and review are provided of the basic process by which economic information is identified, recorded, summarized, and reported in the accounting system. The sequence of steps of this process is referred to as the accounting cycle. To introduce this cycle it is essential to first understand the following concepts:

B. **Double-entry system:**   (AIS) - Accounting Information System - Transactions and other economic events are separately recorded in the accounts, and at least two accounts are affected by these recordings. This practice is called the double-entry system. It is based on the debit-credit convention, which divides accounts into two sides. The debit (dr.) side is always the left-hand side, and the credit (cr.) side the right-hand side of an account. Depending on the type of account, a debit or a credit reflects an increase (+) or a decrease (-) to the specific account as follows:

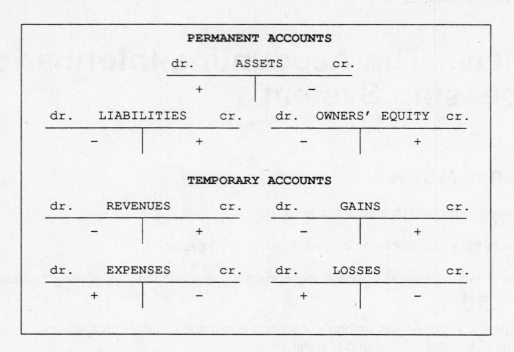

Note that the normal balance of an account is indicated on the side that increases the account. So the normal balances of assets are debit, and those of liabilities and owners' equity are credit. Note also that temporary accounts represent changes in owners' equity. Since revenues and gains increase owners' equity, their normal balances are credit; and since expenses and losses decrease owners' equity, their normal balances are debit.

C.   **Accounts**:   **CICA Handbook,** Section, 1000 considers financial statement elements as the building blocks with which financial statements are constructed. By the same analogy, the building blocks with which financial statement elements are identified, classified and summarized, are **accounts**. Each element consists of a group of accounts, established to record monetary information based on those events having economic consequences to the specific element. Following the categorization of the balance-sheet and the income-statement elements, there are seven major types of accounts which are grouped into two fundamental classifications:

a.   **Permanent (real) accounts (i.e., assets, liabilities**, and **owners' equity):** Permanent accounts appear in the balance sheet, and their balances carry over to future accounting periods. These accounts are inter related and their relationships can be expressed by the following basic accounting equation:

Assets = Liabilities + Owners' Equity

    b.   **Temporary (nominal) accounts (i.e., revenues, expenses, gains and losses):**   Temporary accounts hold the **changes** in permanent accounts and are presented in the income statements. These accounts are established just for periodic measurement of income, and their balances should be reduced to zero through year-end closing entries.

D.   The sequence of steps that are followed each reporting period to process accounting data (i.e., the **accounting cycle**) is presented below:

1.   **Identifying transactions and events:**   The inputs of the accounting information system are events which have economic consequences to the business entity, known as economic events. For financial accounting purposes, economic events may be categorized as follows:

    a.   **Transactions.**   Transactions are transfers or exchanges of something with value between the firm (a specific reporting entity) and one or more independent outside parties. Exchanges are reciprocal if both parties transfer resources and/or assume obligations, e.g., purchases and sales. If, however, only one of the two parties makes the transfer such as payments of cash dividends or receipt of donations, the exchanges are considered nonreciprocal.

    b.   **Other economic events:**

        (1)   Internal events.   These are events which occur within the firm with economic consequences to the firm (e.g., using raw material and depreciable assets).

        (2)   External events: These are events which occur outside of the firm but with economic consequences to the firm (e.g., a flood or an earthquake).

Both transactions and other economic events affect the economic resources or obligations of the entity and must be identified for recording and reporting. As a general rule, if measurable, all transactions are recorded as they occur. Other economic events, however, are recorded selectively, following generally accepted accounting principles, mostly at the year end.

Example:

The Sunny Corporation is a newly established computer retailer. During 1991, its first year of operation, the following transactions and other economic events occurred:

TRANSACTIONS - To be recorded during the period:

1991
January 2:   Sold 2,000 common shares at $5 per share, for cash.

An office building with a useful life of 10 years and a cost of $1,000 was acquired for cash. The building's salvage value is zero.

Purchased $2,000 in merchandise with $1,500 cash and a note of $500.

May 5:   Sold merchandise for $5,000, including $2,000 in credit sales.

October 1:   Paid employees' salaries of $800, for services rendered.

Purchased for cash a four-year fire insurance policy at $96.

Collected $24 from a customer for a two-year service contract.

December 31:   Other expenses of $1,200, incurred and paid.

TRANSACTIONS AND OTHER ECONOMIC EVENTS - To be recorded through period-end adjustments:

December 31   (a) A portion of the unearned service revenue was earned.
($24 x 3/24 = $3)

(b) A portion of the prepaid insurance was expired.
($96 x 3/48 = $6)

(c) Service revenue earned but not yet recorded nor collected, $5.

(d) Employees' salaries incurred but not yet recorded nor paid, $600.

(e) The building had been used and depreciated for the whole year.
($1,000 x 1/10 = $100)

(f) An estimated $40 of the outstanding balances of accounts receivable will not be collectible.

(g) Ending merchandise inventory is determined to be $500.

Note that the above letters, (a), (b), ... (g), are used to identify the specific transactions and other events to be referred to in a later step dealing with adjusting entries.

2. **Journalizing accounting transactions and other events:** Once identified transactions and other economic events are separately recorded chronologically in the general journal by means of journal entries, and each journal entry is expressed in terms of equal debits and credits to accounts affected by the event being recorded.

Example:
Prepare journal entries during the period using the transaction data identified in 1 above:

General Journal		Posting	Amount	
Date 1991	Accounts and Explanations	ref.	Debit	Credit
Jan- 2	Cash	101	10,000	
	Common shares	301		10,000
	Issued 2,000 shares of common for cash.			
	Buildings	106	1,000	
	Cash	101		1,000
	Acquired an office building for cash.			
	Purchases	501	2,000	
	Cash	101		1,500
	Notes payable	201		500
	Purchased merchandise, paid $1,500 cash and issued a note for $500.			
May- 5	Cash	101	3,000	
	Accounts receivable	102	2,000	
	Sales revenue	401		5,000
	To record cash and credit sales.			
Oct- 1	Salaries expense	503	800	
	Cash	101		800
	Paid salaries earned by employees.			
	Prepaid insurance expense	105	96	
	Cash	101		96
	To record payment for a 4-year insurance premium.			
	Cash	101	24	
	Unearned service revenue	211		24
	Collected $24 for a 2-year service contract.			
Dec-31	Other operating expenses	506	1,200	
	Cash	101		1,200
	To record other expenses paid.			
	Totals carried forward to j-2		20,120	20,120

Page j - 1

Note that the "Posting Ref." column (standing for posting reference) is used to enter the identification number of a ledger account indicating the specific amount has been posted to the specific ledger account. This is part of the following step (i.e., posting entries).

3. **Posting entries from journal to ledger:** A ledger is a collection of all of the accounts of a business entity. Each account summarizes the effects of all events on that individual account. Posting is the process of transferring the debits and credits recorded in the journal to the ledger accounts. It periodically reclassifies the information from the chronological format in the journal to an account classification format in the ledger.

Example:

Post the previous journal entries to their respective ledger accounts. For simplicity, the individual ledger accounts are presented in "T" form, known as "T" accounts. The page number in the general journal (i.e., j-1) is entered into the individual accounts as a cross-reference:

General Ledger

CASH

Acct. 101

1991			1991		
Jan-2	j-1	10,000	Jan-2	j-1	1,000
May-5	j-1	3,000		j-1	1,500
Oct-1	j-1	24	Oct-1	j-1	800
				j-1	96
			Dec-31	j-1	1,200
Balance		8,428			

ACCOUNTS RECEIVABLE

Acct. 102

1991		
May-5	j-1	2,000

PREPAID INSURANCE EXPENSE

Acct. 105

1991		
Oct-1	j-1	96

BUILDINGS

Acct. 106

1991		
Jan-2	j-1	1,000

NOTES PAYABLE

Acct. 201

	1991		
	Jan-2	j-1	500

UNEARNED SERVICE REVENUE

Acct. 211

	1991		
	Oct-1	j-1	24

COMMON SHARES

Acct. 301

	1991		
	Jan-2	j-1	10,000

SALES REVENUE

Acct. 401

	1991		
	May-5	j-1	5,000

PURCHASES

Acct. 501

1991			
Jan-2	j-1	2,000	

SALARIES EXPENSE

Acct. 503

1991			
Oct-1	j-1	800	

OTHER OPERATING EXPENSES

Acct. 506

1991			
Dec-31	j-1	1,200	

4. **Preparing an unadjusted trial balance:**   During the accounting period, steps 1 to 3 are repeatedly performed to record daily transactions as they occur. At year end, a trial balance is compiled by listing all account balances on that specific date to detect some of the recording and posting errors. This trial balance is unadjusted because it is prepared prior to year-end adjustments.

Example:

Based on the account balances indicated above, an unadjusted trial balance is compiled as follows:

Sunny Corporation Unadjusted Trial Balance December 31, 1991		
Accounts	Debit	Credit
Cash	8,428	
Accounts receivable	2,000	
Prepaid insurance expense	96	
Buildings	1,000	
Notes payable		500
Unearned service revenue		24
Common stock		10,000
Sales revenue		5,000
Purchases	2,000	
Salaries expense	800	
Other operating expenses	1,200	
	15,524	15,524

5. **Journalizing and posting adjusting entries:**   The objective of adjusting entries is to bring all the permanent and nominal accounts up to date on the accrual basis. Accrual basis accounting requires that revenues are recognized when earned and expenses are recognized when the expenses can be matched against the earned revenues. As illustrated below, any adjusting entry affects both permanent and temporary accounts. Note that the following examples are based on the transactions and other events presented on the earlier pages of this chapter with the identification letters, (a), (b), ..., (g).

   a.   **Deferred items:**   Both revenues and expenses may be deferred as explained below:

   (1)   Deferred revenues: These are revenues having been collected but not yet earned. The collection of unearned revenue should be reported as a liability (i.e., unearned revenue or revenue collected in advance) until the revenue is earned and recognized. In our example, Sunny collected $24 of service revenue in advance and initially recorded it as an unearned revenue. At the end of the period, a portion of that

revenue, i.e., $24 x 3/24 = $3, had been earned. To update the liability and the revenue accounts, the following adjusting entry is appropriate:

(a)   Unearned service revenue   3
             Service revenue   3

(2)   Deferred expenses: Deferred expenses are expenses not yet incurred, but for which cash has already been paid. A deferred expense should be reported as an asset. In our example, the prepaid insurance is a deferred expense. Since Sunny initially recorded this payment as an asset, the amount of expense incurred during the current period (i.e., $96 x 3/48 = $6) should be transferred to the insurance expense account with the following adjusting entry.

(b)   Other operating expenses   6
             Prepaid insurance expense   6

b.   **Accrued items:**   As in the case of deferred items, accrued items may be either revenues or expenses:

(1)   Accrued revenues: Accrued revenues are revenues earned during the period for which cash has not yet been collected. An accrued revenue is recorded at year end with a debit to revenues receivable account and a credit to revenue account. In our example, the $5 service revenue earned, but not yet collected, is an accrued item which calls for the following adjusting entry:

(c)   Accounts receivable   5
             Service revenue   5

(2)   Accrued expenses: Accrued expenses are expenses already incurred during the period but for which cash has not been paid. An accrued expense is an expense payable and should be recognized at the year end together with the incurred expense. In our example, the $600 salaries expense incurred but not yet paid is an accrual item which requires the following adjusting entry:

(d)   Salaries expense   600
             Salaries payable   600

General Journal			j – 2 Page _____	
Date 1991	Accounts and Explanations	Posting ref.	Amount Debit	Credit
	Totals carried from j-1		20,120	20,120
Dec-31	Unearned service revenue Service revenue To recognize service revenue earned. (see Item **(a)**)	211 402	3	3
	Other operating expenses Prepaid insurance expense To recognize expired insurance cost. (see Item **(b)**)	506 105	6	6
	Accounts receivable Service revenue To recognize accrued revenue. (see Item **(c)**)	102 402	5	5
	Salaries expense Salaries payable To accrue salaries expense. (see Item **(d)**)	503 202	600	600
	Depreciation expense Accumulated depreciation To record depreciation expense. (see Item **(e)**)	504 107	100	100

	Bad debt expense
	    Allowance for doubtful
	    accounts
	To record bad debt expense.
	(see Item **(f)**)
		505
		
		103
			40	40

	Inventory Cost of goods sold Purchases To recognize cost of goods sold. (see Item **(g)**)	104 502 501	500 1,500	2,000
	Totals carried forward to j-3		22,874	22,874

After journalizing adjusting entries as shown above, the next step is to post the entries to ledger accounts. Presented next are the updated ledger accounts after posting of adjusting entries. Note that, in our example, all the adjusting entries are posted from j-2 (i.e., page 2 of the general journal).

c.   **Other adjustments:**   In addition to deferred and accrued items, there are two more types of year-end adjustments:

(1)   Estimated items: At the end of the period, expenses should be estimated and recognized for those items which (1) have contribution to and/or can be associated with the current income, and (2) are a function of some future events so that their exact amounts are not yet determinable. In our example, both depreciation and bad debt expenses are estimated items and the following adjusting entries are made:

     (e)   Depreciation expense ($1,000 x 1/10) 100
           Accumulated depreciation   100

     (f)   Bad debt expense   40
           Allowance for doubtful accounts   40

Both accumulated depreciation and allowance for doubtful accounts are contra-asset accounts, which are presented in the balance sheet as reductions in the related asset accounts. Using the accumulated depreciation account is an accounting tradition utilized to disclose more information about the asset, including its original cost and the depreciation expenses recorded to date. The use of the allowance for doubtful accounts is based on the fact that the expense is calculated on an overall estimate, without knowing which of the outstanding accounts will eventually be uncollectible.

(2)   Cost of goods sold: Under the perpetual inventory system the cost of goods sold is determined, and recorded, immediately following the sale. Under the periodic system, however, it is calculated at the end of the period. In the latter case, the cost of goods sold is determined and recorded by (1) closing the purchases and the related return, discount and allowance accounts, (2) closing the beginning inventory, and (3) establishing the ending inventory. In our example, the cost of goods sold is determined and recorded as follows:

     (g)   Inventory (ending, per physical count) 500
          Cost of goods sold ($2,000 - $500) 1,500
            Purchases   2,000

It should be noted that the above entries are just for explanation purpose. In fact, adjusting entries are also journal entries and should thus be formally recorded in the general journal as follows:

General Ledger

CASH

Acct. 101

1991				1991			
Jan-1	j-1	10,000		Jan-2	j-1		1,000
May-5	j-1	3,000			j-1		1,500
Oct-1	j-1	24		Oct-1	j-1		800
					j-1		96
				Dec-31	j-1		1,200
Balance		8,428					

ACCOUNTS RECEIVABLE

Acct. 102

1991			
May-5	j-1	2,000	
Dec-31	**j-2**	**5**	
Balance		2,005	

ALLOWANCE FOR DOUBTFUL ACCOUNTS

Acct. 103

			1991		
			Dec-31	**j-2**	**40**

INVENTORY

Acct. 104

1991			
Dec-31	**j-2**	**500**	

PREPAID INSURANCE EXPENSE

Acct. 105

1991				1991		
Oct-1	j-1	96		**Dec-31**	**j-2**	**6**
Balance		90				

BUILDINGS

Acct. 106

1991			
Jan-2	j-1	1,000	

ACCUMULATED DEPRECIATION

Acct. 107

1991		
Dec–31	**j-2**	**100**

NOTES PAYABLE

Acct. 201

1991		
Jan-2	j-1	500

SALARIES PAYABLE

Acct. 202

1991		
Dec–31	**j-2**	**600**

UNEARNED SERVICE REVENUE

Acct. 211

1991				1991		
Dec–31	**j-2**		**3**	Oct-1	j-1	24
				Balance		21

COMMON SHARES

Acct. 301

1991		
Jan-2	j-1	10,000

SALES REVENUE

Acct. 401

1991		
May-5	j-1	5,000

SERVICE REVENUE

Acct. 402

1991		
Dec–31	**j-2**	**3**
	j-2	**5**
Balance		8

PURCHASES

Acct. 501

1991				1991		
Jan-2	j-1	2,000		**Dec-31**	**j-2**	**2,000**

COST OF GOODS SOLD

Acct. 502

1991		
Dec-31	**j-2**	**1,500**

SALARIES EXPENSE

Acct. 503

1991		
Oct-1	j-1	800
Dec-31	**j-2**	**600**
Balance		1,400

DEPRECIATION EXPENSE

Acct. 504

1991		
Dec-31	**j-2**	**100**

BAD DEBT EXPENSE

Acct. 505

1991		
Dec-31	**j-2**	**40**

OTHER OPERATING EXPENSES

Acct. 506

1991		
Dec-31	j-1	1,200
Dec-31	**j-2**	**6**
Balance		1,206

6.   **Preparing the adjusted trial balance:**   The adjusted trial balance lists all the accounts with the balances which will appear in the financial statements. The purpose of this trial balance is to confirm debit-credit equality after the adjusting journal entries have been made, and to list all the account balances for the preparation of financial statements. Based on the above accounts, an adjusted trial balance is shown as:

```
                        Sunny Corporation
                     Adjusted Trial Balance
                        December 31, 1991

           Accounts                      Debit        Credit

   Cash                                   8,428
   Accounts receivable                    2,005
   Allowance for doubtful accounts                       40
   Inventory                               500
   Prepaid insurance expense                90
   Buildings                             1,000
   Accumulated depreciation                              100
   Notes payable                                         500
   Salaries payable                                      600
   Unearned service revenue                               21
   Common stock                                       10,000
   Sales                                              5,000
   Service revenue                                        8
   Cost of goods sold                    1,500
   Salaries expense                      1,400
   Depreciation expense                    100
   Bad debt expense                         40
   Other operating expenses              1,206

                                        16,269        16,269
```

7. **Preparing financial statements:**   Based on the adjusted trial balance, the following financial statements can be prepared:

a. **The income statement:**   The income statement reports the results of operations of a business entity by presenting the balances of temporary accounts as follows:

```
                     Sunny Corporation
                     Income Statement
             For the year ended December 31, 1991

Revenues:
     Sales revenue                                  $ 5,000
     Service revenue                                      8

          Total Revenues                            $ 5,008
Expenses:
     Cost of goods sold              $ 1,500
     Salaries expense                  1,400
     Depreciation expense                100
     Bad debt expense                     40
     Other operating expenses         1,206

          Total Expenses                              4,246

   Net Income                                       $   762
```

b. **The statement of retained earnings:** This is not a required statement. However, it is often prepared, as illustrated below, to show changes in the retained earnings account during the period, and to provide a linkage between the income statement and the balance sheet:

Sunny Corporation
Statement of Retained Earnings
For the year ended December 31, 1991

Retained earnings, beginning		$ –
Add net income for 1991		762
Less dividends for 1991		–
Retained earnings, ending		$ 762

c. **The balance sheet:** This statement presents the balances of permanent accounts, showing the financial position of a business entity at a point in time, usually the year end. On December 31, 1991, Sunny's balance sheet is:

Sunny Corporation
Balance Sheet
December 31, 1991

Assets			**Liabilities**		
Cash		$ 8,428	Notes payable		$ 500
Accounts receivable	$ 2,005		Salaries payable		600
Less: Allowance for doubtful accounts	40	1,965	Unearned service revenue		21
					$ 1,121
Inventory		500	**Owners' Equity**		
Prepaid insurance exp.		90			
Buildings	$ 1,000		Common shares no par,		
Less: Accumulated depreciation	100	900	2,000 shares issued	$ 10,000	
			Retained earnings	762	10,762
Total Assets		$11,883	Total Liabilities & Owners' Equity		$11,883

8. **Preparing closing entries:** The objective of closing entries is to: (1) close all revenue, expense, gain and loss accounts to a newly established temporary account (i.e., income summary), and (2) close the income summary to retained earnings. In our example, the closing entries are as follows:

General Journal		Page	j — 3	
Date	Accounts and Explanations	Posting	Amount	
1991		ref.	Debit	Credit
	Total carried forward from j-2.		22,874	22,874
Dec-31	Sales	401	5,000	
	Service revenue	402	8	
	Cost of goods sold	502		1,500
	Salaries expense	503		1,400
	Depreciation expense	504		100
	Bad debt expense	505		40
	Other operating expenses	506		1,206
	Income summary	510		762
	To close temporary accounts to income summary.			
	Income summary	510	762	
	Retained earnings	302		762
	To close income summary to retained earnings account.			
	Totals		28,644	28,644

After posting these closing entries to the respective ledger accounts, all temporary accounts have a zero balance and are ready to begin the next period's accounting cycle. In our example, no dividend has been declared for the period. If the company declared dividends, it might debit either directly to retained earnings, or indirectly to the dividends account. Note that **dividends** is a special temporary account, and its balance should be closed to retained earnings.

E. Applying Alternative Recording Methods to Deferred Items

Deferred items are simply prepayments of either revenues or expenses. There are two alternative methods (Standard Recording Method and Expedient Recording Method) to (1) record these prepayments, and (2) make year-end adjustments. Applied properly, these alternative recording methods should produce the same result as in the following illustration:

(1) Deferred revenues: Assume that, on November 1, $3,000 was **collected** from a tenant for 5 months of rent:

a. The amount was initially recorded as a revenue (Expedient Recording Method):

November 1 - Initial recording:

Cash	3,000	
Rent revenue		3,000

December 31 - Year-end adjusting:

Rent revenue	1,800	
Unearned rent (3,000 x 3/5)		1,800

b.   The amount was initially recorded as a liability (Standard Recording Method):

November 1 - Initial recording:

Cash	3,000	
Unearned rent		3,000

December 31 - Year-end adjusting:

Unearned rent	1,200	
Rent revenue (3,000 x 2/5)		1,200

(2)   Deferred expenses: Assume that, on November 1, $3,000 was paid for 5 months of rent:

a.   The amount paid was initially recorded as an expense (Expedient Recording Method):

November 1 - Initial recording:

Rent expense	3,000	
Cash		3,000

December 31 - Year-end adjusting:

Prepaid rent (3,000 x 3/5)	1,800	
Rent expense		1,800

b.   The amount paid was initially recorded as an asset: (Standard Recording Method)

November 1 - Initial recording:

Prepaid rent	3,000	
Cash		3,000

December 31 - Year-end adjusting:

Rent expense	1,200	
Prepaid rent (3,000 x 2/5)		1,200

F. **Worksheet**

At the end of an accounting period, a worksheet is usually prepared to facilitate the preparation of adjusting entries, financial statements, and closing entries. It should be noted that the worksheet is an optional step and is not part of the basic accounting records. A worksheet may be prepared following this procedure:

1.   Set up a worksheet with 6 sets of debit and credit columns, known as 12-column worksheet, and enter the unadjusted trial balance into the first two columns.

2.   Enter the adjusting entries into the next two columns.

3.   Enter the extended account balances into the next two columns to obtain an adjusted trial balance. Make sure the total debit equals the total credit.

4.   Enter the account balances of temporary accounts (other than dividends) into the income statement columns and determine net income for the period.

5.   Enter the beginning balance of retained earnings, current net income as determined in 4 above, and dividends, if any, into the retained earnings columns to determine the ending balance of the retained earnings account.

6.   Enter (a) the account balances of all permanent accounts as presented in the adjusted trial balance except retained earnings, and (b) the ending balance of retained earnings as determined in 5 above into the appropriate balance sheet columns. Make sure again the debit total equals the credit total.

Using our example, a worksheet is presented on the following page:

Worksheet for Sunny Corporation for the year ended December 31, 1991

Accounts	Unadjusted Trial Balance		Adjusting Entries		Adjusted Trial Balance		Income Statement		Retained Earnings		Balance Sheet	
	Debit	Credit	Debit	Credit	Debit	Credit	Debit	Credit	Debit	Credit	Debit	Credit
Cash	8,428				8,428						8,428	
Accts. receivable	2,000		(c) 5		2,005						2,005	
Allowance for doubtful accounts		–		(f) 40		40						40
Inventory	–		(g) 500		500						500	
Prepaid insurance	96			(b) 6	90						90	
Buildings	1,000				1,000						1,000	
Acc. depreciation	–			(e) 100		100						100
Notes payable		500				500						500
Salaries payable				(d) 600		600						600
Unearned service revenue		24	(a) 3			21						21
Common stock		10,000				10,000						10,000
Retained earnings		–				–				–		
Sales revenue		5,000				5,000		5,000				
Service revenue				(a) 3		8		8				
				(c) 5								
				(g) 2,000		–						
Purchases	2,000											
Cost of goods sold	–		(g) 1,500		1,500		1,500					
Salaries expense	800		(d) 600		1,400		1,400					
Depreciation exp.	–		(e) 100		100		100					
Bad debt expense	–		(f) 40		40		40					
Other operating expenses	1,200		(b) 6		1,206		1,206					
Totals	15,524	15,524	2,754	2,754	16,269	16,269						
Total revenues and expenses							4,246	5,008				
Net income to retained earnings							762			762		
							5,008	5,008				
Dividends									–			
Retained earnings (ending) to balance sheet										762		762
Totals											12,023	12,023

With this worksheet completed, the remaining accounting process is modified as:

1. Preparing the financial statements.
2. Preparing adjusting entries.
3. Journalizing and posting closing entries.

G. Reversing Entries

Some accountants choose to reverse certain adjusting entries made at the end of a period in order to simplify journal entries which occur in the next accounting period. If recorded, the entries are dated the first day of the next period. Reversing entries are appropriate for (1) deferred items initially recorded as revenues or expenses and (2) any accrued revenues and expenses. To illustrate:

1. **Reversing Deferred Items:** If, on October 1, 1991, $1,200 was collected for a one-year service contract, and the service revenue account was used to initially record the transaction:

   Initial recording - October 1, 1991:

Cash	1,200	
Service revenue		1,200

   Adjusting entry - December 31, 1991:

Service revenue ($1,200 x 9/12)	900	
Unearned revenue		900

   Reversing entry - January 1, 1992:

Unearned revenue	900	
Service revenue		900

   Subsequent entry - September 30, 1992:

   None.

   With this reversing entry, the time and effort spent to keep track of the amount of revenue earned during the specific period can be saved.

2. **Reversing Accrued Items:** Suppose a company pays wages every two weeks, and the last payroll of $1,000 of 1991 is to be paid next January together with the first payroll of 1992 which will be $1,800. The company will pay the total wages of $2,800 on January 6, 1992.

   Adjusting entry - December 31, 1991:

Wage expense	1,000	
Accrued wages payable		1,000

   Reversing entry - January 1, 1992:

Accrued wages payable	1,000	
Wage expense		1,000

Subsequent entry - January 6, 1992:

Wage expense	2,800	
Cash		2,800

When recording the payment, reversing entries save the time and effort required to identify separately the amounts of wage expenses incurred in two different accounting periods.

H.   Control Accounts, Subsidiary Ledgers, and Special Journals

To simplify record-keeping for accounts that involve a large amount of detail, (such as accounts receivable and accounts payable), selected general ledger accounts are designated as control accounts to which only summary information is posted. The details related to each control account is maintained in a separate subsidiary ledger (one for each control account). For example, a subsidiary accounts receivable ledger comprises individual receivable accounts for all the company's credit customers.

Special journals are frequently designed to simplify the journalizing and posting of certain types of transactions that occur repeatedly. Those commonly used special journals are (a) the sales journal, (b) the purchases journal, (c) the cash receipts journal, and (d) the cash payments journal.

KEY CONCEPTS

Account   A formal record showing the consequence of transactions and other economic events to a specific element of the financial statements. Each statement element comprises a series of accounts as its building blocks.

Accounting cycle   A series of sequential steps to process financial information for periodic reporting. The necessary steps include journalizing transactions and other events, posting journal entries to ledger accounts, preparing and posting adjusting entries, preparing financial statements and finally closing temporary accounts.

Accrued items   Revenues already earned, but for which cash has not been collected, or expenses already incurred, but for which cash has not been paid.

Adjusting entries   Entries prepared at the period end to update the permanent and the temporary accounts following the accrual concept of accounting.

Credit   To enter an amount to the right hand side of an account. A credit either increases a liability, owners' equity, revenue, or gain account, or decreases an asset, expense or loss account.

Debit   To enter an amount to the left hand side of an account. A debit either increases an asset, expense or loss account, or decreases a liability, owners' equity, revenue or gain account.

Deferred items   Revenues not yet earned, but for which cash has been received, or expenses not yet incurred, but for which cash has been paid.

Double-entry system   An established set of rules for recording transactions and other economic events in accounts, according to which, at least two accounts are affected with totals of debits and credits being equal. This system assures the equality of the basic accounting equation, i.e., Assets = Liabilities + Owners' Equity.

Events (Economic Events)   Happenings affecting the firm's resources or obligations. Events include transactions and other economic events. Other economic events not involving the firm are external, while other economic events not involving outside parties are internal.

Expedient Recording Method   Recording routine transactions for cash flows which expedites the subsequent recording of adjusting entries.

Reversing entries   Entries prepared at the first day of a period to reverse certain adjusting entries recorded at the end of the prior period. Adjusting entries appropriate for reversing entries are (a) deferred items initially recorded as revenues or expenses, and (b) accrued items.

Standard Recording Method   Recording routine transactions for cash flows which recognizes the balance sheet accounts involved.

Transactions   Transfers or exchanges of something with value between two or more independent entities.

REVIEW QUESTIONS AND EXERCISES

TRUE-FALSE

Indicate whether each of the following statements is true or false by circling the correct response.

T   F   1.   The underlying foundation of the balance sheet may be conceptualized by the basic accounting equation, Assets = Liabilities - Owners' Equity.

T   F   2.   Increase in assets and decrease in liabilities are recorded with debits to the appropriate accounts.

T   F   3.   Increase in owners' equity and decrease in revenues are recorded with credits to the appropriate accounts.

T   F   4.   Accounting transactions, if measurable, are generally recorded when they occur.

T   F   5.   Under the double entry system, the recording of any transaction or other economic event always involves two or more accounts with totals of debits and credits being equal.

T   F   6.   The general journal consists of classified accounts and the effects of a transaction or other economic event are directly entered into the respective accounts.

T   F   7.   The ledger is a chronological listing, in debit and credit terms, of the relevant transactions and other economic events affecting the firm.

T   F   8.   The posting process transfers the information contained in journal entries to appropriate ledger accounts.

T   F   9.   An accrual arises when a cash flow takes place prior to the recognition of related revenues or expenses.

T   F   10. Rent collected in advance is an example of accrued item.

T   F   11. Year-end adjusting entries always involve both the permanent (real) and the temporary (nominal) accounts.

T   F   12. If all closing entries are properly prepared and posted, all temporary accounts will have a zero balance.

T   F   13. Preparation of a worksheet is a required step in the accounting cycle.

T   F   14. Reversing entries are prepared in the middle of the accounting cycle to correct recording errors.

EXERCISE 1

Indicate by letter the way in which each of the following is recorded:

____ 1. Indicates an increase in owners' equity.

____ 2. Indicates a decrease in assets.

____ 3. Indicates a decrease in liabilities.

____ 4. Indicates an increase in revenue.

____ 5. Indicates an increase in expense.

D = Debit
C = Credit

EXERCISE 2

Prepare December 31, 1991, **adjusting entries** for the L. C. Bagel Company for each of the following independent items:

a. Bagel Co. paid a 3-year rent expense for $1,200 on January 1, 1991. The payment was initially recorded in the rent expense account.

b. Bagel Co. purchased a 3-year fire insurance policy on July 1, 1990 for $1,200. The payment was initially recorded in the prepaid insurance expense account.

c. Bagel Co. collected $500 from a customer for a 2-year service contract starting July 1, 1991. The amount collected was initially recorded as a service revenue.

d. Bagel Co. collected $600 from a tenant for a 2-year rent starting July 1, 1990. The amount collected was initially recorded as an unearned rent revenue.

e. Bagel Co. borrowed $10,000 from its bank on April 1, 1991. The original entry included a credit to loan payable for $10,000. The annual interest rate is 12%.

f. An inventory of office supplies on hand reveals a value of $800. The ledger reflects a balance in the office supplies inventory account of $2,450.

g. Bagel reported credit sales for 1991 of $50,000, 2% of which was estimated as uncollectible.

EXERCISE 3

For each of the above entries (a-g), indicate the effect on the elements of the 1991 financial statements **if the adjusting entry is inadvertently omitted.** Indicate your response by entering **O** (overstated), **U** (understated), or **N** (no effect) in the blanks provided:

	Assets	Liabilities	Owners' Equity	Revenues	Expenses
a.					
b.					
c.					
d.					
e.					
f.					
g.					

MULTIPLE CHOICE

Enter the letter corresponding to the response which **best** completes each of the following statements or questions.

_____ 1. An accrued revenue can best be described as an amount:

    a. received, but not yet earned.
    b. earned, but not yet received.
    c. received and earned.
    d. neither received nor earned.

_____ 2. Which of the following is most likely an accrued expense?

    a. Cost of goods sold
    b. Dividends declared
    c. Wages and salaries
    d. Acquisition of a tract of land

_____ 3. Which of the following is most likely a prepaid expense?

    a. Cost of goods sold
    b. Dividends declared
    c. Acquisition of municipal bonds
    d. Fire insurance

_____ 4. Of the following cash outflows, the one most likely to require an adjusting entry is:

    a. paid accounts payable.
    b. purchased municipal bonds at a discount.
    c. acquired a tract of land.
    d. paid cash dividends.

_____ 5. Adjusting entries:

    a. involve both the real and the nominal accounts.
    b. involve real accounts only.
    c. involve nominal accounts only.
    d. may be characterized by any of the above.

_____ 6. The first-year transactions of a company included the acquisition of $4,000 in office supplies initially recorded as an asset (i.e., office supplies inventory). If supplies on hand at the end of the year amount to $1,500, the adjusting entry for office supplies will include:

    a. a credit to office supplies inventory of $2,500.
    b. a debit to office supplies expense of $1,500.
    c. both of the above.
    d. none of the above.

_____ 7. On April 1, 1991, a company purchased 10% Hydro bonds of $10,000 at face value. If the bond interest is payable annually on July 1, the company would report the following in its balance sheet on December 31, 1991:

    a. an accrued interest revenue of $500.
    b. a deferred interest revenue of $500.
    c. an accrued interest revenue of $750.
    d. a deferred interest revenue of $750.

_____ 8. On January 1, 1991, Kelso Company purchased a 3-year insurance policy for $3,000. If the payment was initially recorded as an asset and no adjusting entry was made on December 31, 1991:

    a. the prepaid insurance expense is overstated by $1,000.
    b. the insurance expense is overstated by $1,000.
    c. the accrued expense is overstated by $2,000.
    d. the total asset is not affected.

_____ 9. The closing process can be described as a means of:

    a. updating account balances prior to the preparation of financial statements.
    b. creating zero balances in nominal accounts.
    c. transferring revenue and expense data to retained earnings.
    d. both b and c.

_____ 10. A year-end adjusting entry should **never** consist of:

    a. an asset account and a liability account.
    b. an asset account and an owners' equity account.
    c. a revenue account and an expense account.
    d. all of the above.

_____ 11. A year-end adjusting entry is **not** required for which of the following?

    a. Cost of goods sold under the perpetual inventory system
    b. Cost of goods sold under the periodic inventory system
    c. All of the above
    d. None of the above

_____ 12. Which of the following adjusting entries creates an increase in **assets**?

    a. Accruing unrecorded interest expense
    b. Accruing unrecorded interest revenue
    c. Recording depreciation expense
    d. Recording the earned portion of rent collected in advance

_____ 13. When a worksheet is prepared, the amount of a certain item appears in both the retained earnings and the balance sheet columns. This item is most likely to be:

    a. beginning retained earnings.
    b. ending retained earnings.
    c. net income for the period.
    d. dividends declared during the period.

_____ 14. A reversing entry is appropriate for:

    a. all types of adjusting entries.
    b. all deferred and accrued items.
    c. all accruals and those deferred items initially recorded as assets or liabilities.
    d. all accruals and those deferred items initially recorded as revenues or expenses.

SOLUTIONS TO REVIEW QUESTIONS AND EXERCISES

TRUE-FALSE

1.	F	5.	T	9.	F	13.	F
2.	T	6.	F	10.	F	14.	F
3.	F	7.	F	11.	T		
4.	T	8.	T	12.	T		

EXERCISE 1

1.	C	4.	C
2.	C	5.	D
3.	D		

EXERCISE 2

a.	Prepaid rent	800	
	Rent expense		800

$1,200 x 2/3 = $800.

b.	Insurance expense	400	
	Prepaid insurance		400

$1,200 x 1/3 = $400.

c.	Service revenue	375	
	Unearned service revenue		375

$500 x 3/4 = $375.

d.	Unearned rent revenue	300	
	Rent revenue		300

$600 x 1/2 = $300.

e.	Interest expense	900	
	Accrued interest payable		900

$10,000 x 12% x 9/12 = $900.

f.	Office supplies expense	1,650	
	Office supplies inventory		1,650

$2,450 - $800 = $1,650.

g.	Bad debt expense	1,000	
	Allowance for doubtful accounts		1,000

$50,000 x 2% = $1,000.

EXERCISE 3

	Assets	Liabilities	Owners' Equity	Revenues	Expenses
a.	U	N	U	N	O
b.	O	N	O	N	O
c.	N	U	O	O	U
d.	N	O	U	U	N
e.	N	U	O	N	U
f.	O	N	O	N	U
g.	O	N	O	N	U

MULTIPLE CHOICE

1.	b	5.	a	9.	d	13.	b
2.	c	6.	a	10.	d	14.	d
3.	d	7.	a	11.	a		
4.	b	8.	a	12.	b		

CHAPTER 4

Review: The Income Statement and Statement of Retained Earnings

CHAPTER OBJECTIVES

This chapter is designed to enable students to:

A.   Discuss the nature of accounting income, including the defining of accounting income and relate accounting income to other definitions of income.

B.   Understand the basic role of the income statement and the statement of retained earnings.

C.   Define the basic elements of the income statement.

D.   Describe and illustrate the single- and multiple-step forms of the income statement.

E.   Illustrate special areas of reporting and disclosures on the income statement governed by accounting pronouncements, including extraordinary items, unusal or infrequent items, discountinued operations, changes in accoutning estimates and accounting principles, and prior period adjustments.

F.   Explain the composition and purpose of the statement of retained earnings.

G.   Illustrate the computation and presentation of earnings per share on the income statement.

CHAPTER OVERVIEW

A.   Income Concepts

Business income can be measured in various ways based on the underlying income concepts. There are two widely accepted concepts of income (also referred to as approaches to income measurement) representing two distinct points of view:

1.   **Economic concept of income.**   To some economists, income represents a change in wealth. Income for a period is the amount that an entity could distribute to its owners during the period and still leave the entity's wealth intact at the end of the

period as it was at the beginning. Since a business entity's wealth is represented by its net assets, which are, in turn, considered as capital, this economic concept of income is known as the **capital maintenance** or **net asset approach**. Under this approach, economic income is measured as follows:

```
Net assets, December 31, 1991                  $50,000
Less: Owners' investments during 1991          (10,000)
Add:  Dividends distributed during 1991          8,000
                                               --------
Adjusted net assets, December 31, 1991         $48,000
Less: Net assets, January 1, 1991              (45,000)
                                               --------
Net income for 1991                            $ 3,000
                                               ========
```

The capital maintenance approach gives rise to the controversy over the valuation methods of net assets, e.g., historical cost, replacement cost, net present value, etc., with or without adjustments for inflation. It also fails to report detailed information about the components of income, which are considered useful in predicting future cash flows.

2. **Accounting concept of income.**   The income concept generally adopted by accountants is known as accounting income. Accounting income is measured continuously throughout the reporting period as revenue, expense, gain or loss transactions occur. Under this approach, commonly called the **transaction approach**, net income for a period is calculated using the following equation:

Net income = Revenues - Expenses + Gains - Losses

The transaction approach has been adopted as a generally accepted accounting standard on the grounds that this approach emphasizes arms' length transactions which are objectively verifiable and thus reliable. Under this approach, furthermore, the components of income are to be reported in detail on the income statement to provide useful and essential information for, among other objectives, predicting future cash flows.

B. A complete set of financial statements must include (1) **an income statement**, (2) **a statement of financial position (balance sheet)**, and (3) **a statement of cash flows**. In addition, however, **a statement of retained earnings** is often included to provide full disclosure.

C. **Definitions of the Elements on the Income Statement (CICA Handbook, Sec. 1000)**

Revenues

Revenues are increases in economic resources, either by way of inflows or enhancements of assets or reductions of liabilities, resulting from the ordinary activities of an entity, normally from the sales of goods, the rendering of services or the use by others of entity resources yielding rent, interest, royalties, or dividends.

Expenses

Expenses are decreases in economic resources, either by way of outflows or reductions of assets or incurrences of liabilities, resulting from the ordinary revenue-earning activities of an entity.

Gains

Gains are increases in equity from peripheral or incidental transactions and events affecting an entity and from all other transactions, events, and circumstances affecting the entity except those that result from revenues or equity contributions.

Losses

Losses are decreases in equity from peripheral or incidental transactions and events affecting an entity and from all other transactions, events, and circumstances affecting the entity except those that result from expenses or distributions for equity.

D. Formats of the Income Statement

The components of income may be organized and presented on the income statement in either of the following two ways, usually referred to as the formats of income statement:

1. **Single step.**   In a single-step income statement, (a) all the revenues and gains are added together; (b) all the expenses and losses are added together; and (c) net income is derived by subtracting the total expenses and losses from the total revenues and gains in a single step:

```
                             ABC COMPANY
                           Income Statement
                   For the year ended Dec. 31, 1991

      Revenues and Gains:

      Sales revenues                                        $100,000
      Gain on sale of land¹                                    5,000
                                                            _____

         Total revenues and gains                           $105,000

      Expenses and Losses:

      Cost of goods sold                    $ 40,000
      Operating expenses                      30,000
      Fire loss¹                               2,000
      Income tax expenses                      8,000
                                            _____

         Total expenses and losses                            80,000

      Net income                                            $ 25,000
```

¹--Not considered "Extraordinary" items as per CICA Handbok, Sec. 3480.

2.   Multiple step.   The multiple-step format distinguishes between the major and minor operating activities and provides multiple classifications of income as follows:

```
                        ABC COMPANY
                      Income Statement
                For the year ended Dec. 31, 1991

    Sales revenue                              $100,000
    Less: Cost of goods sold                    (40,000)

    Gross margin                               $ 60,000
    Less: Operating expenses                    (30,000)

    Income from (primary) operations           $ 30,000
    Other revenues and gains:
       Gain on sale of land¹                       5,000

    Other expenses and losses:
      Fire loss¹                                   (2,000)

    Income before taxes                        $ 33,000
    Less: Income tax expenses                    (8,000)

    Net income                                 $ 25,000
```

[1]--Not considered "extraordinary" items as per CICA Handbook, Sec. 3480.

Note that the **other** revenues, expenses, gains and/or losses result from minor and incidental operating and non-operating activities such as interest revenues, interest expenses, dividends revenues, and gains or losses from investment, disposal of equipment, fire loss, etc.

It is apparent that by separating results achieved through various activities, the multiple-step format provides more information to users than the single-step format. Nevertheless, both of these formats are found in current practice.

3. Special Items and Income Reporting

In addition, there are three types of special items, namely, (1) gains or losses from discontinued operations, (2) extraordinary gains or losses, and (3) cumulative effects of accounting principle changes, each of which has to be presented separately and thus adds one more step to the income statement, regardless of the statement format. For example:

```
                        ABC COMPANY
              Income Statement (Single-step)
              For the year ended Dec. 31, 1991

Revenues and Gains:

Sales revenues . . . . . . . . . . . . . . . . .   $100,000
Gain on sale of land . . . . . . . . . . . . . .      5,000
                                                   _____
Total revenues and gains . . . . . . . . . . . .   $105,000

Expenses and Losses:

Cost of goods sold . . . . . . . .   $ 40,000
Operating expenses . . . . . . . .     30,000
Fire loss . . . . . . . . . . . .       2,000
Income tax expenses . . . . . . .       8,000
                                     _____
Total expenses and losses . . . . . . . . . . .      80,000
                                                   _____
Income from continuing operations . . . . . . .   $ 25,000
Less: Loss from discontinued operations,
        net of tax . . . . . . . . . . . . . . .    (15,000)
                                                   _____
Income before extraordinary items . . . . . . .   $ 10,000
Add:  Extraordinary gains, net of tax . . . . .      24,000
                                                   _____
Net Income . . . . . . . . . . . . . . . . . .     $34,000
                                                   _____
```

E. Special Areas of Reporting

1. Discontinued Operations (Disposal of a Segment of a Business)

The CICA Handbook, Sec. 3475 provides reporting guidelines for discontinuance of a **segment** of a business. A segment is a subsidiary, division, department, or other part of the entity representing a separate major line of business or class of customer. If a segment has been, or is committed to be sold, abandoned, spun off, or otherwise disposed of during the period, any loss or gain on disposal, less the applicable income tax effect, should be reported separately as a component of income before extraordinary items.

To account for the discontinuance of a segment, the following two dates have to be identified:

1. Date of measurement, which is the date on which the entity **formally** commits itself to a plan to dispose of the specific segment. The plan must have all 6 criteria (which follow).

    (1) The major assets to be disposed.
    (2) The expected method of disposal.
    (3) The period expected for completion of the disposal.
    (4) Details of an active program to find a buyer if disposal is to be by sale.
    (5) The estimated results of operations of the segment from the measurement date to the expected disposal date.
    (6) The expected proceeds or salvage value.

2. Date of disposal, which is the date of the actual disposal of the segment's assets.

For the period of measurement, the following two items must be presented separately on the income statement under the heading **Discontinued Operations**:

1. Income (loss) from operations of a discontinued segment, i.e., the current income or loss of the segment up to the date of measurement, net of tax, and

2. Gain (loss) on disposal of discontinued segment:

    a. If the date of measurement is also the date of disposal, this is the actual gain (loss) on the sale of the segment's assets, net of tax.

    b. If the date of disposal is not identical with the date of measurement, but both dates are in the same accounting period, this is the total of the actual earnings of the segment after the date of measurement and the gain (loss) on the sale of the segment's assets.

    c. If the date of disposal is in a subsequent accounting period, it will include:

        (1) the actual earnings of the segment from the date of measurement to the end of current period,
        (2) the expected earnings of the segment for the subsequent period, and
        (3) the expected gain or loss on sale of the segment's assets.

    It is noted that whenever a **phase-out period** and the **expected** gains or losses are involved, the conservatism principle is called for. That is, for the year of measurement, losses should be provided for as estimated. If a gain is expected, it should be recognized only to the extent of the losses actually incurred since the date of measurement. Any remainder should be recognized when realized. The following set of general rules has been developed:

```
GENERAL RULES TO DETERMINE GAIN/LOSS ON DISPOSAL OF SEGMENT

Let:      a = current actual earnings after the measurement date.
          b = Expected earnings for the subsequent period plus
              Expected gain or loss on sale of assets.

          G/L = gains (losses) on disposal of segment.

If b =< 0,  G/L = a + b

If b > 0, and:

    If a > 0,  G/L = a

    If a =< 0, and:

          If a + b < 0,  G/L = a + b
          If a + b >= 0,   G/L = 0
```

When a segment is disposed of in a later period, the difference between the total gains (losses) on disposal **realized** since the date of measurement and the gains (losses) on disposal previously **recognized**, net of tax effect, should be presented on the income statement for that period as gains (losses) from discontinued operations.

Example:

Cole Corporation concluded an agreement on October 1, 1991 to dispose of its Clovis Division on April 1, 1992 with an expected loss of $20,000. The Division reports an operating income of $10,000 for the first three quarters of 1991, and an operating loss of $10,000 for the last quarter. During its phase-out period, an additional loss of $5,000 is estimated for the first three months of 1992. The applicable tax rate is 40%. Based on this information and assume that income from continuing operations for 1991, net of tax, is $25,000, a partial income statement of 1991 would be as follows:

Income from continuing operations	$25,000
Discontinued operations:	
Income from operations of Clovis Division prior to date of measurement, net of tax [$10,000 x (1 - 40%)]	6,000
Loss on disposal of Clovis Division, net of tax	(21,000)*
Total loss from discontinued operations	$15,000
Income before extraordinary items	$10,000

* Actual current loss	$(10,000)
Expected operating loss	(5,000)
Expected loss on sale of assets	(20,000)
Total losses, gross	$(35,000)
Less: Tax effect, 40%	14,000
Total loss, net of tax	$(21,000)

Further assume that, in 1992, the operating loss of the division and the loss on sale of its assets were $6,000 and $24,000, respectively, then the loss from discontinued operations reported in 1992 would be the **total realized loss less those loss reported in 1991**, net of tax, as shown below:

```
Loss realized (Oct. 1 1991 - Dec. 31, 1991)     $10,000
Loss realized (Jan. 1 1992 - Mar. 31, 1992)       6,000
Loss realized on disposal of assets              24,000

Total realized loss on disposal                 $40,000
Less: Loss recognized in 1991                   (35,000)

Loss recognized for 1992                           5,000
Less: tax effect, 40%                              2,000

Loss from disc. operations, 1992, net of tax    $ 3,000
```

2.   Extraordinary Items

For decades, there has been controversy over the **current operating approach** vs. the **all inclusive approach** to the determination of income. The advocates of the **current operating approach** place stress on the normal earning power of a business, and maintain that the income statement should report only the regularly recurring items related to business operations. Non-recurring items are incidental in nature and should thus be closed directly to the retained earnings account. The proponents of the **all inclusive approach**, on the other hand, are concerned with the possibility of income manipulation by allowing direct adjustments to retained earnings, and contend that any items affecting owners' equity, except contributions by or distributions to owners, should be part of current income and presented on the income statement.

The CICA Handbook, Sec. 3480 adopted a compromise approach and prescribed that, (1) net income for a period should reflect all items of profit and loss recognized during the period **except for** certain prior year adjustments, and (2) **extraordinary items** should be segregated from the results of ordinary operations. Following **Sec. 3480**, extraordinary items are results of events or transactions that meet **all** of the following criteria:

1.   They are not expected to occur frequently over several years.

2.   They do not typify the normal business activities of the entity.

3.   They do not depend primarily on decision or determinations by management or owners.

Certain gains or losses such as follows should **not** be reported as extraordinary items because they are either usual in nature or may be expected to recur:

1.   Write-down or write-off of receivables, inventories or intangible assets.

2.   Gains or losses from exchange or translation of foreign currencies.

3. Gains or losses from sale or abandonment or property, plant, or equipment used in the business.

4. Effects of strike, including those against competitors and major suppliers.

Items that meet only one of the two criteria should be reported as a separate component of income from continuing operations. It should be noted, however, that the environment in which the business operates has to be considered in determining whether an underlying event or transaction is extraordinary. In any event, material gains or losses from **early extinguishment of long-term debts** must be classified as extraordinary **(CICA Handbook, Sec 3480)** in order to alert the users of financial statements to the unusual nature of the transaction. Any extraordinary items, if material, should be shown separately in the income statement, net of tax effect, as follows:

```
Income before extraordinary items          $10,000
Extraordinary gains (net of tax)            24,000

Net income                                 $34,000
```

3. **Accounting Changes.**   The CICA Handbook, Sec. 1506 defines three types of accounting changes, all of which will be discussed in Chapter 24 in detail. The present purpose is to present a brief summary of these changes with an emphasis on changes in accounting principle:

1. **Change in estimate.**   On the accrual basis, estimates are used extensively in the determination of income, e.g., estimated useful life and salvage value of a depreciable asset, estimated allowance rate of uncollectible accounts receivable, estimated product warranty expenses, etc. As a sound practice, estimates have to be periodically reviewed and revised in light of recent experiences and new information. Prior accounting results are not to be disturbed by a change in estimate. Instead, the new estimate should be applied to the current and subsequent periods (Prospectively).

2. **Change in reporting entity.**   This type of change occurs when there is a business combination, e.g., two or more companies are combined into a single reporting entity. The **CICA, Sec. 1506** requires a restatement of prior accounting results to reflect such a change.

3. **Change in accounting principle.**   This is a change from one GAAP to another GAAP. The **CICA, Sec. 1506** requires that the cumulative effect of the change, net of tax, be reported in the period of change, and presented separately on the statement of retained earnings (with fully descriptive footnotes).

    To illustrate, assume that, on January 1, 1991, Jason Company changed its depreciation method from the straight-line method to the sum-of-the-years-digits method for equipment, acquired on January 1, 1988 with a cost of $9,000, salvage value of zero and an estimated life of 5 years. The applicable tax rate was 40%,

a.   To determine the cumulative effect of the change:

```
Accumulated depreciation under the
sum-of-the-years-digits method:
($9,000 / 15) x (5 + 4 + 3)                      $ 7,200

Accumulated depreciation under the
straight-line method: ($9,000 x 3/5)             (5,400)

Cumulative effect before tax                     $ 1,800
Less: Income tax effect (40%)                      (720)

Cumulative effect, net of tax                    $ 1,080
```

b.   Statement of retained earnings presentation: (See Section F)

4.   Intraperiod Income Tax Allocation

Income tax expense is reported on the income statement in a manner to relate the tax effects to the causes of tax. Following **CICA Handbook,Sec 3470**, the total income tax for the current accounting period should be allocated to various components on the current income statement, including income from continuing operations and of special items as discussed above. The tax effect of prior year adjustments, on the other hand, should be separately allocated to the respective adjustments and presented on the statement of retained earnings. This process, referred to as **intraperiod income tax allocation,** is summarized as follows:

Change in depreciation method in Canada is reflected in the Statement of Retained Earnings.

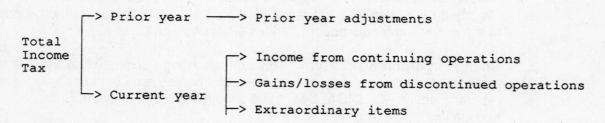

Intraperiod Income Tax Allocation

F.   The Statement of Retained Earnings

The main purpose of this statement is to reconcile the balance of the retained earnings account from the beginning to the end of the period, and thus to provide a connecting link between the income statement and the balance sheet. The typical format of the statement is shown on the following page:

```
                      ABC COMPANY
          The Statement of Retained Earnings
            For the year ended Dec. 31, 1991

Retained earnings, beginning balance              $10,000
Prior year adjustment, net of tax                  (1,080)

Retained earnings, as restated                    $ 8,920
Add: Net income for the year                       33,000
Less: Dividends declared during the year          (15,000)

Retained earnings, ending balance                 $26,920
```

Prior period adjustments must be reported on the statement of retained earnings. Prior period adjustments must possess the characteristics set out in paragraphs 3600.02-03 of the *CICA Handbook*; they do not flow through the income statement. Prior period adjustments are rare and essentially limited to:

(1) Nonrecurring adjustments or settlements or income taxes;

(2) Settlements of claims resulting from litigation.

(3) Correction of an error in the financial statement of a prior period, and

(4) Adjustments that result from realization of income tax benefits of preacquisition operating loss carryforwards of purchased subsidiaries.

Assume that Campbell Company discovered that the ending inventory of the previous year was overstated by $7,500, which caused net income for that year, and thus the retained earnings, to be overstated. Further assume that the applicable tax rate was 40%. The appropriate journal entries to correct the error would be:

```
Prior year adjustment -Inventory error          4,500
     Inventory [$7,500 x (1 - 40%)]                        4,500
To restate beginning inventory, net of tax.

Retained earnings                               4,500
     Prior year adjustment-Inventory error                 4,500
To close prior year adjustment.
```

G. Earnings Per Share (EPS)

Earnings per share is an integral part of the income statement. It is a ratio relating the income of a firm to the firm's outstanding common stock. It is used extensively by financial analysts and investors to evaluate the relative profitability of various business entities. The basic equation of computing earnings per share is:

EPS = Earnings / Number of common shares

Where (1) earnings is the reported income less dividends to preferred stockholders, and (2) number of common shares is the weighted-average number of common shares outstanding during the period.

Following **The CICA Handbook, Sec. 3500**, earnings per share disclosure should include the following, if applicable:

Income before extraordinary items and discontinued operations per share,
Net income for the period per share.

To illustrate, assume the weighted-average number of common shares outstanding is 10,000. Then, based on the example given in **D**, the earnings per share would be presented on the income statement or notes to income statements as follows:

Although not required by the CICA Handbook, many corporations would present EPS as:

```
Income from continuing operations per share           $2.50
Loss from discontinued operations per share          (1.50)
Extraordinary gain                                     2.40

Net income per share                                  $3.40
```

KEY CONCEPTS

All inclusive approach   A concept of income under which any transactions or events affecting owners' equity, other than investments from, and distributions to owners during the period, are included in the measurement of income.

Current operating approach   A concept of income under which only normal, ordinary, recurring operating activities would be included in the measurement of income.

Earnings per share   An integral part of the income statement (or the notes to financial statements cross-referenced disclosing various components of earnings on a per common share basis.

Extraordinary items   Transactions or events having effects on the entity's net assets which are both unusual in nature and infrequent in occurrence.

Intraperiod income tax allocation   The procedure whereby the total tax for a period is separately associated with specific items on the income statement and the statement of retained earnings.

Prior year adjustments   Adjustments directly increase or decrease retained earnings without passing through the income statement. These include the tax effect of a certain business combination and corrections of prior period errors.

Income statement   A required financial report which measures the results of business operations for a given period of time.

Statement of retained earnings   A statement showing the changes in the retained earnings account during a given period, including prior year adjustments, current income, and currently declared dividends.

REVIEW QUESTIONS AND EXERCISES

TRUE-FALSE

Indicate whether each of the following statements is true or false by circling the correct response.

T   F   1.   Economic income is the algebraic sum of revenues, gains, expenses, and losses, each recognized on the accrual basis.

T   F   2.   Gains and losses differ from revenues and expenses in that they arise from the entity's peripheral or incidental transactions and events, whereas revenues and expenses are from the entity's ongoing major operations.

T   F   3.   The transaction approach to the determination of income provides information about the components of income which is useful to external decision makers.

T   F   4.   Under the transaction approach, the distribution of dividends is irrelevant to the determination of income.

T   F   5.   In view of environmental factors, a particular gain or loss might be classified as extraordinary by one company but not by another.

T   F   6.   Extraordinary items are defined in general as gains and/or losses which are **either** unusual in nature **or** infrequent in occurrence.

T   F   7.   A segment of a business is defined as a subsidiary, division, department, or other part of the entity representing a separate major line of business or class of customer.

T   F   8.   When a segment is to be discontinued, the measurement date is the date when the segment's assets are disposed of.

T   F   9.   The cumulative effect of a change in depreciation methods must be adjusted directly to the retained earnings account.

T   F   10. Prior period adjustments as well as gains or losses from discontinued operations must be classified as extraordinary items.

T   F   11. Gains or losses not qualified as extraordinary items must be excluded from the income statement.

T   F   12. Intraperiod tax allocation requires that income tax for the current period be allocated among components of the current income statement and the statement of retained earnings so that the income tax effect is reported with the result of the transaction that caused the tax.

T   F   13.   Earnings per share is computed for both common stock and preferred stock.

T   F   14.   A statement of retained earnings details the changes in the balance of retained earnings from the beginning to the end of the accounting period.

EXERCISE 1

For each of the transactions and events below, indicate in the space provided the appropriate income statement classification:

_____   1.   Interest accrued on investment in bonds.

_____   2.   Sales of merchandise on credit.

_____   3.   Cost of goods sold.

_____   4.   Loss on the sale of investments.

_____   5.   Direct casualty loss (unusual, infrequent and not dependent on management)

_____   6.   Prepaid rental expense.

_____   7.   Cash dividends declared.

_____   8.   Unpaid wages earned by employees.

_____   9.   Unusual fire loss (not rare for the company).

_____   10.   Income tax effect of error in a prior period.

A.   Revenue

B.   Expense

C.   Gain or loss (ordinary)

D.   Gain or loss (unusual or infrequent)

E.   Extraordinary gain or loss

F.   Not reported on the income statement

EXERCISE 2

Heally Company decides to sell its Investment Service Division in 1991. The following data are available:

1991:

Operating loss of the division from beginning to measurement date, $200,000.
Operating loss of the division from measurement date to end of 1991, $50,000.
Expected operating loss of the division for 1992, $35,000.
Expected gain on sale of the division's assets in 1992, $100,000.
Applicable tax rate, 40%.

1992:

Realized earnings of the division for 1992, $30,000.
Realized loss on sale of the division's assets in 1992, $80,000.

Required:

1. Determine gain or loss from discontinued operations for 1991.

2. Determine gain or loss from discontinued operations for 1992.

EXERCISE 3

Presented below is information about the Millbrook Company for 1991. Prepare the income statement in (1) single-step format, and (2) multiple-step format.

Sales revenue	$25,000
Finished goods inventory:	
January 1, 1991	9,000
December 31, 1991	13,000
Cost of goods manufactured	14,000
Operating expenses:	
Selling expenses	5,000
General and administrative expenses	4,000
Nonoperating revenues and gains:	
Interest revenue	3,000
Dividends revenue	2,000
Nonoperating expenses and losses:	
Interest expense	1,000
Extraordinary items:	
Earthquake loss	5,000
Common shares outstanding (weighted average):	2,000 shares
Income tax rate:	40%

MULTIPLE CHOICE

Enter the letter corresponding to the response which **best** completes each of the following statements or questions.

_____ 1. An item not typically reported in the **Income from (primary) Operations** section of an income statement is:

    a. cost of goods sold.
    b. gain from discontinued operations.
    c. sales returns and allowance.
    d. advertising expenses.

_____ 2. A loss resulting from damage to a productive facility would be reported **separately, net of tax**, on the income statement if the event causing the damage is:

    a. infrequent but not unusual.
    b. unusual but not infrequent.
    c. both unusual and infrequent.
    d. either unusual or infrequent.

_____ 3. In 1991, Ashlander Company's plant was destroyed by an unusual and infrequent earthquake. The casualty loss was $25,000. Assume the applicable tax rate was 40%, the amount of extraordinary loss, net of tax, reported in the 1991 income statement should be:

    a. $15,000.
    b. $10,000.
    c. $25,000.
    d. $0.

_____ 4. In 1991, McKinley Corporation reported a gain from discontinued operations of $40,000, net of tax. This item should be **separately** presented on the Income Statement in:

    a. single-step format only.
    b. multiple-step format only.
    c. both single-step and multiple-step format.
    d. none of the above.

_____ 5. Which of the following would not have an effect on income under the all inclusive approach:

    a. dividends revenues.
    b. cumulative effect from accounting principle changes.
    c. extraordinary gains or losses.
    d. dividends declared.

_____ 6. In the application of intraperiod income tax allocation, income tax is separately apportioned to each of the following *except*:

    a. the effect of the correction of a prior year's error.
    b. gain or loss due to an unusual and infrequent event.
    c. cumulative effect of accounting principle changes.
    d. gross margin on sales.

_____ 7. Net income for 1991 is $120,000, and the reported extraordinary gain (net of tax) is $60,000. Assuming a tax rate of 40%, the amount reported as **income tax expense**, as a component of income before extraordinary items is:

    a. $40,000.
    b. $60,000.
    c. $80,000.
    d. $100,000.

_____ 8. Fun Corporation changed from the sum-of-the-years-digit method to the straight-line method of depreciation for a building acquired for $120,000 with an estimated residual value of $10,000 and useful life of 10 years. Assume the old method has been applied for 5 years, and the applicable tax rate is 40%, the cumulative effect of the change, net of tax, should be:

    a. $40,000.
    b. $25,000.
    c. $15,000.
    d. $14,500.

_____ 9. If the disposal of a segment involves a phase-out period, and there is an **expected** gain on the disposal of the segment,

    a. the expected gain should be totally excluded from the current income statement.
    b. the expected gain should be totally included in the current income statement.
    c. the expected gain should be used to offset current realized loss since the measurement date, and the remainder, if any, recognized when realized.
    d. none of the above.

_____ 10. The income concept adopted by accountants is known as the:

    a. current operating approach.
    b. net asset approach.
    c. capital maintenance approach.
    d. transaction approach.

_____ 11. Which of the following transactions or events is most likely to be classified as an extraordinary item:

   a. A branch of the company was disposed of during the year.
   b. A branch in a foreign country was expropriated during the year.
   c. A foreign subsidiary was acquired during the year.
   d. A customer declared bankruptcy during the year.

_____ 12. The following information is available for Burlingame Corporation at the end of 1991:

   Net income for 1991 $210,000
   Prior year adjustment, net of tax   10,000
   Common stock issued and outstanding   100,000 shares

   Earnings per share for 1991 would be:

   a. $3.10.
   b. $2.20.
   c. $2.10.
   d. none of the above.

_____ 13. Given the data for Burlingame Corporation in Question 12 above, and assume that the Corporation had preferred stock outstanding and declared preferred dividends during the year, earnings per share for 1991 would be:

   a. $3.10.
   b. $2.20.
   c. $2.10.
   d. none of the above.

_____ 14. The balance in the retained earnings account at the end of the current fiscal year is $69,000. For the year, dividends of $20,000 were declared and net income of $40,000 was reported. A prior year adjustment of $5,000 (net of tax) was made during the period to correct the overstated beginning inventory. The beginning balance in the retained earnings account was:

   a. $64,000.
   b. $54,000.
   c. $89,000.
   d. $39,000.

SOLUTIONS TO REVIEW QUESTIONS AND EXERCISES

TRUE-FALSE

1.	F	5.	T	9.	T	13.	F
2.	T	6.	F	10.	F	14.	T
3.	T	7.	T	11.	F		
4.	T	8.	F	12.	T		

EXERCISE 1

1.	A	4.	C	7.	F	10.	F
2.	A	5.	E	8.	B		
3.	B	6.	F	9.	D		

EXERCISE 2

1. Determine gain or loss from discontinued operations for 1991:

   Discontinued Operations:

Loss from operations of Investment Division, up to date of measurement, net of tax	$120,000
Loss from discontinued operations	$120,000

   Note that loss on disposal of the segment is zero because the expected gain (100,000 − $35,000 = $65,000), exceeds the actual loss from the measurement date to the end of current period ($50,000).

2. Determine gain or loss from discontinued operations for 1992.

   Discontinued Operations:

Loss on disposal of Investment Division, net of tax [($50,000 − $30,000 + $80,000) − 0] x 60%	$60,000
Loss from discontinued operations	$60,000

EXERCISE 3

1. Single-step Format:

```
                        Millbrook Company
                   Income statement (Single-step)
                  For Year Ended December 31, 1991
                            (in $000)

Revenues:
   Sales                                                    $25,000
   Interest                                                   3,000
   Dividends                                                  2,000

     Total Revenue                                          $30,000
Expenses:
   Cost of goods sold
      ($9,000 + $14,000 - $13,000)           $10,000
   Selling expenses                            5,000
   General and administrative expenses         4,000
   Interest expense                            1,000
   Income tax expense, ($30,000 - $20,000) x 40%  4,000

     Total Expense                                         (24,000)

Income before extraordinary item                           $ 6,000
Extraordinary item:
   Earthquake loss                           $ 5,000
   Less: Income tax saving, $5,000 x 40%      (2,000)       (3,000)

Net Income                                                 $ 3,000
```

Earnings per share (2,000 shares outstanding):

```
   Income before extraordinary item per share,
      $6,000 / 2,000 shares                                 $3.00
   Extraordinary loss per share, $3,000 / 2,000 shares     (1.50)
   Net income per share, $3,000 / 2,000 shares             $1.50
```

2. Multiple-step Format:

Millbrook Company
Income statement (Multiple-step)
For Year Ended December 31, 1991
(in $000)

Sales revenue			$25,000
Finished goods inventory, Jan. 1, 1991	$ 9,000		
Add: Cost of goods manufactured	14,000		
Less: Finished goods inventory, Dec. 31, 1991	(13,000)		
Cost of goods sold			(10,000)
Gross margin on sales			$15,000
Operating expenses:			
Selling expenses	$ 5,000		
General and administrative expenses	4,000		
Total operating expenses			(9,000)
Income from primary operations			$ 6,000
Other revenues and gains:			
Interest revenue	$3,000		
Dividends revenue	2,000	$5,000	
Other expenses and loss			
Interest expense		(1,000)	4,000
Income before tax and extraordinary item			$10,000
Income tax expense, $10,000 x 40%			(4,000)
Income before extraordinary item			$ 6,000
Extraordinary item:			
Earthquake loss	$ 5,000		
Less: Income tax saving, $5,000 x 40%	(2,000)		(3,000)
Net income			$ 3,000

Earnings per share (2,000 shares outstanding):

Income before extraordinary item per share,	
$6,000 / 2,000 shares	$3.00
Extraordinary loss per share, $3,000 / 2,000 shares	(1.50)
Net income per share, $3,000 / 2,000 shares	$1.50

MULTIPLE CHOICE

1.	b	5.	d	9.	c	13.	d
2.	c	6.	d	10.	d	14.	b
3.	a	7.	a	11.	b		
4.	c	8.	c	12.	c		

Computations:

3.   (a) $25,000 x (1 - 40%) = $15,000.

7.   (a)   ($120,000 - $60,000) x 40% / 60% = $40,000.

8.   (c)   Accumulated depreciation (SYD):

($120,000 - $10,000) x 40/55	$80,000
Less: Accumulated depreciation (SL):	
($120,000 - $10,000) x 5/10	(55,000)
Cumulative effect before tax	$25,000
Less: Income tax effect, 40%	(10,000)
Cumulative effect, net of tax	$15,000

14.   (b) $69,000 + $20,000 - $40,000 + $5,000 = $54,000.

CHAPTER 5

Review: The Balance Sheet and the Statement of Changes in Financial Position

CHAPTER OBJECTIVES

This chapter is designed to enable students to:

A.   Describe balance sheet formats and how each format reflects the basic accounting identity between assets and equities.

B.   Explain the different methods used to value assets, liabilities, and equities.

C.   Understand the importance of terminology, comparative statements, reporting subsequent events, and footnote disclosure in communicating accounting information and the financial status of a company.

D.   Understand the uses and limitations of the balance sheet.

E.   Describe two alternative formats for structuring a statement of changes in financial position.

F.   Know the major elements of the statement of changes in financial position.

G.   Explain the usefulness of the statement of changes in financial position.

CHAPTER OVERVIEW

PART I.   THE BALANCE SHEET FORMAT

A.   The balance sheet (also known as the statement of financial position) presents a list of assets, liabilities and owners' equity of a firm which shows its resources, claims to, and the residual interest in those resources as of a particular date. Prior to the 1920s, such a list had been the paramount financial report of a business. The balance sheet lost its preeminent position to the income statement during the half-century starting about 1920, due mainly to the growing concern with (1) the operating effectiveness of a firm, and (2) the correlation between past performance, as indicated in the reported income, and the future dividend payments. In recent decades, it has regained a measure of respectability as the external decision makers have redirected their interest to the financial position of a firm, while the accounting profession has devoted considerable efforts to improve the balance sheet and thus to make it more useful.

B.   Bases (methods) of valuation

Any asset or liability item presented on the balance sheet must have a monetary value, and the monetary value is determined by the selected valuation basis. Presented below are the major bases used by accountants:

1.   **Historical cost.**   This is the most commonly used valuation method based on the exchange price of the item at the time of the original transaction, reduced by any recorded depreciation, depletion, or amortization to date, as appropriate.

2.   **Market value.**   This is the current market (or fair) value of the item. Depending on whether the item is to be acquired or disposed of, it is subdivided into:

   a.   **Current cost.**   This is the amount of cash necessary to acquire the same item at the balance sheet date, generally referred to as the replacement cost or reproduction cost.

   b.   **Current exit value.**   This is the amount of cash that may be obtained at the balance sheet date from selling the item in an orderly, instead of forced, liquidation.

3.   **Net realizable value.**   This is the net amount of cash into which the item is expected to be converted in an ordinary operations of the firm (e.g., selling price of the item less estimated cost to complete and sell), also referred to as the expected exit value.

4.   **Present value** (or net present value).   This is the future value discounted to the balance sheet date.

The balance sheet primarily reports historical cost because it is available, objective, and verifiable. The market value, on the other hand, often can be known reliably only when the item is bought or sold in a completed transaction, whereas the net realizable value involves future events with even greater degree of uncertainty. Therefore, these values are used only under limited circumstances mainly for purposes of conservatism (e.g., cost or market rule), and supplementary disclosure (e.g., current cost accounting). The present value, however, is used extensively to determine the initial value of certain long-term items such as bonds, capital leases and pension plans at the time of the original transaction.

5.   **Assets**

   1.   **Current assets.**   Current assets are assets that can reasonably be expected to be realized in cash, or to be sold or consumed during the normal operating cycle of the business or within one year from the balance sheet date, whichever is longer. The major categories of current assets are

presented on the balance sheet in the order of their decreasing liquidity as follows:

a. Cash.
b. Temporary investments or investments in marketable securities.
c. Receivables.
d. Inventories.
e. Prepaid expenses.

Receivables are often reported at net realizable value, while short-term investments and inventories are usually valued at lower of cost or market. Prepaid expenses are valued at cost. Note that a prepaid expense is classified as a current asset on the grounds that an investment is made by paying cash in advance, thereby reducing cash outlays for the next reporting period. Note also that, in theory, long-term prepayments should be classified as noncurrent. In practice, however, such a prepayment is relatively minor in amount and presented as a current asset.

2. **Investments and Funds.** This classification includes:

a. Noncurrent investments in, (1) the capital stock of another company, (2) bonds of other entities, and (3) tangible assets, such as land, buildings, etc.

b. Cash set aside in special purpose funds (e.g., sinking funds and plant expansion funds) for long-term future use as needed.

c. Cash surrender value of life insurance policies carried by the company.

The common characteristics of this group of assets include: (1) the items are not used in the ongoing major operations of the company, and (2) management plans to retain the items beyond one year from the balance sheet date, or the operating cycle if it is longer. Most long-term investments are reported at their original cost while a fund is reported at the accumulated amount in the fund. A cash surrender value is usually reported at its realizable value.

3. **Operational or Capital Assets.** Operational or capital assets are long-term assets used in the continuing operations of the company. These assets are subclassified as:

a. Tangible. Tangible assets are those assets used in operating the business that have physical substance, such as land, buildings, machinery, equipment, etc.

b. Intangible. Intangible assets are those assets used in operating the business that do not have physical substance but have value because of the rights conferred by their ownership, such as patents, copyrights, leasehold, goodwill, etc.

Operational assets are reported at historical cost basis, i.e., at their original costs less accumulated depreciation, depletion, or amortization, as appropriate. (*CICA, Sec. 3060*)

4.   **Intangible Capital Assets.**   Intangible capital assets are reported as a separate element on the balance sheet. Major items should be listed separately, and the accumulated amount of amortization also should be disclosed in the notes or elsewhere in the financial statements. By convention, the contra account, accumulated amortization, seldom is separately listed. This contrasts to the usual treatment given depreciation and depletion related to tangible operational assets.

5.   **Other assets.**   This classification includes assets that do not fit any of the other categories. Examples include long-term receivables from employees and idle operational assets. They are usually reported at realizable value or historical cost.

6.   **Deferred charges.**   Long-term prepayments are grouped under this category. The only conceptual difference between a prepaid expense (classified as a current asset) and a deferred charge is the length of time over which the amount is amortized. Typical examples of deferred charges include machinery rearrangement costs, pension costs paid in advance, etc. Organization cost is sometimes presented as a deferred charge, although some would prefer to report it as an intangible operational asset. A deferred charge should originally be recorded at cost, which then is amortized as its future benefit expires.

6.   **Liabilities**

1.   **Current liabilities.**   Current liabilities are obligations expected to be satisfied with current assets or by the creation of other current liabilities. Examples of current liabilities include:

a.   Accrued expenses such as salaries payable and taxes payable.
b.   Accounts payable.
c.   Short-term notes payable.
d.   Currently maturing portion of long-term debts such as bonds.
e.   Unearned revenues.

The above items are usually classified in the order in which they will be paid. Current liabilities are valued at the amount due during the current period. For financial ratio analysis, the difference between current assets and current liabilities is called working capital:

Working capital = Current assets - Current liabilities

Further, the quotient between current assets and current liabilities is known as current ratio, or working-capital ratio:

Current (or working-capital) ratio = Current assets / Current liabilities.

Both working capital and current ratio are used to evaluate the reporting entity's liquidity, i.e., the ability to meet its short-term obligations.

2.   **Noncurrent liabilities.**   Obligations not classified as current are noncurrent, or long-term liabilities, including long-term notes payable, bonds payable, obligations under capital lease, pension obligations, and deferred credits. As a general rule, noncurrent liabilities are presented at their present values.

7.   Owners' equity

For a corporation, owners' equity is called shareholders' equity; for a partnership, partners' equity; and for a sole proprietorship, proprietor's equity. It represents the owners' residual interest in the entity. Owners' equity is classified mainly in terms of the sources of capital, namely, contributed, earned and unrealized.

1.   **Contributed capital.**   Contributed capital is capital contributed by owners as an investment. For a corporation, it is subclassified as:

   a.   Capital stock.   This classification reports the stated value, of capital stock issued and outstanding. Stated capital is the amount specified by law as the amount of the consideration received for the stock.

   b.   Contributed capital in excess of par is applicable only in jurisdictions that permit par value stock. This classification reports the excess of resources received by the corporation over the par value of the capital stock issued; or, in the case of stock dividends, the excess of retained earnings capitalized over the par value of the stock.

   c.   Other contributed capital.   This classification includes donations of assets, contributions resulting from treasury stock transactions, and the conversion or retirement of stock.

   Note that, in practice, items **b** and **c** are usually combined and presented under the caption entitled additional contributed capital.

2.   **Retained earnings.**   This classification reports the corporation's accumulated net earnings and prior period adjustments, less dividends since its inception.

3.   **Unrealized losses and gains.**   Unrealized losses mainly result from recording long-term equity investments at lower of cost or market. On certain rare occasions an asset may be written up to market value, resulting in an unrealized gain.

C.   **Additional Reporting Issues**

1.   **Loss and gain contingencies.**   A contingency is defined in **The CICA Handbook, Sec. 3290** as an existing condition, situation, or set of circumstances involving uncertainty as to possible loss or gain to an enterprise that will ultimately be resolved when one or more future events occur or fail to occur. It requires firms to accrue and disclose any contingent loss that meets two basic conditions:

a.   Information available prior to issuance of the financial statements indicates that it is probable an asset has been impaired or that a liability has been incurred.

b.   The amount of the loss can be reasonably estimated.

If a contingent loss meets only one of the two conditions, footnote disclosure without accrual is acceptable. For a contingency related to a legal case, usually firms refrain from reporting the expected loss on the grounds that the firm will prevail in the case, and/or that no material adverse judgment will occur.

Unlike loss contingencies, gain contingencies may at most be disclosed in footnotes if there is a high probability of realization and the amount can be reasonably estimated.

2.   **Comparative statements.**   The CICA, **Sec. 1500** states that the presentation of comparative financial statements in annual and other reports enhances the usefulness of such reports. In order to help predict the future success of a business, comparative financial statements for two or more periods should be reported. In 1980, the SEC began requiring three-year comparative statements for listed companies.

3.   **Subsequent events.**   *Subsequent events* are important material events that occur after the balance sheet date but prior to the actual issuance of the financial statements, which ordinarily is one to four months later. Subsequent events must be reported because they involve information that could influence the statement users' interpretation and evaluation of the future prospects of the business.

Auditing standards define these events and specify that they must be reported either in the tabular portion of the statements (balance sheet, income statements, etc.) or in the notes to the statements, depending on the nature of the events. The effects of subsequent events should be reported in the tabular portion of the statements if they (1) provide additional evidence about conditions that existed at the balance-sheet date, (2) affect estimates inherent in the process of preparing the financial statements, and (3) require adjustments to the financial statements resulting from the estimates.

4.   **Full disclosure.**   Full disclosure requires complete reporting of all information relating to the economic affairs of the enterprise to avoid misleading interested parties. **The CICA Handbook, Sec 1500 and 1505** requires that information about important accounting policies adopted by the enterprise be disclosed in a separate summary or as notes to the financial statements. In addition, supplementary disclosure in parenthetical notes, footnotes or supporting schedules are normally required for:

a.   Long-term commitments and obligations such as lease contracts and pension plans.

b.   Owners's equity such as the number of shares of each class of capital stock authorized, issued and outstanding, as well as the par value, dividend rate and conversion term of the stock.

c.   Accounting changes including changes in estimates, principles, and reporting entities.

d.   The effects of price level changes (optional).

5.   **The Auditors' Report.**   The auditors' report also is called the *accountants' report* or the *public accountants' report*. It is typically the last item presented in the financial statements, although its presentation can, instead, precede the financial reports.

The auditors' primary function is to express the *auditors' professional opinion* on the financial statements. Although the auditors have sole responsibility for all opinions expressed in the auditors' report, company management has the primary responsibility for the financial statements themselves, including the supporting notes.

The auditors' report is structured to include (1) an introductory paragraph, (2) a scope paragraph, and (3) an opinion paragraph. The general look and standard format of an auditors' report has the following seven key elements:

1.   Date.
2.   Salutation.
3.   Identification of the statements examined.
4.   Statement of scope of the examination.
5.   Opinion introduction.
6.   Reference to fair presentation in conformity with generally accepted accounting principles.
7.   Signature of the public accountant.

When an audit is finished, the auditors are required to draft an opinion paragraph that best communicates their professional opinion about the company's financial statements. One of the following four types of opinions is given:

1. *Unqualified opinion*   An unqualified opinion is given when the auditor has formed the opinion that the statements (*a*) present fairly the results of operations, financial position, and cash flows; (*b*) in conformance with GAAP; and (*c*) provide reasonable assurance that the financial statements are free of material misstatement.

2. *Qualified opinion*

3. *Adverse opinion*

4. *Denial of opinion*

D.   Usefulness and Limitations of the Balance Sheet

1. The **usefulness** of the balance sheet can be summarized as follows:

    a.   It provides information about a firm's financial strength as reflected in measures of both liquidity and financial flexibility. **Liquidity** describes expected time before an asset is realized or converted into cash or until a liability has to be paid; whereas **financial flexibility** is the ability of the firm to alter its cash flows in order to respond to unexpected needs and opportunities.

    b.   It furnishes data needed to calculate a firm's profitability ratios such as return on assets, and return on equity.

    c.   It presents information about a firm's **net worth** and **capital structure** which are often analyzed using financial ratios such as book value per share, debt to total assets ratio, and long-term debt to equity ratio.

2. The major **limitations** of the balance sheet are:

    a.   The assets and liabilities presented on the balance sheet are mainly based on historical cost, which may not be relevant to the assessment of the firm's current value.

    b.   The balance sheet relies heavily on estimates such as allowance for uncollectible receivables, accumulated depreciation and provisions for warranty expenses, and these estimates may be arbitrary.

    c.   Certain important assets and liabilities are omitted entirely from the balance sheet. Examples are human assets, the value of research and development activities, and liabilities related to off-balance-sheet financing such as sales of receivables with recourse.

E.   **Forms (formats) of the Balance Sheet**

Two forms of the balance sheet are available:

1.   Report balancing form.   In this form, the balance-sheet elements are presented vertically as follows:

```
                   The Balance Sheet
        ─────────────────────────────────────────
        Assets                            xxxxx
        Less: Liabilities                (xxxx)

        Yields:  Owners' equity           xxxx
                                         ═══════
```

This form reflects the owner's point of view that the value of the firm to the owners is what remains after the liabilities are subtracted from the assets, i.e., **Assets - Liabilities = Owners' equity.**

2.   Financial (account) form.   In this form, balance-sheet elements are separately presented on the two sides of the statement, with assets on the left-hand side, and liabilities and owners' equity on the right-hand side as shown below:

```
                   The Balance Sheet
        ──────────────────────┬──────────────────────
        Assets         xxxx   │  Liabilities      xxxx
                              │
                              │  Owners' equity   xxxx
                      ──────  │                  ──────
        Total          xxxx   │  Total            xxxx
                      ══════  │                  ══════
```

This form reflects the general accounting equation, i.e., **Assets = Liabilities + Owners' equity,** and the equality of the two sides of the balance sheet would always be maintained. A balance sheet based on this form represents the entity's viewpoint that the entity is separated from its owners, and both the creditors and the owners provide the means of financing the entity's assets.

3.   **Classified Balance Sheet**

To aid decision makers, the balance sheet delineates the entity's resource structure (major classes and amounts of assets) and its financing structure (major classes and amounts of liabilities and equity). The common classifications of balance sheet items as found in current reporting practice are listed in account form as follows:

```
                        ABC Corporation
                        BALANCE SHEET
                        Dec. 31, xxxx
```

ASSETS	Liabilities
1. Current assets.	1. Current liabilities (including short-term deferred credits).
2. Investments and funds.	2. Long-term (or noncurrent) liabilities (including long-term deferred credits).
3. Operational assets – tangible (often called capital or fixed assets or property, plant and equipment).	**Owners' equity**
4. Operational assets – intangible.	1. Contributed capital:
5. Other assets.	a. Capital stock.
6. Deferred charges.	b. Other contributed capital.
	2. Retained earnings.
	3. Unrealized losses and gains.

F.   THE STATEMENT OF Changes in Financial Position

1.   The statement of changes in financial position is a cash basis report. It provides information about the cash inflows and cash outflows of the company. It is intended to help investors and creditors project their own prospective cash flows from investments in, and loans to, the company. For cash flow purposes, cash is defined in the **CICA, Sec. 1540** as cash and cash equivalents (i.e., short-term highly liquid investments). The statement of changes in financial position, along with the other financial statements, should provide (1) feedback about cash flows for each major activity of a business, and (2) information to aid decision makers in assessing the financial strength of a business including its ability to generate positive future cash flows with which it will meet its future obligations, pay dividends, and support future growth.

2.   Business Activities and Cash Flows

The **CICA, Sec. 1540** specifies four business activities to be separated for the purpose of reporting cash flows:

1.   Operating activities.   The *CICA Handbook* (paragraph 1540 specifies that the SCFP should disclose at least the following items : **a.** Cash from operations: the amount of cash from operations should be reconciled to the income statement or the components of cash from operations should be disclosed. **b.** Cash flows resulting from discontinued operations. **c.** Cash flows resulting from extraordinary items. **d.** Outlays for acquisition and proceeds on disposal of assets, by major category, not included in (**a**), (**b**) or (**c**) above. All cash increases and decreases

directly related to net income should be included in this classification. However, cash flows related to gains or losses of an extraordinary nature, discontinued operations, or disposal of fixed assets must be removed from operating activities in order to associate their full cash effect with investing or financing activities, whichever is the dominant source of the gain or loss.

2. **Investing activities.**   This major classification reports cash inflows and outflows related to (a) the acquisition and disposal of property, plant and equipment, (b) loans made by the enterprise, and (c) investment in debt or equity securities of other enterprises.

3. **Financing activities.**   These activities involve cash flows related to (a) cash obtained to finance the enterprise, and (b) cash used to pay back the owners and creditors for their prior cash-providing activities.

4. **Noncash financing and investing activities.**   These activities involve important events which do not involve cash.

3. **Formats of the Statement of Cash Flows**

Cash flows may be reported using either the **direct** or the **indirect** approach. Their difference is in the presentation of cash flows related to operating activities. Under the direct approach, the various sources and uses of cash are itemized on the statement, whereas those income items not affecting current cash flows are excluded from the presentation. Under the indirect approach, the net cash flow from operating activities is obtained by making adjustments to income for (1) those income items not affecting current cash flows (e.g., bad debt expenses, depreciation expenses and amortization expenses), (2) those changes in current assets and liabilities related to business operations (e.g., accounts receivable, inventory, prepaid expense, accounts payable, and accrued expenses), and (3) those gains or losses resulting from investing or financing activities (e.g., gain on disposal of investments and losses on early extinguishment of long-term debts). As indicated in the **CICA Handbook, Sec. 1540**, both formats are acceptable, yet the indirect approach is preferable. The typical formats under these approaches are separately shown as follows:

1. **The direct approach:**

```
                          ABC Corporation
        STATEMENT OF CHANGES IN FINANCIAL POSITION (DIRECT APPROACH)
                   For Year Ended December 31, xxxx

Cash flows from operating activities:
   Cash flow from customers                      $ 20,000
   Cash payments for purchases of merchandise      (8.000)
   Cash payments for operating expenses            (2,000)
   Cash payments for taxes                         (1,000)
   Net cash provided by operating activities                 $ 9,000

Cash flows from investing activities:
   Cash paid for the acquisition of buildings    $ (6,000)
   Cash received from sale of equipment             2,000
   Net cash used in investing activities                      (4,000)

Cash flows from financing activities:
   Cash received from issuance of common stock   $ 25,000
   Cash paid for dividends                         (5,000)
   Net cash provided by financing activities                 20,000
Net increase in cash                                        $25,000
Add: Cash balance at beginning of xxxx                       10,000

Cash balance at end of xxxx                                 $35,000
```

2. The indirect approach:

```
                              ABC Corporation
           STATEMENT OF CHANGES IN FINANCIAL POSITION (INDIRECT APPROACH)
                      For year ended December 31, xxxx

Cash flows from operating activities:
   Income from operations                        $  7,500
   Adjustment for depreciation expenses             2,000
   Adjustment for gain on sale of equipment          (500)
   Net cash provided by operating activities                   $ 9,000

Cash flows from investing activities:
   Cash paid for the acquisition of buildings    $ (6,000)
   Cash received from sale of equipment             2,000
   Net cash used in investing activities                        (4,000)

Cash flows from financing activities:
   Cash received from issuance of common stock   $ 25,000
   Cash paid for dividends                         (5,000)
   Net cash provided by financing activities                   20,000

Net increase in cash                                           $25,000
Add: Cash balance at beginning of xxxx                          10,000

Cash balance at end of xxxx                                    $35,000
```

G.   Usefulness of the Statement of Changes in Financial Position

A SCFP is useful in providing investors, creditors, and other interested parties feedback about cash inflows and outflows for each major activity--operating, investing, and financing. Decision makers are particularly interested in the amount of cash a company generates from its operating activities. The operating activities necessarily must be the primary cash source because operations must eventually pay for the company's debts, dividends, and provide for growth. Also, the SCFP provides useful information about a company's borrowing patterns and subsequent repayments (its financing activities), new investments by owners, and dividends.

The SCFP also helps decision makers assess the financial strength of a business which is evidenced by the relationship between the company's assets and liabilities and the company's credit standing with financial institutions and other lenders as reflected in the balance sheet.

The SCFP is an indispensable complement to the balance sheet. In any one year, unusual events can occur that might be interpreted incorrectly or yield inaccurate evaluations of the company's longer-term financial position; therefore, a series of cash flow statements covering several years is essential. Further, there is no substitute for a careful analysis based on a complete set of financial statements, plus whatever else is known about a particular company. Annual reports are but one source of information.

KEY CONCEPTS

Current assets   Assets that can be reasonably expected to be realized in cash, or to be sold or consumed during the normal operating cycle or within one year, whichever is longer.

Current cost   The amount of cash necessary to acquire the same item at the balance sheet date.

Current exit value   The amount of cash that may be obtained at the balance sheet date from selling the item in an orderly liquidation.

Current liabilities   Obligations expected to be satisfied with current assets or by the creation of other current liabilities.

Deferred charges   Long-term prepayments of expenses.

Financing activities   Obtaining resources from owners and providing them with a return on, and a return of, their investment; and borrowing money and repaying amounts borrowed.

Full disclosure   Complete reporting of all information relating to the economic affairs of the entity to avoid misleading interested parties.

Investing activities   Making and collecting loans and acquiring and disposing of debt or equity instruments and plant assets held for or used in the production of goods, or services by the firm.

Loss and gain contingencies   Existing condition, situation, or set of circumstances involving uncertainty as to possible loss or gain that will ultimately be resolved when one or more future events occur or fail to occur.

Net realizable value   The net amount of cash into which an asset is expected to be converted (e.g., the expected selling price less cost of disposal).

Operating activities   All transactions and events not defined as investing or financing activities.

Operational assets   Long-term assets used in the continuing operations of the company.

Present value   The future value discounted to the balance sheet date.

Subsequent events   Important occurrences after the balance sheet date but prior to the actual issuance of the financial statements.

REVIEW QUESTIONS AND EXERCISES

TRUE-FALSE

Indicate whether each of the following statements is true or false by circling the correct response.

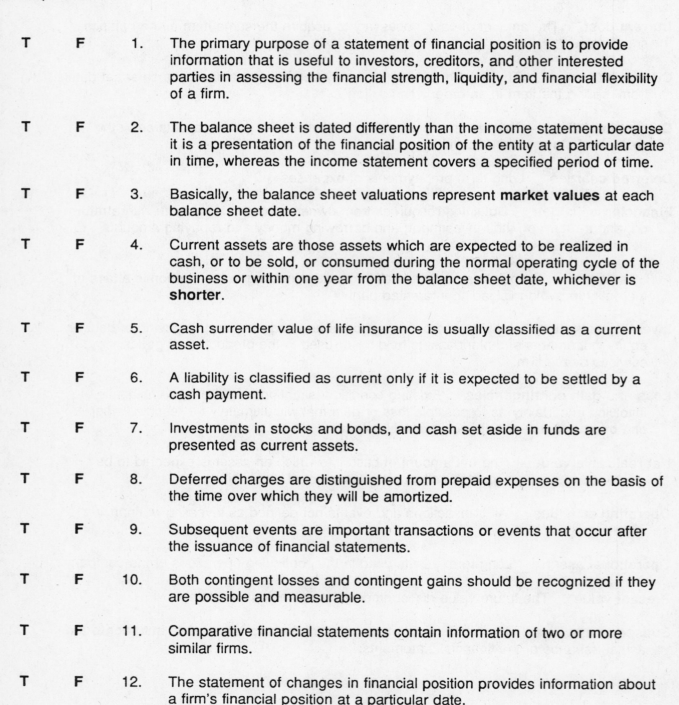

T   F   1.   The primary purpose of a statement of financial position is to provide information that is useful to investors, creditors, and other interested parties in assessing the financial strength, liquidity, and financial flexibility of a firm.

T   F   2.   The balance sheet is dated differently than the income statement because it is a presentation of the financial position of the entity at a particular date in time, whereas the income statement covers a specified period of time.

T   F   3.   Basically, the balance sheet valuations represent **market values** at each balance sheet date.

T   F   4.   Current assets are those assets which are expected to be realized in cash, or to be sold, or consumed during the normal operating cycle of the business or within one year from the balance sheet date, whichever is **shorter**.

T   F   5.   Cash surrender value of life insurance is usually classified as a current asset.

T   F   6.   A liability is classified as current only if it is expected to be settled by a cash payment.

T   F   7.   Investments in stocks and bonds, and cash set aside in funds are presented as current assets.

T   F   8.   Deferred charges are distinguished from prepaid expenses on the basis of the time over which they will be amortized.

T   F   9.   Subsequent events are important transactions or events that occur after the issuance of financial statements.

T   F   10.   Both contingent losses and contingent gains should be recognized if they are possible and measurable.

T   F   11.   Comparative financial statements contain information of two or more similar firms.

T   F   12.   The statement of changes in financial position provides information about a firm's financial position at a particular date.

T   F   13.   The statement of changes in financial position is an accrual basis report.

T   F   14.   The statement of changes in financial position reports cash flows from operating, investing, and financing activities.

EXERCISE 1

Indicate the usual balance sheet classification of each item below by entering the appropriate identifying letter in the space provided. When the item is a contra account, place a minus sign before the identifying letter as illustrated in Item 0 below:

Document	**Source**
-A 0. Allowance for doubtful accounts	A. Current asset
___ 1. Land (held for speculation)	B. Investments and funds
___ 2. Plant expansion fund	C. Tangible operational asset
___ 3. Accumulated depreciation	D. Intangible operational asset
___ 4. Rent revenue	E. Current liabilities
___ 5. Rent revenue collected in advance	F. Long-term liabilities
___ 6. Prepaid insurance	G. Unrealized gain or loss
___ 7. Accrued income taxes payable	H. Contributed capital
___ 8. Patents	I. Not reported on the balance sheet
___ 9. Preferred stock outstanding	
___ 10. Unrealized loss from recording long-term investment at lower of cost or market.	

EXERCISE 2

The comparative adjusted trial balance of Miniwawa Corporation and other related data are given below:

| | 1991 | | 1990 | |
	Debit	Credit	Debit	Credit
Cash	$12,000		$13,000	
Accounts receivable	4,500		6,000	
Allowance for doubtful accounts		$ 500		$ 600
Inventory	5,000		4,000	
Investments in bonds (long-term)	2,000		2,000	
Plant assets	20,000		15,000	
Accumulated depreciation		9,000		6,000
Patents (net)	1,200		1,500	
Accounts payable		3,000		3,200
Notes payable (long-term)		1,800		500
Bonds payable (long-term)		8,000		10,000
Common stock		10,000		10,000
Retained earnings, beginning		11,200		11,200
Sales		16,000		13,000
Cost of goods sold	8,000		6,000	
Wages and salaries	2,000		1,800	
Depreciation expenses	3,000		3,000	
Patent amortization expense	300		300	
Other operating expenses	500		1,900	
Income tax expense	1,000		0	
	$59,500	$59,500	$54,500	$54,500

Additional data for 1991:

1. At December 31, plant assets were acquired for $5,000 cash.
2. At December 31 long-term notes were issued for $1,300 cash.
3. Retired long-term bonds of $2,000, at face value.
4. The number of outstanding common shares for 1991 was 1,000.

Required:

1. Prepare a statement of income (single step) for 1991.
2. Prepare a balance sheet as of December 31, 1991 in account form.
3. Prepare a statement of changes in financial position for 1991 using:
    a. The direct approach.
    b. The indirect approach.

MULTIPLE CHOICE

Enter the letter corresponding to the response which **best** completes each of the following statements or questions.

_____ 1. Each of the following is an essential characteristic of a liability, *except*

    a. It is a result of past transactions or events.
    b. The dollar amount of the obligation is **known for certain**.
    c. It represents a probable future sacrifice of economic benefits.
    d. It represents an obligation to transfer assets or provide services to another entity in the future.

_____ 2. The basis used to classify assets as current or noncurrent is:

    a. the operating cycle or one year, whichever is shorter.
    b. the operating cycle or one year, whichever is longer.
    c. whether the asset is used currently in the company's operations.
    d. whether the dollar amount is fixed.

_____ 3. An item not generally classified as a current asset is:

    a. the cash surrender value of life insurance.
    b. trade notes receivable.
    c. prepaid expenses.
    d. marketable securities.

_____ 4. A valuation method typically used to value operational assets is:

    a. historical cost.
    b. replacement cost.
    c. selling price.
    d. present value.

_____ 5. Each of the following is classified as a current liability, *except*:

    a. obligations expected to require the creation of other current liabilities.
    b. bonds payable currently due.
    c. deferred credit.
    d. accrued expenses.

_____ 6. Current assets minus current liabilities is referred to as:

    a. net assets.
    b. working capital.
    c. current cash equivalent.
    d. cash surrender value.

____ 7. Investments and funds include all of the following, *except*:

    a. a bond sinking fund.
    b. a cash surrender value.
    c. land in use.
    d. investment in land.

____ 8. An item not reported in the owners' equity section of the balance sheet is:

    a. retained earnings appropriated for plant expansion.
    b. donated capital.
    c. working capital.
    d. capital stock.

____ 9. Which of the following is not a primary objective of the statement of changes in financial position:

    a. to disclose the increase or decrease in cash during the reporting period.
    b. to help investors and creditors assess the firm's financial position.
    c. to help investors and creditors assess the firm's future cash flows.
    d. to help investors and creditors assess their own future cash flows.

____ 10. A loss contingency should be recognized if it is:

    a. probable that a liability was incurred and the amount of loss can be reasonably estimated.
    b. probable that a liability was incurred or the amount of loss can be reasonably estimated.
    c. reasonably possible that a loss will occur and the amount of loss can be reasonably estimated.
    d. reasonably possible that a loss will occur or the amount of loss can be reasonably estimated.

____ 11. Tanka Corporation sold a fully depreciated equipment for $1,000. This transaction would be reported on the statement of changes in financial position as a(n):

    a. operating activity.
    b. investing activity.
    c. financing activity.
    d. None of the above.

____ 12. If, during the accounting period, sales revenue is $20,000 and accounts receivable increases by $5,000, cash received from customers for the period:

    a. is $25,000.
    b. is $20,000.
    c. is $15,000.
    d. depends on the proportion of cash and credit sales.

____ 13. Selected information from Lenda Company's accounting records is as follows:

Cash paid to retire common stock	$12,000
Proceeds from issuance of preferred stock	$15,000
Cash dividends paid	$ 5,000
Proceeds from sale of equipment	$25,000

On the statement of changes in financial position for the year, Lenda should report net cash flow from financing activities as:

a. $2,000, net outflow of cash.
b. $13,000, net outflow of cash.
c. $23,000, net outflow of cash.
d. $25,000, net inflow of cash.

____ 14. Based on the same information as in Item 13, Lenda should report net cash flow from investing activities as:

a. $2,000, net outflow of cash.
b. $13,000, net outflow of cash.
c. $23,000, net outflow of cash.
d. $25,000, net inflow of cash.

SOLUTIONS TO REVIEW QUESTIONS AND EXERCISES

TRUE-FALSE

1. T	5. F	9. F	13. F
2. T	6. F	10. F	14. T
3. F	7. F	11. F	
4. F	8. T	12. F	

EXERCISE 1

1. B	4. I	7. E	10. G
2. B	5. E	8. D	
3. - C	6. A	9. H	

EXERCISE 2

1. **Income statement.**

Miniwawa Corporation
Income Statement
For Year Ended December 31, 1991

Sales revenues		$16,000
Expenses:		
Cost of goods sold	$ 8,000	
Wages and salaries	2,000	
Depreciation expenses	3,000	
Patent amortization expense	300	
Other operating expenses	500	
Income tax expense	1,000	
Total expenses		14,800
Net Income		$ 1,200
Earnings per share		$1.20

2. **Balance sheet.**

Miniwawa Corporation
Balance Sheet
December 31, 1991

Assets			Liabilities		
Current assets:			Current liabilities:		
Cash		$12,000	Accounts payable		$ 3,000
Accounts receivable	$4,500				
Less: Allowance for doubtful accounts	500	4,000	Noncurrent liabilities:		
			Notes payable	$ 1,800	
Inventory		5,000	Bonds payable	8,000	
Total current assets		$21,000	Total noncurrent liab.		9,800
Investment and funds:			Total liabilities		$12,800
Investment in bonds		2,000	Shareholders' equity		
Property, plant, and equipment:			Contributed capital:		
Plant assets	$20,000		Common stock	$10,000	
Less: Accumulated depreciation – plant assets	9,000		Retained earnings:		
Total property, plant, and equipment		11,000	Retained earnings: Unappropriated	12,400	
Intangible assets:					
			Total shareholders' equity		22,400
Patents (net)		1,200			
Total assets		$35,200	Total liabilities and shareholders' equity		$35,200

3. **Statements of Cash Flows:**

a. **Direct approach:**

Miniwawa Corporation
STATEMENT OF CHANGES IN FINANCIAL POSITION (DIRECT APPROACH)
For Year Ended December 31, 1991

Cash flows from operating activities:		
Cash flow from customers	$ 17,400 (1)	
Cash payments for purchases of merchandises	(9,200) (2)	
Cash payments for operating expenses	(2,500)	
Cash payments for taxes	(1,000)	
Net cash provided by operating activities		$ 4,700
Cash flows from investing activities:		
Cash paid for the acquisition of plant assets	$ (5,000)	
Net cash used in investing activities		(5,000)
Cash flows from financing activities:		
Cash paid for retirement of bonds	$ (2,000)	
Cash received from issuance of bonds	1,300	
Net cash provided by financing activities		(700)
Net decrease in cash		$(1,000)
Add: Cash balance at beginning of 1991		13,000
Cash balance at end of 1991		$12,000

Notes: (1) Cash flows from customers = Sales + Decrease in accounts receivable
= $16,000 + 1,400
= $17,400.

(2) Cash payments for purchases of merchandise = Cost of goods sold + Increase in inventory + Decrease in accounts payable
= $8,000 + $1,000 + $200
= $9,200.

b. **Indirect approach:**

Miniwawa Corporation
STATEMENT OF CHANGES IN FINANCIAL POSITION (INDIRECT APPROACH)
For Year Ended December 31, 1991

Cash flows from operating activities:		
Net income for 1991	$ 1,200	
Adjustment for depreciation expenses	3,000	
Adjustment for patents amortization	300	
Adjustment for decrease in accounts receivable (net)	1,400	
Adjustment for increase in ending inventory	(1,000)	
Adjustment for decrease in accounts payable	(200)	
Cash increase from operating activities		$4,700
Cash flows from investing activities:		
Cash paid for the acquisition of plant assets	$ (5,000)	
Net cash used in investing activities		(5,000)
Cash flows from financing activities:		
Cash paid for retirement of bonds	$ (2,000)	
Cash received from issuance of bonds	1,300	
Net cash provided by financing activities		(700)
Net decrease in cash		$(1,000)
Add: Cash balance at beginning of 1991		13,000
Cash balance at end of 1991		$12,000

MULTIPLE CHOICE:

1. b	5. c	9. b	13. a
2. b	6. b	10. a	14. d
3. a	7. c	11. b	
4. a	8. c	12. c	

Computations:

12.   (c) Cash received from customers = Sales - Increase in accounts receivable
     = $20,000 - $5,000
     = $15,000.

13.   (a) Net cash flow from financing activities
     = Proceeds from stock issue - Cash paid to retire stock
      - Cash dividends
     = $15,000 - $12,000 - $5,000
     = $(2,000), net cash outflow.

14.   (d) Net cash flow from investing activities
     = Proceeds from sale of equipment
     = $25,000.

CHAPTER 6

Interest: Concepts of Future and Present Value

CHAPTER OBJECTIVES

This chapter is designed to enable students to:

A. Explain the concept of the time value of money, which underlies all interest calculations and a wide range of accounting functions.

B. Discuss the difference between simple and compound interest.

C. Explain the difference between future value and present value as these terms apply to both single payment amounts and annuities.

D. Accounting for the distinction between an ordinary annuity and an annuity due.

E. Compute the following values, using *future* and *present value tables*:
    a. Future value of a single payment.
    b. Present value of a single payment.
    c. Future value of an annuity.
    d. present value of an annuity.

F. Solve complex time value problems that involve multiple elements by combining present and future value computations for both single-payment and annuity amounts.

CHAPTER OVERVIEW

A. **Interest** is the rent paid for the use of money over time, often referred to as the **time value** of money. Measurement of interest involves the basic concepts of the **future** and **present** value of a dollar, which are essential considerations in a number of accounting situations. These concepts and the related calculation procedures are discussed in this chapter. Present and future values of **single amounts** and **annuities** are considered separately, and then shown to be related.

B. **Simple Interest vs. Compound Interest**

    1. **Simple Interest** (i.e., the interest earned on the principal only) is computed as follows:

Interest amount = P x i x n

where:

P = principal
i = interest rate
n = number of interest periods

For example, if $1,000 is invested at 12% for one year, the interest would be $1,000 x 12% x 1 year = $120. This interest would increase the investment to $1,120, referred to as the **future value** or **future amount (F)** of $1,000 at 12% at the end of 1 year as calculated below:

$$F = P(1 + i \times n)$$
$$= \$1,000 (1 + 12\% \times 1)$$
$$= \$1,120$$

Reciprocally, given the future amount, the principal *(P)* may be determined as:

$$P = F / (1 + i \times n)$$
$$= \$1,120 / (1 + 12\% \times 1)$$
$$= \$1,000$$

The principal, as determined above, is referred to as the **present value** of the future amount. For accounting purposes, however, neither the future amount, nor the present value, is normally calculated on the simple interest basis. Rather, the typical interest computation is based on compound interest, known as the **effective interest method**.

2.   **Compound Interest** involves the determination of interest on not only the principal, but also the interest previously earned but unpaid. Knowledge of compound interest is essential, because it is applied to a variety of accounting problems whenever the **future value** or **present value** of any long-term item is involved.

Based on the compound interest, there are six future and present values as shown in the following diagram:

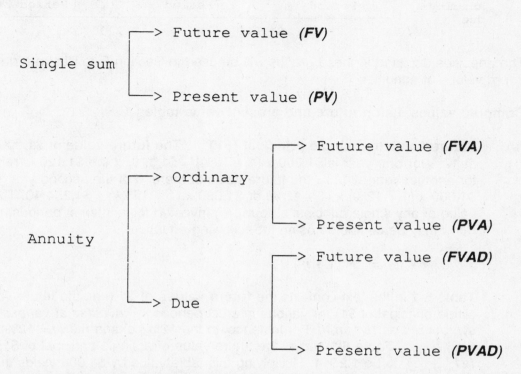

As is illustrated below, each of these values may be computed using a specific interest table in the text.

C.   Basic Concepts

Given the alternative of receiving $1,000 now or receiving $1,000 one year from now, the rational choice would be to receive the money now. If the $1,000 is received now, it could be invested to make money and thus to receive more than $1,000 a year from now. The difference between the $1,000 now (its **present value**) and its value one year from now (its **future value**) is known as the interest. The following three variables are fundamental to the computation of interest: (1) **principal**, the amount loaned or borrowed, (2) **interest rate**, expressed as a percentage of principal for a specified period (usually a year), and (3) **time,** the number of interest periods that the principal is outstanding.

D.   Ordinary annuity and annuity due compared.

A series of equal, periodic payments, or rents, to be paid or received at uniform intervals in time, is referred to as an **annuity.** If payments are made at the **end** of each payment period, the designation is an **ordinary annuity.** When the equal payments are made at the **beginning** of each period, the designation is an **annuity due.** The distinction between an ordinary annuity and an annuity due is shown graphically below:

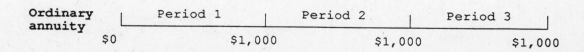

Annuity due	Period 1	Period 2	Period 3
$1,000	$1,000	$1,000	$0

The annuities depicted in these graphs will be used in Section E to illustrate present and future values of annuities.

E.   Compute values, using future and present value tables

(a)   Future value of a single principal (*FV*).   The **future value** of $1,000 invested at 12% for **one** year is $1,000 x (1 + 12%) = $1,120. If the $1,120 is reinvested for another year at 12%, the future value at the end of the second year would be $1,000 x (1 + 12%) x (1 + 12%) or $1,000 x $(1 + 12\%)^2$ = $1,254.40. The future value of any single principal amount *(P)* invested for *n* interest periods, at interest rate *i* may be computed using the following equation:

$$FV \quad = \quad P \, (1 + i)^n.$$

Table 6-1 in the text contains the **future values of $1** (i.e., the future values of a single principal of $1) for various interest periods, *n, invested at various rates, i,* symbolized as *(fv1, n, i)*. For instance, in the 12% column (i.e., *i* = 12%), row 2 (i.e., *n* = 2), **Table 6-1** shows the future value of a single principal of $1, *(i.e.,* $fv1_{n=2, i=12\%}$*)*, to be 1.2544. Multiplying this table value by $1,000 yields the future value of a single principal of $1,000:

$$
\begin{aligned}
FV \quad &= \quad \$1,000 \times fv1_{n=2, i=12\%} \\
&= \quad \$1,000 \times 1.2544 \text{ (from \textbf{Table 6-1})} \\
&= \quad \$1,254.40
\end{aligned}
$$

If interest is compounded **semiannually**, the rate *(i)* used in the computation should be the **semiannual rate,** determined by **dividing** the **annual rate** by two. Similarly, the number of interest periods *(n)* should be the number of semiannual periods, calculated as the number of years multiplied by two. By the same token, if interest is compounded quarterly, *i* would be obtained by dividing the annual rate by four, whereas *n* would be determined by multiplying the number of years by four, etc.

(b)   Present value of a single future amount (*PV*).   Since the future value of a single principal amount is the principal **times** $(1 + i)^n$, the computation can be reversed to find the principal (i.e., the **present value** of the single future amount) by taking the future amount and dividing it by $(1 + i)^n$. For example, since the **Table 6-1** value at $(1 + 12\%)^2$, or $fv1_{n=2, i=12\%}$, is 1.2544, the present value of $1,254.40 to be received two years from now, **discounted** at 12%, is $1,254.40 / 1.2544, or $1,000.

Note that **dividing** by the **Table 6-1** value is equivalent to **multiplying** by its reciprocal, so:

$$
\begin{aligned}
\textbf{\textit{PV}} \quad &= \quad \$1,254.40 \; / \; 1.2544 \\
&= \quad \$1,254.40 \times (1 \; / \; 1.2544) \\
&= \quad \$1,254.40 \times .79719 \\
&= \quad \$1,000
\end{aligned}
$$

Reciprocals of **Table 6-1** values [i.e., $1 / (1 + i)^n$] are presented in **Table 6-2** showing the present values of a single future amount of $1, for various future periods (*n*) discounted at various rates (*i*), symbolized as $pv1_{n,i}$. Accordingly, the **present value** of $1,254.40 to be received two years from now, **discounted** at 12% can be found using **Table 6-2**, as follows:

$$
\begin{aligned}
\textbf{\textit{PV}} \quad &= \quad \$1,254.40 \times \textbf{\textit{pv1}}_{n=2, i=12\%} \\
&= \quad \$1,254.40 \times .79719 \text{ (from \textbf{Table 6-2})} \\
&= \quad \$1,000
\end{aligned}
$$

To better understand the relationship between future value and present value, consider the following two illustrations:

ILLUSTRATION 1:   Future value of a single principal amount

Assume that, on January 1, 1991, you deposit $1,000 in a savings account which pays 6% interest at the end of each year on both principal and previously earned interest. What will be your **account balance** at the end of year 1993?

Computation:

$$
\begin{aligned}
\textbf{\textit{FV}} \quad &= \quad \$1,000 \times \textbf{\textit{fv1}}_{n=3, i=6\%} \\
&= \quad \$1,000 \times 1.191 \text{ (from \textbf{Table 6-1})} \\
&= \quad \textbf{\$1,191}
\end{aligned}
$$

A **fund accumulation schedule** as follows may be prepared to demonstrate the accuracy of the above computation:

Date	Beginning Balance	Interest earned	Ending Balance
Jan. 1, 1991	1,000		
Dec. 31, 1991	1,000	1,000 x 6% = 60	1,060
Dec. 31, 1992	1,060	1,060 x 6% = 64	1,124
Dec. 31, 1993	1,124	1,124 x 6% = 67	**1,191**

ILLUSTRATION 2:   Present value of a single future amount

Assume you are offered a stereo system for which the salesperson says you can pay $1,191, after three years, which includes interest at 6% annually. What price would you pay for the stereo system if you accept the offer?

Computation:

$$PV = \$1,191 \times pv1_{n=3,i=6\%}$$
$$= \$1,191 \times .83962 \text{ (from \textbf{Table 6-2})}$$
$$= \$1,000$$

By paying $1,191 for the $1,000 stereo after three years, you would be paying the remaining $191 for the three year's **interest.**

In some situations, the **interest rate** or the **number of interest periods** may not be known. To solve for the unknown variable, the **future value** is divided by the **present value** (or vice versa) to derive a **table value**. Locating this table value in **Table 6-1** (or **Table 6-2**) relative to the known variable (*n* or *i*) determines the corresponding **unknown** variable (i or n).

(c) Future value of ordinary annuity *(FVA).*

Table 6-3 contains **future values** of ordinary annuities of $1 invested at the end of each of *n* periods at various rates of interest (*i*), symbolized as $fva_{n,i}$. These values are used as the factors for determining the future value of an ordinary annuity of any amount. For example, the **future value at the end of year 3** of the **ordinary annuity** above (i.e., $1,000 at the end of each of the three years) can be found as follows, assuming an interest rate of 12%:

$$FVA = \$1,000 \times fva_{n=3,i=12\%}$$
$$= \$1,000 \times 3.3744 \text{ (from \textbf{Table 6-3})}$$
$$= \$3,374.40$$

Note that this same value can be found by determining the future value at the **end of year 3** for each of the three individual payments using **Table 6-1**, and summing those values:

Annuity Payment Number	Amount	*n*	Table 6-1 $fv1_{n,i=12\%}$	Future Value
1	$1,000	2	1.25440	$1,254.40
2	1,000	1	1.12000	1,120.00
3	1,000	0	1.00000*	1,000.00
Total Future Value			3.37440	$3,374.40

* $fv1_{n=0,i=12\%} = (1 + 12\%)^0 = 1.$

(d) Present value of ordinary annuity (PVA):

In a number of accounting applications it is desirable to know the **present value** of an annuity. In later chapters you will determine the present value of a series of lease payments, pension obligations, and future interest payments associated with a bond.

Table 6-4 contains **present values** of ordinary annuities of **$1** invested at the end of each of n periods at various rates of interest (i), symbolized as $pva_{n,i}$. The present value **at the beginning of year 1** of the **ordinary annuity** above (i.e., $1,000 at the end of each of the three years) can be found as follows, assuming an interest rate of 12%:

$$PVA = \$1,000 \times pva_{n=3, i=12\%}$$
$$= \$1,000 \times 2.40183 \text{ (from \textbf{Table 6-4})}$$
$$= \$2,401.83$$

Note that this same value can be found by determining the present value at the **beginning of year 1** of each of the three individual payments using **Table 6-2**, and summing those values:

Annuity Payment Number	Amount	n	Table 6-2 $pv1_{n, i=12\%}$	Present Value
1	$1,000	1	.89286	$ 892.86
2	1,000	2	.79719	797.19
3	1,000	3	.71178	711.78
Total Present Value			2.40183	$2,401.83

Future value of annuity due *(FVAD):*

Table 6-5 contains **future values** of annuities due of **$1** invested at the beginning of each of the n interest periods at various rates of interest (i), symbolized as $fvad_{n,i}$. The **future value at the end of year 3** of the **annuity due** above (i.e., $1,000 at the beginning of each of the three years) can be found as follows, assuming an interest rate of 12%:

$$FVAD = \$1,000 \times fvad_{n=3, i=12\%}$$
$$= \$1,000 \times 3.77933 \text{ (from \textbf{Table 6-5})}$$
$$= \$3,779.33$$

Note that this same value can be found by determining the **future value at the end of year 3** of each of the three individual payments, using **Table 6-1**, and summing those values:

```
Annuity Payment      Amount        n      Table 6-1    Future Value
   Number                                 fvl_n,i=12%

     1              $1,000         3       1.40493      $1,404.93
     2               1,000         2       1.25440       1,254.40
     3               1,000         1       1.12000       1,120.00
                                                        ─────────
  Total Future Value                      3.77933      $3,779.33
                                          ═══════      ═════════
```

It should be noted that an annuity due differs from an ordinary annuity by an additional period of interest for each of the payments. Take the first payment, the annuity due would earn **three** periods of interest, whereas the ordinary annuity earns only **two**. Therefore, the future value of an annuity due can be calculated by multiplying $(1 + i)$ by the future value of an ordinary annuity:

$$\textbf{\textit{FVAD}} \quad = \quad \textbf{\textit{FVA x (1 + i)}}$$
$$= \quad \$3,374.40 \times (1 + 12\%)$$
$$= \quad \$3,779.33$$

Present value of annuity due *(PVAD)*.

Table 6-6 contains **present values** of annuities due of **$1** invested at the beginning of each of the n periods at various rates of interest (i), symbolized as $\textbf{\textit{pvad}}_{n,i}$. The present value at the beginning of year 1 of the **annuity due** above (i.e., $1,000 at the beginning of each of the three years) can be found as follows, assuming an interest rate of 12%:

$$\textbf{\textit{PVAD}} \quad = \quad \$1,000 \times \textbf{\textit{pvad}}_{n=3,i=12\%}$$
$$= \quad \$1,000 \times 2.69005 \text{ (from \textbf{Table 6-6})}$$
$$= \quad \$2,690.05$$

Note that this same value can be found by determining the **present value at the beginning of year 1** of each of the three individual payments, using **Table 6-2**, and summing those values:

```
Annuity Payment      Amount        n      Table 6-2    Future Value
   Number                                 pvl_n,i=12%

     1              $1,000         0       1.00000*     $1,000.00
     2               1,000         1        .89286         892.86
     3               1,000         2        .79719         797.19
                                                        ─────────
  Total Future Value                      2.69005      $2,690.05
                                          ═══════      ═════════
```

* $pvl_{n=0,i=12\%} = 1 / (1 + 12\%)^0 = 1.$

It should again be noted that an annuity due differs from an ordinary annuity by **one** period of interest for each of the payments. Take the first payment, under the annuity due it is not **discounted**, whereas under the ordinary annuity it should be discounted for **one** period. Therefore, the present value of annuity due can be obtained by multiplying $(1 + i)$ by the present value of ordinary annuity:

$$
\begin{aligned}
\textit{PVAD} &= \textit{PVA x (1 + i)} \\
&= \$2,401.83 \times (1 + 12\%) \\
&= \$2,690.05
\end{aligned}
$$

To better understand the relationship between future value and present value and between an ordinary annuity and annuity due, consider the following four illustrations:

ILLUSTRATION 3:   Future value of ordinary annuity *(FVA)*

Assume you deposit $1,000 at the end of each of the next 4 years to a savings account which pays annual interest at the rate of 6%. What will be your account balance after four years?

Computation:

$$
\begin{aligned}
\textit{FVA} &= \$1,000 \times \textit{fva}_{n=4, i=6\%} \\
&= \$1,000 \times 4.37462 \text{ (from \textbf{Table 6-3})} \\
&= \mathbf{\$4,374.62}
\end{aligned}
$$

ILLUSTRATION 4:   Future value of annuity due *(FVAD)*

Assume your annual deposits in the previous illustration are made at the beginning of each period. What will be your account balance after four years?

Computation:

$$
\begin{aligned}
\textit{FVAD} &= \$1,000 \times \textit{fvad}_{n=4, i=6\%} \\
&= \$1,000 \times 4.63709 \text{ (from \textbf{Table 6-5})} \\
&= \mathbf{\$4,637.09}
\end{aligned}
$$

Note that the future value of annuity due can also be obtained by multiplying the future value of ordinary annuity by *(1 + i)*:

$$
\begin{aligned}
\textit{FVAD} &= \textit{FVA x (1 + i)} \\
&= \$4,374.62 \times (1 + 6\%) \\
&= \$4,637.09
\end{aligned}
$$

ILLUSTRATION 5: Present value of ordinary annuity

Assume you are offered a personal computer for which you can pay installment payments of $1,000 (which include interest at 6%) at the end of each of the next four years. What price would you pay for the computer if you accept this offer?

Computation:

$$
\begin{aligned}
\textbf{\textit{PVA}} \quad &= \quad \$1,000 \times pva_{n=4,i=6\%} \\
&= \quad \$1,000 \times 3.46511 \text{ (from \textbf{Table 6-4})} \\
&= \quad \textbf{\$3,465.11}
\end{aligned}
$$

Since you pay $4,000 (i.e., $1,000 x 4) for the $3,465.11 computer, the remaining $534.89 represents interest paid for financing the purchase over the four years.

ILLUSTRATION 6: Present value of annuity due

Assume your installment payments in the previous illustration are made at the beginning of each year (i.e., one $1,000 payment now). What would be the effective purchase price of the computer?

Computation:

$$
\begin{aligned}
\textbf{\textit{PVAD}} \quad &= \quad \$1,000 \times pvad_{n=4,i=6\%} \\
&= \quad \$1,000 \times 3.67301 \text{ (from \textbf{Table 6-6})} \\
&= \quad \textbf{\$3,673.01}
\end{aligned}
$$

Note that the present value of annuity due can also be obtained by multiplying the present value of ordinary annuity by $(1 + i)$:

$$
\begin{aligned}
\textbf{\textit{PVAD}} \quad &= \quad \textbf{\textit{PVA}} \times \textbf{\textit{(1 + i)}} \\
&= \quad \$3,465.11 \times (1 + 6\%) \\
&= \quad \textbf{\$3,673.01}
\end{aligned}
$$

In some cases, the present value (or future value) is known and the periodic payments are to be determined. For example, in a later chapter you will determine the lease payments required in each of a specified number of periods to recover a specified investment, a present value. In these cases, the known present (or future) value is **divided by** the table value (for the appropriate number of interest periods and the appropriate interest rate) to derive the required periodic payments.

In other situations, the **interest rate** or the **number of interest periods** may be the unknown value. The solution requires that the present (or future) value be divided by the amount per payment to derive a **table value**. Locating this table value in **Table 6-4** (or **Table 6-3**) relative to the known value, n or i, determines the corresponding unknown value, i or n.

F. Miscellaneous Issues

1. **Linear interpolation of table values.** To determine the unknown interest rate (or number of interest periods), linear interpolation is often necessary. Linear interpolation is a method to compute how far between two table values does the factor corresponding to the implicit rate lie. Assume $2,000 is deposited in a savings account at the end of each year for three years. In order to accumulate to $7,500 at the end of the third year, what is the implicit interest rate, assuming annual compounding?

Computation:

a. To find the future value **factor** of ordinary annuity *(fva)* corresponding to the implicit interest rate:

$fva_{n=3,i=?}$ = $7,500 / $2,000 = 3.7500

b. Using the appropriate table and the given number of annuity payments, to find two nearest **table values** *(fva)* between which the above computed factor lies:

From **Table 6-3** with $n = 3$:

At interest rate = 22%, $fva_{n=3,i=22\%}$ = 3.7084
At interest rate = 24%, $fva_{n=3,i=24\%}$ = 3.7776

By inspection, the implicit interest rate is between 22% and 24%.

c. Linear interpolation:

```
22%   =   3.7084 ─┐
                  ├─> .0416 ─┐
 ?    =   3.7500 ─┘         ├─> .0692
                            │
24%   =   3.7776 ──────────┘
```

Implicit interest rate (**i**)
= 22% + (.0416 / .0692) x (24% - 22%)
= 22% + [.0416 / .0692] x 2%
= 22% + 1.2%
= 23.2%

2. **Deferred annuity.** When the first payment of an annuity occurs after two or more interest periods have elapsed (deferred), it is a deferred annuity. The future value of a deferred annuity is identical with that of an annuity not deferred. So it does not cause any computation problem. To calculate the present value of a deferred annuity, however, a certain adjustment is to be made to take care of the deferral.

Given:

n = number of annuity payments
n' = number of interest periods deferred
n" = number of interest periods deferred + number of annuity payments
   = n' + n

R = Rent (amount per payment)

Then the present value of a deferred ordinary annuity (PVA_d) can be calculated using the following equation:

$$PVA_d = R (pva_{n",i} - pva_{n',i})$$

To illustrate, you plan to deposit $1,000 in a savings account at the end of each year for three years beginning the end of the third year (1993). Assume the annual interest rate is 12%:

To determine the present value of the deferred ordinary annuity payments at the beginning of the first year (1991):

$$
\begin{aligned}
PVA_d &= \$1,000 \times (pva_{n"=5, i=12\%} - pva_{n'=2, i=12\%}) \\
&= \$1,000 \times (3.60478 - 1.69005) \text{ (from \textbf{Table 6-4})} \\
&= \$1,000 \times 1.91473 \\
&= \$1,915
\end{aligned}
$$

Alternatively, the same result may be obtained by first determine the future amount at the end of the fifth year, which is then discounted back to the beginning of the first year:

$$
\begin{aligned}
PVA_d &= \$1,000 \times fva_{n=3, i=12\%} \times pv1_{n"=5, i=12\%} \\
&= \$1,000 \times 3.3744 \times .56743 \\
&= \$1,915
\end{aligned}
$$

Note that when a series of payments becomes highly irregular, each payment may be considered as an independent single amount. Compute separately the future or present value of each of these single amounts, and sum them up to obtain the total future or present value of the payment series.

3. Multiple present and future value amounts

Careful analysis is required when a problem involves two or more present and future amounts. For example, you deposit $10,000 in your savings account which earns 10% interest annually. You will withdraw from this account three equal annual amounts, the first withdrawal to be made at the end of the fifth year. Compute the amount of each withdrawal.

a. Determine the future value of the single principal of $10,000 at 10% for 5 years:

$$FV = \$10,000 \times fv1_{n=5, i=10\%}$$
$$= \$10,000 \times 1.61051 \text{ (from } \textbf{Table 6-1}\text{)}$$
$$= \$16,105.10$$

b. The future value of the deposit becomes the present value of the withdrawals at the end of the fifth year (i.e., FV => PVAD). At that point in time, the withdrawals constitute an annuity due because the first withdrawal is on that date.

So:

Let: R   = the amount per withdrawal

$$PVAD = FV = R \times pvad_{n=3, i=10\%}$$

$$\$16,105.10 = R \times 2.73554 \text{ (from } \textbf{Table 6-6}\text{)}$$
$$R = \$16,105.10 / 2.73554$$
$$= \$5,887.35$$

Summary of Interest Concept:

Type of payments	Value to be computed	Symbol of value	Table to be used	Symbol of table value	Formula
Single principal (P)	Future value	FV,n,i	6-1	fv1,n,i	FV = P x fv1
Single future value (F)	Present value	PV,n,i	6-2	pv1,n,i	PV = F x pv1
Ordinary annuity (R)	Future value	FVA,n,i	6-3	fva,n,i	FVA = R x fva
Ordinary annuity (R)	Present value	PVA,n,i	6-4	pva,n,i	PVA = R x pva
Annuity due (R)	Future value	FVAD,n,i	6-5	fvad,n,i	FVAD = R x fvad
Annuity due (R)	Present value	PVAD,n,i	6-6	pvad,n,i	PVAD = R x pvad

KEY CONCEPTS

Annuity   A series of equal payments or receipts (usually called rents) at uniform intervals in time.

Annuity due   An annuity with each payment or receipt occurring at the beginning of a period.

Compound interest   Interest computed on the principal amount and all previously earned but unpaid interest.

Deferred annuity   An annuity with the first payment occurring two or more periods from the start.

Future value   The value at a specific future date, which includes the principal sum or periodic payments and the compound interest accrued up to that date.

Interest   The cost of using money over time, representing a time value of money.

Ordinary annuity   An annuity with each payment or receipt occurring at the end of a period.

Present value   The value of a fixed future amount discounted to the present time.

Simple interest   Interest computed on the principal only.

REVIEW QUESTIONS AND EXERCISES

TRUE-FALSE

Indicate whether each of the following statements is true or false by circling the correct response.

T   **F**   1.   The difference between an amount borrowed and the amount repaid generally is known as interest.

T   **F**   2.   By taking into account the time value of money, present value analysis allows a comparison of decision alternatives at a common point in time.

T   **F**   3.   The computation of simple interest includes both unpaid principal and unpaid interest.

T   **F**   4.   If interest is compounded semiannually, the rate used in the computation is the annual rate divided by 2, and the number of interest periods used is the number of years divided by 2.

T   **F**   5.   The present value of a future amount discounted at 15% is less than if discounted at 20%.

T   **F**   6.   The present value of an amount to be received 10 years hence is less than if the amount were to be received 5 years hence.

T   **F**   7.   An annuity is a series of equal periodic payments (or receipts) occurred at uniform intervals in time.

T   **F**   8.   In an ordinary annuity, equal payments are made at the beginning of each period.

T   **F**   9.   The present value of an annuity due is greater than the present value of an ordinary annuity.

T   **F**   10.   Given a specified interest rate, determining the future value of a series of year-end deposits utilizes the concept of the future value of an annuity due.

T   **F**   11.   Mike Hart wishes to make four equal year-end deposits to be able to withdraw $12,000 at the end of the fourth period. He should consult tables containing present values of an annuity due to calculate the amount per deposit.

T   **F**   12.   If Static Elect Ltd. is considering the purchase of a $10,000 computer by making monthly payments of $250 for 48 months, a table containing present values of an annuity can be used to solve for the applicable interest rate.

T   F   13. The future value of annuity table can be used to calculate an annuity's future value, the periodic rent, the interest rate, or the number of periods, if the other three values are known.

T   F   14. In all present and future value problems, n is always equal to the number of years.

EXERCISE 1

Several different business situations related to the concept of the time value of money are listed below. Indicate by letter the compound interest concept to be used in solving for the unknown amount in each situation.

Situation

___ 1. Amount that must be deposited at the end of each month to accumulate $10,000 at the end of five years, assuming the investment will earn a 12% rate of return.

___ 2. Amount required now to pay a $2,000 obligation due in 3 years.

___ 3. Amount necessary to prepay a 4-year insurance policy that would otherwise require $100 installments at the beginning of each year.

___ 4. Balance on deposit after 6 years as a result of a deposit of $4,000 today in a savings account.

___ 5. Balance on deposit after 5 years as a result of an annual year-end deposit of $1,000 in a savings account.

___ 6. Equal amounts required to be paid at the end of each month to purchase a $9,000 automobile on a 3-year loan at 10.9% interest.

Concepts

A. Future value of 1.

B. Present value of 1.

C. future value of an ordinary annuity of 1.

D. Present value of an ordinary annuity of 1.

E. Future value of an annuity due of 1.

F. Present value of an annuity due of 1.

EXERCISE 2

Abbey Company desires at least a 10% return on its investments. Determine the amount Abbey would be willing to pay for a bond with a face value of $5,000, a stated interest rate of 12% payable semiannually, and a ten-year term to maturity. (The present value of $1.00 discounted at 5% for 20 periods is .37689; the present value of an ordinary annuity of $1.00 at 5% for 20 periods is 12.4622.)

EXERCISE 3

Park Place Corporation acquired a truck for $75,000, agreeing to make payments in three equal, annual installments. The installment payments are to include payment for the truck, plus interest at 12% annually. The present value of an ordinary annuity of $1.00 for three periods at 12% is 2.40183. Calculate the amount of the three year-end installments.

MULTIPLE CHOICE

Enter the letter corresponding to the response which **best** completes each of the following statements or questions.

_____   1.   Presented below are four compound interest table values (factors) with the same interest periods (n) and interest rate (i). Which one is the table value (factor) for the present value of a single future amount?

      a.   3.79079.
      b.   4.16986.
      c.   6.10510.
      d.   0.62092.

_____   2.   Presented below are four compound interest table values (factors) of the present value of ordinary annuities with different numbers of payments at the same annual interest rate of 10%. Which one would be used to calculate the present value of an ordinary annuity with three annual payments?

      a.   0.90909.
      b.   2.48685.
      c.   3.16986.
      d.   4.86842.

_____   3.   Right-On Company purchased a truck on January 1, 1991. It was agreed that Right-On would pay the total amount due, $15,000, on January 1, 1992. Assuming a 12% rate of interest, the calculation of the purchase price of the truck would involve multiplying $15,000 by the:

      a.   present value of 1 (pv1).
      b.   future value of 1 (fv1).
      c.   present value of ordinary annuity of 1 (pva).
      d.   future value of ordinary annuity of 1 (fva).

_____   4.   Cindy Plower wants to calculate how much money she needs to deposit today into a savings account which earns 10% in order to be able to withdraw $5,000 at the end of each of the next 5 years. She should use which present value concept?

      a.   present value of an annuity due of $1 for 5 periods.
      b.   present value of an ordinary annuity of $1 for 5 periods.
      c.   present value of $1 for 5 periods.
      d.   future value of $1 for 5 periods.

_____ 5. The method that should be used to compute the interest rate necessary on a given amount deposited today in order to withdraw a fixed amount at the beginning at each year for the next 5 years is the:

    a.   future amount of an ordinary annuity.
    b.   future amount of an annuity due.
    c.   present value of an ordinary annuity.
    d.   present value of an annuity due.

_____ 6. If the present value is to be calculated on monthly payments over 3 years, discounted at an annual rate of 12%, the interest periods (n) and the interest rate (i) used to find the appropriate table value (factor) would be:

    a.   3 periods, 12%.
    b.   3 periods, 1%.
    c.   36 periods, 12%.
    d.   36 periods, 1%.

_____ 7. In which of the following circumstances would a company not be concerned about future/present value concepts?

    a.   computing how much to deposit into a fund today in order to have the necessary cash in 10 years to repay bonds.
    b.   computing how much must be deposited into a pension fund today to cover the estimated future retirement payments.
    c.   calculating whether to buy a machine which will save $5,000 in each of the next 5 years or a machine that will save $6,000 per year for 4 years, when the cost of each machine is the same.
    d.   computing the payroll for the following payday including all related federal tax, CPP, and unemployment insurance cost considerations.

_____ 8. Molten Ltd. is involved in a two-year project in which its expected rate of return is 10%. Molten is investing $40,000 today and will invest another $50,000 one year from today. The present value of $1 for one period at 10% is .909 and for two periods is .826. For comparison with projected benefits, Molten should consider the cost of the investment at today's value to be:

    a. $74,340.
    b. $77,660.
    c. $85,455.
    d. $90,000.

_____ 9. Margaret Brown plans to make semiannual deposits of $1,000 in her savings account over the next three years. The annual interest rate is 12% compounded semiannually. The first deposit will be made immediately. How much will Margaret have accumulated by the end of the third year?

   a. $3,779.33.
   b. $7,393.84.
   c. $2,690.05.
   d. $5,212.36.

_____ 10. Quick Company purchased a truck and agreed to pay for it in five equal annual payments of $5,000 at the end of each of the next five years. If the annual interest rate is 10%, how much should be recorded as the cost of the truck?

   a. $18,953.95.
   b. $25,000.00.
   c. $61,051.00.
   d. $20,849.35.

_____ 11. On January 1, 1991, Futura Corporation decides to make five annual deposits in order to accumulate a fund of $500,000 to be available at the beginning of 1996. If the fund will earn interest at 12%, compounded annually, and the first deposit will be made at the end of 1991, how much should be the annual deposit amount (rounded to the nearest dollar)?

   a. $100,000.
   b. $ 90,496.
   c. $ 85,436.
   d. $ 78,705.

_____ 12. Assume the same data as in Item 11, except that the first payment is made on January 1, 1991, the annual deposit amount would be (rounded to the nearest dollar):

   a. $90,496.
   b. $85,436.
   c. $78,705.
   d. $70,272.

_____ 13. Henry purchased a personal computer and agreed to pay $4,000 today, $5,000 one year from today and $6,000 two years from today. If the annual interest rate is 10%, the acquisition cost of the computer is:

   a. $15,000.00.
   b. $13,504.15.
   c. $13,636.35.
   d. $12,434.25.

_____ 14. Based on the same information as in Item 13, except that J & J is offered the option to make equal installment payments of $5,000 at the end of the next three years. The acquisition cost of the computer would then be:

a. $15,000.00.
b. $13,504.15.
c. $13,636.35.
d. $12,434.25.

SOLUTIONS TO REVIEW QUESTIONS AND EXERCISES

TRUE-FALSE

1.	T	5.	F	9.	T	13.	T
2.	T	6.	T	10.	F	14.	F
3.	F	7.	T	11.	F		
4.	F	8.	F	12.	T		

EXERCISE 1

1.	C	4.	A
2.	B	5.	C
3.	F	6.	D

EXERCISE 2

Abbey would be willing to pay as much as $5,623.11 to yield 10% on the investment. This is the total of the present value of the $5,000 principal payment to be received in 10 years ($1,884.45) and the present value of the semiannual interest payments ($3,738.66).

Calculations:

```
PV of single future amount ($5,000 x .37689)        $1,884.45
Present value of ordinary annuity ($300 x 12.4622)   3,738.66
                                                    _____
         Total present value of the bond            $5,623.11
                                                    ==========
```

EXERCISE 3

The annual payment amount (R) is $31,226.

Calculations:

$$R = PVA / pva_{n=3, i=12\%}$$

$$= \$75,000 / 2.40183$$

$$= \$31,226.$$

MULTIPLE CHOICE:

1.	d	5.	d	9.	b	13.	b
2.	b	6.	d	10.	a	14.	d
3.	a	7.	d	11.	d		
4.	b	8.	c	12.	d		

Computations:

8.   (c)   Cost of investment $= \$40,000 + \$50,000 \times pv1_{n=1, i=10\%}$
$$= \$40,000 + \$50,000 \times .90909$$
$$= \$85,455.$$

9.   (b)   FVAD (the accumulated amount) $= \$1,000 \times fvad_{n=6, i=6\%}$
$$= \$1,000 \times 7.39384$$
$$= \$7,393.84.$$

10.   (a)   PVA (the acquisition cost of truck) $= \$5,000 \times pva_{n=5, i=10\%}$
$$= \$5,000 \times 3.79079$$
$$= \$18,953.95.$$

11.   (d)   R (rent or annual deposit amount) $= FVA / fva_{n=5, i=12\%}$
$$= \$500,000 / 6.35285$$
$$= \$78,705.$$

12.   (d)   R (rent or annual deposit amount) $= FVAD / fvad_{n=5, i=12\%}$
$$= \$500,000 / 7.11519$$
$$= \$70,272.$$

13.   (b)   PV (the acquisition cost of computer)
$$= \$4,000 \times 1.000 + \$5,000 \times .90909 + 6,000 \times .82645$$
$$= \$4,000 + \$4,545.45 + \$4,958.70$$
$$= \$13,504.15.$$

14.   (d)   PVA (the acquisition cost of computer) $= \$5,000 \times pva_{n=3, i=10\%}$
$$= \$5,000 \times 2.48685$$
$$= \$12,434.25.$$

CHAPTER 7

Revenue and Expense Recognition

CHAPTER OBJECTIVES

This chapter is designed to enable students to:

A.   Explain the theory and conceptual framework underlying current revenue recognition practices.

B.   Explain the revenue and matching principles for expenses and apply them to income determination for most sales transactions.

C.   Apply the acceptable methods of accounting for revenue for long-term contracts and identify the circumstances where each is appropriate.

D.   Use the installment and cost recovery methods of revenue recognition and identify the circumstances where each is appropriate.

E.   Properly account for revenue when the right of return exists.

F.   Apply the principles of revenue recognitition for service sales using four different methods: (a) specific performance, (b) proportional performance, (c) completed performance, and (d) collection.

G.   Apply the theory and conceptual framework linking expense to revenue recongnition.

CHAPTER OVERVIEW

A.   As presented in Chapter 2, **revenues** are inflows of assets or settlements of liabilities whereas **expenses** are outflows of assets or incurrence of liabilities, from activities that constitute the entity's ongoing major or central operations. To provide guidelines for implementing the definitions of these and other elements of the financial statements, the following **fundamental criteria** which should be the basis to recognizing any item for accounting purposes are presented:

1.   The item meets the definition of an **element of financial statements.**
2.   The item has relevant attribute that is reliably **measurable.**
3.   The information about the item is **relevant.**
4.   The information about the item is **reliable.**

In addition, there are specific implementation principles with respect to the recognition of revenues:

1. **Revenue recognition principle**:   Theoretically, revenues are earned through a continuous earning process, involving the receipt of an order, the production of a product, a sale and the subsequent collection of cash. Yet, in order to provide timely information, a decision must be made concerning the point during or after this process at which revenues should be recognized. Following the **CICA, Sec. 1000**, revenues are recognized when:

    a. The item has an appropriate basis of measurment and a reasonable estimate can be made of the amount involved.

    b. For items involving obtaining or giving up future economic benefits, it is probable that such benefits will be obtained or given up.

    Thus, revenues are normally recognized when performance is achieved and reasonable assurance exists with respect to measurement and collectability of the consideration. Gains are recognized when realized.

B. **Expense recognition principle:**

1. Expenses incurred in generating revenues are matched with those revenues. More specifically, expenses are generally recognized when an entity's economic benefits are used up in delivering or producing goods, rendering services or other activities that constitute its ongoing major or central operations. The following three classes of expenses are identifiable:

    a. **Direct expenses** (e.g., cost of goods sold, sales commissions and service labor) are recognized for the reporting period in which the related sales revenue is recognized.

    b. **Period expenses** (e.g., advertising expenses, general and administrative expenses, and research and development expenses) are recognized during the period in which cash is spent or liabilities are incurred.

    c. **Allocated expenses** (e.g., depreciation and insurance) are apportioned by systematic and rational procedures to the periods expected to benefit from the incurrence of these expenses.

2. **Points of Revenue Recognition**

    For most firms, merchandise is normally exchanged for cash or for a short-term promise of cash payment with revenues recognition at delivery. In these cases, sales revenues are recognized on the date the merchandise is delivered or the services have been performed, generally referred to as the point of sale (or delivery). The related expenses, on the other hand, may be recognized at the sale point, or at the end of the accounting period in which the revenues are recognized.

Due to the complexity of sales transactions and different degrees of uncertainty regarding the collection of accounts receivable and the related costs after sales, there are special applications of these recognition principles:

3. **Revenue recognition before delivery.**   This includes (a) accounting for long-term contracts under the **percentage-of-completion method**, under which revenues are recognized even when work on the product is still in process; and (b) accounting for the production of certain precious metals or agricultural products with assured prices and insignificant distribution costs under the **completion-of-production method**, under which revenues are recognized when the production process is completed, even if the product is not yet sold.

4. **Revenue recognition after delivery**.   This includes (a) **the installment method** and (b) the **cost recovery method,** under which revenues are deferred even sales are made and merchandise is physically delivered. These (2) two methods are covered in section D.

C.   Accounting for Long-Term Construction Contracts

In the construction industry a project often spans **more than one accounting period**. The question arises as to whether to recognize revenues and expenses only at the completion, or **throughout** the earning process of the construction. The completed-contract method is both more objective and more conservative. Income is recognition is delayed until all income is earned. The percentage-of-completion method recognizes income as it is earned over the life of the contract.

Either of these two estimations can result in errors and potentially misleading information. Section 3400 of the *CICA Handbook* allows either method depending on the relationship to the work accomplished. Thus, it is still necessary to apply professional judgment.

1. **The completed-contract method:**   Before the construction project is completed, neither revenue, nor expense, is recognized. Construction costs are initially debited to an inventory account entitled construction in process inventory. When the project is completed, the total contract price is recognized as sales (or revenues from contracts), and the inventory is transferred to the cost of sales (or cost of construction). The difference between these two numbers is the realized gross profit for the year of completion.

2. **The percentage-of-completion method:**   Under this method, revenues, expenses and gross profit are recognized in each year during the construction period in proportion to the percentage of total project completed during the specific year. The following steps are pertinent:

Step 1:   Compute cumulative percentage of completion based on actual and estimated costs.

Step 2:   Compute cumulative gross profit to be recognized to date by multiplying cumulative percentage of completion by the estimated total gross profit of the project (i.e., contract price minus the estimated total costs).

Step 3: Determine gross profit to be recognized in the year by subtracting previously recognized gross profit from the cumulative gross profit to be recognized to date.

Step 4: Record the transactions for the year:

a. To record construction costs as incurred:

Construction in process inventory   xxxx
    Cash, accounts payable, etc.   xxxx

b. To recognize current gross profit:

Construction in process inventory   xxxx
Costs of Construction   xxxx
    Revenues from long-term contracts   xxxx

The above entries show that (1) construction costs incurred continue to accumulate in the inventory account, (2) the recognized gross profit is added to the inventory account, and (3) two nominal accounts, namely, costs of construction (i.e., construction costs currently incurred) and revenues from long-term contracts are created to record and report current gross profit. Note that the amount of revenues is the sum of construction costs currently incurred and gross profit currently recognized.

Under either method, progress billings are recorded with a debit to receivable and a credit to **billings on contracts**. The credit balance of billings on contracts account is reported on the balance sheet to offset the debit balance of the **construction in process inventory**. They are both closed when the construction is completed. Until then they are presented as current assets if their net balance is a debit, or as current liabilities if their net balance is a credit.

It should be noted that, regardless of the method applied, if a **loss** is indicated for any year of the construction period, it should be recognized for that year as a reduction in construction in process inventory. Under the percentage-of-completion method, a loss incurred when the previously recognized gross profit exceeds the cumulative gross profit to be recognized to date.

ILLUSTRATION 1: Accounting for Long-term Construction Contracts

Solid Construction Ltd. contracted to build a city hall for the City of New Hills for $2,000,000. The construction costs of the contract were initially estimated to be $1,200,000. Data relevant to the project are shown below (in $000):

	1991	1992	1993	Total
Contract price				$2,000
Costs incurred	$ 300	$ 900	$ 450	1,650
Estimated additional costs	1,200	514	0	
Progress billings	270	810	920	2,000
Collections on billings	223	675	1,102	2,000

Additional information:

1. Contract price remained unchanged throughout the construction.
2. Costs incurred were actual costs for each of the construction years. Note that actual costs deviated from the estimates.
3. Additional costs to complete were estimates at the end of each of the construction years, and the estimated total costs (including cumulative actual costs and estimated additional costs to complete) were revised from year to year.
4. Progress billings were based on the construction contract.

Required: Based on the above information:

1. Determine gross profit to be recognized under:

   a. The completed-contract method; and
   b. The percentage-of-completion method.

2. Prepare journal entries under:

   a. The completed-contract method; and
   b. The percentage-of-completion method.

SOLUTION:

1. DETERMINE GROSS PROFITS:

   a. Completed-contract method:

	1991	1992	1993
Total contract price			$2,000
Total costs incurred			(1,650)
Gross profit from construction			$ 350

b. Percentage-of-completion method:

Total contract price	$2,000	$2,000	$2,000
Actual costs to date (cumulative)	$ 300	$1,200	$1,650
Estimated costs to complete	1,200	514	0
Estimated total costs	$1,500	$1,714	$1,650

Percentage of completion to date:

$300/$1,500	20%		
$1,200/$1,714		70%	
$1,650/$1,650			100%

Estimated total gross profit:

$2,000 - $1,500	$ 500		
$2,000 - $1,714		$ 286	
$2,000 - $1,650			$ 350

Gross profit to be recognized to date:

$500 x 20%	$ 100		
$286 x 70%		$200	
$350 x 100%			$ 350
Less: Gross profit recognized in previous years	0	100	200
Gross profit in current year	$ 100	$ 100	$ 150

2. JOURNAL ENTRIES:

	Completed -Contract	Percentage-of- Completion

1991:

a. To record costs of construction:

Construction in process inventory	300		300
Cash, payable, etc.		300	300

b. To record progress billings:

Accounts receivable	270		270
Billings on contracts		270	270

c. To record collections on billings:

Cash	223		223
Accounts receivable		223	223

d. To recognize gross profit:

Construction in process inventory	n/a		100
Costs of construction			300
Revenues from contracts			400

1992:

a. To record costs of construction:

Construction in process inventory	900		900	
Cash, payable, etc.		900		900

b. To record progress billings:

Accounts receivable	810		810	
Billings on contracts		810		810

c. To record collections on billings:

Cash	675		675	
Accounts receivable		675		675

d. To recognize gross profit:

Construction in process inventory	n/a		100	
Costs of construction			900	
Revenues from contracts				1,000

1993:

a. To record costs of construction:

Construction in process inventory	450		450	
Cash, payable, etc.		450		450

b. To record progress billings:

Accounts receivable	920		920	
Billings on contracts		920		920

c. To record collections on billings:

Cash	1,102		1,102	
Accounts receivable		1,102		1,102

d1. To recognize revenues and expenses:

Billings on contracts	2,000	
Costs of construction (expenses)	1,650	
Revenues from contracts		2,000
Construction in process inventory		1,650

d2. To recognize gross profit and to close offsetting accounts:

Construction in process inventory	150	
Costs of construction	450	
Revenues from contracts		600
Billings on contracts	2,000	
Construction in process inventory		2,000

D. Installment Method

An installment sale occurs when a contract is signed calling for the purchaser to make payments in accordance with a plan over a period of time. Most installment sales result in revenue recognition at the point of sale. However, if, and only if, (1) receivables are to be collected over an extended period of time, and (2) because of the terms of the contract and other conditions, there is no reasonable basis for estimating the degree of collectibility, either the installment method or the cost recovery method may be used.

Under the installment method, both sales and cost of sales are recorded in the period of sale, but the related gross profit is deferred to those periods in which cash is collected. The accounting procedures are outlined as follows:

1. Record installment sales and cost of installment sales as incurred, and cash as collected.

2. At the end of the year, close installment sales and cost of installment sales to deferred gross profit and compute the gross profit rate for current installment sales as sales less cost of sales divided by sales.

3. Apply the gross profit rate to cash collected from current installment sales to determine gross profit from current installment sales realized and to be recognized in the year.

4. For cash currently collected from installment sales made in any prior year, apply that year's gross profit rate to the collected amount to determine gross profit from that year's installment sales realized and to be recognized in the current year.

5. The recognized gross profit is reported on the income statement; whereas the unrealized gross profit is deferred and presented on the balance sheet as a deduction from the related installment accounts receivable. Note that the ending balance of the deferred gross profit and the related accounts receivable should always reflect the appropriate gross profit rate.

6. In case of repossession of merchandise resulting from a customers' default, both the installment accounts receivable and the related deferred gross profit should be written off and the repossessed merchandise is recorded at its fair or net realizable value. A gain or loss is recognized to balance the repossession entry.

ILLUSTRATION 2:   Installment Method

Kern-Valley Company uses the installment method in accounting for installment sales. In 1991, Clement made installment sales of $150,000, of which $60,000, $60,000 and $30,000 were collected in 1991, 1992 and 1993, respectively. The cost of the merchandise sold was $90,000.

Required: Based on the above information, prepare journal entries for 1991, 1992 and 1993.

SOLUTION:

1991:

a.   **To record installment sales:**

Installment accounts receivable – 1991	150,000	
Installment sales		150,000

b.   **To record cost of installment sales:**

Cost of installment sales	90,000	
Inventory		90,000

c.   **To record collection of cash:**

Cash	60,000	
Installment accounts receivable – 1991		60,000

d.   **To record deferred gross profit:**

Installment sales	150,000	
Cost of installment sales		90,000
Deferred gross profit – 1991		60,000

Note that gross profit rate of current installment sales is:
($150,000 – $90,000) / $150,000 = 40%.

e.   **To recognize realized gross profit ($60,000 x 40% = $24,000):**

Deferred gross profit – 1991	24,000	
Realized gross profit – 1991		24,000

1992

a.   **To record collection of cash:**

Cash	60,000	
Installment accounts receivable – 1991		60,000

b.   **To recognize realized gross profit ($60,000 x 40% = $24,000):**

Deferred gross profit – 1991	24,000	
Realized gross profit – 1991		24,000

1993:

a.   **To record collection of cash:**

Cash	30,000	
Installment accounts receivable – 1991		30,000

b.   **To recognize realized gross profit ($30,000 x 40% = $12,000):**

Deferred gross profit – 1991	12,000	
Realized gross profit – 1991		12,000

ILLUSTRATION 3:   Repossession of merchandise

Assume the same fact as in **ILLUSTRATION 2,** except that the amount collected in 1993 was $28,000. The remaining balance of accounts receivable ($2,000) was defaulted and Clement repossessed the merchandise which was estimated to have a fair value of $1,000.

Required: Prepare journal entry to record the transactions in 1993.

SOLUTION:

1993:

a. **To record collection of cash:**

Cash	28,000	
Installment accounts receivable - 1991		28,000

b. **To recognize realized gross profit**
    ($28,000 x 40% = $11,200):

Deferred gross profit - 1991	11,200	
Realized gross profit - 1991		11,200

c. **To record repossession of merchandise:**

Inventory of repossessed merchandise	1,000	
Deferred gross profit-1991 ($2,000 x 40%)	800	
Loss on repossession of merchandise	200	
Installment accounts receivable - 1991		2,000

2.   Cost Recovery Method

The installment method is based on the assumption that, even there is no reasonable basis for estimating the degree of collectibility, the degree of the uncertainty is moderate so that partial recognition of income with each dollar collected is appropriate. However, if there is a **very high degree of uncertainty**, it seems justifiable to view every dollar received as representing recovery of product cost until the cost is fully recovered. This is the cost recovery method, under which equal amounts of revenue and expense are recognized as collections are made until all costs have been recovered, postponing any recognition of profit until that time.

The **CICA, Sec. 3400** states that, for sales of **real estate**, if (1) recovery of cost of the property is not reasonably assured, (2) the buyer defaults, or (3) cost has already been recovered and collection of additional amount is uncertain, the cost recovery method (or the deposit method) shall be used. Under the deposit method, cash received from the buyer is reported as a deposit on the sales contract, and the property under the sales contract is still reported as an asset in the financial statements of the seller until the cost is fully recovered.

E.   Revenue Recognition When Right of Return Exists

Following the **CICA, Sec. 3400**, if an enterprise sells its product but gives the buyer the right to return the product, revenue from the sale shall be recognized at the time of sale only if all the following conditions are met:

1.   The price is substantially fixed or determinable at the date of sale.

2.   The buyer has paid the seller, or the buyer's obligation to pay the seller is not contingent on the buyer's resale of the product.

3.   The buyer's obligation to the seller would not be changed in the event of theft or physical destruction of or damage to the product.

4.   The buyer has economic substance apart from that provided by the seller.

5.   The seller does not have significant obligations to directly bring about resale of the product by the buyer.

6.   The amount of future returns can be reasonably estimated.

If one or more of these conditions are not met, a variation of the installment method is used. i.e., both sales and cost of goods sold are closed to deferred gross profit, which will then be recognized when either the return privilege expires, or all the above conditions are finally met.

F.   Service Sales

When services are sold, recognition of the revenue depends on the nature of the service performed, particularly as it relates to the point at which the service is **substantially performed**. The four methods of revenue recognition for service sales are described as follows:

1.   The **specific performance method** is used when service revenue is earned by performing a **single act**, such as a doctor performing surgery for a fee. Revenue is recognized **when the act is performed** (or when all material services or conditions relating to the sale have been substantially performed).

      Franchise fees received, for which the franchisor has additional services to perform, should be **deferred** until commencement of operations by the franchisee (presumed to be the earliest point at which substantial performance has occurred).

2.   The **proportional performance method** is used when service revenue is earned by **performance of more than one act**. Revenue is recognized based on the proportional performance of each act, similar to the percentage-of-completion method illustrated above. Determining the proportional performance depends on the nature of the acts performed, as follows:

      a.   If the acts are **similar**, such as monthly maintenance services, recognize an **equal** amount of revenue for each act.

b.   If the acts are **dissimilar**, such as periodic tax preparation services, recognize revenue in proportion to the seller's direct costs to perform each act.

c.   If the acts are **similar with a fixed period of performance,** such as computer maintenance services for a fixed annual fee, recognize revenue on a **straight-line basis** over the fixed period.

3.   The **completed-performance method** is used when service revenue is earned by performing a series of acts, in which the final act is so important to the service that revenue cannot be considered as having been earned until the final act occurs.

4.   The **collection method** is used when there is significant **uncertainty** regarding the collection of fees or the amount of related expenses. Revenue is not recorded until the cash is collected.

RECOGNITION OF GAINS AND LOSSES

G.   Gains and losses result fro peripheral or incidental transactions, events, and circumstances. Whether an item is a gain or loss of an ordinary revenue or expense depends on the primary activities or businesses of the reporting entity. Gains and losses are distinguished from revenues ad expenses. Most gains and losses are recognized when the related transaction is completed.

Estimated loses, but not gains, are recognized prior to their ultimate realization. For example, unrealized losses on (1) write-downs of short-term investments to market value below cost, (2) disposal of a segment of the business, (3) pending litigation; and expropriation of assets are recognized if they both are likely and can be reasonably estimated (*CICA Handbook*, section 3290). If both conditions are not met, the nature and estimated amount of the contingent loss must be disclosed in a note to the financial statements.

In contrast, gains are almost never recognized prior to the completion of a transaction that establishes the existence and amount of the gain.

KEY CONCEPTS

Accounting for long-term contracts -- Completed-contract method   Revenues and expenses are recognized when the long-term project is completed and the product delivered. Construction costs are accumulated in an inventory account and progress billings are accumulated in a contra inventory account. When the project is completed, these two accounts are closed to costs (expense) and revenues accounts, respectively, and their difference reflects the gross profit of the project.

Accounting for long-term contracts -- Percentage-of-completion method   Gross profit is recognized annually based on the percentage of the project completed during the year. Before the completion of the project, construction costs incurred and gross profit recognized are recorded in an inventory account, which is closed against billings on contracts when the project is completed.

Cost recovery method   Gross profit on sales is not recognized until the cost of goods sold is fully recovered. This method is an alternative to the installment method, but is more appropriate when the uncertainty about the collectibility is very high.

Expense recognition principle   Expense is recognized as incurred. Expenses may directly or indirectly match with revenues. Indirect expenses, which match indirectly with revenues, may be recognized by relating them to a time period or by means of systematic and rational allocation.

Installment method   Gross profit on installment sales is recognized in proportion to the relative amount of cash collected during a specific period, based on the appropriate gross profit rate. This method is appropriate if accounts receivable are collectible over an extended period of time and there is no reasonable basis for estimating the degree of collectibility.

Recognition principle (general)   An accounting item is recognized if (1) the item meets the definition of an element of financial statements, (2) it is measurable, (3) the information about the item is relevant, and (4) the information about the item is reliable.

Revenue recognition (service sales)   Revenue recognition is based on the nature of the service performed. Revenue should be recognized when the service has been substantially performed. If the service involves more than one performance, recognize revenue based on the number of performance if the acts are similar, based on the relative direct costs incurred if the acts are dissimilar. If the collection is highly uncertain, revenue is not recognized until cash is collected.

Revenue recognition principle (general)   Revenue should be recognized when it is (1) earned and (2) realized or realizable. Revenue is realized when products or other assets are sold for cash. Revenue is realizable when products or other assets are sold and claims for cash, which are readily convertible to known amount of cash, are received.

REVIEW QUESTIONS AND EXERCISES

TRUE-FALSE

Indicate whether each of the following statements is true or false by circling the correct response.

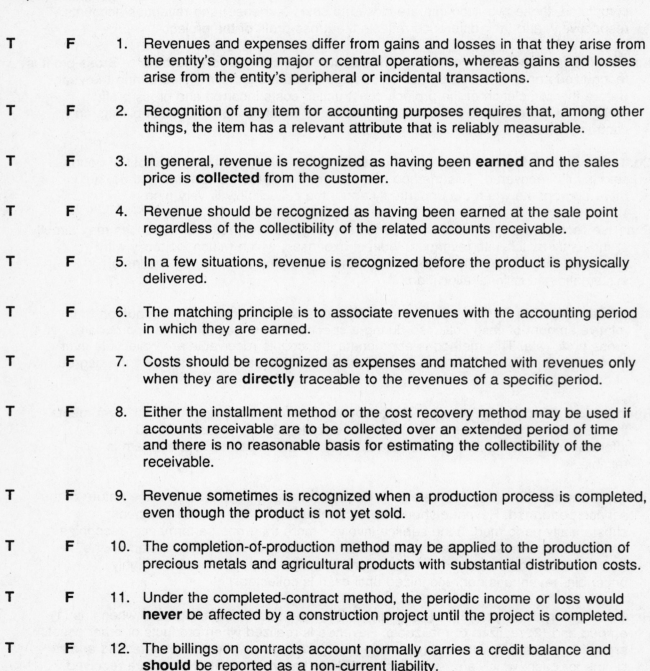

T   F   1. Revenues and expenses differ from gains and losses in that they arise from the entity's ongoing major or central operations, whereas gains and losses arise from the entity's peripheral or incidental transactions.

T   F   2. Recognition of any item for accounting purposes requires that, among other things, the item has a relevant attribute that is reliably measurable.

T   F   3. In general, revenue is recognized as having been **earned** and the sales price is **collected** from the customer.

T   F   4. Revenue should be recognized as having been earned at the sale point regardless of the collectibility of the related accounts receivable.

T   F   5. In a few situations, revenue is recognized before the product is physically delivered.

T   F   6. The matching principle is to associate revenues with the accounting period in which they are earned.

T   F   7. Costs should be recognized as expenses and matched with revenues only when they are **directly** traceable to the revenues of a specific period.

T   F   8. Either the installment method or the cost recovery method may be used if accounts receivable are to be collected over an extended period of time and there is no reasonable basis for estimating the collectibility of the receivable.

T   F   9. Revenue sometimes is recognized when a production process is completed, even though the product is not yet sold.

T   F   10. The completion-of-production method may be applied to the production of precious metals and agricultural products with substantial distribution costs.

T   F   11. Under the completed-contract method, the periodic income or loss would **never** be affected by a construction project until the project is completed.

T   F   12. The billings on contracts account normally carries a credit balance and **should** be reported as a non-current liability.

T   F   13. Under the percentage-of-completion method, the construction in process inventory account is debited for both construction costs and the recognized gross profit.

T   F   14. Under the installment method, any amount of cash received indicates a portion of realized revenue.

EXERCISE 1

Indicate with the appropriate letter the point during the earning process at which revenue and gross profit generally are recognized in each of the following situations:

Situation	Stage of the Earning Process
___ 1. Completed-contract method for long-term projects.	A. An order is received or production is scheduled.
___ 2. Credit sales of merchandise (short term).	B. During the production process.
___ 3. Percentage-of-completion method	C. Production is completed.
___ 4. Installment sales of merchandise in which a reasonable basis for estimating uncollectible accounts is lacking, but uncertainty about the collectibility is considered moderate.	D. Sale. E. Cash is collected. F. Cost is fully recovered.
___ 5. Noncash sales of merchandise (an exchange).	
___ 6. Real estate sales with a very high degree of uncertainty about the collectibility of accounts receivable.	

EXERCISE 2

F. & F. Builders LTD. contracted to costruct a building for $5,000,000. Data relevant to the project are shown below for the construction period, 1991 and 1992 (in $000).

	1991	1992	Total
Contract price			$5,000
Costs incurred during the year	$1,200	$1,800	$3,000
Estimated additional costs	$2,000	0	

Required: Determine the construction income that F & F should recognize in both 1991 and 1992 using (1) the completed-contract method, and (2) the percentage-of-completion method.

1. **Completed-contract method:**

	1991	1992
Total contract price		
Total costs incurred		
Gross profit from construction		

2. **Percentage-of-completion method:**

	1991	1992
Total contract price		
Actual costs to date (cumulative)		
Estimated costs to complete		
Estimated total costs		
Percentage of completion to date		
Estimated total gross profit		
Gross profit to be recognized to date		
Less: Gross profit recognized in previous years		
Gross profit in current year		

EXERCISE 3

In 1991, Dan Willms Company sold an office computer for $50,000, received a down-payment of $10,000 and required the balance be paid by two installments of $20,000 each, due in 1992 and 1993. Willms collected $20,000 in 1992, and repossessed the computer (estimated net realizable value, $8,000) in 1993 as the customer failed to pay the remaining $20,000 when due. The merchandise sold cost Willms $23,000.

Required: Prepare the required entries for 1991, 1992, and 1993, respectively, assuming the installment method is used.

1991:   To record the sale.

To record the cost of sales.

To record the receipt of down-payment.

To record deferred gross profit.

To record the realized gross profit.

1992:   **To record the collection.**

To record the realized gross profit.

1993:   **To record the repossession of merchandise.**

MULTIPLE CHOICE

Enter the letter corresponding to the response which **best** completes each of the following statements or questions.

____ 1. The **CICA, Sec. 1000** Statement of Concepts No. 6 defines the **elements** of financial statements. In defining **revenues**, the Handbook identified each of the following attributes **except:**

    a. may be settlements of liabilities.
    b. may be proceeds from selling the entity's own stock.
    c. may be inflows of assets.
    d. result from activities that constitute the entity's ongoing major operations.

____ 2. Each of the following is an essential characteristic of an expense, **except:**

    a. It is a result of activities that constitute the entity's ongoing major operations.
    b. It represents distributions to the stockholders of the entity.
    c. It represents an outflow of assets or the incurrence of a liability.
    d. It represents actual or expected cash outflows (or the equivalent).

____ 3. Each of the following is a criterion for the recognition of an item in the financial statements **except:**

    a. The information about the item must be reported on the same valuation basis as those of the prior periods.
    b. The information about the item is relevant.
    c. The item must meet the definition of an element of financial statements.
    d. The item has a relevant attribute that is reliably measurable.

____ 4. In general, revenue is recognized when the earning process is virtually complete, and

    a. the sales price has been realized or is realizable.
    b. the sales price has been collected.
    c. production is completed.
    d. a purchase order has been received.

____ 5. The **primary** justification for the cost recovery method is to:

    a. assure consistent treatment of sales revenues.
    b. provide uniform measurement of income.
    c. comply with the conservatism constraint.
    d. apply the cost principle.

____ 6. When using the percentage-of-completion method to account for a long-term contract, the gross profit recognized in the first year of a three-year construction project generally is the estimate of total gross profit from the project multiplied by the ratio of:

a. estimated costs to complete to estimated total costs.
b. estimated costs to complete to actual costs incurred to date.
c. estimated total costs to estimated costs to complete.
d. actual costs incurred to date to estimated total costs.

____ 7. Gross profit on a long-term contract is recognized when billings are sent under the:

	Completed-contract method	Percentage-of-Completion method
a.	No	No
b.	Yes	No
c.	Yes	Yes
d.	No	Yes

____ 8. Under the installment method:

a. Gross profit is measured by the difference between the cash collection and the cost of installment sales.
b. Gross profit is recognized at the point of sale.
c. Gross profit is deferred until the cost is fully recovered.
d. Gross profit is recognized proportional to the amount of sales price collected during the period.

____ 9. Green Company uses the percentage-of-completion method of accounting for long-term contracts. During 1991, Green began work on a construction project with a fixed contract price of $100,000. The project was completed in 1995. The following accounting data are pertinent:

	Cumulative Contract costs incurred	Estimated additional cost to complete
1991	$ 10,000	$50,000
1992	24,000	36,000
1993	39,000	26,000

In 1993, Green should have recognized gross profit on this contract of:

a. $ 5,000.
b. $ 6,000.
c. $ 8,000.
d. $ 4,000.

___ 10. Henry's Computer Store appropriately uses the installment method of accounting. The following data are available for 1991:

Installment sales	$250,000
Cost of sales	$150,000
Cash collections	$100,000

The gross profit on installment sales realized in and deferred at the end of 1991 should be:

	Realized	Deferred
a.	$20,000	$80,000
b.	$30,000	$70,000
c.	$40,000	$60,000
d.	$60,000	$40,000

___ 11. Gerry Ko Company uses the installment method of accounting for installment sales. The following data are obtained from its accounting records:

	1991	1992
Installment sales	$250,000	$360,000
Cost of installment sales	$175,000	$288,000
Amount collected from:		
1991 installment sales	$150,000	$ 50,000
1992 installment sales	0	$216,000

The realized gross profits for 1991 and 1992 are:

	1991	1992
a.	$105,000	$207,800
b.	$ 75,000	$164,600
c.	$135,000	$216,000
d.	$ 45,000	$ 58,200

___ 12. In 1991 FFF Construction Corporation contracted to build a motel. The contract price is $300,000 and the total cost is estimated as $200,000. Over the construction period there is no change in either the contract price, or the estimated total cost. Costs incurred for 1991 and 1992 are $100,000 and $80,000, respectively.

How much gross profit should be recognized in 1991 under the percentage-of-completion method:

    a. $40,000
    b. $50,000
    c. $60,000
    d. $80,000

___ 13. Based on the same data as in Item No. 12, what should be the balance of the construction in process inventory account at the end of 1991 under the percentage-of-completion method:

    a. $100,000.
    b. $120,000.
    c. $140,000.
    d. $150,000.

___ 14. Based on the same data as in Item No. 12, what should be the ending balance of construction in process inventory at the end of 1992 under the percentage-of-completion method:

    a. $100,000
    b. $200,000.
    c. $250,000.
    d. $270,000.

SOLUTIONS TO REVIEW QUESTIONS AND EXERCISES

TRUE-FALSE

1.	T	5.	T	9.	T	13.	T
2.	T	6.	F	10.	F	14.	T
3.	F	7.	F	11.	F		
4.	F	8.	T	12.	F		

EXERCISE 1

1.	C	4.	E
2.	D	5.	D
3.	B	6.	F

EXERCISE 2

1. Completed-contract method:

	1991	1992
Total contract price	0	$5.000
Total costs incurred	0	3,000
Gross profit from construction	0	$2,000

2. Percentage-of-completion method:

	1991	1992
Total contract price	$5,000	$5,000
Actual costs to date (cumulative)	$1,200	$3,000
Estimated costs to complete	2,000	0
Estimated total costs	$3,200	$3,000
Percentage of completion to date	37.5%	100%
Estimated total gross profit	$1,800	$2,000
Gross profit to be recognized to date	$ 675	$2,000
Less: Gross profit recognized in previous years	0	(675)
Gross profit in current year	$ 675	$1,325

EXERCISE 3

1991:   **To record the sale.**

Installment accounts receivable – 1991	50,000	
Installment sales		50,000

To record the cost of sales.

Cost of installment sales	23,000	
Inventory		23,000

To record the receipt of down-payment.

Cash	10,000	
Installment accounts receivable – 1991		10,000

To record deferred gross profit.

Installment sales	50,000	
Cost of installment sales		23,000
Deferred gross profit – 1991 sales		27,000

To record the realized gross profit.

Deferred gross profit – 1991 sales	5,400	
Gross profit – 1991 sales		5,400

1992:   **To record the collection.**

Cash	20,000	
Installment accounts receivable – 1991		20,000

To record the realized gross profit.

Deferred gross profit – 1991 sales	10,800	
Gross profit – 1991 sales		10,800

1993:   **To record the repossession of merchandise.**

Repossessed merchandise inventory	8,000	
Deferred gross profit – 1991 sales	10,800	
Loss on repossession of merchandise	1,200	
Installment accounts receivable		20,000

MULTIPLE CHOICE

1.	b	5.	c	9.	a	13.	d
2.	b	6.	d	10.	c	14.	d
3.	a	7.	a	11.	d		
4.	a	8.	d	12.	b		

Computations:

9. (a)

Cumulative cost incurred	$24,000	$39,000
Estimated additional cost	36,000	26,000
Estimated total cost	$60,000	$65,000
Total gross profit	100,000	100,000
Gross profit	$40,000	$35,000
Gross profit rate	40%	60%
Realized gross profit to date	$16,000	21,000
Previously recognized gross profit	0	16,000
Realized gross profit for the year	$16,000	**$ 5,000**

10. (c)

Total gross profit of installment sales ($250,000 - $150,000)	$100,000
Gross profit realized in 1991 ($100,000 x $100,000 / $250.000)	**40,000**
Gross profit deferred	**$ 60,000**

11. (d)

1991: Gross profit realized from 1991 sales
       [$150,000 x ($250,000 - $175,000) / $250,000]   **$45,000**

1992: Gross profit realized from 1991 sales
       ($50,000 x $75,000 / $250,000) $15,000

       Gross profit realized from 1992 sales
       ($216,000 x ($360,000 - $288,000) / $360,000)   43,200

       Total realized in 1992   **$58,200**

12.   (b)

```
            Total gross profit ($300,000 - $200,000)      $100,000
            Gross profit rate ($100,000 / $200,000)            50%

            Gross profit realized in 1991                  $50,000
```

13.   (d)

```
            Actual cost incurred to date                   $100,000
            Gross profit recognized to date                  50,000

            Construction in process -- 1991                $150,000
```

14.   (d)

```
            Cost incurred to date                          $180,000
            Estimated additional cost                        20,000

            Total estimated cost                           $200,000
            Contract price                                  300,000

            Total gross profit                             $100,000
            Percentage of completion                           90%

            Recognized gross profit to date               $ 90,000
            Cost incurred to date                           180,000

            Construction in process -- 1992                $270,000
```

CHAPTER 8

Cash and Receivables

CHAPTER OBJECTIVES

This chapter is designed to enable students to:

A. Explain the composition of cash and receivables accounts.

B. Prepare a bank reconciliation and explain other internal control procedures for cash.

C. Determine the conditions under which receivables may be recorded.

D. Perform the adjustments to accounts receivable for uncollectible accounts, discounts, and returns and allowances.

E. Explain factoring, assignment, and pledging of accounts receivable and account for the transfer of receivables whether the transfer is recorded as a sale or a liability.

F. Explain and apply appropriate valuation concepts to the reporting of notes receivable; in particular by using present value techniques.

CHAPTER OVERVIEW

Accounting for cash and receivables is the topic of this chapter. Cash and cash equivalents are defined, and procedures for the internal control of cash (including petty cash funds and bank reconciliations) are presented first. Accounting for accounts receivable, bad debt expense and notes receivable follow.

A. Characteristics of Cash and Cash Equivalents

Cash is the medium of exchange for many transactions and is measured in dollar terms. **The cash account includes only those items immediately available as a medium of exchange.** It consists of coin, currency, petty cash and certain negotiable instruments that are acceptable to financial institutions for immediate deposit and withdrawal. These instruments include certified cheques, money orders, cashier's cheques, ordinary cheques, and many market funds with cheque cashing privileges. The company's own cheques not yet delivered to the payees should not be deducted from the balance of the cash account, whereas an overdraft should be reported as a current liability. However, if the depositor has more than one account in the same bank, it is appropriate accounting to offset the negative balance in one account against the positive balances in the other accounts.

Other near cash items called **cash equivalents** are **excluded from the cash account**, because a delay or penalty may result upon conversion of cash equivalents to cash. These items, including compensating balance (minimum balance that must be retained in the account against short-term borrowing arrangements, treasury bills, commercial paper and certificates of deposit, are usually recorded as short-term investments. Also excluded from the cash account are postage stamps (a prepaid expense), cash advances paid to employees and other parties (receivables) and postdated customer's cheques (receivables).

For external reporting, practices vary. Many companies combine cash and cash equivalents. The trend toward such a combination is likely to accelerate because section 1540 requires a cash and cash equivalent basis for the statement of changes in financial position.

B.   **Internal Control of Cash**

A system of internal control is a plan designed to (1) safeguard assets, (2) promote accurate accounting records, (3) evaluate performance, and (4) ensure compliance with company policies and law. A well-designed internal control system is particularly important for cash because it is the asset most vulnerable to errors and irregularities. The following control procedures are essential:

1.   **General control:**

* Separate custody and accounting for cash.
* Account for all cash transactions.
* Maintain only the minimum cash balance needed.
* Perform periodic test counts of cash balances.
* Reconcile ledger and bank cash account balances.
* Achieve an adequate return on idle cash balances.
* Physically control cash.

2.   **Control of Cash Receipts**   Cash inflows have many sources and cash control procedures vary across companies. However, the following procedures apply in most situations:

1. Separate the responsibilities for handling cash, recording cash transactions, and reconciling cash balances. This separation reduces the possibility of theft and of concealment through false recording.
2. Assign cash-handling and cash-recording responsibilities to different persons to ensure a continuous and uninterrupted flow of cash from initial receipt to deposit in an authorized bank account. This control requires (*a*) immediate counting, (*b*) immediate recording, and (*c*) timely deposit of all cash received.
3. Maintain continuous and close supervision of all cash-handling and cash-recording functions. This control includes both routine and surprise cash counts, internal audits, and daily reports of cash receipts, payments, and balances.

3. **Control of Cash Disbursements** Most firms disburse to a large number of different payees. The following fundamentals apply to most cases:
1. Separate the responsibilities for cash disbursement documentation, cheque writing, cheque signing, cheque mailing, and recordkeeping.
2. Except for internal cash funds (petty cash), make all cash disbursements by prenumbered cheques.
3. If petty cash funds are employed, develop tight controls and authorization procedures for their use.
4. Prepare and sign cheques only when supported by adequate documentation and verification.
5. Supervise all cash disbursements and recordkeeping functions.

4. **Petty Cash Fund (or Imprest Cash System)**

A petty cash fund frequently is established to make routine payments of relatively small expenses. It is an amount of cash segregated and physically controlled by immediate disbursements upon proper authorization. The custodian of this fund maintains in the fund (1) cash and (2) receipts for expenses, that usually sum to a specified total. The receipts are the basis for recording appropriate expenses when the fund is replenished.

ILLUSTRATION 1:

(1) **To establish a petty cash imprest fund of $500:**

Petty cash	500	
Cash		500

(2) **To record expenses and replenish the imprest fund:**

Postage expenses	150	
Supplies expenses	190	
Miscellaneous expenses	128	
Cash short and over	12	
Cash		480

Note that cash short and over is an expense (debit) or a revenue (credit) resulting from normal human error.

5. **Reconciliation of Book and Bank Cash Accounts Balances**

Control of Cash through Bank Accounts The use of accounts with banks or other financial institutions is an important means of cash control. Bank accounts provide several advantages:

* Cash is physically protected off the company premises.
* A separate record of cash is maintained by the bank.
* Cash handling and theft risk is kept to a minimum.
* Customers may remit payments cash management services such as chequing privileges, investment advice, and interest revenue on accounts.

Large companies with widely dispersed activities often use multiple bank accounts in diverse locations to facilitate cash collection and to take advantage of float. Float consists of uncollected or undeposited cheques in transit between companies. Firms attempt to (1) maximize payment float to increase interest earned on the funds supporting cheques written to other firms, and (2) minimize collection float to reduce interest lost on cheques received from other firms.

Lockbox systems can reduce collection float. Customers mail their payments to a local bank or post office box. A local bank is authorized (for a fee) to empty the box daily and deposit the funds to the company's account with the local bank.

Electronic funds transfer (EFT) is a means of transferring funds between banks and firms by telephone, wire, or computer linkages for immediate posting of transactions to accounts. The advantages of EFT include reduced paperwork, fewer errors, and lower transaction costs. The chief disadvantages are the cost of new equipment and internal control system required in the new EFT environment.

The bank maintains a totally separate record of cash transactions and presents monthly statements which can be used to reconcile the book and the bank cash balances in order to identify discrepancies and correct errors.

A monthly bank reconciliation may be constructed in a variety of ways, depending on the immediate purpose, A commonly used format is to reconcile both the bank and the book cash balances to the true or correct cash balance as shown on the following page:

ILLUSTRATION 2:

Balance per bank	$35,000
Transactions recorded by the firm but not by the bank:	
+ Deposits outstanding	7,000
− Cheques outstanding	(15,000)
Errors made by the bank:	
+ Errors understate bank balance	0
− Errors overstate bank balance	(300)
True or correct cash balance	$26,700
Balance per book	$25,000
Transactions recorded by the bank but not by the firm:	
+ Notes collected by bank	2,000
− Service charges	(300)
− Not-Sufficient-fund cheques	(800)
Errors made by the firm:	
+ Errors understate book balance	800
− Errors overstate book balance	0
True or correct cash balance	$26,700

Note that (1) both reconciliations should come up to the same correct cash balance, and (2) all the adjustments appear in **book balance reconciliation** require formal **journal entries** in order to adjust the cash account to the correct balance.

An alternative format is called **comprehensive bank reconciliation** as shown in **Illustration 3**. This approach uses four columns with upper and lower sections for bank balance and book balance reconciliations, respectively. Per bank statement line is a summary of current cash transactions taken from the bank statement, whereas per cash account is a summary of current cash transactions as recorded in the books. The first column presents prior balances as indicated in the last reconciliation. The middle two columns are used to determine the correct cash receipts and payments for the specific month. The last column shows the result of current reconciliation, which is identical with the consolidation result of **Illustration 2**. Note that any previous discrepancies affecting current cash transactions are **removed**, whereas any current discrepancies affecting future cash transactions are **added** to the current receipts and payments columns.

ILLUSTRATION 3:

Comprehensive Bank Reconciliation

August 31, xxxx

	July 31 balances	August receipts	August payments	August 31 reconciled balances
Bank:				
Per bank statement	$27,000	$165,000	$157,000	$35,000
Deposits outstanding				
July 31	12,000	(12,000)		
Aug 31		7,000		7,000
Cheque outstanding				
July 31	(18,000)		(18,000)	
Aug 31			15,000	(15,000)
Understated cash payments				
Aug 31			300	(300)
Correct cash balance	$21,000	$160,000	$154,300	$26,700
Books:				
Per cash account	$21,000	$158,000	$154,000	$25,000
Note collected by bank				
Aug 31		2,000		2,000
Service charges				
Aug 31			300	(300)
NSF cheques				
Aug 31			800	(800)
Overstated cash payments				
Aug 31			(800)	800
Correct cash balance	$21,000	$160,000	$154,300	$26,700

C. Receivables include all of a firm's claims for money, goods, services, and other noncash assets from other firms. The most important receivables are accounts receivable and notes receivable, and the main accounting issues pertaining to receivables are recognition and valuation.

Accounts Receivable

Accounts receivable arise from the sale of goods and services to customers on credit in the firm's ordinary course of business. They include amounts that are expected to be collected either during the year following the balance sheet date or within the operating cycle of the entity, whichever is longer.

1. **Recognition of accounts receivable.** Accounts receivable can be recognized only when the revenue recognition principle has been fulfilled. In general, they are initially valued at the original exchange price less trade discounts. To encourage customers to pay promptly, however, cash discounts are often offered. Cash discounts can be accounted for by either the gross or the net approach.

Conceptually the net approach is more appealing because the sales revenue and accounts receivable are initially recorded at cash equivalent (i.e., selling price less cash discount), and the forfeited cash discount is properly viewed as a charge for late payment. To illustrate:

ILLUSTRATION 4:

Prepare journal entries using (a) the gross approach, and (2) the net approach to record the following:

(1) Sold merchandise for $5,000, terms **2/10, n/60** (i.e., the credit period is 60 days, but there will be a 2% cash discount if payment is made within the discount period of the first 10 days.)

(2) 60% of the receivable was collected within the ten-day discount period.

(3) 30% was collected without cash discount.

(4) 10% past due.

a. Gross Approach

(1) **To record sales at the gross invoice price:**

Accounts receivable	5,000	
Sales		5,000

(2) **To record collection within the discount period:**

Cash	2,940	
Sales discount ($5,000 x 60% x 2%)	60	
Accounts receivable		3,000

(3) **To record collection beyond the discount period:**

Cash ($5,000 x 30%)	1,500	
Accounts receivable		1,500

(4) **To record forfeited cash discount of past due accounts:**

none.

b. Net Approach

(1) **To record sales at the invoice price net of cash discount:**

Accounts receivable ($5,000 x 98%)	4,900	
Sales		4,900

(2) **To record collection within the discount period:**

Cash	2,940	
Accounts receivable ($4,900 x 60%)		2,940

(3) **To record collection beyond the discount period:**

Cash ($5,000 x 30%)	1,500	
Accounts receivable ($4,900 x 30%)		1,470
Sales discount forfeited		30

(4) **To record forfeited cash discount of past due accounts:**

Accounts receivable ($5,000 x 10% x 2%)	10	
Sales discount forfeited		10

Note that sales discount forfeited is similar to interest revenue, but may not be recorded if its economic effect is immaterial.

2. **Measuring uncollectible accounts receivable.** When a company sells on credit, it is unlikely that all receivables will actually be collected. In theory, the uncollectibles should be recorded in a contra-sales account because sales are overstated. However, they are generally recorded as an operating expense (i.e., bad debt expense). If there is little basis for estimating what will be uncollectible, or the amount involved is immaterial, the **direct write-off method** may be applied to recognize bad debt expense and to reduce accounts receivable when the accounts become uncollectible. In practice, most firms use the **allowance method**, under which bad debt expense is recognized when an allowance is provided for the estimated uncollectibles, and the uncollectible accounts are written off against the allowance, when confirmed. The following two approaches are common:

a. **Credit sales (or the income statement) approach.** This approach is to estimate **directly** the amount of bad debt expense with an emphasis on the matching principle and the income statement. An average bad debt rate based on credit sales is first computed using historical records. It is then applied to current credit sales to estimate current bad debt expense. This method is simple and easy to implement. However, it is criticized for being unable to assure the adequacy of the balance of the allowance account in order to report accounts receivable at their net realizable value and to enable users to assess reasonably future cash flows.

b. **Accounts receivable (or the balance sheet) approach.** Under this approach, the primary focus is on the net realizable value of accounts receivable, regardless of whether the expense matches sales revenue. Bad debt expense is estimated using the following three steps: (1) Compute a historical bad-debt rate on outstanding receivables, (2) Determine the **required** balance of the allowance account by applying the rate to the current outstanding balance of receivables, and (3) Adjust the allowance account to this required balance, and, in the meantime, recognize the adjustment amount as current bad debt expense.

Note that, instead of using a single rate, an aging schedule may be set up using different bad debt rates for different age groups of outstanding receivables. This procedure is referred to as the **aging method.**

In recent years, the accounts receivable approach, especially the aging method, has been gaining in popularity. It is because computer software has lowered the cost of implementation of this method, and cash flow problems have prompted companies to monitor the age of their receivables more closely than ever before.

ILLUSTRATION 5:

Fred Company made credit sales of $500,000 during 1991. Selected account balances at the end of the year were: Accounts receivable, $100,000; Allowance for doubtful accounts, $600 (credit).

a. **Credit sales (or the income statement) approach:** Assuming bad debt expense is estimated as 2% of credit sales, the appropriate adjusting entry would be:

Bad debt expense ($500,000 x 2%)	10,000	
Allowance for doubtful accounts		10,000

b. **Accounts receivable (or the balance sheet) approach:** Assuming the bad debt rate is 5% of the outstanding receivables, the required balance of the allowance account would be $5,000 ($100,000 x 5%), and current bad debt expense would be $4,400 ($5,000 - $600). The appropriate journal entry is:

Bad debt expense	4,400	
Allowance for doubtful accounts		4,400

Under the allowance method, any account which is confirmed to be uncollectible would be written off against the allowance account. Note that a reversing entry would be required if an account previously written off turns out to be collectible.

E.   Use of accounts receivable to obtain immediate cash

Many companies use their accounts receivable to secure immediate financing. If material, the economic effects of these arrangements have to be measured and disclosed. There are three major arrangements in this regard:

a.   **Factoring accounts receivable.**   Factoring is a financing arrangement to transfer receivables to a financial institution, known as the factor, for cash. Usually, the factor retains a certain percentage (e.g., 10% or 20%) of the transferred receivables to protect against sales returns, allowances and discounts. The debtors of these transferred accounts are usually notified to make their payments to the factor (notification basis). A factoring may be with or without recourse:

Factoring without Recourse   A non-recourse factoring arrangement generally constitutes an ordinary sale of receivables because the factor has no recourse against the transferor for uncollectible accounts. Control over the receivables passes to the factor. The factor typically assumes (1) legal title to the receivables, (2) the cost of uncollectible accounts, and (3) collection responsibilities. However, any possible adjustments or defects in the receivables (sales discounts, returns, and allowances) are borne by the transferor because these represent preexisting conditions.

Factoring without recourse is treated as a sale of receivables because most of the risks and rewards are transferred.

ILLUSTRATION 6:

Assume that, on July 5, 1991, the Company sold $6,000 accounts receivable without recourse to a local bank. The bank paid a net amount of 90% of the factored accounts less 3% commission on the amount of accounts receivable. On August 1, there was a sales return of $200 related to the factored accounts. The bank collected $5,700 from the customers and remitted $400 to Constoner on October 10. The remaining $100 was uncollectible.

July 5, 1991 – to record the sale of receivable:

Cash [($6,000 X (100% - 10% - 3%)]	5,220	
Receivable from factor ($6,000 X 10%)	600	
Loss (commission) on sale of receivables	180	
Accounts receivable		6,000

August 1 – To record sales return:

Sales returns and allowances	200	
Receivable from factor		200

October 10, 1991 -- To record cash remitted from factor:

Cash	400	
Receivable from factor		400

Note that since the factor was without recourse, the $100 uncollectible should be recognized by the **factor** as a bad debt expense.

Factoring with recourse.   When receivables are factored with recourse, the firm retains the ownership risks associated with the receivables, and thus guarantees payment to the factor. A factoring as such may be either a sale, or a borrowing and has to have the following three criteria:

i) The transferor surrenders control of the future economic benefits of the receivables.

ii) The transferor's obligation under the recourse provisions can be reasonably estimated.

iii) The transferee cannot require the transferor to repurchase the receivables except under the recourse provisions.

Any factoring with recourse that meets **all** the three criteria should be recorded as a sale. Otherwise, it must be treated as a loan:

(a) **A sale.**   For a factoring with recourse qualified as a **sale**, the appropriate journal entries would be the same as a factoring without recourse, except that, the firm, instead of the factor, should recognize the bad debt expense. Use the same data as in **ILLUSTRATION 6**, but assume that the remaining amount remitted from the factor to the firm is $300 (i.e., the retained amount less sales returns and **bad debt**). The **October 10** journal entry recording the receipt of cash would be changed to:

October 10, 1991 -- to record cash remitted from factor:

Cash	300	
Bad debt expense	100	
Receivable from factor		400

(b) A loan. If one or more of the above criteria is not satisfied, the transfer should be treated as a loan:

July 5, 1991 -- To record borrowing:

Cash	5,220	
Receivable from factor	600	
Discount on sale of receivables*	180	
Payable to factor		6,000

* The discount on transferred receivables is a prepaid interest which will be amortized over the loan term as interest expenses.

August 1, 1991 -- To record sales return:

Sales returns and allowances	200	
Accounts receivable		200

Payable to factor	200	
Receivable from factor		200

October 10, 1991 -- To record final settlement:

Cash	300	
Bad debt expense	100	
Receivable from factor		400

Interest expense	180	
Discount on sale of receivables		180

Payable to factor	5,800	
Accounts receivable		5,800

The last two entries are pertinent only to a borrowing, i.e., the amortized discount is charged to interest expense, whereas the liability is closed against the receivable.

b. Assignment and pledging of accounts receivables. Both assignment and pledging use receivables as collateral for a loan:

(1) Assignment. In an assignment of accounts receivable, the assignor assigns the rights to certain specific receivable accounts to the assignee. The assignor usually issues a formal promissory note, retains title to the receivables, and continues to receive payments from customers. Cash collected from these accounts will be used **specifically** for the payments of the principal and interest of the loan. The accounts assigned are **reclassified** as Accounts Receivable Assigned, which is presented separately on the balance sheet as a current asset and is offset by the related Notes Payable account. The excess of accounts receivable assigned and notes payable is usually labelled as Equity in Accounts Receivable Assigned. Presented below are some typical entries recording assignment transactions:

To record the assignment:

Cash	4,800	
Financing fees	200	
Notes payable		5,000
Accounts receivable assigned	6,000	
Accounts receivable		6,000

To record the collection:

Cash	5,700	
Accounts receivable assigned		5,700

To record the payment:

Notes payable	5,000	
Interest expense	500	
Cash		5,500
Accounts receivable	300	
Accounts receivable assigned		300

(2) **Pledging.** Pledging arrangements also use receivables as a means of financing, but the rights to **specific** receivables are not formally assigned. There is thus no need for any journal entry to reclassify the accounts. Nevertheless, appropriate footnote disclosure may still be required.

F. Notes Receivable

A note receivable is a written promise to pay the payee (or holder) a specified amount at a specified future date, or dates. The end of the note's term is called the maturity date, at which the final payment is normally due. Except for some short-term notes, notes explicitly or implicitly carry interest.

1. **Notes receivable with or without stated interest.** A note carrying interest (i.e.,

with a stated interest rate) is called an interest-bearing note which requires the payment of both face value and interest. A noninterest-bearing note, on the other hand, does not state any interest rate but commands interest through its face value which exceeds the principal amount. Journal entries pertinent to these two types of notes receivable are illustrated separately below:

ILLUSTRATIONS 7:

Assume that, on November 1, 1991, Lundar sold $5,000 of merchandise on credit and received a six-month note receivable.

a. **Interest-bearing notes.**   Assuming the note stated a 10% interest rate to be received at maturity:

November 1, 1991 -- To record the sale:

Notes receivable	5,000	
Sales		5,000

December 31, 1991 -- To accrue earned interest:

Interest receivable ($5,000 x 10% x 2/12)	83	
Interest revenue		83

January 1, 1992 -- To reverse previous adjusting entry:

Interest revenue	83	
Interest receivable		83

May 1, 1992 -- To record the collection:

Cash	5,250	
Notes receivable		5,000
Interest revenue ($5,000 x 10% x 6/12)		250

b. **Noninterest-bearing notes.**   Assuming the note was without a stated rate, but 10% interest is included in the face of the note:

November 1, 1991 -- To record the sale:

Notes receivable [$5,000 (1 + 10% x 6/12)]	5,250	
Sales		5,000
Discount on notes receivable		250

December 31, 1991 -- To amortize note discount:

Discount on notes receivable ($250 x 1/3)	83	
Interest revenue		83

May 1, 1992 -- To record the collection:

Cash	5,250	
Notes receivable		5,250

May 1, 1992 -- To amortize note discount:

Discount on notes receivable ($250 x 2/3)	167	
Interest revenue		167

2. **Interest-bearing notes with unreasonable interest rates.**   When a note does not carry interest or the stated interest rate of the note is unreasonable, the note and the sale should be recorded at the fair value of the goods or service provided, or at the market value of the note, whichever is the more clearly determinable. The market value of the note is generally its present value determined by discounting all future payments on the note using an imputed interest rate, normally the prevailing interest rate for similar instruments of issuers with similar credit rating. This pronouncement was to enforce the substance over the form principle, and to eliminate overstatement of notes receivable and sales. It should be noted that, when a note is received (or issued) solely for cash, the present value of the note is measured by the cash proceeds exchanged.

ILLUSTRATION 8:

On January 1, 1991, Franker Company sold merchandise on credit and received a three-year, $50,000 note, with a stated annual rate of 5% to be paid at the end of each year. The market rate of interest is 10%.

To compute the present value of the note:

PV of face value of the note = Face Value x $pv1_{n,i}$
= $50,000 x $pv1_{n=3, i=10\%}$
= $50,000 x .75132 (from **Table 6-2**)   = $37,566

PV of annual interest payments
= Rent (interest) per payment x $pva_{n,i}$
= $2,500 x $pva_{n=3, i=10\%}$
= $2,500 x 2.48685 (from **Table 6-4**)   = $ 6,217

PV of the note at 10% = $37,566 + $6,217   = $43,783

Journal entries (Assuming the effective interest method):

January 1, 1991 -- To record sales:

Notes receivable	50,000	
Sales		43,783
Discount on notes receivable		6,217

December 31, 1991 -- To record interest revenue for 1991:

Cash	2,500	
Discount on notes receivable	1,878	
Interest revenue		4,378

December 31, 1992 -- To record interest revenue for 1992:

Cash	2,500	
Discount on notes receivable	2,066	
Interest revenue		4,566

December 31, 1993 -- To record interest revenue for 1993:

Cash	2,500	
Discount on notes receivable	2,273	
Interest revenue		4,773

December 31, 1993 -- To record the collection:

Cash	50,000	
Notes receivable		50,000

Note that under the effective interest method, interest revenue for a period is determined by multiplying the beginning carrying value of the note by the market (effective) interest rate as indicated in the following note discount **amortization schedule:**

Year	Cash interest 5%	Interest revenue 10%	Note Receivable Increase	Balance
0				43,783
1	2,500	43,783 x 10% = 4,378	1,878	45,661
2	2,500	45,661 x 10% = 4,566	2,066	47,727
3	2,500	47,727 x 10% = 4,773	2,273	50,000

Further note that, if the effect is immaterial, discount on note may also be amortized using the straight-line method. In that case, the annual interest revenue would be $4,572.33 ($2,500 + $6,217 / 3).

3. **Discounting notes receivable.** Cash also can be generated from a note receivable by **selling (or discounting)** the note to a bank. The cash proceeds from the note are its **maturity value** (principal plus interest to maturity) less a specified **discount** (maturity value x discount rate x time to maturity) charged by the bank.

ILLUSTRATION 9:

Assume a $3,000, 10%, nine-month note, dated January 1, 1991, is sold on April 1, 1991 at a discount rate of 16%.

To determine cash proceeds:

Maturity value of the note [$3,000 x (1 + 10% x 9/12)]	$3,225
Discount charge ($3,225 x .16 x 6/12)	258
Cash proceeds	$2,967

To record the discounting (sale) of the note:

Cash	2,967	
Loss on sale of note (plug)	108	
Notes receivable		3,000
Interest revenue ($3,000 x 10% x 3/12)		75

The gain/loss on sale of note is supported by the CICA, sec. 3290. Since the total interest revenue is not really earned and the amounts involved are usually immaterial, the following alternative recording is common:

Cash	2,967	
Interest expense	33	
Notes receivable		3,000

Note that if the note is endorsed by the company **with recourse**, it is contingently liable for the payment of the note at maturity. This contingency usually is disclosed by a footnote. In case the note is dishonored, the company will make the payment at the note's maturity value with the following entry:

Dishonored notes receivable (or accts. receivable)	3,225	
Cash		3,225

KEY CONCEPTS

Accounts receivable   Amounts owed by customers for goods and services sold in the firm's ongoing major operations. Accounts receivable are recognized only when the revenue recognition principle has been fulfilled.

Assignment   In an assignment of accounts receivable, the assignor assigns the rights to specific accounts receivable to the assignee for cash. Under this arrangement the assignor usually retains title to the receivables, and continues to receive payments. The amount collected, however, is used to make payment(s) to the assignee.

Bad debt expense   Bad debt expense is usually estimated using the allowance method, which is based on either credit sales or accounts receivable. Under the credit sales approach bad debt expense is a certain percentage of credit sales. Under the accounts receivable approach, the allowance provided for uncollectible accounts is a certain percentage of outstanding accounts receivable.

Cash   Items which are immediately available as a medium of exchange, measured in dollar terms.

Cash equivalent   Near cash (highly liquid) items such as compensating balance, treasury bills, commercial paper and certificates of deposit, which could be converted into cash in short term.

Factoring   A financing arrangement to transfer receivables to a financial institution for cash. A factoring may be without or with recourse. A factoring without recourse is an ordinary sale of receivables. If a factoring is with recourse and if the firm surrenders control over the receivables and its obligation can be reasonably estimated, it is also accounted for as a sale. Otherwise, the factoring should be recorded as a borrowing.

Internal control   A system designed to safeguard assets, promote accurate accounting records, evaluate performance and ensure compliance with company policies and law.

Notes receivable   A written promise issued by a customer to pay the firm a specified amount at a specified future date or dates. A long-term note without a stated interest rate or with an unreasonable stated interest rate should be measured at its present value using the prevailing market rate.

Petty cash fund   Cash segregated and physically controlled for immediate disbursements for miscellaneous items upon proper authorization.

Receivables   Claims for money, goods, services and other noncash assets from other parties.

REVIEW QUESTIONS AND EXERCISES

TRUE-FALSE

Indicate whether each of the following statements is true or false by circling the correct response.

T   F   1. To be classified as cash, a bank deposit must have no restrictions on its use or availability.

T   F   2. The replenishment of a petty cash fund generally will not involve debits to expense accounts because expenses are recorded at the time incurred.

T   F   3. An important motivation for internal control is the prevention of theft.

T   F   4. The accuracy of accounting records has nothing to do with internal control.

T   F   5. In connection with reconciliations of bank and book balances, journal entries are required for adjustments to the book balance but not for adjustments to the bank balance.

T   F   6. The gross approach to accounting for receivables is conceptually preferable because cash discount is properly viewed as an interest charge for late payment by customers.

T   F   7. With the net approach to recording accounts receivable, payments made within the cash discount period require a debit to the sales discount account.

T   F   8. Under the aging method, bad debt expense estimation is not affected by the existing balance of the allowance for uncollectible accounts.

T   F   9. The focus of the credit sales (or the income statement) approach to the estimation of bad debt expense is on the matching principle and the income statement.

T   F   10. A factoring without recourse is essentially an ordinary sale of receivables and should be treated as such.

T   F   11. Both assignment and pledging require a reclassification of accounts receivable.

T   F   12. Notes receivable generally should be recorded at their present values, but certain short-term notes may be recorded at their face values.

T   F   13. For long-term notes without stated interest or with an unreasonable stated rate, the imputed interest rate(s) should be used to determine their present value(s).

T   F   14. When a note is discounted with the bank, the cash proceeds are the face value of the note less discount charges.

EXERCISE 1

Given the following data for Trippa Corporation:

CASH ACCOUNT		
Bal. May 31 5,000		
June deposits 22,500	June cheques 25,000	

Other data (June 30):
Outstanding cheques $150
Deposits in transit $650

BANK STATEMENT SUMMARIZED

Balance, May 31, 1991 ....$ 5,500	
Deposits, June 1991 15,500	
Cheques, June 1991.........(19,000)	
Customer's NSF cheques....... (300)	
Notes receivable collected 1,000	
Bank service charges (50)	
Balance, June 30, 1991 2,650	

Required:

1. Prepare a bank statement reconciliation using the following format:

BANK	
Bal. per bank, June 30	
Add:	
Less:	
Correct balance	

BOOKS	
Bal. per books, June 30	
Add:	
Less:	
Correct balance	

2. Prepare adjustment entries for Trippa:

EXERCISE 2

Given the following year-end unadjusted balances of selected accounts of the Silver Co.:

Accounts receivable	$35,000
Notes receivable (arose out of sales)	5,000
Sales revenues (gross, 80% on credit)	100,000
Sales returns and allowances	8,000
Allowance for uncollectibles	200 credit

In addition, assume that the uncollectible accounts just confirmed but not yet recorded amount to $1,500.

Required: Based on the above information complete the following:

1.   Journal entry: To write off uncollectible accounts:

2.   Assume 5% of the outstanding accounts and notes receivables would not be collectible.

   a.   Determine bad debt amount:

   b.   Record bad debt expense:

3.   Assume bad debts would be 2% of net credit sales.

   a.   Determine bad debt amount:

   b.   Record bad debt expense:

EXERCISE 3

On January 1, 1991, HP Sales, Inc. made a credit sale and received a three-year trade note, face value $5,000, 4% stated interest to be paid annually at year end. The market interest rate on the date of sale was 12%.

Required: Based on the above information complete the following:

1. Determine the present value of the note:

2. Record the sale:

MULTIPLE CHOICE

Enter the letter corresponding to the response which **best** completes each of the following statements or questions.

_____ 1. Which of the following should be classified as cash?

    a. an employee's IOU.
    b. a chequeing account compensating balance.
    c. a money order.
    d. dividend cheques mailed, but not yet cashed.

_____ 2. Which of the following operations ideally should not be performed all by the same person?

    a. review journal entries and review bank reconciliations.
    b. order departmental supplies, file correspondence, type memos and type cheques.
    c. receive invoices from suppliers, compare invoices to purchase orders, prepare cheque requisitions for payment to suppliers.
    d. type, sign, and mail cheque, and prepare the bank reconciliation.

_____ 3. Reconciliation of the bank balance with the book balance provides all but which of the following benefits?

    a. It checks the accuracy of the records of both the company and the bank.
    b. It insures that all cash disbursements are legitimate payments.
    c. It provides the correct cash balance for the balance sheet.
    d. It provides information for adjusting entries to the company's accounts.

_____ 4. In a bank reconciliation, outstanding cheques are:

    a. subtracted from the bank balance.
    b. added to the bank balance.
    c. subtracted from the book balance.
    d. added to the book balance.

_____ 5. A company uses the net approach to account for cash discounts offered to its customers. In the case of payment after the discount period, which of the following would be appropriate?

    a. a debit to sales discounts for the amount of the discount.
    b. a debit to accounts receivable for the amount of the discount.
    c. a credit to accounts receivable for the full amount received.
    d. a credit to a revenue account for the amount of the discount.

_____ 6. Which of the following is an advantage of the net approach over the gross approach to record sales?

    a. The net approach is simpler since discounts are ignored.
    b. There will be no discounts since all receivables will be collected on a timely basis.
    c. The net approach does not overstate receivables.
    d. None of the above.

_____ 7. Camper Retails extends credit to its customers. Since uncollectible accounts are immaterial, management has decided to use the direct write-off method to account for bad debt expenses. Which of the following would be true:

    a. Receivables likely will be overstated.
    b. The matching principle is violated if the write-off occurs in the period the receivable is created.
    c. The direct write-off method is more costly from an operational standpoint.
    d. All of the above are true.

_____ 8. Which of the following statements is true regarding the accounts receivable approach to the estimation of uncollectibles?

    a. It emphasizes the matching principle and the income statement.
    b. It recognizes bad debt expense when the accounts are confirmed as uncollectible.
    c. It highlights the net realizable value of accounts receivable and the balance sheet.
    d. It determines current bad debt expense directly as an average rate of accounts receivable.

_____ 9. Given the following information:

Balance per books, August 31, 1991	$ 16,640
Deposits in transit, August 31, 1991	800
Cheques outstanding, August 31, 1991	1,200
Bank service charges, August	50
Customer's NSF cheque	100

A customer's cheque of $150 was erroneously recorded by the firm as $510,

The correct balance of the cash account should be:

    a. $18,140.
    b. $18,410.
    c. $16,850.
    d. $16,130.

_____ 10. Based on the information given in Item 9, the cash balance per bank statement on August 31 is likely to be:

    a. $18,100.
    b. $16,490.
    c. $16,530.
    d. $16,130.

_____ 11. Conby Company uses the allowance method of accounting for uncollectible accounts. During 1991, Conby had charges to bad debt expense of $5,000 and wrote off as uncollectible accounts receivable totalling $600. Conby's working capital (current assets - current liabilities) would be increased (decreased) by:

    a. $5,000.
    b. $4,400.
    c. $(4,400).
    d. $(5,000).

_____ 12. Which of the following is a means of using receivables to obtain immediate cash?

    a. factoring.
    b. pledging.
    c. assignment.
    d. all of the above.

_____ 13. Metremaid, Inc. received a 6-month note with a face value of $30,000 and a stated interest of 4%. Three months later, Metremaid discounted the note at a bank at a discount rate of 10%. The cash amount received by Metremaid from the bank would be:

    a. $30,199.
    b. $28,080.
    c. $28,800.
    d. $29,835.

_____ 14. On January 1, 1991, Salmon sold a used personal computer and received a noninterest-bearing 1-year note with a face value of $10,000. Given the prevailing market rate was 12%. Salmon would report interest revenue for 1991 for:

    a. $1,000.
    b. $1,200.
    c. $1,071.
    d. $1,152.

SOLUTIONS TO REVIEW QUESTIONS AND EXERCISES

TRUE-FALSE

1. T	5. T	9. T	13. T
2. F	6. F	10. T	14. F
3. T	7. F	11. F	
4. F	8. F	12. T	

EXERCISE 1

1. Prepare a bank statement reconciliation using the following format:

BANK	
Bal. per bank, June 30	$2,650
Add:	
Deposits in transit	650
Less:	
Outstanding cheques	(150)
Correct balance	$3,150

BOOKS	
Bal. per books, June 30	$2,500
Add:	
Notes collected by bank	1,000
Less:	
Customers' NSF cheques	(300)
Service charges	(50)
Correct balance	$3,150

2. Prepare adjusting entries for Trippa:

a.	Cash	1,000	
	Notes receivable		1,000
b.	Accounts receivable	300	
	Service charges	50	
	Cash		350

EXERCISE 2

1. To write off uncollectible accounts:

Allowance for uncollectible accounts	1,500	
Accounts receivable		1,500

2.. Assume 5% of the outstanding receivables would not be collectible.

    a. Determine bad debt amount:

Required balance of allowance account [($35,000 + $5,000 - $1,500) x 5%]	$1,925
Plus: Existing **debit** balance of allowance account ($1,500 - $200)	1,300
Bad debt expense	$3,225

    b. Journal entry: Record bad debt expense:

Bad debt expense	3,225	
Allowance for uncollectible accounts		3,225

3. Assume bad debts would be 2% of net credit sales.

    a. Determine bad debt amount:

    Bad debt expense
    = ($100,000 - $8,000) x 80% x 2% = $1,472

    b. Journal entry: Record bad debt expense:

Bad debt expense	1,472	
Allowance for uncollectible accounts		1,472

EXERCISE 3

1.   Determine the present value of the note:

PV of face value of the note = Face Value x $pv1_{n,i}$
= \$5,000 x $pv1_{n=3, i=12\%}$
= \$5,000 x .71178 (from **Table 6-2**)   \$3,559

PV of annual interest payments
= Rent (interest) per payment x $pva_{n,i}$
= \$200 x $pva_{n=3, i=12\%}$
= \$200 x 2.40183 (from **Table 6-4**)   480

PV of the note at 12%   \$4,039

2.   Record the sale:

Notes receivable	5,000	
Sales		4,039
Discounts on notes receivable		961

MULTIPLE CHOICE

1. c	5. d	9. d	13. d
2. d	6. c	10. c	14. c
3. b	7. a	11. d	
4. a	8. c	12. d	

Computations:

9.   (d) Correct cash balance
          = \$16,640 - \$50 - \$100 - \$510 + \$150
          = \$16,130.

10.   (c) Balance per bank statement
          = \$16,130 + \$1,200 - \$800
          = \$16,530.

11.   (d) **Decrease** in working capital
          = \$5,000 + \$600 - \$600
          = \$5,000.

13.   (d) Maturity value of the note
          = \$30,000 × (1 + 4% × 6/12)
          = \$30,600.

          Discount charge
          = \$30,600 × 10% × 3/12
          = \$765.

          Cash proceeds
          = \$30,600 - \$765
          = \$29,835.

14.   (c) PV of the note
          = \$10,000 × $pv1_{n=1, i=12\%}$
          = \$10,000 × .89286
          = \$8,929.

          Interest revenue
          = PV × i
          = \$8,929 × 12%
          = \$1,071.

CHAPTER 9

Inventory Measurement, and Cost of Goods Sold

CHAPTER OBJECTIVES

This chapter is designed to enable students to:

A. Explain the characteristics of inventories.

B. Describe the components of inventory costs.

C. Apply the periodic or perpetual inventory method.

D. Explain the various cost flow assumptions used to value inventory including their effect on reported income and the reasons for management's choice among the alternatives.

CHAPTER OVERVIEW

A. Inventories are assets particularly important to both trading and manufacturing companies. In general, inventories are classified as:

1. Merchandise inventories -- goods purchased by a trading company for resale in the company's ordinary course of business.

2. Manufacturing inventories -- items purchased by a manufacturing company for use, or to be manufactured for sale. They are subclassified as:

   a. Raw materials inventory -- tangible goods purchased for direct use in the manufacture of goods for sale.

   b. Work in process inventory -- manufactured items requiring further processing before completion and sale.

c.   Finished goods inventory -- manufactured goods completed and ready for sale.

d.   Supplies inventory -- items purchased for indirect use in the manufacture of goods for sale.

3.   Miscellaneous inventories -- items such as office supplies, janitorial supplies, and shipping supplies which are typically used in the near future and recorded as selling or general expense when used.

B.   Composition of Inventory -- Items to Be Included in Inventory

Inventory should consist of all items for which the firm has legal title. This determination has particular significance at the end of an accounting period at which time ownership and possession may not coincide. For example, merchandise in transit should be included in the inventory of the buyer if the merchandise was shipped F.O.B. shipping point. Items shipped F.O.B. destination legally belong to the seller during transit and should not be included in the buyer's inventory. Likewise, merchandise on consignment remains the property of the consignor and therefore is included in the consignor's inventory.

C.   Measuring the Quantity of Inventory -- Inventory Recording Systems

Keeping a record of the quantity of inventory may be accomplished by either of the following two inventory systems:

1.   **Periodic inventory system.**   Acquisitions of merchandise are debited to a purchases account. Records are not maintained for withdrawals (sales) of inventory during the period. A determination of inventory quantities and a computation of cost of goods sold are made only at the end of each accounting period, after a physical count of inventory. This system saves costly accounting procedure for keeping track of daily inventory flows and assigning inventory costs. It may be appropriate for firms with large volume and a great variety of low-priced inventory items.

2.   **Perpetual inventory system.**   It requires a debit to the inventory account for any merchandise acquisition. Also, after each sale or issue, the inventory account is credited with a corresponding debit to cost of goods sold or work in process. A periodic physical count of inventory is required only to verify the balance generated by this procedure. This system provides continuing record on the inflows and outflows of inventory items and makes available the up-dated information about the items on hand and the cost of goods sold or used. It is appropriate for firms with high-cost inventory items for which a formal accounting process to monitor the continuous physical as well as cost flows is

crucial. Due to advanced computer technology, the popularity of the perpetual inventory system has been growing.

The typical journal entries under these two systems are presented below:

Transaction or Event	Periodic Inventory System	Perpetual Inventory System

Routine purchases of inventory items	Purchases xxxx
	   Cash, etc. xxxx
		Inventory xxxx
		   Cash, etc. xxxx

Routine sales	Cash, etc. xxxx
	   Sales xxxx
		Cash, etc. xxxx
		   Sales xxxx

	n/a	Cost of sales xxxx Inventory xxxx

Year-end adjustment	Inventory, ending xxxx
	Cost of sales xxxx
	   Inventory, beginning xxxx
	   Purchases xxxx
		n/a

Year-end closing	Sales xxxx
	   Cost of sales xxxx
	   Income summary xxxx
		Sales xxxx
		   Cost of sales xxxx
		   Income summary xxxx

D.   Measuring the Cost of Inventory

Inventories should be recorded at cost. The cost is measured by the **total cash equivalent outlay** made to acquire the goods, to transport them and to prepare them for sale or for use. Therefore, the purchase price, freight-in charges, and handling, storage, insurance and all other necessary expenditures to get the inventory to a condition and location ready for sale or for use should all be included in the inventory cost.

Many companies are offered cash discounts on purchases to encourage early payments. The following two methods are generally acceptable to account for purchases and the related discounts:

1.   **Net method.**   The cost of inventory is recorded net of cash discounts. Any available discounts not taken are reported as either **purchase discount lost** or **interest expense**. This method is based on cash equivalent concept and is considered conceptually preferable.

2.   **Gross method.**   Inventory acquisition is recorded at the gross cost. Discounts taken are credited to the **purchase discounts** account, which is then reported as either a financial revenue or a reduction in cost of goods sold. This method is widely used partly because management may want to avoid disclosure of the company's failure to take cash discounts.

To illustrate, assume that Golden Handshake Merchandisers purchased merchandise on credit. The invoice price was $8,000, with a 2% cash discount if paid within ten days. The journal entries under the gross and the net methods are presented as follows:

Transaction or Event	Gross Method	Net Method

To record the purchase	Purchases (Inventory) 8,000
	   Accounts payable 8,000
		Purchases (Inventory) 7,840
		   Accounts payable 7,840

To record payment within the discount period	Accounts payable 8,000
	   Cash 7,840
	   Purchase discounts 160
		Accounts payable 7,840
		   Cash 7,840

To record payment beyond the discount period	Accounts payable 8,000
	   Cash 8,000
		Accounts payable 7,840
		Purchase discounts lost
		(or Interest expense) 160
		   Cash 8,000

3. Inventory Cost Flow Methods

The cost of goods available for sale is allocated between goods sold during the period and inventory on hand at the end of the period. Since the unit costs of inventory items acquired at different time typically vary, in allocating cost it must be determined which portion of the goods available was sold, and which portion remains in inventory. This creates a need for management to select an explicit **cost flow** method (assumption) which most clearly reflects periodic income under the circumstances. The *CICA Handbook*, sec. 3030 states:

The method selected for determining cost should be one which results in the fairest matching of costs against revenues regardless of whether or not the method corresponds to the physical flow of goods.

The following cost flow methods conform to the cost principle:

1. **Specific identification.**   This method identifies actual flow of physical items and traces their actual costs. Each item stocked is specifically marked so that its unit cost can be identified and related to the specific flow of physical goods at any time.

    This method assures exact matching of costs and revenues. It is appropriate where individual units have high costs and unique characteristics. Its limited applicability is due to the requirement of detailed records, and the opportunity to manipulate income by arbitrary selection of items at time of sale.

2. **Average cost methods.**   These methods assign costs on the basis of weighted-average unit cost of items available for sale. It can be applied in two ways:

a.   **Weighted-average cost.**   This method is used with the **periodic inventory system**. The unit cost is computed only at the end of each period by dividing the total cost of goods by the total number of units available for sale. Cost of goods sold is computed as the unit cost multiplied by the number of units sold. Likewise, inventory is computed as the unit cost multiplied by the number of units remaining.

b.   **Moving-average cost.**   This method is designed for the **perpetual inventory** system, under which a new weighted-average cost is calculated after each purchase. When goods are sold or issued, the moving-average unit cost **at that time** is used to determined the cost of those goods sold or issued.

The average methods are generally viewed as objective, consistent, and not subject to easy manipulation. However, under these methods, the **average costs** of the period, instead of current costs, are matched against current revenues, and the ending inventories are reported on the basis of **average costs**, instead of actual costs.

3.   **First-in, first-out method (FIFO).**   The FIFO method assumes that inventory items are sold in the order in which they are acquired. The costs associated with the earliest units acquired are the first costs recorded as cost of goods sold or used, and the goods remaining in inventory are valued at the most recent unit costs.

FIFO can be easily applied to either a periodic or a perpetual inventory system. It produces an inventory value that approximates current cost. It is systematic and objective, usually consistent with the physical flow of goods, and not subject to income manipulation. The primary criticism against FIFO is the mismatch of the oldest unit costs with current revenues.

4.   **Last-in, first-out method (LIFO).**   The LIFO method assumes that the inventory items are sold in the reverse order in which they are acquired. The costs associated with the latest units acquired (last cost in) are first costs recorded as cost of goods sold (first cost out), and the oldest costs available remain in the ending inventory. Depending on whether the periodic or the perpetual system is used, LIFO may result in different inventory and cost of goods sold numbers, because in a perpetual system, a LIFO determination is made with each sale, whereas in a periodic system, it is made only once a year (i.e., at the end of the accounting period).

The LIFO method achieves a better matching of current costs and current revenues. In a period of **rising prices** this method will reduce net income, and may improve cash flows. LIFO is not an acceptable inventory costing method for tax purposes in Canada.

ILLUSTRATION -- INVENTORY COST FLOW METHODS

The following information is obtained from Rapid Corporation's financial records:

			Units	Unit Cost	Total Cost
Jan.	1	Beginning inventory	100	$10	$1,000
Mar.	1	Purchases	400	$12	$4,800
Mar.	5	Sales	(250)		
May	2	Purchases	100	$15	$1,500
Aug.	1	Sales	(150)		
Oct.	3	Purchases	100	$25	$2,500
Dec.	31	Ending inventory (physical count)	300	?	?

Required: Determine (1) cost of goods sold, and (2) ending inventory value under:

   (a) Specific identification method (assuming the units sold during the period were those purchased on March 1).
   (b) Average cost methods.
   (c) FIFO method.
   (d) LIFO method.

SOLUTION:

(a) **Specific identification method:**

   To calculate cost of goods sold:

		Units	Unit Cost	Total Cost
Mar. 5	Sales	250	$12	$3,000
Aug. 1	Sales	150	$12	1,800
Total cost of goods sold		400		**$4,800**

   To calculate ending inventory:

	Units	Unit Cost	Total Cost
From beginning inventory	100	$10	$1,000
From May 2 purchases	100	$15	1,500
From Oct. 3 purchases	100	$25	2,500
Total ending inventory	300		**$5,000**

(b)   Average cost methods:

(i)   Periodic inventory system -- Weighted-average method:

Beginning inventory	100	$10	$1,000
Mar. 1 purchases	400	$12	4,800
May 2 purchases	100	$15	1,500
Oct. 3 Purchases	100	$25	2,500
Total available	700		$9,800

Weighted-average unit cost = $9,800 / 700 = $14

Cost of goods sold ($14 x 400)	**$5,600**
Ending inventory ($14 x 300)	**$4,200**

(ii)   Perpetual inventory system -- Moving-average method:

	Purchases			Sales (issues)			Inventory Balance		
	Units	Unit cost	Total cost	Units	Unit cost	Total cost	Units	Unit cost	Total cost
Jan. 1	100	10	1,000				100	10.00[1]	1,000
Mar. 1	400	12	4,800				500	11.60[2]	5,800
Mar. 5				250	11.60	2,900	250	11.60	2,900
May 2	100	15	1,500				350	12.57[3]	4,400
Aug. 1				150	12.57	1,886	200	12.57	2,514
Oct. 3	100	25	2,500				300	16.71[4]	5,014
Total	700		9,800	400		4,786	300		5,014

[1] $1,000 / 100 = $10.
[2] $5,800 / 500 = $11.60.
[3] $4,400 / 350 = $12.57.
[4] $5,014 / 300 = $16.71.

So:

Cost of goods sold	$4,786
Ending inventory	$5,014

(c) FIFO method -- Applicable to both the periodic and perpetual systems:

Cost of goods sold:

100 units x $10	$1,000
300 units x $12	3,600
Total	**$4,600**

Ending inventory:

100 units x $25	$2,500
100 units x $15	1,500
100 units x $12	1,200
Total	**$5,200**

(d) LIFO method.

(i) Periodic inventory system:

Cost of goods sold:

100 units x $25	$2,500
100 units x $15	1,500
200 units x $12	2,400
Total	**$6,400**

Ending inventory:

100 units x $10	$1,000
200 units x $12	2,400
Total	**$3,400**

(ii) Perpetual inventory system:

	Purchases			Sales (issues)			Inventory Balance		
	Units	Unit cost	Total cost	Units	Unit cost	Total cost	Units	Unit cost	Total cost
Jan. 1	100	10	1,000				100	10.00	1,000
Mar. 1	400	12	4,800				100 400	10.00 12.00	1,000 4,800
Mar. 5				250	12.00	3,000	100 150	10.00 12.00	1,000 1,800
May 2	100	15	1,500				100 150 100	10.00 12.00 15.00	1,000 1,800 1,500
Aug. 1				100 50	15.00 12.00	1,500 600	100 100	10,00 12.00	1,000 1,200
Oct. 3	100	25	2,500				100 100 100	10.00 12.00 25.00	1,000 1,200 2,500
Total	700		9,800	400		5,100	300		4,700

So: Cost of goods sold   **$5,100**
       Ending inventory   **$4,700**

F.   **LIFO Inventory Problems and Dollar-Value LIFO**

The inventory methods presented above are based on the unit cost approach. To apply this approach to LIFO, there are several problems:

1.   **Initial adoption of LIFO.**   Firms may switch from FIFO (or some other methods) to LIFO. In this case the year in which the switch is made is generally specified as the base year, and the opening inventory of that year becomes the base layer, LIFO inventory. Base layer LIFO inventory is recorded at cost regardless of the prior method used. So, if inventory had been written down previously, it must now be written up to cost, with an offsetting credit to change in accounting principle account.

2.   **LIFO inventory liquidation.**   After LIFO is initially adopted, the firm may voluntarily or involuntarily reduce its base layer LIFO inventory, generally referred to as LIFO inventory liquidation. In this case, some old costs would become part of cost of goods sold to be matched against current revenues. This distortion of income can be avoided by recording cost of goods sold at its replacement cost. To illustrate, assume that the liquidated base layer LIFO cost is $1,500 and the estimated replacement cost is $2,000:

When LIFO inventory is liquidated:	Cost of goods sold	2,000	
	Inventory		1,500
	Temporary liability --		
	LIFO inventory liquidation		500
When replacement takes place:	Inventory	1,500	
	Temporary liability --		
	LIFO inventory liquidation	500	
	Accounts payable		2,000

Note that cost of goods sold is recorded at the estimated replacement cost, and a temporary liability is recorded for the difference between the estimated cost and the base layer LIFO cost. When the inventory items are replaced, the base layer LIFO cost is restored, and the temporary liability is closed. If the actual replacement cost differs from the original estimate, the difference is treated as a change in accounting estimate and debited or credited to the cost of goods sold for the year of replacement.

KEY CONCEPTS

Average method   This method assigns costs on the basis of the weighted-average unit cost of items available for sale. It can be applied in two ways, namely, weighted-average cost which is applied to the periodic inventory system, and moving-average cost, which is applied to the perpetual inventory system.

Cost of inventory   The acquisition cost of inventory measured by the total cash equivalent outlay which is necessary to get the inventory to a condition and location ready for sale or use.

FIFO method   This method assumes that the inventory items are sold or used in the order in which they are acquired. The costs associated with the oldest units are first recorded as cost of goods sold.

Inventory   Goods purchased and held for resale, goods manufactured for sale, and materials purchased for use to produce goods for sale.

LIFO method   This method assumes that the inventory items are sold or used in the reverse order in which they are acquired. The costs associated with the latest units acquired are first costs recorded as cost of goods sold. This method would produce different results as it is applied to different inventory costing systems (i.e., periodic and perpetual).

Perpetual inventory system   Any increase (e.g., purchases) or decrease (e.g., sales or issues) in the physical units of inventory items is immediately and formally recorded in the inventory account. Cost of goods sold and inventory figures are both available at any time. A periodic physical count is required only to verify the balance of the account.

Periodic inventory system   A determination of inventory quantities and a computation of cost of goods sold are made only periodically, usually at the end of each accounting period, after a physical count of inventory. This system saves costly accounting procedure for keeping track of daily inventory flows and assigning costs.

Specific identification   This method identifies actual flow of physical items and traces their actual costs. It is appropriate if the inventory consists of high-cost and low-volume items with unique characteristics.

REVIEW QUESTIONS AND EXERCISES

TRUE-FALSE

Indicate whether each of the following statements is true or false by circling the correct response.

T   F   **1.**   Merchandise in transit shipped F.O.B. destination is included in the inventory of the buyer even if the buyer does not yet have possession.

T   F   **2.**   Goods on consignment are included in the inventory of the consignor even though the merchandise is physically held by the consignee.

T   F   **3.**   When a perpetual inventory system is employed, a sale transaction usually requires a journal entry to record the cost of **that** sale.

T   F   **4.**   Periodic inventory system is typically used by firms with inventory items which are relatively expensive and have a low turnover rate.

T   F   **5.**   Physical inventory counts are a necessary part of a perpetual inventory system, but are not required in a periodic system.

T   F   **6.**   When purchase discounts are available but not taken, the lost discounts are recorded as an expense when accounted for by the net method.

T   F   **7.**   If ending inventory is understated because of the inadvertent exclusion of an item of inventory and the error is undetected, the balance in retained earnings at the end of the **subsequent** year will be understated.

T   F   **8.**   The choice of a cost flow assumption refers to the movement of costs through an accounting system, not the physical movement of the inventory.

T   F   **9.**   The FIFO method may be used in either a periodic or perpetual inventory system, but the amounts produced for inventory and cost of goods sold will differ depending on the system in use.

T   F   **10.**   During an inflationary period, FIFO will result in a higher net income than will LIFO.

T   F   **11.**   For purposes of income determination, LIFO produces a close matching of current costs and current revenues since the most recent costs are the first expensed.

T   F   12.   If the LIFO method is used in conjunction with a perpetual inventory system, a LIFO determination of inventory cost must be made after each sale.

T   F   13.   LIFO is an acceptable method of costing ending inventory according to Revenue Canada.

T   F   14.   If the average cost method is used in conjunction with a perpetual inventory system, a new average cost must be calculated after each purchase.

EXERCISE 1

Harry Crown Corporation purchased a product with a list price of $5,000 and terms of 2/10, n/60.

Required: Prepare the appropriate Journal entries to record the purchase and the payment under each of the following methods:

Transaction or Event	Gross Method	Net Method
To record the purchase		
To record payment within the discount period		
To record payment beyond the discount period		

EXERCISE 2

The following data were obtained from the inventory record of AB Brown Company for the month of June:

Inventory, June 1	200 units	@ $20
Purchase, June 10	600 units	@ $30
Purchase, June 20	400 units	@ $40
Inventory, June 30	300 units	

Required: Assuming the periodic inventory system, determine (1) the cost to be assigned to the ending inventory, and (2) the cost of goods sold for the month of June, under each of the following cost flow methods:

a.   **FIFO method:**

(1)   Ending inventory cost =

(2)   Cost of goods sold =

b.   **LIFO method:**

(1)   Ending inventory cost =

(2)   Cost of goods sold =

c.   **Average method:**

(1)   Ending inventory cost =

(2)   Cost of goods sold =

EXERCISE

3.   Below is a list of statements relating to inventory systems. Each statement describes a characteristic of the periodic and/or perpetual systems. Some statments relate to only one system, some statements relate to both systems, and some relate to neither system. Enter check marks in the blanks to indicate the appropriate system; therefore, a statement may require one, two, or no checkmarks.

		Perpetual Inventory System	Periodic Inventory System
(a)	When an item is sold, two concurrent accounting entries are made for different amounts.	_____	_____
(b)	Cost of goods sold is determined as a residual amount.	_____	_____
(c)	At the end of the accounting period, two inventory entries usually must be made in the accounts.	_____	_____
(d)	A physical inventory count rarely, if ever, is taken.	_____	_____
(e)	More effective inventory control (such as of theft) is possible.	_____	_____
(f)	The amount (balance) in the inventory account throughout the accounting period usually is the beginning inventory amount.	_____	_____
(g)	Each purchase is debited to the inventory account throughout the accounting period.	_____	_____
(h)	Inventory amounts are determined by actual count.	_____	_____
(i)	Purchases of merchandise are not debited to the inventory account throughout the period.	_____	_____
(j)	The method which usually involves more detailed recordkeeping.	_____	_____
(k)	Inventory amounts are determined from the detailed inventory records.	_____	_____
(l)	Only one accounting entry is made when an item is sold.	_____	_____

(m)   An inventory control account with a changing
        balance is maintained.   _____   _____

(n)   Only one accounting entry is made to record a
        purchase of merchandise.   _____   _____

MULTIPLE CHOICE

Enter the letter corresponding to the response which **best** completes each of the following statements or questions.

_____ 1.   Based on the cash equivalent concept, the available purchase discount is preferably to be:

a.   reported as other income, whether taken or not.
b.   reported as other income, only if taken.
c.   reported as a reduction in inventory, whether taken or not.
d.   reported as a reduction in inventory, only if taken.

_____ 2.   Under the periodic inventory system, the determination of cost of goods sold involes:

a.   subtract puchases from beginning inventory.
b.   subtract purchases from ending inventory.
c.   add purchases to ending inventory.
d.   subtract ending inventory from total available for sale.

_____ 3.   If the beginning inventory is overstated and the ending inventory understated, then:

a.   Net income is overstated.
b.   Net income is understated.
c.   Net income is unaffected.
d.   none of the above.

_____ 4.   Which of the following firms would be most likely to use the specific identification method to value its inventory?

a.   an automobile dealership.
b.   a mail order house.
c.   a department store.
d.   a parts manufacturer.

_____ 5.   Identify the **untrue** statement below concerning inventory flow methods:

a.   Under either the periodic or the perpetual inventory system, the FIFO method will produce the same results.
b.   In the absence of price changes, the results of using FIFO would be identical to those obtained by LIFO.
c.   FIFO will provide a close matching of current revenues with current costs since the most recent costs are expensed first.
d.   When the inventory turnover is rapid, the ending inventory under FIFO will tend to approximate the replacement cost of the inventory.

_____ 6.   The choice of the LIFO inventory cost method for financial reporting purposes may be supported on the following basis:

a.   In a period of rising prices LIFO produces more realistic asset measurement than either FIFO or the average method.
b.   In most situations the LIFO assumption of cost flows approximates actual physical flows of goods.
c.   LIFO provides a closer matching of current revenues and current costs than FIFO and the average method.
d.   LIFO cannot be supported on a conceptual basis. Its advantage lies solely with its closer matching of current assets with current expenses.

_____ 7.   In a period of falling prices, the reported income under the LIFO method will be:

a.   higher than the reported income under the FIFO method.
b.   the same under either the perpetual or the periodic system.
c.   Less than the reported income under the moving-average method.
d.   less than the reported income under the FIFO method.

_____ 8.   Assume that a company records purchases net of discount. If the company bought merchandise valued at $5,000 on credit terms 3/15, n/30, the entry to record a payment for half of the purchase within the discount period (it qualifies for the discount) would be a debit to:

a.   Accounts payable for $2,500 and credit to cash for $2,500
b.   Accounts payable for $2,425 and a credit to cash for $2,425
c.   Accounts payable for $2,425 and to interest expense for $75, and a credit to cash for $2,500
d.   Accounts payable for $2,500, and credits to interest revenue for $75 and to cash for $2,500
e.   None of the above.

____ 9. Kracker Company incurred the following costs during 1991:

Merchandise purchased for resale	$20,000
Sales commissions	$ 4,000
Interest on accounts payable	$ 1,000
Freight in	$ 500

How much should be included in the cost of the merchandise inventory:

a. $20,000.
b. $24,000.
c. $21,000.
d. $20,500.

____ 10. The following information is available for George Corporation for 1991:

Sales	$250,000
Beginning inventory	$ 50,000
Purchases	$160,000
Ending inventory	$ 60,000

Under the periodic inventory system, George's cost of goods sold for 1991 is:

a. $160,000.
b. $210,000.
c. $160,000.
d. $150,000.

____ 11. In 19C, a company's records contained the following information about inventory. The company uses a periodic inventory system and records puchases using the net method. (in 000's)

Beginning inventory (at net)	$ 80
Purchases (at invoice price)	100
Purchase terms, 5/10, n/30	
Purchase returns (at invoice price)	10
Discounts lost	5
Ending inventory (at net)	33

What was the amount of 19C cost of goods sold:

a. $127.5
b. $132.0
c. $132.5
d. $137.0
e. None of the above

The following information is pertinent to questions 12, 13 and 14:

Graham Company had 400 units of inventory on hand at **July 1**, 1991, costing $20 each. Purchases and sales of goods during the month were as follows:

July 12, 1991 Sales:	200 units	@ $40
July 15, 1991 Purchases:	100 units	@ $26
July 25, 1991 Purchases:	300 units	@ $28
July 30, 1991 Sales:	200 units	@ $40

Assuming Graham does not maintain perpetual inventory records, and according to a physical count, 400 units were on hand at **July 31**, 1991.

____ 12.   The cost of inventory at July 31, 1991, under the FIFO method is:

   a. $11,000.
   b. $9,000.
   c. $8,000.
   d. $9,500.

____ 13.   The cost of inventory at July 31, 1991, under the LIFO method is:

   a. $11,000.
   b. $9,000.
   c. $8,000.
   d. $9,500.

____ 14.   The cost of inventory at July 31, 1991, under the weighted-average cost method is:

   a. $11,000.
   b. $9,000.
   c. $8,000.
   d. $9,500.

SOLUTIONS TO REVIEW QUESTIONS AND EXERCISES

TRUE-FALSE

1.	F	5.	F	9.	F	13.	F
2.	T	6.	T	10.	T	14.	T
3.	T	7.	F	11.	T		
4.	F	8.	T	12.	T		

EXERCISE 1

Transaction or Event	Gross Method	Net Method

To record the purchase	Purchases (inventory) 5,000
	   Accounts payable 5,000
		Purchases (Inventory) 4,900
		   Accounts payable 4,900

To record payment within the discount period	Accounts payable 5,000
	   Cash 4,900
	   Purchase discounts 100
		Accounts payable 4,900
		   Cash 4,900

To record payment beyond the discount period	Accounts payable 5,000
	   Cash 5,000
		Accounts payable 4,900
		Purchase discounts lost
		(or Interest expense) 100
		   Cash 5,000

EXERCISE 2

	Units	Units cost	Total cost
June 1	200	$20	$ 4,000
June 10	600	30	18,000
June 20	400	40	16,000
Total available	1,200		$38,000

a.   **FIFO method:**

(1)   Ending inventory cost = 300 units x $40 = $12,000.

(2)   Cost of goods sold = $38,000 - $12,000 = $26,000.

b.   **LIFO method:**

(1)   Ending inventory cost
      = 200 units x $20 + 100 units x $30 = $7,000.

(2)   Cost of goods sold = $38,000 - $7,000 = $31,000.

c.   **Average method:**

(1)   Ending inventory cost = 300 x ($38,000 / 1,200) = $9,500.

(2)   Cost of goods sold = $38,000 - $9,500 = $28,500.

EXERCISE 3

	Perpetual	Periodic
(a)	✓	—
(b)	—	✓
(c)	—	✓
(d)	—	—
(e)	✓	—
(f)	—	✓
(g)	✓	—
(h)	—	✓
(i)	—	✓
(j)	✓	—
(k)	✓	—
(l)	—	✓
(m)	✓	✓
(n)	✓	✓

MULTIPLE CHOICE

1. c
2. d
3. b
4. a
5. c
6. c
7. a
8. b
9. d
10. d
11. c
12. a
13. c
14. d

Computations and explanations:

9.   (d)   Total cost included in inventory = $20,000 + $500 = $20,500.

10.   (d)   Cost of goods sold (1991) = $50,000 + 160,000 - $60,000
= $150,000.

11.   (b)   Cost of Goods sold (19C)
= 80 + 95 - 9.5 - 33 = 132.5

12.   (a)   Ending inventory cost under FIFO = 100 units x $26 + 300 units x $28
= $11,000.

13.   (c)   Ending inventory cost under LIFO = 400 units x $20
= $8,000.

14.   (d)   Ending inventory cost under weighted average method
= 400 units x [($8,000 + $2,600 + $8,400) / 800 units]
= $9,500.

CHAPTER 10

Alternative Inventory Valuation Methods

CHAPTER OBJECTIVES

This chapter is designed to enable students to:

A.   Determine inventory values using the lower-of-cost-or-market approach.

B.   Explain and apply the gross margin method of estimating inventories.

C.   Explain and apply the retail inventory method.

D.   Explain and apply the relative sales value method.

E.   Account for losses on purchase commitments.

F.   Explain the effect of inventory errors on the income statements of the current and succeeding years.

CHAPTER OVERVIEW

A.   1.   The previous chapter described the nature and measurement of inventories based on the historical cost principle. However, when the market value of inventory declines below its cost, the historical cost principle is abandoned in favor of the **lower-of-cost-or-market rule** in order to comply with the conservatism constraint. The *CICA Handbook*, Sec. 3030 provides the following; in view of the lack of precision in meaning, it is desirable that the term *market* not be used in describing the basis of valuation. A term more descriptive of the method of determining market, such as *replacement cost, net realizable value* or *net realizable value less normal profit margin* would be preferable.

2.   **Lower-of-Cost-or-Market (LCM) Rule.**   Under GAAP, inventories must be valued at cost or current market value, whichever is lower. Once inventory is written down to market, the market value becomes the new cost, and any later recovery of the market price is generally ignored. In applying the LCM rule, the following terms are essential:

1.   **Cost** is the inventory value determined under one of the historical cost methods, including specific identification, FIFO, LIFO and average cost.

2.   **Net realizable value (NRV)** is the estimated selling price of the goods in the ordinary course of business less reasonably predictable costs of completion and disposal.

In Canada, the **market value** is the **net realizable value**. It is then compared with cost, and the inventory should be valued at the **lower** of cost or the "designated market value". To illustrate:

	Case			
	I	II	III	IV
NRV	6	8	4	5
Designated market value	6	8	4	5
Cost	7	7	7	7
LCM value chosen	6	7	4	5

The LCM rule may be applied (a) to each item of inventory, (b) to total inventory, or (c) to major categories of inventory. Most firms prefer the first approach because it is more conservative than its alternatives.

When market is lower than cost, the difference reflects an **inventory holding loss**. This loss may be dealt with by either of the following methods:

1.   **Direct inventory reduction method.**   Ending inventory is reduced **directly.** That is, the LCM amount is both reported on the balance sheet and used in the calculation of cost of goods sold. Inventory holding loss is not separately presented. Rather it is included in a higher cost of goods sold to reduce net income.

2.   **Inventory allowance method.**   Ending inventory is reported at acquisition cost. A decline in market value is recorded by debiting inventory holding loss and crediting allowance to reduce inventory to LCM. The allowance account is presented on the balance sheet to reduce inventory **indirectly** from cost to market.

In the subsequent year, the allowance from the prior year should be closed to the beginning inventory if the merchandise is still on hand, or to cost of goods sold if it is sold. A new allowance is set up at the year end based on a new LCM calculation. An alternative is to leave the allowance account on the books, and adjust the account at year end to its new balance based again on a new LCM calculation. If the beginning allowance is greater than the ending allowance, the difference would be recorded by debiting allowance and crediting holding gain (or gain due to market recovery).

Both methods derive exactly the same income and total asset amounts. However, the allowance method is generally preferred because it separately reports inventory holding loss on the income statement, and keeps the cost data rather undistorted. In any event, the LCM rule is generally criticized for its inconsistent treatments of holding loss and holding gain, and for its use of a variety of market values.

B. Gross Margin (or Gross Profit) Method

The gross margin method is based on the assumption that an average gross margin based on **historical** records can be used to estimate inventory values from **current** sales. This method is not generally acceptable for external reporting. Nevertheless, it is useful in (1) testing (by auditors) the reasonableness of the reported inventory value, (2) preparing interim financial reports, (3) budgeting and forecasting, and (4) estimating the cost of inventory when the inventory has been destroyed (e.g., in fire). The following steps are pertinent to the application of the gross margin method:

```
┌─────────────────────┐   ┌─────────────────────┐   ┌─────────────────────┐   ┌─────────────────────┐
│ Gross margin rate   │   │ Estimated current   │   │ Estimated current   │   │ Estimated ending    │
│ = Gross margin/sales│   │ gross margin        │   │ cost of goods sold  │   │ inventory           │
│ (based on historical│──>│ = Current sales x   │──>│ = Current sales -   │──>│ = Total available   │
│  data)              │   │   gross margin      │   │   estimated current │   │   for sale -        │
│                     │   │   rate              │   │   gross margin      │   │   estimated cost    │
│                     │   │                     │   │                     │   │   of goods sold     │
└─────────────────────┘   └─────────────────────┘   └─────────────────────┘   └─────────────────────┘
```

The above procedure is based on the gross margin rate, referred to as the mark-up rate on sales. Occasionally, however, mark-ups are quoted on cost. In this case, the quoted mark-up on cost can be converted into the mark-up on sales, and vice versa.
To illustrate, given the following:

Historical data		Percentages	
		On sales	On cost
Sales	$125	100%	125%
Cost (of sales)	$100	80%	100%
mark-up	$ 25	20%	25%

The mark-up rates on sales and on cost are 20% and 25%, respectively. To convert:

Mark-up rate on sales   = Mark-up rate on cost / (1 + Mark-up rate on cost)
       = 25% / (1 + 25%) = 20%.

Mark-up rate on cost   = Mark-up rate on sales / (1 - Mark-up rate on sales)
       = 20% / (1 - 20%) = 25%.

C.   Retail (or Retail Inventory) Method

The retail method is a generally accepted method used to estimate inventory cost primarily by retailers who maintain inventory records at selling prices. This method tends to result in a more accurate estimation of inventory cost than the gross margin method because it uses the **current** cost to retail ratio instead of the **historical** gross profit percentage. Like the gross margin method, it does not require physical count of inventory items and saves considerable clerical work.

Terms used in the application of the retail method are defined as follows:

Original sales price -- Sales price first marked on the purchased merchandise.
Additional Markup -- An increase above the original sales price.
Additional Markup Cancellation - The cancellation of part or all of an additional markup.
Net markup -- The difference between additional markups and additional markup cancellations.
Markdown -- A decrease below the original sales price.
Markdown Cancellation -- The cancellation of part or all of a markdown.
Net markdown -- The difference between markdowns and markdown cancellations.

Under the retail method inventory cost is generally estimated as follows:

1.   Determine total goods available for sale at retail price.

2.   Calculate ending inventory at retail by subtracting sales from the total goods available for sale at retail price.

3.   Compute cost to retail ratio, also known as the cost ratio.

4.   Convert ending inventory at retail to cost using the appropriate cost ratio.

Depending on how the cost ratio is calculated and applied, the retail method can be used to approximate various cost flow methods including average cost, FIFO and LIFO as illustrated on the following page:

1. **Retail method -- Average cost basis**: Under this method, beginning inventory, current purchases, net markups and net markdowns are **all** included in the calculation of the average cost ratio as demonstrated below:

	At cost	At retail
Inventory, January 1, 1991	$ 2,000	$ 4,000
Purchases	45,000	77,000
Purchase returns	(1,000)	(2,000)
Freight-in	4,000	-
Add: Net markups	-	5,000
Less: Net markdowns	-	(4,000)
Total available for sale	**$50,000**	**$80,000**
Less: Sales at retail		(60,000)
Ending inventory at retail		$20,000
Ending inventory at cost ($20,000 x 62.5%*)	(12,500)	
Cost of goods sold	$37,500	

* The average cost ratio = $50,000 / $80,000 = 62.5%.

2. **Retail method -- FIFO basis:** Under the FIFO assumption, the beginning inventory is assumed to be sold first, and the cost of the ending inventory comes from the purchases of the current period. Accordingly, the cost and retail amounts of the beginning inventory are excluded from the computation of current cost ratio. To illustrate:

	At cost	At retail
Purchases	$45,000	$77,000
Purchases return	(1,000)	(2,000)
Freight-in	4,000	-
Add: Net markups	-	5,000
Less: Net markdowns	-	(4,000)
Current addition (purchases)	**$48,000**	**$76,000**
Inventory, January 1, 1991	2,000	4,000
Total available for sale	$50,000	$80,000
Less: Sales at retail		(60,000)
Ending inventory at retail		$20,000
Ending inventory at cost ($20,000 x 63%*)	**(12,600)**	
Cost of goods sold	**$37,400**	

* The current cost ratio = $48,000 / $76,000 = 63%.

Note that if the beginning inventory retail is greater than current sales, the excessive beginning inventory would be carried as a layer of the ending inventory, and converted from retail to cost using the beginning cost ratio.

3. **Retail method -- LCM rule:** When the retail method is used to approximate the lower-of-cost-or-market rule, **net markdowns,** which reflect a decline in the utility of the inventory, are excluded from the cost ratio computation. Such an exclusion reduces the cost ratio, decreases ending inventory cost, and thus increases the cost of goods sold, indicating an inventory holding loss. An application of the retail method on the average cost basis under the LCM rule, generally known as the **conventional retail method,** is demonstrated as follows:

	At cost	At retail
Inventory, January 1, 1991	$ 2,000	$ 4,000
Purchases	45,000	77,000
Purchases return	(1,000)	(2,000)
Freight-in	4,000	-
Add: Net markups	-	5,000
Total available excluding markdowns	$50,000	$84,000
Less: **Net markdowns**		(4,000)
Total available for sale		$80,000
Less: Sales at retail		(60,000)
Ending inventory at retail		$20,000
Ending inventory at cost ($20,000 x 60%*)	(12,000)	
Cost of goods sold	$38,000	

* The average cost (LCM) ratio = $50,000 / $84,000 = 60%.

Note that the net markdowns can also be excluded from the computation of current cost ratio under the retail FIFO method in order to approximate the FIFO (LCM) inventory valuation.

4.   Special Items Related to the Retail Inventory Method

Six factors may complicate computation of the ending inventory by the retail inventory method. The way each is usually treated, follow:

1. **Freight-in.** Expenditures for freight add to the cost of merchandise, therefore, freight-in is added to goods available for sale (or directly to purchases) at cost but not at retail.

2. **Purchase returns.** Purchase returns, as distinguished from allowances, reduce the amount of goods available for sale, therefore, they are deducted from goods available for sale at both cost and retail.

3. **Abnormal casualty losses** and missing merchandise arising from unusual or infrequent events (such as a fire or theft) are deducted from goods available for sale at both cost and retail because they cannot be sold; removal from both cost and retail eliminates their effect on the cost ratio as if they had not been purchased in the first place. The damaged merchandise is set up in a special inventory account at its net realizable value.

4. **Sales returns and allowances.** Because this is a contra account to the sales revenue account, sales returns and allowances are deducted from gross sales. If the returned merchandise is placed back into inventory for resale, no change in the at cost column is needed because its cost is already properly included in the purchases amount. However, if the merchandise is not returned to inventory (because of damages, for example), then its cost should be deducted in the at cost column on the sales line after the cost ratio. (Because net sales has been reduced, the cost also should be reduced.)

5. **Discounts to employees and favoured customers.** Employee and customer discounts result from selling merchandise below the normal sales price and are not caused by market value decreases. Therefore, they are different from markdowns. Such discounts are deducted below the cost ratio, which means they reduce ending inventory at retail but not the total cost of goods available for sale. Net sales include sales made to employees at discount prices thus understating the retail value of goods sold. They are added back to determine ending inventory at retail.

6. **Normal spoilage.** Normal spoilage includes shrinkage and breakage. This amount is deducted below the cost ratio, along with sales, because the expected cost of normal spoilage implicity is included in determining the selling price and it does not reflect market value changes. Normal spoilage, then, is not included in the cost-to-retail ratio calculation. Deduction of normal spoilage in arriving at the cost ratio would overstate the cost ratio and the estimated cost of ending inventory. Abnormal spoilage and theft are deducted from the total cost of goods available for sale because they are not included in determining selling prices. Failure to deduct abnormal spoilage in arriving at the cost ratio would understate the cost ratio and the estimated cost of ending inventory.

D.   Additional Inventory Issues

1.   **Used item valuation.**   Sometimes inventory includes items, such as repossessed, obsolete, or damaged goods, that are not in "brand new" condition. These items are generally measured at **replacement costs** when their market values can be reliably determined. Otherwise, they should be reported at **net realizable value.** As a general rule, whenever an inventory item is written down from its original cost, the difference is debited to a loss account (e.g., loss on repossession, casualty loss, loss on obsolescence, etc.)

2.   **Interchangeable and marketable item valuation.**   Ordinarily, inventory cannot be valued above cost. An exception is permitted for inventories for which units are interchangeable and immediate marketable at quoted prices, such as certain agricultural and mineral products and commodities with government controlled markets. When an inventory item is valued at **selling price**, a holding gain or loss due to price changes is recognized and reported.

3.   **Lump sum acquisition.**   When different inventory items are acquired for a single price, the lump sum cost is allocated to these items on the basis of their **relative sales values.** For example, if $90 is paid for merchandise A (sales value = $70) and merchandise B (sales value = $30), the acquisition cost is allocated as follows:

Merchandise	Sales value	Allocation	Inventory cost
A	$70	(70/100) x $90	$63
B	30	(30/100) x $90	27
	$100		$90

E.   Purchase commitments.   Companies sometimes make commitments with their suppliers to purchase merchandise in the future at a specified price. If such a purchase commitment is **subject to revision or cancellation**, and a material loss is possible and can be reasonably estimated, it must be disclosed in the footnotes. If the purchase commitment is **not subject to revision or cancellation** and a material loss is probable and can be reasonably estimated, the loss should be recognized and recorded as follows:

Estimated loss on purchase commitment   xxxx
     Estimated liability on purchase commitment   xxxx

A recovery of previously recognized loss is recorded as a "gain" in the period during which the recovery takes place:

Estimated liability on purchase commitment   xxxx
      Recovery of loss on purchase commitment   xxxx

This treatment records the loss in the period when it became likely and is consistent with the provisions of *CICA Handbook*, section 3290, "Contingencies".

F.   Inventory Errors

Inventory errors may be caused by a misstatement of (1) beginning inventory, (2) current purchases, and/or (3) ending inventory. Any of these misstatements affects both the cost of goods sold (an income statement item) and the ending inventory (a balance sheet item). Considering beginning inventory and current purchases as inflows, and cost of goods sold and ending inventory as outflows of inventory, these elements may be related as follows:

The above diagram indicates that the total inflow equals the total outflow. Based on this equality, the effect of inventory errors on cost of goods sold can be easily identified:

1.   Cost of goods sold is overstated, and net income is understated, if:

    a.   Beginning inventory is overstated,
    b.   Purchases are overstated, and/or
    c.   Ending inventory is understated.

2.   Cost of goods sold is understated, and net income is overstated, if:

    a.   Beginning inventory is understated,
    b.   Purchases are understated, and/or
    c.   Ending inventory is overstated.

To illustrate, assume that beginning inventory is overstated by $1,000, the current purchase is understated by $2,500, and ending inventory is overstated by $1,750, the net effect of these errors is an understatement of cost of goods sold by $3,250 [($1,000 - $2,500) - $1,750 = - $3,250] as shown below:

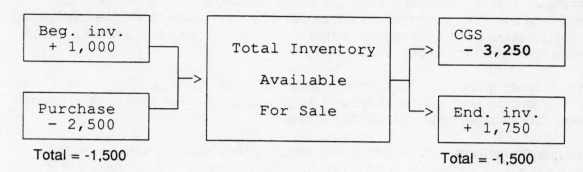

Total = -1,500   Total = -1,500

Note that as the cost of goods sold is understated by $3,250, the net income is overstated by $3,250. Note also that since the ending inventory is overstated, the beginning inventory of the subsequent period is also overstated by the same amount (i.e., $1,750).

KEY CONCEPTS

Lower-of-cost-or-market (LCM) rule (method)   Inventory is valued at cost or market value, whichever is lower. A loss on inventory valuation is recognized when the inventory is written down to market. The loss is included in the cost of goods sold under the direct reduction method, but presented as a separate item (inventory holding loss) under the indirect (allowance) method. Once written down to market, the market value becomes the new cost of the inventory.

Market value of inventory   The market value of inventory is measured by its replacement or reproduction cost, within a range with the net realizable value as the ceiling and net realizable value less normal profit as the floor.

Gross margin method   This method is used to estimate inventory value when it is impracticable or impossible to trace historical cost and to take physical count. It is useful for inventory testing (by auditors), forecasting, interim reporting and estimating inventory damage. It uses historical gross margin rate to estimate first the gross margin of current net sales, then the cost of current sales, and finally the ending inventory cost.

Retail method   This method is used extensively by retailers such as department stores. Inventory at retail price is first determined, which is then converted to cost using a cost to retail ratio. It can be applied to approximate various inventory flow assumptions as well as the LCM rule.

REVIEW QUESTIONS AND EXERCISES

TRUE-FALSE

Indicate whether each of the following statements is true or false by circling the correct response.

T   F   1.   In the application of the lower-of-cost-or-market rule, "market" refers to the net realizable value of the inventory.

T   F   2.   If the utility of inventory declines below its original cost and the LCM rule is used to reflect the loss, total assets and net income will be reduced in the period of loss.

T   F   3.   The LCM rule may be applied to individual inventory items, the total inventory, or major components of inventory.

T   F   4.   The gross margin method is a frequently used alternative to the LIFO, FIFO and average cost methods of inventory valuation for external reporting purposes.

T   F   5.   In the application of the retail method the cost of goods sold can be determined without knowing the retail price of goods purchased.

T   F   6.   The retail method permits a determination of inventory cost without a physical count.

T   F   7.   When using the retail method on FIFO basis, the beginning inventory is excluded from the computation of the current cost to retail ratio.

T   F   8.   A lower-of-cost-or-market approximation by the retail method excludes net markups but includes net markdowns in the computation of the cost to retail ratio.

T   F   9.   A markup cancellation cannot exceed a previous increase above the original selling price.

T   F   10.   A net markdown is the excess of total markdowns over total markups.

T   F   11.   In the retail method abnormal casualty losses are deducted from goods available for sale.

T   F   12.   Discounts to employees and favoured customers are deducted from goods available for sale in the retail method.

T   F   13.   If beginning inventory is understated and the error is undetected, net income for the period is overstated.

T   F   14.   If ending inventory is understated and the error is undetected, ending balance of retained earnings is overstated.

EXERCISE 1

The following data are available concerning various inventory items of a discount store. For each inventory circle the appropriate inventory valuation under the lower-of-cost-or-market rule:

Inventory Item	Cost	Replacement Cost	Net realizable value (Ceiling)	Net realizable value less normal profit (Floor)
A	$150	$140	$180	$120
B	150	160	140	100
C	100	160	180	120
D	100	110	140	90
E	80	70	90	75

EXERCISE 2

Kropko Corporation experienced a warehouse fire on July 2, 1991, at which time the records indicated the following:

Merchandise inventory, January 1, 1991	$ 2,350
Purchases to date	18,500
Freight-in	1,000
Sales to date	25,000

Required: Assuming the gross margin percentage has averaged 35% of sales for the past three years, estimate the cost of inventory destroyed in the fire.

EXERCISE 3

Salmon Company decided to adopt the retail method to value its inventory. The following information is available for 1991:

	Cost	Retail
Merchandise inventory, January 1, 1991	$ 5,500	$ 20,000
Purchases	82,500	125,000
Purchase returns	3,000	4,200
Freight-in	5,000	
Net additional markups		11,742
Net markdowns		2,542
Net sales		120,000

Required: Determine the December 31, 1991 inventory cost under:

1. Retail method -- average cost basis.
2. Retail method -- average cost (LCM) basis (conventional retail).
3. Retail method -- FIFO basis.

MULTIPLE CHOICE

Enter the letter corresponding to the response which **best** completes each of the following statements or questions.

____ 1. In applying the lower-of-cost-or-market rule, "market" refers to:

   a. net realizable value.
   b. replacement cost.
   c. sales price.
   d. sales price less normal profit.

____ 2. When applying the LCM rule, "market" should not be more than:

   a. replacement cost.
   b. net realizable value.
   c. net realizable value plus normal profit.
   d. replacement cost plus normal profit.

____ 3. If the beginning inventory and current purchases are both overstated:

   a. Net income is overstated.
   b. Net income is understated.
   c. Net income is unaffected.
   d. none of the above.

____ 4. The gross margin method is least likely to be used in which of the following situations?

   a. determining the inventory valuation for the annual financial statements.
   b. forecasting and budgeting.
   c. costing inventory destroyed by a tornado.
   d. costing inventory for a quarterly report.

____ 5. Which of the following is generally thought to be an advantage of the retail method:

   a. It allows estimates of inventory to be made without the necessity of a physical count.
   b. It saves considerable clerical work.
   c. It results in a more accurate estimation of ending inventory cost than the gross margin method.
   d. All of the above.

6. In calculating the cost to retail ratio for the conventional retail method:

   a. beginning inventory is excluded.
   b. current purchase is excluded.
   c. net markups are excluded.
   d. net markdowns are excluded.

7. Which of the following is *not* a use of the retail inventory method:

   a. To provide inventory cost data for external financial reports.
   b. To provide inventory cost data for income tax purposes.
   c. To provide a test of the overall reasonableness of a physical inventory costed in the normal manner
   d. To provide the actual amount for the inventory value which will appear in the financial statements.

8. To compute cost to retail ratio and the ending inventory at retail, respectively, under the retail method on FIFO (LCM) basis, net markdowns are to be:

Cost to retail ratio	**Ending inventory at retail**
a. Excluded	Excluded
b. Included	Excluded
c. Excluded	Included
d. Included	Included

9. The following data refer to an item of inventory held by Franco Retailers at December 31, 1991:

Cost	$ 1,300
Estimated selling price	2,000
Estimated disposal costs	200
Normal profit margin	600
Replacement cost	1,100

   Following the lower-of-cost-or-market rule, this item should be valued at:

   a. $1,100
   b. $1,800
   c. $1,300
   d. $1,400

____ 10.   The following information is available from the records of the Kilcona Corporation for the year ended December 31, 1991:

Sales	$250,000
Beginning inventory	$ 50,000
Purchases	$150,000
Historical gross margin ratio	40%
Year-end physical inventory	$ 30,000

Assume that all sales and purchases have been properly recorded and the gross margin ratio has always been maintained, how much might the company reasonably estimate as missing inventory at the year end?

a. $10,000
b. $20,000
c. $60,000
d. $50,000

____ 11.   The following information is available from the records of Bill & Pay Company for the year ended December 31, 1991:

	At Cost	At Retail
Inventory, January 1, 1991	$24,000	$ 54,000
Purchases	48,000	90,000
Net additional markups		12,000
Net markdowns		6,000
Sales		100,000

Under the average cost retail method, Bill & Pay's inventory cost on December 31, 1991 is:

a. $24,000
b. $25,000
c. $30,000
d. $45,000

____ 12.   Based on the same information as in question 11 except that the company uses the retail method on FIFO basis, the inventory cost on December 31, 1991 is:

a. $24,000
b. $25,000
c. $30,000
d. $40,000

____13.   Midnight Grocers Co. purchased 2,000 baskets of Grade AA, and 1,000 baskets of Grade A apples for $3,200. The selling prices are $3 and $2 per basket for AA and A grades, respectively. Using the relative sales value method, the valuation of AA graded apples is:

    a. $2,000
    b. $2,200
    c. $2,300
    d. $2,400

____14.   Merchandise purchased on December 31, 1991 for $1,200 was included in the ending inventory. The purchase was not recorded because the invoice from the supplier has not been received. The ending inventory also included goods consigned by a consignor at their total selling price of $600. As a result of these errors:

    a.   Net income is overstated by $600.
    b.   Net income is understated by $600.
    c.   Net income is overstated by $1,800.
    d.   Net income is understated by $1,800.

SOLUTIONS TO REVIEW QUESTIONS AND EXERCISES

TRUE-FALSE

1.	T	5.	F	9.	T	13.	T
2.	T	6.	T	10.	F	14.	F
3.	T	7.	T	11.	T		
4.	F	8.	F	12.	F		

EXERCISE 1

A. $150 (cost)
B. $140 (net realizable value)
C. $100 (cost)
D. $100 (cost)
E. $80   (cost)

EXERCISE 2

Merchandise inventory, January 1, 1991	$ 2,350
Purchases	18,500
Freight-in	1,000
Total goods available for sale	$21,850
Less: Cost of goods sold ($25,000 x 65%)	16,250
Inventory lost in fire	$ 5,600

EXERCISE 3

1. Retail method - average cost basis:

	At Cost	At Retail
Inventory, January 1, 1991	$ 5,500	$ 20,000
Purchases	82,500	125,000
Purchases return	(3,000)	(4,200)
Freight-in	5,000	
Add: Net additional markups		11,742
Less: Net markdowns		(2,542)
Total goods available for sale	**$ 90,000**	**$150,000**
Less: Sales at retail		(120,000)
Ending inventory at retail		$ 30,000
Ending inventory at cost ($30,000 x 60%*)	**(18,000)**	
Cost of goods sold	$ 72,000	

*Average cost ratio = $90,000 / $150,000 = 60%.

2. Retail method - average cost (LCM) basis (conventional retail):

	At Cost	At Retail
Inventory, January 1, 1991	$ 5,500	$ 20,000
Purchases	$ 82,500	$125,000
Purchases return	(3,000)	(4,200)
Freight-in	5,000	
Add: Net additional markups		11,742
Total available excluding markdowns	**$ 90,000**	**$152,542**
Less: Net markdowns		(2,542)
Total goods available for sale		$150,000
Less: Sales at retail		(120,000)
Ending inventory at retail		$ 30,000
Ending inventory at average cost (LCM) ($30,000 x 59%*)	**(17,700)**	
Cost of goods sold	$ 72,300	

*Average cost (LCM) ratio = $90,000 / $152,542 = 59%.

3. Retail method - FIFO basis:

	At Cost	At Retail
Purchases	$ 82,500	$125,000
Purchases return	(3,000)	(4,200)
Freight-in	5,000	
Add: Net additional markups		11,742
Less: Net markdowns		(2,542)
Current increase in inventory	**$ 84,500**	**$130,000**
Inventory, January 1, 1991	5,500	20,000
Total goods available for sale	$ 90,000	$150,000
Less: Sales at retail		(120,000)
Ending inventory at retail		$ 30,000
Ending inventory at FIFO cost ($30,000 x 65%*)	**(19,500)**	
Cost of goods sold	$ 70,500	

*Current cost ratio = $84,500 / $130,000 = 65%

MULTIPLE CHOICE

1.	a	5.	d	9.	c	13.	d
2.	b	6.	d	10.	b	14.	c
3.	b	7.	d	11.	a		
4.	a	8.	c	12.	b		

Computations and explanations:

9. (b) Since the cost ($1,300) is greater than both the replacement cost ($1,100) and the floor ($2,000 - $200 - $600 = $1,200), and the floor is greater than the replacement cost, the LCM value is the floor value.

10. (b)

```
Beginning inventory                                        $ 50,000
Purchases                                                   150,000

Total available for sale                                   $200,000
Less: Cost of goods sold, $250,000 x (1 - 40%)              150,000

Estimated ending inventory                                              $ 50,000
Physical inventory                                          30,000

Inventory loss                                             $ 20,000
```

11. (a)

	At Cost	At Retail
Inventory, January 1, 1991	$24,000	$ 54,000
Purchases	48,000	90,000
Net additional markups		12,000
Net markdowns		(6,000)
Total available	$72,000	$150,000
Sales		(100,000)
Ending inventory at retail		$ 50,000
Ending inventory at cost ($50,000 x $72,000 / $150,000)	(24,000)	
Cost of goods sold	$ 48,000	

12. (b)

	At Cost	At Retail
Purchases	$ 48,000	$ 90,000
Net additional markups		12,000
Net markdowns		(6,000)
Current increase in inventory	$ 48,000	$ 96,000
Inventory, January 1, 1991	24,000	54,000
Total available	$ 72,000	$150,000
Sales		(100,000)
Ending inventory at retail		$ 50,000
Ending inventory at cost ($50,000 x $48,000 / $96,000)	(25,000)	
Cost of goods sold	$ 47,000	

13. (d) Inventory cost (AA grade)
= $3,200 x [(2,000 x $3) / (2,000 x $3 + 1,000 x $2)]
= $2,400.

14. (c) Overstated income
= Understated cost of goods sold
= Understated purchases + Overstated ending inventory
= $1,200 + $600 = $1,800.

CHAPTER 11

Capital Assets: Acquisition, Disposal and Exchange

CHAPTER OBJECTIVES

This chapter is designed to enable students to:

A.   Determine the value of plant assets at acquisition.

B.   Distinguish expenditures that should be capitalized to plant assets from those that should be expensed.

C.   Determine the value of plant assets acquired by means other than cash.

D.   Present the arguments for and against the capitalization of interest during construction of plant assets, and explain the effect of interest capitalization on financial statements.

E.   Determine the amount of interest to be capitalized during construction of plant assets.

F.   Account for the disposal of plant assets including any gains or losses on disposal.

G.   Account for exchanges of non-monetary assets.

H.   Account for post-acquisition costs in conjunction with plant assets.

"CHAPTER OVERVIEW"

A.   The Nature of Capital Assets

Capital assets are acquired for active use in the operation of a business, and provide measurable benefits beyond the current accounting period. For accounting purposes capital assets usually are classified into **tangible** and **intangible**, depending on whether these assets have physical substance or not. Tangible capital assets, generally referred to as fixed assets, plant assets, or property, plant, and equipment, may be further classified into:

1.   Those subject to depreciation, such as buildings, equipment, etc.

2.   Those subject to depletion, such as mineral deposits, timber tracts and other natural resources.

3.   Land, which is not subject to either depreciation or depletion.

This chapter provides a discussion of the acquisition, disposal and exchange of these plant assets except natural resources which will be discussed in Chapter 13.

B.   Capital Assets Acquired by Purchase

The acquisition cost of a capital asset (in accordance with CICA, Sec 3060) includes the invoice price net of discount, sales taxes, freight, installation, break-in costs, and other expenditures necessarily incurred to bring it to the condition and location for its intended use. This cost provides benefits to the business beyond the period of acquisition and is thus capitalized (i.e., debited to the appropriate asset account). Not all costs which might appear to be associated with the acquisition, however, are included in the acquisition cost. For example, interest on debt incurred to purchase capital assets, post acquisition property tax and insurance premiums are expensed when incurred.

If two or more capital assets are acquired for a **lump-sum** purchase price, the cost is allocated to the appropriate asset accounts on the basis of their relative market values. Assume $21,000 is paid for an office computer with a fair value of $16,000 and a printer with a fair value of $8,000, the lump-sum cost would be allocated as follows:

Assets acquired	Fair value	Allocation	Acquisition cost
Computer	$16,000	$21,000 x $16,000 / $24,000	$14,000
Printer	8,000	$21,000 x $8,000 / $24,000	7,000
Total	$24,000		$21,000

A capital asset acquired **on credit** should be recorded at its cash equivalent price. The difference between this price and the total payment under the debt agreement is recorded as interest expense over the term of the debt. If the cash equivalent price is indeterminable, the asset and related liability are recorded at the present value of the cash payment(s). The discount rate used in computing the present value should be realistic, reflecting the risk and duration of the debt.

C.   1.   Capital assets acquired by means other than cash. When a capital asset is acquired for **consideration other than cash,** its recorded cost is either the market value of the consideration given for the exchange, or the market value of the asset acquired, whichever is more objectively determinable. For instance, when equity securities (common or preferred stock) are exchanged for a plant asset, the transaction should be recorded at the fair market value of the securities given, provided that the market could absorb additional securities without affecting the established price. If the market value of the securities cannot be determined reliably, the fair market value of the assets acquired should be used. In the absence of any reliable fair market value, it may be approximated by an independent appraisal.

2. **Capital Assets Acquired by Donation**

The donation of a plant asset is an example of a nonreciprocal transfer, i.e., a transfer of resources in one direction. The **CICA, Sec. 3830** requires that a nonmonetary asset received in a nonreciprocal transfer be recorded at the fair market value of the asset. If the donation is unconditional, both the asset and the additional paid-in capital from donation should be increased by the fair market value. If conditions are imposed by the donor on the use of the donated asset, the expected cost of complying with those restrictions should be estimated and deducted from the market value of the asset. If the donation is contingent upon the fulfillment of a contractual obligation by the recipient, the asset should be treated as a contingent asset until the conditions have been met. **CICA HB 3800** requires that such a donated asset be disclosed in the footnotes **only**, until the contingency is eventually removed.

Instead of being donated directly, assets are often acquired with the assistance of various levels of governments. Often these programs require the firm to maintain certain employment levels or pollution control levels, for example, for the assistance (or loan) to be forgivable. If the conditions of the assistance are not met, the firm may be required to refund the amounts received to the granting agency.

CICA Handbook, section 3800 uses the income approach in that (1) the receipt of assistance confers a benefit to the firm and should be reflected in income, (2) the assistance received generally offsets costs and thus should be reflected, (3) the assistance is a factor in the overall results of the operation and the statement of income should report this factor, and (4) most assistance is not entirely gratuitous and thus, in some sense, is earned.

3. **Plant Assets Acquired by Self-construction:** Companies often construct plant assets for their own use. In this case, all incremental costs closely associated with the construction, including material, labor and certain overhead costs (e.g., utility costs, maintenance on equipment and supervision) should be capitalized as the acquisition costs of the constructed assets. Following the conservatism principle, the amount of construction cost to be capitalized should never exceed the cost of acquiring a similar asset of equal capacity and quality from outsiders, and the excessive construction cost, if any, should be recognized immediately as a loss.

Construction cost capitalization gives rise to two accounting issues:

1. **General overhead allocation:** The capitalization of general overhead costs such as depreciation and taxes has been controversial. No official pronouncement provides guidelines on whether and how to allocate general overhead costs to self-constructed assets. Many accountants are of the opinion that, in the absence of idle capacity, a reasonable portion of general overhead should be assigned to the self-constructed asset.

2. **Interest capitalization**

D.   Interest Capitalization During Construction

In general interest incurred on debt used to acquire an asset is expensed as incurred because it is a financing cost which does not increase the utility of the asset acquired. For years, however, there had been disagreement among accountants over the capitalization of interest expenditures during the construction period. This issue was then clarified by the CICA. According to **Sec. 3060**:

   a.   **Qualifying assets.**   Assets qualifying for interest capitalization are limited to those constructed for a firm's own use (e.g., self-constructed buildings, equipment, plant, etc.), or constructed as discrete projects for sale or lease (e.g., real estate developments and ships).

   b.   **Avoidable interest.**   The amount of interest to capitalize in any period is limited to that portion of the interest cost incurred during the period that could have been avoided if expenditures for the assets had not been made.

   c.   **Qualifying expenditures.**   Expenditures qualifying for interest capitalization are limited to those that have required the payment of cash, the transfer of other assets or the incurring of a liability on which interest is recognized (in contrast to liabilities, such as trade payable and accruals).

E.   Amount of Interest to Be Capitalized

Based on the above guidelines, interest is capitalized as follows:

   a.   **Capitalization period**:   The period begins when the following conditions are present:

      (1)   Qualifying expenditures have been made.

      (2)   Construction and related activities occurred for substantially the entire period

      (3)   Interest cost was incurred.

   The capitalization period shall end when the asset is substantially complete and ready for the intended use.

   b.   **Capitalization amount**:   The following steps are pertinent to the calculation the amount of capitalized interest:

      (1)   Determine actual interest cost (**AIC**) for the construction period.

      (2)   Compute average accumulated expenditures (**AAE**).   This is the weighted average of accumulated qualifying expenditures during the construction period.

(3) Compute the interest potentially capitalizable (**IPC**). This is determined by applying the appropriate interest rate to the **AAE** amount. Two methods are allowed:

(a) **Specific method.** Apply the interest rate of **specific** construction debt to the **AAE**. If the **AAE** exceeds the principal amount of the specific debt, the weighted-average interest rate on all other interest-bearing debt is applied to the excess.

(b) **Weighted-average method.** The weighted-average interest rate on **all** interest-bearing debt is applied to the **AAE**.

(4) Capitalize the lesser of **AIC** and **IPC**.

ILLUSTRATION 1: INTEREST CAPITALIZATION

Happy Go Lucky Company decided to construct its own warehouse. For 1991, expenditures for the building totaled $500,000. Assume that $100,000 was paid on January 2, 1991, and the remaining amount of $400,000 was paid evenly throughout the year. A 10% note directly related to the project was issued on January 2, 1991, with a face value of $200,000. Debt not directly related included a $500,000 long-term note at 12%, and another note of $200,000 at 8.5%, both issued in 1990.

Required: Determine the amount of capitalized interest in 1991 using (1) the specific method, and (2) the weighted-average method.

SOLUTION:

1. The specific method:

Step 1: Compute actual interest cost:

10% Note:	$200,000 x 10%	$20,000
12% Note:	$500,000 x 12%	60,000
8.5% Note:	$200,000 x 8.5%	17,000
AIC		$97,000

Step 2: Compute average accumulated expenditures:

$100,000 x 1/1	$100,000
$400,000 x 1/2	200,000
AAE	$300,000

Step 3: Compute interest potentially capitalizable:

On specific borrowing: $200,000 x 10%	$20,000
On general borrowing: [$100,000 x 11%]*	11,000
IPC	$31,000

Step 4: Determine capitalized interest:

IPC	$31,000
AIC	97,000
Capitalized interest -- the lesser	$31,000

* AAE financed by general debt
= AAE – Specific borrowing
= $300,000 – $200,000 = $100,000.

Weighted–average interest rate of general debt
= Interest expense of general debts / Principal of general debt
= [$500,000 x 12% + $200,000 x 8.5%] / [$500,000 + $200,000]
= $77,000 / $700,000 = 11%.

2.   **Weighted–average method:**

Steps 1 and 2:   Same as the specific method.

Step 3:   Compute interest potentially capitalizable:

IPC = $300,000 x [$97,000 / $900,000]* $32,333

Step 4:   Determine capitalized interest:

IPC	$32,333
AIC	97,000
Capitalized interest – the lesser	$32,333

* $97,000 and $900,000 are the total interest expenses and the
total debt, respectively, as indicated in Step 1.

Financial Statement Disclosure of Interest   The *CICA Handbook*, section
1520, requires that the amount of interest expense be disclosed in the
financial statements or footnotes. In periods of interest capitalization,
section 3850 requires the interest capitalized to be disclosed.

F.   Disposal of Capital Assets:

The disposal of plant assets may be **voluntary** (sale, abandonment, etc.), or **involuntary** (fire, flood, earthquake, condemnation, etc.). In any case, the asset and its accumulated depreciation up to the date of disposal are removed from the records, and, if indicated, a gain or loss on disposal should be recorded.

The recorded gain or loss should be classified as either **ordinary** or **extraordinary.** A gain or loss is extraordinary if it is both **unusual in nature** and **infrequent in occurrence.** Obviously, an involuntary disposal is more likely to result in an extraordinary gain or loss than is a voluntary disposal.

G. **Exchange of Capital Assets:**

Plant assets are often exchanged for other plant assets. The proper accounting for the exchange transaction depends on whether the asset surrendered is "similar" or "dissimilar" to the asset acquired. Assets are considered similar if they are held for resale in the same line of business, or they are productive assets used for comparable purposes. (CICA, sec. 3830)

1. **Exchange of dissimilar assets:** When dissimilar assets are exchanged (e.g., land exchanged for a new machine), the earnings process is culminated. The market value of the asset surrendered is recorded as the cost of the asset received, and a gain or loss is **fully** recognized for the difference between the market value and book value of the surrendered asset.

    To illustrate, assume land with a book value of $50,000 and a market value of $80,000 was exchanged for equipment. The transaction would be recorded as:

Equipment	80,000	
Land		50,000
Gain on disposal of land		30,000

    If cash was paid or received to even the exchange, cash account would be credited or debited, and the cost of equipment would be increased or decreased by the cash amount. If the fair value of land is not reliably determinable, the market value of the equipment may be used to record the exchange.

2. **Exchange of similar assets:** In an exchange of similar assets (e.g., an old machine exchanged for a new machine), accounting treatment depends on whether the transaction involves cash:

    a. **Exchange not involving cash.** The exchange transaction is viewed as a continuation of the earnings process. The new asset is recorded at the book value of the old asset, or the market value of the new asset, whichever is lower. A loss is recognized if the market value of the new asset is lower.

    Assume Tatoo Company acquires a new machine in exchange for an old machine. The old machine originally cost $18,000 and has a book value of $12,000.

    Case 1: The fair market value of the new machine is $15,500:

Machine (new)	12,000	
Accumulated depreciation (old)	6,000	
Machine (old)		18,000

    Case 2: The fair market value of the new machine is $11,000:

Machine (new)	11,000	
Accumulated depreciation (old)	6,000	
Loss on exchange	1,000	
Machine (old)		18,000

b.   Exchange involving cash payment.   If cash payment is involved in the exchange, the cost of the new asset is the sum of the book value of the old asset and the amount of cash paid, or the market value of the new asset, whichever is lower. Thus, if $2,500 cash plus the old machine were given in the previous example:

Case 3:   The fair market value of the new machine is $15,500:

Machine (new)	14,500	
Accumulated depreciation (old)	6,000	
Cash		2,500
Machine (old)		18,000

Case 4:   The fair market value of the new machine is $11,000:

Machine (new)	11,000	
Accumulated depreciation (old)	6,000	
Loss on exchange	3,500	
Cash		2,500
Machine (old)		18,000

c.   Exchange involving cash receipt.   When cash is received in an exchange of similar assets, The earnings process is continuing.

For example, Orange Company exchanged an old equipment for a new equipment, and **received** $4,000 from the exchange. The old equipment had a cost of $24,000 and accumulated depreciation of $16,000. The fair value of the new equipment is $10,000.

Cash received	$ 4,000
"Fair" value of new equipment	10,000
Total "fair" value received	$14,000

To record the exchange:

Cash	4,000	
Equipment (new) (8,000 - 4,000)	4,000	
Accumulated depreciation (old)	16,000	
Equipment (old)		24,000

However, the exchange may result in a **loss**, i.e., the book value of old machine exceeds the total "fair" value received. The entire loss should be recognized, and the new machine should be recorded at its "market value". To illustrate, using the above example except the "fair" value of the new equipment is $3,000, the exchange would result in a total loss of $1,000 as shown below:

Total "fair value" received ($4,000+$3,000)		$7,000
Less: Book value of asset surrendered		
Cost of equipment (old)	$24,000	
Less: Accumulated depreciation	16,000	8,000
Loss on exchange		($1,000)

To record the exchange:

Cash	4,000	
Equipment (new)	3,000	
Accumulated depreciation (old)	16,000	
Loss on exchange	1,000	
Equipment (old)		24,000

H. Expenditures Subsequent to Acquisition:

Expenditures relating to an asset are classified into revenue expenditures and capital expenditures as follows:

1. **Revenue expenditures** include maintenance and ordinary repairs, which are incurred to maintain an asset in the original condition, but neither extend its useful life nor increase its productivity above original expectation. Therefore, these expenditures benefit current period only and are **expensed** currently to match against the revenues of that period. Two approaches may be used: The incurred approach and the allocation approach.

2. **Capital expenditures** are those expenditures which extend the useful life of the asset, increase the productivity of the asset, or enhance the quality of the product. Expenditures meeting any of these conditions usually benefit the current and future periods and are therefore **capitalized** (recorded as an asset) and allocated over a number of periods they benefit.

   a. **Betterments, improvements, replacements and renewals.**   Betterments are costs incurred to enhance the service potential of capital assets. A betterment occurs when there is an increase in physical output capacity, operating costs are lowered, useful life is extended, or the quality of output is improved. Betterments should be recorded at cost.

   An improvement involves substituting a major component of a plant asset with a significantly improved component. (the replacement of an old shingle roof with a modern fireproof tile roof)

A replacement involves substituting a major component of a plant asset with a one of comparable quality. (Replacement of a truck engine with a similar engine)

Renewals involve large expenditures, are not recurring in nature, and usually increase the utility or the service life of the asset beyond the original estimate. (Major overhauls of equipment)

Each of these categories of expenditures increases the useful life or productivity of the original asset. Three different approaches have evolved to account for these expenditures, all of which cause the book value of the original asset to increase.

1.   *Substitute for the old asset*. The substitution approach removes the cost of the old component and related accumulated depreciation, recognizes a loss equal to the remaining book value, and increases the original asset account in the amount of the expenditure.

This approach is applied only when the cost of the old subunit and the related accumulated depreciation amount are known or can reliably be estimated.

2.   *Increase asset account*. Use the increased asset account approach when the old costs and related accumulated depreciation amounts are not known. The cost of the betterment is debited to the primary asset account under the historical cost principle. The cost and accumulated depreciation of the unit replaced are not removed from the accounts because they cannot be determined reliably.

3.   *Reduce accumulated depreciation*. Reducing accumulated depreciation is the traditional approach used when the primary effect is to lengthen the remaining life of the related asset. The expenditure is debited to the related accumulated depreciation account as a recovery of previously recognized depreciation on the grounds that some of the useful life is restored. The cost of the unit replaced and related accumulated depreciation are not removed from the accounts.

b.   **Additions.**   The cost of extending, expanding or enlarging existing assets (e.g., adding a wing to a building) should be capitalized. If the addition is an integral part of the existing asset, the cost is added to that asset account. Otherwise the cost is debited to a separate asset account and depreciated over its own useful life.

c.   **Rearrangements of assets.**   These costs include expenditures for moving or rearranging existing assets or changing the layout of the plant. Such costs are debited to a separate asset account (a deferred charge) and written off over the period expected to be benefited, if determinable.

d.   Disclosure of Plant Assets

Publicly-held firms generally disclose plant assets by major classes in the balance sheet, and information about significant accounting policies relating to the assets in footnotes.The CICA, sec. 3060 sets out the disclosure requirements.

KEY CONCEPTS

Capital expenditures   Expenditures that are expected to yield benefits beyond the current accounting period and are thus capitalized and then amortized over a number of years.

Exchange of dissimilar assets   An exchange of assets which are dissimilar in their type, or in the purpose of which they are used. The earnings process of a dissimilar assets exchange is considered culminated, and any gain or loss is recognized in full. The Ceiling Value of the asset acquired is its market value. With these circumstances it is possible to recognize gains or losses on these exchanges.

Exchange of similar assets   An exchange of assets which are considered to be similar (in productive function) is treated as a continuation of the earnings process. The operations of the business are not changed. Therefore gains or losses are not recognized on these exchanges. However, since the ceiling value of the asset acquired is its known market value it may be possible to recognize a loss on the exchange.

Interest capitalization   Interest during the construction period may be capitalized if (1) Qualifying expenditures have been made, (2) Construction and related activities are in progress, and (3) Interest cost is being incurred.

Qualifying assets for interest capitalization   Interest may be capitalized on assets constructed for a company's own use or as discrete projects for sale or lease.

Revenue expenditures   Expenditures that are expected to yield benefits only in the current accounting period and are thus expensed as incurred.

Tangible capital assets (plant assets, fixed assets or property, plant and equipment)   Assets with physical substance that are acquired for use in operation and provide measurable benefits beyond the current accounting period.

REVIEW QUESTIONS AND EXERCISES

TRUE-FALSE

Indicate whether each of the following statements is true or false by circling the correct response.

T   F   1.   Theoretically, **all** available discounts, whether taken or not, should be deducted from the cost of an acquired plant asset.

T   F   2.   If cash price is not determinable for an asset acquired on credit, the asset and related liability should be recorded at the **present value** of debt payments, discounted at a market rate of interest.

T   F   3.   The purchase price for three assets acquired as a group usually is allocated among the assets on the basis of their previous **book values**.

T   F   4.   When **similar** assets are exchanged, the earning process is considered to have been culminated (completed).

T   F   5.   When **dissimilar** assets are exchanged and cash is also received in the exchange, the new asset is recorded at the market value of the asset surrendered plus the cash received.

T   F   6.   The asset acquired in an exchange of similar assets in which cash is received is recorded at the difference between the market value of the **new** asset less the cash received.

T   F   7.   The fair value of a donated asset is debited to an asset account and credited to a **revenue** account.

T   F   8.   The primary difference between a capital expenditure and a revenue expenditure is the **magnitude** of the cost incurred.

T   F   9.   Self constructed assets should include, at a minimum, direct material, direct labor, incremental overhead, and interest on debt specifically related to the construction.

T   F   10.   Assets intended for sale or lease that are produced in large quantities on a **repetitive** basis qualify for interest capitalization.

T   F   11.   A firm's **incremental** borrowing rate should be used to calculate interest capitalization for assets financed with general borrowing.

T   F   12.   The **book value** of an asset is increased when accounting for a betterment, but not when accounting for a replacement.

T   F   13. An addition of a new wing to a building should be recorded by adding the cost to the building and depreciated over the life of the building or the addition, whichever is **longer**.

T   F   14. A loss should be recognized when an asset is abandoned or when its value to the firm becomes permanently impaired.

EXERCISE 1

Indicate in the space provided the most appropriate classification of each expenditure listed below:

Expenditures Incurred

____ 1. Tires on delivery truck repaired.

____ 2. Air conditioner repaired.

____ 3. New wing of office space added to an office building.

____ 4. Warehouse roof replaced, adding 5 years to warehouse life.

____ 5. Office building repainted.

____ 6. Repair of worn floor with new longer-lasting materials.

____ 7. Tune-up on delivery truck.

____ 8. Body work on delivery truck because of auto accident.

____ 9. Major overhaul of motor of construction machinery, increasing its productivity.

____ 10. Conveyer belt on factory equipment is replaced with a new, improved speedier belt.

Classification

A. Ordinary Repair - debit an expense.

B. Betterment - debit an asset.

C. Replacement - debit an asset and remove old costs.

D. Rearrangement - debit an asset.

E. Addition - debit an asset.

EXERCISE 2

Butter Flutta Corporation decided to build a warehouse for its own use. Construction began on January 1, 1991, at which time Butter borrowed $25,000 at 7% to finance the construction. Butter had outstanding at the time a $50,000 note at 10% and another note of $200,000 at 8%. A total cost (not including interest) of $120,000 was incurred evenly throughout 1991.

Required: Using the following schedules, determine the interest of the warehouse to be capitalized in 1991 under (1) the specific method, and (2) the weighted average method.

1. The specific method:

    Step 1. Compute actual interest cost (AIC):

            7% Note:
            10% Note:
            8% Note:

            AIC

    Step 2. Compute average accumulated expenditures (AAE):

    Step 3: Compute interest potentially capitalizable (IPC):

            On specific borrowing:
            On general borrowing:

            IPC

    Step 4: Determine capitalized interest:

            IPC
            AIC

            Capitalized interest

2. Weighted average method:

    Steps 1 and 2: Same as the specific method.

    Step 3: Compute interest potentially capitalizable (IPC):

            IPC

    Step 4: Determine capitalized interest:

            IPC
            AIC

            Capitalized interest

EXERCISE 3

Unsung Corporation trades a used machine for a similar new machine. The used machine has an original cost of $45,000 and accumulated depreciation of $30,000. The new machine has a list price of $20,000, and a fair value of $18,000.

Required: Prepare the appropriate journal entry to record the exchange transaction in each of the following cases:

1. The exchange does not involve cash.

2. Unsung paid $4,000 for the exchange.

3. Unsung received $5,000 from the exchange.

MULTIPLE CHOICE

Enter the letter corresponding to the response which **best** completes each of the following statements or questions.

_____ 1. A characteristic common to all operational assets is:

    a. used in operation with measurable future benefits.
    b. subject to depreciation.
    c. physical substance.
    d. acquired for resale.

_____ 2. The acquisition cost of a machine typically would **not** include:

    a. sales taxes.
    b. interest on financing the machine acquisition.
    c. in-transit insurance cost.
    d. costs of assembly, installment and testing.

_____ 3. When office equipment is purchased:

    a. freight charges paid would not be included in its cost.
    b. installation charges would not be included in its cost.
    c. the cost should be reduced by a cash discount available.
    d. all costs incurred in connection with the acquisition should be expensed in the period.

_____ 4. When a plant asset is constructed by a firm for its own use, general overhead costs may be:

    a. charged to the asset on a basis proportional to that charged to normal production.
    b. excluded from the cost of the plant.
    c. either a. or b.
    d. neither a. and b.

_____ 5. Which of the following conditions is **not** necessary for interest capitalization for a self-constructed asset?

    a. all funds used in construction are from directly-related debt.
    b. expenditures for the construction have been made.
    c. interest cost is being incurred.
    d. construction activities are in progress.

____ 6. The amount of interest which is capitalized on a self-constructed asset may not exceed total interest cost actually incurred:

    a. on general debt.
    b. during the construction period.
    c. on directly-related debt.
    d. during the accounting period.

____ 7. In an exchange of capital assets:

    a. gains are recognized entirely regardless of whether the assets are similar.
    b. gains are recognized only if the assets are similar.
    c. losses are recognized regardless of whether the assets are similar.
    d. losses are recognized only if the assets are similar.

____ 8. In an exchange of capital assets without involving cash an earnings process culminates if the plant assets are:

    a. dissimilar.
    b. similar.
    c. Both a. and b. are true.
    d. Neither a. nor b. is true.

____ 9. A used machine with a book value of $25,000 and a market value of $33,000 was exchanged for a used delivery truck with a list price of $36,000. The old machine plus $2,000 in cash were given in the exchange. The firm should record:

    a. a gain of $10,000.
    b. a gain of $8,000.
    c. no gain or loss.
    d. the truck at $36,000.

____ 10. Assume the same fact as in question 9 except, instead of **paying** $2,000 in the exchange, the firm received $2,000 cash. The firm should record:

    a. a gain of $10,000.
    b. a gain of $8,000.
    c. no gain or loss.
    d. the truck at $36,000.

____ 11. Garner Pharmaceutical was given a tract of land on which to build a new plant by Somerville as an inducement to locate in the community. The land had been acquired three years ago by Somerville at a cost of $50,000, but was appraised currently at $60,000. Garner's entry to record the donation will include a(n):

    a. extraordinary gain of $60,000.
    b. ordinary gain of $50,000.
    c. debit to the asset of $50,000.
    d. credit to paid-in-capital at $60,000.

____12. Happy Company started construction of a plant on January 2, 1991. Construction expenditures incurred in 1991 is $180,000, $40,000 of which was borrowing by issuing a 10% note on the same date when the construction began. Assume expenditures incurred evenly throughout the year, and the company did not have any other debt outstanding during the construction period, the amount of interest cost capitalized in 1991 is:

   a. $4,000.
   b. $2,000.
   c. $3,000.
   d. $6,000.

____13. Company Smith and Company Green exchange similar delivery trucks as follows:

	Company Smith	Company Green
Original cost of truck	$18,000	$22,000
Accumulated depreciation	$ 9,000	$15,000
Current market value	$12,000	$ 8,000
Cash received (paid)	$ 4,000	$(4,000)

What amount should Company Smith record for the truck received?

   a. $5,000.
   b. $6,000.
   c. $9,000.
   d. $8,000.

____14. Assume the same fact as in question 13, what amount should Company Green record for the truck received?

   a. $7,000.
   b. $10,000.
   c. $11,000.
   d. $12,000.

SOLUTIONS TO REVIEW QUESTIONS AND EXERCISES

TRUE-FALSE

1.	T	5.	F	9.	T	13.	F
2.	T	6.	F	10.	F	14.	T
3.	F	7.	F	11.	F		
4.	F	8.	F	12.	F		

EXERCISE 1

1.	A	5.	A	9.	B
2.	A	6.	B	10.	B
3.	E	7.	A		
4.	C	8.	A		

EXERCISE 2

1. The specific method:

Step 1: Compute actual interest cost (AIC):

7% Note: $25,000 x 7%		$ 1,750
10% Note: $50,000 x 10%		5,000
8% Note: $200,000 x 8%		16,000
AIC		$22,750

Step 2: Compute average accumulated expenditures (AAE):

$120,000 x 1 / 2	$60,000

Step 3: Compute interest potentially capitalizable (IPC):

On specific borrowing: $25,000 x 7%	$ 1,750
On general borrowing: [$35,000 x 8.4%]*	2,940
IPC	$ 4,690

Step 4: Determine capitalized interest:

IPC	$ 4,690
AIC	$22,750
Capitalized interest - the lesser	$ 4,690

* Average accumulated expenditures financed by general debt
  = Average accumulated expenditures - Specific borrowing
  = $60,000 - $25,000 = $35,000.

  Weighted-average annual interest rate of general debt
  = Interest expense of general debt / Principal of general debt
  = [$50,000 x 10% + $200,000 x 8%] / [$50,000 + $200,000]
  = $21,000 / $250,000 = 8.4%.

2. **Weighted-average method:**

   Steps 1 and 2: Same as the specific method.

   Step 3: Compute interest potentially capitalizable:

IPC = $60,000 x [$22,750 / $275,000]*	$ 4,964

   Step 4: Determine capitalized interest:

IPC	$ 4,964
AIC	$22,750
Capitalized interest - the lesser	$ 4,964

   * The weighted-average annual interest rate is calculated using
      the annual interest expenses ($22,750) and the total debt
      amount ($275,000) as indicated in Step 1.

EXERCISE 3

1. The exchange does not involve boot.

Machine (new), plug	15,000	
Accumulated depreciation (old)	30,000	
Machine (old)		45,000

2. Unsung paid $4,000 for the exchange.

Loss on exchange of plant assets	1,000	
Machine (new), ceiling	18,000	
Accumulated depreciation (old)	30,000	
Machine (old)		45,000
Cash		4,000

3. Unsung received $5,000 from the exchange.

Machine (new), plug	**10,000**	
Cash	5,000	
Accumulated depreciation (old)	30,000	
Machine (old)		45,000

1. Cash received	5,000	
Fair value of new equipment	18,000	
Total fair value received	23,000	

MULTIPLE CHOICE

1.	a	5.	a	9.	b	13.	a
2.	b	6.	b	10.	b	14.	c
3.	c	7.	c	11.	d		
4.	c	8.	a	12.	a		

Computations and explanations:

9. (b) Exchange of dissimilar assets, recognize gain in its entirety:
         Boot does not affect gain recognition.

Market value of old	$33,000
Book value of old	25,000
Gain	$ 8,000

10. (b) Same as question 9.

11. (d) Garner should record the donation by a debit to the asset account, and a credit to the paid-in capital account, at the market value of the donated asset.

12. (a)

Actual interest incurred ($40,000 x 10%)	$4,000
AAE ($180,000 / 2)	$90,000
IPC ($40,000 x 10% + $50,000 x 0)	$4,000
Interest capitalized	$4,000

13. (b) **Company Smith:** In the exchange of similar nonmonetary asset involving cash receipt.

Acquisition cost of new asset
= Book value of old - Cash received
= $9,000 - $4,000
= $5,000.

14. (c) **Company Green:** In the exchange of similar nonmonetary assets involving cash payment, the acquisition cost of new asset is the sum of the book value of old asset plus the amount of cash paid:

Acquisition cost of new asset
= Book value of old + Cash paid
= ($22,000 - $15,000) + $4,000
= $11,000.

CHAPTER 12

Capital Assets: Depreciation and Impairment

CHAPTER OBJECTIVES

This chapter is designed to enable students to:

A. Describe the nature of depreciation and explain the factors that affect the determination of depreciation expense.

B. Use several depreciation methods and explain the rational and incentives for using each.

C. Explain the relationships between depreciation, taxes, cash flows, and dividends.

D. Account for fractional year depreciation and depreciation of post-acquisition costs.

E. Explain and account for changes in depreciation estimates, depreciation methods, and depreciation errors.

F. Explain and use special depreciation systems.

G. Account for and report impairments in asset values.

H. Explain the capital cost allowance system and calculate depreciation for tax purposes (refers to Appendix 12A)

I. Account for depreciation using the annuity and sinking fund methods (refers to Appendix 12B).

J. Account for casualty losses (refers to Appendix 12C).

CHAPTER OVERVIEW

An attribute common to all tangible capital assets is their revenue producing potential through use. They can be viewed as a bundle of economic service potential consumed over time as revenues are earned. The costs of these assets, except for land, are therefore matched against revenue over their useful life in a process of amortization which traditionally has been termed, depreciation, depletion or amortization depending on the nature of the capital asset. This chapter focuses on depreciation processes and other issues related to depreciable assets.

A. The Nature of Depreciation

Depreciation is a process of allocating the cost of a depreciable asset, in a systematic and rational manner, to the accounting periods which benefit. It is a process of **cost allocation**, **not** of **asset valuation**.

Causes of Depreciation The decline in usefulness or useful life of plant assets is caused by physical factors (including wear and tear from operations, action of time or other elements, and deterioration and decay) and obsolescence, which is the result of new technology making older assets less efficient and therefore more expensive to operate. Obsolescence also occurs when facility expansion renders certain assets unusable under new operating conditions, or when facility expansion renders certain assets unusable under new operating conditions, or when demand for the product or services supplied by the asset declines. Assets rendered obsolete are typically in good condition and still capable of supplying the service originally expected of it. Depreciation accounting considers all predictable factors that limit the usefulness and useful life of plant assets.

The depreciation process requires consideration of the following four factors of a depreciable asset:

1. Acquisition cost of the asset, and capitalized post-acquisition costs as discussed in Chapter 11.

2. Residual (salvage) value of the asset. This is an estimate of the net amount recoverable from the asset at the end of its expected service life. The depreciable cost of an asset (also referred to as the depreciation base) is its acquisition cost less estimated residual value. In practice, however, residual values are often ignored.

3. Service (useful or economic) life of the asset. This is the estimated number of years, machine hours or units of output that the asset is expected to perform or to produce. It is the expected life of the asset (a) to its present owner or user, (b) for the purpose for which it was acquired, and (c) assuming a specific repair and maintenance policy.

4. Method of depreciation.

B. Depreciation Methods and Depreciation Systems

1. Depreciation methods: A depreciation method is a pattern of allocating the depreciable cost of **an individual asset** over its expected service life. Theoretically, any method is generally acceptable as long as it is justifiable (rational) and consistently applied (systematic). Nevertheless, the following depreciation methods are common:

   a. Straight-Line Method (SL): This method is based on equal allocation of cost to each time period.

   b. Activity (or input and output) Methods: These methods are based on service input or productive output of the assets:

    (1)   Service (or Machine) Hours Method (SH).
    (2)   Productive Output (or unit-of-production) Method (PO).

c.   Accelerated Methods: Like the SL method, these methods are time based. However, they are designed to recognize greater amounts of depreciation early in the useful life of the asset, and lesser amounts later:

    (1)   Sum-of-the-Years'-Digits Method (SYD).
    (2)   Declining-Balance Methods (DB).

2.   Depreciation systems: These are cost allocation patterns applied to certain classes of, instead of individual, assets:

    a.   Inventory (appraisal) system.
    b.   Group and composite systems.
    c.   Retirement and replacement systems.

The above listed depreciation methods are separately discussed in this section. For illustration, assume a machine with the following factors was acquired on January 1, 1991 for use in operation:

Cost (**C**)	$100,000
Estimated salvage value (**S**)	$10,000
Estimated useful life (**L**)	4 years

Service hours (**H**):

1991	2,000 machine hours
1992	3,000 machine hours
1993	4,000 machine hours
1994	1,000 machine hours
Total	10,000 machine hours

Units of output (**U**):

1991	15,000 units
1992	25,000 units
1993	20,000 units
1994	40,000 units
Total	100,000 units

1. **Straight-line method.** The depreciable cost is divided by the service life expressed in **years** to produce equal annual depreciation charges:

Annual depreciation rate ($) = (C - S) / L

Depreciation expense = ($100,000 - $10,000) / 4 years
= $22,500 per year.

The SL method is the most popular method in use. It is straight forward, rational and systematic. It is particularly appropriate when the use, and the decline in service potential of the asset are approximately the same each period, and repair and maintenance expenditures are stable.

2. **Service Hours Method.** This method assumes that the decrease in useful life of an asset is directly related to the amount of time the asset is used:

Hourly depreciation rate ($) = (C - S) / H
= ($100,000 - $10,000) / 10,000 hours
= $9 per hour

Depreciation expense = Depreciation rate x Actual hours used

1991	= $9 x 2,000 hours = $18,000
1992	= $9 x 3,000 hours = $27,000
1993	= $9 x 4,000 hours = $36,000
1994	= $9 x 1,000 hours = $ 9,000

This method usually produces a logical matching of expense and revenue if the asset's service potential can be reliably measured in terms of service time. For assets such as buildings and furniture, however, it is impossible to apply.

3. **Productive Output Method.** The service life is expressed in terms of expected productive capacity. A depreciation rate per unit is calculated as the depreciable cost divided by expected capacity:

Unit depreciation rate ($) = (C - S) / U
= ($100,000 - $10,000) / 100,000 units
= $0.90 per unit

Depreciation expense = Depreciation rate x Actual units produced

1991	= $0.90 x 15,000 units = $13,500
1992	= $0.90 x 25,000 units = $22,500
1993	= $0.90 x 20,000 units = $18,000
1994	= $0.90 x 40,000 units = $36,000

This method is particularly appealing when actual output can be measured reliably and the useful life in units of output can be reasonably estimated. It is obviously not applicable to firms that do not produce goods.

4. **Sum-of-the-Years'-Digits Method.**   A decreasing fraction each year is multiplied by the depreciable cost. The denominator of the fraction each year is the sum of the digits of the years involved. A useful formula for calculating the denominator of the fraction is **n(n + 1) / 2**, where n is the estimated service life of the asset in years. The numerator is **n** for the first year and declines by one each year thereafter.

Sum of the years' digits	$= 4 + 3 + 2 + 1 = 10$
	or
	$= n(n + 1) / 2$
	$= 4(4 + 1) / 2 = 10$
Depreciation rate ($ per digit)	$= (C - S) / SYD$
	$= (\$100,000 - \$10,000) / 10$
	$= \$9,000$ per digit
Depreciation expense	$=$ Depreciation rate x digits for the year
1991	$= \$9,000 \times 4 = \$36,000$
1992	$= \$9,000 \times 3 = \$27,000$
1993	$= \$9,000 \times 2 = \$18,000$
1994	$= \$9,000 \times 1 = \$\ 9,000$

The Sum-of-the-Years'-Digits method is appropriate for assets, such as computers and other high-technology equipment, supplying proportionately greater benefits early in their useful life, and then gradually or suddenly become obsolete as technology changes. The same argument is applicable to declining balance and other accelerated depreciation methods.

5. **Declining-Balance Methods:**   A fixed depreciation rate is calculated by dividing a certain percentage (e.g., 120%, 150% or 200%) by the useful life of the asset. This rate is then multiplied by the beginning book (or carrying) value of the asset to derive the depreciation charge for the year. As the book value declines over time, the annual depreciation charge decreases year after year. The accumulated depreciation, however, must not exceed the depreciable cost of the asset. The most used percentage is 200%, referred to as the **Double-Declining-Balance Method (DDB)**, as illustrated below:

Depreciation rate (**R**)	$= 200\% / L$
	$= 200\% / 4$
	$= 50\%$

Depreciation expense	= R x Beginning book value	
	= R x (Cost - Beginning accumulated depreciation)	
1991	= 50% x ($100,000 - 0)	= $50,000
1992	= 50% x ($100,000 - $50,000)	= $25,000
1993	= 50% x ($100,000 - $75,000)	= $12,500
1994	= ($100,000 - $87,500) - $10,000	= $ 2,500*

* Just like any other depreciation method, the book value of the asset should never be less than the estimated salvage value. Therefore, depreciation expense for 1994 is the difference between the beginning book value and the estimated salvage value.

C. 1. **Depreciation and income taxes.**   Businesses report depreciation not only for financial accounting, but also for tax purposes. For tax purposes, a firm is allowed to take tax advantage by deducting greater amounts of depreciation in early years. Before the Income Tax Act, companies usually adopted certain accelerated depreciation methods such as those discussed in this chapter. Under this system: (a) **residual value** is disregarded, and (b) assets are assigned to a class with a **specified life** (e.g., 3-year, 5-year, or 10-year assets). In addition, the annual CCA deduction is determined by multiplying the undepreciated capital cost of the asset by a **maximum statutory percentage** pertinent to the asset's class.

2. **Depreciation and cash flow.**   Depreciation for financial accounting purposes is a noncash expense. It does not guarantee that sufficient cash will be available for asset replacement. However, since it affects both tax liabilities and retained earnings, it does save current tax payment, and, in certain cases, may reduce dividends otherwise paid.

D. **Fractional Year Depreciation**

Most capital assets are not placed in service at the beginning of an accounting period, nor is a disposal typically made at the period end. Therefore, under time-based depreciation methods, some adjustment is often needed to account for the depreciation of the fractional year of service:

1. **Straight-line method.**   When **SL** method is used, monthly depreciation is calculated simply as the annual amount divided by 12. This monthly rate is then multiplied by the number of months the asset is in use during the reporting period (usually to the nearest month).

2. **Accelerated methods.**   Accelerated methods calculate a depreciation charge for each **12-month** service period. If the calculated 12-month charge falls into two reporting periods, the charge is usually allocated to these two reporting periods on the straight-line basis. For example, if the machine in the previous illustration is acquired on April 1, 1991:

a. Sum-of-the-years'-digits method.

The following yearly service charges are obtained from the above example under the **SYD** method:

Depreciation expense for the first 12-month period	= $36,000
Depreciation expense for the second 12-month period	= $27,000
Depreciation expense for the third 12-month period	= $18,000
Depreciation expense for the fourth 12-month period	= $ 9,000

Then the cost is allocated to the **five** reporting periods as follows:

1991	= $36,000 x 9/12	= $27,000
1992	= $36,000 x 3/12 + $27,000 x 9/12	= $29,250
1993	= $27,000 x 3/12 + $18,000 x 9/12	= $20,250
1994	= $18,000 x 3/12 + $ 9,000 x 9/12	= $11,250
1995	= $ 9,000 x 3/12	= $ 2,250

b. Double-declining-balance method.

Under this method, adjustment for fractional year depreciation is explicitly made for the year of acquisition, i.e., 1991. After that year, depreciation expense is calculated by multiplying depreciation rate by the beginning book value of the asset except for the last year, in which depreciation expense is the difference between the beginning book value and the estimated salvage value of the asset:

Depreciation expense:

1991	= 50% x ($100,000 - 0) x 9/12	= $37,500
1992	= 50% x ($100,000 - $37,500)	= $31,250
1993	= 50% x ($100,000 - $68,750)	= $15,625
1994	= ($100,000 - $84,375) - $10,000	= $ 5,625*

Note that depreciation expense for 1994, $5,625, is less than 50% of the beginning book value ($15,625 x 50% = $7,812.50). It is because the book value of the asset should never be reduced below its salvage value. That is, the total depreciation expense should not exceed the asset's depreciable cost.

3. **Depreciation of post-acquisition costs.** Capitalized post-acquisition cost of plant assets also must be depreciated as follows:

a. If the new item is an integral part of the original asset, and is expected to be retired with, or extend the life of the original asset, depreciation on the original asset is recognized through the date of the post-acquisition expenditure. The resulting carrying value of the asset is then combined with the post-acquisition expenditure to be depreciated over the remaining life of the asset.

b. If the post-acquisition costs are not combined with the original asset, the costs should be depreciated separately.

E.   Depreciation and Accounting Changes

1.   **Changes in estimate.**   Revisions of estimates used in calculating depreciation (service life or residual value) require depreciation to be recalculated for the **remaining service life** of the asset. The carrying value of the asset, less newly estimated salvage value, is depreciated over the remaining life based on the new estimate. (CICA Handbook, sec. 1506)

To illustrate, assume a machine with an acquisition cost of $100,000, an estimated salvage value of zero and useful life of 4 years had been depreciated for two years by the straight-line method when the firm changed the estimated total useful life to 6 years and salvage value to $10,000. The annual depreciation for the remaining 4 years is recalculated as follows:

```
Cost                                         $100,000
Less: Accumulated depreciation                (50,000)
                                             _____

Carrying value                               $ 50,000
Less: Newly estimated residual value          (10,000)
                                             _____

Remaining depreciable cost                   $ 40,000
Divided by: Remaining useful life                   4   years
                                             _____

Recalculated annual depreciable expense       $10,000
```

2.   **Changes in principle.**   A change from a generally accepted depreciation method to another generally accepted depreciation method (e.g., SYD to SL) is a change in accounting principle. Most accounting changes, including changes in depreciation method, are treated on a current and prospective basis. According to sections 1506 and 3060 of the **CICA Handbook**, the new method is used in the period of change and in subsequent periods; no retroactive changes are made.

To illustrate, assume a machine with a cost of $200,000, residual value of $35,000 and useful life of 10 years had been depreciated for 2 years by the SYD method before the firm decided to change to the straight line method. The cumulative effective of this change would be (ignore taxes):

USE PROSPECTIVE METHOD

Accumulated depreciation under SYD:
= ($200,000 - $35,000) x {(10 + 9) / [10 x (10 + 1) / 2]}
= $165,000 x 19 / 55
= $57,000.

Cost	$200,000
- Accumulated Depreciation	- 57,000
= Book Value	$143,000

Book Value	$143,000
- Salvage	- 35,000
= Amount to be depreciated	108,000

Remaining Life   10 - 2 = 8 years

Annual Depreciation
 Straight line method - Years 3 to 10

$$\frac{\$108,000}{8} = \$13,500 \text{ per year}$$

3. **Correction of depreciation errors.** Depreciation errors are GENERALLY caused by arithmetic mistakes or omission of assets from depreciation calculations. Corrections of depreciation errors affecting prior period(s) involve prior year adjustments, i. e., adjustments made to retained earnings for the effect of the errors on the net income of prior years affected.

For example, the machine as described in part 1 was mistakenly expensed when acquired in 1991. The error was discovered in 1992. The following correcting entry would be recorded in 1992, assuming 40% tax rate and SL depreciation:

Machine	100,000	
Accumulated depreciation		25,000
Deferred income tax		30,000
Prior period adjustment		45,000

Note that prior period adjustment net of tax is determined as follows:

Acquisition cost of machine expensed	$100,000
Depreciation expense for 1991 not provided (SL)	25,000
Understated income before tax	$ 75,000
Less: Tax effect (40%)	30,000
Adjustment to retained earnings	$ 45,000

F. Special Depreciation Systems

1. **Retirement and replacement systems**: These systems are used primarily by railroads and utilities for similar items with small individual values such as poles, tracks, etc. The **retirement method** is similar to the **FIFO** concept of inventory costing. The earliest acquisition cost is the first to be charged to depreciation expense. The **replacement system**, in contrast, is based on the **LIFO** assumption that the most recent acquisition cost is the first to be expensed. Under either system, (1) depreciation expense is provided whenever there is physical retirement of the asset items, (2) the salvage value of the retired items is credited to depreciation expense, and (3) accumulated depreciation account is not used.

To illustrate, assume the following:

	Units acquired	Unit cost	Units retired	Residual value
1991	20,000	$10	–	–
1992	2,000	$15	2,500	$2,000
1993	1,000	$20	500	$ 600

Journal entries to record the acquisition and disposal of the assets, and depreciation expenses under these two systems are presented respectively below:

	Retirement System (FIFO)		Replacement System (LIFO)	

1991

Assets	200,000		200,000	
Cash		200,000		200,000

1992

Assets	30,000		30,000	
Cash		30,000		30,000
Depreciation exp.	25,000*		35,000**	
Assets		25,000		35,000
Cash	2,000		2,000	
Depreciation exp.		2,000		2,000

1993

Assets	20,000		20,000	
Cash		20,000		20,000
Depreciation exp.	5,000***		10,000****	
Assets		5,000		10,000
Cash	600		600	
Depreciation exp.		600		600

```
   *   2,500 units x $10 = $25,000.
  **   2,000 units x $15 + 500 x $10 = $35,000.
 ***   500 units $10 = $5,000.
****   500 units x $20 = $10,000.
```

2. **Composite and group systems:** The **composite system** is to deals with a group of **dissimilar assets** (e.g., an entire operating assembly consisting of different types of equipment). These assets are combined in a single control account, and only one accumulated depreciation account is maintained for the entire group. The procedure pertinent to this system include:

(a) Compute annual depreciation expense for each asset in the group using the straight-line method.

(b)   Establish a composite depreciation rate by dividing the total depreciation expense of the group as computed above by their total cost.

(c)   Determine current depreciation expense by multiplying the established composite rate to the balance in the asset control account.
In the subsequent years, the original rate may still be maintained and applied to new balances of the asset account if the change in the account is insignificant. Otherwise a new composite rate may be needed.

(d)   The retirement of any asset in the group is recorded by debiting cash, if any, crediting asset at its cost. Their difference is entered to the accumulated depreciation account.

On the other hand, the **group system** is applicable to a group of **similar assets** (e.g., small trucks), that are recorded in the same account and treated as a single asset. A group rate is determined using the average life of the assets in the group. The retirement of any item in the group is treated the same way as under the composite system. Any addition to the group would require the recalculation of the group depreciation rate.

3.   **Inventory (appraisal) system**:   This system is used in instances of numerous, inexpensive asset items such as hand tools and utensils. These items are treated much like a supplies inventory. That is, depreciation expense each period is the recorded balance of the items on hand at the beginning of the period, plus current acquisition cost, and less cash received on disposal and the appraised replacement cost of items on hand at the end of the period. The calculated depreciation expense is usually credited directly to the asset account.

Strictly speaking, this system is a process of asset valuation, rather than cost allocation. Since it is not systematic and objective, it is generally considered as unacceptable.

G.   **Impairment of value** -- plant assets.   Plant asset impairments are caused by casualty, obsolescence, negligence, or mismanagement. A permanent impairment in the value of a plant asset leads to a write-down of the asset to market value, by a debit to a nonrecurrent loss, and a credit to the accumulated depreciation account. It is argued that the recognition of an impairment loss is a departure from the historical cost principle, and that arbitrary write-downs of plant assets erode confidence in financial statements. Furthermore, recognizing loss when an asset decreases in value but not a gain when an asset increase in value results in inconsistencies in practice. (CICA, Sec. 3060)

H.   **Depreciation and Income Taxes**

1.   Depreciation under GAAP rules and depreciation under the Income Tax Act are different matters. Under both authorities, depreciation acts to reduce income before tax, and total depreciation over the life of an asset is limited to original cost. But there the similarity ends. Under GAAP, depreciation guidelines are intended to allocate an asset's historical cost to the accounting periods in which the asset is used, in accordance with the matching principle.

In contrast, tax depreciation is geared to the revenue needs of the federal government, which change in response to economic conditions and the fiscal policies of Parliament. For example, tax depreciation currently provides an incentive for replacement, modernization, and expansion of industrial facilities through accelerated depreciation schedules.

2. The Income Tax Act does not allow the deduction of depreciation expense in the determination of taxable income. Instead it provides that a taxpayer may deduct a **capital cost allowance** as specified by the Act. Therefore, depreciation expense is added to, and capital cost allowance is deducted from income before income taxes to determine taxable income.

The capital cost allowance system (CCA) relies on the grouping of assets into various classes established by the Act. Most classes provide a rate to use in calculating the equivalent of declining balance depreciation, although some classes use the equivalent of straight-line depreciation.

3. The basic rules for the capital cost allowance system can be explained for most classes as follows:

   1. When assets are purchased, their purchase price (**capital cost**) is added to the balance (**undepreciated capital cost**) of the appropriate asset class.

   2. When assets are sold, the lesser of the proceeds or the capital cost is deducted from the balance in that asset's class.

   3. Assets are considered to be purchased in the middle of the taxation year (half-year rule).

   4. The maximum capital cost allowance deductible for a particular class is the balance of undepreciated capital cost, after adjusting for the half-year rule, multiplied by the CCA rate for that class.

I. Annuity and Sinking Fund Methods of Depreciation

The annuity and sinking fund methods of depreciation are based on the same concepts that underlie an annuity investment. Investment is made and returns are received. Each periodic return includes two separate elements: (a) a return of principal and (b) investment revenue. For each period, the return of principal becomes larger (this represents depreciation) and the periodic interest element becomes smaller as the asset diminishes in value with use. The annuity and sinking fund methods yield the same overall effect on the income statement and balance sheet; their differences relate to the reporting of depreciation expense and imputed interest revenue on the income statement. Either method is acceptable under current GAAP, according to paragraph 3060.35 of the *CICA Handbook*.

J. **Insured casualty loss.** Losses from disasters such as fires and storms may be covered by a casualty insurance policy. In case of loss, the amount recoverable from the insurance company is recorded by debiting a receivable account and crediting a loss account. If the recoverable amount exceeds the book value of the asset destroyed or damaged, the difference is recognized as a gain.

Many casualty insurance policies carry a **coinsurance clause** requiring that the owner be a coinsurer of the property. In this case, the amount recoverable from the insurance company is the **lowest** of the following:

a. the **F**ace **V**alue of the insurance policy (**FV**).
b. the amount of the **L**oss (**L**).
c. the **I**ndemnity **F**ormula **V**alue (**IFV**) as determined below:

IFV $= (FV / CR) \times L$

where:

CR = **C**oinsurance **R**equirement
= Replacement cost of the property x Coinsurance rate (e.g., 80%)

KEY CONCEPTS

Changes in depreciation estimate   Revision of estimates used in calculating depreciation requires current and future depreciation to be recalculated using the carrying value of the asset, and its newly estimated remaining life and salvage value.

Changes in depreciation method   A change from a generally accepted depreciation method to another generally accepted depreciation method (e.g., SYD to SL) is a change in accounting principle. Most accounting changes, including changes in depreciation method, are treated on a current basis. According to sections 1506 and 3060 of the *CICA Handbook*, the new method is used in the period of change and in subsequent periods; no retroactive changes are made.

Depreciation   An accounting process of allocating the cost of a certain tangible capital asset over its expected service life in a rational and systematic manner. It is a process of cost allocation, not of valuation.

Depreciation methods   A pattern of allocating the depreciable cost of **an individual asset** over its expected service life. The straight-line, activity, and accelerated methods are common in practice.

Depreciation systems   A pattern of allocating the depreciable cost of **a class of** depreciable assets. Several depreciation systems are available, namely, the inventory appraisal, group, composite, replacement and retirement systems.

Impairment of property value   Capital asset impairment in value, if permanent, leads to an recognition of a nonrecurrent loss, and a credit is usually made to accumulated depreciation. No specific accounting principle governing their timing, recognition or measurement is currently available.

REVIEW QUESTIONS AND EXERCISES

TRUE-FALSE

Indicate whether each of the following statements is true or false by circling the correct response.

T F 1. Depreciation is a systematic and rational method of measuring an asset's decline in value over its service life.

T F 2. Residual value is the estimated recoverable amount of an asset at the end of its estimated service life.

T F 3. The SYD method will create a higher depreciation charge in the first year of an asset's life than will the straight-line method.

T F 4. The activity methods are preferred when depreciation is caused primarily by the passage of time.

T F 5. The SYD method differs from other methods in part due to the use of acquisition cost as the depreciation base.

T F 6. The retirement method expenses the cost of assets purchased to replace existing assets in the year the replacement occurs.

T F 7. The capital cost allowance (i.e., depreciation) deduction under Revenue Canada is determined by applying a statutory percentage to cost less residual value.

T F 8. Composite depreciation combines dissimilar assets, and group depreciation combines similar assets together for depreciation purpose.

T F 9. Under a casualty insurance policy with a coinsurance clause, the amount recoverable from the insurance company is equal to the amount of loss.

T F 10. A change in depreciation estimate is an example of a change in accounting principle.

T F 11. No correcting entry is made for a change in the estimated service life of a depreciable asset.

T F 12. The **book value** of a plant asset should always be the same as the market value of the asset.

T F 13. Since the composite system combines dissimilar assets in a single account for depreciation purpose, it is not generally acceptable.

T F 14. If a machine is purchased in connection with a copper mine and cannot be moved to another site, it should be depreciated over the estimated life of the copper mine if the expected useful life of the machine is longer.

EXERCISE 1

Different Company acquired a machine on April 1, 1991 at a total cost of $16,000 with an estimated salvage value of $4,000 after a service life of 4 years.

Required: Determine the appropriate depreciation expense for 1991 and 1992 under each of the following methods:

		1991		**1992**
Straight-line method	(a)	—————	(b)	—————
SYD method	(c)	—————	(d)	—————
DDB method	(e)	—————	(f)	—————

EXERCISE 2

Given the following data:

	Units acquired	Unit cost	Units retired	Residual value
1991	10,000	$20	–	–
1992	5,000	$15	600	$800

Required: Complete the following journal entries to record the acquisition, disposal and depreciation expense provision of the assets under the retirement and the replacement systems:

	Retirement System (FIFO)	Replacement System (LIFO)
	-------------------	-------------------

1991

Assets
    Cash

1992

Assets
    Cash

Depreciation exp.
    Assets

Cash
    Depreciation exp.

SHORT EXERCISE 3

At the beginning of 1991, Altona Company adopted the composite method of depreciating the assets listed below:

Asset	Cost	Service Life	Residual Value
A	$100,000	10 years	$20,000
B	70,000	6	10,000
C	50,000	4	2,000

Required:

(1) Compute the depreciation expense for individual assets in the group under the SL method.

(2) Establish composite depreciation rate:

(3) Determine and record depreciation expense for 1991 under the composite system:

(4) Assume Asset C is disposed at the end of 1991 for $45,000, record the disposition:

MULTIPLE CHOICE

Enter the letter corresponding to the response which **best** completes each of the following statements or questions.

____ 1. Depreciation:

    a. is a process of asset valuation.
    b. affects only the income statement.
    c. allocates an asset's cost to periods benefited, in a rational and systematic manner.
    d. is a cash expense.

____ 2. Which of the following is not used for the calculation of depreciation expense?

    a. normal maintenance expense of the asset.
    b. residual value of the asset.
    c. useful life of the asset.
    d. acquisition cost of the asset.

____ 3. When the productive output method of depreciation is used:

    a. Depreciation expense will vary directly with sales.
    b. Depreciation expense will vary directly with output.
    c. Depreciation rate per unit will vary directly with sales.
    d. Depreciation rate per unit will vary directly with output.

____ 4. The depreciation method which will produce the **least** depreciation expense in the **second** year for an asset with 10-year useful life is:

    a. straight-line.
    b. SYD.
    c. DDB.
    d. Capital Cost Allowance.

____ 5. Which of the following methods does not give rise to the problem of fractional year depreciation?

    a. straight-line.
    b. SYD.
    c. DDB.
    d. productive output.

_____ 6. Which of the following is not a time based depreciation method?

    a. straight-line.
    b. SYD.
    c. DDB.
    d. productive output.

_____ 7. The depreciation system frequently used for numerous low unit cost assets is the:

    a. inventory appraisal system.
    b. group depreciation system.
    c. composite depreciation system.
    d. capital cost allowance system.

_____ 8. A change in depreciation method requires:

    a. the cumulative effect of the change be presented as an extraordinary item.
    b. the new method be used to recalculate depreciation expenses for all prior years.
    c. the cumulative effect of the change be ignored.
    d. the cumulative effect of the change be recorded as a prior year adjustment.

_____ 9. A machine that was acquired on January 1, 1991 for $35,000 has been depreciated on a straight-line method assuming a service life of 5 years and a residual value of $5,000. At the beginning of 1994, it was decided that the remaining service life would be 3 years, and the residual value should remain unchanged. The depreciation expense for 1994 should be:

    a. $6,000
    b. $3,000
    c. $4,000
    d. $5,000

_____10. In the previous question, assume the asset has been depreciated under the SYD method, the depreciation expense for the fourth year should be:

    a. $6,000
    b. $3,000
    c. $4,000
    d. $5,000

_____11. In question 9, assume the asset was originally depreciated using the straight-line method, and during 1994 (in addition to changing the service life), the firm changed from the SL to the SYD method, depreciation expense for 1994 should be:

    a. $6,000
    b. $4,000
    c. $5,000
    d. $3,000

____12. In the previous question, the cumulative effect of the change in depreciation method (from SL to SYD) should be (ignore tax):

a. $5,000
b. $4,000
c. $3,000
d. $0

____13. A machine with an estimated service life of 5 years and an estimated residual value of $2,500 was acquired on January 1, 1991 for $25,000. The depreciation expense for 1992 under the DDB method would be:

a. $9,000
b. $6,000
c. $7,000
d. $8,000

____14. In the previous question, assume the machine was disposed for $4,000 on January 1, 1994. The loss to be recognized from the disposal should be (ignore tax):

a. $3,000
b. $1,400
c. $1,600
d. $1,200

SOLUTIONS TO REVIEW QUESTIONS AND EXERCISES

TRUE-FALSE

1.	F	5.	F	9.	F	13.	F
2.	T	6.	F	10.	F	14.	T
3.	T	7.	F	11.	T		
4.	F	8.	T	12.	F		

EXERCISE 1

	1991		**1992**	
Straight-line method	$2,250		$3,000	
	(a) _____		(b) _____	
SYD method	$3,600		$3,900	
	(c) _____		(d) _____	
DDB method	$6,000		$5,000	
	(e) _____		(f) _____	

Computations:

Straight-line method:

Depreciation rate per year = ($16,000 - $4,000) / 4
= $3,000

Depreciation expense for 1991 = $3,000 x 9/12
= $2,250

Depreciation expense for 1992 = $3,000

SYD method:

Depreciation rate per digit = ($16,000 - $4,000) / (4+3+2+1)
= $12,000 / 10
= $1,200

Depreciation expense for 1991 = $1,200 x 4 x 9/12
= $3,600

Depreciation expense for 1992 = $1,200 x 4 x 3/12 +
$1,200 x 3 x 9/12
= $1,200 + $2,700
= $3,900

DDB method:

Depreciation expense for 1991   = $16,000 x 2/4 x 9/12
   = $6,000

Depreciation expense for 1992   = ($16,000 - $6,000) x 2/4
   = $5,000

EXERCISE 2

	Retirement System (FIFO)		Replacement System (LIFO)	
1991				
Assets	200,000		200,000	
Cash		200,000		200,000
1992				
Assets	75,000		75,000	
Cash		75,000		75,000
Depreciation exp.	12,000		9,000	
Assets		12,000		9,000
Cash	800		800	
Depreciation exp.		800		800

EXERCISE 3

(1)   Compute depreciation expenses for individual assets under the SL method:

Asset	Original cost	Salvage value	Service life	Annual SL depreciation
A	$100,000	$20,000	10 years	$ 8,000
B	70,000	10,000	6	10,000
C	50,000	2,000	4	12,000
Total	$220,000			$30,000

(2)   Establish composite depreciate rate:

Composite rate
= Total annual straight-line depreciation / Total cost of asset group
= $30,000 / $220,000
= 13.63%

(3)   Determine and record depreciation expense for 1991:

Depreciation expense
= Total cost x composite depreciation rate
= $220,000 x 13.63%
= $30,000

Journal entry:

Depreciation expense	30,000	
Accumulated depreciation		30,000

(4)   Record the disposal of asset C:

Cash	45,000	
Accumulated depreciation	5,000	
Assets		50,000

MULTIPLE CHOICE:

1.	c	5.	d	9.	c	13.	b
2.	a	6.	d	10.	b	14.	b
3.	b	7.	a	11.	a		
4.	a	8.	c	12.	d		

Computations and explanations:

9.   (c)   Depreciation expense for 1994 based on the new estimate is computed by dividing the beginning carrying value of the asset less residual value, which is still $5,000, by the remaining service life as shown below:

Depreciable value = Cost - Residual value
= $35,000 - $5,000
= $30,000.

Depreciation expense for 1994 (SL)
= ($30,000 x 2/5) / 3
= $4,000

10.   (b)   Same as question 9 except that the SYD method is being used:

Depreciation expense for 1994 (SYD)
= ($30,000 x 3/15) x 3/6
= $3,000

Note that the sum of the years' digits of the originally estimated service life is 15 [i.e., 5 x (5 + 1) / 2], and that of the remaining life based the new estimated is 6 (i.e., 3 + 2 + 1).

11.   (a)   Depreciation expense for 1994 under the SYD method
35,000 - 18,000 = 17,000
17,000 - 5,000 = 12,000   12,000 x $\frac{3}{6}$ = $6,000
  1 + 2 + 3 = 6

Note that a change to the SYD method requires the new method be used to recalculate depreciation for all the prior years.

12.   (d)   Accumulated depreciation at the end of 1993 under SL
= $30,000 x 3/5 = $18,000.

Recalculated depreciation up to the end of 1993 using SYD
= $30,000 x 12/15 = $24,000.

The cumulative effect of the change from SL to SYD
= $18,000 - $24,000 = $(6,000), Debit.

13.   (b)   Depreciation expense for 1992 (under DDB)
= [$25,000 - ($25,000 x 2/5)] x 2/5 = $6,000.

14.   (b)   Gain or loss on disposal is the difference between the carrying value of the asset and cash proceeds as shown below:

Depreciation expenses under DDB:

```
1991: $25,000 x 2/5                      $10,000
1992: ($25,000 - $10,000) x 2/5            6,000
1993: ($25,000 - $16,000) x 2/5            3,600

Total                                    $19,600

Carrying (book) value
= $25,000 - $19,600
= $5,400

Loss on disposal
= $5,400 - $4,000
= $1,400.
```

CHAPTER 13

Intangible Assets and Natural Resources

CHAPTER OBJECTIVES

This chapter is designed to enable students to:

A.   Explain the concepts and characteristics of intangible assets.

B.   Describe the general accounting treatment for intangible assets.

C.   Account for intangible assets including deferred charges, leaseholds, and licensing agreements.

D.   Explain how goodwill arises; measure, record, and amortize goodwill.

E.   Explain the accounting treatment for research and development costs.

F.   Explain the accounting treatment for computer software costs.

G.   Explain the accounting issues and reporting requirements for natural resources.

H.   Explain the accounting issues and requirements for oil and gas exploration costs. (Refers to the chapter appendix.)

CHAPTER OVERVIEW

A.   The Nature of Intangible Assets

For accounting purposes, **intangible assets** are defined in the same terms as other capital assets. That is, they are held for the use of the entity, have been acquired with the intention of being used on a continuing basis, and are not intended for sale in the ordinary course of business. Section 3060 *(CICA Handbook)* defines intangible properties as

> "capital assets that lack physical substance. Examples of intangible properties include brand names, copyrights, franchises, licences, patents, software, subscription lists and trademarks."

There is considerable similarity in the problems of accounting for tangible and intangible assets. However, it is more difficult to identify, measure, and estimate the periods of benefit for intangible assets. In particular, the intangible asset's lack of physical substance makes its value difficult to estimate and may make its useful life indeterminable.

B. Accounting for Intangible Assets – General Rules

1. **Acquisition of intangible assets.** Intangible assets can be generated internally in the ordinary course of operations. They can also be acquired externally by purchase from another entity. As a general rule, the expenditures related to **internally generated** intangible assets are expensed as incurred, whereas the acquisition cost of **an externally purchased** intangible asset is capitalized. Just as the acquisition of tangible operational assets, the cost to be capitalized includes cash paid plus the current market value of any noncash consideration given on the date of acquisition, or the fair value of the intangible asset received if it is more clearly determinable. The following entry is pertinent to the acquisition of intangible assets:

Intangible assets	xxxx	
Cash		xxxx

2. **Amortization of intangible assets.** The costs of intangible assets must be allocated to expense in a rational and systematic manner over a period of time. This allocation process is referred to as **amortization.** Straight-line amortization generally should be applied unless a company demonstrates that another acceptable method is more appropriate. Because of their very nature, intangible assets seldom have a residual value. The journal entry to record the amortization is as follows:

Amortization expense	xxxx	
Intangible assets		xxxx

    The amortization period of an intangible asset is the asset's expected economic life, which may be limited by legal, contractual or other provisions, or by economic factors such as obsolescence or competition. As required in the CICA, Sec. 3060, in no instance should the amortization period of any intangible asset exceed 40 years.

    A revision of the estimate of the useful life of an intangible asset is accounted for as a change in accounting estimate. The unamortized balance is amortized over the remainder of the revised estimated life.

3. **Impairment of the value of intangible assets.** An impairment of the value of an intangible asset occurs when its use value (economic utility) falls below its book value. In such cases, the balance should be written down and a loss recognized as indicated in the following entry:

Loss on reducing intangible assets to market	xxxx	
Intangible assets		xxxx

4.   **Disposal of Intangible assets.**   The disposal of an intangible asset (by sale, exchange, or otherwise) is recorded in the same manner as the disposal of a tangible asset. That is, the asset account is removed from the books and a gain or loss on disposal is recorded. The following entry is to record a sale of an intangible asset at a loss:

Cash	xxxx	
Loss on disposal of intangible assets	xxxx	
Intangible assets		xxxx

5.   **Summary of Accounting Treatments for Various Intangible Assets.**

<u>How Obtained</u>

Type	Purchased	Internally Generated
Identifiable intangible asset	1. Capitalize 2. Amortize over the legal life or the estimated useful life, whichever is shorter, with a maximum of 40 years.	1. Expense or capitalize depending on the specific intangible. 2. If capitalized, amortize as for purchased intangibles.
Unidentifiable intangible asset	1. Capitalize. 2. Amortize over the legal life or the estimated useful life, whichever is shorter, with a maximum of 40 years.	1. Expense as incurred. 2. There is no option to capitalize.

C.   Identifiable Intangible Assets -- Legal (or Contractual) Rights

Many intangible assets such as those which follows are exclusive legal or contractual rights which can be separately identified apart from the firm and are separately exchangeable:

1.   **Patents.**   A patent represents an exclusive **legal right** to a product or process for a period of 17 years. The cost of purchasing or successful legal defenses of a patent should be capitalized. Costs of an internally developed patent other than legal fees, registration fees, and other expenditures incidental to the registration must be expensed as incurred. The capitalized costs should be amortized over the legal life or the useful life of the patent, whichever is shorter.

2.   **Copyrights.**   A copyright gives the authors of literary, musical, or other artistic works the exclusive **legal right** to print, reprint and copy the work, to sell or distribute copies, and to perform and record the work. These rights can be sold or contractually assigned to other persons. The capitalized cost of a copyright includes legal and other registration fees if the right is internally generated, or the acquisition price and any related expenditure if the right is purchased. The legal life of a copyright is the life of the author plus 50 years. However, the capitalized cost of a copyright should be amortized over its useful life, not to exceed 40 years.

3.   **Trademarks** or **tradenames.**   **A trademark or a tradename** (e.g., Pepsi) is a symbol, name or any other distinctive identity for a product. If registered, the original user has the **legal right** to use the trademark or the tradename exclusively for a legal life of 20 years. Once registered, the life can be renewed for an unlimited number of 20-year periods. Therefore, the maximum amortization period allowed is 40 years. The costs of a purchased trademark or tradename that should be capitalized include cash equivalent amount paid for the purchase, and other expenditures directly related to the acquisition and protection of the right. For an internally developed trademark or tradename, the attorney's fees, registration fees, design costs, consulting fees and other related expenditures may all be capitalized. The capitalized costs should be amortized over the useful life of the asset or 40 years, whichever is shorter.

4.   **Franchises**.   A franchise is an agreement which grants the franchisee the exclusive right to sell a product or service (e.g., McDonalds) in a certain geographical area. Amounts **initially** paid to the franchisor (another business or a governmental unit) to acquire the franchise should be debited to an intangible asset account and amortized over its useful life, not to exceed 40 years. **Annual payments** for products, services, etc. made under a franchise agreement should be expensed as incurred.

5.   **Industrial Design Registrations**

     An **industrial design registration** is similar to a patent but applies to the shape, pattern, or ornamentation applied to an article of manufacture. A patent protects function while industrial design registration protects appearance. Once registered at the Canadian Industrial Design Office of Consumer and Corporate Affairs Canada, the design is protected for five years and may be renewed for an additional five years.

6.   **Organization cost.**   Expenditures incurred in connection with the formation of a business, including legal fees, accounting fees, incorporation fees, promotional expenditures and underwriting fees for handling of stock issues, are **organization costs** that are capitalized and amortized over a reasonable period of time, not to exceed 40 years. Often, the amortization period selected is five years -- the minimum required for tax purposes. Note that stock issuance costs may alternatively be treated as a reduction of the paid-in capital.

7.   **Leasehold prepayments and leasehold improvement.**   For an operating lease (i.e., a lease that does not, in form or in substance, transfer the ownership of the leased asset), the lessee may make rental payments in advance. Such an advance

payment should be amortized to the entire lease term. The cost of improving the leased asset (known as leasehold improvement) is usually reported as an intangible asset because, under operating lease, the asset does not belong to the lessee. Leasehold improvement should be capitalized and then amortized over the remaining term of the lease or the life of the improvement, whichever is **shorter**.

8.   **Deferred charges.**   A deferred charge is a long-term prepayment for a service that will contribute to the generation of future revenues. Deferred charges have no physical substance, and can rarely be sold to others. Many accountants prefer to classify deferred charges separately as **deferred charges**, rather than **intangible assets**. Examples are machinery rearrangement costs, long-term prepaid insurance and leaseholds (prepaid rent expenses). Deferred charges are generally amortized over their respective useful lives.

9.   **Development stage companies.**   Companies in the development stage usually incur significant startup costs before they have significant revenues. Companies in this stage present financial statements prepared on essentially the **same basis** as other businesses. Capitalization or deferral of costs is subject to the same assessment of recoverability that would be applicable in an established operating enterprise. In addition, (a) the statements must be identified as those of a company in the development stage, and (b) the balance sheet must report the **operating deficit accumulated** during the development stage in the stockholders' equity section.

10.   **Stock issuance costs.**   Expenditures associated with the issuance of capital stock are called *stock issuance costs*. Such costs include printing stock certificates and related items, professional fees, commissions paid for selling capital stock, and the costs of filing with securities commissions. Stock issuance costs, as opposed to organizational costs, are accounted for either as an offset to the issuance price of the capital stock to which they relate or they are treated as a deferred charge, which is amortized to expense in conformity with the matching principle (usually on a conservative basis).

D.   Unidentifiable Intangible Asset -- Goodwill

Goodwill represents the expected value of a firm's future "above normal" earning power. This expectation arises when there are favorable characteristics or factors relating to the firm or its operating environment that make it likely to produce higher than average earnings. It is the most common and important **unidentifiable** intangible asset. It is unidentifiable because it derives value from its association with other assets of a firm. It does not exist independent of the firm and cannot be sold separately.

Following the **CICA, Handbook, Sec. 1580,** goodwill is **recognized** only when it is purchased in connection with the acquisition of a company as a unit, generally referred to as a business combination. The purchase price, which is believed to be the only objective means of measuring the acquisition cost of a goodwill, reflects the results of the negotiations between the seller and the buyer, and may be greatly influenced by the negotiation skills of the parties at the bargaining table. In any event, both parties must estimate a value for the firm. One of the most appealing methods for such an estimation is the excess earnings approach.

Under the **excess earnings approach**, the expected average annual earnings are estimated on the basis of the company's past annual earnings and the anticipated future operation and market conditions. The present value of these expected future excessive earnings is the estimated goodwill. To apply this approach, it is often difficult to determine the discount rate (or normal rate of return), and the number of periods over which excess earnings should be discounted. An alternative is to multiply the expected average excessive earnings by a specified number of years. In this case, however, the selection of an appropriate **number** of years is always a controversial issue.

Under GAAP goodwill is **measured** by the excess of the purchase price of the acquired business as a unit over the fair value of its net assets (i.e., the sum of the fair values of individual assets less current values of existing liabilities). The excessive amount is recorded as goodwill and amortized over a period of no longer than 40 years. In case the acquisition cost is less than the fair value of net assets acquired, the difference (referred to as negative goodwill) should be **allocated** to noncurrent assets other than long-term investment in marketable securities proportional to their relative fair values until these values are all reduced to zero. Any remaining unallocated amount is recorded as **deferred credit** (i.e., the **recognized negative goodwill**). Just like the purchased goodwill, the recorded deferred credit should be amortized over the period estimated to be benefited, but no longer than 40 years.

ILLUSTRATION:

Assume that the Hotwax Corporation purchases both Ski Company and Hill Company on January 1, 1991. Based on the following data, determine the acquired goodwill or deferred credit under each of the cases:

	Ski Co. Fair value	Hill Co. Fair Value
Current assets	$10,000	$ 80,000
Marketable security investment	25,000	55,000
Land	50,000	75,000
Liabilities	(35,000)	(10,000)
Net assets	$50,000	$200,000
Purchase price	$70,000	$ 70,000

Solution:

1. Acquisition of Ski Company:

Purchase price	$70,000
Less: Fair value of net assets acquired	(50,000)
Goodwill acquired	**$20,000**

2. Acquisition of Hill Company:

Purchase price	$ 70,000
Less: Fair value of net assets acquired	(200,000)
Negative goodwill	$(130,000)
Less: Negative goodwill allocated to land	75,000
Deferred credit acquired	**$(55,000)**

E.   Research and development costs.   The CICA Handbook, Section 3450 definitions are:

Research is planned investigation undertaken with the hope of gaining new scientific or technical knowledge and understanding. Such investigation may or may not be directed toward a specific practical aim or application.

Development is the translation of research findings or other knowledge into a plan or design for new or substantially improved materials, devices, products, processes, systems, or services prior to the commencement of commercial productions or use. Development includes the conceptual formulation, design, and testing of product alternatives; construction of prototypes; and operation of pilot plants. It does not include routine or periodic alterations to existing products, production lines, manufacturing processes, and other ongoing operations. It may also include market research or market testing activities.

The main provisions of *CICA Handbook* section 3450 are:

1. Research costs should be charged as an expense of the period in which they are incurred.

2. Development costs should be charged as an expense of the period in which they are incurred.

3. Development costs should be deferred to future periods if all of the following criteria are satisfied:

a. The product or process is clearly defined and the costs attributable thereto can be identified.
b. The technical feasibility of the product or process has been established.
c. The management of the enterprise has indicated its intention to produce and market, or use, the product or process.
d. The future market for the product or process is clearly defined or, if it is to be used internally rather than sold, its usefulness to the enterprise has been established.
e. Adequate resources exist, or are expected to be available, to complete the project.

4. Financial statements must disclose the amounts or research and development costs charged to expense for the period, the amount of deferred development costs charged to expense for the period, development costs deferred during the period and the unamortized deferred development costs.

5.   The section does not apply to specialized activities such as work done for others, enterprises in the development stage and those unique to enterprises in the extractive industries.

F.   **Computer software.**   Developers of computer software (e.g., Lotus, Wordperfect) incur significant costs in connection with both (a) the development and (b) the production of their software. Costs incurred to establish the technological and economic feasibility of a software product are deemed research and development (R & D) and, accordingly, are expensed as incurred. Technological feasibility is established when all planning, designing, coding, and testing activities necessary to establish that the product can be produced to meet its design specifications are completed. Subsequently, costs of producing and duplicating product masters, preparing documentation, and packaging products are capitalized as inventory of computer software. The annual amortization of the capitalized software cost is the **greater** of the following:

   a.   The ratio of current period's gross revenues from the product to total current and anticipated gross revenues from the product over its remaining estimated economic life; or

   b.   The amount determined by the straight-line method of amortization over the remaining estimated economic life of the product.

G.   Natural resources are operational assets which are physically consumed in production. Examples are timberland, oil and gas, and various types of mineral deposits such as gold, silver, copper, and coal.

1.   **Cost Determination**

   The costs of natural resources include the following three categories:

   1.   **Acquisition costs.**   Costs incurred to purchase, lease or otherwise acquire the rights to property for purposes of exploring and producing a natural resource.

   2.   **Exploration costs.**   Costs incurred to identify areas that may warrant testing, or actually examining and testing specific areas for the presence of the natural resource, if the exploration effort results in the discovery of the natural resource in sufficient quantities to be economically extracted.

   3.   **Development costs.**   All costs incurred after discovery to build the producing system, including the costs of tunnels, shafts, wells and other drilling activities.

   In the exploration and development of natural resources, certain buildings and equipment may be acquired. The costs of these **physical** facilities are capitalized and reported as depreciable plant assets. Otherwise all the costs indicated above should be capitalized as natural resources. Note that to capitalize those exploration costs related to a successful discovery of natural resources is referred to as the **successful efforts approach.** In contrast, many accountants prefer the **full cost approach** and capitalize all the exploration costs, whether the related projects are successful or unsuccessful.

2. **Depletion**

   Depletion is the process of allocating the costs of natural resources. The calculation of depletion is similar to the productive output method of depreciation. A unit depletion rate is derived by dividing the cost of the natural resources, less residual value, by an estimate of the number of units (tons, barrels, cubic feet, etc.) to be produced. The depletion amount in a given year is calculated by multiplying the rate per unit by the number of units produced that year.

   The depletion amount is debited to an inventory account (coal inventory, oil inventory, etc.) with a corresponding credit to the natural resource account. As the inventory is sold, its cost (including depletion) is expensed as cost of goods sold.

3. **Liquidating dividend:**   Federal and provincial laws often permit cash dividends paid by certain natural resource companies in an amount equal to income plus the amount of depletion. This practice is common when the company has no plans to replace the natural resource in kind, and operations are to cease when the natural resource has been exhausted. The excessive dividend is a liquidating dividend, and should be recorded as a reduction in the owners' equity.

H. **Accounting Issues for Oil and Gas Exploration Costs**

Accounting for the extraction of natural resources in the oil and gas industry is a difficult area. The major issue focusses on the appropriate accounting measurement and treatment of exploration costs.

Oil and gas companies incur large costs in the process of exploring for oil and gas deposits. Individual firm exploration activities are the result of management's decision that there is a reasonable expectation the firm will earn an acceptable rate of return on its overall exploration program. There is risk, however, because at the time the exploration efforts are made, the firm does not know which exploration efforts will be successful and which will be unsuccessful. The situation faced by the company is similar to the issue faced by a firm electing to engage in R & D activities. For the same reasons, the accounting issues are similar to those in accounting for R & D costs.

There have been two quite different methods of accounting for exploration costs. The choice results in a different flow of costs through the financial statements. The most frequently used method results in the capitalization of only those exploration costs associated with successful exploration and the immediate expensing of all exploration costs associated with unsuccessful efforts. This approach is called the **successful efforts method** and was used most frequently by the larger oil companies. The second method, called the **full-cost method**, capitalizes all exploration costs so long as the value of the estimated recoverable units from producing wells is expected to exceed the total capitalized costs.

This controversy has been resolved by allowing oil and gas companies to choose either the successful-efforts or the full-costing method. Paragraph 3060.25 of the *CICA Handbook* states that:

> For an oil and gas property, the cost of the capital asset comprises acquisition costs, development costs and certain exploration costs depending on whether the enterprise accounts for its oil and gas properties using the full cost method or the successful efforts method. An enterprise applies the method of accounting for acquisition, exploration, and development costs that it considers to be appropriate to its operations and applies the method consistently to all its properties.

Apparently, the method used is not as important as its appropriateness to the enterprise and the application of the chosen method on a consistent basis.

KEY CONCEPTS

Amortization of intangible assets   The capitalized costs of intangible assets must be allocated rationally and systematically to their estimated useful lives, not to exceed 40 years. The useful lives of exclusive rights are subject to legal or contractual constraint. Intangible assets rarely have residual value, and the amortization is mostly based on the straight-line method.

Depletion   An accounting process of allocating the cost of natural resources to the productive outputs. The calculation of depletion is similar to the productive output method of depreciation.

Goodwill   Goodwill is the most important unidentifiable intangible asset of a firm, representing the firm's future "above normal" earning power. However, goodwill is not recognized unless it is purchased in connection with an acquisition of a company as a unit, and is measured by the excessive price paid over the fair value of the net assets acquired.

Identifiable intangible assets   These are intangible assets which can be separately identified apart from other assets of the firm. Most of identifiable intangible assets are exclusive legal or contractual rights and can be separately sold or purchased. For a purchased right the purchase price and expenditures directly related to the protection of the right are capitalized. Costs incurred internally to develop intangible assets are expensed except those costs which are directly related to registration of a legal right.

Intangible assets   Intangible assets are similar to other operational assets in that (1) they represent a long-term economic benefits, and (2) they are acquired for operational purposes. Unlike other operational assets, however, they are characterized by a lack of physical substance.

Negative goodwill   Negative goodwill arises when the price paid for the acquisition of a company as a unit is less than the fair value of net assets acquired. Negative goodwill is recognized only if it exceeds the total fair value of the acquired noncurrent assets other than long-term investment in marketable securities. The recognized negative goodwill is credited to a deferred credit account.

Natural resources   Natural resources are operational assets which are physically consumed in production. The related acquisition costs, exploration costs, and development costs should be capitalized and then depleted.

Research and Development   Research is planned search aimed at discovery of new knowledge useful in developing a new product (or process) or improving an existing product (or process). Development is the translation of research findings into a plan or design for the new or existing product (or process). In general, research and development costs should be expensed when incurred.

REVIEW QUESTIONS AND EXERCISES

TRUE-FALSE

Indicate whether each of the following statements is true or false by circling the correct response.

T   F   1.   The primary distinguishing feature of intangible assets is a lack of physical substance.

T   F   2.   Intangible assets, whether purchased from others or developed internally, must be capitalized and reported on the balance sheet.

T   F   3.   Costs capitalized as intangible assets should be amortized systematically over a period of 40 years.

T   F   4.   The straight-line method is generally more appropriate for tangible assets such as property, plant and equipment than for intangible assets.

T   F   5.   The recorded costs of an internally generated patent include legal fees and registration fees directly associated with the patent.

T   F   6.   The cost of defending a patent in court against infringement by others, if successful, should be charged to the patent account.

T   F   7.   Registration of a trademark gives the owner the exclusive right to its use for a nonrenewable period of **17** years.

T   F   8.   If a municipality grants a private enterprise the exclusive right to provide garbage collection to the city, the cost of acquiring the right should be debited to a franchise account and amortized over its useful life or 40 years, whichever is **longer**.

T   F   9.   Annual payments made under a franchise agreement should generally be capitalized to the franchise account.

T   F   10.   Goodwill developed internally should be recorded as an intangible asset based on the expected excessive earnings and amortized over a period no longer than 40 years.

T   F   11.   Goodwill is recognized only if it is purchased in connection with the acquisition of a company as a unit, and is measured by the excess of acquisition price over the fair value of net assets acquired.

T   F   12.   Negative goodwill should be recognized as long as the fair value of the acquired net assets exceeds the price paid for the acquisition of a company as a unit.

T   F   13. In general research and development costs are not recorded as intangible assets, but expensed when incurred.

T   F   14. Depletion of natural resources is generally based on a flat annual rate under the straight-line method.

EXERCISE 1

Match each of the partial descriptions below with the term to which it best relates. Terms may be used more than once.

Descriptions	Related Phrases
_____ 1. Life plus 50 years	A. Intangible assets
_____ 2. Long-term prepaid expense	B. Research and development costs
_____ 3. Exclusive right to an invention	C. Patents
_____ 4. Right to conduct business in an area	D. Copyrights
_____ 5. Generally expensed as incurred	E. Franchise
_____ 6. 17 years	F. Goodwill
_____ 7. Exclusive right to literary or artistic products	G. Negative goodwill
_____ 8. Above average earning power	H. Deferred charges
_____ 9. Deferred credit	
_____ 10. Operational assets lack of physical substance	

EXERCISE 2

Given the following information on David Manufacturing Company during its first year of operation and assume that all the costs are incurred on January 1:

Transaction Description	Amount
Incorporation fees	$ 3,000
Cost of developing a new product	2,400
Legal fees related to organization	1,000
Advertising costs (product promotion)	800
Cost of designing a trademark	1,600
Cost of purchasing a tradename	1,200
Research and development on new patent	3,500
Purchase of a patent for a new process	3,400
Acquisition cost of a franchise to sell a product in the area for 20 years	3,600
Cost of the purchased goodwill	20,000

Required: Assuming that any amount allocated to organization costs should be amortized over five years, and all other intangible assets are amortized over the maximum time allowed, complete the following:

	Acquisition Cost	Amortization for the year	Unamortized balance
1. Organization costs			
2. Patents			
3. Trademarks			
4. Tradenames			
5. Franchise			
6. Goodwill			
Total			

MULTIPLE CHOICE

Enter the letter corresponding to the response which **best** completes each of the following statements or questions.

_____ 1. Goodwill:

   a. can have value only in conjunction with an enterprise as a whole.
   b. should not be recorded if generated internally, unless the market value of the firm exceeds the fair value of its identifiable net assets.
   c. should be amortized over no more than 40 years unless its benefits are expected to continue longer than that.
   d. if negative, should be disregarded.

_____ 2. Which of the following would **rarely** be considered for the amortization of an intangible asset?

   a. residual value.
   b. legal life.
   c. expected actions of competitors.
   d. obsolescence.

_____ 3. The cost of designing and registering a trademark should be:

   a. expensed when incurred.
   b. capitalized as an intangible asset that should **not** be amortized.
   c. capitalized and amortized over its useful life, not to exceed 20 years.
   d. capitalized and amortized over its useful life, not to exceed 40 years.

_____ 4. Which of the following should not be accounted for as an intangible asset?

   a. a franchise to sell Manitoba Fried Chicken.
   b. the cost of developing a new manufacturing process.
   c. the cost of designing a trademark.
   d. provincial incorporation fees for a new corporation.

_____ 5. Payroll expenditure directly related to a research project:

   a. should be capitalized and amortized over the period benefited.
   b. should always be expensed as incurred.
   c. Should generally be expensed as incurred unless the project contributes to the development of a new product for sale.
   d. should generally be expensed as incurred unless it is directly related to projects done by contract for others.

_____ 6. Which of the following expenditures related to research and development projects should be **expensed** as incurred?

   a. conceptual formulation and design of possible equipment for sale.
   b. purchase of equipment having future alternative uses.
   c. laboratory research under contract aimed at developing a new process for a governmental entity.
   d. acquisition of materials to be used in a variety of research projects.

_____ 7. Which of the following should be **expensed** as incurred by the franchisee for a franchise to sell a product in the specified area for five years?

   a. amount paid for the franchise.
   b. legal fees paid to obtain the franchise.
   c. annual payments to the franchisor for sales made under the franchise agreement.
   d. none of the above.

_____ 8. Which of the following should **not** be capitalized **as natural resources**?

   a. costs incurred to identify areas that may warrant testing.
   b. costs incurred to purchase rights to property for purposes of exploring a natural resource.
   c. costs incurred to built the producing system.
   d. costs incurred to acquire physical facilities.

_____ 9. Bowling Company acquired a patent at a cost of $59,500 on January 1, 1991. At the same time, Bowling spent another $8,500 to successfully defend the patent against infringement. It is expected that the patent would have an economic life of 10 years. Patent amortization expense for 1991 should be:

   a. $5,950
   b. $6,800
   c. $5,100
   d. $850

_____ 10. In 1991, Toyko Manufacturing Company developed a new product to be marketed in 1992. The following costs were incurred during 1991:

Research and development departmental costs	$350,000
Materials and supplies consumed	120,000
Compensation paid to research consultants	250,000
Total	$720,000

These costs are expected to be totally recovered by 1994. What amount should be recognized as an intangible asset in 1991?

a. $0
b. $350,000
c. $600,000
d. $720,000

_____ 11. Tricky Corporation incurred $350,000 of costs to develop a patent which was granted on January 1, 1991. Registration fees of the patent totaled $35,000. Tricky estimates the useful life of the patent will be seven years. What amount should Tricky charge to patent amortization expense for the year ended December 31, 1991:

a. $7,000
b. $5,000
c. $55,000
d. $0

_____ 12. The following data are obtained from Ready Company's records, which was recently incorporated, and is still at development stage:

legal fees related to registration	$2,400
Registration fees	3,000
merchandise	3,400
Accumulated operating deficit	5,000
Stock issuance costs	2,000

The amount that may be capitalized as organization costs is:

a. $5,400
b. $2,400
c. $7,400
d. $12,400

_____ 13. Right Ltd. paid $800,000 to acquire Left Company as a unit. The book value and fair value of Left's assets and liabilities were as follows:

	Book Value	Fair Value
Current assets	$250,000	$280,000
Plant assets	350,000	520,000
Patents	100,000	80,000
Liabilities	(200,000)	(200,000)
Total	$500,000	$680,000

The amount of goodwill purchased by Right is:

a. $0
b. $300,000
c. $120,000
d. $180,000

_____ 14. Assuming the same data as in question 13, except that Right paid only $250,000 for the acquisition, what is the negative goodwill **recognized** by Right from that acquisition?

a. $0
b. $25,000
c. $35,000
d. $20,000

SOLUTIONS TO REVIEW QUESTIONS AND EXERCISES

TRUE-FALSE

1.	T	5.	T	9.	F	13.	T
2.	F	6.	T	10.	F	14.	F
3.	F	7.	F	11.	T		
4.	F	8.	F	12.	F		

EXERCISE 1

1.	D	4.	E	7.	D	10.	A
2.	H	5.	B	8.	F		
3.	C	6.	C	9.	G		

EXERCISE 2

	Acquisition Cost	Amortization for the year	Unamortized balance
1. Organization costs	$4,000	$800	$3,200
2. Patents	3,400	200	3,200
3. Trademarks	1,600	40	1,560
4. Tradenames	1,200	30	1,170
5. Franchise	3,600	180	3,420
6. Goodwill	20,000	500	19,500
Total	**$33,800**	**$1,750**	**$32,050**

MULTIPLE CHOICE

1.	a	5.	d	9.	b	13.	c
2.	a	6.	a	10.	a	14.	a
3.	d	7.	c	11.	b		
4.	b	8.	d	12.	c		

Computations and explanations:

9.   (b)   Patent cost   = Purchase price + legal fees
                                 = $59,500 + $8,500
                                 = $68,000.

             Annual amortization = $68,000 / 10
                                 = $6,800.

10.   (a)   All the expenditures are research and development costs and
             should be expensed as incurred.

11.   (b)   For an internally developed patent, only expenditures directly related to
             registration may be capitalized.

             Annual amortization = $35,000 / 7
                                 = $5,000.

12.   (c)   Organization costs = Legal fees + Registration fees
                                   + Stock issuance costs
                                 = $2,400 + $3,000 + $2,000
                                 = $7,400.

13.   (c)   Goodwill   = Acquisition cost - Fair value of net assets
                                 = $800,000 - $680,000
                                 = $120,000.

14.   (a)   None of the negative goodwill is recognized, because the fair value of plant and other assets is greater than the indicated negative goodwill as shown below:

Purchase price	$250,000
Less: Fair value of net assets acquired	(680,000)
Negative goodwill	$(430,000)
Allocate negative goodwill:	
to plant assets	372,667*
to patents	57,333**
Deferred credit acquired	0

Notes: Negative goodwill is allocated to plant and other assets in proportion to their fair values as follows:

  * Negative goodwill allocated to plant
    = $430,000 x 520 / 600
    = $372,667.

  ** Negative goodwill allocated to patents
    = $430,000 x 80 / 600
    = $57,333.

CHAPTER 14

Investments -- Temporary and Long Term

CHAPTER OBJECTIVES

This chapter is designed to enable students to:

A. Explain the reasons why a firm might invest in debt and equity securities.

B. Apply the classification criteria and record the initial acquisition of investment securities.

C. Discuss the conceptual basis for accounting for various types of investments.

D. Account for temporary investments using the allowance method.

E. Account for temporary investments using the direct write-off method.

F. Account for long-term investments in equity securities using the (a) cost method, (b) equity method, and (c) the market value method.

G. Explain the disclosure requirements for investment securities.

H. Account for stock dividends, stock splits, and stock warrants received by an investor.

I. Prepare consolidated financial statements (Appendix 14A)

J. Explain the use of special purpose funds; account for the cash surrender value of life insurance; and, account for futures contracts. (Appendix 14B)

A. Introduction

In addition to their major courses of business, many companies make a variety of **investments**, such as acquiring land or other properties for speculation, setting up special purpose long-term funds, buying life insurance policies for their executives and building up cash surrender values. However, the most important of all is probably purchasing securities issued by other entities. The motivation for such security investments might be to (1) earn a return on temporarily idle cash, or (2) to acquire the voting stock of another firm (perhaps a major customer, supplier or competitor) in order to gain influence, control, business expansion or some other business advantages.

B. Nature of Securities and Classification of Security Investments

The appropriate accounting for a security investment depends upon the nature of the securities and the classification of security investments as follows:

1. **Equity or debt securities.** An equity security is defined as any instrument representing ownership shares (e.g., a common stock or a preferred stock) or the right to acquire ownership shares (e.g., stock options). This term, however, does not encompass callable or redeemable preferred stock, treasury stock and convertible bonds. A debt security, on the other hand, is an instrument representing creditors' claim with a fixed amount and usually some interest obligation (e.g., a note or a bond).

2. **Marketable or nonmarketable.** An equity or a debt security is considered marketable if the sales price of the security is currently available on a national securities exchange or in the over-the-counter market.

3. **Current or noncurrent:** A security investment is classified as **current** (or **short-term**) if the security is (1) readily marketable, and (2) intended to be converted to cash within an accounting period or operating cycle, whichever is longer. Otherwise, it should be classified as **noncurrent** (or **long-term**).

4. **Significant influence.** Investor's ability to exercise significant influence over operating and financial policies of an investee may be indicated in several ways (such as representation in the board of directors, material intercompany transactions, etc.). In general, however, in the absence of evidence to the contrary, significant influence should be presumed if an investor holds 20% or more of the investee's voting stock.

C. 1. Accounting methods applicable to specific circumstances are summarized in the following diagram and will be individually discussed thereafter:

```
Given:    C   = Cost method
          E   = Equity method
          LCM = Lower-of-cost-or-market method
          MV  = Market value method
```

	Equity Securities	Debt Securities
Current (or Short-term)	LCM	LCM
Noncurrent (or Long-term)	C, E or MV * (mutually exclusive)	C

Note: * **Long-term** investments in equity securities should be accounted for using:

    (1) the **cost** method,
    (2) the **equity** method, or
    (3) the **market value** method.

2. **Accounting Methods for Investment in Equity Securities**

  1. **Cost method.** This method is applicable if the investor does not have significant influence, and the securities are not marketable. Under this method:

    a. The investment is initially recorded at cost.

    b. Investment income (revenue) is recognized whenever dividends are received, unless the dividends are liquidating (i.e., the total dividends received exceed the investor's cumulative share in the investee's earnings since the investment). Liquidating dividends are considered a return of the original investment and should be credited to the investment account.

    c. Gain or loss on the investment is recognized only when realized (i.e., the acquired securities are sold).

    d. At any time, if a decline in market value of any individual security is **other than temporary**, investment in the specific security should be written down to market directly, and a loss is recognized (CICA Handbook, Sec 3050). The market value then becomes the new cost of the investment.

  3. **Lower-of-cost-or-market (LCM) method.** Following the **CICA Handbook, sec 3010**, the LCM method is applied to (a) investments classified as current. Under this method:

    a. The investment is initially recorded at cost.

    b. The securities shall be grouped separately into a current portfolio. The carrying amount of the portfolio shall be the lower of its **aggregate** cost or market value. The requirement for an aggregate comparison allows unrealized gains of some securities to offset unrealized losses of some other securities in the portfolio.

    When the market value of the portfolio is less than its cost at the balance sheet date and the decrease in market value is considered temporary, an **unrealized loss** is recorded. There are (2) methods of recognizing such a decline in value on the balance sheet; the allowance method and the direct write off method.

D. **Allowance Method** The allowance method for temporary investments is similar to that used for accounts receivable. The investment or portfolio of investments is carried on the balance sheet at cost and, should the market value of the portfolio decline to an amount below the cost at the balance sheet date, an allowance is established to reduce the cost value to market.

1. In the **subsequent** years, the allowance account should be adjusted up and down to reflect changes in the excess of cost over current market value. If the market value goes further down, the above procedures still apply (i.e., the unrealized loss is debited, and the allowance account credited for the current change in market value). If the market value goes up, the allowance account should be debited. The **recovery of market value** account is credited, which is reported on the income statement as an other operating gain.

2. When an individual security is **reclassified** between the **current** and **noncurrent** portfolios, the security is transferred at the **lower of cost or market** at the date of transfer. If its market value is less than cost, the market value becomes the **new cost** basis, and the difference between the "old" and the "new" costs is recorded as a loss as if the security were sold and a loss realized.

3. When a decline in market value of a security is considered permanent, the unrealized loss is recognized, the investment account is written down to market, and the market value becomes the new cost for subsequent cost or market application.

4. When a security is sold, investment is credited at the original cost of the security, and the realized gain or loss is recognized. The allowance account should be adjusted, usually at the year end, to reflect the excess of cost over market value of those **securities remaining in the investment.**

ILLUSTRATION 1 -- LCM METHOD, TEMPORARY EQUITY INVESTMENT

On January 2, 1991, Parker Industries invested temporarily idle cash in two common stocks as follows: Spider Corporation, $12,000, and Peter Corporation, $25,000. During 1991, a cash dividend of $1,000 was received from Spider Corporation. On December 31, 1991 the market prices of those investments were: Spider Corporation, $12,500, and Peter Corporation, $20,000.

1991.

The following journal entries and financial statement presentation for 1991 are appropriate: (Assume the allowance method)

(1)   To record the investment:

```
   Investment in equity securities              37,000
        Cash ($25,000 + $12,000)                         37,000
```

(2)   **To record cash dividend received:**

```
Cash                                            1,000
        Investment income (or dividend income)          1,000
```

(3)   **To adjust the investment to LCM at the year end:**

```
Unrealized loss on investments                  4,500*
        Allowance to reduce investments to market       4,500
```

*Aggregate difference is calculated as follows:

	Cost	Market	Difference
Spider Corporation	$12,000	$12,500	$ (500)
Peter Corporation	25,000	20,000	5,000
Aggregate (Cost − Market)	$37,000	$32,500	$ 4,500

(4)   To close unrealized loss account:

```
Income summary                                  4,500
        Unrealized loss on investment                   4,500
```

(5)   **To present investment on the balance sheet:**

```
Investment in equity securities                 $37,000
Less: Allowance to reduce
        investment to market                    (4,500)   $32,500
```

1992.

Assume that at the end of 1992, the aggregate market value increased to $35,000.

(1) To adjust allowance to the new required balance
    [($37,000 − $35,000) − $4,500]:

```
Allowance to reduce investments to market       2,500
        Recovery of unrealized loss on investment       2,500
```

(2) To close the cost recovery account:

```
Recovery of unrealized loss on investment       2,500
        Income summary                                  2,500
```

(3)   To present investment on the balance sheet:

```
Investment in equity securities                 $37,000
Less: Allowance to reduce
        investment to market                    (2,000)   $35,000
```

E. 1.   Direct Write-Off Method   The direct write-off method treats each investment in like shares as a separate account. Therefore, if at the balance sheet date the carrying value of those shares is greater than the market value, they are written down to market and a loss is recognized. The new carrying value is not adjusted if the shares subsequently increase in market value.

ILLUSTRATION 2 -- LCM METHOD, TEMPORARY EQUITY INVESTMENT

On January 2, 1991, Parker Industries invested temporarily idle cash in two common stocks as follows: Spider Corporation, $12,000, and Peter Corporation, $25,000. During 1991, a cash dividend of $1,000 was received from Spider Corporation. On December 31, 1991 the market prices of those investments were: Spider Corporation, $12,500, and Peter Corporation, $20,000.

1991.

The following journal entries and financial statement presentation for 1991 are appropriate: (Assume the direct write-off method)

1991 - Journal Entries

(1)   **To record the investment:**

Investment in equity securities	37,000	
Cash ($25,000 + $12,000)		37,000

(2)   **To record cash dividend received:**

Cash	1,000	
Investment income (or dividend income)		1,000

(3)

Unrealized loss on investments	5,000	
Investment in equity securities		5,000

To write down to market the value of Peter Corporation (25,000 - 20,000=)

(4)   To close unrealized loss account:

Income summary	5,000	
Unrealized loss on investment		5,000

(5)   **To present investment on balance sheet:**

Investment in equity securities	$32,000
(at LCM)	

1992.

Assume that at the end of 1992, the aggregate market value increased as follows:

Spider Corporation	$13,000
Peter Corporation	22,000
	$35,000

Note: - No Entries would be made to change the $32,000 carrying value.

- The investment on the balance sheet would be:

Investment in Equity Securities

(Market, $35,000) at cost $32,000

2. Accounting Methods for Investments in Debt Securities

Investment in debt securities is accounted for using the **cost method**. The investment is carried at cost, interest revenue is recognized as accrued, and a gain or loss is recognized only if realized. If the decline in market value is significant and not due to temporary conditions, the investment account is directly adjusted to market, and the unrealized loss is recognized and included in the determination of income. Any subsequent recovery in market value is disregarded. Two possible exceptions:

1. If the debt securities are **marketable** and the investment is classified as **current**, the **lower-of-cost-or-market method** may also be applied.

2. For any other debt securities, the cost method must be applied. However, if a long-term investment in a debt security was acquired at a premium or discount, the premium or discount is amortized over the remaining term of the security. This topic is covered in Chapter 16.

F. Cost Method of Accounting for Long-Term Investments in Equity Securities

(a) The cost method of accounting is used for long-term investments in equity securities when the investor is not able to exercise significant influence or control over the investee company. The investment is valued at cost when acquired and is carried at this value unless there is an "other than temporary decline" in its market value. Examples of value impairment include bankruptcy, depressed market price for a prolonged period, continued losses for a period of years, or severe losses by the investee in the current and prior years. The investment should not be written up if there is a subsequent increase in value.

The gain or loss on disposal of the investment is based on the difference between the proceeds of disposal and the average carrying value of the shares. Therefore, unrealized losses would be recognized when there is an other than temporary impairment, but unrealized gains are not recognized. Gains would only be recognized when realized through the disposal of all or part of the investment held.

In some cases, the dividends received by an investor may be greater than the investor's proportionate share of earnings since the date of purchase. These preacquisition (or liquidating) dividends should be accounted for as a return of capital rather than investment revenue. That is, the dividend (all or part) is credited to the investment account.

(b) Equity method. For the investor, the cost and the LCM methods discussed above are based on the two-entity concept. That is, the investor considers the investee as a separate business entity. In contrast, the equity method views the investor and the investee as a special type of **single entity.** Under this concept, the investee is a part of the investor's entity, and the income of the investee is part of the investor's earnings.

The equity method is required when the investor's long-term investment in the investee's common stock enables the investor to exercise significant influence over the investee. Under this method:

a.   The investment is initially recorded at cost.

b.   The investment is increased by the recognized investment income, which is measured as:

Investment Income   = Proportionate share of investee's income
+/- Adjustments

where the **adjustments** include an:

(1)   amortization of the differences between the fair and book values of individual assets acquired and liabilities assumed,
(2)   amortization of the purchased goodwill, and
(3)   elimination of profits or losses from intercompany transactions (known as intercompany profits or losses).

In the event that the investor's investment losses **exceed** the carrying amount of the investment, it ordinarily should **discontinue** applying the equity method and the **excessive losses** should not be recognized. Application of the equity method should be resumed when the investment income of subsequent periods has equaled the unrecognized investment losses.

c.   The investment account is decreased whenever cash dividends are declared by the investee. Under the equity method, there is no concern with the issue whether a certain dividend is liquidating or not.

d.   When the investor's level of influence changes, a change in accounting method may be required. If the change is from the equity method to another method, **no adjustment** is made to the carrying amount of the investment. However, when a change to the equity method is appropriate, **retroactive adjustments** are required to the investment account, the income statement and retained earnings. The adjusted amounts should be those which would have occurred if the equity method always had been used.

e.   A gain or loss on security investment is recognized when realized, and the **LCM** rule does not apply.

f.   The equity basis method is a modified cost basis method. The investment account is carried at the original cost plus the investor's equity in the undistributed earnings of the investee. While the notion of lower of cost or market does not appear to be applicable, nonetheless, some firms do indicate that their equity basis investments are carried at the lower of cost or market. A permanent impairment in the market value of the investee's shares would require a write down by the investor to the extent that market value was below carrying value.

ILLUSTRATION 3 -- THE EQUITY METHOD

Parent Company purchased **55%** of Subsidiary Company's outstanding common stock for $45,000 on January 2, 1991. On that date, the balance sheet of Subsidiary and estimated market values of its assets and liabilities were as follows:

	Book Value	Market Value	Difference
Cash and receivables	$ 10,000	$ 10,000	
Equipment (net)	20,000	25,000	$ 5,000
Land	30,000	41,000	11,000
Total Assets	$ 60,000	$ 76,000	
Liabilities	$ 20,000	$ 20,000	
Owners' equity	40,000	56,000	
Total liab. & owners' equity	$ 60,000	$ 76,000	

Further assume that, on the date of acquisition, Subsidiary's equipment had a useful life of 5 years. For the year Subsidiary reported $8,000 of net income, and declared and paid $5,000 dividends. Any purchased goodwill is amortized over 40 years.

Required: Prepare journal entries to record the investment.

SOLUTION:

(1)   **To record the investment:**

Investment in Subsidiary	45,000	
Cash		45,000

(2)   **To record dividends received:**

Cash ($5,000 x 55%)	2,750	
Investment in Subsidiary		2,750

(3)   **To record share of Subsidiary's reported income:**

Investment in Subsidiary ($8,000 x 55%)	4,400	
Investment income		4,400

(4)   **To amortize the difference between the fair and book values of equipment:**

Investment income ($5,000 x 55% / 5)	550	
Investment in subsidiary		550

(5)   **To amortize goodwill:**
(goodwill = $45,000 − $56,000 x 55% = $14,200)

Investment income ($14,200 / 40)	355	
Investment in Subsidiary		355

Note that:

(1) Only a real account (investment in subsidiary) and a nominal account (investment income) are used to record the investment transactions.

(2) The difference between the fair and the book values of the equipment acquired by Parent was $2,750 [($25,000 - $20,000) x 55%], which was to be amortized (depreciated) over the remaining useful life of the equipment at $550 ($2,750 / 5) per year.

(3) The acquired goodwill must be amortized over a period of no longer than 40 years, and adjusted to investment income.

(c) Market value method.   Unlike any other methods, the market value method is based on the current value concept, instead of the cost principle. This method is not generally accepted except that, following specialized industry accounting practices (i.e., industry peculiarities), certain **specialized industries** (e.g., an investment company, mutual fund, pension fund or insurance company) may use it to account for their investments in **marketable** securities. Under this method:

a.   The investment is initially recorded at cost.

b.   Dividends received are recognized as investment income.

c.   A change in the market value of each individual security is directly adjusted to the investment account, and an unrealized gain or loss is recorded. Then:

   (1)   under the **current approach**, the unrealized gain or loss is included in current income, or

   (2)   under the **deferral approach**, the unrealized gain or loss is deferred and reported as a contra owners' equity account.

d.   When the investment is sold, the carrying value of the investment (including the deferred unrealized gain or loss, if applicable) is closed and a resulting realized gain or loss is recognized.

To summarize, in accounting for both temporary and long-term investments, you must carefully distinguish between realized and unrealized gains and losses.

Realized gains and losses usually relate to the sale of an asset. Unrealized gains and losses relate to the comparison of the market value of the asset to its carrying value. When market value is greater than the carrying value, there is an unrealized gain. When market value is less than the carrying value, there is an unrealized loss. In the context of temporary investments, the following relationships exist:

1.   *Realized gain.* If at date of sale, the net proceeds are greater than the carrying value of the securities sold, a **realized gain** in the amount of the difference is recognized.

2. *Realized loss.* If at date of sale, the net proceeds are less than the carrying value of the securities sold, a **realized loss** in the amount of the difference is recognized.

3. *Unrealized loss.* An unrealized loss occurs when the market value of securities is less than their carrying value. An **unrealized loss** is recognized:

   a. At the end of an accounting period, if the current market value of the securities is less than their carrying value.

   b. When individual securities are transferred between the long-term and temporary portfolios and the market value at date of transfer is lower than the carrying value.

4. *Unrealized gain.* An unrealized gain occurs when the market value of the securities is greater than their carrying value. **Unrealized gains** are normally not recognized. When the allowance method is used, however, unrealized gains are recognized when the allowance to reduce to market account is reduced. The unrealized gain can be recorded only to the extent of the write-downs for unrealized losses. For this reason it is often called an *unrealized loss recovery.* That is, under the allowance method, the valuation of the portfolio can never exceed the original cost of the total portfolio. An unrealized gain (i.e., reduction of prior unrealized losses) is recorded in an adjusting entry at the end of the accounting period. Normally, under the direct method, previously recorded write-downs are not reversed and unrealized gains are not recognized. Recognition comes about when they are realized through the sale of the securities.

G. Disclosure Requirements in Accounting for Equity Security Investment

An investor firm must disclose the following for its investments in equity securities:

1. Aggregate costs of the **current** and **noncurrent** portfolios, respectively.

2. Aggregate market values of the Portfolios.

3. Gross unrealized gains and losses.

4. Net realized gain or loss, the basis for determining this gain or loss, and the change in the valuation allowance that is included in the determination of income. Refer to CICA Handbook, Sec. 3050 for the Candian requirements under the heading "Disclosures Required for Long-Term Investments in Equity Securities).

H. Special Problems in Accounting for Equity Investment

1. **Stock dividends and stock split.** A **stock dividend** is a capitalization of a part of retained earnings and does not increase or decrease the net assets of the issuing corporation. The investor neither receives assets from, nor owns more of the issuing corporation. Therefore it should make no entry for the dividends other than a

memorandum record for the number of additional shares received. Nevertheless, the new cost per share should be recalculated to take the additional shares into consideration.

To the issuer a **stock split** is different from a **stock dividend**. However, the two are virtually identical from the point of view of the investor.

2. **Stock rights.** The privilege given shareholders (investors) of purchasing additional shares from the issuing corporation at a specific price and by a specified future date is commonly known as a stock right. The certificate evidencing one or more rights often is called a stock warrant.

The term *stock right* is usually interpreted as one right for each share of old stock. Stock rights are rights to acquire a specified number of shares of certain stock at a specified price within a specified period of time. When a right is issued by an investee to its stockholders (investors), the investor usually does not record the right unless it is detachable from the shares it holds. If the right is separable (detachable) from the original shares and the market value of the right is available, an entry is prepared to debit a separate account such as **investment in stock right**, with a counter credit to **investment income**. When the right is disposed of:

(1) If the right is sold, cash less the carrying value of investment in stock right, if any, is recorded as a gain (loss).

(2) If the right is exercised and new shares are acquired, the acquisition cost of these new shares should include cash paid and the carrying value of investment in stock right, if any.

(3) If the right is expired, the carrying value of the right, if any, is closed to a loss account.

I. **Prepare Consolidated Financial Statements**

The appendix presents the fundamental concepts of **Consolidated financial statements**. The complexities involved are deferred to advanced texts that develop this topic. The *CICA Handbook*, section 3050, provides the basic accounting guidelines for consolidated financial statements. Consolidation of the financial statements of a parent company and a (subsidiary is only a reporting procedure; therefore, it does not affect the accounts of either the parent company or the) subsidiary. Consolidation is done only by the parent company, not by the subsidiary.

When an investor company owns over 50% of the outstanding voting stock of another company, in the absence of overriding constraints, a controlling interest exists. The investor company is called the parent company. The second (or investee) company is called a subsidiary company. In a parent-subsidiary relationship, both corporations continue as separate legal entities; therefore, they are separate accounting entities. As separate entities, they have separate accounting systems and separate financial statements. The parent company prepares two sets of financial statements: one set as a separate entity and another set as a consolidated entity. To prepare consolidated financial statements, the separate financial statements of the parent and the subsidiary are combined each period by the parent company into one overall (i.e., consolidated) set of financial statements as if they were one single entity. The income statements, balance sheets, and statements of changes in financial position (SCFP) are also consolidated in this manner.

J. Special-Purpose Funds as Long-Term Investments

1. Companies often set aside cash, and sometimes other assets, in special funds (special-purpose funds) to be used in the future for a specific, designated purpose. Although a special-purpose fund can be a current asset, it is more commonly a non-current asset. As such, it is not directly related to current operations. Long-term funds are reported on the balance sheet under the non-current classification under the caption "investments and funds."

   Funds may be set aside (1) by contract, as in the case of a bond sinking fund; (2) by law, as in the case of rent deposits; or (3) voluntarily, as in the case of a plant expansion fund.

2. Cash Surrender Value of Life Insurance

When a firm insures the lives of its top executives, with itself as the beneficiary, the firm is in essence making an investment. Some insurance policies allow the firm to build up a cash surrender value while the policy is in force. A cash surrender value is the amount that would be refunded should the policy be terminated at the request of the insured.

Cash surrender value increases over time as the firm pays the insurance premium. Therefore, a periodic premium payment covers not only the firm's insurance expense for the period, but also current contribution to the cash surrender value. The cash surrender value is recorded as an asset and usually reported on the balance sheet under **investments and funds**.

3. Accounting for Futures Contracts

Business entities and other investors often purchase **futures contracts** as an investment or as a hedge to offset the risks of future price changes. A futures contract is a contract between a buyer and seller of a commodity or financial instrument and the clearing- house of a future exchange. Futures contracts vary; however, such contracts have three common characteristics:

1. They obligate the buyer (seller) to accept (make delivery of) a commodity or financial instrument at a specified time, or they provide for cash settlement periodically rather than delivery.

2. They can be effectively canceled before the specified time by entering into an offsetting contract for the same commodity or financial instrument.

3. All changes in the market value of open contracts are settled on a regular basis, usually daily.

For recording and reporting futures contracts, the two approaches are the market-value approach and the hedge-deferral approach. The primary issue in accounting for a futures contract is whether changes in the market value of a futures contract should be recognized as a gain or loss in the reporting period when the market price changes take place, or whether the gain or loss should be deferred to a later date. Two criteria for determining the accounting approach for futures contracts are:

1.   The item to be hedged exposes the company to market price or interest rate risk.

2.   The futures contract reduces that risk and is designated as a hedge.

The market-value approach must be used when the hedge fails to meet both of these criteria. The market-value approach requires that all gains and losses due to market price changes be recognized in the reporting period when the market price changes.

The hedge-deferral approach must be used when one or both criteria are met. The hedge-deferral approach requires that all gains or losses due to market price changes be deferred and recognized at the termination of the futures contract as an adjustment to the cost (or price) in the subsequent terminating transaction.

KEY CONCEPTS

Debt securities   Instruments representing creditors' claim on a fixed amount and usually some interest obligation (e.g., notes and bonds).

Equity securities   Any instrument representing ownership shares (e.g., common stock, or preferred stock), or the right to acquire ownership shares. Callable or redeemable preferred stock, treasury stock or convertible bonds are not considered as equity securities.

Marketable equity securities   An equity security for which sales price is currently available on a national securities exchange or in the over-the-counter market.

Realized gain or loss   The difference between the net proceeds from the sale of a security and its cost.

Significant influence   Investor's ability to influence the investee's operating and financial policies. An investment of 20% or more of the voting stock of an investee should lead to a presumption that the investor has the ability to exercise the influence, unless there is evidence to the contrary.

The cost method   An accounting method applied to investments in most debt securities and certain nonmarketable equity securities, under which the investment is initially recorded at cost, interest accrued or dividends received are recognized as income, and the investment account continues to carry the original cost unless there is a liquidating dividend, a substantial and permanent decline in market value, or a disposal of the security investment.

The equity method   The accounting method required to be applied to long-term investment in the equity securities of another firm (the investee) over which the investor has significant influence. This method is based on the single-entity concept. Investment is initially recorded at cost. The investment account increases by the investor's investment income, and decreases by its share in dividends declared by the investee.

The lower-of-cost-or-market method   An accounting method primarily applied to investments in marketable equity securities in which the investor does not have significant influence. This method is basically the same as the cost method, except that a valuation allowance is established to account for the unrealized loss of a portfolio at the end of an accounting period. The allowance method or the direct write off method may be used.

The market value method   The only valuation method based on the current value concept. It is not generally acceptable, except for some specialized industries such as investment and insurance companies. Under this method, investment in marketable securities is initially recorded at cost. The investment account is then adjusted directly to the market value, and both the unrealized gain and loss are recorded.

Unrealized gain or loss   The difference between the market value of a security and its cost at any given date.

Valuation allowance   The **net** unrealized loss in a portfolio of marketable equity security investment (i.e., the amount by which aggregate cost exceeds market value of a portfolio).

REVIEW QUESTIONS AND EXERCISES

TRUE-FALSE

Indicate whether each of the following statements is true or false by circling the correct response.

T   F   1. Regardless of the accounting method used, stock investments should **initially** be recorded at the total cost of the investment, including brokerage fees and commissions.

T   F   2. Using the **cost method** the investor does not adjust the investment account to reflect temporary market value changes.

T   F   3. The use of **lower-of-cost-or-market (LCM)** requires that marketable equity investments be classified into a current portfolio.

T   F   4. When the market value of temporary investments has declined below the carrying value, they should be carried at market.

T   F   5. Once the aggregate carrying value of a **specific current portfolio** has been written down following **LCM** (direct write off method), the carrying value may not be written back up for subsequent recovery of market value.

T   F   6. The market value method is not in accordance with GAAP, and should thus never be applied to accounting for security investment.

T   F   7. Using the equity method, the investor's share of investee's dividends should not be recorded as investment income.

T   F   8. The equity method is required for long-term equity investment, regardless of whether the investor is able to exercise significant influence or not.

T   F   9. Using the equity method the investor company records the amortization of goodwill by debiting amortization of goodwill (expense) and crediting goodwill.

T   F   10. The unrealized loss from writing down short-term security investment to LCM (Allowance Method) is reported as a component of income from continuing operations.

T   F   11. An investment in common stock is accounted for using the equity method only if the stock is marketable.

T   F   12. Equity securities include common stock, preferred stock and stock rights, but exclude callable and redeemable preferred stock, treasury stock and convertible bonds.

T   F   13. When a change in the level of ownership requires that an investor change from the equity method to the LCM, the investment account should be adjusted retroactively to reflect the new method.

T   F   14. When the fair value of a depreciable asset exceeds its book value at acquisition, the equity method requires a periodic increase in both the investment account and investment income.

EXERCISE 1

On January 2, 1991, Michael Corporation purchased 5,000 shares of Basket Company's common stock from a national stock exchange for $290,000. The investment represents 40 percent of Basket's equity interest and is to be held as a long-term investment. Michael received dividends of $2.5 per share on December 10, 1991, and Basket reported net income of $120,000 for the year. At December 31, 1991, the market value of Basket's common stock was $53 per share.

Additional information:

1. Immediately before the acquisition, Basket reported a book value of its net assets as $500,000, and the fair value of an equipment was $50,000 above its book value. The equipment had a remaining useful life of 5 years.

2. The remainder of the excess of the cost of the investment over the book value of net assets purchased was attributable to goodwill, amortized over 20 years.

Required: Prepare the required journal entries for Michael Corporation to record the investment.

1. January 2, 1991:

2. December 10, 1991:

3. December 31, 1991:

   a.   To record Michael's share in Basket's reported income:

   b.   To amortize the difference between the fair value and the book value of depreciable assets:

   c.   To amortize the purchased goodwill:

EXERCISE 2

Based on the same data as in **Exercise 1** except that the acquired common stock represents a 10% of Basket's equity interest.

Required: Prepare the journal entries required by Michael for the investment.

   1.   January 2, 1991:

   2.   December 10, 1991:

   3.   December 31, 1991:

EXERCISE 3

Golf Corporation purchased common shares of Club Company and Ball Company for temporary investment purposes as follows:

a.   On January 2, 1991, purchased 300 shares of Club Company's stock at $25 per share, plus a brokerage fee of $150.

b.   On March 5, 1991, purchased 500 shares of Ball Company's stock at $65 per share, plus a brokerage fee of $500.

c.   On June 20, 1991, purchased additional 200 shares of Club Company's stock at $28 per share, plus brokerage fee of $110.

d.   On October 15, 1991, received from Ball Company cash dividends of $1 per share. The dividends were not liquidating.

e.   On November 1, 1991, sold 100 shares of Club's common at $32 per share. Incurred brokerage fee of $100.

f.   On December 31, 1991, market prices were: Club's common, $28 per share, and Ball's common, $62 per share.

g.   On December 31, 1992, market prices were: Club's common, $21 per share, and Ball's common, $60 per share.

Required:

Give an entry to record each of the investment transactions and year-end adjustments, applying the **allowance** method:

a.   January 2, 1991:

b.   March 5, 1991:

c.   June 20, 1991:

d.   October 15, 1991:

e.   November 1, 1991:

f.   December 31, 1991: (year-end adjustment)

g.   December 31, 1992: (year-end adjustment)

MULTIPLE CHOICE

Enter the letter corresponding to the response which **best** completes each of the following statements or questions.

_____ 1. For market value to be used as the basis for valuation of a firm's marketable equity securities (held as a temporary investment) under the allowance method:

   a. management's intention must be to dispose of the securities within one year.
   b. the market value must be less than cost for each equity security in the portfolio.
   c. the market value must approximate historical cost.
   d. the aggregate market value must be less than the aggregate cost of a portfolio.

_____ 2. Which of the following statements is **untrue** regarding investments in equity securities?

   a. If the investor owns less than 20% of the investee's marketable voting stock for temporary investment, the **LCM method** generally is required.
   b. If the investor owns more than 20% of the investee's nonmarketable voting stock for long-term investment, the **equity method** is generally required.
   c. If the investor owns less than 20% of the investee's common stock for long-term investment, the **equity method must** be used.
   d. If the investor owns 50% of the investee's voting stock for temporary investment, the **LCM method** is appropriate.

_____ 3. Corporations invest in the securities of other companies for each of the following reasons *except*:

   a. to earn a return on otherwise idle cash.
   b. to ensure a supply of a required raw material.
   c. to expand their business operations.
   d. to report intercompany profit.

_____ 4. The unrealized loss on **current** investment in marketable equity securities due to a decline in market price is:

   a. reported in the shareholders' equity section of the balance sheet.
   b. included in the determination of income from operations.
   c. reported as extraordinary items.
   d. reported in the liability section of the balance sheet.

_____ 5. In the application of the equity method, dividends from the investee should be accounted for as:

   a. an increase in the investment account.
   b. a reduction in the investment account.
   c. dividend revenue.
   d. an extraordinary item.

6. What is the most appropriate basis for recording the acquisition of 40% of the voting stock of another corporation in a noncash transaction?

   a. at the book value of the stock acquired.
   b. at the par value of the stock acquired.
   c. at the book value of the consideration given.
   d. at the market value of the consideration given.

7. A marketable equity security is transferred from a current portfolio to a noncurrent portfolio, the security should be transferred at the:

   a. carrying value of the security, if higher than cost.
   b. original cost of the security, regardless of the market.
   c. market value of the security, regardless of the cost.
   d. lower of cost or market.

8. When the equity method is changed to the allowance method:

   a. no adjustment to the carrying amount of the investment is required.
   b. the investment account should be adjusted to the original cost of the investment.
   c. the investment account should be adjusted to the lower of cost or market.
   d. the investment account should be adjusted to the market, regardless of the cost.

9. Primary Investment Company purchased marketable equity securities for temporary investment. The cost and market value on December 31, 1991 of its current portfolio were as follows:

	Cost	Market
Alpha common	$1,000	$1,200
Beta common	5,450	5,000
Theta common	3,000	2,800
Total	$9,450	$9,000

   Assuming that, at the beginning of 1991, Primary's valuation allowance account had a balance of $500, Primary should report in its 1991 financial statements:

   a. unrealized loss of $450.
   b. unrealized loss of $650.
   c. unrealized gain of $500, and unrealized loss of $450.
   d. recovery of unrealized loss of $50.

10. Based on the same data as in question 9, except that Primary sold its holding of Theta's common on December 31, 1991 for $3,500, and paid commission of $50. Primary should report in its 1991 financial statements:

   a. a realized gain of $450, and a recovery of unrealized loss of $250.
   b. realized gain of $700.
   c. unrealized loss of $50.
   d. recovery of unrealized loss of $150.

_____ 11. On January 2, 1991, Hawk Inc. bought 40% of the outstanding common stock of Dove Company for $400,000 cash. Hawk accounts for this investment by the equity method. At the date of acquisition of the stock, Dove's net assets had a book value as well as a fair value of $800,000. Any purchased goodwill should be amortized over 40 years. Dove's net income for the year ended December 31, 1991, was $20,000. During 1991, Dove paid cash dividends of $10,000.

Hawk should recognize investment income for 1991 of:

a. $4,000
b. $6,000
c. $8,000
d. $7,800

_____ 12. Based on the same data as in question 11, Hawk's investment account should have a balance on December 31, 1991 of:

a. $400,000
b. $478,800
c. $438,800
d. $402,000

_____ 13. Based on the same data as in question 11 except that, at the acquisition of the stock, Dove's book value of net assets was $700,000. The difference between the book value and the fair value was attributable to a building, which had a remaining useful life of 10 years.

Hawk should recognize investment income for 1991 of:

a. $2,000
b. $3,400
c. $7,400
d. $7,800

_____ 14. During 1991, its first year of operation, Twin Investment Company purchased several marketable equity securities, and at December 31, 1991, had the following investments:

	Cost	Market *
Short-term:		
Security A	$1,000	$1,500
Security B	5,000	3,000
Total	$6,000	$4,500
Long-term:		
Security X	$4,000	$3,600
Security Y	4,400	3,000
Total	$8,400	$6,600

Using the LCM approach Twin should establish a valuation allowance at December 31, 1991 with a corresponding charge against:

Income

a. $0
b. $3,300
c. $1,500
d. $1,800

*Non permanent decline in market

SOLUTIONS TO REVIEW QUESTIONS AND EXERCISES

TRUE-FALSE

1.	T	5.	T	9.	F	13.	F
2.	T	6.	F	10.	T	14.	F
3.	T	7.	T	11.	F		
4.	T	8.	F	12.	T		

EXERCISE 1

1. January 2, 1991:

Investment in common stock, long-term	290,000	
Cash		290,000

2. December 10, 1991:

Cash (5,000 Shares x $2.5)	12,500	
Investment in common stock, long-term		12,500

3. December 31, 1991:

    a. To record Michael's share in Basket's reported income:

Investment in common stock, long-term	48,000	
Investment income ($120,000 x 40%)		48,000

    b. To amortize the difference between the fair value and the book value of depreciable assets:

Investment income ($50,000 x 40% / 5)	4,000	
Investment in common stock, long-term		4,000

    c. To amortized the purchased goodwill:

Investment income {[[$290,000-($550,000 x 40%)]/20}	3,500	
Investment in common stock, long-term		3,500

EXERCISE 2

1.   January 2, 1991:

Investment in marketable equity securities	290,000	
Cash		290,000

2.   December 10, 1991:

Cash (5,000 shares x $2.5)	12,500	
Dividends income		12,500

3.   December 31, 1991:

No entry as cost method is used for long term investment

EXERCISE 3

a.   January 2, 1991: To record investment in Club's common:

Investment in stock, short-term	7,650	
Cash (300 shares x $25) + $150		7,650

b.   March 5, 1991: To record investment in Ball's common:

Investment in stock, short-term	33,000	
Cash (500 shares x $65) + $500		33,000

c.   June 20, 1991: To record investment in Club's common:

Investment in stock, short-term	5,710	
Cash (200 shares x $28) + $110		5,710

d.   October 15, 1991: To record receipt of Ball's cash dividends:

Cash (500 shares x $1)	500	
Dividends income		500

e.   November 1, 1991: to record disposal of Club's common:
                         (FIFO cost = 100 shares x $25 x 102%)

Cash (100 shares x $32 - $100)	3,100	
Investment in stock, short-term		2,672
Realized gain on investment		428
[(7650 + 5710) / 500] x 100		

f. December 31, 1991: To record unrealized loss:

Unrealized loss on investment   1,488*
   Allowance to reduce investment to market   1,488

* Unrealized loss is calculated as follows:

	Cost	Market	Difference
Club's stock	$10,688	$11,200	$ (512)
Ball's stock	33,000	31,000	2,000
Total	$43,812	$42,200	$1,488

g. December 31, 1992: To record incremental unrealized loss:

Unrealized loss on investment   3,800 *
   Allowance to reduce investment to market   3,800

* Accumulated unrealized loss is calculated as follows:

	Cost	Market	Difference
Club's stock	$10,688	$ 8,400	$2,288
Ball's stock	33,000	30,000	3,000
Total	$43,812	$38,400	$5,288

Adjustment to allowance = $5,288 - $1,488 = **$3,800**.

MULTIPLE CHOICE

1.	d	5.	b	9.	d	13.	a
2.	c	6.	d	10.	a	14.	c
3.	d	7.	d	11.	b		
4.	b	8.	a	12.	d		

Computations and explanations:

9.   (d)   To determine change in valuation allowance:

        January 1, 1991 $500
        December 31, 1991 ($9,450 - $9,000)   450

        Adjustment for recovery of unrealized loss $ 50

10. (a)

   (1) To determine realized gain on investment:

Cash proceeds	$3,500
Less: Commission	50
Cost of investment	3,000
Realized gain	$ 450

   (2) To determine change in valuation allowance:

January 1, 1991	$500
December 31, 1991 ($6,450 - $6,200)	250
Adjustment for recovery of unrealized loss	$250

11. (b) To calculate investment income:

Share in reported income ($20,000 x 40%)	$8,000
Amortization of goodwill:	
[($400,000 - $800,000 x 40%) / 40]	(2,000)
Investment income	$6,000

12. (d) To calculate the carrying value of investment account:

Initial cost of investment	$400,000
Recognized investment income	6,000
Dividends received ($10,000 x 40%)	(4,000)
Balance, December 31, 1991	$402,000

13. (a) To calculate investment income:

Share in reported income ($20,000 x 40%)	$8,000
Amortization for difference between fair and book value of building	
($100,000 x 40%) / 10	(4,000)
Amortization of goodwill	
[($400,000 - $800,000 x 40%) / 40]	(2,000)
Investment income	$2,000

14.   (c)   To calculate unrealized losses:

	Short-term	Long-term
Aggregate cost	$6,000	$8,400
Aggregate market	4,500	6,600
Unrealized loss	$1,500	$1,800

Note that the unrealized loss of short-term investment is closed to income summary, and that of the long-term investment is not recorded (the decline in market value is temporary).

CHAPTER 15

Short-Term Liabilities

CHAPTER OBJECTIVES

This chapter is designed to enable students to:

A.   Define a liability and specify its characteristics.

B.   Distinguish between short-term (current) and long-term liabilities.

C.   Explain when it is appropriate to recognize a liability in a firm's accounts and how to measure the value attached to the liability.

D.   Properly account for interest-bearing and noninterest-bearing current liabilities as well as for notes with unrealistic interest rates.

E.   Explain why cash collected in advance of delivery of a good or service creates a liability for the firm.

F.   Properly account for the incurrence and payment of short-term liabilities.

G.   Define contingent and estimated liabilities and appropriately account for or provide disclosure.

CHAPTER OVERVIEW

A.   The *CICA Handbook*, has defined a **liability** as the "obligation of an entity arising from past transactions or events, the settlement of which may result in the transfer or use of assets, provision of services or other yielding of economic benefits in the future." Thus a liability possesses three essential characteristics:

*   An obligation exists that can be satisfied only by the transfer of an asset or a service to another entity.
*   The obligation must be unavoidable.
*   The event that gave rise to the obligation has occurred.

For financial reporting, liabilities are classified as current (short-term) or noncurrent (long-term). This chapter discusses the concept of and items typically classified as current liabilities.

B.   **Current (short-term) liabilities** are defined as "amounts payable within one year from the date of the balance sheet or within the normal operating cycle, where this is longer than a year. Current assets are those assets expected to be converted to cash or used in normal operations during the operating cycle of the business, or one year from the balance date, whichever is longer. Because of the association between current assets and current liabilities, the time dimension that applies to current assets also generally applies to current liabilities. Liabilities that do not conform to this definition are called *long-term*, or noncurrent, liabilities.

The usual types of current liabilities are discussed as follows:

C.   When a liability is incurred in conformity with the definition, it should be immediately recognized and recorded. The *Handbook* definition of a liability is important because it is specific about the essential distinctions defining a debt. The amount of a liability conceptually should be measured as the present value of all future cash payments (or the cash equivalent of non-cash assets and services), discounted at an interest rate consistent with the risks involved. A liability involves a principal amount that is subject to interest, whether specific or not, and interest on the principal amount, which is incurred as time passes.

Accounting recognition of a liability should take place on the date the liability is incurred. The transaction that creates a liability usually identifies the date when the obligation comes into existence. However, the recognition date of a liability is not always clear cut, such as in the case of an injury to an employee, or outsider, when the final determination of the existence of a liability depends on the legal decision of a court of law.

Furthermore, current liabilities can influence operations in a way that long-term liabilities generally do not because current liabilities represent a claim on current resources that resources that are thereby unavailable for day-to-day operations. These claims differ from long-term liabilities, such as bonds, that mature years into the future. The distinction is critical to the classification of liabilities as either current or long-term.

Measurement of the amount of a liability sometimes is difficult. The transaction that creates a liability usually provides the basis for measuring its amount. Measuring the amount of a liability is directly related to its cause.

The usual types of current liabilities are discussed as follows:

1.   Accounts Payable (or Trade Accounts Payable)

Accounts payable are obligations to suppliers of goods or services that arise from ongoing business operations including the acquisition of merchandise, materials, supplies, and services which are used in the production and/or sale of goods and services.

In general, accounts payable are recognized when legal title to the goods passes or when the services are received. They are typically recorded at the amount due. If a cash discount is involved, the related accounts payable may be recorded using either the **gross** or the **net approach** similar to their counterparts in accounts receivable as discussed in Chapter 8. It is noted that the amount of cash discount is usually immaterial and the issue is relatively minor.

2. Dividends Payable

The declaration of cash, scrip or property dividends by the board of directors creates a legal obligation for a corporation and should be recorded and reported as a current liability if they are to be paid within the coming year, or operating cycle, whichever is longer. Undeclared dividends of any kind are not recorded because the corporation has no obligation to its stockholders. Nevertheless, undeclared dividends on cumulative preferred stock, known as preferred dividends in arrears, should be disclosed in the notes. A declared stock dividend, on the other hand, is a transfer of retained earnings to contributed capital without sacrificing any future economic benefit, and should thus be reported in the owners' equity section of the balance sheet.

D. Short-Term Notes Payable

A short-term note payable might be a **trade note payable** that arises from the same source as an account payable, or a **nontrade note payable** that arises from other sources including the current maturity of a certain long-term debt. A trade note is customarily recorded at its **face amount**. A nontrade note, on the other hand, should be reported at its **present value**. The present value of a note issued solely for cash is the cash amount received, whereas the present values of other notes are calculated in terms of the respective types of notes and the applicable interest rates. Basically, accounting procedures which deal with notes payable are similar to their counterparts dealing with notes receivable as introduced in Chapter 8.

Depending on whether a rate of interest is explicitly stated, notes are generally classified as interest-bearing and noninterest-bearing. The stated interest rate of an interest-bearing note, furthermore, may or may not be realistic (i.e., the same as the market interest rate). In any case the calculation of the present value of a note is based on the following general equations:

Maturity value (MV) = Face value $(1 + r \times n)$

Present value (PV) = MV $/ (1 + i \times n)$
= Face value $(1 + r \times n) / (1 + i \times n)$

where:
I = Effective (market) interest rate
r = Stated interest rate
n = Term of the note

1. **Interest-bearing note with a realistic stated interest rate:** Assume that Borman Bakery acquired a machine by issuing a six-month note with a face value of $8,000 and a stated interest rate of 10% to be paid at maturity. Further assume that the stated interest rate is realistic (i.e., the stated and the market interest rates are identical), and that the note is issued and matures in the same accounting period:

a. **To determine the present value of the note:**

Since i = r:

Present value = $8,000 (1 + 10% x 6/12) / (1 + 10% x 6/12)
                = **$8,000**

b. **To record the issuance of the note:**

Machinery	8,000	
Notes payable		8,000

c. **To record the payment of the note at maturity:**

Notes payable	8,000	
Interest expense ($8,000 x 10% x 6/12)	400	
Cash		8,400

2. **Interest-bearing note with unrealistic stated interest rate:**   Assume that when Borman Bakery issued the above note, the market interest rate is 16%:

a. **To determine the present value of the note:**

Present value = $8,000 (1 + 10% x 6/12) / (1 + 16% x 6/12)
                = **$7,778**

b. **To record the issuance of the note:**

Machinery	7,778	
Discount on notes payable	222	
Notes payable		8,000

c. **To record the payment of the note at maturity:**

Notes payable	8,000	
Interest expense ($8,000 x 10% x 6/12)	400	
Cash		8,400

d. **To amortize note discount and to adjust interest expense:**

Interest expense	222	
Discount on notes payable		222

3. **Noninterest-bearing note**:   If the note does not bear interest, the face value would include both the cash price of the machine and the implied interest expense. Assuming the $8,000 note does not bear interest and the market interest rate is 16%:

   a. **To determine the present value of the note:**

   Since the note is noninterest-bearing, the maturity value of the note is simply its face value:

   Present value = $8,000 / (1 + 16% x 6/12)
   $$= \$7,407$$

   b. **To record the issuance of the note:**

Machinery	7,407	
Discount on notes payable	593	
Notes payable		8,000

   c. **To record the payment of the note at maturity:**

Notes payable	8,000	
Cash		8,000

   d. **To amortize note discount and to recognize interest expense:**

Interest expense	593	
Discount on notes payable		593

Note that the acquisition cost of the machine is measured by the present value of the note, and the present value of a note is less than its face value if the note does not bear interest or its stated interest rate is unrealistically lower than the market. In these cases the note is discounted. To record a discounted note the following approaches are both acceptable:

1. **The gross approach (as illustrated above):**   The note is recorded at its face value and the excess of the face value over the present value of the note is debited to a contra liability account, i.e., discount on notes payable. The discount is then amortized over the term of the note by making adjustment to interest expense.

2. **The net approach:**   The note is recorded at its present value, note discount is not separately recorded, and the amount paid over the present value of the note is recognized as interest expense.

Note also that if a note is issued in one accounting period and paid in another, a year end adjusting entry to accrue interest expense may be required.

E.   Accrued Liabilities

An expense incurred but for which cash has not been paid is referred to as an accrued expense (liability) and should be recorded by an adjusting entry usually at year end. Accrued liabilities generally due within one year, or an operating cycle, and are classified as short term. Examples of accrued expenses are unpaid salaries earned by employees, unpaid interest owed to creditors and property taxes due to the local government. If salaries of $2,000 incurred but have not been paid by the end of the period, the expense and related liability should be recorded as follows:

Salaries expense	2,000	
Salaries payable		2,000

This adjusting entry may be reversed at the beginning of the following period. With the original adjusting entry reversed, the later payment will be recorded simply by debiting expense, and crediting cash.

1.   Compensated Absences

In addition to an accrual of employees' regular salaries expenses. Any expense due to compensated absences must be recognized (accrued) in the year in which it is earned, provided:

* The absence from work relates to services already rendered.
* The carryover accumulated (or vests).
* The payment is probable (the absence will occur).
* The amount (i.e., cost) can be reliably estimated.

Note that an employer is not required to accrue a liability for **nonvesting** accumulating rights (i.e., can be carried forward) to receive sick pay benefits because of the lower degree of reliability of the estimates and the cost of making those estimates. At the end of each year an adjusting entry should be made to recognize an expense and a liability for those **unused** vacations and holidays earned by employees during the period.

2.   Collection for Third Parties

Provincial and federal laws require businesses to collect current taxes from customers and employees for remittance to designated governmental agencies. These taxes include sales taxes, income taxes withheld from employee paycheques, property taxes, and payroll taxes. Similar collections also are made on behalf of unions, insurance companies, and employee-sponsored activities. When collections are made for third parties, cash and current liabilities both increase. The collections represent liabilities that are settled when the funds are remitted to the designated parties.

A typical entry to record sales revenue and the collection of sales tax is illustrated on the following page, assuming a sale of $200, and a sales tax rate of 8%:

1. **To record the sale:**

Cash [$200 (1 + 8%)]	216	
Sales revenue		200
Sales tax payable ($200 x 8%)		16

2. **To record the remittance:**

Sales tax payable	16	
Cash		16

3. **Advances and Returnable Deposits**

When cash is collected from a customer as an advance payment for products or services or as a deposit which is refundable, the firm is obliged to transfer goods, to render services, or to return the deposits to the customer under certain conditions. Upon receipt of the cash, a liability account (i.e., unearned revenues, or customers deposits) is credited, which is then reported as a current liability if the obligation is expected to be discharged within one year, or an operating cycle if longer. The same rule is applicable to deposits collected from the employees of the firm. Any unclaimed deposits are reported as a miscellaneous revenue.

F. Current Liabilities Conditional to Operating Results

Certain liabilities of a business entity such as follows are based on the results of operations and should be measured and accrued:

1. **Income tax payable.** All the incorporated business entities are legally required to file income tax returns and to pay income taxes. At year end income tax payable is recorded and reported as a current liability. Due to the inevitable discrepancies between tax rules and GAAP, income tax payable as reported in the tax return differs from income tax expense as presented on the financial statements. The accounting procedures used to deal with such discrepancies are covered in Chapter 17 in detail.

2. **Bonus payable.** Many firms pay cash bonuses to selected employees based on revenues, outputs or income. Bonuses increase salaries expenses, which are tax deductible, and establish current liabilities. At year end, bonus expenses should be computed and accrued. Presented below are several commonly employed formulas for computing bonus amounts. Given that:

Income before deducting bonus and tax	**= $10,000**
Bonus rate	**= 10%**
Tax rate	**= 30%**

a. **The bonus is based on income before deducting bonus and tax**

Bonus = Bonus rate x Income before bonus and tax
     = 10% x $10,000
     = $1,000

b. **The bonus is based on income before deducting bonus but after deducting tax:**

Tax = Tax rate x Income before tax but after bonus
= 30% ($10,000 - Bonus)
= $3,000 - 30% x Bonus

Bonus = Bonus rate (Income before bonus and tax - Tax)
= 10% [$10,000 - ($3,000 - 30% x Bonus)]
= $1,000 - $300 + 3% x Bonus
= $700 + 3% x Bonus
= $700 / 97%
= $722

c. **The bonus is based on income after deducting bonus and tax:**

Tax = $3,000 - 30% x Bonus (see b above)

Bonus = Bonus rate (Income before bonus and tax - Bonus - Tax)
= 10% [$10,000 - Bonus - ($3,000 - 30% x Bonus)]
= $1,000 - 10% x Bonus - $300 + 3% x Bonus
= $700 - 7% x bonus
= $700 / 107%
= $654

For the accrual of bonus expenses, the following journal entries are pertinent:

a. **To accrue the bonus:**

Compensation expense	xxxx	
Bonus payable		xxxx

b. **To record the payment:**

Bonus payable	xxxx	
Cash		xxxx

G. Reclassification of Liabilities

1. **Reclassify long-term obligation as current liability.** A long-term obligation generally should be reclassified as a current liability when it becomes payable (or callable) within one year (or operating cycle), **unless** the payment is to be made with a **noncurrent** asset (e.g., if a long-term bond issue is to be paid at maturity with the amounts accumulated in a bond sinking fund). For instance, a 20-year bond is classified as a long-term liability for 19 years, then normally is reclassified as a current liability the 20th year. Furthermore, if the creditor has at the balance sheet date, or will have within one year (or operating cycle, if longer) from that date, the **unilateral right** to demand immediate repayment of the debt under any provision of the debt agreement, the obligation should be reported as a current liability even if its stated maturity date is still years away.

2. **Reclassify current liability as long-term liability.** If a current liability is expected to be **refinanced** with a long-term obligation (e.g., if new bonds will be issued at the maturity of old bonds due within one year, and the proceeds from the second issue will be used to pay the maturity amount of the first issue), the liability should be reported as a **long-term liability** if the following criteria are met:

   1. The agreement must be noncancelable by all parties (except for violations by the debtor) and extend beyond one year from the balance sheet date (or from the start of the operating cycle), whichever is longer.
   2. At the balance sheet date and the issue date, the company must not be in violation of the agreement.
   3. The lender must be financially capable of honoring the agreement.

   If a short-term obligation is to be excluded from current liabilities under a financing agreement, footnote disclosure is required and should include:

   1. A general description of the financing agreement.
   2. The terms of any new obligation to be incurred.
   3. The terms of any equity security to be issued.

J. Contingencies and Estimated Liabilities

A **contingency** is defined in the *CICA Handbook*, paragraph 3290.02, as an existing condition, or situation, involving uncertainty as to possible gain (hereinafter, 'gain contingency') or a loss (hereinafter, 'loss contingency') to an enterprise that will ultimately be resolved when one or more future events occur or fail to occur. Resolution of the uncertainty may confirm the acquisition of an asset of the reduction of a liability or the loss or impairment of an asset or the incurrence of a liability.

This section is divided into three parts:

* Contingent liabilities (loss contingencies) that must be accrued and reported at estimated dollar amounts in the body of the financial statements.
* Contingent liabilities that are reported only in the notes to the financial statements.
* Gain contingencies.

The Handbook specifies particular accounting treatments on the basis of whether the contingency is:

1. **Likely.** The chance of the occurrence (or non-occurrence) of the future event is high.
2. **Unlikely.** The chance of the occurrence (or non-occurrence) of the future event is slight.
3. **Not determinable.** The chance of the occurrence (or non-occurrence) of the future event cannot be determined.

A loss is recognized and a liability is accrued if the loss contingency is **both** likely and reasonable estimated. If the occurrence of the loss is remote, no disclosure is required. If the occurrence of the loss is probable, but the amount cannot be reasonably estimated, or if the occurrence of loss is only reasonably possible, a footnote may suffice to disclose the contingency. These accounting treatments are summarized as follows:

Probabilistic Nature of the Occurrence of the Contingent Event	Amount Can Be Reasonably Estimated	Amount Cannot Be Resonably Estimated
Loss Contingency		
Likely	1. Accrue both a loss and a liability, and report them in the body of the statements.	2. Do not accrue; report as a note in the financial statements.
Unlikely	3. No accrual or note required; however, a note is permitted.	4. No accrual or note required; however, a note is permitted
Gain Contingency		
Likely	5. No accrual except in very unusual circumstances. Note disclosure required.	6. Note disclosure required; exercise care to avoid misleading inferences.
Unlikely	7. Disclosure not recommended.	

Typical loss contingencies include estimated loss on receivables, litigations, claims and assessments, and anticipated losses on the disposal of a segment of the business. In addition, the following transactions are also related to the occurrence of future event(s):

1. **Warranties and guarantees.** Warranties and guarantees are often offered by a seller or a manufacturer to correct deficiencies of or to give refund for the product sold to its customers for a specified period of time. Some firms report warranty and guarantee expenses when the expenditures are made. Theoretically, however, these expenses, if reasonably measurable, should be accrued in the period of the sale. The estimated warranty and guarantee expenses are recorded by debiting an expense account and crediting a liability account (e.g., estimated warranties payable).

   In addition to the manufacturers' warranties and guarantees, many firms sell separately service contracts for the goods sold. In this case, the sales price of the service contract should be recorded as an unearned service revenue, which will then be transferred to a revenue account when earned.

2. **Premiums.** To promote sales, many firms acquire premium items (e.g., dinner ware) and offer to give them away to their customers at no charge, or to sell them at a reduced price below cost upon receiving coupons, box tops, labels, etc. as a proof of their purchase of a certain quantity of a certain product. The cost of such a premium offer over the reduced price, if any, represents an **expense** and should be recognized in the period of sale of the product. At year end the expense of the outstanding claims expected to be redeemed should be estimated, accrued and reported as a current liability. Typical entries pertinent to premium offers are as follows:

1991 -- Year of sale

To record the purchase of $3,000 premium items for cash:

Inventory of premiums	3,000	
Cash		3,000

To record premiums with a cost of $2,000 distributed to customers at a reduced price of $200:

Cash	200	
Premium expense	1,800	
Inventory of premiums		2,000

To accrue estimated premium expense of $900 at year end:

Premium expense	900	
Estimated liability under premium plan		900

1992 -- Year after sale:

To record distribution of premiums with a cost of $1,000 and a reduced price of $100:

Cash	100	
Estimated liability under premium plan	900	
Inventory of premiums		1,000

3. **Purchase contracts.**   Executory (unperformed) contracts or agreements usually are **not** recorded because a transfer of assets or liabilities has not yet occurred. If the anticipated consideration is material, a note disclosure may be sufficient. For a purchase contract, however, if the commitment is firm (i.e., the contract is noncancelable) and the price declines, a loss on the firm commitment is recognized by debiting loss on purchase commitment and crediting a liability account, e.g., estimated liability on purchase commitment. Later price recovery is disregarded and no gain is recognized for the purchase agreement. On the date of purchase, (a) inventory (or purchase) is debited at the market price on the date when the loss was recognized, or on the date of purchase if lower, (b) estimated liability is debited at the existing amount, (c) cash or accounts payable is credited at the contract price, and (d) to balance the entry if necessary, loss on purchase commitment is debited, indicating a further decline in the price.

KEY CONCEPTS

Contingencies   A contingency is an existing condition, situation, or set of circumstances involving uncertainty as to possible gain or loss that ultimately will be resolved when one or more future events occur or fail to occur. A gain contingency is not recorded. A loss contingency should be recognized if it is likely and estimatable.

Current liabilities   Short-term obligations scheduled to mature within one year or operating cycle, if longer, whose liquidation is expected to require the use of existing current assets.

Liabilities   Probable, future sacrifices of economic benefits arising from the present obligations of a particular entity to transfer goods or provide services to other entity in the future resulting from past transactions or events.

Purchase contracts   Unperformed executory contracts which are usually unrecorded. However, if a purchase contract is noncancelable and the market price declines, a liability is recognized for the estimated loss.

Reclassifying long-term liabilities   Long-term liabilities are reclassified as current liabilities if they become due within one year or operating cycle and whose liquidation is expected to require the use of existing current assets.

Refinancing short-term liabilities   Short-term liabilities expected to be refinanced with a long-term obligation are reported as non-current liabilities if (1) the debtor has the intent to refinance, and (2) the debtor has the ability to refinance.

REVIEW QUESTIONS AND EXERCISES

TRUE-FALSE

Indicate whether each of the following statements is true or false by circling the correct response.

T   F   1.   Notes payable generally should be recorded at their present values, but trade notes due within a year may be recorded at their face values.

T   F   2.   Notes payable are distinguished from accounts payable by whether or not they arise in connection with the firm's normal operations.

T   F   3.   A liability may be recognized and reported even though the **exact** amount of the liability is unknown.

T   F   4.   The existence of a legally enforceable claim is not a prerequisite for an obligation to qualify as a liability.

T   F   5.   In order for a liability to be recognized, the event or transaction causing the liability must have occurred.

T   F   6.   Current maturities of long-term debt should always be reclassified as current liabilities.

T   F   7.   A liability payable within one year should always be classified as a current liability.

T   F   8.   A short-term liability should never be reclassified as a long-term liability.

T   F   9.   Dividends in arrears on cumulative preferred stock should be accrued as a current liability.

T   F   10. It is not required to accrue a liability for employees' sick pay that accumulates but is **nonvesting.**

T   F   11. A liability for a loss contingency should be accrued if (a) it is reasonably possible that assets have been impaired and (b) the amount of the loss can be reasonably estimated.

T   F   12. Footnote disclosure is required for those loss contingencies for which an impairment of assets is reasonably possible.

T   F   13. A gain contingency usually is recognized in the statement of income when an increase in assets is reasonably possible and the amount is reasonably measurable.

T   F   14. A noninterest-bearing note does not give rise to the problem of interest expense.

EXERCISE 1

Indicate with the appropriate code the manner in which each of the following usually should be reported on a balance sheet.

ITEMS

____ 1. Accounts payable.

____ 2. Six-month note payable.

____ 3. Preferred dividends in arrears.

____ 4. Cash and property dividends payable.

____ 5. Two-year note payable.

____ 6. Revenues collected in advance.

____ 7. Accrued expenses.

____ 8. Customers' deposits returnable within a year.

____ 9. Unlikely possibility of losing a lawsuit.

____ 10. Likely possibility of loss of $35,000 from pending lawsuit.

____ 11. Likely loss of $53,000 expected to incur in one year.

____ 12. Long-term debt which is subject to creditor's legal right to demand immediate repayment within one year.

____ 13. Short-term obligation expected to be financed on a long-term basis.

____ 14. Bonus payable.

REPORTING

CL = Current liability

LTL = Long-term liability

ND = Note disclosure

NR = Not reported

EXERCISE 2

Holigan Company acquired a piece of equipment by issuing a 8%, one-year, $12,000 note on October 1, 1991.

Required: For each of the following situations determine the present value of the note and prepare journal entries as indicated:

1. **The stated interest rate is realistic:**

    a.   Determine the present value of the note.

    b.   Record the issuance of the note.

    c.   Record year end adjustment.

    d.   Record the payment of the note.

2. **The market interest rate is 14%.**

    a.   Determine the present value of the note.

    b.   Record the issuance of the note.

c.   Record year end adjustment (Straight-line amortization):

d.   Record the payment of the note and amortization of discount:

EXERCISE 3

Berry Corporation entered into an agreement on July 10, 1991 to acquire 10,000 units of merchandise at $12 per unit. On December 31, 1991 the market price of the merchandise fell to $10 per unit. Assume the agreement was noncancelable, and the merchandise was delivered on May 15, 1992, when the market price was (a) recovered to $11, and (b) further declined to $9.

Required: Record the above transactions and year end adjustment as appropriate.

1.   July 10, 1991 -- To record the agreement:

2.   December 31, 1991 -- To record loss on purchase contract:

3.   a.   May 15, 1992 -- To record the purchase (Market price = $11):

     b.   May 15, 1992 -- To record the purchase (Market price = $9):

EXERCISE 4

Green Cereal offers an Almighty Calculator in exchange for 10 return box tops. The cost of the calculator is $15 per piece. In 1991, Green sold 50,000 boxes of cereal at $5 per box, 60% of which will be redeemed. At the end of 1991, 10,000 box tops had been redeemed.

Required: Prepare entry for each of the following:

1. **To record the sale for 1991.**

2. **To record the redemption of box tops in 1991.**

3. **To adjust premiums expense at the end of 1991:**

MULTIPLE CHOICE

Enter the letter corresponding to the response which **best** completes each of the following statements or questions.

_____ 1. The essential characteristics of a liability do **not** include:

   a. It represents an ownership interest.
   b. It is a present duty or responsibility to transfer assets or provide services.
   c. It is an obligation of a particular entity.
   d. The transaction or event obligating the entity has happened.

_____ 2. Which of the following typically would **not** be classified as a current liability?

   a. bonds payable maturing within one year.
   b. a guarantee of the indebtedness of another party.
   c. nontrade notes payable.
   d. rent revenue received in advance.

_____ 3. Which of the following statements concerning dividends is **untrue?**

   a. Once declared, a cash dividend on common stock becomes a liability of the corporation.
   b. Since a dividend is generally paid within a month or so, it usually is classified as current.
   c. Preferred dividends in arrears should not be accrued as a liability.
   d. Once declared, preferred dividends should be disclosed via footnote.

_____ 4. An employer should accrue a liability for compensation of employees' future absences if certain conditions exist. Each of the following is a condition for accrual except:

a. the payment for those benefits is probable.
b. the employee has the right to carry forward the vesting benefits beyond the current period.
c. the amount of payment is known.
d. the benefits have been earned.

_____ 5. Which of the following loss contingencies generally does not require accrual?

a. product warranties.
b. lawsuits with probable negative outcome.
c. premium offers to customers.
d. obligations related to unasserted claims.

6. A loss on a purchase contract should be recognized if:

a. The contract is cancelable.
b. The contract is noncancelable and the market price remains stable.
c. The contract is noncancelable and the market price is higher than the contract price.
d. The contract is noncancelable and the market price is lower than the contract price.

_____ 7. After a loss on a purchase contract is recognized, a later acquisition of the merchandise under the contract should be valued at:

a. the contract price.
b. the market price at the date of purchase.
c. the market price at the date of recognizing the loss.
d. the market price at the date of purchase, or at the date of recognizing the loss, whichever is lower.

_____ 8. The occurrence of a loss contingency is likely, but the amount cannot be reasonably estimated, the loss contingency should be:

a. recorded.
b. disclosed in notes.
c. ignored.
d. either of the above.

____ 9. On January 1, 1991 Prima Pasta Ltd. agreed to grant its employees two weeks vacation each year, with the provision that vacations earned in a particular year could be taken the following year. For the year ended December 31, 1991, all six of Prima's employees earned $600 per week each. Five of these vacation weeks were not taken during 1991. In Prima's statement of income, how much expense should be reported for compensated absences for 1991?

   a. $ 600
   b. $1,200
   c. $7,200
   d. $3,000

____ 10. Marks Taucki Ltd. has $1,000,000 of notes payable due on April 1, 1992. On January 2, 1992, Marks signed an agreement to borrow up to $800,000 to refinance the notes payable on a long-term basis. On the December 31, 1991 balance sheet, Marks should classify:

   a. $200,000 of notes payable as short-term and $800,000 as long-term obligations.
   b. $200,000 of notes payable as long-term and $800,000 as short-term obligations.
   c. $1,000,000 as short-term obligations.
   d. $1,000,000 as long-term obligations.

____ 11. Holly Fabrics borrowed cash from a local bank by issuing a $5,000, 6-month, noninterest-bearing note. Assuming an effective interest rate of 10%, the principal amount that Holly borrowed from the bank is:

   a. $5,000
   b. $4,500
   c. $4,762
   d. $5,500

____ 12. During 1991 Alberta Company introduced a new line of appliances that carry a two-year warranty against manufacturer's defects. Based on industry experience, warranty costs are estimated at 3% of sales in the year of sale and 7% in the year after sale. Sales and actual warranty expenditures for the first two-year period were as follows:

	Sales	Actual warranty expenditures
1991	$30,000	$ 900
1992	$45,000	$3,450

What amount should Alberta report as the warranty expense for 1992?

   a. $3,000
   b. $4,500
   c. $7,500
   d. $3,450

_____ 13. Based on the same data as in Question 12, what amount should Alberta report as estimated warranty liability at December 31, 1992?

    a. $4,050
    b. $3,450
    c. $3,150
    d. $3,300

_____ 14. A company entered into an agreement with its employees to provide bonus at 10% of income before deducting bonus but after deducting tax. Income before tax and bonus for 1991 is $50,000, and the applicable tax rate is 34%. The bonus liability to be accrued for 1991 is:

    a. $3,416
    b. $1,700
    c. $3,300
    d. $4,211

SOLUTIONS TO REVIEW QUESTIONS AND EXERCISES

TRUE-FALSE

1.	T	5.	T	9.	F	13.	F
2.	F	6.	F	10.	T	14.	F
3.	T	7.	F	11.	F		
4.	T	8.	F	12.	T		

EXERCISE 1

1.	CL	5.	LTL	9.	NR	13.	LTL
2.	CL	6.	CL	10.	ND	14.	CL
3.	NR	7.	CL	11.	CL		
4.	CL	8.	CL	12.	CL		

EXERCISE 2

1. **The stated interest rate is realistic:**

    a. **October 1, 1991 -- Determine the present value of the note.**

    Since the stated interest is realistic:

    Present value = Face value = $12,000.

    b. **October 1, 1991 -- Record the issuance of the note.**

Equipment	12,000	
Notes payable		12,000

    c. **December 31, 1991 -- Record year end adjustment.**

Interest expense ($12,000 x 8% x 3/12)	240	
Interest payable		240

    Assuming no reversing entry was made.

d.   **October 1, 1992 – Record the payment of the note.**

Notes payable	12,000	
Interest payable	240	
Interest expense ($12,000 x 8% x 9/12)	720	
Cash		12,960

2.   **The market interest rate is 14%.**

a.   **October 1, 1991 – Determine the present value of the note.**

Present value = $12,000 (1 + 8%)/(1 + 14%)
              = $11,369

b.   **October 1, 1991 – Record the issuance of the note.**

Equipment	11,369	
Discount on notes payable	631	
Notes payable		12,000

c.   **December 31, 1991 -- Record year end adjustment (Straight-line amortization):**

Interest expense	398	
Discount on notes payable ($631 x 3/12)		158
Interest payable ($12,000 x 8% x 3/12)		240

Assuming no reversing entry.

d.   **October 1, 1992 – Record the payment of the note and amortization of discount:**

Notes payable	12,000	
Interest payable	240	
Interest expense	1,193	
Cash ($12,000 x 108%)		12,960
Discount on notes payable ($631 - $158)		473

EXERCISE 3

1. **July 10, 1991 -- To record the agreement:**

    None.

2. **December 31, 1991 -- To record loss on purchase contract:**

Unrealized loss on purchase contract		
[10,000 x ($12 - $10)]	20,000	
Estimated liability on purchase contract		20,000

3. a. **May 15, 1992 -- To record the purchase (Market price = $11):**

Purchases (10,000 x $10)	100,000	
Estimated liability on purchase contract	20,000	
Cash		120,000

    b. **May 15, 1992 -- To record the purchase (Market price = $9):**

Purchases (10,000 x $9)	90,000	
Estimated liability on purchase contract	20,000	
Loss on purchase contract	10,000	
Cash		120,000

EXERCISE 4

1. **To record the sale for 1991.**

Cash	250,000	
Sales (50,000 x $5)		250,000

2. **To record the redemption of box tops in 1991.**

Premium expense [(10,000 / 10) x $15]	15,000	
Inventory of premiums		15,000

3. **To adjust premium expense at the end of 1991:**

Premium expense		
[(50,000 x 60% - 10,000) / 10] x $15	30,000	
Estimated premium liability		30,000

MULTIPLE CHOICE:

1.	a	5.	d	9.	c	13.	c
2.	b	6.	d	10.	a	14.	a
3.	d	7.	d	11.	c		
4.	c	8.	b	12.	b		

Computations:

9. (c) Compensated absence expense
= 6 x 2 weeks x $600
= $7,200.

10. (a) Long-term liability
= $800,000, the amount to be refinanced on long-term basis.

Short-term liability
= $200,000, the amount not to be refinanced.

11. (c) Present value of noninterest-bearing note
= $5,000 / (1 + 10% x 6/12)
= $4,762.

12. (b) Premiums expense for 1992
= Sales in 1992 x total percentage of redemption
= $45,000 (3% + 7%)
= $4,500.

13. (c) Estimated premiums liability at December 31, 1992
= Estimated premiums expense to date - Premiums expenditures to date
= [($30,000 + $45,000) x (3% + 7%)] - ($900 + $3,450)
= $7,500 - $4,350
= $3,150 (or $45,000 x 7% = $3,150).

14. (a) The bonus is on income before deducting bonus but after deducting tax:

Tax = Tax rate x Income before tax but after bonus
= 34% ($50,000 - Bonus)
= $17,000 - 34% x Bonus

Bonus = Bonus rate (Income before bonus and tax - Tax)
= 10% [$50,000 - ($17,000 - 34% x Bonus)]
= $5,000 - $1,700 + 3.4% x Bonus
= $3,300 + 3.4% x Bonus
= $3,300 / 96.6%
= $3,416.

CHAPTER 16

Long-Term Liabilities

CHAPTER OBJECTIVES

This chapter is designed to enable students to:

A.   Define long-term liabilities and value them for financial reporting purposes.

B.   Describe the characteristics of bonds and compute the price of a bond at issuance.

C.   Account for basic and more complex bond situations from the viewpoints of both the issuer and investor.

D.   Discuss the accounting issues surrounding long-term debt instruments issued with equity rights.

E.   Describe the different ways long-term debt may be extinguished.

F.   Calculate the value of long-term notes and measure periodic interest.

G.   Account for serial bonds.

H.   Discuss the issues underlying accounting for troubled debt restructuring.

CHAPTER OVERVIEW

A.   *CICA Handbook*, paragraph 1000.28, defines liabilities as obligations of an entity arising from past transactions or events, the settlement of which may result in the transfer or use of assets, provision of services or other yielding of economic benefits in the future.

Liabilities are characterized by (1) there being a present obligation, (2) of a particular entity to transfer assets or provide services to another entity in the future, and (3) resulting from a transaction or event which has already happened. Any existing obligations whose liquidation will **not** require the use of current assets are reported as long-term liabilities. Typically they include obligations such as bonds, long-term notes, and mortgages which extend beyond one year from the balance sheet date, or an operating cycle if longer.

B.   **Bonds - Characteristics and Computation of Issurance Price**

1.   Many bond issues are offered through a **prospectus**, a document that includes audited financial statements of the issuer and states the offering price; it also

describes (1) the securities offered, (2) the issuing company's business, and (3) the conditions under which the securities will be sold. To announce the bond issue, an advertisement, which indicates the details of the bond issue and includes a list of the underwriters, typically appears in the financial press.

Investors have a wide variety of investment goals, and as a result, many different types of bonds are issued. The following reflects this diversity;

1. Issuing entity
    a. Industrial bonds: issued by private companies.
    b. Government bonds: issued by public entities.
2. Collateral.
    a. Secured bonds: supported by a lien on specific assets; bondholders have first claim on proceeds from sale of secured assets.
    b. Debenture bonds: unsecured; backed only by issuer's credit; on bankruptcy of issuer, bondholders become general creditors.
3. Purpose of issue.
    a. Purchase money bonds: issued in full or part payment for property.
    b. Refunding bonds: issued to retire existing bonds.
    c. Consolidated bonds: issued to replace several existing issues.
4. Payment of interest.
    a. Ordinary (term) bonds: provide cash interest at a stated rate.
    b. Income bonds: interest is dependent on issuer's income.
    c. Registered bonds: pay interest only to the person in whose name the bond is recorded or registered.
    d. Coupon bonds: pay interest on receipt of coupons detached from bonds.
5. Maturity.
    a. Ordinary (term) bonds: mature at a single specified date.
    b. Serial bonds: mature on several installment dates.
    c. Callable bonds: issuer can retire bonds before maturity date.
    d. Redeemable bonds: bondholder can compel early redemption.
    e. Convertible bonds: bondholder can convert bonds into equity securities of the issuer.

2. Present value use

The *CICA Handbook*, section 1000, recognizes that present value techniques can be used for valuation of assets and liabilities except for the following:

1. Payables from ordinary business transactions due in one year or less.
2. Payables arising from advances and deposits not requiring repayment but which will be applied to the price of goods and services in the future.
3. Payables arising from security deposits.
4. Payables arising from cash lending and demand or savings deposits of financial institutions.
5. Payables whose interest rates are affected by the tax attributes or legal restrictions prescribed by government.
6. Payables between a parent company and its subsidiary, or between subsidiaries of a common parent company.

3. **Bond Prices** If the market and stated interest rate are equal, bonds sell at face value. In this case, the interest payments yield a return equal to the market rate for bonds of similar duration and risk. However, the stated and market rates are frequently not the same. Changes in the market rate and issue price are inversely related. If the market rate (12%) exceeds the stated rate (10%), the issue price of the bonds must be below face value to give the investor a return equal to the market rate. Investors are not willing to pay the $1,000 face value per bond (a price that yields 10%) because competing debt securities yield 12%.

When the market interest rate exceeds the stated rate, bonds sell at a **discount** (below face value). When the stated rate exceeds the market rate, the reverse is true and the bonds sell at a **premium** (above face value). In this case, the bonds offer a stated rate above the market rate, making them more attractive. The price of the bonds increases until the yield decreases to the market rate. The terms *discount* and *premium* do not imply negative or positive qualities of the bond issue. They are the result of adjustments to the selling price to bring the yield rate in line with the market rate on similar bonds.

The investor buys two different types of cash flows when purchasing a bond: principal and interest. The price of a bond issue (and valuation of issuance) equals the present value of these payments discounted at the market rate of interest:

Assuming a 20 year, 10% bond with interest paid semiannually the
= ($100,000 x PVI, 5%, 40) + [($100,000 x 5%) x PVA, 5%, 20]

C. **Bond Accounting for the Issuer and the Investor**

Bonds issued at face value present no accounting complications. If they are (purchased) issued at a discount or premium, however, the discount or premium should be amortized over the term of the bonds to adjust (a) the carrying value of the bonds, and (b) the interest expense reported by the issuer and interest revenue reported by the investor. On the balance sheet, any unamortized discount (premium) is deducted from (added to) the face value of the bonds to show the carrying (book) value of the bonds.

1. **Amortization of bond discount or premium:**   Two methods are in use:

   a. **Straight-line method.**   An equal dollar amount of discount or premium is amortized throughout the bond term. Some accountants consider this method conceptually defective because a constant rate of interest is not maintained. Under GAAP it should be used only when the interest amounts obtained are not materially different from those produced under the interest method.

   b. **Interest method.**   A **constant effective rate** of interest is maintained. The dollar amount of interest is calculated by multiplying the effective rate to the beginning book (carrying) value of the bond, i.e., face value - (+) unamortized discount (premium). Since the book value of the bond changes as the discount or premium is amortized, the dollar amounts of amortization vary from period to period.

Under the interest method, an amortization schedule is often prepared showing interest expense (revenue) to be recorded, discount (premium) to be amortized and the carrying value of the bonds over the term of the bonds.

ILLUSTRATION 1 — Bonds issued at a discount:

On January 1, 1991, Jackson & Janet, Ltd. issued $20,000, 10% bonds, which mature in five years. Homer Inc. purchased the entire bond issue. The market rate for bonds of similar risk and maturity is 12%. Interest of $1,000 ($20,000 x 10% x 6/12) is payable **semiannually** on June 30, and December 31.

(1)   To determine the present value (i.e., issuing price) of the bonds:

Price $= \$20,000 \times pv1_{n=10, i=6\%} + \$1,000 \times pva_{n=10, i=6\%}$
                            $= \$20,000 \times .55839 + \$1,000 \times 7.36009$
                            $= \$11,168 + 7,360$
                            $=$ $\$18,528$

Note that, since interest is paid semiannually:

n $= 5 \times 2 = 10$
r $= 10\% / 2 = 5\%$
i $= 12\% / 2 = 6\%$

(2)   To prepare an amortization schedule:

Date	Cash Interest (10% x 6/12)	Effective Interest (12% x 6/12)	Discount Amortization	Unamortized Bond Discount	Carrying Amount of Bond
	(1)	(2)	(3)	(4)	(5)
Jan. 1, 1991				$1,472.00	$18,528.00
June 30, 1991	$1,000	$1,111.68	$111.68	1,360.32	18,639.68
Dec. 31, 1991	1,000	1,118.38	118.38	1,241.94	18,758.06
June 30, 1992	1,000	1,125.48	125.48	1,116.46	18,883.54
Dec. 31, 1992	1,000	1,133.01	133.01	983.45	19,016.55
June 30, 1993	1,000	1,140.99	140.99	842.46	19,157.54
Dec. 31, 1993	1,000	1,149.45	149.45	693.01	19,306.99
June 30, 1994	1,000	1,158.42	158.42	534.59	19,465.41
Dec. 31, 1994	1,000	1,167.92	167.92	366.67	19,633.33
June 30, 1995	1,000	1,178.00	178.00	188.67	19,811.33
Dec. 31,1995	1,000	1,188.67	188.67	0	20,000.00
Total	$10,000	$11,472.00	$1,472.00		

Notes: (1)   Cash interest = Face value x Stated interest rate.

(2)   Effective interest expense (revenue) = Beginning carrying amount x Effective interest rate.

(3)   Discount amortization = Effective Interest - Cash Interest.

(4)   Unamortized discount = Beginning unamortized discount - discount amortization for the interest period.

(5)   Carrying amount (book value) of bonds = Face value - unamortized discount.

The above amortization table shows that the amortization of discount (or premium) adjusts the carrying value of the bonds towards their face value. This table can be used by both the issuer and the investor of the bonds.

(3)   To record bond transactions and report bond liability for the issuer and bond investment for the investor:

Jackson & Janet (Issuer)	Homer Inc. (Investor)

To record issuance of bonds:
 	
Jan. 1, 1991:
 	
   Cash   18,528.00
   Discount on bonds 1,472.00
      Bonds payable   20,000.00
	To record bond investment:
	
	Jan. 1, 1991
	
	   Investment in bonds 18,528.00
	      Cash 18,528.00

To record interest payments:
 	
June 30, 1991:
 	
   Interest expense 1,111.68
      Discount on bonds   111.68
      Cash   1,000.00
 	
Dec. 31, 1991:
 	
   Interest expense 1,118.38
      Discount on bonds   118.38
      Cash   1,000.00
	To record interest receipts:
	
	June 30, 1991:
	
	   Cash 1,000.00
	   Investment in bonds 111.68
	      Interest revenue 1,111.68
	
	Dec. 31, 1991:
	
	   Cash 1,000.00
	   Investment in bonds 118.38
	      Interest revenue 1,118.38

To report bond liability:
 	
Dec. 31, 1991:
 	
  Long-Term Liabilities:
 	
Bonds payable $20,000.00
Less: Discount on bonds   1,241.94
 	
Net book value $18,758.06
	To report bond investment:
	
	Dec. 31, 1991:
	
	  Investment and Funds:
	
	  Investment in bonds $18,758.06

Repeat the above interest entries using the appropriate figures obtained from the amortization table for the remaining term of the bonds.	

To record retirement of bonds:
 	
Dec. 31, 1995:
 	
   Bonds payable   20,000.00
      Cash   20,000.00
	To record disposal of bonds:
	
	Dec. 31, 1995:
	
	   Cash 20,000.00
	      Investment in bonds 20,000.00

Note that while the issuer records bonds payable at face value and uses a separate discount or premium account, the investor usually records bond investment at the net amount [i.e., book (carrying) value]. Note also that if the straight-line method is applied, interest expense (revenue) would be $1,147.20 ($1,000 + $1,472 / 10) every six months.

(4)   Summary Table: Accounting for Bonds (Issuer)

Assume semiannual interest payments.

> *Price of bond issue* = Present value of principal and interest payments
> = (Face value) (*PV1, e, n*) + (face value) (*s*) (*PVA, e, n*)

Where: *e* = effective interest rate per six-month period.
s = stated interest rate/2.
n = number of semiannual periods in bond term.

> *Initial discount* = Face value - Price of bond issue
> (effective rate exceeds stated rate)

> *Initial premium* = Price of bond issue - face value
> (stated rate exceeds effective rate)

> *Net book value of bonds* = Face value + unamortized premium, or
> Face value - unamortized discount

	Premium	Discount
As maturity approaches:		
Unamortized Portion	Declines	Declines
Net book value	Declines	Increases
Annual interest expense*	Declines	Increases

* Under interest method

Two Methods of Amortizing Premium and Discount

	Straight-Line Method	Interest Method
Annual interest expense	Constant over term	Changes each year
Annual interest expense as a percentage of beginning book value	Changes each year	Constant over term

(5)   (a)   Bond issue cost:

Following the *CICA Handbook*, sec. 3070, costs incurred in connection with the issuance of bonds, such as legal costs, printing costs, and underwriting fees, are recorded separately as **deferred charges** and are amortized over the term of the related bonds. The straight-line method of amortization generally is used for materiality reasons.

(b) **Bonds sold between interest dates:** When bonds are sold between interest dates, the bonds will be sold at the appropriate market price **plus** accrued interest. That is, the proceeds from the sale of a bond include the selling price of the bond and interest accrued since the last interest date to the date of issuance.

ILLUSTRATION 2 -- Bonds issued between interest dates:

On March 1, 1991, Golden Ltd. issued $10,000 of 8%, 5-year bonds at face value. Cash interest is payable at year end.

Since the bonds were issued two months after the last interest date, the accrued interest for the two-month period is:

$$\text{Accrued interest} = \$10,000 \times 8\% \times 2/12$$
$$= \$133$$

Golden Ltd. (Issuer)			Investor		
To record issuance of bonds:			To record bond investment:		
Mar. 1, 1991:			Mar. 1, 1991		
Cash	10,133		Investment in bonds	10,000	
Bonds payable		10,000	Interest revenue	133	
Interest expense		133	Cash		10,133
To record the next interest payment:			To record interest receipt:		
Dec. 31, 1991:			Dec. 31, 1991:		
Interest expense	800		Cash	800	
Cash		800	Interest revenue		800
Interest expense (1991) = $800 − $133 = $667.			Interest revenue (1991) = $800 − $133 = $667.		

3. **Accounting period does not coincide with interest period:** When the accounting period ends between interest dates, it is necessary to accrue interest since the last interest date to the end of accounting period. Assume Witch Way Ltd. issued $100,000 of 8%, 5-year bonds for $92,278 on October 1, 1991. Interest is payable each September 30 and March 31. At the end of 1991, three months' interest must be recorded in a year-end adjusting entry, assuming an effective rate of 10%:

Dec. 31, 1991:

Interest expense ($92,278 x 10% x 3/12)	2,307	
Interest payable ($100,000 x 8% x 3/12)		2,000
Discount on bonds payable		307

D.   Long-term debt instruments issued with equity securities

1.   **Bonds with detachable warrants:**   Occasionally bonds are sold with **detachable** stock warrants as part of the security issue. A stock warrant allows the investor to purchase a specified number of shares of common stock at a specified price. Since stock warrants have value and are usually traded in the market separately from bonds, in essence, two different securities, i.e., the bonds (debt) and the warrants (equity), are being sold as a "package."

Accordingly, at issuance, the package price should be allocated between the two different securities on the basis of their relative market values. If the separate market value of only one of the two securities is determinable, the market value determines the allocation.

The allocation is credited to a contributed capital (owners' equity) account and is based on the market values of the two securities on the date of issuance (the proportional method). If only the warrants, for example, have a readily determinable market value, the bonds are valued at the difference between the total bond price and the market value of the warrants(the incremental method).

In contrast, if the stock purchase warrants are not detachable, no separate market for them exists and the entire bond price is allocated to the bonds.

After the issue price is allocated to the bonds and detachable warrants, bond accounting is not affected by the warrants.

ILLUSTRATION 3 -- Bonds with detachable warrants:

On January 1, 1991, Everything Ltd. issued $100,000 of bonds for $109,000. Attached to the bonds were 5,000 detachable stock warrants, exercisable for 5,000 shares of no par common stock at $12 per share. At issuance, the market value of the bonds sold separately was $101,000. Assume that 80% of the warrants were exercised on December 31, 1991, and the remainder forfeited.

Pertinent journal entries are presented as follows:

Everything Ltd. (Issuer)			Investor		
To record issuance of bonds:			To record bond investment:		
Jan. 1, 1991:			Jan. 1, 1991:		
Cash	109,000		Investment in bonds	101,000	
Bonds payable		100,000	Investment in stock warrants	8,000	
Premium on bonds payable		1,000	Cash		109,000
Stock warrants outstanding		8,000			
To record the issuance of stock:			To record the exercise of stock warrants:		
Dec. 31, 1991:			Dec. 31, 1991:		
Cash (4,000 x $12)	48,000		Investment in stock	54,400	
Stock warrant outstanding	6,400		Investment in stock		
Common stock (4,000 x $12)		54,400	warrants ($8,000 x 80%)		6,400
			Cash		48,000
To record forfeited warrants:			To record forfeited warrants:		
Stock warrants outstanding	1,600		Loss on investment in warrants	1,600	
Paid-in capital			Investment in stock		
- from forfeited warrants		1,600	warrants		1,600

2. **Bonds convertible to common stock:**   A convertible bond is one which can be exchanged for a specified number of shares of capital stock of the issuing company. Although the conversion privilege has market value, no **separate** measure of the market value exists for the conversion feature. Thus, the entire sale price of a convertible bond issue is recorded as debt in exactly the same manner as if the bonds were nonconvertible.

If **converted,** the bonds are removed from the accounting records at their current carrying (book) values. The new stock issued in exchange for the bonds is recorded in terms of either (a) the book value of the retired bonds (i.e., **the book value method**), or (b) the market value of the stock issued (i.e., **the market value method**). The book value method, however, appears more popular.

ILLUSTRATION 4 -- Issuance of convertible bonds:

On January 1, 1991, Federated Chicken Ltd. issued $200,000 of 10-year, 10% convertible bonds at 110 (i.e., 110% of face value). Interest was payable on December 31. The conversion privilege specified that at the option of the investor, each $1,000 bond was convertible into 100 shares of Federated's common stock. On December 31, 1991 when the common stock was selling for $11 per share, the bonds were entirely converted. Assume that premium on bonds was amortized using the straight-line method:

Chicken (Issuer)			Investor		
To record issuance of bonds:			To record bond investment:		
Jan. 1, 1991:			Jan. 1, 1991		
Cash ($200,000 x 110%)	220,000		Investment in bonds	220,000	
Bonds payable		200,000	Cash		220,000
Premium on bonds payable		20,000			
Dec. 31, 1991:			Dec. 31, 1991:		
To record interest:			To record interest:		
Interest expense	18,000		Cash	20,000	
Premium on bonds payable	2,000		Investment in bonds		2,000
Cash		20,000	Interest revenue		18,000
To record conversion:			To record conversion of bonds to stock:		
Book value method:			Book value method:		
Bonds payable	200,000		Investment in common stock	218,000	
Premium on bonds payable	18,000		Investment in bonds		218,000
Common stock		218,000			
Market value method:			Market value method:		
Bonds payable	200,000		Investment in common stock	220,000	
Premium on bonds payable	18,000		Investment in bonds		218,000
Loss on conversion	2,000		Gain on conversion of		
Common stock		220,000	bond investment		2,000

3. **Induced conversion.**   To **induce** prompt conversion of the bond, the issuing company may offer cash or other privilege for the conversion. Upon conversion, the fair value of such an inducement (i.e., the fair value of consideration transferred in excess of the fair value of the stock issuable under the original conversion terms) be recognized as an expense if the inducement has only a limited exercisable time.

E.   Extinguishment of Debt

Bonds and long-term notes outstanding are normally retired when due and the debtor is thus relieved of all the obligations related to the debt. The debtor's obligations may also be relieved by means of debt extinguishment. **Extinguishment** of debt is defined as a transaction or event in which any of the following occurs:

1.   The debtor pays the creditor and is relieved of all obligations with respect to the debt.

2.   The debtor is legally released from being the primary obligor under the debt by having the debt (e.g., mortgage) assumed by a third party or having a third party (e.g., an affiliated company) agreed to become the primary obligator for the debt; or

3.   The debtor places cash or other monetary assets in an irrevocable trust to pay the debt. It is referred to as **in-substance defeasance** because the debtor remains legally liable for the debt. However, the possibility that the debtor will be required to make future payments must be remote.

Debt extinguishment may occur before, at or after maturity. Accounting for debt extinguishment involves:

1.   **Updating related accounts.**   Interest expense, discount or premium and related issue costs are updated to the extinguishment date.

2.   **Recording the extinguishment.**   Record (a) the removal of the liability, unamortized discount (or premium) and related issue costs, (b) the transfer of cash and other resources or new issue of debt securities, and (c) the resulting gain or loss on the extinguishment.

3.   **Reporting the extinguishment.**   Gains and losses on extinguishment (e.g., the difference between the reacquisition price and the carrying value of the debt), net of tax, are aggregated and presented on the income statement as an **extraordinary item**, unless they are from cash purchases of debt made to satisfy sinking-fund requirement. In addition, the nature of the transaction including the means used for extinguishment is disclosed in notes.

4. Summary of Gain and Loss Classification on Debt Settlement

Method of Settlement*	Classification of Gain or Loss
1. Conversion of convertible bonds	Ordinary
2. Induced conversion of convertible bonds (gain, loss, and conversion expense)	Ordinary
3. Direct payment of creditors	Ordinary
4. Sinking-fund purchases made within one year of the date of the extinguishment	Ordinary
5. Use of equity securities to settle debt	Ordinary
6. Retirement of convertible debt	Ordinary
7. Call	Ordinary
8. Refunding	Ordinary
9. Legal release from obligation	Ordinary
10. In-substance defeasance	Ordinary

* The word *settlement* includes any means of debt retirement except for troubled debt restructuring.

F. Long-Term Notes and Mortgages

1. **A long-term note** is a formal document that specifies the terms of a debt. Notes generally are not traded in organized exchanges or markets, and have shorter maturities than bonds. The accounting procedures for long-term and short-term notes payable are almost identical, except that most long-term notes are interest-bearing, and that the interest method is usually applied to record interest expenses.

When a long-term note is exchanged for property, goods or services, the transaction is recorded at the market value of the property, goods or services received or the market value of the note, whichever is more clearly evident. If neither market value is known, the transaction is recorded at the present value of the note, discounted at the effective interest rate as illustrated below:

ILLUSTRATION 5 -- Long-term notes payable:

On January 1, 1991, Lundar Lending Ltd. purchased a machine and signed a three-year, $15,000, 6% note. Interest of $900 is payable annually. Assume neither market value is known and the market interest rate is 10%.

(1) Determine the acquisition cost of the machine:

PV (Machine Cost)
$$= \$15,000 \times pv1_{n=3, i=10\%} + (\$15,000 \times 6\%) \times pva_{n=3, i=10\%}$$
$$= \$15,000 \times .75131 + \$900 \times 2.48685$$
$$= \$11,270 + \$2,238$$
$$= \$13,508$$

(2) Record the purchase of the machine and issuance of the note:

January 1, 1991:

Machinery	13,508	
Discount on notes payable	1,492	
Notes payable		15,000

(3) Prepare the amortization schedule:

Date	Cash Interest (6%)	Effective Interest (10%)	Discount Amortiza-tion	Unamortized Note Discount	Carrying Amount of Note
Jan. 1 1991				$1,492.00	$13,508.00
Dec. 31 1991	$900	$1,350.80	$450.80	1,041.20	13,958.80
Dec. 31 1992	900	1,395.88	495.88	545.32	14,454.68
Dec. 31 1993	900	1,445.32*	545.32*	0	15.000.00
Total	$2,700	$4,192.00	$1,492.00		
* rounded					

(4) Record the interest expenses and interest payments:

Dec. 31, 1991:

Interest expense	1,350.80	
Discount on notes payable		450.80
Cash		900.00

Repeat this interest entry for 1992 and 1993, using the appropriate figures presented in the amortization schedule.

(5) Record the payment of the note:

Dec. 31, 1993:

Notes payable	15,000	
Cash		15,000

2. Special kinds of **mortgage notes** are increasingly used to supplement traditional debt arrangements:

a. In a **point-system mortgage**, the lender charges a specified number of "points" at the loan origination, instead of an otherwise higher interest rate. A **point** reduces the amount of cash the borrower receives by 1% of the loan's face value. Thus, for a $200,000 note specifying four points, the borrower would actually receive $192,000 [$200,000 - ($200,000 x 4%)], but would repay $200,000 at maturity, as well as pay periodic interest based on the stated rate and the $200,000 face value.

Periodic interest expense is recorded at the **effective rate** -- the discount rate which provides a present value of future cash flows on the note equal to the net proceeds (i.e., face value minus points).

b.   In a **shared appreciation mortgage**, the interest rate typically is lower than normal. In return for the lower rate, the lender receives a specified share of the appreciation in the value of the mortgaged assets. Similar to a point-system mortgage, periodic interest expense is recorded at the effective rate, which is the discount rate which provides a present value of future cash payments equal to the face value minus an estimate of the current value of the shared appreciation.

c.   In an **adjustable rate (or variable-rate, or floating-rate) mortgage**, the stated rate changes at specified intervals to reflect changes in the market rate. When the interest rate is adjusted, a new payment is computed to equate the note's principal balance to the present value of all remaining payments using the new interest rate. No other complications arise.

3.   Additional Issues -- LT Liabilities

The incentives to issue imaginative financial instruments are diverse. Firms may wish to: (1) reduce interest rate risk, (2) increase the flexibility and attractiveness of financial instruments in a period of increased competition for capital, (3) lower the overall cost of financing, and (4) seek tax advantages.

Accounting for many of these instruments is not yet specified under GAAP and concerns long-term liabilities with respect to: (1) disclosure, (2) recognition and measurement, and 93) distinguishing between liabilities and equity.

The 1990 Statement of Principles, which applies to *all* entities defines a financial instrument as "any contract that gives rise to both a (recognized or unrecognized) financial asset of one entity and a (recognized or unrecognized) financial liability of another entity."

Six fundamental financial instruments have been tentatively identified: (1) unconditional receivable or payable; (2) receivable or payable conditional on the occurrence of an event beyond the control of either party; (3) forward contract, an unconditional right and obligation to exchange financial instruments; (4) option, a right or obligationto exchange ither financial instuments conditional on the occurrence of an event within the control of one party to the contract; (5) guarantee, a right or obligation to exchange financial instruments conditional on an event outside the control of either party; and (6) equity instrument.

Accounting for instruments that have both equity and liability attributes would have special impact on accounting for liabilities.

The CICA and the IASC are working on the project together and both a Canadian and an international set of standards will emerge.

In an effort to reduce current liabilities, some firms refinance them on a long-term basis. The *CICA Handbook*, paragraph 1510.06, stipulated that "Obligations, otherwise classified as current liabilities, should be excluded from the current liability classification to the extent that contractual arrangements have been made for settlement from other than current assets."

G. Serial Bonds

A **serial bond** issue matures in a series of installments, rather than in one maturity amount. The advantages of serial bonds to the issuer include:

* Less need for a sinking-fund.
* Lower perceived risk of the issue.
* Improved marketability.
* Less burdensome debt retirement schedule.

Serial bonds are sold either as separate issues or as one aggregate issue. If the bonds are sold separately, it is possible to identify the yield rate on each, which normally increases with the length of the term to compensate for increased risk. If sold in the aggregate, the entire bond issue carries a single average yield rate. Either way, the price of serial bonds is the sum of the present values of each issue using the appropriate yield rate. Serial bond valuation is consistent with ordinary bond issues.

Three methods of accounting for serial bonds are available:

Interest method: If the yield rate on each issue is known, each issue is treated as an individual bond issue. If not, the entire issue is treated as one bond issue, and the average yield rate is used to recognize interest. The book value of serial bonds payable is reduced by the face amount of serial bonds retired at each maturity date.

Straight-line method: An equal amount of premium or discount is allocated to each reporting period of each separate issue. Then the amounts for each issue are totaled by reporting period. Total amortization for a reporting period reflects each separate issue outstanding that period. This method is permitted only if it produces results not materially different from the interest method.

Bonds outstanding method: The discount or premium for each separate issue need not be identified under this method. A constant rate of discount or premium per dollar of bond outstanding per period is used for amortization. This modified straight-line method is permitted only if it produces results not materially different from the interest method.

All three methods relate the premium or discount to the total face value of bonds outstanding during the period. This amount decreases by the face value of each maturing issue. Consequently, relative to an ordinary bond, discounts and premiums are amortized more quickly.

H.   Troubled Debt Restructuring

A restructure of troubled debt occurs when a debtor encounters difficulties in making payments on debt and its creditor (i.e., lender) **grants a concession** related to the debt obligation to the debtor. A troubled debt restructuring may involve either of the following:

1. **Settlement of debt.**   A debt is settled outright by transferring assets or equity interest of the debtor to the creditor. The debtor will record a **extraordinary gain**, and the creditor will record an **ordinary loss** for the difference between the book value of the debt and the fair value of the assets or equity interest transferred. The debtor may also need to record first an ordinary gain or loss for the difference between the book value and the fair value of the assets prior to the transfer.

2. **Modification of terms.**   Terms of a troubled debt are modified in favor of the debtor. The accounting treatment depends on whether the total **future cash payments** under the modified terms are **less** or **greater than** the carrying amount of the debt before restructuring:

   a.   If the gross amount of future cash payments is less than the carrying value of the debt, the difference is recorded as an extraordinary gain to the debtor and an ordinary loss to the creditor at the date of restructure. No interest should be recorded thereafter. That is, all subsequent cash payments result in a reduction of principal.

   b.   If the gross amount of future cash payments is greater than the carrying value of the debt, no gain or loss is recognized. Instead, a new effective rate of interest is determined (i.e., the rate that discounts the future cash payments to the carrying value of the debt), and that rate is then used to record interest expense by the debtor and interest revenue by the creditor over the modified term of the debt.

KEY CONCEPTS

Bond issue cost   Bond issue costs such as legal fees and printing costs should be separately recorded as a deferred charge, and are amortized using the straight-line method over the term of the related bonds.

Discount (premium) on bonds (notes)   The difference between the face value and the present value of bonds (notes) is either a discount or a premium, arising from the difference between the stated and the effective interest rates. Any discount (premium) should be amortized over the term of the debt, using the interest method. The straight-line method is allowed only if the resulting difference is immaterial.

Extinguishment of debt   The debtor's obligations are relieved before, at or after the maturity date by (1) reacquiring the debt, (2) having a third party assume the debt, or (3) by placing cash or other monetary assets in an irrevocable trust, known as **in-substance defeasance.** Gains and losses on the extinguishment are aggregated and reported as **an extraordinary item**, except those gains or losses from cash purchase of the debt made to satisfy sinking-fund requirements.

Long-term debt   Probable future sacrifice of economic benefits arising from present obligations whose liquidation will not require the use of current assets. Typically it consists of bonds and notes which extend beyond one year or an operating cycle, whichever is longer.

Troubled debt restructuring   A troubled debt restructuring occurs when a debtor encounters difficulties in making payments on debt and the creditor grants a concession to the debtor. If the debt is settled outright, an extraordinary gain is recognized by the debtor, and an ordinary loss is recognized by the creditor. If the concession is made by a modification of debt terms and if the book value of existing debt exceeds the future cash payments under new terms, the difference is recorded as an extraordinary gain to the debtor, and an ordinary loss to the creditor. If the book value is less than the future cash payments under new terms, a new effective rate should be computed and applied to the calculation of interest.

Selling (issuing) price of bonds (notes)   Bonds and notes are sold (issued) at the present value of all the future cash flows of the debt, i.e., the present value of the principal payable at maturity plus the present value of the periodic cash interest payments. The effective interest rate is used in the calculation of the present values.

Serial Bonds   Bonds mature in periodic installment. A serial bond issue may be accounted for as if the bonds represent different issues with separate maturity dates.

Valuation of long-term debt   Long-term debt is valued by the present value of future principal and cash interest payments, discounted at the effective interest rate.

REVIEW QUESTIONS AND EXERCISES

TRUE-FALSE

Indicate whether each of the following statements is true or false by circling the **correct** response.

T   F   1.   In general, liabilities should be valued at their present value. This requires that the future cash outflows needed to discharge the obligation be discounted at the **stated rate** of interest.

T   F   2.   The cash interest payment on bonds should be calculated using the effective interest rate.

T   F   3.   Although a long-term liability is recorded at present value, the carrying value of the liability should not be adjusted for subsequent changes in the market rate of interest.

T   F   4.   A discount related to a bond issue should be recorded as a deferred charge and reported as an intangible asset.

T   F   5.   A reverse relationship exists between the prevailing market rate of interest and the market price of bonds.

T   F   6.   In a typical **point-system mortgage**, the lender assesses a specified number of points, reducing the amount of cash the borrower receives to some amount less than the face value.

T   F   7.   The straight-line method is **required** in amortizing bond discounts or premiums, unless the use of the interest method would not produce materially different results.

T   F   8.   Current GAAP requires that bond issue costs be combined with any discount or premium upon the issuance of bonds.

T   F   9.   Upon the early extinguishment of debt, any gain or loss is classified as an extraordinary item only if the gain or loss is both unusual and infrequent.

T   F   10. The carrying value of a bond increases over the term to maturity if the bond is sold at a discount.

T   F   11. The amortization of a premium by the interest method creates successive increases in interest expense over the life of the bond.

T   F   12. The entire issue price of a convertible bond issue is recorded as debt in exactly the same manner as if the bonds were nonconvertible.

T   F   13. The issue price of bonds sold with detachable stock warrants is recorded entirely as debt if either the market price of the bonds, or the market price of the warrants is not available.

T   F   14. A troubled debt restructuring may involve either an immediate settlement of the debt or a continuation of the debt under modified terms.

EXERCISE 1

On January 1, 1991, Gordon Ltd. issued $100,000 of 4-year, 10% bonds to yield a market rate of 14%. Cash interest is payable on each December 31.

Required:

1. Compute the selling price of the bonds:

2. Prepare journal entry to record the issuance of bonds on January 1, 1991:

3. Record the first cash interest payment on December 31, 1991:

4. Record the second cash interest payment on December 31, 1992:

5. Record the retirement of the bonds on December 31, 1994:

EXERCISE 2

On April 1, 1991, Potatoe Inc. issued $20,000 of 12%, 10-year bonds to yield interest of 8%. Interest was payable on each April 1. The amortization of bond premium was recorded using the effective interest method. The issue cost of the bonds was $500.

Required:

1. **To determine the selling price of the bonds:**

2. **To record the issuance of the bonds on April 1, 1991:**

3. **To record issue cost incurred on April 1, 1991:**

4. **To prepare an amortization schedule:**

Date	Cash Interest (12%)	Effective Interest (8%)	Premium Amortiza-tion	Unamortized Bond Premium	Carrying Amount of Bonds

5. **To amortize bond issue cost on December 31, 1991:**

6. **To accrue interest on December 31, 1991:**

7. **To reverse the above accrual entry on January 1, 1992:**

8. **To record interest payment on April 1, 1992:**

9. **To record early extinguishment of bonds at 115 on April 1, 1993:**
   (Assume interest payment on that date was appropriately recorded)

EXERCISE 3

On April 1, 1991, Henry Ltd. issued $100,000 of 10% convertible bonds, dated January 1, 1991 for $95,320 plus accrued interest. the 10-year bonds mature 9 9/12 (i.e., 9.75) years from date of issuance and pay interest semiannually on June 30 and December 31. The fiscal period for Henry is the calendar year.

The bonds were entirely converted to 8,000 shares of no par common stock on December 31, 1991 when the market price per share of common stock was $11.25.

Required: Prepare all journal entries for Henry during 1991, assuming that the straight-line method of amortization is used.

1.   **To record the issuance of the bonds on April 1, 1991:**

2.   **To record interest payment on June 30, 1991:**

3.   **To record interest payment on December 31, 1991:**

4.   **To record the conversion of the bonds on December 31, 1991:**

      Book value method:

      Market value method:

MULTIPLE CHOICE

Enter the letter corresponding to the response which **best** completes each of the following statements or questions.

_____ 1. Righton Inc. exchanged land with a fair value of $56,000 for Reliance Company's $80,000, noninterest-bearing, 2-year note. For Righton the $24,000 difference represents:

    a. an ordinary gain on the sale of land.
    b. a premium on notes receivable.
    c. a discount on notes to be amortized over two year period.
    d. an extraordinary item.

_____ 2. When bonds are issued between interest dates:

    a. accrued interest since the last interest date is deducted from the market price of the bond issue.
    b. the initial journal entry at issuance is unaffected by the time of sale.
    c. the determination of the price of the bonds is simplified.
    d. the entry to record the issuance of the bonds will include a credit to interest expense.

_____ 3. In an amortization table that amortizes bond discount by the interest method:

    a. the amount of discount amortized decreases with each interest payment.
    b. the carrying value of the bonds decreases gradually to face value.
    c. the total interest expense is equal to the discount on bonds plus the cash interest paid over the term to maturity.
    d. Bond interest expense decreases over the term to maturity.

_____ 4. With respect to the pricing of a bond issue, which of the following statements is true?

    a. The bond issue will sell at a premium if the stated rate exceeds the market rate.
    b. A bond issue will sell at a discount if the stated rate exceeds the market rate.
    c. The price of a bond issue will be equal to the face value if the nominal rate is equal to the stated rate.
    d. As the market interest rate increases, bond prices generally increase.

_____ 5. A gain on the extinguishment of debt:

    a. should be reported as an extraordinary item if it is unusual or occurs infrequently.
    b. should be reported as an extraordinary item if it is unusual and occurs infrequently.
    c. should always be reported as an extraordinary item.
    d. should be reported as an extraordinary item unless it is from a cash purchase of debt made to satisfy sinking fund requirement.

_____ 6. If a corporation issues bonds on January 1, 1991 and uses the straight-line method to amortize the discount on its bonds payable, Its interest expense for 1991 will be:

    a. less than if the interest method were used.
    b. greater than if the interest method were used.
    c. the same as if the interest method were used.
    d. none of the above.

_____ 7. When bonds are issued at a premium, the carrying amount of long-term liability reported on the balance sheet:

    a. decreases or increases each year depending upon the changes in market interest rate.
    b. decreases each year during the life of the bond.
    c. increases each year during the life of the bond.
    d. decreases or increases each year depending upon the method of amortization used.

_____ 8. When a troubled debt restructuring involves only modification of terms (not settled at the date of restructure), the creditor should recognize a loss when the carrying amount of the debt:

    a. exceeds the present value of future cash payments specified by the new agreement.
    b. is less than the total future cash payments specified by the new agreement.
    c. exceeds the total future cash payments specified by the new agreement.
    d. is less than the present value of future cash payments specified by the new agreement.

_____ 9. Given the following:

Face value of bonds	$500,000
Term of bonds	5 years
Stated interest rate	9%
Date of issuance	Jan. 1, 1991
Interest payment dates	June 30 and December 31
Effective interest rate	10%
Present value of 1:	
for 5 periods at 10%	.62092
for 10 periods at 5%	.61391
Present value of an annuity of 1:	
for 5 periods at 10%	3.79079
for 10 periods at 5%	7.72173

The selling price of the bonds is:

a. $482,248
b. $481,046
c. $480,694
d. $500,000

_____ 10. Frank Company Ltd. issued $100,000 of bonds on January 1, 1991 for $101,000 with an effective rate of 11%. If interest is payable on each July 1 and January 1, the interest expense for the first six-month period is:

a. $10,000
b. $11,110
c. $5,555
d. $5,000

_____ 11. On September 1, 1991 Etsell Brothers issued $10,000 of five year bonds with a selling price of $10,675. The bonds were dated January 1, 1991 and had a stated rate of 12% payable on January 1. The cash amount received by Etsell Brothers at issuance is:

a. $11,075
b. $10,675
c. $11,175
d. $11,475

_____ 12. On January 1, 1991, Watch Company Inc. issued 100 of its 10-year, $1,000 bonds for $85,279. The bonds were issued to yield 12% interest. Stated interest rate is 8% payable each June 30 and December 31. Under the interest method, the amount of discount amortized for 1991 is:

a. $1,117
b. $1,184
c. $2,250
d. $2,301

_____ 13. Western Company Ltd. is indebted to the Left Bank through a $15,000 noninterest-bearing note dated December 31, 1991. On December 31, 1993, Left Bank agreed to settle the note for land having a fair market value of $12,000. Western acquired the land at a cost of $5,000. As a result of the troubled debt restructuring, Western should report an (pretax):

	Ordinary Gain	Extraordinary Gain
a.	0	$10,000
b.	$10,000	0
c.	3,000	7,000
d.	7,000	3,000

_____ 14. Nolan Company Ltd. had $250,000 of outstanding convertible bonds. Each $1,000 bond is convertible to 100 shares of Nolan's $10 par common stock. On March 31, 1991 when the bonds had an unamortized premium of $15,000, 80% of the bonds were converted. Under the book value method, paid-in capital in excess of par resulting from the conversion is:

a. $10,000
b. $12,000
c. $15,000
d. $20,000

SOLUTIONS TO REVIEW QUESTIONS AND EXERCISES

TRUE-FALSE

1.	F	5.	T	9.	F	13.	F
2.	F	6.	T	10.	T	14.	T
3.	T	7.	F	11.	F		
4.	F	8.	F	12.	T		

EXERCISE 1

1. **Compute the selling price of the bonds:**

   Pv = $100,000 (Pv1, 4%, 4) + $100,000 (.1) (PVA, 4%, 4)
   = $100,000 x .59208 + $10,000 x 2.91371
   = $59,208 + $29,137
   = $88,345

2. **Jan. 1, 1991 — Record the issuance of bonds:**

Cash	88,345	
Discount on bonds	11,655	
Bonds payable		100,000

3. **Dec. 31, 1991 -- Record the first cash interest payment:**

Interest expense ($88,345 x 14%)	12,368	
Discount on bonds		2,368
Cash		10,000

4. **Dec. 31, 1992 -- Record the second cash interest payment:**

Interest expense [($88,345 + $2,368) x 14%]	12,700	
Discount on bonds		2,700
Cash		10,000

5. **Dec. 31, 1994 -- Record the retirement of the bonds:**

Bonds payable	100,000	
Cash		100,000

EXERCISE 2

1. **To determine the selling price of the bonds:**

   $$PV = \$20,000 \times pv1_{n=10,i=8\%} + (\$20,000 \times 12\%) \times pva_{n=10,i=8\%}$$
   $$= \$20,000 \times .46319 + \$2,400 \times 6.71008$$
   $$= \$9,263.80 + \$16,104.19$$
   $$= \$25,367.99$$

2. **April 1, 1991 — To record the issuance of the bonds:**

Cash	25,367.99	
Premium on bonds		5,367.99
Bonds payable		20,000.00

3. **April 1, 1991 — To record issue cost incurred:**

Bond issue cost (deferred charge)	500.00	
Cash		500.00

4. **April 1, 1991 — To prepare the amortization schedule:**

Date	Cash Interest (12%)	Effective Interest (8%)	Premium Amortization	Unamortized Bond Premium	Carrying Amount of Bonds
Apr. 1 1991				$5,367.99	$25,367.99
Apr. 1 1992	$2,400.00	$2,029.44	$370.56	4,997.43	24,997.43
Apr. 1 1993	2,400.00	1,999.79	400.21	4,597.22	24,597.22
Apr. 1 1994	2,400.00	1,967.78	432.22	4,165.00	24,165.00
Apr. 1 1995	2,400.00	1,933.20	466.80	3,698.20	23,698.20
Apr. 1 1996	2,400.00	1,895.86	504.14	3,194.06	23,194.06
Apr. 1 1997	2,400.00	1,855.52	544.48	2,649.58	22,649.58
Apr. 1 1998	2,400.00	1,811.97	588.03	2,061.55	22,061.55
Apr. 1 1999	2,400.00	1,764.92	635.08	1,426.47	21,426.47
Apr. 1 2000	2,400.00	1,714.12	685.88	740.59	20,740.59
Apr. 1 2001	2,400.00	1,659.41	740.59	0	20,000.00
Total	$24,000.00	$18,632.01	$5,367.99		

5.   December 31, 1991 -- To amortize bond issue cost:

Bond issue expense ($500 x 9/120)	37.50	
Bond issue cost		37.50

6.   December 31, 1991 -- To accrue interest:

Interest expense ($25,367.99 x 8% x 9/12)	1,522.08	
Premium on bonds payable	277.92	
Interest payable ($2,400 x 9/12)		1,800.00

7.   January 1, 1992 -- To reverse the above accrual entry:

Interest payable	1,800.00	
Interest expense		1,522.08
Premium on bonds payable		277.92

8.   April 1, 1992 -- To record interest payment:

Interest expense ($25,367.99 x 8%)	2,029.44	
Premium on bonds payable	370.56	
Cash		2,400.00

9.   April 1, 1993 -- To record early extinguishment of bonds (at 115):

(Assume interest payment on that date was appropriately recorded)

Bonds payable	20,000.00	
Premium on bonds payable (see amort. schedule)	4,597.22	
Bonds issue cost ($500 x 96/120)		400.00
Cash ($20,000 x 115%)		23,000.00
Gain on extinguishment of debt		1,197.22

EXERCISE 3

1. **April 1, 1991 -- To record the issuance of the bonds:**

Cash ($95,320 + $100,000 x 10% x 3/12)	97,820.00	
Discount on bonds payable	4,680.00	
Bonds payable		100,000.00
Interest expense ($100,000 x 10% x 3/12)		2,500.00

2. **June 30, 1991 -- To record interest payment:**

Interest expense ($5,000 + $120)	5,120.00	
Discount on bonds payable [($4,680 / 9.75) x 3/12]		120.00
Cash ($100,000 x 10% x 6/12)		5,000.00

3. **December 31, 1991 -- To record interest payment:**

Interest expense ($5,000 + $240)	5,240.00	
Discount on bonds payable [($4,680 / 9.75) x 6/12]		240.00
Cash ($100,000 x 10% x 6/12)		5,000.00

4. **December 31, 1991 -- To record conversion of the bonds:**

Book value method:

Bonds payable	100,000.00	
Discount on bonds payable ($4,680 - $120 - $240)		4,320.00
Common stock		95,680.00

Market value method:

Bonds payable	100,000.00	
Discount on bonds payable ($4,680 - $120 - $240)		4,320.00
Common stock (8,000 X $11.25)		90,000.00
Gain on conversion of bonds		5,680.00

MULTIPLE CHOICE:

1.	c	5.	d	9.	c	13.	d
2.	d	6.	b	10.	c	14.	b
3.	c	7.	b	11.	d		
4.	a	8.	c	12.	d		

Computations:

9. (c) Bonds selling price
    = $500,000 (PV1, 5%, 10) + $500,000 (.045) (PVA, 5%, 10)
    = $500,000 x .61391 + $22,500 x 7.72173
    = $306,955 + $173,739
    = $480,694

10. (c) Interest expense for the first six months
    = $101,000 x 11% x 6/12
    = $5,555

11. (d) Cash amount received
    = $10,675 + $10,000 x 12% x 8/12
    = $11,475

12. (d)

	Jan 1 to June 30	July 1 to Dec. 31	Total
Beginning carrying value of bonds	$85,279	$86,396	
Effective interest (6%)	$ 5,117	$ 5,184	$10,301
Cash interest (4%)	4,000	4,000	8,000
Discount amortization	$ 1,117	$ 1,184	$ 2,301

13. (d) Ordinary gain
    = Fair value of land - Book value of land
    = $12,000 - $5,000
    = $7,000

    Extraordinary gain
    = Carrying value of debt - Fair value of land transferred
    = $15,000 - $12,000
    = $3,000

14. (b) Paid-in capital in excess of par
    = Book value of bonds converted - Par value of common stock issued
    = ($250,000 + $15,000) x 80%
       - ($250,000 / $1,000) x 80% x 100 x $10
    = $212,000 - $200,000
    = $12,000

CHAPTER 17

Accounting for Income Taxes

CHAPTER OBJECTIVES

This chapter is designed to enable students to:

A.   Explain the concepts of income tax allocation.

B.   Explain and account for interperiod income tax allocation.

C.   Explain and account for intraperiod income tax allocation.

D.   Account for loss carryback tax benefits.

E.   Account for loss carryforward tax benefits with and without the condition of virtual certainty.

CHAPTER OVERVIEW

A.   Concepts of Income Tax Allocation

Taxable income is determined in accordance with tax rules and regulations, whereas the pretax accounting income (also known as financial income) is measured using generally accepted accounting principles.

Under current GAAP, income tax expense is viewed as a deduction on the income statement similar to cost of goods sold, salary expense, and depreciation expense (and, where appropriate, as on offset to an extraordinary item). In this view, income tax expense is measured on the allocation basis and is reported along with all other expenses. This means that income tax expense of a period is based on the pretax income of the period, regardless of when the income tax will be paid. Thus, it causes the reporting of deferred income tax. Section 3470 of the *CICA Handbook* provides the basic guidelines for income tax allocation for financial purposes. This section recognizes two types of income tax allocation:

1.   **Interperiod income tax allocation**--the allocation of income tax expense among two or more accounting periods. The basic principle is to report income tax expense in the period in which the income that caused the tax effect is reported. Interperiod income tax allocation (*a*) requires certain accounting entries and (*b*) is reflected on the financial statements.
2.   **Intraperiod income tax allocation**--the allocation of the current year's income tax amount to the subclassification of the statements of income and retained earnings that caused the tax expense.

Different Interpretations of Income Tax Applications

Deferred tax amounts viewed as:

Assets and Liabilities--Debits are viewed as prepayments, while credits are viewed as estimated liabilities.

Recording Deferred Taxes

1.   **Deferral Method**--The tax rate used in the period when the timing difference originated, is the rate to use to calculate the deferral.
2.   **Liability Method**--Estimate the tax rate which will be used in the period when the timing difference will reverse, is the rate to use to calculate the deferral.

CICA Handbook, Section 3470 requires the use of the deferral method.

Income Tax Allocation

1.   **Comprehensive Tax Allocation**--All timing differences are recognized.

2.   **Partial Tax Allocation**--Indefinite postponement of reversing timing differences is viewed as a permanent difference and therefore no deferral is set up. Deferrals are only to be set up for specific short-term timing differences that would cause material misstatements of reported income if tax allocation were not applied.

CICA Handbook, Section 3470 requires the use of comprehensive tax allocation.

B.   Principles of Interperiod Income Tax Allocation

Interperiod income tax allocation conforms to the matching principle; that is income tax expense should be matched with the income that caused the income tax effect. Some transactions are properly reported in one fiscal period in calculating income for financial accounting purposes (i.e., in the income statement) while they are reported in a different fiscal period for calculation of income tax payable (i.e., in the income tax return). These timing differences result in deferred income tax.

1.   **Accounting Income**--Net income as per the financial statements before the provision for income taxes and after excluding permanent differences.

2.   **Taxable Income**--Accounting income adjusted for timing differences.

Accounting income is used to calculate income tax expense and taxable income is used to calculate income tax payable. The difference between the expense and payable amounts is recorded as deferred income tax.

Timing differences arise when transactions are reported in one period as per accounting procedures based on GAAP, but are reported in another period based on the Income Tax Act.

Timing differences always:

a)   Relate only to items recognized on both the income statement and the tax return;
b)   Cause a deferred income tax debit/credit to be recorded;
c)   and reverse in future periods.

Example of a Timing Difference

Rent Income--For accounting purposes is reported on the accrual basis but for tax purposes is reported on the cash basis.

E.G.   In 1992, the company receives $12,000 cash for the rental of a portion of its building. One-third of the time period is in 1992 and the remaining two-thirds of the time period is in 1993. Assume that all other revenues minus all expenses equal nil, there are no other timing differences and the tax rate is 40%.

	1992	1993
Accounting Income (Pretax)		
Net Income Before Rental Revenue	Nil	Nil
Rental Revenue Earned	$4,000	$8,000
Tax Expense @ 40%	$1,600	$3,200
Taxable Income (Pretax)		
Accounting Net Income before Rental Revenue	Nil	Nil
Rental Revenue Received	$12,000	$ 0
Tax Payable @ 40%	$ 4,800	$ 0

1992

Income tax expense	$1,600	
Deferred income tax	3,200	
Income tax payable		$4,800

1993

Income tax expense	$3,200	
Deferred Income tax		$3,200

Permanent differences arise when transactions cause pretax accounting income and pretax taxable income to be different. This difference will *never* reverse in future periods.

Example of a Permanent Difference

Membership Fees--for accounting purposes is reported as an expense but for tax purposes is not allowed as a reduction of income. This will not reverse in future periods.

Assume Membership Fees in 1993 is the Only Difference

	1993
Revenue	$100,000
Expenses:	
All expenses except membership fees	80,000
Membership fees	10,000
Total Expenses	90,000
Net Income Before Permanent differences	$ 10,000
Add Back Permanent Difference not allowed As per the Tax Act	$ 10,000
Adjusted Net Income	$ 20,000

Tax Expense and Tax
Payable will both be
based on the same amount
$20,000 (no timing differences)

Changes in Income Tax Rates

Timing differences give rise to deferred income taxes which are computed on the basis of tax rates in effect when the timing difference occurred. Subsequently the deferred taxes recognized reverse over the cycle of the timing difference. On this point the *CICA Handbook*, paragraph 3470.18 states:

> Where the difference between accounting and taxable income in a period gives rise to a transfer to income from the tax allocation balance accumulated in prior periods, such transfer will be computed at the rate of accumulation. Where there are practical difficulties in identifying the specific components, the transfer may be calculated at the effective average rate of accumulation; that is, the proportion that the accumulated deferred credit or charge bears to the accumulated difference between taxable and accounting income. This calculation might be made either by types of differences or in the aggregate.

Ideally, the company is able to identify the rate of accumulation for a particular situation and use that rate to transfer the amount(s) out of the deferred tax balance. The following illustration assumes that the rate of accumulation cannot be determined and thus, an average rate is calculated.

To illustrate the accommodation of a change in the tax rates during the timing cycle, assume Air Tight Ltd. had the following data:

	1990	1991	1992
Pretax income	$20,000	$25,000	$30,000
Capital cost allowance	15,000	12,000	9,000
Depreciation	10,000	10,000	10,000
Income tax rate	40%	45%	50%

The entries to record income taxes would be as follows:

1990:

Income tax expenses ($20,000 X .40)	8,000	
Income taxes payable [($20,000 + $20,000 - $25,000) X .40]		6,000
Deferred income taxes [($15,000 - $10,000) X .40]		2,000

1991:

Income tax expense ($25,000 X .45)	11,250	
Income taxes payable [($25,000 + $10,000 - $12,000) X .45]		10,350
Deferred income taxes [($12,000 - $10,000) X .45]		900

1992:

Income tax expense ($15,500 - $414)	15,086	
Deferred income taxes [($10,000 - $9,000) X .414*]	414	
Income taxes payable [($30,000 + $10,000 - $9,000) X .50]		15,500

*($2,000 + $900) ÷ ($5,000 + $2,000) = .414

In the preceding sequence of entries, the timing differences which arose in 1990 and 1991 begin to reverse in 1992. In 1990, 1991, and 1992 the tax liability was based on the tax rate then in effect as required by law. The drawdown of deferred taxes in 1992 is based on the average rate of accumulation up to 1992; that is, the deferred tax balance of $2,900 divided by the accumulated timing difference of $7,000. This ensures that a deferred tax debit does not arise because the reversals are taken out of the deferred tax credit balance at a faster rate than the rate of accumulation when income tax rates change.

Classification of Deferred Income Tax on the Balance Sheet

Deferred income taxes must be reported on the balance sheet (a) if a debit, as a current or noncurrent asset; and (b) if a credit, as a current or long-term liability. On this point the *CICA Handbook* states:

> Accumulated tax allocation credits and/or debits should be segregated in the balance sheet as between current and noncurrent according to the classification of the assets and liabilities to which they relate [paragraph 3470.24].

> Current accumulated tax allocation debits or credits should be shown in current assets or current liabilities [paragraph 3470.26].

Noncurrent accumulated tax allocation debits or credits should be shown as a deferred charge or as a deferred credit outside shareholders' equity [paragraph 3470.27].

Therefore, current debits and credits are offset, and noncurrent debits and credits are not offset.

C.   INTRAPERIOD INCOME TAX ALLOCATION

GAAP specifies two distinctly different types of income tax allocation: (a) interperiod income tax allocation, caused by timing differences among accounting periods resulting from differences between the income statement and the tax return; and (b) intraperiod income tax allocation, which relates total income tax for the period to the various statement components that caused the tax. It is important to understand both types of income tax allocation must be applied; one is not an alternative to the other.

The concept of intraperiod allocation is to report the income tax (or tax saving) associated with a particular kind of item along with that item in the financial statements (i.e., tax expense must follow the item that caused it). Therefore, the tax effect on extraordinary gains and losses, and prior period adjustments is a reduction of the gain or loss. To illustrate intraperiod income tax allocation, assume the following for Manit Limited:

Pretax income before extraordinary items		$40,000
Extraordinary gain (pretax)	10,000	
Total income tax expense, average tax rate 40%		
[($40,000 + $10,000) X .40]	20,000	

Manit Limited would report the results of intraperiod tax allocation of the $20,000 total income tax expense as follows:

Income before income tax and before extraordinary items		$40,000
Less: Income tax expense ($40,000 X .40)		16,000
Income before extraordinary items		24,000
Extraordinary gain (specified)	$10,000	
Less: Applicable income tax ($10,000 X .40)	4,000	6,000
Net income		$30,000

Income Tax Effects of Prior Period Adjustments

Paragraph 3600.05 of the *CICA Handbook* states in part that "The financial statements of prior periods presented for comparative purposes are restated as necessary to reflect the retroactive application of a prior period adjustment, including any related income tax effect." Where the adjustment relates to a period earlier than that presented for comparative purposes, the adjustment is made to the opening balance of retained earnings.

If an error caused a misstatement of reported income of a prior period and if the misstated item had an income tax effect the prior period adjustment would also need to correct for the income tax effect of the error.

To illustrate, assume Tennis Elbow Ltd. inadvertently understated depreciation expense on both the financial statements and the tax return in 1992 by $10,000 when the income tax rate was 40%. In 1994, the company discovered this error when the income tax rate was 45% (there was no error in 1993 or 1994). Two entries (or a single combined entry) would correct the error in 1994:

Prior period adjustment (expense correction)	10,000	
Accumulated depreciation		10,000
Receivable for refund of 1992 income tax		
($10,000 X 40%)	4,000	
Prior period adjustment (tax refund on		
expense correction		4,000

Notice that the tax rate in effect during the year when the error was made (i.e., 40%) was used, rather than the tax rate of the correction year (i.e., 45%). Any interest and/or penalties related to the extra income tax, and any interest related to any tax refunds also would affect the net amount of the prior period adjustment.

The Investment Tax Credit

The **Investment tax credit** is a provision in the income tax laws designed to encourage investments in new productive assets, such as plant, machinery, and equipment. Currently, the law provides that taxpayers who acquire qualified assets can receive an investment tax credit as a direct offset to income tax expense and tax payable. This tax credit is important to investors because they can reduce their income tax payable for the year of purchase of the qualified asset by a portion of its full cost. However, the amount of the investment tax credit deducted from the taxes payable must also be deducted from the capital cost of the asset for tax purposes thus reducing the amount of CCA for tax purposes over the useful life of the asset.

The full amount of the investment tax credit is received through a decrease in income tax payable in the year in which the qualified asset is purchased; however, it relates to the acquired asset which contributes to revenue generation over its useful life.

Section 3805 of the *Handbook*, "Investment Tax Credits," recommends that investment tax credits should be accounted for using the cost reduction approach.

Under this method the total amount of the investment tax credit is either

1. Deducted from the related assets with any depreciation or amortization calculated on the net amount or

2. Deferred and amortized to income on the same basis as the related assets.

Disclosure of Income Tax

Full disclosure of the components of income tax expense (including deferred income tax) is required. In respect to the income statement paragraph 3470.29 of the *CICA Handbook* states that "The amount by which the current income tax provision has been increased or decreased as a result of tax deferrals should be disclosed: either by showing the current and deferred portions of the income tax provision separately on the income statement or by means of a note to the financial statements.

The balance sheet should disclose separately the current and non-current accumulated tax allocation credits and/or debits according to the assets and liabilities to which they relate. The current accumulated tax allocation debits or credits should be included in current assets or current liabilities. The non-current accumulated tax allocations should be shown as a deferred charge or as a deferred credit outside shareholders' equity.

Section 3470 of the *CICA Handbook* requires that a company with shares that trade publicly or one required to file financial statements with a securities commission, "disclose in its financial statements the components of the variation from the basic income tax rate".

Income Tax Loss Carrybacks and Carryforwards

Federal tax laws allow taxpayers to carryback and to carryforward operating losses. The effect is that a corporation may secure a refund of taxes paid in the three years preceding the loss and, if the loss is so large that it is not absorbed when carried back, it may be carried forward and applied against future taxable income for up to seven years.

D.   Loss Carryback

In a period when an operating loss follows periods of net income sufficient to offset the loss, the resultant **loss carryback** gives rise to a refund of income taxes paid in prior periods. The loss is carried back and deducted from the taxable incomes of the prior periods; this results in a reduction of the tax. Paragraph 3470.40 of the *CICA Handbook* states: "Where the loss for tax purposes gives rise to a recovery of income taxes of the previous period, such recovery should be reflected in the income statement for the period of the loss."

The following exhibit illustrates the accounting for loss carryback. The data for 1989 to 1992 includes depreciation expense and capital cost allowances for each year as well as reconciliations between accounting and taxable income (loss). The tax rate is 40%.

These journal entries record the income taxes for 1989 to 1991:

December 31:

	1989	1990	1991
Income tax expense	4,000	3,200	2,000
Income taxes payable	2,800	2,400	1,600
Deferred income taxes	1,200	800	400

These entries reflect the income tax expense based on accounting incomes, income tax payable based on taxable incomes and the deferred tax credit based on the timing difference for each year.

Accounting income for 1992 is a loss of $15,000. Because of the difference between depreciation and CCA, the loss for tax purposes is $15,500; this may be carried back against the taxable incomes reported for the previous three years. The journal entry to record income taxes in 1992 follows:

December 31, 1992:

Tax refund receivable ($15,500 X .4)	6,200	
Income tax expense ($15,000 X .4)		6,000
Deferred income tax ($500 X .4)		200

In this case, the entire benefit is realizable. Therefore, it is recognizable and there is a negative tax expense of $6,000 ($15,000 X .4). The $200 credit to deferred income tax recognizes the effect of the timing difference caused by depreciation and capital cost allowance.

The lower portion of Brick Wall Ltd. income statement would show the following:

Brick Wall Ltd.
Income Statement (in part)
For the Year Ended December 31, 1992

Loss before income taxes	$15,000
Deduct: Recovery of prior years	
income taxes due to loss carryback	6,000
Net loss	$ 9,000

E.   Loss Carryforward

When a company has experienced an operating loss which cannot be absorbed by the profits of the previous three years, it may carry the loss forward and apply it against the profits of the following seven years. This **loss carryforward** creates a recognition problem. The loss carryforward can convey a benefit in the form of a reduction in future income taxes provided that sufficient income is earned in the carryforward period. The determination of the extent of this benefit to be recognized in the year of the loss is the major concern of this section.

Virtual Certainty To recognize the entire benefit of the loss carryforward, requires that there be **virtual certainty**. Paragraph 3470.43 of the *Handbook* states:

> A corporation which has incurred a loss for tax purposes may be virtually certain of realizing the tax benefit resulting from the loss or a portion thereof in the carryforward period prescribed by the tax laws. Virtual certainty of realizing the tax

benefit on a loss other than a capital loss requires all three of the following conditions to be present:

(i)   the loss results from an identifiable and nonrecurring cause;
(ii)   a record of profitability has been established over a long period by the corporation, or a predecessor business, with any occasional losses being more than offset by income in subsequent years; and
(iii)   there is assurance beyond any reasonable doubt that future taxable income will be sufficient to offset the loss carryforward and will be earned during the carryforward period prescribed by the tax laws.

The recognition of the loss carryforward benefit in the year of the loss depends on the assurance that the benefit will be realized within the seven-year carryforward period.

The following exhibit presents the data for accounting for a loss carryback and a loss carry forward with virtual certainty. The Income Tax Act allows loss carrybacks to be applied to any or all of the three preceding years. For simplicity, Elora Co. assumes that the loss in 1992 may be carried back only to 1991 and, that condition for virtual certainty exist. Therefore, the entire benefit of the available loss carryforward may be recognized in 1992, the year of the loss.

Partial Income Statement for Years Ending December 31, Elora Company

	1991	1992
Accounting income (loss)	$ 50,000	$(55,000)
Timing difference:		
Depreciation	$ 15,000	$ 15,000
Capital cost allowance	(25,000)	(22,000)
	(10,000)	(7,000)
Taxable income (loss)	$ 40,000	$(62,000)

Other data:

1.   Income tax rate: 40%
2.   Allocation of taxable loss for 1992:

Total loss available	$ 62,000
Carryback to 1991	40,000
Carryforward available	$ 22,000

The entry to record income taxes for 1992 would appear as follows:

December 31, 1992:

Tax refund receivable ($40,000 X .4)	16,000	
Income tax benefit available ($22,000 X .4)	8,800	
Deferred income tax ($7,000 X .4)		2,800
Income tax expense ($55,000 X .4)		22,000

The tax refund receivable arises because $40,000 of the taxable loss is carried back and applied against the taxable income of 1991 reducing it to zero. The 1991 taxes paid will thereby be refunded. Because the criteria of virtual certainty were assumed to be satisfied, the balance of the 1992 loss will be carried forward and used to reduce future taxable income and taxes payable. Therefore, the benefit of the loss carried forward $8,800 ($22,000 X .4) may be included as an asset on the balance sheet at the end of 1992. The credit to deferred income tax records the effect of the timing difference in 1992 and the credit to income tax expense records the overall reduction in income taxes as a result of the 1992 operating loss.

Partial Financial Statements for 1992, Elora Company

Partial income statement:			
Net loss before income taxes			$55,000
Recovery of income taxes:			
Recovery of prior years' taxes		$16,000	
Recognition of loss carryforward benefit		$ 8,800	
		$24,800	
Less deferred income tax		2,800	22,000
Net loss			$33,000
Partial balance sheet:			
Current assets:			
Tax refund receivable			$16,000
Other assets:			
Tax benefit available for application against future years' income taxes			$ 8,800

Deferred income taxes--$2,800 credited to the existing balance.

Timing Difference Reversals The Income Tax Act regulates the use of capital cost allowances (CCA) by defining the maximum claimable. Therefore, the amount of CCA a firm wishes to use may vary from nil to the maximum allowed.

Unlike loss carryforwards, CCA does not have a time limit. In some cases, a firm may wish to maximize the **benefits of loss carryovers**. In their previous example, Elora could reduce its loss for tax purposes to $40,000 by not claiming any CCA in 1992. then the entire taxable loss of $40,000 could be absorbed by carrying it back to 1991. This is accomplished by reversing previously built up timing differences. The journal entry in 1992 to reflect this would be:

December 31, 1992:

Tax refund receivable ($40,000 X .4)	16,000	
Deferred income taxes ($15,000 X .4)	6,000	
Income tax expense ($55,000 X .4)		22,000

The $6,000 debit to deferred taxes arises because depreciation expense is $15,000 more than the CCA claimed, which is zero. This represents a $15,000 reversal of the timing difference and the tax effect at 40% is $6,000.

Without Virtual Certainty. When the conditions of virtual certainty cannot be met, the value of the loss carryforward benefit as an asset becomes questionable because of the possibility that it will not be realized. As with any other asset, the degree to which it will be realized in the future periods affects the value of the asset in the current period.

Where virtual certainty does not exist, section 3470 of the *Handbook* states that deferred income tax credits (from timing differences in prior periods) may be reduced in the carryforward period by not claiming CCA.

When conditions of virtual certainty do not exist, the *Handbook* does not allow tax carryforward benefits to be set up as an asset. However, the *Handbook* allows the recognition of the carryforward benefit to the extent that deferred tax credits may be reduced. Therefore, the loss carryforward benefit that may be recognized in the year of the loss is limited to the least of the following three amounts:

1.   The tax carryforward benefit itself.
2.   The credit balance in the deferred tax account after adjusting for current period and/or amendment of previous period timing differences.
3.   The total of the available timing difference drawdown during the carryforward period.

The following exhibit presents the data for accounting for a loss carryback and a loss carryforward without virtual certainty. For simplicity Ace Ltd. Assumes that the loss in 1991 may be carried back only to 1990 and that conditions are without virtual certainty. Ace Ltd. will not revise its tax return for 1990.

	1990	1991	1992	1993
Accounting Income (Loss)	$30,000	$(175,000)	$110,000	$50,000
Timing Difference				
Depreciation	15,000	15,000	15,000	15,000
Capital Cost Allowance	(25,000)	—	—	(20,000)
	(10,000)	15,000	15,000	(5,000)
Taxable Income (Loss)	$20,000	$(160,000)	$125,000	$45,000

Other Data

1. Income tax rate 40%

2. Allocation of taxable loss for 1991
   Total loss available $160,000
   Carryback to 1990   20,000

   Carryforward available $140,000

3. Deferred tax - Dec. 31/90 Balance credit of $ 39,000

4. Depreciable assets - balance Dec 31/90
   Net book value $332,500
   Undepreciated capital cost   250,000

   Accumulated timing difference $ 82,500

Journal entries to record income tax

December 31, 1990

Income tax expense ($30,000 X .4)   12,000
    Deferred Income tax ($10,000 X .4)   4,000
    Income tax payable ($20,000 X .4)   8,000

December 31, 1991

Without virtual certainty requires recognition as the least of:

1. Tax carryforward benefit available
   $160,000 - (Carryback to 1990) 20,000 = 140,000 X .4 = $56,000

2. Credit Balance in deferred tax account
   $39,000 - (Deferred tax in 1991) - 6,000   =   33,000

3. Available timing difference drawdown
   $15,000 X 7 years = 105,000 X .4   =   42,000

Tax refund receivable (1990 tax pay.)   8,000
Deferred income tax ($6,000 + 33,000)   39,000
    Income tax expense ($175,000 X .4 - 57,500*)   47,000
* 57,500 is the unrecognized loss carryforward

December 31, 1992
    Entry ignoring loss carryforward
       Income tax expense ($110,000 X .4)   44,000
          Deferred income tax ($15,000 X .4)   6,000
            Income tax payable ($125,000 X .4)   50,000

Entry recognizing loss carryforward
Income tax payable ($125,000 X .4)   50,000
   Deferred income tax*   27,000
   Loss carryforward benefit recognized **   23,000
   * A partial reversal of prior debit to this account
  ** Unrecognized loss carryforward is now recognized

December 31, 1993

Entry ignoring loss carryforward
Income tax expense ($50,000 X .4)   20,000
   Deferred income tax ($5,000 X .4)   2,000
   Income tax payable ($45,000 X .4)   18,000

Entry recognizing loss carryforward
Income tax payable   6,000
   Deferred income tax *   6,000
   * Reversal of the remaining prior debit
   to this account (33,000 - 27,000)

KEY CONCEPTS

Accounting income   Net income as per the financial statements after excluding permanent differences

Available timing difference drawdown   The sum of the annual depreciation expense available to reduce the deferred income tax account for the carryforward period following a taxable loss.

Comprehensive tax allocation   All timing differences are recognized.

Deferral method   The tax rate used in the period when a timing difference originated, is the rate used to calculate the deferred tax.

Deferred tax amount   Tax deferred is reported as an asset or a liability (debit or credit balance)

Intraperiod income tax allocation   The current year's income tax is allocated between the subclassifications of the income and retained earnings statements.

Interperiod income tax allocation   The allocation of income tax among two or more accounting periods.

Investment tax credit   Provision is the income tax laws which allow a percentage of the capital cost of certain qualifying assets to be deducted from income tax payable in the year of purchase.

Loss carryback.   A taxable loss may be carried back to the immediately preceding three years.

Loss carryforward   Any portion of a taxable loss remaining, after applying the loss carryback, may be carried forward to the next seven years.

Permanent differences   Transactions that cause pretax accounting income and pretax taxable income to differ and never reverse in future periods.

Taxable income   Accounting income adjusted for timing differences.

Timing differences   Transactions are reported in one period but taxed in another period.

Virtual certainty   There is no doubt that the total benefit of a loss carryforward will be completely applied against taxable income within the time limit of the loss carryforward period.

Without virtual certainty   It is doubtful that the total benefit of a loss carryforward will be completely applied against taxable income within the time limit of the loss carryforward period.

REVIEW QUESTIONS AND EXERCISES

TRUE-FALSE

Indicate whether each of the following statements is true or false by circling the correct response.

T   F   1. Both accounting income and taxable income are measured in compliance with Generally Accepted Accounting Principles.

T   F   2. A difference between pretax accounting income and taxable income without tax consequences is a permanent difference.

T   F   3. Interperiod tax allocation is mandatory for both permanent and temporary differences.

T   F   4. The investment tax credit (ITC) is an income tax provision that encourages investment in capital assets.

T   F   5. Intraperiod income tax allocation involves deciding how the total income tax amount should be reported in the current financial statements.

T   F   6. A timing difference, once originated, will result in either taxable or deductible amounts in future years when the difference reverses.

T   F   7. In the absence of timing difference, there should be no difference between income tax expense and income tax payable.

T   F   8. The balance in a deferred tax asset account is reported each period as a contra account under liabilities on the statement of financial position.

T   F   9. Prior period adjustment should be shown net of tax effect.

T   F   10. For individual items creating timing differences (e.g., depreciation of a specific asset), a balance will be created in a deferred tax liability (or asset) account and then reduced to zero as the temporary differences reverse.

T   F   11. Intraperiod tax allocation refers to determining the appropriate income tax expense for each reporting period; whereas interperiod tax allocation refers to allocating a given year's tax expense among the financial statement items giving rise to the expense.

T   F   12. A taxable operating loss may first be carried back for 3 years and then forward for up to 7 years.

T   F   13. Under no circumstances should the tax benefits due to a taxable operating loss carried forward be recognized in the year of loss.

T   F   14. Tax benefits due to a taxable operating loss carryback should be measured at the tax rate for the year of loss.

EXERCISE 1

Presented below is a reconciliation of pretax accounting income and taxable income of Patty O'Furniture Ltd. for 1992, the first year of operation, and the differences between pretax accounting and taxable income:

	1992	1993	1994
Pretax accounting income	$8,600		
Timing differences:			
Rental revenue	2,400	$(1,200)	$(1,200)
Depreciation expense	(4,500)	3,000	1,500
Warranty expense	2,000	(1,000)	(1,000)
Permanent difference:			
Tax-exempt dividend income	(1,400)		
Taxable income	$ 7,100		

The current tax rate is 30% which is not expected to change in the foreseeable future.

Required: Complete the following:

Step 1. Analyze tax data:

	1992 (Current year)	Future Years	Effect on Future Taxable Income Deductible	Taxable
1. Schedule timing differences.				
Rental revenue	$ 2,400			
Depreciation expense	(4,500)			
Warranty expense	2,000		___	___
Scheduled timing differences		≡		
2. Determine tax payable.				
Adjusted pretax accounting income	___			
Taxable income				
Tax rate 30%	___		___	
Income tax payable	≡			
3. Determine deferred income taxes.				
Deferred income tax: debit				
credit			≡	
				≡

Step 2. Determine income tax expense:

```
Income tax expense
Deferred Income tax

Income tax payable
```

Step 3. Record income taxes:

```
Income tax expense
Deferred income tax
Income tax payable
```

EXERCISE 2

The applicable tax rate is 40% for 1992-1995.

Required: Complete the following tax schedule and prepare journal entries to record income taxes in each of the four years for Met Cargo Ltd., assuming taxable revenues minus deductible expenses (other than C. C. A. and depreciation deductions) of $100,000 each year, and no deferred income tax at the beginning of 1992.

Year	Depreciation	C.C.A.	Timing Differences (Current)	(Accumulated)	Deferred Income Tax Current Change	Ending Balance
1992	$ 5,000	$ 5,000	$ 0	$ 0	$ 0	$ 0
1993	5,000	7,600				
1994	5,000	7,400				
1995	5,000	0				
	$20,000	$20,000	$ 0			

Journal entries:

1992:

1993:

1994:

1995:

EXERCISE 3

Acme Ltd. reported net income (loss) for the years 1991, 1992, 1993 and 1994 for both tax and accounting purposes as follows:

	Net income	Taxable Income	Tax rate
1991	$ 100,000	80,000	30%
1992	80,000	62,000	30%
1993	90,000	74,000	30%
1994 (current)	(300,000)	(275,000)	40%

There were no deferred income taxes prior to 1991. The only timing difference is between depreciation and capital cost allowance. Annual depreciation is $25,000.

Required:

Give the journal entry to record the income tax for 1994. Acme Ltd will not revise the tax returns for 1991 to 1993.

A: Virtual certainty

B: Without virtual certainty

MULTIPLE CHOICE

Enter the letter corresponding to the response which **best** completes each of the following statements or questions.

_____   1.   Interperiod income tax allocation should be used for:

	Permanent differences	Timing differences
a.	Yes	Yes
b.	Yes	No
c.	No	Yes
d.	No	No

_____   2.   A company, which operated profitably during its first five years, sustained a loss in the sixth year which equalled its pretax income of any four of the first five years of its operations. The company can choose to obtain a refund of income taxes paid by filing an amended return for:

   a.   Any of the first three years of operations.
   b.   the three years immediately preceding the loss.
   c.   Any years before the loss, provided the loss equals or exceeds profits of those years.
   d.   The four most profitable years preceding the loss.
   e.   None of the above.

_____   3.   Transactions and events originating timing differences create the need for:

   a.   taxable loss carryforward.
   b.   taxable loss carryback.
   c.   an adjustment to pretax accounting income in order to make income tax expense equal to income tax payable.
   d.   interperiod tax allocation.

_____   4.   Permanent differences are unlike timing differences in that:

   a.   Permanent differences occur more infrequently than timing differences.
   b.   A permanent difference cannot change its status once designated, but a timing difference may be reclassified in a later period.
   c.   Permanent differences do not reverse themselves in subsequent periods.
   d.   Permanent differences are both unusual and infrequent.

_____ 5. Intraperiod tax allocation:

    a. Involves the allocation of income taxes between current and future periods.
    b. Arises because certain revenues and expenses appear in the financial statements either before or after they are included in the income tax return.
    c. Arises because items included in the determination of taxable income may be presented in different parts of the financial statements.
    d. All of the above are correct.
    e. None of the above are correct.

_____ 6. Intraperiod income tax allocation:

    a. May cause a deferred tax debit or credit.
    b. May cause a deferred tax credit only.
    c. May cause a deferred tax debit only.
    d. Matches the tax effect with the item that caused the tax.
    e. None of the above are correct regarding intraperiod income tax allocation.

_____ 7. Harbin Corporation reports pretax accounting income of $500,000. Its taxable income for the year, however, is $300,000. The difference is due to the use of different depreciation methods. Given that the applicable tax rate is 34%, Harbin's net income for the period is likely to be:

    a. $132,000.
    b. $330,000.
    c. $198,000.
    d. $170,000.

_____ 8. Oshawa Company reported income for the first two years of its operation as follows:

| | December 31 | |
	1992	1993
Pretax accounting income	$1,000,000	$1,200,000
Taxable income	$ 800,000	$1,400,000

The disparity between pretax accounting income and taxable income is attributable to timing differences. What should Oshawa report as income tax expense for 1993, assuming the applicable tax rate for the year is 40%:

    a. $560,000.
    b. $280,000.
    c. $400,000.
    d. $480,000.

____ 9. Using the same data in Question 8 but assume that the differences are permanent, income tax expense for 1993 would be:

    a. $560,000.
    b. $280,000.
    c. $400,000.
    d. $480,000.

____ 10. At the end of its first year of operation, Holstein Ltd. reports the following accounting information:

Pretax accounting income	$300,000
Income tax expense	102,000
Net income	$198,000
Tax on taxable income	$119,000
Deferred income tax*	$ 17,000 (Dr.)

*All due to warranty expense

Holstein estimates its annual warranty expense as a percentage of sales. The amount charged to warranty expense on its books this year was $65,000. Assuming a 34% income tax rate, what amount was actually paid this year on the corporation's warranty?

    a. $15,000.
    b. $50,000.
    c. $40,000.
    d. $42,000.

____ 11. Oak Ltd had taxable income of $4,000 during 1993. Oak used capital cost allowances for tax purposes ($4,200) and straight-line depreciation for accounting purposes ($1,000). Oak had no other timing differences. Oak's pretax accounting income for 19A would be:

    a. $7,200
    b. $800
    c. $8,200
    d. $5,000
    e. None of the above

____ 12. During 1993, Bunt Ltd had pretax accounting income of $4,200. Bunt's only timing difference for 1993 was rent revenue collected in advance of $1,200. Bunt's taxable income for 1993 would be:

a. $3,000
b. $5,400
c. $4,800
d. $4,200 (rent revenue collected in advance is not a timing difference)
e. None of the above

____ 13. Cane Ltd's taxable income was $900 during 1993. Cane had product warranty costs of $360 recognizable for tax purposes and $400 recognizable for financial accounting purposes. Cane had no other timing differences. Cane's pretax accounting income for 1993 would be:

a. $860
b. $940
c. $1,260
d. $900 (warranty costs are not considered timing differences)
e. None of the above

____ 14. Elm Ltd provided the following data related to income tax allocation:

	19A	19B
Pretax accounting income	$1,800	$ 400
Taxable income	400	1,800
Income tax rate	20%	20%

The deferred tax account showed a zero balance at the start of 19A. There was only one timing difference, an expense, which was deductible for tax purposes in 19A, but was recorded for accounting purposes in 19B. There are no carrybacks or carryforwards. The journal entry to record the income tax consequences for 19A would include a:

a. Debit of $280 to Elm's deferred income tax asset account
b. Credit of $280 to Elm's deferred income tax asset account
c. Debit of $80 to Elm's deferred income tax asset account
d. A, B, and C are incorrect, entry is to a tax liability account
e. None of the above are correct

SOLUTIONS TO REVIEW QUESTIONS AND EXERCISES

TRUE-FALSE

1.	F	5.	T	9.	T	13.	F
2.	T	6.	T	10.	T	14.	F
3.	F	7.	T	11.	F		
4.	T	8.	F	12.	T		

EXERCISE 1

Step 1.   Analyze tax data:

	1992 (Current year)	Future Years	Effect on Future Taxable Income Deductible	Taxable
1. Schedule timing differences.				
Rental revenue	$ 2,400	$(2,400)	$(2,400)	
Depreciation expense	(4,500)	4,500		$ 4,500
Warranty expense	2,000	(2,000)	(2,000)	
Scheduled timing differences	$ (100)	$ 100	$(4,400)	$ 4,500
2. Determine tax payable.				
Adjusted pretax accounting income ($8,600 - $1,400)	7,200			
Taxable income	$7,100			
Tax rate 30%				
Income tax payable	$2,130			
3. Determine deferred income taxes.				
Deferred income tax: debit				
credit				$ 30

Step 2. Determine income tax expense: DR(CR)

Income tax expense	$2,160
Deferred income tax	(30)
Income tax payable	$2,130

Step 3. Record income taxes:

Income tax expense	2,160	
Deferred income tax		30
Income tax payable		2,130

EXERCISE 2

Year	Depreciation	C.C.A.	Timing Differences (Current)	(Accumulated)	Deferred Income Tax Current Change	Ending Balance
1992	$ 5,000	$ 5,000	$ 0	$ 0	$ 0	$ 0
1993	5,000	7,600	2,600	2,600	1,040	1,040
1994	5,000	7,400	2,400	5,000	960	2,000
1995	5,000	0	(5,000)	0	(2,000)	0
	$20,000	$20,000	$ 0			

1992:

```
Income tax expense                                        38,000
    Income tax payable [($100,000 - $5,000) x 40%]                  38,000
```

1993:

```
Income tax expense ($36,960 + $1,040)                     38,000
    Deferred income tax ($2,600 x 40%)                              1,040
    Income tax payable [($100,000 - $7,600) x 40%]                 36,960
```

1994:

```
Income tax expense ($37,040 + $960)                       38,000
    Deferred income tax ($2,000 - $1,040)                             960
    Income tax payable [($100,000 - $7,400) x 40%]                 37,040
```

1995:

```
Income tax expense ($40,000 - $2,000)                     38,000
Deferred income tax ($0 - $2,000)                          2,000
    Income tax payable ($100,000 - 0) x 40%]                       40,000
```

Exercise 3

Year	Net Income -	Taxable Income	= A.T.D.	X Tax Rate	= Deferred Tax
1991	$100,000	$ 80,000	$20,000	.30	6,000
1992	80,000	62,000	18,000	.30	5,400
1993	90,000	74,000	16,000	.30	4,800
	$270,000	$216,000	$54,000		$16,200

December 31, 1994

A.   Tax refund receivable *   64,800
      Income tax benefit available**   23,600
      Deferred tax (25,000 X .3)   7,500
          Income tax expense***   95,900
        * 216,000 X .3
       ** (275,000 - 216,000) X .4
      *** 64,800 + 23,600 + 7,500

B.   Loss carryforward $275,000 - 216,000 X .4   23,600
      Credit balance in deferred tax account
          $16,200 - 7,500   8,700
      Available timing difference drawdown
          $25,000 X 7 = 175,000 X .4   70,000

      Tax refund receivable*   64,800
      Deferred tax (7,500 + 8,700)   16,200
          Income tax expense**   81,000
        *216,000 x .3
       **64,800 + 16,200

MULTIPLE CHOICE:

1.	c	5.	c	9.	a	13.	a
2.	b	6.	d	10.	a	14.	a
3.	d	7.	b	11.	a		
4.	c	8.	d	12.	b		

Computations:

7. (b) Net income = $500,000 x (1 - 34%) = $330,000.

8. (d) Income tax expense (1993) = $1,200,000 x 40% = $480,000

9. (a) Income tax expense (1993) = $1,400,000 x 40% = $560,000

10. (a) Warranty expense paid during the year
= Warranty expense - Temporary difference
= $65,000 - ($17,000 / 34%) = $15,000

11. (a) Pretax accounting income =
$ 4,000 + 4,200 - 1,000 = $7,200

12. (b) Taxable income =
$4,200 + 1,200 = $5,400

13. (a) Pretax accounting income =
$900 + 360 - 400 = $860

14. (a) Deferred tax = ($1,800 - 400) X .2 = $280

CHAPTER 18

Accounting for Leases

CHAPTER OBJECTIVES

This chapter is designed to enable students to:

A.   Explain the nature of a lease and why the lessee wishes to keep the lease off the balance sheet, while the lessor prefers to remove the leased asset from its records by considering the lease transaction as a sale or transfer.

B.   Distinguish between a capital lease and an operating lease for the lessee and the lessor.

C.   Account for operating leases for the lessee and lessor.

D.   Account for capital leases for the lessee.

E.   Account for sales-type and direct-financing leases for the lessor.

F.   Account for the special problems relating to leases, including bargain purchase offers; residual value guarantees; different interest rates used by the lessee and lessor; depreciation of the leased asset by the lessee; executory and initial direct costs; and classification of lease receivables and payables.

G.   Describe the requirements and account for sale-leaseback arrangements.

H.   Describe lease disclosure requirements.

I.   Explain the rules for accounting for leases involving real estate.

J.   Explain the additional tax issues involved in leases.

CHAPTER OVERVIEW

A.   1.   A lease is a contractual agreement between a lessor and a lessee that conveys the lessee the right to use a specific asset such as property, plant or equipment, for a specified period of time. In return for this right, the lessee agrees to make specified periodic cash payments during the term of the lease. Accounting for leases is complicated whenever a transfer of ownership in the leased asset is involved or is assumed. This chapter discusses the fundamentals of accounting for **capital leases** and **operating leases** as specified in the *CICA Handbook*, sec. 3065.

2. For the lessee:

    Off-Balance-Sheet Financing   By structuring leasing transactions as operating leases rather than capital leases (in situations where management's intent points to capital lease accounting treatment), *lessees* are able to take possession of and make full use of assets without either capitalizing them or reporting the attending lease payment obligations as balance sheet debt. This accounting treatment is referred to as **off-balance-sheet-financing**. Because most companies routinely take on financing debt in conjunction with asset acquisitions (unless they are cash rich), off-balance-sheet financing is *attractive* to *lessee companies* for two primary reasons:

    *   Debt-equity ratio. Adding more debt to a company's capital structure causes the debt part of the ratio to increase, which is an adverse development if the debt-equity ratio is already considered high. As a result, shareholders might sell their shares, causing the stock price to decline, and creditors may refuse to extend credit (or might call in loans).
    *   Existing debt covenants. If there are bondholders, the bond indenture agreement may include restrictive covenants designed to protect the bondholders' investments. One such covenant prohibits a company from taking on additional debt without the consent of the present bondholders. Bank loans frequently carry similar debt restrictions.

3. For the Lessor:

    (a) **Direct-financing capital lease:** In a **direct-financing lease**, the lessor typically purchases an asset (only to accommodate the leasing transaction) and immediately leases it to the lessee. The lease transaction removes the asset from the books, replacing it with a receivable. The lessor reports a lease receivable on the balance sheet. Because the asset itself is considered sold, no asset depreciation is taken by the lessor. The lessor's profit is derived entirely from interest.

    (b) **Sales-type capital lease: Sales-type leases**, used by manufacturers and dealer/distributors, lease (sell) the asset directly out of finished goods inventory, or a dealer/distributor leases (sells) the asset out of its inventory account. A lease receivable account is opened with entries made to cost of goods sold, sales revenue, and the asset. The lessor's profit is derived partially from selling the asset and partially from interest.

    Therefore, manufacturers and dealers/distributors of industrial equipment use leasing to facilitate sales. For lending institutions and commercial lessors, leasing is simply another addition to their financial services product line.

B.   Capital Leases

A lease must be classified as either a **capital lease** or an **operating lease,** depending on whether substantially all risks and benefits of ownership (equity interest) in the leased asset are transferred from the lessor to the lessee. The following criteria are mandatory:

1.   **Capital lease to the lessee:**   A capital lease to the lessee is a **noncancellable** lease which meets **any** of the following criteria:

   a.   **Criterion 1 – Title transfer:**   The lease agreement specifies that **ownership (title) in the asset transfers** from the lessor to the lessee by the end of the lease term.

   b.   **Criterion 2 – Bargain purchase option (BPO):**   The agreement contains an option that allows the lessee to purchase the leased property for a price that is sufficiently lower than the expected fair value of the asset that, on the date of inception of the lease, exercise of the option appears to be assured.

   c.   **Criterion 3 – Lease term** test: The **lease term** is equal to, or more than **75%** of the estimated **economic life** (remaining useful life) of the leased asset.

   d.   **Criterion 4 – Present value test:**   The present value of the minimum lease payments (MLP) (to be elaborated later) is at least **90% of the fair value** of the leased asset at inception of the lease.

   Note that **criteria 3 and 4** are applicable only if the beginning of the lease term does not fall within the **last 25%** of the **whole life** of the leased asset.

2.   **Capital lease to the lessor:**   Besides meeting any one of the four criteria as stated above, a lease must further meet **the following two additional criteria** to be classified as a capital lease by the **lessor:**

   a.   **Collectibility** of the minimum lease payments is reasonably assured; and

   b.   **No important uncertainties** surround the amount of **unreimbursable costs** yet to be incurred by the lessor.

   Furthermore, the capital leases to the lessor are subclassified as follows:

   a.   **Sales-type lease.**   A capital lease involving manufacturer's or dealer's profit or loss (i.e., difference between the present value of the minimum lease payments and the book value of the leased asset) is specified as a sales-type lease.

   b.   **Direct-financing lease.**   A capital lease to the lessor without involving manufacturer's or dealer's profit or loss is called direct-financing lease.

3.   **Minimum Lease Payments (MLP)**

   The MLP to the lessee are payments that **the lessee** is **obligated** to make or **can be required to make** in connection with the leased property. The **MLP** to the lessor, on the other hand, are payments that **the lessor** expects to collect from the lessee or other parties regarding the leased asset over the term of the lease. Executory costs (e.g., maintenance expenses, property taxes and insurance expenses, etc.). are excluded from the MLP. Depending upon the provisions of a lease contract, the components of the MLP vary:

(a)   Criterion 1 is satisfied:

MLP = Periodic rental payments.

(b)   Criterion 2 is satisfied:

MLP = Periodic rental payments + BPO price.

(c)   Neither Criterion 1, nor Criterion 2 is satisfied: If either Criterion 1 or 2 is satisfied, both the lessee and the lessor would have the same MLP as presented above. However, if a capital lease meets only Criterion 3 and/or 4, then:

(d)   **MLP -- Lessee** includes:

(1)   Periodic rental payments, and
(2)   Residual value of the leased asset guaranteed by the lessee or a third party related to (affiliated with) the lessee.

(e)   **MLP -- Lessor** includes:

(1)   Periodic rental payments, and
(2)   Residual value of the leased asset, whether guaranteed or unguaranteed.

Furthermore, if there is any penalty that the lessee must pay upon failure to renew or extend the lease at the expiration of the lease term, the payment may be included in the MLP to both the lessee and the lessor, in which case, the related renewal period **must not be added** to the lease term.

4. Lease Classification by Lessors and Lessees

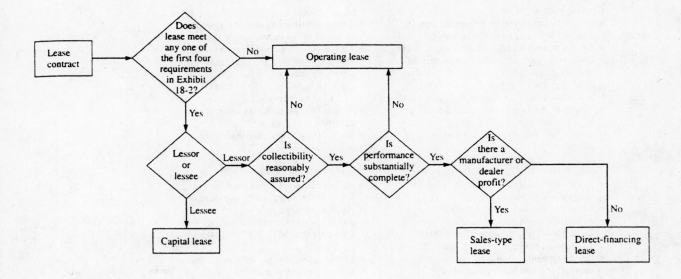

C. Operating lease.

All leases that do not satisfy capital lease criteria as described above are operating leases:

1. **Lessee accounting.** The lessee simply rents the asset from the lessor, and makes periodic rent payments which are accounted for as current operating expenses. The leased asset is not "acquired" and should be returned to the lessor at the end of the lease term. Depreciation expense of the leased asset is not recognized by the lessee.

2. **Lessor accounting.** The lessor continues to own the leased asset and to provide depreciation expenses. Periodic rentals are accounted for as current operating income.

Summary of Basic Lease Accounting Issues for Lessees and Lessors

Lessee

Operating lease
- Lessee is considered to be renting (not owning) the asset from the lessor.
- Lessee makes periodic rent payments to the lessor; these are accounted for as current operating expenses:

Rent expense 000
    Cash   000
- At end of lease term, the asset is returned to the lessor.
- Lessee does not record depreciation expense.

Capital Lease
- Lessee is considered to own the asset for accounting purposes.
- Lease is capitalized on lessee's books as follows:

Leased asset 000
    Lease liability   000
- Lessee recognizes periodic payment as part interest and part reduction of principal:

Interest expense 000
Lease liability. 000
    Cash   000
- At the end of the lease term, the asset generally is retained by the lessee.
- Depreciation expense is recorded on the asset.

Lessor

Operating lease
- Lessor continues to own the asset that is leased to the lessee.
- Lessor collects periodic rent payments that are accounted for as current operating income:

Cash 000
    Leasing income   000
- At end of lease term, the asset is returned to the lessor.
- Lessor records depreciation on the asset.

Direct Financing Lease
- Asset is considered to be sold to the lessee at the inception of the lease.
- Asset is removed from lessor's books and replaced by receivable as follows:*

Lease receivable. 000
    Asset   000
- Lessor recognizes periodic collection of rent as part interest and part as reduction of principal:

Cash 000
    Interest revenue   000
    Lease receivable   000
- At the end of the lease period, the asset is generally retained by the lessee.
- No depreciation expense is taken during the time the asset is out on lease.

D. Accounting for capital leases

1. **Lessee accounting.**   A capital lease is accounted for as if the leased asset were being purchased and paid for by periodic installment payments. Accordingly, both an asset and liability **must be** recorded by the lessee at inception of the lease. The amount recorded (capitalized) is the present value of the minimum lease payments (or fair value of the asset, if lower). The effective interest rate used in the present value computation is the **lower** of:

a. The **lessee's incremental borrowing rate:**   The rate that the lessee would have incurred to borrow, over a similar term, the funds necessary to purchase the leased property; or

b. The **implicit rate** used by the lessor in determining the amount of the periodic payments, if it is known to the lessee.

The **effective interest method** is used to allocate each payment between interest expense and reduction in the lease obligation.

In addition:

a. The lessee is normally required to incur the **executory costs** of the leased asset.

b. The lessee should **depreciate** the "acquisition cost" of the leased asset in a manner consistent with its normal depreciation policy. The following three variables are required:

(1) The acquisition cost of the leased asset. This is the present value of the MLP to the lessee, or the fair value of the leased asset at inception, whichever is lower.

(2) The residual value of the leased asset. A distinction should be made between the residual value used to determine the lessee's MLP, and that used to compute depreciation expense. For depreciation purposes, if a capital lease meets Criterion 1 or 2, the residual value is the estimated market value of the leased asset at the end of **its economic life**. Otherwise, it is limited to the residual value **guaranteed** by the lessee.

(3) The useful life of the leased asset. If the lease meets either Criterion 1 or 2, the depreciable cost should be allocated over the estimated **economic life** of the asset. Otherwise, it is depreciated over the **lease term**.

c. Upon termination of the lease, both the net carrying value of the leased asset and the lease liability are removed from the books. A gain or loss is recognized in the period of termination for any difference.

ILLUSTRATION 1 -- Capital lease (lessee):

Lessor Company leased a piece of equipment to Lessee Company. The following information is pertinent:

. Fair value of leased asset at inception of lease $228,000.00
. Book value of leased asset at inception of lease $185,000.00
. Residual value at end of lease term, guaranteed by lessee $5,000.00
. Lease payment at end of each year $65,846.90
. Executory costs per year paid by lessee $2,500.00
. Estimated economic life of the asset .... 4 years
. Lease term .... 4 years
. Lessee's depreciation method .... Straight-line
. Lessor's implicit interest rate (known to lessee) 12%
. Lessee's incremental borrowing rate 14%
. Bargain purchase option .... none
. Title transfer at the end of lease term .... none
. Date of inception of lease .... January 1, 1992
. Fiscal year coincides with the calendar year

Required: Record the lease transactions for the lessee only.

Solution:

(1) **To classify the lease:**   The lease is a **capital lease** because the lease term (4 years) is more than 75% of the remaining useful life of the asset (Criterion 3). Note that the lease **does not** meet Criterion 4 since the present value of the MLP is less than 90% of the fair value of the leased asset at inception of the lease as shown below:

Present value of minimum lease payments
= $65,846.90 x pva, 12%, 4 + $5,000 x pv1, 12%, 4
= $65,846.90 x 3.03735 + $5,000 x .63552
= $200,000 + $3,177.60
= $203,177.60 < 90% x $228,000.

(2) **To prepare amortization schedule for the lease:**

Lease Amortization Schedule (On Ordinary Annuity Basis)

	Periodic Lease Payments	Periodic Interest Expenses (12%)	Reduction in Liability	Carrying Value of Liability
Jan. 1, 1992	-	-	-	$203,177.60
Dec. 31, 1992	$65,846.90	$24,381.31	$41,465.59	161,712.01
Dec. 31, 1993	65,846.90	19,405.44	46,441.46	115,270.55
Dec. 31, 1994	65,846.90	13,832.47	52,014.43	63,256.12
Dec. 31, 1995	65,846.90	7,590.78*	58,256.12*	5,000.00

* Rounded

(3) **To record lease transactions:**

January 1, 1992

(a) To record capitalization of lease:

Leased equipment	203,177.60	
Lease liability		203,177.60

During 1992

(b) To record executory costs:

Executory expenses	2,500.00	
Cash, payable, etc.		2,500.00

December 31, 1992

(c) To record lease payment:

Lease liability	41,465.59	
Interest expense	24,381.31	
Cash		65,846.90

(d) To record depreciation:

Depreciation expense	49,544.40 *	
Accumulated depreciation		49,544.40

* ($203,177.60 - $5,000) / 4

Entries (b), (c), and (d) are to be repeated each year until December 31, 1995 when the lease term ends.

December 31, 1995

(e) To record termination of the lease and return of leased asset to lessor:

Accumulated depreciation	198,177.60	
Lease liability	5,000.00	
Leased equipment		203,177.60

(4) To present lease asset/liability on the balance sheet:

Balance Sheet
For year ended December 31, 1992

Property plant & equipment:		Current liabilities:	
		Lease liability	$46,441.46
Leased equipment	$203,177.60		
Accumulated depre.	49,544.40	Noncurrent liabilities:	
Net	$153,633.20	Lease liability	$115,270.55

Note that the total carrying value of lease liability of $161,712.01 on December 31, 1992 is broken down into current and noncurrent components based on their relative due dates as indicated in the amortization schedule.

E. Lessor accounting:

a. Sales-type lease.   The lease is treated as an installment sale. The pertinent accounting procedure includes:

(1) At inception of the lease, sales revenues and cost of goods sold are recognized, resulting in a manufacturer's or dealer's profit or loss.

(2) As each rental payment is collected, lease receivable is reduced and interest revenue on the lease receivable is recognized.

(3) If the leased asset is returned to the lessor at the termination of the lease, the asset account is reestablished.

Note:- For a direct financing lease, the lease is treated as a straight inventory transfer-to-a lease receivable at the lease inception.
    - The rest of the lessor accounting is the same as the sales-type lease.

ILLUSTRATION 2 -- Sales-type lease (lessor):

Using the same data as in **ILLUSTRATION 1,** and further assume that the two additional criteria are all met. From the viewpoint of the lessor.

Required: Record the lease transactions for the lessor.

Solution:

(1) **To classify the lease:**   Since the lease meets Criterion 3, and satisfies the two additional criteria, it is a capital lease to the lessor. In addition, the lease involves a dealer's profit of $18,177.60 ($203,177.60 - $185,000.00), so it is a sales-type.

(2) **To prepare amortization schedule:**   The same amortization schedule as shown under the lessee accounting is applicable to the lessor, except that interest expense is changed to interest revenue, and lease liability is changed to lease (or MLP) receivable.

(3) **To record lease transactions:**

January 1, 1992

(a) To record the sale:

Lease receivable	203,177.60	
Cost of goods sold	185,000.00	
Sales revenue		203,177.60
Equipment		185,000.00

December 31, 1992

(b) To record receipt of lease payment:

Cash	65,846.90	
Lease receivable		41,465.59
Interest revenue		24,381.31

Entry (b) is to be repeated each year until the end of the lease term.

December 31, 1995

(c) To reestablish the equipment account:

Equipment	5,000.00	
Lease receivable		5,000.00

(4) To present lease receivable on the balance sheet:

Balance Sheet
As at December 31, 1992

Current assets:	
Lease receivable	$46,441.46
Investment and funds:	
Lease receivable	$115,270.55

Note that the above accounting procedure for the lessor is based on the **net investment method** under which lease receivable is recorded at the present value of the MLP. An alternative is the **gross investment method**, under which the receivable is recorded at the gross amount of the MLP. The excess of the gross amount over the present value of the MLP is credited to the unearned interest account, which is then debited when the revenue is earned.

b.   Direct financing lease.   Accounting for a direct financing lease is the same as for a sales-type lease, except that there is no sales revenue and cost of goods sold, and the lease transaction is recorded by debiting lease receivable and crediting asset.

F. Special Problems Relating to Leases

1. Bargain Purchase Options in Capital Leases

A bargain purchase option (BPO) permits a lessee to purchase the leased property, during a specified period of the lease term, at a price below the expected market value at that time. this price is sufficiently low to reasonably assure that the lessee will take advantage of the bargain. In effect, a BPO is viewed as a sale and transfer of ownership of the leased asset to the lessee at the specified bargain price. If the lease contains a BPO, only the rental payments over the lease term and the BPO payment are included in the minimum lease payments.

Including a BPO in a capital lease contract means that there are two cash flows to the lessor from the lessee; one is from the periodic rentals and the other is from the BPO price. Therefore, the lessor includes the BPO amount in computing the amount of each annual rental. The lessee includes the BPO in computing the cost of the leased asset to be capitalized.

2. Residual Value – (Guaranteed/Unguaranteed)

The residual value of a leased asset is the estimated fair value of the asset at the end of lease term. If the lease satisfies Criterion 1 or 2, the residual value belongs to the lessee, and is simply disregarded in the computation of the MLP.

However, if a capital lease meets only Criterion 3 or 4, the leased asset would eventually be returned to the lessor. In that case the lessee will include the residual value in its MLP only to the extent that it is guaranteed by the lessee. The lessor, however, should include the total residual value, guaranteed or not, in its MLP.

If the residual value is unguaranteed and the lease is a sales type, the leased asset is not **entirely** sold, and the lessor should deduct the present value of the unguaranteed residual value from both the cost of goods sold and the sales revenue. This special adjustment is not required for a direct-financing lease because it assumes no sale. In any event, the total present value of the MLP, which includes unguaranteed residual value, is still carried in the lease receivable account. At the termination of the lease, the lessor restores the asset account and removes the residual value of the leased asset from lease receivable.

Summary of Residual Value Accounting (Assuming the Lessor and Lessee Use the Same Interest Rate)

Situation	Symmetrical Entries and Schedules?	Reason
1. No residual value	Yes	No residual value effect on either party
2. Unguaranteed residual value (Exhibits 18–10 and 18–11)	No	Lessor includes (deducts) the present value of the residual value in lease rental computation. Lessee excludes (does not add) residual value in cost computation.
3. Residual value fully guaranteed by lessee (Exhibit 18–12)	Yes	Lessor includes (deducts) total residual value in lease rental computations. Lessee includes (adds) fully guaranteed residual value in cost computation.
4. Residual value partially guaranteed by lessee	No	Lessor includes (deducts) total residual value in lease rental computations. Lessee includes (adds) the portion of residual value that is partially guaranteed in cost computation.
5. Full or part residual value guarantee by third party (Exhibit 18–13)	No	Lessor includes (deducts) residual value guarantee in lease rental computations. Lessee excludes (does not add) residual value in cost computation (because the residual value is guaranteed by a third party).

ILLUSTRATION 4 -- Sales-type Lease with unguaranteed residual value (lessor)

Given the same data as in **ILLUSTRATION 1**, but assume that (1) lease payments are made at the **beginning** of each year, starting 1992, and (2) residual value of the leased asset is unguaranteed.

Required: Record the lease transactions for the lessor.

(1) **To classify the lease:**   The lease still meets Criterion 3. Since the first lease payment is made on January 1, 1992, instead of the year end, the present value of the MLP should be recalculated in order to conduct Criterion 4 test:

Present value of minimum lease payments
= \$65,846.90 x pvad, 12%, 4 + \$5,000 x pv1, 12%, 4
= \$65,846.90 x 3.40183 + \$5,000 x .63552
= \$223,999.96 + \$3,177.60
= \$227,177.56 > 90% x \$228,000

The lease also meets Criterion 4.

(2) **To prepare amortization schedule:**

Lease Amortization Schedule (On Annuity Due Basis)

	Receipts of Lease Payments	Periodic Interest Revenue (12%)	Reduction in Receivable	Carrying Value of Receivable
Jan. 1, 1992	-	-	-	\$227,177.56
Jan. 1, 1992	\$65,846.90	-	\$65,846.90	161,330.66
Dec. 31, 1992	-	\$19,359.68	(19,359.68)	180,690.34
Jan. 1, 1993	65,846.90	-	65,846.90	114,843.44
Dec. 31, 1993	-	13,781.21	(13,781.21)	128,624.65
Jan. 1, 1994	65,846.90	-	65,846.90	62,777.75
Dec. 31, 1994	-	7,533.33	(7,533.33)	70,311.08
Jan. 1, 1995	65,846.90	-	65,846.90	4,464.18
Dec. 31, 1995	-	535.82*	(535.82)*	5,000.00

* Rounded

(3)   To record lease transactions:

January 1, 1992

(a₁) To record the sale and cost of goods sold:

Lease receivable	227,177.56	
Cost of goods sold	185,000.00	
Sales revenue		227,177.56
Equipment		185,000.00

(a₂) To adjust for the unguaranteed residual value:

Sales	3,177.60	
Cost of goods sold		3,177.60

Note that the present value of unguaranteed residual value is adjusted to both cost of goods sold and sales revenue because it is "unsold." The above two entries may be combined.

(b)   To record receipt of lease payment:

Cash	65,846.90	
Lease receivable		65,846.90

December 31, 1992

(c)   To accrue interest for 1992:

Lease receivable	19,359.68	
Interest revenue		19,359.68

Entries (b) and (c) are repeated on each January 1 and December 31, respectively, until the end of 1995.

December 31, 1995

(d)   To reestablish the asset account:

Equipment		5,000.00
Lease receivable		5,000.00

If the fair value of the equipment is lower than the estimated residual value, a loss is recognized at the termination of the lease.

3. **Different interest rates** The lessor is in the driver's seat and sets whatever rate is considered reasonable and competitive. *CICA*; paragraph 3065.16 instructs lessees to use their incremental borrowing rate, unless the lessor's implicit interest rate is known to the lessee and that rate is lower than the lessee's own borrowing rate.

Although the lessor's interest rate is not explicitly stated in the lease contract, it usually is communicated orally and also may be found in business documents accompanying the lease. In fact, the rate charged by the lessor is frequently subject to negotiation. Thus, in most cases, the lessee simply uses the lower of the incremental borrowing rate or the lessor's implicit interest rate.

4. **Initial Direct Costs**

Initial direct costs are costs incurred by the lessor that are associated directly with negotiating and consummating a completed lease transaction including legal fees, cost of credit investigations, commissions, and clerical costs directly related to initiating the lease. For **operating leases,** such costs are **deferred and amortized** over the lease term to match against rental income. For **direct-financing leases**, the lessor should account for initial direct costs as part of the investment in the leased asset. This means that these costs must be added to the cost of the leased asset to compute the annual rentals. The effect of this treatment is to spread the initial direct costs over the term of the lease and thereby match the expenditures with the related interest revenue. For **sales-type leases,** the initial direct cost is considered as part of selling expenses and should be expensed by the lessor in the year in which the lease is initiated (i.e., the sale is made).

5. **Executory costs** are expenses of ownership and use that include insurance, property taxes, and maintenance. In the case of an operating lease, the executory costs, typically, are paid by the lessor and are recovered by the lessor in the periodic lease rentals. In the case of a capital lease, a major part, if not all, of the executory costs usually are shifted by the lease contract for direct payment by the lessee. Therefore, they are not included in the periodic rentals. They should be excluded by the lessee in computing the present value of the periodic rentals for capitalization purposes.

G. Sales-Leaseback Arrangement

A sale-leaseback arrangement is an agreement in which the seller-lessee sells an asset and then continues to use the asset. The seller-lessee obtains cash while incurring a tax-deductible lease payment. The buyer-lessor receives the lease payments, depreciates the asset for tax purposes, and also may deduct for tax purposes any interest on debt used to finance the asset purchase. The seller-lessee accounts for the transaction as a sale and for the lease as a capital lease. The buyer-lessor accounts for the transaction as a purchase and the lease as a direct-financing lease.

A sale-leaseback transaction is one in which the owner of an asset sells and **immediately** leases it back from the purchaser. The use of the particular asset is thus not interrupted by the transaction. The related accounting procedure is summarized on the next page:

1. **Buyer-lessor.**   For a sale-leaseback transaction, if the lease otherwise qualifies as a capital lease, the buyer-lessor accounts for the transaction first as a **purchase** and then as a **direct-financing** lease. A sales-type lease is not permitted. If the lease is an operating lease, it is first recorded as a purchase and then as an operating lease.

2. **Seller-lessee.**   The seller-lessee should first record the sale and then the capital or operating lease using the criteria indicated earlier. However:

    a. If the fair (market) value of the asset at the time of sale is less than its undepreciated cost, the difference shall be immediately recognized as a loss.

    b. Otherwise, any profit or loss on the sale shall be deferred and amortized in proportion to the amortization of the leased asset, if a capital lease; or in proportion to the related gross rental over the lease term, if an operating lease. Note that, in a sale-leaseback transaction, an artificial loss could incur even if the fair value is above the undepreciated cost of the leased asset.

H. **The *CICA*, sec. 3065 requires the following disclosures with respect to leases:**

Lessee disclosures:

1. For capital leases
    a. *The gross amount of assets under capital leases and related accumulated amortization should be disclosed.*
    b. *Obligations related to leased assets should be shown separately from other long-term obligations. Particulars of obligations related to leased assets, including interest rates and expiry dates, should be shown separately from other long-term obligations. Significant restrictions imposed on the lessee as a result of the lease agreement should be disclosed.*
    c. *Any portion of lease obligations payable within a year out of current funds should be included in current liabilities.*
    d. *Disclosure should be made of the future minimum lease payments in aggregate and for each of the five succeeding years. A separate deduction should be made from the aggregate figures for amounts included in the minimum lease payments representing executory costs and imputed interest.*
    e. *The amount of amortization of leased property included in the determination of net income should be disclosed separately or as part of depreciation and amortization expense for fixed assets. Disclosure should also be made of methods and rates of amortization.*
    f. *Interest expense related to lease obligations should be disclosed separately, or as part of interest on long-term indebtedness.*
    g. *It may be appropriate to disclose the amount of future minimum rentals receivable from noncancelable subleases.*
2. For operating leases
    a. *Disclosure should be made of the future minimum lease payments, in the aggregate and for each of the five succeeding years under operating leases. The nature of other commitments under such leases should also be described. Leases with an initial term of one year or less may be excluded.*
    b. *It may be desirable to disclose the amount of operating lease rentals included in the determination of net income.*

Lessor disclosures

1. For sales-type and direct financing leases:
   a. The net investment in the lease is considered to be distinct from other assets and disclosed separately.
   b. For purposes of statement presentation, the lessor's net investment in the lease would include:
      i. The minimum lease payments receivable, less any executory costs and related profit included therein; plus
      ii. Any unguaranteed residual value of the leased property accruing to the lessor; less
      iii. Unearned finance income remaining to be allocated to income over the lease term.
   c. When income tax factors have been considered in accounting for a direct financing or sales-type lease, any unamortized investment tax credit would either be deducted in computing the net investment in the lease or shown as a deferred credit.
   d. *The lessor's net investment in direct financing and sales-type leases should be disclosed and, in a classified balance sheet, segregated between current and long-term portions. Finance income from direct financing or sales-type leases should be disclosed. Disclosure should be made of how the investment in leases has been computed for purposes of recognizing income.*
2. For operating leases
   a. *Disclosure should be made of the cost of property held for leasing purposes and the amount of accumulated depreciation.*
   b. *Rental income from operating leases should be disclosed.*

I. Real Estate Leases

Leases that involve real estate (land and buildings) are subject to special accounting treatment as summarized below:

1. Lease involving land only.

A lease involving land only is accounted for by the **lessee** as a capital lease if the lease meets Criterion 1 or 2. Otherwise, it is an operating lease. If the lease meets Criterion 1 or 2 and a dealer's profit is involved, the lease is accounted for by the **lessor** as a sales-type lease. The two additional criteria for the lessor are not applicable. The lease is direct financing if it satisfies Criterion 1 or 2 and the two additional criteria but involves no dealer's profit. Note that Criterion 3 is not applicable to land, and that a lease meets Criterion 4 would in all probability also meet Criterion 1.

2. Lease involving both land and building.

For a lease involving both land and building and meeting Criterion 1 or 2, the **lessee's** accounting is unchanged. The **lessor**, on the other hand, treats the land and building as a single unit, using either a sales-type or direct-financing lease, as appropriate.

If the lease meets only Criterion 3 or 4 and the fair value of the land is less than 25% of the total fair value, both the lessee and the lessor treat the land and the building as one unit and as a capital lease.

If, however, the fair value of the land equals or exceeds 25% of the total fair value, the lessee and the lessor treat each separately. The lessor accounts for the building as a sales-type or direct-financing lease and for the land as an operation lease. The lessee accounts for the land as an operating lease and for the building as a capital lease. If none of the four criteria is met, the lessee uses operating-lease accounting.

J.   Tax Considerations for Leases

Tax considerations are an important factor in many leasing arrangements.

The lessee may be unable to use the tax benefits provided in purchasing an asset -- namely, depreciation, interest on debt incurred in connection with the acquisition, and the investment tax credit when available. It may be that the lessee is in a growth phase and has little or no taxable income against which tax benefits could be applied and probably has operating losses being carried forward from previous years. Such companies tend to be short on cash and must borrow heavily to finance new asset acquisitions. The company has ample internal means for sheltering future taxable income; tax benefits from leasing would go to waste.

But tax benefits that the lessee can't use might be extremely valuable to some other company that has a large cash position and is reporting high levels of taxable income. Such a company is probably in the market for tax savings. The solution, of course, is to match the cash-poor company (in the market to acquire assets) with the cash-rich company (in the market for tax savings). Then the task is structuring a lease transaction that meets both parties' needs. The wealthy company with high taxable income becomes the lessor and retains the tax benefits that otherwise would be passed on to the lessee. The needy company benefits by negotiating lease rental terms below the going market rate.

By allowing the use of accelerated depreciation methods (i.e., capital cost allowances). Revenue Canada makes tax incentives more attractive and thereby encourages leasing transactions. Similarly, the existence and extent to which the Income Tax Act allows investment tax credits to be taken also works in favor of leasing.

KEY CONCEPTS

Bargain purchase option   An option that allows the lessee to purchase the leased asset at the end of lease term at a price so low that the exercise of the option is reasonably assured.

Capital lease to the lessee   A noncancellable lease that meets any of the following criteria: (1) ownership transfer, (2) a bargain purchase option, (3) term of the lease is at least 75% of the remaining economic life of the leased asset, or (4) the present value of minimum lease payments is at least 90% of the fair value of the leased asset at inception of the lease.

Capital lease to the lessor   A noncancellable lease that meets any of the four criteria under the capital lease to the lessee, and both of the additional criteria: (1) the collectibility of the lease is assured, and (2) no important uncertainties surround the amount of unreimbursable costs yet to be incurred.

Direct-financing lease   A capital lease to the lessor which does not involve manufacturer's or dealer's profit or loss.

Initial direct costs   Costs incurred by the lessor that are directly associated with accomplishing the lease transaction. Under a sales-type lease, it should be expensed as incurred. Under a direct-financing lease, it should be included in the investment in the leased asset. Under an operating lease, it should be deferred and amortized over the term of the lease.

Lease term   The fixed noncancellable term of the lease plus any period covered by renewal options, the exercise of which are reasonably assured. The lease term should never exceed the date a bargain purchase option becomes exercisable.

Minimum lease payments–lessee   Payments that the lessee is obligated to make in connection with the leased property. They include (1) the amount of periodic rental payments, (2) the amount of bargain purchase option, (3) the residual value guaranteed by the lessee and (4) the amount of penalty for failure to renew the lease. The last two items are considered only if the lease does not meet Criterion 1 or 2.

Minimum lease payments–lessor   Payments that the lessor expects to receive from the lessee and other parties related to the lease. They include the lessee's minimum lease payments plus residual value not guaranteed by the lessee.

Residual value   The estimated market value of the leased property at the end of the lease term. It is included in the minimum lease payments of a capital lease which does not transfer ownership at the end of lease or contain a bargain purchase option.

Sales-type lease   A capital lease to the lessor which involves manufacturer's or dealer's profit or loss.

REVIEW QUESTIONS AND EXERCISES

TRUE-FALSE

Indicate whether each of the following statements is true or false by circling the correct response.

T   F   1. Both lessors and lessees should classify lease transactions as either capital leases or operating leases, and lessees should further subclassify capital leases as sales-type or direct-financing leases.

T   F   2. One sufficient criterion for classification as a capital lease by a lessee is that the present value of the minimum lease payments is equal to 75% or more of the fair value of the leased asset.

T   F   3. In computing the present value of the minimum lease payments, the lessee should use the lower of its incremental borrowing rate or the implicit rate used by the lessor if known to the lessee.

T   F   4. For a lessor to classify a lease agreement as a capital lease, the collectibility of the minimum lease payments must be reasonably assured.

T   F   5. An asset classified as an operating lease should be depreciated by the lessee over the period of time the lessee expects to use the asset.

T   F   6. In a capital lease containing a bargain purchase option, the lessee should depreciate the asset over its economic life even if it is beyond the lease term.

T   F   7. In accounting for a capital lease, the lessor debits a leased asset account for the present value of the minimum lease payments.

T   F   8. If the present value of the minimum lease payments exceeds the carrying value of the leased asset, a capital lease is characterized as a direct-financing lease.

T   F   9. The accounting for a capital lease by the lessee is unaffected by whether the lease is a direct-financing or sales-type lease.

T   F   10. When a bargain purchase option is present, the bargain purchase option price should be part of the minimum lease payments to both the lessee and the lessor.

T F 11. When a residual value is guaranteed by the lessee, the guaranteed residual value should be included in the minimum lease payments to both the lessee and the lessor.

T F 12. When an unguaranteed residual value is present, the minimum lease payments to both the lessee and the lessor should include the unguaranteed residual value.

T F 13. Initial direct costs should be expensed immediately, regardless of whether the lease is a capital or operating lease.

T F 14. In a sale-leaseback transaction, the seller-lessee should recognize gain or loss from the sale immediately regardless of whether the fair value of the leased asset is less than its book value.

EXERCISE 1

Wax Company Ltd. leases a piece of equipment to Johnson Company Ltd. under a three year lease agreement on January 1, 1992. Payments (excluding executory costs) are $20,000 on January 1 of each year starting 1992. The equipment's carrying value is $42,000.

The expected useful life of the equipment is 3 years, and the expected residual value is zero. The lessor's interest rate implicit in the lease, unknown to the lessee, is 7%. The lessee's incremental borrowing rate is 8%. Assume that the collectibility of the lease payments is reasonably assured and there are no important uncertainties surrounding the lessor's unreimbursable costs yet to be incurred.

Required: **Answer the following for the lessee: (round off to the nearest dollar)**

1. What is the appropriate classification of the lease? Why?

2. Determine the present value of the lease:

3. Record the lease contract on January 1, 1992:

4. Record payment on January 1, 1992:

5. Record interest accrued for 1992:

6. Record depreciation expense for 1992:

7. Record payment on January 1, 1993:

EXERCISE 2

Based on the information described in **EXERCISE 1.**

Required: Answer the following for the lessor: (round off to the nearest dollar)

1. What is the appropriate classification of the lease? Why?

2. Determine the present value of the lease:

3. Record the lease contract on January 1, 1992:

4. Record receipt of payment on January 1, 1992:

5. Record interest accrued for 1992:

6. Record receipt of payment on January 1, 1993:

EXERCISE 3

Winnipeg Company Ltd. leased a computer from Western Super Stores Inc. on January 1, 1992. The lease is for a four-year period expiring December 31, 1995. Equal annual payments of $10,000 are due on December 31 of each year. The cost of the computer to Western Super Store was $30,000. The residual value of $1,000 is not guaranteed by either the lessee or any third parties. The lease is properly classified as a capital lease by both the lessee and the lessor. Both companies use straight-line depreciation. The rate of interest contemplated by both firms is 10%.

Required: Answer the following for the lessee:

1. Determine the present value of the lease:

2. Record the lease contract on January 1, 1992:

3. Record payment on December 31, 1992:

4. Record depreciation expense for 1992:

EXERCISE 4

Based on the same data as in **EXERCISE 3.**

Required: Answer the following for the lessor:

1. Determine the present value of the lease:

2. Record the lease contract on January 1, 1992:

3. Record receipt of payment on December 31, 1992:

4. Record termination of lease on December 31, 1995:

MULTIPLE CHOICE

Enter the letter corresponding to the response which **best** completes each of the following statements or questions.

_____ 1.   When a lease transaction is accounted for as an operating lease:

     a.   the leased asset should be depreciated by the lessee over the term of the lease.
     b.   any advance payment by the lessee should be expensed by the lessee immediately.
     c.   the lessee would record a leased asset and a related obligation at the present value of the minimum lease payments.
     d.   the lessor should depreciate the leased asset over its economic life.

_____ 2.   When a lease is classified as a capital lease and the lease contains a bargain purchase option, the leased asset should be depreciated:

     a.   over the term of the lease.
     b.   over the economic life of the leased asset.
     c.   over the term of the lease or the economic life of the leased asset.
     d.   by the lessor.

_____ 3.   Of the following lease arrangements, which would most likely be classified as an operating lease by the lessee?

     a.   The present value of the minimum lease payments is $15,500, and the fair value of the leased asset is $16,000.
     b.   The lease contract contains a clause to transfer the title to the leased asset from the lessor to the lessee.
     c.   The lease contract allows the lessee to buy the leased asset at the market price at the end of the lease term.
     d.   The economic life of the asset is 10 years, and the lease term is 8 years.

_____ 4.   In accounting for a lease transaction classified as a capital lease, over the term of the lease:

     a.   the asset should be depreciated by the lessor in a systematic and rational manner.
     b.   the lease payments by the lessee constitute a payment for lease liability plus interest.
     c.   the gross sum of the lease payments equals the dollar amount that would have been paid by the lessee to purchase the property on the date of the inception of the lease.
     d.   any manufacturer's or dealer's profit or loss should be amortized.

_____ 5. Which of the following conditions is **not** a criterion for classifying a lease as a capital lease:

    a. The present value of the minimum lease payments is at least 75% of the fair value of the leased asset.

    b. The lease transfers ownership in the leased asset to the lessee at the end of the lease term.

    c. The lessee has the option of acquiring the asset at the end of the lease term at a bargain price.

    d. The lease term is greater than three-fourths of the economic life of the asset.

_____ 6. For the lessor to classify a lease agreement as a capital lease, there must be no important uncertainties surrounding the amount of unreimbursable costs yet to be incurred, and:

    a. the lease agreement must transfer ownership to the lessee.

    b. the lessor must be reasonably certain of the collectibility of the lease payments.

    c. the lease term and the economic life of the asset must be approximately the same.

    d. the lessee must guarantee the residual value of the leased asset.

_____ 7. The primary difference between a direct-financing lease and a sales-type lease is that:

    a. in a direct-financing lease, a third party to the transaction supplies a major portion of the financing of the leased asset.

    b. the sales-type lease involves a legal transfer of title to the asset.

    c. the lessor earns both interest income and a manufacturer's or dealer's profit with a sales-type lease.

    d. in a direct-financing lease, the asset is sold by the lessee, who immediately leases the asset back from the purchaser/lessor.

_____ 8. In a sale-leaseback transaction, unless the fair (market) value of the asset at the time of sale is less than its undepreciated cost:

    a. a loss from the sale should be deferred and amortized, but a gain should be recognized immediately.

    b. a gain from the sale should be deferred and amortized, but a loss should be recognized immediately.

    c. any gain or loss from the sale should be deferred and amortized over the term of the lease.

    d. any gain or loss from the sale should be recognized immediately.

____ 9. Lessee Company leased a computer from Lessor Corporation on January 1, 1992, for a ten-year period, the useful life of the asset. Equal rental payments of $5,000 are due on January 1 of each year. The first payment was made on January 1, 1992. The present value of the minimum lease payments over the lease term discounted at 10% was $33,795. The balance in Lessee's lease liability account (including accrued interest) at december 31, 1992 should be:

   a. $26,680
   b. $27,256
   c. $30,392
   d. $31,675

____ 10. Peter Supermarket Inc.leased a piece of equipment from Dewolf Leasing Ltd. on July 1, 1992, for an eight-year period. Equal payments under the lease are $12,000, due on July 1 of each year. The first payment was made on July 1, 1992. The rate of interest is 10%. The selling price of the computer is $70,400 and its cost to Dewolf $56,000. If the lease is appropriately recorded as a sales-type lease, the amount of interest income Dewolf should record for the year ended December 31, 1992 is:

   a. $0
   b. $2,800
   c. $2,920
   d. $3,200

____ 11. On October 1, 1992 Harold Ltd. signed an operating lease for a building with Funk Company for 6 years, at $10,000 per year. At the inception of the lease, Harold paid $20,000, covering rent for the first two years. Harold closed its books on December 31, and correctly reported $20,000 as rent expense on its 1992 income tax return. How much should Harold report in the 1992 income statement as rent expense:

   a. $0
   b. $2,500
   c. $1,667
   d. $3,333

____ 12. Summer Limited leased a new piece of equipment to Winter Inc. on January 1, 1992 for a four-year period. Rental payments of $4,000 are due on January 1 of each year. The first payment was made on January 1, 1992. The fair value of the equipment at the inception of the lease is $14,000 and the cost of the equipment to Summer Ltd. is $10,000. Summer Ltd. properly classified the lease as a sales-type lease. For the year ended December 31, 1992, what amount of profit on the sale and interest income should Summer Ltd. record if the applicable interest rate is 10%?

	Gain on Sale	Interest income
a.	$ 0	$ 995
b.	$3,947	$ 995
c.	$ 995	$3,947
d.	$3,947	$ 0

_____ 13. Short Corporation leased a machine to Shift Limited on January 1, 1992, for a five-year lease. The machine has an economic life of ten years, a residual value at the end of lease term of $50,000, and the residual value at the end of economic life of zero. The lease contains a **bargain purchase option** which allows Shift to purchase the leased machine at the end of the lease term for $25,000. Equal lease payments of $15,000 are made on each January 1, and the first payment is made on January 1, 1992. The applicable interest rate to both the lessee and the lessor is 12%. For the year ended December 31, 1992, Shift should report lease liabilities as:

	Current	Noncurrent
a.	$15,000	$51,916
b.	$15,000	$15,916
c.	$51,746	$15,000
d.	$51,916	$15,000

_____ 14. Based on the same information as in Question 13, Shift should report the following in its financial statements for the year ended December 31, 1992:

	Interest expense	Depreciation expense
a.	$3,585	$14,950
b.	$7,170	$7,475
c.	$7,475	$7,170
d.	$3,585	$7,475

SOLUTIONS TO REVIEW QUESTIONS AND EXERCISES

TRUE-FALSE

1.	F	5.	F	9.	T	13.	F
2.	F	6.	T	10.	T	14.	F
3.	T	7.	F	11.	T		
4.	T	8.	F	12.	F		

EXERCISE 1

Lessee Accounting:

1. **What is the appropriate classification of the lease? Why?**

   The lessee should classify the lease as a capital lease since Criterion 3 is met, i.e., the term of the lease is greater than 75% of the economic life of the leased asset.

2. **Determine the present value of the lease:**

   Present value of MLP to the lessee
   = $20,000 x pvad, 8%, 3
   = $20,000 x 2.78326
   = $55,665.20 = $55,665.000

3. **Record the lease contract on January 1, 1992:**

Leased equipment	55,665.00	
Lease liability		55,665.00

4. **Record payment on January 1, 1992:**

Lease liability	20,000.00	
Cash		20,000.00

5. **Record interest accrued for 1992:**

Interest expense	2,853.00	
Lease liability		2,853.00

   ($55,665.00 - $20,000) x 8% = $2,853.22 = $2853.00

6.   Record depreciation expense for 1992:

Depreciation expense ($55,665.00 / 3)	18,555.00	
Accumulated depreciation		18,555.00

7.   Record payment on January 1, 1993:

Lease liability	20,000.00	
Cash		20,000.00

EXERCISE 2

Lessor Accounting:

1.   What is the appropriate classification of the lease? Why?

The lessor should classify the lease as a sales-type lease since Criterion 3 and the two additional criteria are all met, and the lease involves profit.

2.   Determine the present value of the lease:

Present value of MLP to the lessor
= $20,000 x pvad, 7%, 3
= $20,000 x 2.80802
= $56,160.40 = $56,160.00

2.   Record the lease contract on January 1, 1992:

Lease receivable	56,160.00	
Cost of goods sold	42,000.00	
Sales		56,160.00
Equipment		42,000.00

4.   Record receipt of payment on January 1, 1992:

Cash	20,000.00	
Lease receivable		20,000.00

5.   Record interest accrued for 1992:

Lease receivable [($56,160.00 - $20,000) x 7%]	2,531.00	
Interest revenue		2,531.00

6.   Record receipt of payment on January 1, 1993:

Cash	20,000.00	
Lease receivable		20,000.00

EXERCISE 3

Lessee Accounting:

1. **Determine the present value of the lease:**

   Present value of MLP to the lessee
   = $10,000 x pva, 10%, 4
   = $10,000 x 3.16987
   = $31,698.70

2. **Record the lease contract on January 1, 1992:**

Leased equipment	31,698.70	
Lease liability		31,698.70

3. **Record payment on December 31, 1992:**

Interest expense ($31,698.70 x 10%)	3,169.87	
Lease liability	6,830.13	
Cash		10,000.00

4. **Record depreciation expense for 1992:**

Depreciation expense ($31,698.70 / 4)	7,924.68	
Accumulated depreciation		7,924.68

EXERCISE 4

Lessor Accounting:

1. **Determine the present value of the lessor:**

   Present value of MLP to the lessor
   = $10,000 x pva, 10%, 4 + $1,000 x pv1, 10%, 4
   = $10,000 x 3.16987 + $1,000 x .68301
   = $31,698.70 + $683.01
   = $32,381.71

2. **Record the lease contract on January 1, 1992:**

Lease receivable	32,381.71	
Cost of goods sold	30,000.00	
Sales		32,381.71
Equipment		30,000.00

3. Record receipt of payment on December 31, 1992:

Cash	10,000.00	
Lease receivable		6,761.83
Interest revenue		3,238.17

4. Record termination of lease on December 31, 1995:

Equipment	1,000.00	
Lease receivable		1,000.00

MULTIPLE CHOICE:

1.	d	5.	a	9.	d	13.	a
2.	b	6.	b	10.	c	14.	b
3.	c	7.	c	11.	b		
4.	b	8.	c	12.	b		

Computations:

9. (d) Lease liability (Dec. 31, 1992)
= Acquisition cost - First lease payment + Interest for 1992
= $33,795 - $5,000 + ($33,795 - $5,000) x 10%
= $28,795 + $2,880
= $ 31,675.

To prove:
Lease Amortization Schedule (On Annuity Due Basis)

	Periodic Lease Payments	Periodic Interest Expense (10%)	Reduction in Liability	Carrying Value of Liability
Jan. 1, 1992	–	–	–	$33,795
Jan. 1, 1992	$5,000.00	–	$5,000	28,795
Dec. 31, 1992		2,880	(2,880)	31,675

10. (c) Interest income for the first six months (July 1 to December 31, 1992):
= ($70,400 - $12,000) x 10% / 2
= $2,920

11. (b) Rent expense for the first three months (October 1 to December 31, 1992):
= $10,000 x 3 / 12
= $2,500

12. (b)   Gain on sale = Present value of MLP - Cost
           = $4,000 x pvad, 10%, 4 - $10,000
           = $4,000 x 3.48685 - $10,000
           = $13,947 - $10,000
           = $3,947

           Interest income for 1992
           = ($13,947 - $4,000) x 10%
           = $9,947 x 10%
           = $995

13. (a)

           Present value of MLP
           = $15,000 x pvad, 12%, 5 + $25,000 x pv1, 12%, 5
           = $15,000 x 4.03735 + $25,000 x .56743
           = $60,560.25 + $14,185.75
           = $74,746

Lease Amortization Schedule (On Annuity Due Basis)

	Periodic Lease Payments	Periodic Interest Expense (12%)	Reduction in Liability	Carrying Value of Liability
Jan. 1, 1992	-	-	-	$74,746
Jan. 1, 1992	$15,000	-	$15,000	59,746
Dec. 31, 1992		7,170	(7,170)	66,916
Jan. 1, 1993	15,000	-	15,000	51,916

Total lease liability at Dec. 31, 1992
= $66,916

Current lease liability
= $15,000

Noncurrent lease liability
= $66,916 - $15,000
= $51,916

14. (b)   Interest expense (1992)
           = $7,170

           Depreciation expense
           = $74,746 / 10
           = $7,475

CHAPTER 19

Accounting for Pensions

CHAPTER OBJECTIVES

This chapter is designed to enable students to:

A. Explain the fundamental pension concepts.

B. Explain the basic nature of pension expense and compute the components of pension expense not subject to delayed recognition.

C. Distinguish between projected benefit obligation and accrued pension cost.

D. Explain unrecognized pension costs and their effect on pension expense.

E. Compute and record pension expense and balance sheet pension accounts.

F. Prepare a reconciliation of funded status and the balance in the reported pension account.

G. Explain the concepts of pension plan settlements, curtailments, and termination benefits.

H. Explain the concepts for accounting for pension plans.

CHAPTER OVERVIEW

A. A pension plan is an arrangement whereby a company agrees to provide benefits to employees upon retirement or upon termination of employment for reasons other than retirement based on specified formula. In most cases, the company engages a trustee to receive periodic funding payments, to invest those assets, and to disburse payments to retired employees from the pension fund.

Most pension plains conform to Income Tax Act requirements to qualify for the following tax advantages:

* Employers deduct contributions to the pension fund, subject to certain limitations.
* Employers exclude pension fund earnings from taxable income.

* Employees exclude employer contributions from taxable income, subject to certain limitations
* Employees defer tax on benefits until retirement.

In the process of setting up a pension plan, a time line depicting service and retirement periods similar to this one is used:

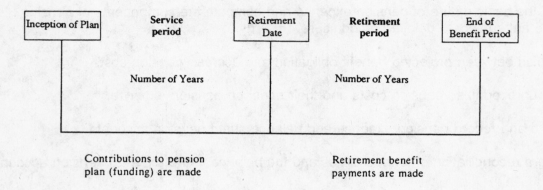

The entities in any pension plan can be shown as follows
Relationships among Entities in a Pension Plan

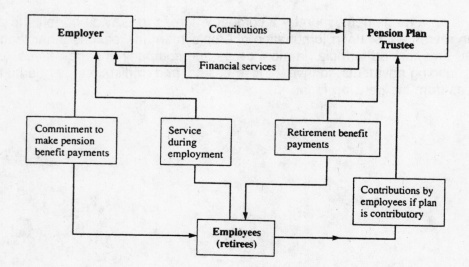

Importance of Actuaries Actuaries--professionals trained in a specific branch of mathematics and statistics--develop the estimates of future retirement benefit payments needed to compute the employer's pension expense and pension obligation. Actuaries use statistical models incorporating several variables, including turnover, inflation, future compensation levels, life expectancy, the interest rate used for discounting benefit payments, final retirement age, and administrative costs.

The actuary works with the employer to develop the historical data and expected changes in the employee population for this estimation process. Actuaries also give advice on the attributes of the plan most appropriate to the employer.

When choosing the discount rate, actuaries consider the following factors:

* Rates implicit in annuity contracts offered by insurance companies.
* Information on interest rates from Statistics Canada.
* Returns on high-quality fixed-income investments expected during the accumulation period.

Firms also consider the average age of employees. For example, the discount rate for a plan covering workers close to retirement might reflect a portfolio of investments with shorter maturities than those of a plan covering a younger work force.

The two (2) types of pension plans are:

1.   Defined contribution plan: A defined contribution plan specifies the formula used to determine the amount of employer's contributions. No promise is made concerning the future benefits to be received by employees.

    The specified (defined) amount of contributions for a period is debited to the pension expense account and credited to the cash account if paid, or to a payable account if accrued. This accounting procedure is straight-forward.

2.   Defined benefit plan: A defined benefit plan, the focus of this chapter, specifies either the amount of benefits to be received by employees upon retirement, or, much more likely, a formula to be used for the determination of these benefits. Note that the defined pension benefits must include **vested benefit**, i.e., the portion of future retirement benefits that an employee is entitled to receive even though that person does not remain an employee of the company until retirement.

B.   **Section 3460 of the *CICA Handbook*, "Pension Costs and Obligations"** The original *CICA Handbook* pronouncement on pensions was issued in December 1968 and revised in October 1973. It offered employers significant latitude in the methods of determining pension expense and required only minimal disclosure. In January 1974, the CICA Accounting Standards Board recognized that section 3460 no longer met the needs of the users of the financial statements.

After some fine-tuning based on comment letters to the exposure drafts, the CICA approved and issued the revised section 3460, "Pension Costs and Obligation," in April 1986.

The revised Section 3460 retained the basic idea that the periodic pension be recognized before the actual payment of benefits to retirees and significantly changed accounting for pensions in three ways:

* The cost of a pension plan is more directly related to the terms of the plan. A projected-benefit method prorated on services for defined benefit plans must be used to determine the retirement benefit.
* Employers now recognized a liability equal to the under funded obligation based on current compensation levels.
* The recommendations expanded disclosure including the actuarial present value of accrued pension benefits attributed to services rendered up to the reporting date, and the value of plan assets (paragraph 3460.60).

C.   **Accrued/Prepaid Pension Cost Account**   This account title is used to indicate that the pension plan is either underfunded (liability) or overfunded (asset).

Employer Pension Obligations   The **projected benefit obligation** (PBO) is the actuarial present value of the benefits attributed to employee service rendered to date, as measured by the pension formula. Service cost increases PBO, while benefit payments reduce PBO.

The AcSB believes that PBO is the most representationally faithful measure of the pension obligation because it is an estimate of a present obligation to make future cash payments as a result of past transactions. The going-concern assumption supports the use of future compensation levels in calculating PBO.

Plan Assets   Plan assets are exclusively restricted for the payment of pension benefits. Except for plan terminations, the employer should not have access to plan assets. Otherwise, a plan's funded status is very uncertain. Plan assets include investments (primarily stocks, bonds, and other securities) and operational assets used in administering the pension fund.

Investment assets are valued at market value or market-related value. The market value is the amount realizable through normal sale. **Market-related value** equals market value or a calculated value that is adjusted to market value of plan investments over a period not exceeding five years. The use of market-related value reduces the volatility of periodic pension expense.

For simplicity, this chapter assumes that the pension fund consists entirely of investments and that market (or fair) value and market-related value are equal.

Funded Status   The funded status of a plan is the difference between PBO and the plan assets at fair value; it indicates whether the plan is underfunded or overfunded. Funded status is the critical measure of a pension plan.

D.   **Amortization of Group 2 Components**

Rationale for Present Accounting Treatment   The unrecognized transition item is actually the result of several components: (1) unrecognized costs of past retroactive plan amendments, (2) unrecognized net gain or loss from previous periods, and (3) the cumulative effect of past accounting principles which were different from the current section 3460. The unrecognized transition item is treated as a change in estimate: currently and prospectively through delayed recognition amortization. This treatment provides yet another source of income smoothing.

E. **Pension Expense**   Pension expense is the net cost of these six components:

1.   *a.*   Service cost.
 b.   Interest cost.
 c.   Actual return on plan assets.
2.   Amortization of unrecognized prior service cost.
3.   Amortization of gains or losses from changes in actuarial assumptions.
4.   Amortization of experience gains or losses.
5.   Transition asset or liability.
6.   Gains or losses on plan settlements or curtailments.

The six components may be classified into two groups as follows:

Group 1 -- The entire amount of each component in this group is **immediately** recognized and included in current pension expense:

1.   **a.**   **Service Cost**   Service cost is the actuarial present value of pension benefits attributed to employee service in a period based on the pension benefit formula.

 b.   **Interest cost:**   The interest cost on projected benefit obligation outstanding during the period, measured by multiplying the beginning balance of projected benefit obligation by the actuary's interest (discount) rate, i.e., the settlement rate at which the pension benefits could be effectively settled. Note that in the year of plan amendment, the resulting prior service cost is added to the beginning PBO for the computation of current interest cost.

 c.   **Expected return on plan assets:**   The return derived by multiplying the beginning market-related value of the plan assets by an expected long-term rate of return, i.e., the average rate of return expected to be realized from the operation of the pension plan.

 Actual Return on Plan Assets   The actual return on plan assets, is the increase or decrease in plan assets at fair value, adjusted for contributions and benefit payments. The following equation shows the changes in the fund during a period:

Beginning fund balance
+ Actual return
+ Employer contributions
- <u>Benefit payments</u>
<u>Ending fund balance</u>

Summary of Relationships among Pension Items

		Effect On:	
Pension Item	Benefit Expense	Projected Plan Obligation	Assets
Service Cost	Increase	Increase	No effect
Interest Cost	Increase	Increase	No effect
Actual return	Decrease	No effect	Increase
Contributions	No effect*	No effect	Increase
Benefit payments	No effect	Decrease	Decrease

*Contributions indirectly reduce future pension expense by increasing plan assets and, therefore, actual return.

Group 2 – The amount of each component in this group, once determined, is subject to **delayed recognition** and has to be amortized over some number of years:

2.   **Prior service cost:**   The cost of retroactive pension benefits caused by either the initial adoption or amendment of a plan attributed to services rendered by employees in periods before the adoption or amendment. In the year of plan adoption or amendment, the related prior service cost should first be deferred and then amortized starting in the same year.

Unexpected gains or losses: Pension cost accounting is based on actuarial cost methods, which are, in turn, based on (1) the expected fund earnings, and (2) actuarial assumptions concerning employee turnover rates, mortality ages, compensation levels, retirement ages, etc. Conceivably, the expectation may not be realized, and/or the assumptions may have to be revised. In these cases, the following gain and/or loss treatments would be resulted: (in #3 and #4)

3.   Gains and losses arising from changes in assumptions are amortized to pension expense over the expected average remaining service life of the employee group.

4.   Experience gains and losses arise because period-end expected values for either the plan assets or the PBO differ from actual period-end values.

The experience gains and losses are thus determined by using the actual balance at the beginning of the period, adding or subtracting the transactions during the period to arrive at the expected values, and comparing the actual values as determined by the trustee and actuary, respectively, to the expected values.

Section 3460 of the *CICA Handbook* allows that the amortization of any adjustments for changes in assumptions or experience gains and losses may commence in the period following their determination.

5. **Transition Asset or Liability** The transition asset or liability equals the difference, at date of transition, between the actuarial present value of the accrued pension benefits, and the value of pension fund assets. The transition asset or liability affects neither PBO nor plan assets. The transition item includes unrecognized gains and losses and unrecognized prior service cost from accounting under the earlier version of section 3460.

When a liability, the transition item is similar to past service cost. It is that part of under funded PBO resulting from benefits promised before transition to the new accounting principles, and may result from past retroactive grants. The amortization of a transition asset is a gain and reduces pension expense.

The transition asset or liability is amortized on a straight-line basis over the average remaining service period of employees expected to receive benefits under the plan.

6. **Gains or losses on plan settlements or curtailments** Employers occasionally make changes to defined benefit plans causing immediate recognition of certain items subject to delayed recognition under section 3460 with guidelines to account for these events.

For example, plan termination or a plant closing resulting in a significant reduction of personnel may require immediate recognition of unrecognized pension items. Future benefit payments and, therefore, projected benefit obligations (PBO) are reduced. The rationale for delayed recognition no longer applies under these circumstances.

Pension plan curtailments, pension plan settlements, and termination benefits are planned changes, as opposed to actuarial or experience gains and losses.

For settlements, curtailments, and termination benefits, the employer discloses the following information: (1) a description of the event and (2) the amount of gain or loss recognized. When the gain or loss from settlements, curtailments, or termination benefits is directly related to the disposal of a business segment, it is included in the total gain or loss reported from discontinued operations (discussed in Chapter 4).

F. A Spreadsheet Approach to Pension Cost Analysis

An amortization spreadsheet is prepared to determine pension expense. The spreadsheet is constructed on the basis of the following relationships:

If	Then	Where
1. Plan fully funded	PBO = PA	PBO = projected benefit obligation PA = pension plan assets
2. Plan underfunded	PBO = PA + APC	APC = accrued pension cost
3. Plan overfunded	PBO = PA − PPC	PPC = prepaid pension cost
4. PSC involved	PBO = PA + PSC	PSC = prior service cost
5. Gain involved	PBO = PA − UEG	UEG = unexpected gain (asset & liab.)
6. Loss involved	PBO = PA + UEL	UEL = unexpected loss (asset & liab.)
7. TC involved	PBO = PA + TC	TC = transition cost

The preceding relationships can be combined and generalized as follows:

$$PBO = PA + PSC +/- UEL/UEG + TC +/- APC/PPC$$

Note that for simplicity unexpected gains are combined with unexpected losses and prepaid pension cost is combined with accrued pension cost.

Each of the above elements is represented by a column on the spreadsheet. One more column, representing **pension expense (PE)**, is added to the spreadsheet to determine current pension expense. Once the expense is determined, it is closed (transferred) to the accrued pension cost. Note that the records on those elements on the spreadsheet are maintained respectively by three parties, namely, the actuary (PBO), the trustee (PA), and the company (all the rest).

Spreadsheet entries include the following:

Components of pension expense:

1.   **Group 1:**

   a.   **Service cost** increases both PBO and PE.

   b.   **Interest cost** increases both PBO and PE.

   c.   **Return** on plan assets increases PA and decreases PE.

2.   **Group 2:**

   a.   **Prior service cost:**

      (1)   PSC arises during the year increases both PBO and PSC.

      (2)   PSC amortized for the year decreases PSC and increases PE.

   b.   **Unexpected loss and gain:**

      (1)   Asset loss arises during the year decreases PA and increases unrecognized pension cost, whereas asset gain increases PA and decreases unrecognized pension cost.

      (2)   Liability loss arises during the year increases both PBO and unrecognized pension cost, whereas liability gain decreases both PBO and unrecognized pension cost.

      (3)   Unexpected loss amortized to the year decreases unrecognized pension cost and increases PE; whereas gain amortization increases unrecognized pension cost and decreases PE.

   c.   **Transition cost** amortized decreases TC and increase PE.

Additional entries:

1.   **Employer's contribution** increases PA and decreases APC/PPC.

2.   **Benefits paid** decreases both PBO and PA.

3.   **Current pension expense** transferred decreases PE and increases APC/PPC.

ILLUSTRATION -- Accounting for pensions

Given the following:

		1992	**1993**	**1994**
1.	Projected benefit obligation:			
	a. Beginning balance	$1,500	$1,550	$1,620
	b. Ending balance	1,550	1,620	1,950
2.	Plan assets (fair value)			
	a. Beginning balance	1,000	1,190	1,350
	b. Ending balance	1,190	1,350	1,460
3.	Service cost	180	200	240
4.	Prior service cost	0	0	180
5.	Unexpected losses (gains):			
	a. Asset loss (gain) occurred	(20)	10	(25)
	b. Liability loss (gain) occurred	(100)	0	130
6.	Unamortized transition cost at Jan. 1, 1992	500		
7.	Employer's contributions	250	335	350
8.	Benefits paid to retirees	180	285	400

9.   Additional information:
   a.   Interest (settlement) rate 10%
   b.   Actual return rate 10%
   c.   Amortization policies:

   (1)   Prior service cost amortized over .... 9 years
   (2)   Unexpected losses (gains):
         Amortization rate
         (applied to beginning unamortized balances) .. 10%
   (3)   Transition cost amortization rate 10%

1. Prepare Pension Plan spreadsheets for the three-year period

Pension Plan Spreadsheet 1992, 1993, 1994

Transition Liability, January 1, 1992:		
PBO Under Revised Section 3460	$1,500	
Fair Value of Plan Assets	1,000	
Transition Liability	$500	

	Memorandum Record			Statement Accounts	
	PBO (Actuary)	Plan Assets (Trustee)	Unrecog- nized Pension Cost	Pension Expense	Accrued/ Prepaid Pension Cost
1992					
Balance, January 1	$1,500	$1,000	$	$	$
Transition Liabilities			500		
Service Cost	180			180 DR	180 CR
Interest Cost (PBO x 10%)	150			150 DR	150 CR
Actual Return (PA x 10%)		100		100 CR	100 DR
Experience Gain		20	(20)		
Actuarial Gain	(100)		(100)		
Contribution		250			250 DR
Benefit Payments	(180)	(180)			
1992 Amortization:					
Transition - 10 Years			(50)	50 DR	50CR
Balance, December 31	$1,550	$1,190	$330	$280 DR	$30 CR
1993					
Service Cost	200			200 DR	200 CR
Interest Cost (PBO x 10%)	155			155 DR	155 CR
Actual Return (PA x 10%)		119		119 CR	119 DR
Experience Loss		(10)	10		
Contribution		335			335 DR
Benefit Payments	(285)	(285)			
1993 Amortization:					
Transition - 10 Years			(50)	50 DR	50 CR
Gain 1992 - 10 Years			12	12 CR	12 DR
Balance, December 31	$1,620	$1,349	$302	$274 DR	$31 DR

	Memorandum Record			Statement Accounts	
	PBO (Actuary)	Plan Assets (Trustee)	Unrecog- nized Pension Cost	Pension Expense	Accrued/ Prepaid Pension Cost
1993					
Balance, December 31	$1,620	$1,349	$ 302	$ 274	$ 31 DR
1994					
Service Cost	240			240 DR	244 CR
Interest Cost (PBO x 10%)	162			162 DR	162 CR
Actual Return (PA x 10%)		135		135 CR	135 DR
Experience Gain		25	(25)		
Actuarial Loss	130		130		
Contributions		350			350 DR
Benefit Payments	(400)	(400)			
Prior Service Cost	180		180		
1994 Amortization:					
Transition - 10 Years			(50)	50 DR	50 CR
Gain 1992 - 10 Years			12	12 CR	12 DR
PSC - 9 Years			(20)	20 DR	20 CR
Loss 1993 - 10 Years			(1)	1 DR	1 CR
Balance, December 31	$1,932	$1,4590	$528	$326 DR	$55 CR

2. Record employer's contributions and pension expenses:

	1992	1993	1994
Pension Expense	280	274	344
Accrued Pension Cost	30	61	6
Cash	250	335	350

G.   Defined Benefit Plans, Settlement, Curtailment and Termination Benefits (*CICA* section 3460):

1.   **Pension plan settlement:**   A settlement is a transaction such as making lump-sum cash payment that relieves the employer of primary responsibility for a pension benefit obligation. The employer is required to include in the income statement a gain (or loss) no more than any unrecognized gain (or loss) and any remaining unrecognized net asset existing at transition date (i.e., when revised *CICA* section 3460 is first applied). The following entry is pertinent:

> Accrued/prepaid pension cost xxxx
> Gain from Settlement   xxxx

2.   **Pension plan curtailment:**   A curtailment is an event such as closing of a plant that significantly reduces the expected years of future service of present   employees or eliminates the accrual of defined benefits of their future services. The employer is required to include in the income statement as a loss the related unrecognized prior service cost associated with years of service no longer expected to be rendered plus any unrecognized net obligation existing at the transition date.

Termination Benefits

When **special termination benefits** are offered as an inducement for employees to retire, both a **loss** and a **liability** should be recorded if (1) the employees accept the offer and (2) the amount of the benefits can be **reasonably estimated.** The amount recognized is the present value of the expected benefits.

When the termination benefits are contractual (contingent on a specific event), the loss and liability are recorded if (1) the entitlement to benefits is probable and (2) the amount can be reasonably estimated.

Disclosure

For settlements, curtailments, and termination benefits, the employer discloses the following information: (1) a description of the event and (2) the amount of gain or loss recognized. When the gain or loss for settlements, curtailments, or termination benefits is directly related to the disposal of a business segment, it is included in the total gain or loss reported from discontinued operations (discussed in Chapter 4).

H.   Financial Reporting by Pension Plans

The *CICA*, section 4100, titled "Pension Plans," establishes standards of financial accounting and reporting for the annual statements of the plan and applies to both defined benefit and defined contribution pension plans.

The financial statements of a pension plan are separate from those of the employer. Pension plan statements report on the amounts available for payment of benefits.

The main objective of plan financial statements is to provide information useful in assessing the present and future ability of the plan to pay benefits when due.

Financial Statement Components

The following three categories of information, measured under the accrual basis of accounting, are required:

1. **Net Assets Available for Benefits** The difference between a plan's assets and its liabilities, or net assets available for benefits, is the participants' equity, that amount available to plan participants. Participant benefits are not liabilities of the plan because the plan exists for the benefit of the employees. Liabilities include normal operating liabilities for plan operations.

    The assets of a plan include contributions receivable from the employer (and employees if the plan is contributory), investments, and operating assets. Contributions receivable are included in assets if a formal commitment is made by the employer to make a future contribution. Investments are measured at fair value (not a forced or liquidation sale value). Operating assets are measured at cost less accumulated depreciation or amortization.

2. **Changes during the Year in the Net Assets Available for Benefits** Minimum disclosure includes:

    *   Investment income by type of investment, excluding changes in market values of investment assets.
    *   Changes during the period in the market value of investment assets.
    *   Contributions from employer and participants.
    *   Administrative expenses.
    *   Benefit payments.
    *   Refunds and transfers.
    *   Net assets available for benefits at the beginning and the end of the period.

    This category provides a much more detailed picture of pension plan assets than is required of the employer.

3. **The Actuarial Present Value of Accumulated Plan Benefits** Accumulated plan benefits are the future benefit payments attributable to employee service rendered, to the financial statement date, as measured under the plan's provisions. The present value of benefits is another measure of the total obligation of the employer. Both the time value of money and probability of payment are considered in this measurement.

    Changes in actuarial assumptions and experience are treated as estimate changes. For example, if the discount rate used to measure the present value of benefits is decreased, the actuarial present value of accumulated benefits increases. Information about factors causing changes in the actuarial present value of accumulated plan benefits should also be disclosed. This information explains why the present value of accumulated benefits changed during the period and includes plan amendments, changes in actuarial assumptions, benefits earned in the period, and benefits paid. This facilitates an assessment of the plan's ability to pay benefits on a continuing basis, and supplements the disclosures as of a particular date.

Additional required disclosures to supplement the financial statements include the methods used to determine investment fair value, assumptions used to determine the actuarial present value of accumulated benefits, including changes in assumptions, the plan agreement including vesting and benefit provisions, and plan amendments.

Financial Statement Presentation:

1. Income statement presentation: Pension expense is presented in the income statement as an operating expense. *CICA* section 3460 further requires the disclosure of its components. Gain or loss from a single occurrence not directly related to the operation of the pension plan and not in the ordinary course of the employer's business should be recognized immediately, but not as a pension expense, e.g., the pension related gain or loss due to plant closing should be included in the gain or loss from discontinued operations.

2. Balance sheet presentation: Accrued/prepaid pension cost is either a current liability or a current asset depending on whether its ending balance is a credit or debit. Additional pension liability is presented as a noncurrent liability. Deferred pension cost is considered as an intangible asset, while unrealized pension cost should be included as a stockholders' equity adjustment.

KEY CONCEPTS

Accumulated benefit obligation   The actuarial present value of all the benefits attributed to employee service rendered to date on the basis of **existing** salary levels.

Defined benefit plan   A plan that specifies either the amount of benefits to be received by employees upon retirement, or a formula to be used for the determination of these benefits.

Interest cost   Interest cost on the projected benefit obligation, measured by multiplying the actuary's discount rate by the beginning balance of the projected benefit obligation.

Liability gain or loss   Gain or loss resulting from changes in actuarial assumptions with respect to a pension plan. This gain or loss is subject to delayed recognition.

Plan assets   Assets that have been segregated from the employer and restricted to providing future benefits to the retired employees.

Prior service cost   Cost of retroactive benefits attributed to service rendered prior to the initiation or amendment of a pension plan. Prior service cost must be amortized over the expected remaining years of service, starting in the year of plan adoption or amendment.

Projected benefit obligation   The actuarial present value of all the benefits attributed to employee service rendered to date on the basis of projected **final** salary levels.

Return on plan asset   Return on plan asset investment may be expected or actual. The expected return for a period is fully included in the pension expense of that period, while the recognition of the difference between the expected return and the actual return, known as asset gain or loss, must be delayed.

Service cost   The actuarial present value of benefits attributed by the pension benefit formula to services rendered by employees during the current period.

Transition cost   The changeover cost to revised *CICA* section 3460 measured by the difference between projected benefit obligation and plan asset, adjusted for the existing accrued (prepaid) pension cost on the beginning of the changeover year. Transition cost must be amortized using the straight-line method.

REVIEW QUESTIONS AND EXERCISES

TRUE-FALSE

Indicate whether each of the following statements is true or false by circling the correct response.

T   F   1.   Pension expense is recognized only when pension benefits are paid to retired employees.

T   F   2.   A defined benefit pension plan is a plan that specifies either the amount of benefits to be paid upon employees' retirement or a formula used for the determination of these benefits.

T   F   3.   A projected benefit obligation is the actuarial present value of all the benefits attributed to employee's service on the basis of current salary levels.

T   F   4.   To determine periodic pension expense, all the six components have to be amortized over the expected future service years of participating employees.

T   F   5.   The interest cost component of pension expense is generally calculated by multiplying the beginning balance of projected benefit obligation by the actuary's discount rate.

T   F   6.   Unexpected gain or loss must be amortized using the straight-line method.

T   F   7.   Transition cost must be amortized over the expected future years of service of participating employees using the straight-line method.

T   F   8.   The difference between actual return and the expected return on plan assets may be combined with gains and losses from assumption changes for possible future amortization to pension expense.

T   F   9.   In order to reduce the wide fluctuation of pension expenses, it is acceptable that some or all the unexpected gains or losses may be excluded from the computation of periodic pension expense.

T   F   10.   The employer must recognize as a minimum liability an amount equal to the excess of projected benefit obligation over the fair value of pension plan assets.

T   F   11.   Amortization of a net gain **increases** pension expense, and amortization of a net loss **decreases** pension expense.

T   F   12.   Prior service cost is amortized over the average remaining service life of employees, and it may commence in the year **after** the prior service cost arises.

T   F   13. The PBO minus the sum of the fair value of plan assets and unrecognized (unamortized) prior service cost, unexpected loss/gain and transition cost must equal the balance in accrued/prepaid pension cost.

T   F   14. In accounting for additional pension liability, if the additional pension liability exceeds the unrecognized prior service cost, the excess should be reported as an unrealized pension cost.

EXERCISE 1

Match the terms with the most appropriate description by entering the corresponding letters in the blanks provided.

ITEMS

____ 1. Additional pension liability

____ 2. Vested benefit obligation

____ 3. Prepaid pension cost

____ 4. Noncontributory plan

____ 5. Defined contribution plan

____ 6. Interest cost

____ 7. Pension plan assets

____ 8. Projected benefits obligation

____ 9. Net periodic pension expense

____ 10. Pension benefit formula

DESCRIPTIONS

A. Determines the retirement benefits based on a defined benefit pension plan.

B. Actuarial present value of all future pension benefits on the basis of projected future compensation levels.

C. Formula used to determine the amount of employer's contribution. No promise is made concerning employees' future benefits.

D. A pension liability that may cause a debit to an intangible asset.

E. Cumulative employer's contributions in excess of recognized pension expense.

F. Computed by the employer; comprised of up to six components.

G. Pension obligation that is not contingent on future employment of employees.

H. A pension plan where only the employer provides funding.

I. Beginning PBO multiplied by the actuary's discount rate.

J. Funds related to the pension that usually are administered by an independent trustee.

EXERCISE 2

Assume that Hero Company Ltd. made the following information available:

1.   At beginning of year -- Jan. 1 1992:

    a.   Projected benefit obligation $800,000
    b.   Plan assets (Fair value) $750,000
    c.   Unamortized transition cost $50

2.   For the year -- 1992:

    a.   Service cost $100,000
    b.   Liability gain (due to assumption changes) ...... $ 50,000
    c.   Employer's contribution $190,000
    d.   Benefits paid to the retirees $115,000

3.   At the year-end -- Dec. 31 1992:

    a.   Plan assets (Fair value) $900,000
    b.   PBO $890,000

4.   Additional information:

    a.   Interest (settlement) Rate 10%
    b.   Actual rate of return 10%
    c.   Amortization policies
        (1) Unexpected Losses (gains)
            Amortization rate applied
            To beginning unamortized balance 10%
        (2) Transition cost .... 5 Years

Required: For 1992:

    1.   Prepare amortization spreadsheet.
    2.   Prepare journal entries to record:
        a.   Cash contribution to pension plan.
        b.   Pension expense.

EXERCISE 3

Smooth-Sailing Ltd. sponsored a defined benefit pension plan for its employees at the beginning of 1992. The following data relate to the operation of the plan for 1992 and 1993:

	1992	1993
Service cost for the year	6,000	7,000
Cash contribution to the plan	5,000	6,000
Benefits paid	1,000	1,250
Liability loss during the year	0	1,200
Beginning balance:		
Projected benefit obligation	0	6,635
Plan assets -- Fair value	0	4,000
Prior service cost	$1,500	$?
Ending balance:		
Projected benefit obligation	6,635	14,182
Plan assets -- Fair value	4,000	9,150
Interest (Settlement) rate	9%	9%
Actual rate of return	10%	10%
Prior service cost and unexpected loss amortization rate	12%	12%

Required: For 1992 and 1993:

1. Prepare pension plan spreadsheets.
2. Prepare journal entries to record:
   a. Cash contribution to pension plan.
   b. Pension expense.

MULTIPLE CHOICE

Enter the letter corresponding to the response which **best** completes each of the following statements or questions.

____ 1. Which of the following is not relevant for the calculation of periodic pension expense for the current year?

a. Pension benefits paid during the current year.
b. Projected benefit obligation.
c. Pension plan asset.
d. Expected rate of return on pension plan asset.

____ 2. Pension related estimates (not funding data), are provided by the:

a. Independent actuary.
b. Employer company.
c. Pension fund trustee.
d. A and C.
e. None of the above.

____ 3. Net periodic pension expense is computed by the:

a. Employer company.
b. Actuary.
c. Fund trustee.
d. All of the above.
e. None of the above.

____ 4. The interest component of net periodic expense is computed by multiplying the:

a. Ending PBO by the expected rate of return on plan assets.
b. Beginning PBO by the actuary's discount rate.
c. Ending PBO by the actuary's discount rate.
d. Beginning PBO by the current market rate of interest.
e. None of the above.

____ 5. The pension expense reported by a company will be increased by **interest cost** when:

a. Projected benefit obligation exists at the beginning of the year.
b. Amounts funded are greater than pension cost accrued.
c. Pension plan asset exists at the beginning of the year.
d. The plan is fully vested.

____ 6.   Pension data for ABC for three separate cases were:

	Case 1	*Case 2*	*Case 3*
PBO	$300,000	$300,000	$300,000
Plan assets at fair value	262,500	300,000	315,000

The funding status of the PBO for each case is:

	Case 1	*Case 2*	*Case 3*
a.	Fully funded	Overfunded	Underfunded
b.	Underfunded	Fully funded	Overfunded
c.	Overfunded	Underfunded	Fully funded
d.	Overfunded	Fully funded	Underfunded
e.	None of the above.		

____ 7.   In the computation of pension expense, which of the following component is likely to be **negative** (i.e., reduce pension expense):

a.   service cost.
b.   interest cost.
c.   amortization of prior service cost.
d.   Amortization of net asset gain.

____ 8.   Costs related to a new pension plan that are necessary to "catch up" for services rendered prior to the inception of the pension plan are classified as:

a.   actuarial losses.
b.   prior service costs.
c.   retroactive deferred charge.
d.   service costs.
e.   none of the above.

___ 9. The projected benefit obligation on January 1, 1992 was $160,000. During 1992 pension benefits paid by the trustee were $20,000. The actuary's discount rate was 10%. Service cost for 1992 is $60,000. Pension plan assets (at fair value) increased during 1992 by $30,000 as expected. There had been no liability gain or loss. The amount of the PBO at December 31, 1992 was:

    a. $176,000.
    b. $196,000.
    c. $216,000.
    d. $246,000.

___ 10. Desparado Inc.'s records revealed the following related to its defined benefit pension plan:

Plan assets at fair value, January 1, 1992	$3,000
Expected return on plan assets during 1992	300
Actual return on plan assets during 1992	200
Contributions to the pension fund during 1992	500
Amortization of unexpected loss for 1992	10
Pension benefits paid during 1992	520
Pension expense, 1992	360

The December 31, 1992 amount of pension plan assets at fair value is:

    a. $2,480.
    b. $2,980.
    c. $3,180.
    d. $3,200.

___ 11. Plumfull Ltd. had $50,000 unrecognized prior service cost when it amended a defined benefit plan on January 1, 1992. The number of employees participating in the plan was 200 with average retirement rate 25% per year.

Based on the above information, what would be the amount of prior service cost amortized for 1992 under each of the two amortization methods?

	Expected-Future- Years-of-Service	Straight-Line
a.	$10,000	$12,500
b.	$10,000	$20,000
c.	$20,000	$12,500
d.	$20,000	$20,000

The following information is pertinent to Items 12 to 14:

Mustard Company Ltd. adopted a defined benefit pension plan on January 1, 1992. Data presented below relate to the operation of the plan for 1992 and 1993:

		1992	1993
Service cost		$600,000	$700,000
Cash contribution to the plan		500,000	500,000
Beginning balance:			
Projected benefit obligation		0	600,000
Plan assets -- Fair value		0	500,000
Ending balance			
Projected benefit obligation		600,000	1,360,000
Plan assets -- Fair value		500,000	1,045,000
Interest (settlement) rate		10%	10%
Rate of return (expected and actual)		9%	9%

____ 12. What is the recognized periodic pension expense for the year?

	1992	**1993**
a.	$500,000	$700,000
b.	$600,000	$715,000
c.	$500,000	$500,000
d.	$600,000	$700,000

____ 13. What is the balance of the accrued pension cost as of December 31?

	1992	**1993**
a.	$0	$600,000
b.	$600,000	$700,000
c.	$100,000	$150,000
d.	$100,000	$315,000

____ 14. What is the additional pension liability as of December 31?

	1992	**1993**
a.	$0	$0
b.	$100,000	$200,000
c.	$100,000	$150,000
d.	$100,000	$315,000

SOLUTIONS TO REVIEW QUESTIONS AND EXERCISES

TRUE-FALSE

1.	F	5.	T	9.	T	13.	T
2.	T	6.	T	10.	F	14.	T
3.	F	7.	T	11.	F		
4.	F	8.	T	12.	T		

EXERCISE 1

1.	D	5.	C	9.	F
2.	G	6.	I	10.	A
3.	E	7.	J		
4.	H	8.	B		

EXERCISE 2

1. **Prepare pension plan spreadsheet:**

Pension Plan Spreadsheet, 1992

	Memorandum Record			Statement Account Accrued/ Prepaid	
	PBO (Actuary)	Plan Assets (Trustee)	Unrecognized Pension Cost	Pension Expense	Pension Cost
1992					
Balance, January 1	$ 800	$ 750	$	$	$
Transition Liabilities			50		
Service Cost	100			100 DR	100 CR
Interest Cost (PBO x 10%)	80			80 DR	80 CR
Actual return (PA x 10%)		75		75 CR	75 DR
Actuarial Gain	(50)		(50)		
Contribution		190			190 DR
Benefit Payments	(115)	(115)			
1992 Amortization:					
Transition 5 years			10	10 DR	$ 10 CR
Balance, December 31	$ 815	$ 900	$ 10	$ 115 DR	$ 75 DR

2. **Record Employer's Contributions and Pension Expense**

Pension Expense	115	
Accrued Pension Set	75	
Cash		190

EXERCISE 3

1. **Prepare pension plan spreadsheets:**

Pension Plan Spreadsheets

	Memorandum Record			Statement Account Accrued/Prepaid	
	PBO (Actuary)	Assets (Trustee)	Unrecognized Pension Cost	Pension Expense	Pension Cost
Balance, January 1	$ 0	$ 0	$ 0	$ 0	$ 0
Prior Service Cost	1,500		1,500		
Service Cost	6,000			6,000 DR	6,000 CR
Contribution		5,000			5,000 DR
Benefit Payments	(1,000)	(1,000)			
1992 Amortization					
PSC – 12%			(180)	180 DR	180 CR
Balance, December 31	$ 6,500	$ 4,000	$ 1,320	$ 6,180 DR	$ 1,180 CR
Service Cost	7,000			7,000 DR	7,000 CR
Interest Cost (PBO x 9%)	585			585 DR	585 CR
Actual Return (PA x 10%)		400		400 CR	400 DR
Actuarial Loss	1,200		1,200		
Contribution		6,000			6,000 DR
Benefit Payments	(1,250)	(1,250)			
1993 Amortization					
PSC – 12%			(180)	180 DR	180 CR
Balance, December 31	$ 14,035	$ 9,150	$ 2,340	$ 7,365 DR	$ 2,545 CR

2. **To prepare journal entries:**

	1992		1993	
Pension Expense	6,180		7365	
Accrued Pension Cost		1,180		1,365
Cash		5,000		6,000

MULTIPLE CHOICE:

1.	a	5.	a	9.	c	13.	d
2.	a	6.	b	10.	c	14.	a
3.	a	7.	d	11.	d		
4.	b	8.	b	12.	b		

Computations:

9.   (c)   PBO -- Beginning balance $160,000
           Interest cost (10%)   16,000
           Service cost   60,000
           Benefits paid   (20,000)

           PBO -- Ending balance $216,000

10. (c)   PA -- Beginning balance $3,000
           Actual return   200
           Cash contribution   500
           Benefits paid   (520)

           PA -- Ending balance $3,180

11. (d)

a. Expected-future-years-of-service method:

$$N = P \times (1 + R) / 2R$$
$$= 200 \times 1.25 / .50$$
$$= 500$$

$$r_{1992} = p_{1992} / N$$
$$= 200 / 500$$
$$= 40\%$$
where p_{1992} = Number of active employees during 1992.

PSC amortized = $50,000 x 40% = $20,000

b. Straight-line method:

$$r = 2R / (1 + R)$$
$$= .50 / 1.25$$
$$= 40\%$$

PSC amortized = $50,000 x 40% = $20,000

12. (b) The information indicates that there is neither prior service cost, nor transition cost. It is also implied that there is no experience gain/loss. Therefore, pension expense is determined by the three major components as follows:

	1992	1993
Service cost	$600,000	$700,000
Interest cost ($600,000 x 10%)	0	60,000
Expected return ($500,000 x 9%)	0	(45,000)
Pension expense	$600,000	$715,000

13. (d) Accrued pension cost

	1992	1993
Beginning balance	$ 0	$100,000
Pension expense	600,000	715,000
Cash contribution	(500,000)	(500,000)
Ending balance	$100,000	$315,000

14. (a)

	1992	1993
Accumulated benefit obligation	$450,000	$1,000,000
Plan asset, Fair value	(500,000)	(1,045,000)
Accrued pension cost	(100,000)	(315,000)
Additional pension liability *	0	0

* There is no additional pension liability since the accumulated benefit obligation was overfunded.

CHAPTER 20

Corporations: Contributed Capital

CHAPTER OBJECTIVES

This chapter is designed to enable students to:

A. Explain the characteristics, advantages and disadvantages of the corporate form of business organization.

B. Describe the different types of shareholders' investments and the various rights that attach to each.

C. Describe and demonstrate accounting and reporting practices for the issuance of various forms of share capital, both for cash and for noncash consideration.

D. Apply prescribed accounting and reporting practices for the issuance of subscribed shares.

E. Apply the accounting and reporting practices for the retirement of shares, including callable and redeemable shares, and for the conversion of convertible preferred shares.

F. Explain donations and additional contributed capital.

G. Apply the accounting and reporting practices for treasury shares.

CHAPTER OVERVIEW

A. A **corporation,** which is by far the dominant form of business organization in terms of total capital investment, is characterized by the following:

1. **Limited liability** -- The shareholders (owners) are **not** personally liable for debt of the entity.

2. **Transferability** -- Ownership interest is easily transferable.

3. **Continuity** -- The entity continues when ownership changes.

While the above characteristics are conceived as advantages, there are also disadvantages of a corporation, e.g.:

1. **Double taxation** -- Corporate earnings are first taxed on the corporation as earned, and then taxed on the shareholders when distributed as dividends.

2. **Separation of management** -- Since the ownership of a corporation is separable from its management, small shareholders may lose control.

B.   Shareholders' Equity

In a business enterprise, the **equity** is the ownership interest. It ranks after liabilities as a claim to or interest in the assets of the enterprise, and is thus a **residual** interest measured by the difference between the enterprise's assets and its liabilities, i.e., net assets.

Since the owners of a corporation are shareholders, their equity is generally referred to as the shareholders' equity, which includes contributed (paid-in) capital, retained earnings and unrealized capital. **Unrealized capital,** as a category of shareholders' equity, is not widely used in practice. It arises when assets are written up above cost or net book value. Because of adherence to the cost principle and the concept of conservatism, assets rarely are written up from cost to fair market value. In the past, the most common example of such write-ups was writing up capital assets from cost to market values in *unusual* circumstances, like a change in control. An upward adjustment of the asset account requires an offsetting credit to unrealized capital increment. This is called an appraisal increase credit. Starting in 1991, this is no longer permitted by the *CICA Handbook.*

Life insurance and mutual fund companies, required to carry certain assets at market value, will report an unrealized capital increment.

The **contributed capital** is generally divided into:

1. **Share capital,** representing (a) the minimum initial share price, (b) the minimum amount of net assets the corporation must maintain, and (c) the basis on which dividends are declared. Since share capital is legally restricted from being impaired, it is referred to as legal capital.

2. **Other contributed capital,** or **additional paid-in capital:**

    a. **from shareholders** such as paid-in capital in excess of par when the stock is issued, and **other stock transactions** subsequent to the issuance of stock, e.g., the reacquisition and the retirement of stock.

    b. **from other parties** such as land, machinery or building donated to the company by a third party, e.g., the city.

It may be useful to define the following terms:

1. **Authorized share capital** -- the maximum number of shares that can be legally issued. Under the Canada Business Corporations Act, a corporation is entitled to issue an unlimited number of shares. The corporation may choose to place a limit on authorized shares. Such a limit must be stated in the articles of incorporation. Certain provincial incorporation acts impose authorized share limits on corporations.
2. **Issued share capital** -- the number of shares that have been issued to shareholders to date.
3. **Unissued share capital** -- the number of shares of authorized share capital that have not been issued; that is, the difference between authorized and issued shares.
4. **Outstanding share capital** -- the number of shares that have been issued and are currently owned by shareholders.
5. **Treasury stock** -- shares issued and later reacquired by the corporation and that are still held by the corporation; that is, the difference between issued shares and outstanding shares. Under the Canada Business Corporations Act and most provincial legislation, shares reacquired by a corporation must be *retired,* and treasury stock cannot exist. In these jurisdictions, issued and outstanding shares will be equal.
6. **Subscribed shares** -- unissued shares set aside to meet subscription contracts (i.e., shares sold on credit and not yet paid for). Subscribed shares are usually not issued until the subscription price is paid in full.

3. **Classification of Share Capital**

Share capital of a corporation may include both **common shares** or **preferred shares**. As determined in the corporate charter and federal or provincial law, each share certificate conveys to the shareholders certain rights such as follows:

Common shares – the primary issue of shares which normally carries the following rights:

a. the right to vote for directors.
b. the right to share profits.
c. the right to share in the distribution of assets in the event the company is liquidated.
d. the preemptive right to acquire additional shares in proportion to existing holdings if the total shares outstanding is increased.

Preferred shares.   An issue of share which may confer certain preferences or features not possessed by common shares such as:

a. The preference to specified amount of **dividends** (stated dollar amount per share or rate of par value). That is, if the board of directors declares dividends, preferred shareholders will receive the stated dividends before any dividends are paid to common shareholders. (see next psge)

b. The right of conversion which allows preferred shareholders to exchange their shares for common share at a specified conversion ratio.

c. A redemption privilege which allows preferred shareholders the option, under specified conditions, to return their shares for a predetermined redemption price.

d. A preference as to the distribution of assets in the event the corporation is liquidated.

Dividend Preferences

In terms of dividends distribution, a preferred share may be either:

1. **Cumulative or noncumulative.**   Typically, a preferred share is cumulative, which means that if the specified preferred dividends are not paid in a given year, the unpaid dividends, referred to as **dividends in arrears**, accumulate and must be made up in later years before any dividends are paid to common shares. Preferred dividends in arrears, furthermore, should be paid when the shares are retired or converted into common shares. In any event, however, they are not considered as liabilities, and should only be reported in the notes. If the preferred share is noncumulative, any unpaid dividends are simply disregarded.

2. **Participating or nonparticipating.**   A participating preferred share allows investors to receive additional dividends **beyond the specified amount**, whereas the dividends on nonparticipating preferred shares are limited to the stated rate. The distribution of additional dividends is a pro rata allocation based on the relative contributed capital amounts of common and preferred shares outstanding. If the share is fully participating, the pro rata allocation is without upper limit. If the share is partially participating, on the other hand, there is a ceiling imposed on the preferred participation. Dividend distribution with cumulative and participating preferred share outstanding is based on the following **priority**:

   a. preferred dividends in arrears.
   b. preferred current dividends.
   c. common dividends at preferred dividend rate, known as current matching.
   d. participation:

      (1) If **fully participating** -- all the remainder is allocated to preferred and common on pro rata basis.

      (2) If **partially participating** -- Allocate the remainder on a pro rata basis to preferred and common **up to** the maximum participation rate, and allocate all the rest to common.

ILLUSTRATION 1 -- Common and preferred dividends

Given: The balance sheet of Karson Corporation Ltd. included the data shown below for 1992. No dividends were declared in 1992. During 1993, Young declared cash dividends of $300,000:

Common shares, no par value, 60,000 shares issued, @ $10 $600,000
50¢ Preferred shares, no par value, 80,000 shares issued, @ $5   400,000

Note: When the preferred shares are participating (cases 3, 4 & 5), the common shareholders will receive a matching dividend of $1.00 per share, before the participating clause is activated.

Required: Allocate the declared dividends in each of the following cases:

Case 1: The preferred shares are **noncumulative** and **nonparticipating**.
Case 2: The preferred shares are **cumulative** and **nonparticipating**.
Case 3: The preferred shares are **noncumulative** and **fully participating**.
Case 4: The preferred shares are **cumulative** and **fully participating**.
Case 5: The preferred shares are **cumulative** and **partially participating**, with a maximum participation rate of 25¢ above the stated rate of 50¢.

SOLUTION:

	Preferred	Common	Total
Case 1	$40,000 [1]	$260,000	$300,000
Case 2	80,000 [2]	220,000	300,000
Case 3	120,000 [3]	180,000	300,000
Case 4	144,000 [4]	156,000	300,000
Case 5	100,000 [5]	200,000	300,000

[1]   Preferred dividends (1993) = $80,000 x 50¢ = $40,000.

[2]   Preferred dividends (1992 and 1993) = $80,000 x 50¢ x 2 = $80,000.

* Matching ratio for no par value shares
Preferred shares – Current dividend
60,000 x $1 = $60,000

Preferred share ratio of total
$40,000/$(40,000 + 60,000) = 40%

Common share ratio of total
$60,000/$(40,000+ 60,000) = 60%

		Balance to be Distributed
3.	Amount decalred available for dividends	300,000
	Preferred current dividend 80,000 x $.50	40,000
	Subtotal	260,000
	Common matching dividend 60,000 x $1	60,000
	Available for participation	200,000
	Preferred participating dividend $200,00 x 40%*	80,000
	Subtotal	120,000
	Common participating dividend $200,000 x 60%	120,000
	Preferred 40,000 + 80,000 = 120,000	
	Common 60,000 + 120,000 = 180,000	0
4.	Amouunt declared available for dividend	300,000
	Preferred dividend in arrears 80,000 x $.50	40,000
	Subtotal	260,000
	Preferred current dividend 80,000 x $.50	40,000
	Subtotal	220,000
	Common matching dividend 60,000 x $1	60,000
**	Available for participation	160,000
	Preferred participating dividend 160,000 x 40%*	64,000
	Subtotal	96,000
	Common participating dividend 160,000 x 60%*	96,000
	Preferred 40,000 + 40,000 + 64,000 = 144,000	
	Common 60,000 + 96,000 = 156,000	0
5.	** Available for participation	160,000
	Lesser of participating calculation $160,000 x 40%* = 64,000	
	OR maximum participation 80,000 x $.25 = 20,000	20,000
	Remainder to common	140,000
	Common participating dividend	140,000
	Preferred 40,000 + 40,000 + 20,000 = 100,000	
	Common 60,000 + 140,000 = 200,000	0

C. Issuance of Shares

1. Shares issued for cash. When no par shares are issued for cash, the share capital account (common or preferred) is credited for the total proceeds received.

Some provinces permit corporations to issue par value shares. The share capital issued is recorded at the par value, and the excess of any proceeds received in excess of the par value amount is credited to contributed capital in excess of par.

2. Shares issued for noncash consideration. If shares are issued for considerations other than cash, the transaction is recorded at the fair value of the shares or of the consideration, whichever is more reliably determinable. The issuance of shares for noncash consideration sometimes involves questionable valuations. Some companies have disavowed market values and independent appraisals in order to permit the governing authority of the company to set arbitrary values in these non-cash transactions. In some cases, companies are motivated to overvalue shareholders' equity. This condition is often referred to as *watered stock:* the value of the resources received for the issued shares is less than the value of the shares issued (i.e., they are watered down). On the other hand, some companies are motivated to understate shareholders' equity -- a condition often called *secret reserves*. Secret reserves are also created intentionally and/or in error by depreciating or amortizing a properly recorded asset over a period less than its useful life.

D. 1. Shares issued on subscription basis. Frequently shares are issued on a subscription basis. That is, prospective shareholders sign a contract to purchase a specified number of shares at a specified price to be paid by installment. Because a legal contract is involved, accounting recognition must be given when these transactions occur. The following entries are typical:

a. On date of subscription:

Subscriptions receivable (at subscription price)	xxxx	
Common shares subscribed (no par)		xxxx

b. On date of collection:

Cash	xxxx	
Subscriptions receivable		xxxx

c. On date of issuance of shares:

Common shares subscribed	xxxx	
Common shares		xxxx

Common or preferred shares subscribed is presented on the balance sheet as an addition to the respective share capital. Subscriptions receivable preferably are presented as a contra equity account (i.e., to be deducted from the total shareholders' equity), although some accountants treat it as a current asset like other receivables.

2. In case a subscriber **defaults** after partial fulfillment of the subscription contract, the corporation should comply with federal and provincial law or follow the contract to (1) return all the collected payments to the subscriber, (2) issue shares proportional to the amount collected, (3) retain all the payments collected from the subscriber, or (4) resell the subscribed shares to a third party under a lien whereby the subscriber is responsible for maintaining the original subscription price.

ILLUSTRATION 2 -- Issue shares on subscription basis

Given: On July 1, 1992, Raw Meats Ltd. sold 1,000 shares of its no par common shares to Mr. Mara and another 2,000 shares to Mr. Oran for $15 per share with 40% down payments. the remainder is due on December 31, 1992. Subscribed shares will be issued upon collection of the subscribed price in full.

On the due date, Mr. Mara paid the additional $9,000 and Raw Meats issued 1,000 shares to Mr. Mara upon receipt of the payment. Mr. Oran, however, defaulted the subscription contract.

Required: Record the share transactions.

Solution:

a. *** July/1/1992 -- To record subscription of shares:**

Subscriptions receivable (3,000 shares x $15)	45,000	
Common shares subscribed		45,000

b. *** July/1/1992 -- To record collection of down payments:**

Cash ($45,000 x 40%)	18,000	
Subscriptions receivable		18,000

* May be combined into one entry

c. **Dec./31/1992 -- To record collection of additional payments made by Mr. Mara:**

Cash ($15,000 x 60%)	9,000	
Subscriptions receivable		9,000

d. **Dec./31/1992 -- To record issuance of shares to Mr. Mara:**

Common shares subscribed	15,000	
Common shares, (1,000 shares, at $15)		15,000

e. **Dec./31/1992 – To record defaulted subscriptions:**

Case 1: Return all the amounts collected from Mr. Oran:

Common shares subscribed	30,000	
Subscriptions receivable ($30,000 x 60%)		18,000
Due to defaulting subscriber		12,000

Case 2: Issue shares proportional to the amounts collected, i.e., 40%:

Common shares subscribed	30,000	
Subscriptions receivable ($30,000 x 60%)		18,000
Common shares, (800 shares, @ 15)		12,000

Case 3: Retain all payments collected from Mr. Oran:

Common shares subscribed	30,000	
Subscriptions receivable ($30,000 x 60%)		18,000
Contributed capital from defaulted subscriptions		12,000

Case 4: Resell the forfeited shares at Mr. Oran's cost:

(1) Cancel the original subscription contract:

Common shares subscribed	30,000	
Subscriptions receivable ($30,000 x 60%)		18,000
Due to defaulting subscriber		12,000

(2) Resell the forfeited shares, assuming the shares were sold for **$12.50** per share:

Cash ($12.50 x 2,000 shs.)	25,000	
Due to defaulting subscriber	5,000	
Common shares		30,000

Note that the defaulting subscriber is responsible for the decline in price as well as resale cost. To avoid the incentive of default, the amount to be refunded to the defaulting subscriber cannot exceed the amount paid to the date of default less resale cost. No resale cost is assumed in the above example.

3. **Share issue costs.** Costs incurred in connection with the issuance of share capital are generally treated as a **reduction** in the **proceeds** received. Some companies, however, record share issue costs as a deferred charge (e.g., **organization costs**) and amortize the costs over a reasonable period of time.

4.   "Donations" by shareholders

Shareholders occasionally donate shares back to the corporation.

a.   When donated shares are received and retired, the share capital account is reduced by the average price per share credited to the account to date, and a contributed capital account, "donated capital," is created.

b.   When donated shares are received and will be reissued, they are handled as treasury stock. (see section F) Shareholders may donate cash as well. The credit goes to "Contributed Capital-Shareholders Donation."

5.   Convertible preferred shares: Corporations issue *convertible* preferred shares, which are similar to convertible bonds. These shares give the shareholder an option, within a specified time period, to exchange the convertible preferred shares currently held for other classes of share capital, usually common shares, at a specified rate. The accounting treatment for conversion of preferred shares is analogous to the book value method for convertible bonds. The converted shares are formally retired when received by the corporation. Conversion privileges require the issuing corporation to set aside a sufficient number of units of the other security to fulfill the conversion privileges until they are exercised or expire.

At date of conversion, all account balances related to the converted shares are removed and the new shares issued are recorded at the same amount.

ILLUSTRATION 3 -- Convertible preferred shares

Assume that on January 1, 1992, Gew Inc. issued 10,000 share of $.80, no par convertible preferred shares for $15 per share. The conversion privilege specified the issuance of five shares of no par common shares for each share of preferred. All outstanding preferred shares are converted to common shares on January 1, 1993.

January 1, 1992:

To record issuance of preferred shares:

Cash	150,000	
$.80 Preferred shares		150,000

January 1, 1993:

To record conversion of preferred to common:

$.80 Preferred shares	150,000	
Common shares		150,000

2.   Preferred shares with detachable warrants.   When a preferred share is issued with detachable share warrants, it is accounted for in the same manner as the issuance of bonds with detachable warrants, except that preferred shares are used instead of bonds payable and premium (or discount) on bonds.

E. Reacquisition of Shares

Shares previously issued is often reacquired by the issuing corporation. Accounting procedures dealing with such reacquisition depends upon whether the reacquired shares are intended to be retired or to be reissued in the future.

Formal retirement. When shares are reacquired and retired, all capital items relating to the specific shares are removed from the accounts. If the shares are cumulative preferred and there are dividends in arrears, such dividends are paid and charged to retained earnings in the normal manner. Where the cost of the acquired shares is different from the average original issuance price, the CICA recommends that the cost be allocated as follows for nopar shares:

1. When the reacquisition cost is *higher* than the average price per share issued to date:

   a. To share capital, in the amount of the average price per share credited to the share capital account to date.
   b. Any excess, to contributed capital if contributed capital has been created by any prior reacquisition transaction of the same class of shares.
   c. Any excess, to retained earnings.

2. When the reacquisition cost is *lower* than the average price per share issued to date:

   a. To share capital, in the amount of the average price per share credited to the capital account to date.

   b. Any excess, to contributed capital.

Legislation restricts purchases by requiring a solvency test or restriction or appropriations of retained earnings equal to the cost of the shares. For example, the Canada Business Corporations Act, Section 32, provides that:

A corporation shall not make any payment to purchase or otherwise acquire shares issued by it if there are reasonable grounds for believing that

   a. the corporation is, or would after the payment be, unable to pay its liabilities as they become due; or
   b. the realizable value of the corporation's assets would after the payment be less than the aggregate of its liabilities and stated capital of all classes.

Restriction or appropriation of retained earnings equal to the cost of the purchased shares is based on the view that the purchase of shares has the same impact as the payment of a cash dividend.Therefore, the retained earnings should be appropriated or frozen.

This legislation also applies to treasury stock (which follows) in section F.

ILLUSTRATION 3 -- Retirement of shares

Sutcha Corporation Ltd. had the following shares outstanding:

Preferred shares, nopar, 6,000 shares (originally sold at $25)	$150,000
Common shares, nopar, 20,000 shares (originally sold at $15)	300,000

The following transactions were completed (in this order):

a.   Purchased and retired 50 shares of the common shares at $17 per share.
b.   Purchased and retired 20 shares of the preferred shares at $27.
c.   Purchased and retired 30 shares of the common shares at $14.
d.   Purchased and retired 10 shares of the preferred shares at $20.

Required:

1.   Give entries for all of the above transactions.

a.   Purchase and retirement of 50 shares of common stock at $17:

Common shares (50 shares X $15)	750	
Retained earnings	100	
Cash (50 shares X $17)		850

b.   Purchase and retirement of 20 shares of preferred stock at $27:

Preferred shares (20 shares X $25)	500	
Retained earnings	40	
Cash (20 shares X $27)		540

c.   Purchased and retired 30 shares of common stock at $14:

Common shares (30 shares x $15)	450	
Contributed capital--retirement of common shares		30
Cash (30 shares x $14)		420

d.   Purchased and retired 10 shares of preferred stock at $20:

Preferred shares (10 shares X $25)	250	
Contributed capital--retirement of preferred shares		50
Cash (10 shares x $20)		200

F.   Donation.

Shareholders sometimes donate a corporation's shares back to the corporation. Shares received by donation are classified as treasury stock unless formally retired. Neither total assets nor total equity are changed by the donation of treasury stock. Three methods have been employed in recording the receipt of donated treasury stock:

1.   When the donated shares are received, debit the treasury stock account for the current market value of the shares and credit "contributed capital, donated treasury stock," for the same amount. Upon subsequent sale, any gains or losses (i.e., net asset increases or decreases) would be accounted for as illustrated in part F for the single-transaction method.

2.   When the donated shares are received, debit the treasury stock account for the average paid in (or in the case of par value shares, the par) and credit an appropriately designated donated capital account. Subsequent sales would be recorded as illustrated in part F for the two transaction method.

3.   When donated shares are received, a memorandum entry is made on the basis that there was no cost. Subsequent sales amounts would be credited to contributed capital for the full sales price. This method is seldom used.

Additional Contributed Capital

Contributed capital is created by a number of events that involve the corporation and its shareholders. Several accounts for additional contributed (paid-in) capital were introduced in this chapter, such as contributed capital on share repurchase or donations. The Exhibit below summarizes some of the transactions that may cause increases or decreases in additional contributed capital.

Some Transactions That May Affect Additional Contributed Capital

Increase In Additional Contibuted Capital	**Decrease In Addtional Contributed Capital**
1. Receipt of donated shares or assets.	1. Retirement of shares at a price greater than average issue price to date, when previous contributed capital has been recorded.
2. Retirement of shares at a price less than average issue price to date.	
3. Issue of par value shares at a price or assigned value higher than par. Shares may be issued for cash, noncash consideration, or by subscription on bond conversion on conversion of preferred shares; and as a stock dividend.	2. Issue of par value shares at a discount--a rare event.
	3. Treasusry stock transactions, shares issued below cost, when previous contributed captial has been recorded.
4. Treasury stock transactions, shares reissued above cost.	4. On a quasi reorganizaiton.

G.   Treasury Stock - These are reacquired shares that are not retired, but rather intent of management is to reissue them in the near future.

There are two methods of accounting for treasury stock. These are (1) the single-transaction method and (2) the two-transaction method. The difference between these methods rests on whether the acquisition and subsequent resale are regarded as a single transaction or as two separate transactions.

1.   Under the single-transaction method, a treasury stock account is debited for the *cost* of the shares acquired upon the purchase of treasury stock. When the shares are resold, the treasury stock account is credited for the cost, and the difference, which is the gain or loss, affect various equity accounts. The single-transaction method is based on the view that the purchase and subsequent resale are one continuous transaction. Purchase is the initial step, involving the use of assets to effect a temporary contraction of total capital. The final step in the transaction is the resale of treasury shares and a consequent expansion of assets and total capital. Under this method, the balance in the treasury stock account is logically shown as a deduction from the total of shareholders' equity.

When treasury stock is resold at a price in excess of its cost, and the single-transaction method is used, the excess should be recorded as contributed capital in a special contributed capital account. Where the shares are sold at less than their cost, the deficiency should be charged as follows:

1.   First, to capital arising from prior resale or cancellation of shares of the same class.
2.   Second, to retained earnings after the balance in (1) above has been exhausted.

2.   Under the two-transaction method, the objectives to be accomplished are:

1.   To make a final accounting with the retiring shareholders from whom the treasury shares were acquired.
2.   To record precisely the capital contributed by the new shareholder, the purchaser of treasury shares.

The final accounting with the retiring shareholder involves removal of the amount originally invested by the shareholder, computed on an average basis for all shares issued. When the shares are resold, the entire proceeds of the sale are treated as capital invested by the new shareholder, that is, as if the shares were an original issue.

The CICA recommends, the following:

The Committee is of the opinion that the single-transaction method as set out above is the preferable method of accounting for the acquisition by a company of its own shares.

When treasury stock is **retired**, the treasury stock and the related share capital, both recorded at average per share paid in, are removed from the books.

The following entries illustrate both methods of accounting for treasury stock.

ILLUSTRATION 4 -- Treasury stock transactions

Given: On December 31, 1992, the shareholders' equity section of the balance sheet of Golson Inc. included the following:

Common shares, 20,000 shares	$25,000
Retained earnings	100,000

During 1993:

a. Reacquired 4,000 shares of treasury stock at $2.25 per share.
b. Sold 2,000 shares of treasury stock at $2.50 per share.
c. Sold 1,000 shares of treasury stock at $.50 per share.
d. Retired 1,000 shares of treasury stock.

Required: Record the treasury stock transactions using:

(1) Single-transaction method and
(2) Two-transaction method.

SOLUTION:

```
          Single- Transaction Method                       Two-Transaction Method

a.  To record acquisition of treasury stock:

    Treasury stock (at cost)      9,000       Treasury stock                  5,000
      Cash (4,000 shs. x $2.25)        9,000  Retained earnings               4,000
                                                Cash (4,000 shs. x $2.25)           9,000

b.  To record sale of treasury stock:

    Cash (2,000 shs. x $2.50)     5,000       Cash (2,000 shs. x $2.50)       5,000
      Treasury stock (at cost)        4,500     Treasury stock, (at par)           2,500
      Contributed  capital                      Contributed capital in excess of par 2,500
        from TS trans.                 500

c.  To record sale of treasury stock:

    Cash (1,000 shs. x $0.50)       500       Cash (1,000 shs. x $0.50)         500
    Contributed capital from TS trans. 500    Contributed capital from TS trans. 750
    Retained earnings             1,250         Treasury stock (at par)            1,250
      Treasury stock (at cost)        2,250

d.  To record retirement of treasury stock:

    Common shares (1,000 shs. x $1.25) 1,250  Common shares                   1,250
    Retained earnings             1,000         Treasury stock (at par)            1,250
      Treasury stock (at cost)        2,250
```

Under the single-transaction method, treasury stock is presented on the balance sheet as a contra shareholders' equity account. Under the two-transaction method, it is presented as a contra capital share account.

KEY CONCEPTS

Callable and redeemable preferred shares   Preferred shares that the issuing company has the option to retire at a specified price is known as **callable**. Preferred shares that the shareholders have the option to return to the corporation at a specified price is known as **redeemable.**

Common shares   Primary issue of shares that entitle the holders of the shares the right to vote, share profit and acquire new shares.

Convertible preferred shares   Preferred shares that allows the shareholders to exchange their shares for common shares at a specified conversion ratio.

Cumulative preferred shares   Preferred shares on which the undeclared dividends accumulated as dividends in arrears should be paid before any dividends are paid on common shares.

Participating preferred shares   Preferred share that has the right to receive additional dividends on top of the stated amount or rate. A participation with upper limit is known as partially participating, whereas a participation without an upper limit is termed fully participating.

Preferred shares   Share that confers preferences and rights that the common share does not possess. Typical preferences include dividends distribution, asset distribution and conversion.

Share subscription   A contractual commitment that the prospective shareholders will purchase a specified number of shares at a specified price within a specified time period. The corporation shall issue subscribed shares upon collection of the subscription price in full.

Shareholders' equity   Equity of a corporation consisting of contributed capital, retained earnings and unrealized capital. Shareholders' equity represents the residual interest in the business entity measured by the difference between assets and liabilities.

Treasury stock   Issued share is reacquired and temporarily held by the issuing corporation. Treasury shares may be accounted for using either the single transaction or two transaction method.

REVIEW QUESTIONS AND EXERCISES

TRUE-FALSE

Indicate whether each of the following statements is true or false by circling the correct response.

T   F   1. An advantage of a corporation over a partnership is that transfer of ownership generally is unrestricted.

T   F   2. Legal capital is the portion of shareholders' equity that is legally required to be maintained for the protection of creditors.

T   F   3. Owners of common shares are more likely to possess voting rights than owners of preferred shares.

T   F   4. The dividend preference of preferred share generally is a fixed percentage of its market price.

T   F   5. If preferred shares are participating, unpaid current dividends must be paid in subsequent years prior to dividend payments to common shareholders.

T   F   6. Common shareholders always have a right over preferred shareholders to assets of a corporation in the event of **liquidation**.

T   F   7. If preferred shares are callable, preferred shareholders have an option to acquire a specified number of shares of common stock within a specified time period, at a specified call price.

T   F   8. At the time a common share subscription for no-par shares contract is signed, the issued common shares account is credited for the issue price of the shares.

T   F   9. When a corporation reacquires shares of its own stock, for retirement, an "investment in shares" account is set up.

T   F   10. Retirement of common shares reduces the dividend requirements of the corporation but this action always will increase book value per common share.

T   F   11. A solvency test or restriction of retained earnings equal to the cost of the retired shares must be done to protect creditor interests.

T   F   12. When preferred shares are called and retired, the excess of call price over the original contributed capital of those shares should be debited to retained earnings.

T   F   13. The balance sheet presentation of treasury stock is the same under either the single transaction method or the two transaction value method.

T   F   14. Share issue cost must be recorded as a deferred charge and amortized over 40 years.

EXERCISE 1

The board of directors of Carter Corporation declared cash dividends of $6,000, $21,000, and $90,000 in 1992, 1993 and 1994, respectively. In each of the three years, Carter's shares consisted of the following:

$8 Preferred, 1,000 shares, nopar   150,000
Common, 20,000 shares, nopar $350,000

Determine the amount of dividends to be paid to preferred and common shareholders in each of the three years:

1. The preferred shares are noncumulative and nonparticipating:

	Preferred	Common
1992	_____	_____
1993	_____	_____
1994	_____	_____

2. The preferred shares are cumulative and fully participating: (Common shares to receive matching $.80 dividend):

	Preferred	Common
1992	_____	_____
1993	_____	_____
1994	_____	_____

EXERCISE 2

Mowman Grass Ltd. received articles of incorporation authorizing the issuance of 100,000 shares of common with no par value. Give journal entries to record the following transactions.

a. To record subscriptions of 10,000 shares each for Mr. A and Mr. B, at $20 per share.

b. To record collection of 50% of the subscription price.

c. To record collection of balance of subscription receivable from Mr. A.

d. To record issuance of the subscribed shares to Mr. A.

e. Mr. B defaulted on the contract. To record the forfeited transaction assuming that Mowman refunded the previously collected amount to Mr. B.

EXERCISE 3

O'Shock Electrical Ltd. originally issued 40,000 shares of its nopar common at $16 per share. Give the appropriate journal entry for each of the following transactions in 1992.

1. On January 10, O'Shock reacquired and retired 5,000 shares at $10 per share.

2. On April 5, O'Shock reacquired and retired 1,000 shares at $21 per share.

3. On October 14, O'Shock reacquired and retired 2,000 shares at $35 per share.

MULTIPLE CHOICE

Enter the letter corresponding to the response which **best** completes each of the following statements or questions.

_____ 1. Which of the following is **not** one of the characteristics of the corporate form of business organization?

    a. Income is taxed only when distributed as dividends.
    b. Ownership is easily transferable.
    c. Liability is limited to resources of the corporate entity.
    d. It is not necessary to reorganize the business when ownership changes.

_____ 2. The basic rights of common share ownership generally do **not** include:

    a. the right to vote for directors.
    b. the right after preferred shares to receive dividends.
    c. the right to share in the distribution of assets in the event of liquidation.
    d. the right to maintain a proportional share of ownership in the company by purchasing a proportional share of any new shares issued.

_____ 3. The excess of the fair value of the consideration received over the par value of common shares issued should be credited to:

    a. a liability account.
    b. common shares.
    c. other contributed capital.
    d. retained earnings.

_____ 4. A donated operational asset for which the fair value, if known, should be recorded as a debit to operational assets and a credit to:

    a. other contributed capital.
    b. retained earnings.
    c. a deferred charge.
    d. other income.

_____ 5. When a corporation sells some of its own common shares, all on credit, there should be a debit to the account:

    a. stock subscriptions receivable-common shares.
    b. accounts receivable.
    c. cash.
    d. stock notes receivable-common shares.
    e. common shares subscribed.

_____ 6. Dividends in arrears:

    a. are reported in a note to the financial statements.
    b. arise in connection with fully participating preferred shares.
    c. are reported as a current liability.
    d. are reported as a noncurrent liability.

_____ 7. When all of the preferred shares are purchased and formally retired by the issuing corporation for less than its original issue price, accounting for the retirement increases:

    a. retained earnings.
    b. contributed capital unrealized.
    c. net income for the period.
    d. contributed capital from shares retirement.
    e. none of the above.

_____ 8. HOC has the following shares outstanding:

    $1.80 preferred noncumulative, nonparticipating, 10,000 shares
    Common, 10,000 shares

    Dividends are two years in arrears, excluding the current year. Total dividends of $90,000 will be paid. The total amounts that will be received by the (a) preferred shareholders and (b) common shareholders are:

	(a) *Preferred Shareholders*	(b)*Common Shareholders*
a.	$36,000	$54,000
b.	$18,000	$72,000
c.	$90,000	$ 0
d.	$54,000	$36,000
e.	None of the above.	

_____ 9. A company reacquires and retires shares of its own shares at the weighted average issue price and reports the transaction in the theoretically correct manner. What effect will this transaction have on shareholders' equity and earnings per share, respectively?

    a. increase and decrease.
    b. decrease and decrease.
    c. increase and no effect.
    d. decrease and increase.
    e. none of the above.

_____ 10. During 1992 BXO issued for $110 per share, 5,000 shares of $10 convertible preferred. One share of preferred can be converted into three shares of BXOs common at the option of the preferred shareholder. On December 31, 1993, all of the preferred was converted into common. The market value of the common shares at the conversion date was $40 per share. What amount should be credited to the common shares account on December 31, 1993?

    a. $375,000.
    b. $500,000.
    c. $550,000.
    d. $600,000.
    e. $660,000.

_____ 11. Based on the same data as in Question 10, if the preferred had been issued at $120, shareholders' equity would **decrease** by:

    a. $0.
    b. $150,000.
    c. $375,000.
    d. $600,000.
    e. $660,000.

_____ 12. Constant Corporation reported shareholders' equity on its balance sheet at December 31, 1992 as follows:

Common, 20,000 shares,	$300,000
Retained earnings	200,000
Total shareholders' equity	$500,000

In 1993, Constant's earned income of $25,000, declared cash dividends of $15,000 and retired 2,000 shares of its outstanding stock for $20 per share. At the end of 1993, Constant's retained earnings should have the following balance:

    a. $200,000
    b. $110,000
    c. $210,000
    d. $225,000

_____ 13. Based on the same data as in Question 12, except that Constant retired 2,500 shares at $5 per share, Constant's retained earnings at the end of 1993 should have the following balance:

    a. $200,000
    b. $110,000
    c. $210,000
    d. $225,000

_____ 14. The shareholders' equity section of PTO's statement of financial position at December 31, 1988, was as follows:

Common shares, (authorized 1,000,000 shares,
issued and outstanding, 900,000 shares) $11,700,000
Retained earnings   1,300,000

Total shareholders' equity $13,000,000

On January 2, 1989, PTO purchased and retired 100,000 shares of its own shares for $1,800,000. Immediately after retirement of these 100,000 shares, the balance in the retained earnings account should be:

a. $1,100,000
b. $ 800,000
c. $1,300,000
d. $ 500,000
e. none of these

SOLUTIONS TO REVIEW QUESTIONS AND EXERCISES

TRUE-FALSE

1.	T	5.	F	9.	F	13.	F
2.	T	6.	F	10.	F	14.	F
3.	T	7.	F	11.	T		
4.	F	8.	T	12.	T		

EXERCISE 1

1. **The preferred shares are noncumulative and nonparticipating:**

	Preferred	Common
1992	$ 6,000	$ 0
1993	$ 8,000	$13,000
1994	$ 8,000	$82,000

2. **The preferred shares are cumulative and fully participating:**

	Preferred	Common
1992	$ 6,000	$ 0
1993	$10,000[1]	$11,000
1994	$30,000[2]	$60,000

Notes:

[1] Preferred dividends in arrears ($2,000) and current preferred dividends ($8,000). The remainder ($11,000) was totally distributed to common shares, which was less than the matching dividend rate of $.80. There was thus no participation.

[2] Current preferred dividends plus participation = ($90,000 x 1 / 3) = $30,000.

EXERCISE 2

a. **To record subscriptions of 10,000 shares each for Mr. A and Mr. B, at $20 per share.**

Subscriptions receivable (20,000 shs. x $20)	400,000	
Common shares subscribed (20,000 shs. x $20)		400,000

b. **To record collection of 50% of the subscription price.**

Cash ($400,000 x 50%)	200,000	
Subscriptions receivable		200,000

c. **To record collection of balance of subscription receivable from Mr. A.**

Cash ($200,000 x 50%)	100,000	
Subscriptions receivable		100,000

d. **To record issuance of the subscribed shares to Mr. A.**

Common shares subscribed (10,000 shs. x $20)	200,000	
Common shares		200,000

e. **Mr. B defaulted on the contract. To record the forfeited transaction assuming that Mowman refunded the previously collected amount to Mr. B.**

Common shares subscribed (10,000 x $20)	200,000	
Subscriptions receivable		100,000
Due to defaulting subscriber (Mr. B)		100,000

EXERCISE 3

<u>1992</u>

1. January 10   Common Shares (5,000 X $16)   80,000
                    Cash (5,000 X $10)   50,000
                    Contributed Capital-Retirement
                       of Common Shares   30,000

2. April 5   Common Shares (1,000 X $16)   16,000
                  Contributed capital-retirement
                     of common shares   5,000
                      Cash (1,000 X $21)   21,000

3. October 14 Common Shares (2,000 X $16)   32,000
                  Contributed capital-retirement
                     of common shares (balance)   25,000
                  Retained earnings (plug)   3,000
                      Cash (2,000 X $35)   70,000

MULTIPLE CHOICE:

1.	a	5.	a	9.	d	13.	a
2.	d	6.	a	10.	c	14.	b
3.	c	7.	d	11.	a		
4.	a	8.	b	12.	a		

COMPUTATIONS

10. (c) $110 x 5,000 shares = $550,000

12. (a) Opening balance $200,000
        Earned income   + 25,000
        Cash dividends   - 15,000
        Retirement [2,000 x (5-15)]   0
                                         $200,000

13. (c) Opening balance $200,000
        Earned income   + 25,000
        Cash dividends   - 15,000
        Retirement [2,000 x (5-15)]   0
                                         $210,000

14. (b) $11,700,000 ÷ 900,000 = $13
13 x 100,000 = $1,300,000
1,300,000 - (1,800,000 - 1,300,000)
= $800,000

CHAPTER 21

Corporations: Retained Earnings and Stock Options

CHAPTER OBJECTIVES

This chapter is designed to enable students to:

A. Explain the nature of retained earnings and dividends.

B. Prepare the proper accounting entries for cash dividends, property dividends, liquidating dividends, and scrip dividends.

C. Accounting for stock dividends and stock splits.

D. Explain the nature of an appropriation of retained earnings and how it should be reported.

E. Apply the appropriate accounting and reporting standards for stock option plans, rights, and warrants.

F. Apply the appropriate accounting treatment for stock appreciation rights.

G. Recognize a quasi reorganization, explain when it is appropriate, and apply the accounting procedures that are applied in a quasi reorganization.

CHAPTER OVERVIEW

Part I – Retained Earnings

A. **Retained earnings** represent a corporation's accumulated net income (or net loss) and prior period adjustments, less dividends and other amounts transferred to the contributed capital accounts. The sources and uses of retained earnings are summarized in the following T account:

Retained Earnings

Decreases (debits)	Increases (credits)
* Net loss (including extraordinary items) * Prior period adjustments (primarily correc- tion of accounting errors of prior periods * Cash dividends * Property dividends * Scrip dividends * Stock dividends * Share retirement transactions	* Net income (including extraordinary items) * Prior period adjustments (primarily correc- tion of accounting errors of prior periods * Removal of deficit by quasi-reorganization

A credit balance in this account indicates the amount of net assets previously earned and retained by the firm. A debit balance is referred to as a **deficit**. Note that dividends generally are declared only to the extent of retained earnings available for distribution. In some jurisdictions, however, dividends may be paid on the basis of contributed capital also.

B.   Nature of Dividends

Corporations are not required to pay dividends. Dividends are distributions of cash, noncash assets, or the corporation's own shares to the shareholders in proportion to the number of outstanding shares held by each of them. The following sequential events are typical:

1.   On the **date of declaration**, the board of directors formally announces (declares) the dividend distribution. A declared dividend constitutes an enforceable contract between the corporation and its shareholders. A journal entry is required to record the dividend declared on this date in the books of both the declarer and the investor.

2.   On the **date of record,** a list of **shareholders of record** is prepared to identify those who hold shares at this specified date and are thus entitled to receive the declared dividends. No entry is made.

3.   To provide time for transfer of the shares, the stock exchanges advance the effective **ex-dividend date** by three or four days beyond the date of record. In that case, one who holds the shares on the day prior to the stipulated ex-dividend date receives the dividend. No entry is made.

3.   On the **date of payment**, cash, noncash asset, or the corporation's shares are distributed to those shareholders who are entitled to the dividend. This date typically follows the declaration date by four to six weeks, and a journal entry is required to record the payment.

C.   Forms (Types) of Dividends

Dividends may take the following forms:

1.   **Cash dividends.**   Cash dividends are the usual form of distributions to shareholders. The board of directors may declare cash dividends if both retained earnings and cash are available. To record cash dividends:

a.   On date of declaration:

Retained earnings   xxxx
    Cash dividends payable   xxxx

b.   On date of payment:

Cash dividends payable   xxxx
    Cash   xxxx

Cash dividends are usually reported on the balance sheet as a current liability. In the rare situations that a corporation has enough retained earnings but is temporarily short of cash, it may choose to declare a **scrip (or liability) dividend.** In essence, a scrip dividend is also a cash dividend except that a future date longer than ordinary (e.g., one year) is specified as the date of payment. Promissory notes, called scrip, are often issued to stockholders prior to the payment date. Once issued the notes are treated as ordinary notes. Any interest accrued and paid should be debited to interest expense.

2. **Property dividends.**   A **property dividend** involves the distribution of noncash assets (property) to shareholders. The dividend is recorded at the fair market value of the property to be distributed in accordance with *CICA Handbook*, sec. 3830. The property should be revalued and a gain or loss on the revaluation should be recognized prior to recording the dividend. The most commonly used property for dividend purpose is an investment in equity securities. Note that when a property is revalued, it is limited to that portion of the property that is used for dividends distribution. The remainder should still be maintained at cost. To record a property dividend:

a.   On date of declaration:

(1)   To record revaluation of the property:

Investment in equity securities   xxxx
    Gain on disposal of security investment   xxxx

(2)   To record the dividend:

Retained earnings   xxxx
    Property dividends payable   xxxx

b.   On date of payment

To record the payment:

Property dividends payable	xxxx	
Investment in equity securities		xxxx

Like cash dividends, property dividends are usually reported on the balance sheet as current liabilities.

A similar transaction to a property dividend is a *spin-off*. In a spin-off, the shares of wholly or substantially owned subsidiary are distributed to the parent company's shareholders such that the shareholders now directly own the subsidiary rather than exercise control indirectly through the corporation. When a transaction is a spin-off, it is usually valued at the book value of the spun off shares, not the market value.

3.   **Stock dividends.**   A **stock dividend** is a proportional distribution of additional shares of common or preferred stock to the stockholders of the corporation. It is a transfer of certain amount of retained earnings to permanent capital account(s), and the assets, liabilities and the total shareholders' equity of the firm are not affected by the transfer. The primary reasons for the issuance of stock dividends include (a) to retain earnings permanently in the business, and (b) to increase the number of shares outstanding so as to reduce the market price per share and to make it more affordable to small investors.

When a stock dividend is of the same class as that held by the recipients, it is called an *ordinary stock dividend.* When a class of share capital other than the one already held by the recipients is issued, such a dividend is called a *special stock dividend* (e.g., preferred shares issued to the owners of common).

Accounting Issues Related to Ordinary Stock Dividends   The three primary issues in accounting for stock dividends are the value that should be recognized, the accounts and dates that should be used, and the manner of disclosure in the financial statements.

The shares issued for the dividend could be recorded at market value, at stated (or par) value, or at some other value.

The CICA has made no recommendation on the matter; however, the Canada Business Corporations Act, 1975, requires shares to be issued at fair market value.

There are three alternatives: market value, stated value, and memo disclosure.

Situation 1 -- Market Value Method   Consistent with the Canada Business Corporations Act, a corporation's board of directors should require capitalization of the current market value of the additional shares issued. The market value of the stock dividend should be measured on the basis of the market price per share immediately after the stock dividend is issued.

Situation 2 -- *Stated Value Method* The board of directors in certain jurisdictions may decide to capitalize a stated amount per share -- average paid in per share to date, or par value, if applicable.

Situation 3 -- *Memo entry* Since a large stock dividend may be issued for the primary purpose of reducing market price per share, it is obvious that the shareholder has received nothing of value. A memo entry should recorded to identify the number of shares issued, outstanding, and subscribed. No change is made in any capital account. This parallels the treatment of a stock split.

ILLUSTRATION 1 -- Stock dividends

N-Gauge-Clutch Inc. declared a stock dividend of 10,000 common shares. The outstanding common shares had been issued for $10 per share, on average. The market price of the stock **at the declaration and issuance** of the new shares was $50. The board used $10 as the stated value, if appropriate.

Required:

(1)   **Recording stock dividends on date of issuance:**

```
┌─────────────────────────────────────────────────────────────────────────┐
│                    ORIGINAL ENTRY AT DATE OF ISSUANCE                     │
├────────────────────────────────┬──────────────────────────────────────────┤
│       Market Value Method      │           Stated Value Method            │
│       ─────────────────        │           ──────────────────             │
│                                │                                          │
│  On date of declaration:       │   On date of declaration:                │
│    None                        │     None                                 │
│                                │                                          │
│  On date of issuance:          │   On date of issuance:                   │
│    Retained earnings  500,000* │     Retained earnings   100,000 **       │
│      Common stock      500,000 │       Common stock       100,000         │
│                                │                                          │
│    * 10,000 shs. x $50 = $500,000  │  ** 10,000 shs. x $10 = $100,000      │
└────────────────────────────────┴──────────────────────────────────────────┘
```

(2)   **Recording stock dividend on date of declaration:**

```
┌─────────────────────────────────────────────────────────────────────────┐
│                   ORIGINAL ENTRY AT DATE OF DECLARATION                   │
├────────────────────────────────┬──────────────────────────────────────────┤
│       Market Value Method      │           Stated Value Method            │
│       ─────────────────        │           ──────────────────             │
│                                │                                          │
│  On date of declaration:       │   On date of declaration:                │
│    Retained earnings   500,000 │     Retained earnings    100,000         │
│      Stock dividends distributable  500,000 │  Stock dividends distributable  100,000 │
│                                │                                          │
│  On date of issuance:          │   On date of issuance:                   │
│    Stock dividends distributable  100,000 │  Stock dividends distributable  100,000 │
│      Common stock      100,000 │       Common stock       100,000         │
├─────────────────────────────────────────────────────────────────────────┤
│  Note: Stock dividends distributable is reported as an increase in contributed capital. │
└─────────────────────────────────────────────────────────────────────────┘
```

When a corporation issues stock dividends (e.g., 10% stock dividends), some shareholders may be entitled only to a fractional number of shares (e.g., 3/10 of a share). In this case, the company may either distribute cash for those fractional shares based on current share market price, or issue stock warrants which may be exchanged for shares such as 10 warrants for a share. Stock warrants issued are recorded by crediting stock warrants outstanding at the market value of equivalent number of whole shares. Stock warrants outstanding will then be transferred to common shares when the warrant rights are exercised. As the exercise period is over, any outstanding warrants become unexercisable and are closed to contributed capital from lapsed warrant rights.

ILLUSTRATION 2 -- Stock dividends with fractional shares

On October 10, 1992 2-Market Ltd. declared 10% stock dividends of 25,000 shares on its no par common shares. On November 10, 24,500 shares of common and stock warrants equivalent to 500 whole shares were distributed to shareholders. On December 10, 80% of the warrant rights were exercised, and the remaining rights became unexercisable at the year end. Market price of the shares on date of declaration and issuance was $10 per share.

October 10, 1992:

No entry.

November 10, 1992 -- To record stock and warrants distributed:

Retained earnings	250,000	
Common stock (24,500 shs. X $10)		245,000
Stock warrants outstanding (500 shs. X $10)		5,000

December 10, 1992 -- To record exercise of stock warrants:

Stock warrants outstanding (400 shs. X $10)	4,000	
Common shares		4,000

December 31, 1992 -- To record lapse of warrant rights:

Stock warrants outstanding (100 shs. X $10)	1,000	
Contributed capital from lapsed warrants rights		1,000

4. **Liquidating dividends.**   A **liquidating dividend** is a return of the contributed capital instead of a distribution of earnings. Liquidating dividends may be either intentional or unintentional. Intentional liquidating dividends occur when the board of directors knowingly declares dividends as returns of investment to the shareholders. In most jurisdictions, such a dividend is not allowed unless creditors' claims have been met. Intentional liquidating dividends are recorded by debiting contributed capital and crediting dividends payable.

Unintentional liquidating dividends, on the other hand, occur when retained earnings are improperly overstated, and the board of directors unknowingly declared dividends based on the overstated amount. Unintentional liquidating dividends are recorded as ordinary dividends until the error is discovered. A correcting entry would then be required by debiting contributed capital and crediting retaining earnings.

5. Stock Splits

A **stock split** is similar to a stock dividend in that **additional shares** are distributed. The primary purpose of a stock split is to increase the number of shares, reduce the market price per share, and improve the marketability of the shares. Unlike a stock dividend, a stock split involves no capitalization of retained earnings and does not affect the balance of any account. It is recorded in a memo entry only.

D. Appropriations (Restrictions) of Retained Earnings

An **appropriation of retained earnings** restricts a portion of retained earnings from being distributed as dividends. Appropriations may be made (a) to comply with federal and provincial laws, (b) to satisfy a contractual requirement, or (c) to indicate a specific purpose for a specified portion of retained earnings (management intent). A formal journal entry may be used to reclassify retained earnings with a debit to "unappropriated retained earnings" and a credit to "appropriated retained earnings". This entry should be reversed when the need for the restriction no longer exists. Many firms disclose the appropriations in the notes instead of presenting them in the balance sheet.

E. Stock Rights and Options

Evidence of ownership of one or more stock rights is a certificate called a *stock warrant*. Stock rights sometimes are simply referred to as stock warrants, a stock warrant typically specifies (1) the number of rights represented by the warrant, (2) the option price (which may be zero) per share of the specified shares, (3) the number of rights to obtain a share (4) the expiration of the rights, and (5) instructions for exercising the rights.

Three dates are important regarding stock rights: (1) *announcement date* of the rights offering, (2) *issuance date* of the rights, and (3) *expiration date* of the rights. Between the announcement date and the issuance date of the rights, the related shares will sell *rights on*. That is, the price of the shares will include the value of the rights because the shares and the rights are not separable during that period of time. After the issuance date of the rights and until expiration of the rights, the shares and rights sell separately. That is, the shares sell *ex rights* during this period of time. The rights will have a separate market price.

Stock rights received by a shareholder may be (1) *exercised* by purchasing additional shares, as specified, from the corporation, (2) *sold* at the market value of the rights, or (3) allowed to *lapse* on the expiration date.

Corporations issue stock rights and options for the following reasons:

1. To give existing shareholders the first chance to buy additional shares when the corporation decides to raise additional equity capital by selling a large number of unissued shares. Stock rights are evidence of shareholders' preemptive right to maintain their existing level of ownership in the firm even if new shares are issued.
2. As compensation to outsiders (such as underwriters, promoters, and professionals) for services provided to the corporation.
3. As a "poison pill" to make the corporation less attractive as a take-over target.
4. To represent fractional shares when a stock dividend is declared and issued.
5. As additional compensation to officers and other employees of the corporation. These rights often are referred to as stock options or stock incentive plans.
6. To enhance the marketability of other securities issued by the corporation. These include issuing common stock rights with convertible bonds payable (in Chapter 16) and convertible preferred shares (in Chapter 20).

4. Stock Rights to Employees -- Stock Option Incentive Plans

1. **Stock option plans** allow employees of a corporation the option of purchasing a specified number of shares of the firm's capital at a specified price within a specified period of time. A stock option plan may be **noncompensatory** if it possesses **all** the following characteristics:

   (1) Substantially all full-time employees meeting limited employment criteria are included.

   (2) The shares are offered to eligible employees equally, or is based on a uniform percentage of salaries or wages.

   (3) The time permitted for exercise of an option is limited to a reasonable period.

   (4) The discount from the market price does not exceed 15%.

   If these conditions are met, then,

   (1) There is no additional cost to the company

   (2) There is no additional compensation to the employees

   A noncompensatory plan is not recorded until the option privilege is exercised by the employees. When it is exercised, the following entry is pertinent:

Cash	xxxx	
Common shares		xxxx

2. **Compensatory stock option plans.**   If a stock option plan does not contain **all** of the six characteristics above, it is classified as **compensatory.** Compensatory plans require the **measurement** of the total compensation and its allocation to compensation expense in the appropriate accounting period. The following dates are essential:

   a.   **Date of grant.**   This is the date on which a certain option privilege is officially granted to specific employee(s).

   b.   **Date of measurement.**   This is the first date that (1) the **option price** per share and (2) the **number of shares** obtainable are known, so that the total compensation cost can be measured.

   c.   **Date of exercise.**   This is the date that the option privilege is exercised and the shares are issued.

The total compensation cost is measured by multiplying the number of shares obtainable and the difference between the option price and the market price of the stock on the date of measurement. This total cost should be allocated to compensation expense in the period(s) **benefitted** by the expected employees' service for which the options are granted:

   a.   If the date of measurement is also the date of grant, the total cost is measured on that date and recorded as deferred compensation cost, which is then allocated to the benefitted years.

   b.   If the date of measurement is subsequent to the date of grant, compensation expense must be accrued each period prior to the date of measurement based on an **estimate** of either the option price, or the number of shares, or both. On the date of measurement, the excess of the measured total compensation cost over the estimated compensation expense recognized to date is to be allocated to the remaining number of benefitted years.

When options are exercised, the shares issued are recorded at the sum of the cash received and the recorded value of the stock options tendered.

ILLUSTRATION 4 -- Compensatory stock option plan

On January 1, 1992, Kutless Company granted John Kutless, the president, an option to purchase 2,000 shares of his common stock. The period of expected service, for which the options are being given, is five years. The options were exercised on December 31, 1996.

The quoted market prices of Kutless's common shares were as follows:

January 1, 1992	$30
December 31, 1992	$35
December 31, 1994	$40

Case 1:   Option price of $20 per share is known at the date of grant:

a.   January 1, 1992 (date of grant and also date of measurement):

To record total compensation cost – [2,000 x ($30 - $20)]:

Deferred compensation cost	20,000	
Stock rights outstanding		20,000

b.   At the end of each of the five years:

To allocate deferred compensation cost – ($20,000 / 5):

Compensation expense	4,000	
Deferred compensation cost		4,000

c.   December 31, 1996 (date of exercise):

To record issuance of stock:

Cash (2,000 x $20)	40,000	
Stock rights outstanding	20,000	
Common shares (2,000 x $30)		60,000

Case 2: Option price of $20 per share is not known until the end of 1994. At the end of 1992, the option price is estimated to be $18 per share.

a.   January 1, 1992 (date of grant):

No entry.

b.   December 31, 1992:

To record compensation cost based on estimated option price:

Deferred compensation cost [2,000 x ($35 - $18)]	34,000	
Stock rights outstanding		34,000

c.   At the end of each of 1992 and 1993:

To record compensation expense:

Compensation expense ($34,000 / 5)	6,800	
Deferred compensation cost		6,800

d.   December 31, 1994 (date of measurement):

To adjust deferred compensation cost:
[2,000 x ($40 - $20) - $34,000]

Deferred compensation cost	6,000	
Stock rights outstanding		6,000

e.   At the end of each of 1994 to 1996:

To record compensation expense:
{[2,000 x ($40 - $20) - $6,800 x 2] / 3]}

Compensation expense	8,800	
Deferred compensation cost		8,800

f.   December 31, 1996 (date of exercise):

To record exercise of stock options:

Cash (2,000 x $20)	40,000	
Stock rights outstanding ($34,000 + $6,000)	40,000	
Common shares		80,000

SHARES ISSUED TO EMPLOYEES--SUMMARIZED

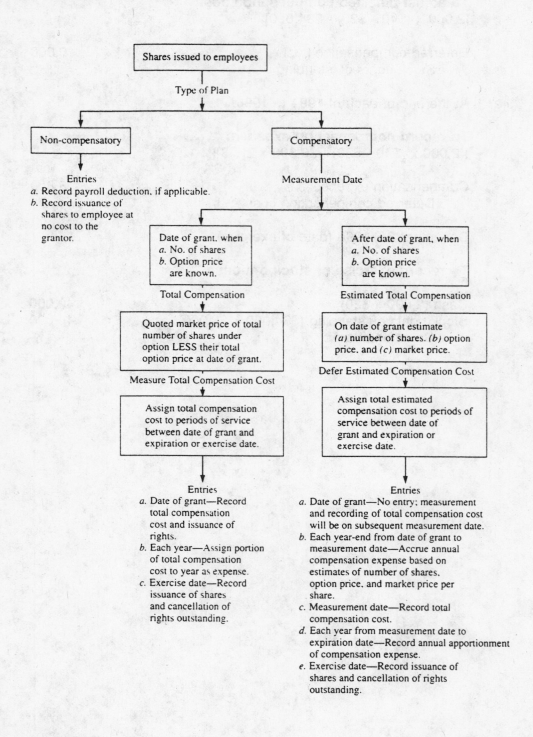

Shares issued to employees

Type of Plan

Non-compensatory

Entries
a. Record payroll deduction, if applicable.
b. Record issuance of shares to employee at no cost to the grantor.

Compensatory

Measurement Date

Date of grant, when
a. No. of shares
b. Option price
are known.

Total Compensation

Quoted market price of total number of shares under option LESS their total option price at date of grant.

Measure Total Compensation Cost

Assign total compensation cost to periods of service between date of grant and expiration or exercise date.

Entries
a. Date of grant—Record total compensation cost and issuance of rights.
b. Each year—Assign portion of total compensation cost to year as expense.
c. Exercise date—Record issuance of shares and cancellation of rights outstanding.

After date of grant, when
a. No. of shares
b. Option price
are known.

Estimated Total Compensation

On date of grant estimate (a) number of shares. (b) option price, and (c) market price.

Defer Estimated Compensation Cost

Assign total estimated compensation cost to periods of service between date of grant and expiration or exercise date.

Entries
a. Date of grant—No entry; measurement and recording of total compensation cost will be on subsequent measurement date.
b. Each year-end from date of grant to measurement date—Accrue annual compensation expense based on estimates of number of shares. option price, and market price per share.
c. Measurement date—Record total compensation cost.
d. Each year from measurement date to expiration date—Record annual apportionment of compensation expense.
e. Exercise date—Record issuance of shares and cancellation of rights outstanding.

Specific issues on accounting for compensatory stock option plans:

a. **Service period.** Total compensation cost should be allocated over a service (benefitted) period that extends from the date of grant to the date on which the employee has no further option obligations, usually the first date that the option is exercisable. Sometimes, service period is specified in the plan.

b. **Forfeited plan.** Failure of an employee to fulfill the option obligations is treated as a change in estimate. The related stock options outstanding and the unamortized deferred compensation cost should both be removed and the difference accounted for as a reduction in current compensation expense.

c. **Lapsed plan.** If the exercise period lapsed, any outstanding stock options became unexercisable. Then the credit balance of the stock options outstanding may be either transferred to paid-in capital from lapsed stock options, or recognized as compensation expenses for the current and a reasonable number of future periods as a change in estimate.

d. **Disclosure.** On the balance sheet, stock options outstanding, offset by the unamortized deferred compensation cost, is presented as an element of contributed capital.

F. Stock Appreciation Rights (SAR's)

These rights are awards entitling employees to receive cash, shares or a combination of the two in an amount equivalent to any excess of **the market value on the date of exercise** of a stated number of shares of the employer company's shares over a stated price. The form of payment may be specified when the rights are granted or may be determined when they are exercised.

Under a stock appreciation plan, the amount of cash or the number of shares an employee is entitled to receive becomes known only when the employee exercises his (her) appreciation rights. Therefore, prior to the date of exercise, estimates must be used each year to recognize annual compensation expense. If cash is to be paid, the expense should be accrued against a liability account, e.g., "stock appreciation plan liability." If shares are issued, it is accounted for similarly as a stock option plan, except that (1) the date of measurement is the date of exercise, and (2) the number of shares issued is based on their market value equivalent to the amount of share appreciation.

$$\begin{array}{l}\text{Stock appreciation} \\ \text{rights liability} \\ \text{(to date)}\end{array} = \begin{array}{l}\text{No. of} \\ \text{SARs granted}\end{array} \times \left[\begin{array}{l}\text{Market price} \\ \text{per share at} \\ \text{end of} \\ \text{current year}\end{array} - \begin{array}{l}\text{Market price} \\ \text{per share at} \\ \text{grant date}\end{array}\right] \times \begin{array}{l}\text{Percent of} \\ \text{period of} \\ \text{service} \\ \text{completed} \\ \text{to date}\end{array}$$

G.   Quasi-Reorganizations

A firm undergoing financial difficulties, but with favorable prospects, may use a quasi-reorganization to write down inflated asset values and eliminate an accumulated deficit (debit balance in retained earnings). To effect the reorganization the following procedure is pertinent:

1.   The firm's assets (and perhaps liabilities) are **revalued** (up or down) to reflect fair market values, with corresponding credits or debits to retained earnings. This process typically increases the deficit.

2.   The deficit is eliminated against additional paid-in capital. If additional paid-in capital is not sufficient to absorb the entire deficit, a reduction in capital stock may be necessary.

3.   The retained earnings account is dated to show the date the deficit was eliminated and when the accumulation of earnings began.

Listed are certain associated safeguards or conditions:

1.   Retained earnings immediately after the quasi reorganization must be zero.
2.   Upon completion of the quasi reorganization, no deficit shall remain in any corporate capital account.
3.   The effects of the whole procedure shall be made known to all shareholders entitled to vote and appropriate approval in advance obtained from them.
4.   A fair and conservative balance sheet shall be presented as of the date of the reorganization, and the readjustment off values should be reasonably complete, in order to obviate as far as possible future readjustments of like nature.

KEY CONCEPTS

Dividends   Distributions of earnings of the corporation to its shareholders in proportion to their respective share holdings. A dividend that is a return of the contributed capital is known as a liquidating dividend. Dividends may take various forms such as cash, scrip, property or shares.

Quasi reorganization   A special procedure to write down inflated assets and to remove accumulated deficit in order to reestablish a new accounting basis of a company which has a significant deficit but appears to have favorable prospects.

Retained earnings   Accumulated, undistributed net income or net loss. It is mainly used to distribute dividends. Appropriations are sometime made to restrict a specified portion of retained earnings from being distributed to the shareholders of the corporation. Such appropriations may be made with or without a journal entry.

Stock appreciation rights   A right which allows the employees to receive share appreciation of a certain number of common shares in cash or in shares.

Stock dividends   A distribution of additional shares to the shareholders of the corporation. The three primary issues in accounting for stock dividends are the value that should be recognized, the accounts and dates that should be used, and the manner of disclosure in the financial statements.
There are three alternatives in accounting for stock dividends: market value, stated value, and memo disclosure.

Stock option plans   A plan that grants employees the option to purchase a certain number of common shares at a specified option price within a specified period. A stock option plan is **noncompensatory** if (1) substantially all full-time employees are included, (2) the stock is offered to all eligible employees equally, (3) the exercise period is reasonably short, and (4) the discount from the market price is reasonably small, (5) there is no additional cost to the company, (6) there is no additional compensation to the employees. Plans that do not possess all these characteristics are classified as **compensatory**.

Stock split   Additional shares distributed to existing shareholders resulting in a reduction in the weighted average issue price per share. The primary intent is to increase the number of shares outstanding in order to improve the marketability of the shares. A stock split does not require any entry as it does not affect the balance of any account, however, a memorandum entry may be made.

Stock warrants   Certificates that entitle the holders to purchase a specified number of shares at a specified price within a specified period of time. Stock warrants may be issued for the fractional shares of stock dividends distribution, to attach to bonds or preferred shares issued, or to grant stock option privileges to employees.

REVIEW QUESTIONS AND EXERCISES

TRUE-FALSE

Indicate whether each of the following statements is true or false by circling the correct response.

T   F   1. The existence of a credit balance in unappropriated retained earnings indicates that a corporation has cash available for paying dividends.

T   F   2. The declaration of a cash dividend creates a legal obligation to pay the dividend which does not exist prior to the declaration.

T   F   3. A dividend may involve the distribution of cash, investment in securities, or some other asset.

T   F   4. A property dividend is recorded at the carrying value (book value) of the assets to be distributed.

T   F   5. A stock dividend does not affect assets, liabilities, or total shareholders' equity.

T   F   6. Accounting for a stock dividend generally involves a reduction of retained earnings and an increase in contributed capital equal to the market value of the shares distributed.

T   F   7. In the case of stock split, there is no change in the total number of shares issued, nor in the total amount of the shareholders' equity.

T   F   8. A dividend that reduces the contributed capital is a liquidating dividend.

T   F   9. An appropriation of retained earnings assures the availability of cash or other assets for some legal, contractual, or discretionary purposes.

T   F   10. Generally, a quasi-reorganization results in an adjustment of inflated asset balances and an elimination of a deficit in retained earnings.

T   F   11. When convertible preferred shares are issued, the package price of the issue should be allocated to both the preferred shares and the common share accounts.

T   F   12. Stock option plans that require the employees to pay cash as consideration for the shares they receive are referred to as compensatory plans.

T   F   13. The measurement date for a compensatory stock option plan is the first date on which both the option price and the market price are known for the shares available under the plan.

T   F   14. When the date of grant and the measurement date of a stock option plan differ, no entry is required at the date of grant.

EXERCISE 1

The shareholders' equity of Catch Up Corporation Ltd. on June 30, 1992, is presented below:

Common shares, 200,000 shares issued,	$3,600,000
Retained earnings	9,400,000

On August 15, 1992, the board of directors declared a 10% stock dividend on common shares, to be distributed on October 15, 1992. The market price of the common shares was $30 on August 15, 1992, and $35 on October 15, 1992, respectively. No entry was made on the declaration date. The stated value (if appropriate) is established by the board of directors as the average amount paid in to date.

Required:

1. Use the market value method to record the distribution on October 15, 1992:

2. Use the stated value method to record the distribution on October 15, 1992:

EXERCISE 2

For each of the transactions below, indicate the effect on **total retained earnings,** using +
for increase, - for decrease, or **0** for no effect. Consider each transaction separately.

_____   1.   Declaration and distribution of stock dividend (memo entry method not used to
record this)

_____   2.   An appropriation for plant expansion.

_____   3.   A net loss for the year.

_____   4.   Declaration of a property dividend.

_____   5.   A purchase and retirement of shares at a price in excess of the weighted
average issue price.

_____   6.   A stock split.

_____   7.   Conversion of bonds into common shares, no par value (at book value).

_____   8.   Declaration of a cash dividend.

_____   9.   Net income for the year.

_____   10. Receipt of land as a donation.

EXERCISE 3

On September 1, 1992, Muddy Track Shoes declared a property dividend to be paid on October 1, 1992 with 2,000 shares of common shares of Betty Windmill Corporation, currently held as an investment. The investment shares were purchased five years ago at a cost of $15 per share. The market value of the shares on September 1, 1992 was $21 per share.

Required:

Prepare journal entries for Muddy relative to the declaration and payment of the property dividend.

1. September 1, 1992 (date of declaration):

2. October 1, 1992 (date of payment):

EXERCISE 4

On January 2, 1992, Fabulous Sport granted Kee Allen, the president, an option to purchase 10,000 shares of Fablan's no par value common shares at $35 per share. The option becomes exercisable on January 2, 1994 after Allen has completed two years of service, for which the options are being granted.

The quoted market price of Fablan's common shares was as follows:

January 2, 1992	$40
December 31, 1992	$45
January 2, 1994	$60

Requires:

Prepare journal entries for Fablan relative to the stock option agreement:

1. January 2, 1992 (date of grant):

2. December 31, 1992:

3. December 31, 1993:

4. January 2, 1994 (date of exercise):

MULTIPLE CHOICE

Enter the letter corresponding to the response which **best** completes each of the following statements or questions.

_____ 1. Which of the following does not affect retained earnings?

    a. cash dividends.
    b. property dividends.
    c. stock dividends.
    d. intentional liquidating dividends.

_____ 2. Which of the following is not affected by stock dividend?

    a. contributed capital.
    b. retained earnings.
    c. total shareholders' equity.
    d. number of shares outstanding.

_____ 3. Both stock dividend and stock split affect which of the following?

    a. contributed capital.
    b. retained earnings.
    c. total shareholders' equity.
    d. number of shares outstanding.

_____ 4. A stock dividend does not cause which of the following?

    a. an increase in contributed capital.
    b. an increase in total shareholders' equity.
    c. a decrease in retained earnings.
    d. an increase in number of shares outstanding.

_____ 5. Any compensation cost involved in a compensatory employee stock option plan should be expensed:

    a. in the period containing the date of grant.
    b. in the period containing the measurement date.
    c. in the period(s) benefitted by the expected employee's service.
    d. in the period in which the options are exercised.

_____ 6. The measurement date in accounting for compensatory stock option plans is:

a. The date on which options are granted to employees.
b. The earliest date on which both the number of shares to be issued and option price are known.
c. The date on which the options are exercised.
d. The date the corporation forgoes alternative use of the shares to be sold under option.

_____ 7. Under a stock appreciation plan, the date of measurement is also:

a. the adoption date of the plan.
b. the date of grant.
c. the earliest date when the right becomes exercisable.
d. the date of exercise.

_____ 8. Chambers Corporation had investment in Chavez Company's bonds with a face value of $200,000 and an unamortized discount of $10,000. Eighty percent of the investment bonds is to be distributed as property dividends. On the declaration date, the investment has a total market value of $240,000. How much gain should Chambers recognize as a result of this property dividend?

a. $50,000.
b. $40,000.
c. $30,000.
d. $0.

_____ 9. The shareholders' equity section of Ball Corporation as of December 31, 1992, included:

Common shares, (10,000 shares)	$50,000
Retained earnings	70,000

On May 1, 1993, the board of directors declared a 10% stock dividend, and accordingly 1,000 additional shares were issued. The market price of the stock was $10 a share when the dividend was declared. For the year ended December 31, 1993, Ball sustained a net loss of $15,000. Ball's retained earnings at December 31, 1993 should be: (board used market value method)

a. $45,000.
b. $50,000.
c. $55,000.
d. $60,000.

_____ 10. Based on the same data as in Question 9, except that the board of directors used the stated value method where the stated value equal "average paid in per share" to date. Ball's retained earnings at December 31, 1993 should be:

    a. $40,000.
    b. $45,000.
    c. $50,000.
    d. $55,000.

_____ 11. On January 2, 1993, the board of directors of Dapper Corporation declared a cash dividend of $400,000 to shareholders on record on January 8, 1993, and payable on February 20, 1993. Dapper's December 31, 1992 balance sheet reveals the following:

    Common shares $900,000
    Unappropriated retained earnings 300,000

    The $400,000 dividend includes a liquidating dividend of:

    a. $400,000.
    b. $300,000.
    c. $200,000.
    d. $100,000.

_____ 12. On July 1, 1992, the Tall Corporation granted stock options to certain of its key employees as additional compensation. The options permitted the purchase of 10,000 shares of Tall's common at a price of $40 per share. On the date of grant, the market value of the shares was $52 per share. The options were exercisable beginning January 1, 1993, and expire on December 31, 1994. On February 1, 1993, when the shares were selling for $55, the options were exercised. How much total compensation cost should Tall record for these options?

    a. $120,000.
    b. $150,000.
    c. $420,000.
    d. $450,000.

_____ 13. Based on the same data as in Question 12, except that under the plan adopted by Tall the grantee will receive cash for the difference between the market price value and grant price per share on the date of exercise. How much total compensation cost should Tall record with respect to the stock appreciation rights plan?

    a. $120,000.
    b. $150,000.
    c. $420,000.
    d. $450,000.

_____ 14. A stock option plan is a compensatory plan if:

    a. the employee must have worked for the company for one year.
    b. the employee must report the option on the employee's current tax return.
    c. the employee must work for the company until retirement.
    d. it involves a cost to the grantor.
    e. none of the above.

SOLUTIONS TO REVIEW QUESTIONS AND EXERCISES

TRUE-FALSE

1.	F	5.	T	9.	F	13.	F
2.	T	6.	T	10.	T	14.	T
3.	T	7.	F	11.	F		
4.	F	8.	T	12.	F		

EXERCISE 1

October 15, 1992 -- To record stock dividends issued:

1. Market value

Retained earnings (20,000 shs. x $35)	700,000	
Common shares		700,000

2. Stated value

Retained earnings (20,000 shs. x $18)	360,000	
Common shares		360,000

EXERCISE 2

1.	-	5.	-	9.	+	
2.	0	6.	0	10.	0	
3.	-	7.	0			
4.	-	8.	-			

EXERCISE 3

1. September 1, 1992 (date of declaration):

Investment in equity securities [2,000 shs. x ($21 - $15)]	12,000	
Gain on disposal of investment		12,000
Retained earnings (2,000 shs. x $21)	42,000	
Property dividends payable		42,000

2. October 1, 1992 (date of payment):

Property dividends payable	42,000	
Investment in equity securities		42,000

EXERCISE 4

Prepare journal entries for Fablan relative to the stock option agreement:

1. January 2, 1992 (date of grant and also date of measurement):

Deferred compensation cost [10,000 shs. ($40 - $35)]	50,000	
Stock options outstanding		50,000

2. December 31, 1992:

Compensation expense ($50,000 x 1/2)	25,000	
Deferred compensation cost		25,000

3. December 31, 1993:

Compensation expense ($50,000 x 1/2)	25,000	
Deferred compensation cost		25,000

4. January 2, 1994 (date of exercise):

Cash (10,000 shs. x $35)	350,000	
Stock options outstanding	50,000	
Common shares		400,000

MULTIPLE CHOICE:

1.	d	5.	c	9.	a	13.	b
2.	c	6.	b	10.	c	14.	d
3.	d	7.	d	11.	d		
4.	b	8.	b	12.	a		

Computations:

8. (b) Market value of investment in bonds $240,000
Book value of investment in bonds:
     Face value of bonds $200,000
       Less: Unamortized discount   10,000

                                                (190,000)

     Excess of market value over book value $ 50,000
     Percentage to be distributed   80%

     Gain recognized $ 40,000

9. (a) Retained earnings -- December 31, 1992 $ 70,000
Less: Stock dividend (1,000 shs. x $10)   (10,000)
        Net loss -- 1993   (15,000)

     Retained earnings -- December 31, 1993 $ 45,000

10. (c) Retained earnings -- December 31, 1992 $ 70,000
Less: Stock dividend (1,000 shs. x $5)   (5,000)
        Net loss -- 1993   (15,000)

     Retained earnings -- December 31, 1993 $ 50,000

11. (d) Dividend declared $400,000
Unappropriated retained earnings   (300,000)

     Liquidating dividend $100,000

12. (a) Compensation cost
= 10,000 shs. ($52 - $40)
= $120,000.

13. (b) Compensation cost
= 10,000 shs. ($55 - $40)
= $150,000.

CHAPTER 22

Earnings per Share

CHAPTER OBJECTIVES

This chapter is designed to enable students to:

A.   Explain why financial statements users pay close attention to a company's reported earnings per share (EPS) and why EPS is difficult to interpret.

B.   Calculate basic EPS for firms with simple capital structures.

C.   Calculate fully diluted EPS for firms with complex capital structures.

D.   Calculate adjusted EPS and explain when its use is appropriate.

E.   Calculate pro forma EPS and explain when its use is appropriate.

CHAPTER OVERVIEW

A.   Section 3500 of the *CICA Handbook*, "Earnings per Share," requires that:

All enterprises, except for the following, should show earnings per share for the current and preceding period in the financial statements covered by the auditor's report:
a.   business enterprises which do not have share capital;
b.   government owned companies;
c.   wholly-owned subsidiaries;
d.   companies with few shareholders.

Earnings per share applies only to common shares, the mainstay equity investment medium that corporations use to raise business capital. Investors evaluate companies and make decisions to buy, sell, or hold (or sometimes to sell short) based on many factors. Cash flows, future prospects, the state of the economy, the nature of the corporation's competitive market, assessment of the abilities of key employees, and so on, all play a major role. Past performance is viewed as an objective base on which to predict future performance. The company's EPS on common shares is a commonly quoted performance statistic, as it relates past performance to the unit (the share) being traded.

B.   Simple Capital Structure

EPS applies only to common shares. For a firm with a simple capital structure (i.e., without potentially dilutive security or rights), a single presentation is appropriate. The following formula is applied to the calculation of a **basic EPS**.

Let: E = Earnings to common stockholders for the period
         S = Weighted average of common shares outstanding during the
           period

EPS = E / S

1. To determine **E, preferred dividends** are deducted from net income. If the preferred shares are cumulative, an amount equal to the current-period preferred dividends is deducted, regardless of whether the dividends have been declared. If the preferred shares are noncumulative, only declared dividends are deducted. Note that the deduction must be made even if there is a net loss.

2. To calculate **S,** any increases (e.g., issued new shares) or decreases (e.g., purchased and retired stock) are weighted by the fraction of the period from the date of increase/decrease to the end of period and then added to or subtracted from those shares outstanding for the entire period. Stock dividends and splits should be retroactively applied to those shares previously issued or reacquired.

ILLUSTRATION 1 -- Simple capital structure and basic earnings per share

At the end of 1992 the records of Hottman Ltd. reflect the following:

Common shares, no par value, authorized 100,000 shares:

Jan. 1 1992	Outstanding	30,000 shs.
April 1 1992	Sold and issued	6,000 shs.
June 1 1992	Declared stock dividends	10%
July 1 1992	Purchased and retired	(1,000) shs.
Aug. 5 1992	Declared stock split	2 for 1
Oct. 1 1992	Sold and issued	2,000 shs.

$1.00 Preferred shares, cumulative and nonconvertible,
   no par value, 50,000 shs. outstanding for the whole year $500,000

Net income $120,000

Required:

1. **To identify capital structure:**

   The capital structure is simple because the preferred stock is nonconvertible and there is no dilutive stock rights outstanding during the period.

2. **To compute earnings to common:**

   E = Net income - Preferred dividends
   = $120,000 - (50,000 X $1)
   = $70,000

3. **To compute weighted average outstanding common shares:**

Date	No. of Shs.		Stk Div.		Stk Split		WA factors		WA No. of shs.
Jan.1 1992	30,000	x	1.1*	x	2**	x	12/12	=	66,000
April 1 1992	6,000	x	1.1*	x	2**	x	9/12	=	9,900
July 1 1992	(1,000)			x	2**	x	6/12	=	(1,000)
Oct. 1 1992	2,000					x	3/12	=	500

   S (Weighted average number of outstanding common shares)   75,400

   * Retroactive adjustment for 10% stock dividends declared on June/1/1992.
   ** Retroactive adjustment for 2 for 1 stock split declared on Aug./5/1992.

4. **To compute EPS:**

   EPS = E / S
   = $70,000 / 75,400 shs.
   = $.93

5. **To present earnings per share:**

   To comply with *CICA Handbook*, Section 3500, earnings per share should be calculated and presented for (a) income before extraordinary items and (b) net income. To extend the above illustration, assume the following:

Income before extraordinary loss	$140,000
Extraordinary loss (net of tax)	(20,000)
Net income	$120,000

EPS figures are presented as follows:

Earnings per common share:
Income before extra. loss ($90,000* / 75,400 shs.) $1.19
Extraordinary loss ($20,000 / 75,400 shs.) **   (.26)

Net income $ .93

*Income before extraordinary loss to common
  = Income before extraordinary loss - Preferred dividends
  = $140,000 - $50,000
  = $90,000.

  **The per-common share amount of any extraordinary items is shown as a matter of convenience.

C.   Complex Capital Structures

Complex capital structures constitute *all* capital structures except those described as simple. A capital structure is not simple if the corporation has outstanding convertible securities or rights that are *potentially dilutive;* potentially dilutive securities are securities that may be converted to common shares and thus cause an increase in the number of outstanding common shares. Diluted securites that may increase the outstanding common shares include convertible preferred shares, convertible bonds payable, and stock rights, stock options stock warrants, and other securities that provide for conversion into or purchase of common shares. For *complex capital structures,* Section 3500 prescribes a *dual EPS presentation* that reports the dilutive effects in two sets of EPS amounts. The actual EPS known as basic EPS and the potentially lowest EPS if the dilutive securities had been converted at the start of the fiscal period known as fully diluted EPS.

Potentially dilutive securities and rights are generally classified into two categories, namely, equity contracts, and convertible securities. These securities and rights should be separately identified and individually analyzed.

Before analyzing individual securities and rights, it is often convenient to calculate the **EPS** as if the capital structure were simple.

A Simplified Overview of EPS Computations Follows:

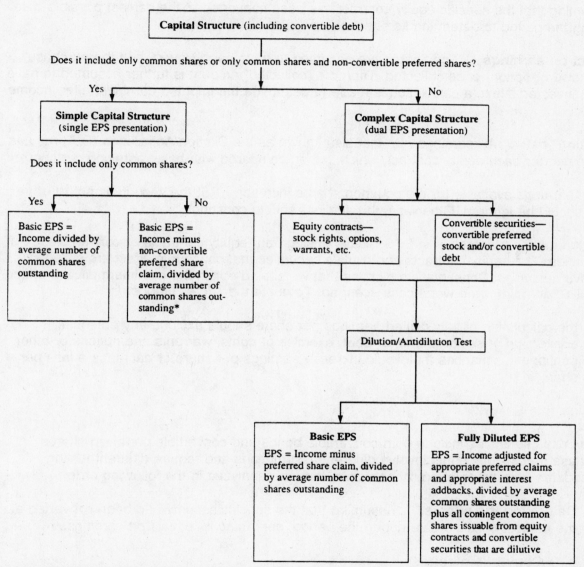

```
┌─────────────────────────────────────────┐
│ Capital Structure (including convertible │
│ debt)                                    │
└─────────────────────────────────────────┘

Does it include only common shares or only common shares and non-convertible preferred shares?

   Yes                                              No

┌────────────────────────┐          ┌────────────────────────┐
│ Simple Capital Structure│          │ Complex Capital Structure│
│ (single EPS presentation)│         │ (dual EPS presentation) │
└────────────────────────┘          └────────────────────────┘

Does it include only common shares?

  Yes            No                Equity contracts—    Convertible securities—
                                   stock rights, options, convertible preferred
┌──────────────┐ ┌──────────────┐ warrants, etc.       stock and/or convertible
│ Basic EPS =  │ │ Basic EPS =  │                      debt
│ Income divided│ │ Income minus │
│ by average   │ │ non-convertible│
│ number of    │ │ preferred share│       Dilution/Antidilution Test
│ common shares│ │ claim, divided │
│ outstanding  │ │ by average     │
└──────────────┘ │ number of      │
                 │ common shares  │
                 │ out-           │
                 │ standing*      │
                 └──────────────┘
```

Basic EPS

EPS = Income minus preferred share claim, divided by average number of common shares outstanding

Fully Diluted EPS

EPS = Income adjusted for appropriate preferred claims and appropriate interest addbacks, divided by average common shares outstanding plus all contingent common shares issuable from equity contracts and convertible securities that are dilutive

* If the preferred shares are cumulative, deduct the dividends for the current year whether declared or not; if non-cumulative, deduct for current year only if declared during the current year.

D. Equity Contracts

Equity contracts include common stock rights, options, warrants, other common share purchase contracts, and subscribed common shares. These contracts give the holders the right to purchase common shares at a specified price for a specified number of shares. Assuming that the specific equity contract has been converted at the earliest possible date during the period to determine its effect on earnings.

Effect on earnings   The shares are assumed to have been issued, and the purchase (exercise or option) price collected. Then the "collected" amount is further assumed to have been invested. Next, a calculation is made to determine the imputed earnings, after income taxes.

Dilution test: An earnings rate test also known as the Dilution/Antidilution (D/A) ratio, is computed for each equity contract, which is then compared with basic earnings per share:

If the earnings available for the common shares increase EPS, the security is not **dilutive** and should be ignored. Otherwise, the analysis should continue.

Dilution means a decrease in EPS results arising from equity contracts or convertible securities. The equity contracts and dilutive securities that cause this effect are called *dilutive securities*. Conservatism dictates that we should obtain the maximum dilutive effect on EPS, or look for the worst case scenario. To quote the *CICA Handbook*:

> the calculation of fully diluted earnings per share should exclude any potential conversion of senior shares or debt, exercise of rights, warrants and options or other contingent issuances that would increase earnings per share or decrease a loss per share.

E. Convertible Securities

Convertible securities include both convertible bonds and convertible preferred shares. Because these stock rights involve different assumptions and require different testing procedures from those of equity contracts, they are analyzed in the following order:

1.   **Determine the effects.**   Assuming that the specific security had been converted at the earliest possible date during the period, determine its effects on earnings.

   a.   **Convertible bonds:**

   (1)   **Effect on earnings.**   If the bonds had been converted into common shares, current interest on bonds would have been saved. Since the interest is tax deductible, the net effect on earnings is:

   Earnings = Interest savings net of taxes, therefore,
   Increased earnings = Net interest expense (1 - Tax rate) saved

   (2)   **Effect on shares.**   If the bonds had been converted, the additional shares of common would have been issued:

Number of bonds outstanding x Conversion rate (in common shares)

b. **Convertible preferred shares:**

(1) **Effect on earnings.**   If the preferred shares had been converted into common shares, current preferred dividends (as discussed under the basic EPS) would have been saved. Note that preferred dividends are not tax deductible, so the effect on earnings is increased by **Preferred dividends savings**

(2) **Effect on shares.**   If the preferred shares had been converted, the additional shares of common would have been issued:

Number of preferred shares outstanding x Conversion ratio (in common shares)

2. **Dilution test:**   An earnings rate test, also known as the Dilution/Antidilution (D/A) ratio, is computed for each convertible security, which is then compared with basic earnings per share:

If the earnings available for the common shares increase EPS, the security is not **dilutive** and should be ignored. Otherwise, the analysis should continue.

F. **Overall Dilution/Antidilution test.**   When multiple dilutive securities and rights are present, an overall D/A test is applied in order from the maximum dilution effect to the minimum dilution effect.

It is not entirely clear from Section 3500 of the *CICA Handbook* how the D/A test is to be applied. One alternative is to examine the EPS effect of each item individually. If it is lower than basic EPS, then the item is considered dilutive and included in fully diluted EPS.

The alternative approach is a bottom-line approach. Calculate the effect of each item on fully diluted EPS, starting with the most dilutive item (measured individually). As illustrated in exhibit 22-6 in the text, it appears that the bottom-line approach is preferable.

The previous procedures are applied to obtain the lowest possible EPS presented in the income statement.

Summary of Computation of Basic EPS (for your study)

Numerator	Denominator
1. Income before discontinued operations and extraordinary items:	
$\dfrac{\text{Income before discontinued operations and extraordinary items}} {} - \text{Dividend claims of preferred shares}^{\dagger}$	Weighted average number of common shares outstanding
2. Extraordinary items: Extraordinary gain or loss (net of tax)	Same as above.
3. Discontinued operations: Gain or loss (net of tax)	Same as above.
4. Net income: Same as (1) plus or minus extraordinary items and gain or loss from discontinued operations.	Same as above.

Summary of Computation of Fully Diluted EPS*

Numerator				Denominator	
1. Income before discontinued operations and extraordinary items:					
Income before discontinued operations and extraordinary items	− Dividend claims of *non-convertible* preferred shares[†]	+ Interest expense (net of tax) on all convertible debt	+ Interest revenue (net of tax) on proceeds from shares issued under existing options	Weighted average number of common shares outstanding	+ All other common shares that would be issued on convertible securities or options
2. Extraordinary items: Extraordinary gain or loss (net of tax).				Same as above.	
3. Discontinued operations: Gain or loss (net of tax)				Same as above.	
4. Net income: Same as (1) plus or minus extraordinary items and gain or loss from discontinued operations.				Same as above.	

* Excluding all antidilutive securities.

[†] If preferred shares are cumulative, subtract the dividends for the current year whether declared or not; if non-cumulative, subtract the dividends for the current year only if declared during the current year.

G.   Reporting Earnings Per Share

Section 3500 of the *CICA Handbook* recommends that:

Basic EPS figures should be shown either on the face of the income statement or in a note to the financial statements cross-referenced to the income statements. . . for (*a*) income before discontinued operations and extraordinary items; (*b*) net income for the period

and

where the effect of potential conversions of senior shares or debt, exercises of rights, warrants and options and contingent issuances on EPS would be materially dilutive, fully diluted EPS figures for "income before discontinued operations and extraordinary items" and "net income for the period," should be disclosed, for the current period, in a note to the financial statements, cross-referenced to the income statement. Such figures should be described as fully diluted.

ILLUSTRATION 2 – Complex capital structure and dual presentation

At the end of 1992, the record of the Biggar Co. Ltd. reflected the following:

Common shares, authorized 100,000 shares
Outstanding at beginning of year, 20,000 shares $200,000
Sold and issued on April 1, 1992, 5,000 shares $60,6000

$9 Preferred stock, cumulative, 1,000 shares
Issued on January 1, 1991 at 120
Each share convertible into 4 shares of common $100,000

10% Convertible bonds, due Dec. 31, 1996,
Interest payable on June 30 and Dec. 31
Each $1,000 par bond convertible into 50 shares of common
200 bonds issued on January 1, 1992:

Face value $200,000
Initial discount on bonds $14,720
Effective yield 12%

Stock options, 12,000 shares granted on September 30, 1991:
Option price per share $40
Exercisable in 1992

Stock warrants, 5,000 shares issued on October 31, 1992
Stated purchase price per share 0
Exercisable in 1998

Additional information:

1.   Net income reported for 1992 .... $45,000
2.   Applicable tax rate 34%
3.   Assume rate of return on cash invested 8%

Required: Determine and present basic and fully diluted earnings per share.

Solutions:

Step 1 -- Compute basic earnings per share (EPS):

E   = Net income - Current preferred dividends
         = $45,000 - ($9 X 1,000)
         = **$36,000**

S   = 20,000 + 5,000 x 9/12
         = **23,750 shs.**

EPS   = $36,000 / 23,750 shs.
         = **$1.52**

Step 2 -- Equity contract

A)   Stock option

Proceeds on exercising option
            = Option price X shares Issued
            = $40 X 12,000
            = 480,000

Earnings (E) = Proceeds X Rate, net of tax (1-tax rate)
                = $480,000 X 8% X (1 - 34%)
                = $480,000 X .08 X .66
                = $25,344

Shares Issued(s) = 12,000 shares

Earnings Ratio (ER) = E ÷ S
                            = $25,344 ÷ 12,000
                            = $2.11

Since ER > EPS, the stock option is antidilutive, and should thus be ignored.

B) Stock warrant

Proceeds on exercising warrant
- = warrant price X shares issued
- = 0 X 5,000
- = 0

E = Proceeds X Rate, net of tax (1- tax rate)
 = 0 X .8% X (1 - 34%)
 = 0 X .08 X .66
 = 0

S = 5,000 shares

ER = E ÷ S
 = 0 ÷ 5,000 shares
 = 0

Since ER > EPS, the stock warrant is dilutive

Step 3 – Convertible securities:

A. Convertible preferred shares:

= Preferred dividends which would have been saved
= Current preferred dividends
= **$9,000**

= Additional common shares assumed to have been issued
= Shares of preferred x conversion ratio
= 1,000 shs. x 4
= **4,000 shs.**

ER = $9,000 / 4,000 shs.
 = **$2.25**

Since ER > EPS, the convertible preferred share is **antidilutive**, and should thus be ignored.

B. Convertible bonds:

= Bond interest expense (net of tax) which would have been saved.
= Beginning carrying value x effective yield x (1 - Tax rate)
= ($200,000 - $14,720) x 12% x (1 - 34%)
= **$14,674**

= Additional common shares assumed to have been issued
= Number of bonds x conversion rate
= 200 shs. x 50
= **10,000 shs.**

ER = $14,674 / 10,000 shs.
    = **$1.47**

Since ER < EPS, the convertible bond is **dilutive**, and the analysis should continue.

Step 4 -- Overall Dilution/Antidilution Test:

1. **Determine:**

    a. Ranking -- Common share equivalents:

	E	S	ER	Rank
(1) Stock warrants	$ 0	2,400	$ 0	1
(2) Convertible bonds	14,674	10,000	1.47	2

    b. Recompute earnings per share based on the basic earnings per share:

    EPS (E = $36,000, S = 23,750) $1.52

    (1) Include the No. 1 ranked stock options in the computation:

        EPS (1)
        = [E + ^E(1)] / [S + ^S(1)]
        = ($36,000 + 0) / (23,750 + 2,400)
        = $36,000 / 26,150
        = $1.38

    (2) Since the ER of No. 2 ranked convertible bonds ($1.47) was greater than the recomputed EPS(1), the bonds, should be excluded, and:

        Fully diluted EPS = $1.38

Step 5 -- Financial statement presentation (partial income statement):

Earnings per share:

	Basic	Fully diluted
Net income	$1.52	$1.38

D. Adjusted Basic EPS

Paragraph 3500,28 of the *CICA Handbook* recommends that "where common shares have been issued on conversion of senior shares or debt during the period, **adjusted basic EPS** should be calculated as though the conversion had taken place at the beginning of the period." Therefore, in calculating the weighted average shares outstanding, the shares that had been issued on conversion would be considered to have been outstanding for the entire 12 months and weighted accordingly.

The income figure (i.e., the numerator) would be increased by:

1.   The amount of dividend applicable to the senior shares converted.
2.   The amount of interest expensed during the period, after income taxes, on debt converted.

Adjusted basic EPS would be disclosed in the financial statements if the resulting EPS figures are materially different from basic EPS. When disclosed, the adjusted basic EPS should be presented for income both before and after extraordinary items and discontinued operations.

Items are included in fully diluted EPS calculations only if they pass the D/A test and reduce reported EPS figures. This is not true of adjusted EPS items, which must be included whether they increase or decrease basic EPS. The rationale behind this requirement is that adjusted EPS builds on a transaction--the conversion of securities or retirement of debt--that has *actually* taken place. Fully diluted EPS considers transactions that *might* take place.

ILLUSTRATION 3 - Adjusted Basic EPS

Mutchmore Close Ltd. had a $500,000 net income in 1992 and had the following capital structure:

		Shares	Months Affected
1.	*Common* shares	50,000	Jan. 1 to Oct. 1
2.	*Common* shares - Additional issued as a result of a Conversion of preferred shares	10,000	Oct. 1 to Dec. 31
3.	$8 Preferred shares (each convertible into 20 common shares)	20,000	Jan. 1 to Oct. 1
4.	$8 Preferred shares	19,500	Oct. 1 to Dec. 31

Note: Preferred dividends for the year were paid quarterly.

Calculations:
1. For numerator (income):
    Preferred dividend claim:

March 31	20,000 X $8/4	$40,000
June 30	20,000 X $8/4	40,000
Sept. 30	20,000 x $8/4	40,000
Dec. 31	19,500 X $8/4	39,000
		159,000

2.   For denominator (shares)

Actual Shares Outstanding	Months Outstanding	Weighted Shares Outstanding

January 1-October 1

INSERT REST OF GRAPH

E.   Pro Forma EPS

Where transactions occur after the balance sheet date involving the issue of common shares, the EPS figures previously presented may not be relevant for users' needs. When common shares are issued subsequent to the balance sheet date

  i.   for cash where the proceeds are to be used to retire senior shares or debt outstanding at the balance sheet date;
  ii.   on the conversion of senior shares or debt outstanding on the balance sheet date; or
  iii.   in a reorganization (par. 3500.39)

pro forma basic EPS for the current period using the altered share capital for income before and after extraordinary items and discontinued operations should be disclosed in the financial statements. In addition, if the entity has disclosed fully diluted EPS, then a revised ratio, **pro forma fully diluted EPS** must also be calculated.

The pro forma EPS figures are calculated as if the common shares (actually issued after the balance sheet date) had been issued at the beginning of the current period, or at the date of issuance of the senior shares or debt, if later. The income figure is increased by

  i.   the amount of dividend for the period applicable to the senior shares to be retired or converted; and
  ii.   the amount of interest expensed for the period, after income taxes, on the debt to be retired or converted. (par. 3500.40)

The purpose of these calculations is to show how current fiscal year's results will project into the following fiscal year, with a different capital structure.

ILLUSTRATION 4 Pro Forma EPS

Using the same data as in Illustration 3. Assume that after the 1992 fiscal year ended, on January 31, 1993, 100,000 common shares were issued for $1,100,000. The proceeds were used to retire $1,000,000 of 12% debenture bonds payable. The bonds were not convertible and thus did not affect any prior fully diluted EPS calculations. A 40% tax rate has been assumed. Mutchmore Close would be required to calculate pro forma basic EPS and pro forma fully diluted EPS, as follows:

Calculations:
1.   For numerator (income):
      Interest avoided $1,000,000 X .12 $120,000
      Tax Effect (40%)   48,000

      Net impact on income $ 72,000

2.   For denominator (shares):
      Shares issued   100,000

Pro forma basic:

$$EPS = \frac{341{,}000^* + 72{,}000}{52{,}500^* + 100{,}000}$$

$$= \$2.71$$

Pro forma fully diluted:

$$EPS = \frac{\$500{,}000 + 72{,}000}{255{,}000^* + 100{,}000}$$

$$= \$1.61$$

* As previously calculated in Illustration 3

KEY CONCEPTS

Adjusted Basic EPS   Where common shares have been issued on conversion of senior shares or debt during the period, adjusted basic EPS should be calculated as though the conversion had taken place at the beginning of the period. Therefore, shares that had been issued on conversion would be considered to have been outstanding for the entire 12 months and weighted accordingly.

Antidilutive securities and stock rights   A convertible security or a common stock right that would increase earnings per share if it is converted, or exercised. Antidilutive securities and common stock rights should be ignored in the calculation of earnings per share.

Complex capital structure   A capital structure that consists of common stock and potentially dilutive securities and stock rights. A complex capital structure is required to report two types of earnings per share (i.e., the basic and the fully diluted earnings per share), known as dual presentation.

Dilutive securities and stock rights   A convertible security, equity contract or other common stock right that would reduce earnings per share if converted or exercised. Dilutive securities and stock rights should be included in the computation of earnings per share.

Earnings per share   A primary indicator of a company's success measured by dividing earnings to common shareholders by the weighted average common shares outstanding.

Fully diluted earnings per share   Earnings per share figures that are calculated as if all the **common share equivalents and other dilutive securities** had already been converted and/or exercised, and the related common shares issued.

Pro Forma earnings per share   Earnings per share figures that are calculated as if all the common shares (actually issued after the balance sheet date) had been issued at the beginning of the current period, or at the date of issuance of the senior shares or debt, if later.

Simple capital structure   A capital structure that does not involve convertible securities or stock rights that would materially dilute the reported earnings per share. A simple capital structure is required to report single (or basic) earnings per share.

REVIEW QUESTIONS AND EXERCISES

TRUE-FALSE

Indicate whether each of the following statements is true or false by circling the correct response.

T   F   1. When a firm's capital structure includes securities **other than common stock** the firm is said to have a complex capital structure.

T   F   2. The Melvin Company Ltd. began the calendar-year accounting period with 100,000 shares of common stock outstanding and on October 1 sold 10,000 additional shares. Its weighted average number of shares outstanding would be 105,000.

T   F   3. In computing the weighted average number of common shares outstanding, shares issued as **stock dividends** are weighted by the fraction of the period that these additional shares are outstanding.

T   F   4. If a firm declares no dividends on cumulative preferred stock, no adjustment of the earnings to common is required in earnings per share calculations.

T   F   5. For public corporations, reporting earnings per share is not required.

T   F   6. The current dividends of a cumulative preferred share should be ignored in computing earnings per share if the company incurred a net loss for the period and no dividend was declared during the period.

T   F   7. If the capital structure is simple, neither stock dividends, nor stock splits, would be considered in the computation of earnings per share.

T   F   8. All the outstanding stock rights should be included in EPS computations, regardless of when the rights are exercisable.

T   F   9. All the dilutive securities and stock rights should be included in EPS computation, regardless of whether the overall dilution effect is material.

T   F   10. A simple capital structure refers to a stockholders' equity section which only has common stock and no potentially dilutive securities that, upon their conversion or exercise in the aggregate, would dilute earnings per share.

T   F   11. In computing EPS for a simple capital structure, net income is reduced by cumulative preferred dividends on nonconvertible preferred stock, whether dividends are declared or not.

T   F   12. Basic EPS and fully diluted EPS must always be represented for a complex capital structure.

T   F   13. Pro Forma EPS figures show the effect of the issuance of senior shares or debt or common shares as if they had been issued at the start of the current period.

T   F   14. Adjusted basic EPS would not be disclosed in the financial statements if the resulting EPS figures are materially different from basic EPS.

EXERCISE 1

Better Built Ltd. is authorized to issue 500,000 shares of no par common shares. Shares activities during 1992 are listed as follows:

January 1 -- Outstanding ....100,000 shs.
April   1 -- Sold and issued ....20,000 shs.
May   1 -- Issued 20% stock dividends ....24,000 shs.
July   1 -- Reacquired treasury stock .... 5,000 shs.
August   1 -- Declared stock split .... 2 to 1
October 1 -- Sold treasury stock .... 4,000 shs.

Required:

1. Compute the weighted average common shares outstanding during 1992:

2. Further assume that Better Built declared and issued another 20% stock dividend on May 1, 1993. Determine the weighted average common shares to be used in computing earnings per share for 1992 and 1993 on the 1993 **comparative income statement**.

EXERCISE 2

On January 1, 1992, Land of Gauze Ltd. had outstanding 220,000 shares of no par common stock that was sold originally at $20, and 10,000 shares of $1.40 nonconvertible, cumulative preferred stock. The preferred stock was sold originally at $28. No dividends had been declared since 1990.

On October 1, 1992, Land sold and issued an additional 80,000 shares of common stock at $80.

(after tax) Net income for 1992 was $254,000. The tax rate for the year was 40%.

Required: Compute EPS for the year ended December 31, 1992:

EXERCISE 3

Extend **EXERCISE 2** and further assume that on January 1, 1992, Land issued common stock options for 20,000 shares of common stock, exercisable two years after the date of issuance. The option price was $20. Interest rate on investments was 6%.

Required: For the year ended December 31, 1992:

Compute fully diluted EPS:

EXERCISE 4

Gordo Company's net income for 1992 is $260,000. At the end of 1992, Gordo reported 200,000 common shares, outstanding for the entire year, and 8% bonds payable of $100,000. The bonds were convertible into 20,000 shares of common stock. The bonds were issued at par. The applicable tax rate was 30%.

Required: Compute EPS and fully diluted EPS:

EXERCISE 5

Shevrolet Ltd. had a net income of $420,000 in 1992. At the end of 1992, Shevrolet had $500,000 of 11% convertible (each $1,000 bond into 100 common shares) bonds due on Dec. 31, 1999

: $3.00 no par preferred shares, of which 10,000 are outstanding and
; 200,000 common shares outstanding at year end.

On December 31, 1002, 10,000 common shares were issued on the conversion of 100 bonds (face value of $100,000)

Required: Compute the EPS and the adjusted EPS: (Assume a 40% tax rate)

EXERCISE 6

Orange Trucks Ltd. had the following capital structure at the end of 1992:

12% Bonds payable, due in 2002 $700,000

Share capital:
  Authorized: 10,000 $3, cumulative,
 no par value preferred shares, and 200,000 common
 shares, no par value
Issued and fully paid: 5,000 preferred shares
              and 90,000 common shares

John's net income for the current year before interest and income tax of 40% is $100,000. One month after the end of 1992, Orange Trucks Ltd. issued 100,000 common shares and used the proceeds to retire all of the bonds payable.

Required:

Calculate all required EPS disclosures for the 1992 financial statements.

MULTIPLE CHOICE

Enter the letter corresponding to the response which **best** completes each of the following statements or questions.

____ 1. In computing the weighted average number of shares outstanding, the number of shares should be weighted by the fraction of the period they are (are not) outstanding for each of the following **except:**

a. new shares of common sold during the period.
b. shares reacquired as treasury stock.
c. shares represented by a option plan initiated in mid-year.
d. shares of common stock issued during the period pursuant to a stock dividend.

____ 2. A firm is considered to have a complex capital structure if it has outstanding:

a. nonconvertible cumulative preferred shares.
b. a compensatory employee stock option plan.
c. nonconvertible bonds.
d. more than five types of securities.

____ 3. Concerning earnings per share for a complex capital structure, which of the following statements are correct?

a. basic earnings per share must be based on the weighted average number of common shares outstanding plus all common share equivalents.
b. both basic and fully diluted earnings per share must be presented for income before extraordinary items and for net income.
c. a "common stock warrant" is a security which is not, in form, a common share but which contains provisions to enable its holder to become a common shareholder.
d. "primary earnings per share" is never reported at less than "fully diluted earnings per share."
e. all four statements (a, b, c, and d) are correct.

____ 4. When calculating EPS for a complex capital structure, which of the following is generally considered an equity contract?

	Nonconvertible preferred shares	Stock warrants
a.	Yes	No
b.	Yes	Yes
c.	No	Yes
d.	No	No

_____ 5.   In determining basic earnings per share (EPS), dividends on nonconvertible cumulative preferred shares should be:

      a.   deducted from net income whether declared or not.
      b.   deducted from net income only if declared.
      c.   added back to net income whether declared or not.
      d.   disregarded.

_____ 6.   Basic earnings per share presents the amount of earnings attributable to:

      a.   all common shares and dilutive securities.
      b.   common shares, preferred shares, common shares warrants, and all dilutive securities.
      c.   each share of common outstanding, including common shares subscribed.
      d.   each share of common shares outstanding.
      e.   none of the above.

_____ 7.   When determining earnings per share, interest expense, net of income taxes, on convertible bonds that are dilutive should be:

      a.   deducted from net income for FDEPS calculation.
      b.   not deducted from net income for FDEPS calculation.
      c.   added back to net income for FDEPS calculation.
      d.   not added back to net income for FDEPS calculation.

_____ 8.   When computing fully dilute earnings per share, convertible securities are:

      a.   recognized only if they are dilutive.
      b.   recognized only if they are antidilutive.
      c.   ignored.
      d.   recognized whether they are dilutive or antidilutive.
      e.   none of the above.

_____ 9.   At December 31, 1991, Capture Corp. had outstanding 200,000 shares of common and 2,000 shares of $10 nonconvertible but cumulative preferred shares. No dividends were declared on either the preferred or the common shares in 1992. Net income for 1992 was $100,000 (net of tax). For 1992, EPS was:

      a. $.40.
      b. $.50.
      c. $.60.
      d. $2.00.

_____ 10. Greener Company's balance sheet at December 31, 1992 included the following:

                                                        Shares issued and outstanding

        Common shares, no par   400,000
        Preferred shares, $2.50, no par
            noncumulative and
            nonconvertible   200,000

On October 1, 1993, Greener issued a 25% stock dividend on its common and paid $500,000 cash dividends on preferred. Net income for the year ended December 31, 1993 was $2,000,000. Greener's 1993 EPS should be:

a. $3.00.
b. $3.53.
c. $4.00.
d. $5.00.

_____ 11. Stock options exercisable at $25 each to obtain 6,000 shares of common were outstanding during a period when the average market price of the common was $30. In computing fully diluted earnings per share, the assumed exercise of these options will increase the weighted average number of shares outstanding by:

a. 1,000.
b. 3,000.
c. 5,000.
d. 6.000.

_____ 12. On December 31, 1992, Whit, Inc., had 600,000 shares of common issued and outstanding. Whit issued a 10% stock dividend on July 1, 1993 and on October 1, 1993, purchased and retired 48,000 shares of its common stock. The number of shares that Whit should use in computing earnings per share for the year ended December 31, 1993 is:

a. 612,000.
b. 618,000.
c. 648,000.
d. 660,000.

_____ 13.   Basic earnings per share is $15. Including a stock option and other dilutive securities will result in an EPS of $14.62. The EPS data should be presented as:

	EPS	FDEPS
a.	$15.00	$ -
b.	$15.00	$14.62
c.	$ -	$14.62
d.	$14.62	$ -

_____ 14.   Hodges Company Ltd. had 100,000 shares of common outstanding at the beginning of 1992. On July 1, 1992, Hodges issued 20% bonds at face value of $500,000. The bonds were convertible into 20,000 shs. of common. Assuming net income of $185,000 and a tax rate of 30%, what should be Epperson's fully diluted earnings per share for 1992?

a. $2.00.
b. $1.00.
c. $1.50.
d. $1.85.

SOLUTIONS TO REVIEW QUESTIONS AND EXERCISES

TRUE-FALSE

1.	F	5.	F	8.	F	13.	T
2.	F	6.	F	10.	F	14.	F
3.	F	7.	F	11.	F		
4.	F	8.	F	12.	F		

EXERCISE 1

1. Compute the weighted average common shares outstanding during 1992:

```
                                  Retroactive Restatement
    Date      No. of Shs.      Stk Div.    Stk Split    WA factors      WA No. of shs.

Jan/1/1992     100,000    x     1.2*   x     2**    x    12/12    =       240,000
Apr/1/1992      20,000    x     1.2*   x     2**    x     9/12    =        36,000
Jul/1/1992      (5,000)                x     2**    x     6/12    =        (5,000)
Oct/1/1992       4,000                             x     3/12    -         1,000

S (Weighted average common shares outstanding)                           272,000
```

* Retroactive adjustment for 20% stock dividends declared on May/1/1992.
** Retroactive adjustment for 2 to 1 stock split declared on Aug/1/1992.

2. Compute weighted average common shares outstanding for 1993 comparative EPS reporting:

Weighted average common shares outstanding (1992) adjusted for 1993 stock dividends
= 272,000 x 1.2
= 326,400 shs.

Weighted average common shares outstanding (1993):
= 282,000* x 1.2
= 338,400 shs.

* Number of shares outstanding at January 1, 1993:

Jan/1/1992	100,000 x 1.2 x 2	240,000
Apr/1/1992	20,000 x 1.2 x 2	48,000
Jul/1/1992	(5,000) x 2	(10,000)
Oct/1/1992	4,000	4,000
Jan/1/1993		282,000

EXERCISE 2

EPS = E / S

= (Net income - Preferred dividends) / Weighted average common shares outstanding

= ($254,000 - $200,000 X 7%) / (220,000 shs. + 80,000 shs. x 3/12)

= $240,000 / 240,000

= $1

EXERCISE 3

Proceeds = Option Price X Shares Issued

= $20 X 20,000

= 400,000

E = Proceeds X Investment rate (net of tax [1 - tax rate])

= $400,000 X 6% X (1 - 40%)

= $400,000 X .06 X .6

= $14,400

S = 20,000 shares

ER = E ÷ S

= $14,400 ÷ 20,000

= $.72

ER < EPS thus the option was dilutive

FDEPS

$$\frac{\$240,000 + 14,400}{240,000 + 20,000}$$

= 254,400 ÷ 260,000

= $.98

Note that the FDEPS ($.98) is more than 97% of BEPS ($1), the dilution effect is material and a dual presentation of EPS figures is not required.

EXERCISE 4

Data analysis:

Step 1. Compute EPS:

EPS
= E / S
= $260,000 / 200,000
= **$1.30**

Step 2. Convertible bonds analysis:

    a. Determine the effects:

        $^E = \$100,000 \times 8\% \times (1 - 30\%)$
          = **$5,600**

        $^S = 20,000$ shs.

    b. Dilution test:

        ER = ^{E} / ^{S}
        = $5,600 / 20,000 shs.
        = **$.28**

        Since **ER < EPS**
        The bonds were dilutive

EXERCISE 5

Basic EPS:

$$\frac{420,000 - 30,000\ ^1}{190,000\ ^2} = \$2.05$$

[1] Preferred dividend requirement
    10,000 X $2 = $20,000

[2] Weighted average common shares o/s
    Jan. 1 - Dec. 31 $190,000 X $\frac{12}{12}$ = $190,000
    Dec. 30 - Dec. 31 $10,000 X $\frac{0}{12}$ = $\underline{\qquad 0 \qquad}$
                                     $\underline{\$190,000}$

FDEPS

$$= (E + {}^\wedge E) / (S + {}^\wedge S)$$
$$= (\$260{,}000 + \$5{,}600) / (200{,}000 + 20{,}000)$$
$$= \$265{,}600 / 220{,}000$$
$$= \mathbf{\$1.21}$$

Adjusted EPS:

$$\frac{426{,}600^{\;3} - 30{,}000^{\;1}}{200{,}000\;\underline{4}} = \$1.98$$

[3] Net Income $420,000
  Add: Bond interest avoided
  if Jan. 1 conversion is
  assumed
    $100,000 X .11 = $11,000
  Less: Income tax
    $11,000 X 40% =   4,400
                                6,600
                             $426,600

[4] Weighted average common shares 0/s
  Jan. 1 - Dec. 31 $190,000 X $\frac{12}{12}$ = 190,000

        assumed)
  Jan. 1 - Dec. 31 $10,000 X $\frac{10{,}000}{12}$
                                200,000

Note: Fully diluted EPS should be shown in addition to the above but was not asked for in this exercise.

EXERCISE 6

Basic EPS:

<u>Net income available to common shareholders</u>
  Number of common shares outstanding

$$\frac{\$100{,}000 - \$15{,}000^{\;1}}{90{,}000} = \$.94$$

[1] Preferred dividend requirement
    5000 X $300 = 15,000

Basic Pro forma:

$$\frac{\$100,000 - \$15,000 \,^1 + \$50,400 \,^2}{90,000 + 100,000 \,^3} = \$.71$$

[2] Net income increase from avoided bond interest

700,000 X .12 =		$84,000
Less: Income		
tax (84,000 X .4) =		33,600
		$50,400

[3] Additional common shares issued

MULTIPLE CHOICE:

1.	d	5.	a	9.	a	13.	a
2.	b	6.	d	10.	a	14.	a
3.	e	7.	c	11.	d		
4.	c	8.	a	12.	c		

Computations:

9. (a) EPS = E / S = ($100,000 - $200,000 x 10%) / 200,000 shs.
        = $.40

10. (a) EPS = E / S = ($2,000,000 - $500,000) / 400,000 shs. x 1.25
        = $1,500,000 / 500,000 shs.
        = $3

        ^S = 6,000 shs.

11. (c) Weighted average common shares outstanding
        = 600,000 x 1.1 - 48,000 shs. x 3 / 12
        = 648,000 shs.

13. (a) Single presentation (i.e., EPS) is justified because the dilution effect is not
        material:

        EPS = $15
        FDEPS = $14.62

        $14.62 > 97% x $15

14. (a) FDEPS = [$185,000 + ($500,000 x 20% x 6 / 12) x (1 - 30%)]
        / (100,000 shs. + 20,000 shs. x 6 / 12)
        = $220,000 / 110,000 shs.
        = $2

CHAPTER 23

Statement of Changes in Financial Position

CHAPTER OBJECTIVES

This chapter is designed to enable students to:

A. Recognize the usefulness of the statement of changes in financial position, or statement of cash flows.

B. Explain the major provisions of Section 1540 of the *CICA Handbook*, "Statement of Changes in Financial Position.

C. Analyze transactions to identify necessary disclosures in the statement of changes in financial position.

D. Prepare a statement of changes in financial position by analyzing transactions.

E. Prepare a statement of changes in financial position by using a spreadsheet.

F. Prepare a statement of changes in financial position using the T-account approach.

CHAPTER OVERVIEW

A. Following *CICA Handbook,* Section 1540, a business enterprise that provides a set of financial statements that reports both financial position and results of operations could also provide a statement of changes in financial position (SCFP) for each period for which results of operations are provided. The primary purpose of this statement is to provide relevant information about cash receipts and payments of the enterprise during the period in order to help investors, creditors and management for the following purposes:

Assessment by Investors and Creditors of	Uses within the Firm
Ability of finance operations	Cash forecasting
Ability to pay dividends	Monitoring liquidity and changes in financial position
Ability to pay interest	
Cash consequence of deferred taxes	Budgeting
Liquidity	Strategic planning
Ability to adapt to changing conditions	Evaluating operating peformance
The quality of earnings	Monitoring working capital and fixed asset investment
A firm's general performance	

B. Cash and Cash Equivalents Basis

The assessment of a firm's cash flows in incomplete without considering the net cash position. Typically, firms invest a substantial portion of idle cash in cash equivalent securities to earn a return higher than is available from savings accounts. Firms with cash flow shortages routinely borrow from banks on a short-term basis. Components of cash and cash equivalents may vary according to the nature of industry. In addition to cash itself, the category may include some or all of the company's temporary investments (called *cash equivalents*), and, as a reduction in cash, short-term bank debt.

In the United Stated, the cash definition excludes bank debt. **Cash equivalents** are strictly defined as investments readily convertible into known amounts of cash that are close to their maturity dates. This would include Treasury bills, notes, and bonds receivable, if maturity date is not more than three months away. In Canada, the components of temporary investments included in cash equivalents are left to professional judgment and thus may include marketable securities and longer term money market investments. The components *must* be disclosed.

C. Classifications on the SCF:

CICA Handbook, section 1540 requires companies to report cash flows in terms of **operating, investing,** and **financing activities,** as summarized below:

1. **Operating activities:**

    a. Cash receipts and payments related to the operating cycle.

    b. Cash flows from other transactions may appear to be investing or financial flows, but are classified as operating if related to the main business activity.

2.   **Investing activities:**

   a.   Making and collecting loans.

   b.   Acquiring and disposing of long-term investments in debt or equity securities of other enterprises.

   c.   Acquiring and disposing of property, plant, equipment and other long-term assets.

3.   **Financing activities:**

   a.   Issuing and reacquiring equity securities, and paying dividends.

   b.   Borrowing money and repaying money borrowed on a long-term basis.

   c.   Obtaining and paying for other resources provided by creditors on long-term basis.

4.   **Non-Cash Activities**   Significant *non-cash* investing and financing activities must be disclosed in a manner that clearly identifies them as non-cash transactions. They may be listed as separate items in the SCFP, identified and cross-referenced as non-cash transactions, or disclosed in a note.

   Non-cash investing and financing transactions may be completely cash-free or involve a partial cash payment.

D.   **Presentation Methods and the SCFP**

1.   **Cash flows from operating activities:**   The following two methods are both allowed:

   a.   **Direct method:**   This method involves presenting the major classes of operating cash receipts and payments such as:

   (1)   Operating cash inflows -- cash received from:

   Customers.
   Interest on receivables.
   Dividends from investments.
   All other sources of cash that do not stem from investing and financing activities.

(2)   Operating cash outflows -- cash paid for:

Purchase of goods for resale.
Interest on liabilities.
Income taxes, duties, and fines.
Salaries and wages.
All other uses of cash that do not stem from investing and financing activities.

To determine cash flows from operating activities under the direct method, it may be necessary to convert accounting data from the accrual basis to the cash basis. The following equations are usually used:

(1)   **Cash received from customers**
= Sales revenue
+/- Decrease/Increase in accounts receivable

(2)   **Cash received from interest, dividends or other revenues**
= Interest revenue, dividend revenue, etc.
+/- Decrease/Increase in the respective receivable account
+/- Increase/Decrease in the respective unearned revenue account

(3)   **Cash paid for purchase of goods for resale**
= Cost of goods sold
+/- Increase/decrease in inventory
+/- Decrease/Increase in accounts payable

(4)   **Cash paid for salaries and wages, interest, taxes or other expenses**
= Salaries and wages, interest, income taxes, and other expenses
+/- Decrease/Increase in the respective payable accounts
+/- Increase/Decrease in the respective prepaid expense accounts

b.   **Indirect method:**   This method starts with the reported net income and converts it to the cash basis with the following adjustments:

(1)   **Revenues.**   **Remove** from net income those revenues that did not generate cash, e.g., credit sales, income from equity security investments under the equity method and current revenues collected in prior period(s). **Add back** to income those revenues collected but not yet earned.

(2)   **Expenses.**   **Add back** to net income those expenses that did not use cash, e.g., bad debt expenses, depreciation expenses, amortization expenses including the amortization of goodwill, bonds discounts. **Reduce** net income for those expenses paid but not yet expensed and the amortization of bonds premiums.

(3) **Gains/Losses.** **Remove** from net income those incidental gains, and **add back** to net income those incidental losses directly pertaining to investing or financing activities, e.g., gains or losses from disposal of operational assets.

2. **Cash flows from investing and financing activities:**

a. All investing and financing activities affecting cash flows should be presented. Note that:

(1) Changes in non-cash equivalent marketable security investments, either current or noncurrent, should be treated as investment activities.

(2) Changes in long-term debt reclassified as short-term should be included in the financing activities.

(3) Cash proceeds or payments arose from investing or financing activities giving rise to the incidental gains or losses, after taxes, should be reported in its **entirety** as investing or financing activities, as appropriate.

(4) Income taxes should be allocated according to the cause of the item: Ordinary taxes in operations, tax paid or reduction with proceeds of extraordinary items, discontinued operations, prior period adjustment, etc. in investing activities, etc.

b. **Noncash investing and financing activities** that do not result in cash receipts or cash payments **in the period** may be presented on the **SCFP**. They may be disclosed separately in a supplementary schedule or elsewhere in the financial report. Examples are:

(1) Obtaining plant assets by issuing debt or equity securities.

(2) Settlement of debt by issuing new debt or equity securities.

(3) Cash or other dividends declared but remaining unpaid.

(4) Granted stock options under a compensatory option plan.

(5) Converted preferred stock to common shares.

Noncash transactions involving **related accounts**, e.g., declared stock dividends, write off fully depreciated plant assets and noncollectible accounts receivable, are not required to be disclosed on the **SCFP**.

Note further that an investing or financing transaction may involve part cash and part noncash items, such as paying cash and issuing a long-term note for the acquisition of a piece of equipment. In this case, the cash amount could be reported under the caption "Cash flow from investing activities" and the noncash amount would be separately reported as a noncash investing or financing transaction, or the entire amount of the transaction can be shown in the SCFP with appropriate cross-referencing to the related transaction.

E.   Preparing the Statement of Cash Flows

1.   **Schedule approach.**   This approach is neither systematic nor comprehensive. Nevertheless, it is appropriate for companies with small number of transactions and accounts. Accounting data are analyzed to identify transactions during the period and determine their effects on cash flows. These effects are then organized using a schedule as presented below. For demonstration purposes, both the direct method and the indirect method are presented on the same schedule.

Schedule to Prepare a Statement of Changes in Financial Position

	Cash Flows	
	Direct Method	Indirect Method
Operating activities:		
Cash basis:		
Revenues received	+	
Expenses paid	−	
Accrual basis:		
Net income/loss		+ (−)
Adjustments to income/loss:		
Estimated expenses		+
Gains (Losses)		− (+)
Increase/Decrease in current assets (excluding marketable securities)		− (+)
Increase/Decrease in current debt (excluding reclassified short-term bank debt)		+ (−)
Investing activities:		
Cash acquisition of investment items	−	
Cash received from disposal of investment	+	
Financing activities:		
Issuance of debt or equity securities	+	
Retired debt or equity securities	−	
Distribution of cash dividends	−	
Increase (Decrease) in cash (current)	+ (−)	
Beginning cash balance	+	
Ending cash balance	+	

ILLUSTRATION 1 -- The schedule approach to preparing a SCF:

To illustrate, given the following accounting records of the Solid Company Ltd. at the end of 1992:

Income Statement:

Sales	$ 60,000
Cost of sales	(22,000)
Depreciation expenses	(14,000)
Other expenses	(8,000)
Loss on sale of plant assets (*not* extraordinary)	(1,000)
Net income	$ 15,000

Comparative balance sheet:

	December 31 1991	December 31 1992	Increase (decrease)
Debits			
Cash	$ 20,000	$ 26,000	$ 6,000
Accounts receivable	28,000	41,000	13,000
Inventory	22,000	43,000	21,000
Plant assets	120,000	150,000	30,000
Total debits	$190,000	$260,000	$ 70,000
Credits			
Accumulated depreciation	$ 40,000	$ 50,000	$ 10,000
Accounts payable	25,000	30,000	5,000
Accrued expenses	60,000	65,000	5,000
Notes payable	0	10,000	10,000
Common shares	50,000	80,000	30,000
Retained earnings	15,000	25,000	10,000
Total credits	$190,000	$260,000	$ 70,000

Additional information:

a. A machine with a cost of $10,000 and accumulated depreciation of $4,000, was disposed of for $5,000.
b. A note was issued for the acquisition of plant assets of $10,000.

A schedule to prepare a statement of changes in financial position is presented as follows:

Schedule to Prepare a Statement of Changes in Financial Position

	Cash Flows	
Operating activities:	Direct Method	Indirect Method
Cash basis:		
Cash received from customers	$ 47,000 (1)	
Cash paid for purchase of goods	(38,000) (2)	
Cash paid for other expenses	(3,000) (3)	
Accrual basis:		
Net income		$15,000
Adjustments to reconcile net income with cash flows:		
Depreciation expenses		14,000
Loss on sale of plant assets		1,000
Increase in accounts receivable		(13,000)
Increase in inventory		(21,000)
Increase in accounts payable		5,000
Increase in accrued expenses		5,000
Net cash inflow from operating activities	$ 6,000	$ 6,000
Investing activities:		
Cash acquisition of plant assets	$ (30,000)	
Cash received from disposal of plant assets	5,000	
Acquired plant assets by issuing note	(10,000)	
Net cash outflow from investing activities	$ (35,000)	
Financing activities:		
Issued common shares for cash	$ 30,000	
Paid cash dividends	(5,000) (4)	
Issued note to acquire plant assets	10,000	
Net cash inflow from financing activities	$ 35,000	
Net increase in cash ($6,000 − $25,000 + $25,000)	$ 6,000	
Beginning cash balance	20,000	
Ending cash balance	$ 26,000	

(1)   **Cash received from customers**
= Sales revenue − increase in accounts receivable
= $60,000 − $13,000 = $47,000.

(2)   **Cash paid for purchase of goods for sale**
= Cost of sales + Increase in inventory − Increase in accounts payable
= $22,000 + $21,000 − $5,000 = $38,000.

(3)   **Cash paid for other expenses**
= Other expenses − Increase in accrued expenses
= $8,000 − $5,000 = $3,000.

(4)   **Cash dividends paid**
= Net income − Increase in retained earnings
= $15,000 − $10,000 = $5,000.

As indicated in the above schedule, under the indirect method, the adjustments consist of (1) amortization items, (2) gains and losses, and (3) changes in current assets and current liabilities **not** directly pertaining to investing and financing activities. It is noted that these current item changes reflect the leads and lags between income and cash flows from operating activities.

Based on the above schedule, a statement of changes in financial position is prepared as follows:

```
                          Solid Company
              Statement of Changes In Financial Position
                  For the Year Ended December 31, 1992
                             (in $000s)

Cash Flows From Operating Activities: (Indirect method)

   Net income                                              $ 15

   Adjustments to reconcile net income with cash flows:

       Depreciation expenses                                14
       Loss on disposal of plant assets                      1
       Increase in accounts receivable                     (13)
       Increase in inventory                               (21)
       Increase in accounts payable                          5
       Increase in accrued expenses                          5

           Net cash inflow from operating activities                $  6

Cash Flows From Investing Activities:

   Acquisition of plant assets                            $(30)
   Disposal of plant assets                                  5
   Acquisition of Plant Assets (Note A)                    (10)
           Net cash outflow from investing activities               (35)

Cash Flows from Financing Activities:

   Issuance of common shares                              $ 30
   Paid cash dividends                                      (5)
   Issuance of Note (Note A)                                10

       Net cash inflow from financing activities                   $ 35

Net increase in cash, 1992                                         $  6

Cash balance, January 1, 1992                                        20

Cash balance, December 31, 1992                                    $ 26

Note A:  Noncash Investing and Financing Activities:

      *Acquired $10,000 of plant assets by issuing a 10%, 5-year note.
```

* Alternatively, this noncash transaction could have been reported only as a note and not included in the body of the statement.

If the **direct method** is applied, cash flows from operating activities would be presented differently as follows:

```
Cash Flows From Operating Activities: (Direct method)

           Received from customers                          47
           Paid for purchases of goods                     (38)
           Paid for other expenses                          (3)

               Net cash inflow from operating activities           $  6
```

2. Spreadsheet (or work sheet) approach.   This approach offers a more systematic method of analyzing the changes in **all account balances** (in the income statement and balance sheet) for evidence of cash inflows and outflows. The following steps are pertinent:

a.   Set up a spreadsheet with the upper section presenting the comparative balance sheet, and the lower section showing the effects of changes in balance sheet accounts on cash flows.

b.   For each balance sheet account other than cash, construct debit=credit entries to (1) explain the changes in the account during the year, and (2) determine the effects of these changes on cash flows.

c.   To construct spreadsheet entries, it is preferable to follow a sequential order such as:

(1)   Starting with the **additional information items**;

(2)   Analyze the **income statement accounts**, enter first the reported net income, and then search for, from top to bottom, (a) items not affecting cash flows and (b) gains and losses; and

(3)   Complete the explanation for the change in each of the balance sheet accounts starting with the account next to cash.

d.   After the changes in all balance sheet accounts other than cash and cash equivalents are fully explained, the net cash flow from the three business activities should be identical with the net increase (or decrease) in cash and cash equivalent accounts. Enter these changes and complete the spreadsheet.

ILLUSTRATION 2 -- The spreadsheet approach to preparing a SCFP (indirect method):

Using the same data as in **ILLUSTRATION 1**, a typical spreadsheet under the indirect method is presented below:

```
                              Solid Company

          Spreadsheet to Prepare the Statement of Changes in Financial Position

                    For the year ended December 31, 1992
                             (Indirect method)
```

Comparative Balance Sheet	Dec/31/1991	Analysis of Changes Debit		Credit		Dec/31/1992
Cash	$ 20,000	(1)	6,000			$ 26,000
Accounts receivable	28,000	(e)	13,000			41,000
Inventory	22,000	(f)	21,000			43,000
Plant assets	120,000	(b-1)	10,000	(a)	10,000	
		(g)	30,000			150,000
Less: Accumulated depreciation	(40,000)	(a)	4,000	(d)	14,000	(50,000)
Total assets	$150,000					$210,000
Accounts payable	$ 25,000			(h)	5,000	$ 30,000
Accrued expenses	60,000			(i)	5,000	65,000
Notes payable	0			(b-2)	10,000	10,000
Common shares	50,000			(j)	30,000	80,000
Retained earnings	15,000	(k)	5,000	(c)	15,000	25,000
Total Liabilities and OE	$150,000		$ 89,000		$ 89,000	$210,000

Statement of Cash Flows	Inflows (Dr.)		Outflows (Cr.)		Sub total
Cash flows from operating activities:					
Net income	(c)	15,000			
Adjustment to net income:					
Loss on disposal of plant assets	(a)	1,000			
Increase in accounts receivable			(e)	13,000	
Increase in inventory			(f)	21,000	
Depreciation expenses	(d)	14,000			
Increase in accounts payable	(h)	5,000			
Increase in accrued expenses	(i)	5,000			$ 6,000
Cash flows from investing activities:					
Disposal of plant assets	(a)	5,000			
Acquisition of plant assets			(g)	30,000	(35,000)
Acquired plant assets by issuing note payable			(b-1)	10,000	
Cash flows from financing activities:					
Issued common shares for cash	(j)	30,000			
Paid cash dividends			(k)	5,000	35,000
Issued note payable to acquire plant assets	(b-2)	10,000			
Net increase in cash during 1992			(1)	6,000	$ 6,000
Total		$ 85,000		$ 85,000	
```
```

Explanation of spreadsheet entries:

Spreadsheet entries based on the additional information:

a. **Disposal of assets.**   The cost of the assets which were disposed of and the related accumulated depreciation are removed from the accounts, the recognized loss is added back (debit) to cash flow from operating activities, and the **entire proceeds** are included in the cash inflows from investing activities (debit):

Disposal of plant assets	5,000	
Loss on disposal of plant assets	1,000	
Accumulated depreciation	4,000	
Plant assets		10,000

b. **Noncash investing and financing transaction.**   A noncash investing and financing transaction is debited and credited to the appropriate balance sheet accounts without affecting cash flows:
To report in the body of the statement

b-1 Plant assets	10,000	
Acquired plant assets by		
issuing note payable		10,000
b-2 Issued note payable to		
acquire plant assets	10,000	
Notes Payable		10,000

Alternative disclosure - only report by way of a footnote to the statement

b Plant assets	10,000	
Notes payable		10,000

Spreadsheet entries based on the income statement:

c. **Net income.**   Net income is entered as an increase in retained earnings (credit) and an increase in cash flows from operating activities (debit):

Net income	15,000	
Retained earnings		15,000

d. **Depreciation expenses.**   The net change of $10,000 in the accumulated depreciation account reflects a reduction of the $4,000 accumulated depreciation associated with the disposal of plant assets, and a current increase in depreciation of $14,000, which is debited to cash flows from operating activities.

Depreciation expense	14,000	
Accumulated depreciation		14,000

Spreadsheet entries based on the balance sheet:

e. **Accounts receivable.** An increase in accounts receivable implies a credit sale during the period. Accounts receivable is debited, and cash flows from operating activities is credited for the increase:

Accounts receivable	13,000	
Increase in accounts receivable		13,000

f. **Inventory.** Inventory changes are resulted from operating activities and an inventory increase implies a cash outflow exceeding cost of goods sold. The inventory account is debited, and cash flows from operating activities is credited:

Inventory	21,000	
Increase in inventory		21,000

g. **Acquisition of plant asset.** The net change of $30,000 in plant assets reflects a deduction of $10,000 for the assets disposed of, an addition of $10,000 new assets acquired through a noncash exchange transaction, and another addition of $30,000 new assets currently acquired for cash:

Plant assets	30,000	
Acquisition of plant assets		30,000

h. **Accounts payable.** Increase in accounts payable implies an excess of current merchandise purchases over payments. Accounts payable is credited, and cash flows from operating activities is debited:

Increase in accounts payable	5,000	
Accounts payable		5,000

i. **Accrued expenses.** An increase in accrued expenses indicates an excess of the recognized expenses over cash payments. The amount is thus credited to accrued expenses, and debited to cash flows from operating activities:

Increase in accrued expenses	5,000	
Accrued expenses		5,000

j. **Common shares.** Increase in common shares indicates the issuance of new shares for cash, a financing activity:

Issued common shares for cash	30,000	
Common shares		30,000

k. **Dividends.**   The $10,000 net increase in retained earnings reflects the $15,000 current net income and a cash dividends of $5,000. Paying cash dividends reduces retained earning and increase cash outflow from financing activity:

Retained earnings	5,000	
Paid cash dividends		5,000

l. **Cash account.**   As the final entry, $6,000 is entered to explain the net change in cash account on the one hand, and to balance the total cash inflows and outflows on the other hand:

Cash	6,000	
Net increase in cash (during 1992)		6,000

After all the changes in the balance sheet accounts are fully explained and the spreadsheet completed, a **SCFP** can be prepared using the information provided in the lower section of the spreadsheet.

ILLUSTRATION 3 -- The spreadsheet approach to preparing a SCFP (direct method):

If the direct method is desired, the spreadsheet may be modified to include income statement items. As an alternative, a reconciliation schedule such as follows may be used to convert income components under the accrual basis to cash flows from operating activities under the cash basis, i.e., the direct method:

Reconciliation Schedule to Determine
Cash Flows from Operating Activities
Direct Method

	Income Statement	Reconciliation Adjustments Dr.	Cr.	Cash Flows from Operating Activities
Sales (Cash received from customers)[1]	$ 60,000		$ 13,000 (1)	$ 47,000
Cost of sales (Cash paid to suppliers)[2]	(22,000)	$ 5,000 (2)	21,000 (3)	(38,000)
Depreciation expenses[3]	14,000	14,000 (4)		0
Other expenses (Cash paid for expenses)[4]	(8,000)	5,000 (5)		(3,000)
Loss on sale of plant assets[5]	(1,000)	1,000 (6)		0
Net income	$ 15,000	$ 25,000	$ 34,000	$ 6,000

Notes:

[1] Cash received from customers = Sales revenue – Increase in accounts receivable.
[2] Cash paid to suppliers = Cost of goods sold + increase in inventory – increase in accounts payable.
[3] Depreciation expenses are removed under the direct method.
[4] Cash paid for other expenses = Other expenses – Increase in accrued expenses.
[5] Loss is removed from operating activities.

F. **The T-account approach.**   The T-account approach is similar to the spreadsheet approach. The constructed entries are directly entered into a complete set of T-accounts, which replace the columnar format of the spreadsheet. This approach is particularly efficient for simple problems. T-accounts may also be established selectively and used in conjunction with any other approaches under either the direct or the indirect method. A T-account to summarize cash transactions as indicated in **ILLUSTRATION 2** is presented on the next page:

Cash

Inflows		Outflows	
Jan/1/1992	20,000		
Operating activities			
(a) Loss on disposal of assets	1,000	(e) Increase in accounts receivable	13,000
(b) Net income	15,000	(f) Increase in inventory	21,000
(d) Depreciation expenses	14,000		
(h) Increase in accounts payable	5,000		
(i) Increase in accrued expenses	5,000		
	40,000		34,000
Investing activities		(b) Acquisition of plant assets by issuing note payable	10,000
(a) Disposal of plant assets	5,000	(g) Acquisition of plant assets	30,000
	5,000		40,000
Financing activities			
(j) Issuance of common stock	30,000	(k) Paid cash dividends	5,000
(b) Issued note payable to acquire plant asets	10,000		
	40,000		5,000
Dec/31/1992	26,000*		

* Ending cash balance

$$= \$20,000 + (\$40,000 - \$34,000) + (\$5,000 - \$30,000)$$
$$+ (\$30,000 - \$5,000)$$
$$= \$26,000.$$

G. Statement of Cash Flows and Additional Disclosure.   Whichever approach is used, the statement of changes in financial position is the same as presented earlier in this chapter (see page 579).

Disclosure Requirements of Section 1540, *CICA Handbook*

The statement of changes in financial position should disclose at least the following items:

a. Cash from operations: the amount of cash from operations should be reconciled to the income statement or the components of cash from operations should be disclosed.
b. Cash flows resulting from discontinued operations.
c. Cash flows resulting from extraordinary items.
d. Outlays for acquisition and proceeds on disposal of assets, by major category, not included in (*a*), (*b*) or (*c*) above.
e. The issue, assumption, redemption, and repayment of debt not included in (*a*), (*b*), or (*c*) above.
f. The issue, redemption, and acquisition of share capital, and
g. The payment of dividends, identifying separately dividends paid by subsidiaries to minority interests.

KEY CONCEPTS

Statement of changes in financial position   A required primary financial statement designed to help users to assess an entity's ability to generate positive future cash flows, to pay dividends, and to meet obligations, and to project the entity's needs for external financing. In the statement, cash flows are classified in terms of business activities, including operating, investing and financing activities.

Operating activities   All transactions and other events that are not defined as investing or financing activities. They generally involve producing and delivering goods and providing services. Cash flows from operating activities are generally measured by the cash effects of transactions and other events that enter into the determination of income.

Investing activities   Making and collecting loans, and acquiring and disposing of investments and operational assets.

Financing activities   Obtaining resources from owners and providing them with a return on their investment; borrowing money and repaying amounts borrowed, and obtaining and paying for other resources obtained from creditors on long-term basis.

Cash equivalents   Short-term and highly liquid investments which are (a) readily convertible to cash, and (b) so near their maturity that they present insignificant risk of changes in value because of changes in interest rates.

Noncash investing and financing transactions   Investing or financing transactions not affecting cash flows are noncash exchanges which may be included in the SCFP, if properly cross-referenced and described. Alternatively they may be disclosed separately in a schedule or note to the SCFP.

Direct method and indirect method   The net cash flow from operating activities may be calculated **directly** or **indirectly.** Under the direct method, the calculation involves a listing of major classes of cash receipts and cash payments. Under the indirect method, the calculation starts with net income and then making adjustments to net income for those items not affecting cash in order to reconcile net income to net cash flow from operating activities.

REVIEW QUESTIONS AND EXERCISES

TRUE-FALSE

Indicate whether each of the following statements is true or false by circling the correct response.

T   F   1. One of the objectives of the SCFP is to determine and present the cash flow from operations.

T   F   2. Cash flows from investing and financing activities include both inflows and outflows of cash that are directly related to transactions and events reported in the income statement.

T   F   3. The full cash effect of a transaction involving an **extraordinary gain or loss**, net of tax, is reported in the SCFP as either an investing or financing activity.

T   F   4. The payment of cash for the retirement of shares is reported as an investing activity in a SCFP.

T   F   5. Investing (or financing) activities that include both cash and noncash components, such as the purchase of equipment by paying partially cash and issuing a note for the difference, should be reported with either cash flows from investing (financing) activities or noncash investing (financing) activities, depending on whether the cash or noncash component is dominant.

T   F   6. The operating activity sections of both the indirect and direct SCFPs convert accrual income to cash-basis income, the net cash flow from operations.

T   F   7. The appropriation of retaining earnings for future plant expansion should be reported on a SCFP as a noncash financing and investing activity.

T   F   8. The net increase or decrease in cash as reported in a SCFP must be identical with the difference between the beginning and the ending cash (and cash equivalents) balances as indicated in the comparative balance sheet.

T   F   9. An increase in accounts receivable for the period means that the cash collected from customers is more than the reported sales amount.

T   F   10. A decrease in inventory should be a deduction from net income in deriving cash flows from operating activities (indirect method).

T   F   11. Amortization of bond payable premium should be added to net income in deriving cash flows from operating activities (indirect method).

T   F   12. When a current liability, directly related to an operating expense, decreases during a reporting period, the cash outflow related to the expense exceeds the expense as reported on the income statement.

T   F   13. Cash payments for interest or taxes should be classified in a **SCFP** as an operating, investing, or financing activity depending upon the classification of the item that caused the interest or tax.

T   F   14. When reporting cash flows from operating activities by the indirect method, net income should be (a) reduced by increases in current assets and (b) increased by increases in current liabilities, if those current accounts are directly related to activities reported on the income statement.

Exercises 1 through 6 are based on the following data provided by the accounting record of Ovenready Company at December 31, 1992:

Income statement

Sales	$ 280
Cost of sales	(168)
Depreciation expenses	(20)
Other expenses	(72)
* Gain on sale of investment	12
* Loss on sale of plant assets	(4)
Net income	$ 28

* *Not* extraordinary

Comparative balance sheet:

	December 31 1991	1992	Increase (decrease)
Debits			
Cash	$ 136	$ 138	$ 2
Accounts receivable (net) ..	48	64	16
Inventory	64	56	(8)
Long-term investment in shares of AB Ltd.	24	0	(24)
Long-term investment in shares of XYZ Ltd.	0	46	46
Plant assets	320	392	72
Total debits	$ 592	$ 696	$ 104
Credits			
Accumulated depreciation ..	$ 192	$ 156	$ (36)
Accounts payable	76	48	(28)
Long-term notes payable ..	40	120	80
Common shares	200	260	60
Retained earnings	84	112	28
Total credits	$ 592	$ 696	$ 104

Additional information:

a. Purchased plant assets for cash, $36.
b. Sold plant assets for $24 cash; cost, $84, and two thirds depreciated.
c. Purchased plant assets by issuing a note payable of $120 in payment.
d. Sold the long-term investment in shares of AB Ltd. for $36 cash.
e. Purchased long-term investment in shares of XYZ Ltd. for cash, $46.
f. Retired notes payable at maturity date by issuing common shares, $40.
g. Sold unissued common shares for cash, $20.

EXERCISE 1

Complete the following schedule to compute cash flows from operating activities using (a) the direct method and (b) the indirect method:

Schedule to Prepare the Statement of changes in financial position -- 1992		
Operating activities:	a. Direct method	b. Indirect method
Cash basis:		
Cash received from customers		
Cash paid for purchase of goods		
Cash paid for other expenses		
Accrual basis:		
Net income		
Adjustments to reconcile net income with cash flow:		
Depreciation expenses		
Gain on sale of investments		
Loss on sale of plant assets		
Increase in accounts receivable		
Decrease in inventory		
Decrease in accounts payable		
Net cash inflow from operating activities		

(1) **Cash received from customers**
= Sales revenue - increase in accounts receivable
=

(2) **Cash paid for purchase of goods for sale**
= Cost of sales - Decrease in inventory + Decrease in accounts payable
=

(3) **Cash paid for other expenses**
= Other expenses - Increase in accrued expenses
=

EXERCISE 2

Complete the following schedule to compute cash flows from investing activities:

Investing activities:	
Cash received from:	
Sale of plant assets	
Sale of long term investment in shares of AB Ltd.	
Cash paid for:	
Purchase of plant asset	
Purchase of long term investment in shares of XYZ Ltd.	
Acquisition of plant assets by issuing a note payable	
Net cash outflow from investing activities	

EXERCISE 3

Complete the following schedule to compute cash flows from financing activities:

```
Financing activities:

Cash received from:
    Issuing note payable to acquire plant assets
    Issuing common shares for cash
    Issuing common shares to retire notes payable

Cash paid for:
    Notes payable retired by issuing common shares

    Net cash outflow from financing activities
```

EXERCISE 4

Complete the following abbreviated statement of cash flows using your answers from the previous exercises:

```
                Statement of Changes in Financial Position
                        For year ended Dec/31/1992

Cash flow from operating activities

Cash flow from investing activities

Cash flow from financing activities

Net increase in cash

Beginning cash balance

Ending cash balance
```

EXERCISE 5

Give the alternative method of disclosing noncash investing and financing activities, by completing the following disclosure note.

Note: Noncash investing and financing activities:

1.

2.

EXERCISE 6

Complete the following spreadsheet (indirect method) for Ovenready Company.

```
┌──────────────────────────────────────────────────────────────────────────────────────┐
│                              Ovenready Company                                         │
│                                                                                        │
│        Spreadsheet to Prepare the Statement of Changes in Financial Position           │
│                                                                                        │
│                      For the year ended December 31, 1992                              │
│                              (Indirect method)                                         │
│                                                                                        │
│ Comparative Balance Sheet                           Analysis of Changes                │
│                                 Dec/31/1991        Debit        Credit     Dec/31/1992  │
│                                                                                        │
│ Cash                              $ 136                                       $ 138     │
│ Accounts receivable                  48                                          64     │
│ Inventory                            64                                          56     │
│ Investments, long-term shares AB Ltd. 24                                          0     │
│ Investments, long-term shares XYZ Ltd. +                                         46     │
│ Plant assets                        320                                         392     │
│                                                                                        │
│ Less: Accumulated depreciation     (192)                                       (156)    │
│                                                                                        │
│     Total assets                  $ 400                                       $ 540     │
│                                   ======                                      ======     │
│                                                                                        │
│ Accounts payable                  $  76                                       $  48     │
│ Notes payable, long-term             40                                         120     │
│ Common shares                       200                                                 │
│                                                                                 260     │
│ Retained earnings                    84                                         112     │
│                                                                                        │
│     Total Liabilities and OE      $ 400                                       $ 540     │
│                                   ======                                      ======     │
│                                                                                        │
│ Statement of Cash Flows                       Inflows (dr.)  Outflows (Cr.)  Sub total  │
│                                                                                        │
│ Cash flow from operating activities:                                                   │
│                                                                                        │
│     Net income                                                                         │
│     Adjustment to net income:                                                          │
│         Loss on sale of plant assets                                                   │
│         Gain on sale of investments in shares of AB Ltd                                │
│         Depreciation expenses                                                          │
│         Increase in accounts receivable                                                │
│         Decrease in inventory                                                          │
│         Decrease in accounts payable                                                   │
│                                                                                        │
│ Cash flow from investing activities:                                                   │
│                                                                                        │
│     Acquisition of plant assets by issuing a note payable                              │
│     Acquisition of plant assets                                                        │
│     Sale of plant assets                                                               │
│     Sale of long-term investments                                                      │
│     Purchase of long term investment in shares of XYZ Ltd                              │
│                                                                                        │
│ Cash flow from financing activities:                                                   │
│                                                                                        │
│     Issued note payable to acquire plant assets                                        │
│     Issued common stock for cash                                                       │
│     Issued common shares to retire notes payable                                       │
│     Retired notes payable by issuing common shares                                     │
│                                                                                        │
│ Net increase in cash during 1992                                                       │
│                                                                                        │
│     Total                                                                              │
└──────────────────────────────────────────────────────────────────────────────────────┘
```

MULTIPLE CHOICE

Enter the letter corresponding to the response which **best** completes each of the following statements or questions.

_____ 1. Which of the following is not a primary objective of the SCFP?

    a. to provide alternative to net income as an indicator of the firm's overall performance.
    b. to help investors and creditors assess the firm's ability to generate positive future cash flows.
    c. to help investors and creditors assess the firm's ability to meet its obligations.
    d. to help investors and creditors assess the reasons for differences between net income and associated cash flows.

_____ 2. Which of the following is **not** an appropriate adjustment to reconcile net income with net cash flow from operating activities (indirect method):

    a. an addition for patent amortization.
    b. a deduction for bonds payable discount amortization.
    c. an addition for a loss on sale of land.
    d. an addition for depreciation expense.

_____ 3. Which of the following is a cash transaction and would be presented as an inflow (or outflow) of cash in a SCFP: (non-cash transactions are disclosed in a supporting schedule.)

    a. an acquisition of a long-term investment in shares of X Ltd.
    b. an acquisition of a building with a long-term note.
    c. a property dividend.
    d. common shares issued for a tract of land.

_____ 4. A SCFP is required to be presented:

    a. by the Canada Business Corporations Act for federally incorporated entities.
    b. whenever a set of financial statements including balance sheet and income statement are provided.
    c. as an alternative to comparative balance sheet.
    d. as an alternative to a statement of retained earnings.

_____ 5. Receipts from sale of equity securities of other enterprises should be reported as cash inflow from which of the following business activities:

    a. operating activities.
    b. investing activities.
    c. financing activities.
    d. some other activities.

_____ 6.   A stock dividend declared in the period should be reported as which of the following:

    a.   a cash outflow from investing activities.
    b.   a cash outflow from financing activities.
    c.   a cash outflow from operating activities.
    d.   none of the above.

_____ 7.   When using the indirect method, an increase in inventory for 1992 should be reported in the 1992 SCFP as:

    a.   an addition to net income in the computation of cash flows from operating activities.
    b.   a deduction from net income in the computation of cash flows from operating activities.
    c.   a financing activity.
    d.   an investing activity.

_____ 8.   Which of the following is **not** an adjustment to net income to determine the net cash flow from operating activities under the indirect method:

    a.   Increase in accounts receivable.
    b.   Increase in inventory.
    c.   Increase in investment in marketable securities.
    d.   Increase in prepaid expenses.

_____ 9.   If sales revenue was $100,000, accounts receivable decreased by $4,000, and inventory increased by $3,000, cash received from customers should be:

    a. $98,000.
    b. $100,000.
    c. $104,000.
    d. $101,000.

_____ 10.   The following entry was recorded by Captain Morgan Ltd.:

Cash	30,000	
Loss on sale of plant assets	4,000	
Accumulated depreciation	11,000	
Plant assets		45,000

Captain Morgan's SCFP would include which of the following:

    a.   a cash inflow from investing activities of $26,000.
    b.   a cash inflow from investing activities of $30,000.
    c.   a cash inflow from operating activities of $26,000.
    d.   deduction of $4,000 from net income in using the indirect method of determining cash flows from operating activities.

_____ 11. Selected information from Bulldozer Ltd's accounting records and financial statements for 1992 is as follows:

Cash paid to retire common shares	$ 4,000
Cash dividends paid	1,500
Proceeds from sale of land (cost $6,000)	7,000
Issued bonds payable	10,000
Interest paid on bonds	1,000

On the SCFP for the year ended December 31, 1992, Bulldozer should report net cash inflow from financing activities in the amount of:
a. $4,500.
b. $5,000.
c. $10,000.
d. $12,000.

_____ 12. Assume the following data from the accounting records of Home Day Care Center:

Cost of goods sold	$84,000
Accounts receivable decrease	6,000
Accounts payable decrease	8,000
Inventory increase	14,000

The cash paid to suppliers of goods should be:

a. $64,000.
b. $90,000.
c. $100,000.
d. $106,000.

_____ 13. The net income for the Off 'n On Company Ltd. for the year ended December 31, 1992 was $80,000. Additional information follows:

Depreciation expense	$16,000
Decrease in trade notes payable	2,000
Decrease in accounts receivable	3,000
Increase in bonds payable	10,000
Sale of common shares for cash	25,000
Amortization of discount on bonds payable	200
Dividend paid	10,000

The net cash flow from operating activities for 1992 should be reported as:

a. $96,000.
b. $96,800.
c. $97,000.
d. $97,200.

_____ 14. Selected information from Clear Lake Company's accounting records and financial statements for 1992 is as follows:

Net cash flow from operating activities	$1,500
Cash paid to acquire land and building	1,800
Common shares issued for cash	500
Proceeds from sale of equipment	400
Cost of office equipment purchased	200

Clear Lake's SCFP would present net cash outflow for investing activities of:

a. $1,600.
b. $1,800.
c. $2,000.
d. $2,400.

SOLUTIONS TO REVIEW QUESTIONS AND EXERCISES

TRUE-FALSE

1.	T	5.	F	9.	F	13.	F
2.	F	6.	T	10.	F	14.	T
3.	T	7.	F	11.	F		
4.	F	8.	T	12.	T		

EXERCISE 1

Schedule to Prepare the Statement of Changes in Financial Position -- 1992		
Operating activities:	a. Direct method	b. Indirect method
Cash basis:		
Cash received from customers	$ 264 (1)	
Cash paid for purchase of goods	(188) (2)	
Cash paid for other expenses	(72) (3)	
Accrual basis:		
Net income		$ 28
Adjustments to reconcile net income with cash flow:		
Depreciation expenses		20
Gain on sale of investments		(12)
Loss on sale of plant assets		4
Increase in accounts receivable		(16)
Decrease in inventory		8
Decrease in accounts payable		(28)
Net cash inflow from operating activities	$ 4	$ 4

(1) **Cash received from customers**
      = Sales revenue - increase in accounts receivable
      = $280 - $16
      = $264.

(2) **Cash paid for purchase of goods for sale**
      = Cost of sales - Decrease in inventory + Decrease in accounts payable
      = $168 - $8 + $28
      = $188.

(3) **Cash paid for other expenses**
      = Other expenses - Increase in accrued expenses
      = $72 - 0
      = $72.

EXERCISE 2

```
Investing activities:

Cash received from:
  Sale of plant assets                         $  24
  Sale of long term investments in shares
    of AB Ltd                                     36

Cash paid for:
  Purchase of plant asset                        (36)
  Purchase of long term investment in shares
    of XYZ Ltd                                   (46)
  Acquisition of Plant assets by issuing a
    note payable                               (120)

Net cash inflow from investing activities      $ (142)
```

EXERCISE 3

```
Financing activities:

Cash received from:
  Issuing note payable to acquire plant assets    120
  Issuing common shares for cash             $  20
  Issuing common shares to retire notes payable    40

Cash paid for:
  Notes payable retired by issuing common shares  (40)

Net cash inflow from financing activities       $ 140
```

EXERCISE 4

```
              Statement of Changes in Financial Position
                     For year ended Dec/31/1992

Cash flow from operating activities             $   4

Cash flow from investing activities              (142)

Cash flow from financing activities               140

Net increase in cash                            $   2

Beginning cash balance                            136

Ending cash balance                             $ 138
```

EXERCISE 5

Note: Noncash investing and financing activities:

1. Plant assets were acquired by issuing a long-term note payable of $120.

2. Common shares were issued to retire notes payable of $40.

EXERCISE 6

```
                              Ovenready Company

       Spreadsheet to Prepare the Statement of Changes in Financial Position

                       For the year ended December 31, 1992
                                (Indirect method)
```

Comparative Balance Sheet	Dec/31/1991	Analysis of Changes Debit		Credit		Dec/31/1992
Cash	$ 136	(m)	2			$ 138
Accounts receivable	48	(j)	16			64
Inventory	64			(k)	8	56
Investments, long-term shares AB Ltd	24			(d)	24	0
Investments Long-term – shares in XYZ Ltd	+	(e)	46			46
Plant assets	320	(a)	36	(b)	84	
		(c-1)	120			392
Less: Accumulated depreciation	(192)	(b)	56	(i)	20	(156)
Total assets	$ 400					$ 540
Accounts payable	$ 76	(l)	28			$ 48
Notes payable, long-term	40	(f-1)	40	(c-2)	120	120
Common shares	200			(f-2)	40	
				(g)	20	260
Retained earnings	84			(h)	28	112
Total Liabilities and OE	$ 400		$ 344		$ 344	$ 540

Statement of Cash Flows	Inflows (dr.)		Outflows (Cr.)		Sub total
Cash flow from operating activities:					
Net income	(h)	28			
Adjustment to net income:					
Loss on sale of plant assets	(b)	4			
Gain on sale of investments shares AB Ltd			(d)	12	
Depreciation expenses	(i)	20			
Increase in accounts receivable			(j)	16	
Decrease in inventory	(k)	8			
Decrease in accounts payable			(l)	28	$ 4
Cash flow from investing activities:					
Acquisition of plant assets by issuing a note payable			(c-1)	120	
Acquisition of plant assets			(a)	36	
Sale of plant assets	(b)	24			
Sale of long-term investments	(d)	36			(142)
Purchase of long term investment in shares XYZ Ltd			(e)	46	
Cash flow from financing activities:					
Issued note payable to acquire plant assets	(c-2)	120			
Issued common stock for cash	(g)	20			
Issued common shares to retire notes payable	(f-2)	40			(140)
Retired notes payable by issuing common shares			(f-1)	40	
Net increase in cash during 1992			(m)	2	$ 2
Total		$ 300		$ 300	

MULTIPLE CHOICE

1.	a	5.	b	9.	c	13.	d
2.	b	6.	d	10.	b	14.	a
3.	a	7.	b	11.	a		
4.	a	8.	c	12.	d		

Computations:

9. **(c)** Cash received from customers
= Sales revenues + Decrease in accounts receivable
= $100,000 + $4,000
= $104,000.

11. **(a)**

Retirement of common shares	$(4,000)
Cash dividends paid	(1,500)
Bonds issued	10,000
Net cash inflow from financing activities	$ 4,500

12. **(d)**

Cost of goods sold	$ 84,000
Decrease in accounts payable	8,000
Increase in inventory	14,000
Cash paid to suppliers	$106,000

13. **(d)**

Net income	$80,000
Depreciation expenses	16,000
Decrease in notes payable	(2,000)
Decrease in accounts receivable	3,000
Amortization of bonds payable discount	200
Net cash inflow from operating activities	$97,200

14. **(a)**

Acquisition of land and building	$(1,800)
Disposal of equipment	400
Acquisition of office equipment	(200)
Net cash outflow for investing activities	$(1,600)

CHAPTER 24

Accounting Changes and Error Corrections

CHAPTER OBJECTIVES

This chapter is designed to enable students to:

A. Explain the causes of, and reporting issues involves in, accounting changes and error corrections.

B. Describe accounting changes, both changes in accounting principle, and changes in estimate. Describe prior period adjustments and error corrections, and the proper accounting treatment for each.

C. Prepare the required entries and disclosures for the retroactive approach to accounting principle changes and prior period adjustments.

D. Prepare the required entries and disclosures for the current approach to accounting principle changes.

E. Prepare the required entries and disclosures for the prospective approach to accounting principle changes and changes in estimate.

F. Recognize several types of accounting errors and be able to make corrections, including the proper treatment for a prior period adjustment.

G. Prepare financial statements from incomplete records.

CHAPTER OVERVIEW

A. Reasons for change

New *CICA Handbook* pronouncements often require changes in accounting principle. Firms also change accounting principles to adapt to changing macroeconomic conditions. Technological changes and obsolescence induce changes in estimates of the useful lives of plant assets. Merger and acquisition activity caused many accounting changes as subsidiary companies adopted the principles of the parent company.

B.   Types of accounting changes:

Accounting changes are classified into three categories as follows:

The CICA developed Section 1506 of the *CICA Handbook*, which deals with two types of **accounting changes** and **correction of error** in previously issued financial statements.

1.   *Accounting changes:*
   a.   A **change in accounting principle** is a change from one generally accepted accounting principle to another. A change from completed contract to percentage-of-completion for revenue from long-term contracts is an example.
   b.   A **change in accounting estimate** is a change from one good faith estimate to another, justified by new information or conditions. A change in the estimated useful life or estimated residual value of a depreciable asset is an example.
2.   *Correction of error:*
   Error corrections to rectify accounting errors made in prior periods require special treatment. Errors are distinct from estimate changes. Estimate changes result from new information; error corrections require only information known at the time of the error. Error corrections are not accounting changes.

C.   Approaches to reporting accounting changes:

Three approaches to reporting accounting changes are provided. These approaches vary in the extent to which they achieve financial statement consistency comparability and integrity:

   a.   **Retroactive Approach**   This reporting method restates all prior financial statements on a comparative basis to conform to the new principle. The cumulative income difference (net of tax), is an adjustment to the current (and comparative) opening *retained earnings* balance. The retroactive portion of the change does not effect current income. Error corrections affecting prior years' income also use this approach; we call the cumulative difference a **prior period adjustment.**

   b.   **Current Approach**   This reporting method also recognizes the cumulative difference ("catch-up" adjustment) between the expense or revenue under the old and new accounting principles through the beginning of the current period. The *retained earnings statement* discloses this amount, net of tax effect, as a line item entitled **cumulative effect of change in accounting principle.** In some circumstances, while the *total* effect of a change in accounting policy on prior periods can be determined, the effect with respect to *specific prior periods may not be reasonably determinable.* In such cases, the retroactive effect of the change in the accounting policy is accounted for as a cumulative adjustment of the opening balance of retained earnings of the period in which the change is made.

   c.   **Prospective Approach**   This reporting approach applies revised accounting principles or estimates only to current and future periods affected by the change. Prior financial statements remain unchanged, and no cumulative effect on prior years' income is computed. Estimate changes are the most common example of this treatment. Estimates, by their nature, are subject to error and periodic revision over time. Firms are expected to report financial statements that reflect the most current information.

Prospective treatment is appropriate for:

1. Changes in accounting principle, under certain circumstances.
2. Changes in estimates.

As discussed, a change in accounting principle is to be applied retroactively or as retroactively as possible. A change in principle may be applied *prospectively* if full retroactive restatement is impossible, and even restatement of opening balances and retained earnings *cannot be accomplished*.

d. Annual reports generally include financial statements for the current year and for one or two previous years for comparative purposes. Trends in earnings and financial ratios can be observed.

Comparative financial statements are required by GAAP, and the *CICA Handbook*, sec. 1500 generally must disclose a five-year summary of key financial data. The Canada Business Corporations Act also requires comparative financial statements.

Reporting Guidelines: Retroactive Approach

The following guidelines are applied to accounting principle changes subject to the retroactive approach:

1. Prior financial statements included for comparative purposes are restated to conform to the new accounting principle. All affected account balances are restated. Therefore, all periods presented reflect the new accounting principle.
2. The cumulative income difference between the two methods for prior periods is recorded as an adjustment to the beginning retained earnings balance for the current period, net of tax. The entry to record the cumulative adjustment involves retained earnings and a real (balance sheet) account, and often an income tax account.
3. For *each year* presented in the financial statements, the beginning retained earnings balance is adjusted by the after-tax effect of the change attributable to *prior years* (whether or not presented).
4. The effect of the change on the financial statements of current and prior periods should be disclosed for all periods presented if they are affected by the change. This would include, if appropriate, net income, earnings per share, and working capital.
5. The fact that prior year's financial statements have been restated must be disclosed.
6. Subsequent financial statements need not repeat the disclosures.

Although they appear similar to accounting changes, the following are *not* changes in accounting principles:

a. Initial adoption of an accounting principle for new transactions or transactions that were previously immaterial. For example, immaterial advertising costs were previously expensed but are now capitalized.
b. Adopting a new accounting principle for a new group of assets or liabilities that

are clearly different in substance from those already in existence. For example, a firm adopts the percentage-of-completion method for its first long-term construction contract.

c.   A change from an inappropriate accounting principle to an allowed method. For example, switching from capitalizing research costs to immediate expensing.

d.   A change in depreciation methods (say, from declining balance to straight line) *if based on changed circumstances, experience or new information is not considered a change in policy*, effective in fiscal years beginning on or after December 1, 1990. Section 3060 of the *CICA Handbook*, specifies that the amortization method should be regularly reviewed and, by implication, regularly changed if appropriate. Of course, if a change in depreciation policy is based on something *other* than a change in circumstances, experience or new information, it should be applied retroactively.

The retroactive approach applies to all accounting principle changes *except* those for which sufficient information is not available.

ILLUSTRATION 1 -- Change in accounting principle (retroactive approach)

Manitoba Ltd. purchases a piece of equipment on January 1, 1990 with a cost of $10,000, a useful life of 5 years and an estimated salvage value of $1,000. During 1992, Manitoba decided to change from the straight-line method to the sum-of-the-years-digit method of depreciation. The applicable income tax rate is 40%.

Note: The change was made to conform to a long-standing industry norm and was not based on new information. Therefore, the chance qualifies for retroactive restatement.

Required:

(1)   Determine the cumulative effect:

Depreciation expenses up to January 1, 1992:

New method (SYD) ($10,000 - $1,000) x (5 + 4) / 15	$5,400
Old method (SL) ($10,000 - $1,000) x 2 / 5	3,600
Cumulative effect before tax	$1,800
Tax effect (40%)	720
Cumulative effect, net of tax	$1,080

(2)   Record the cumulative effect:

Cumulative effect on accounting principle changes	1,080	
Deferred income taxes	720	
Accumulated depreciation		1,800

(3) Record current depreciation expense based on the new method:

Depreciation expense ($10,000 - $1,000) x 3 / 15   900
    Accumulated depreciation   900

Since the effect of the sum-of-the-years digits method can be traced back to specific years, the previous years income statements can be restated.

D. Reporting Accounting Principle Changes: Current Approach

The current approach applies to accounting principle changes for which it is possible to restate the financial statements as of the beginning of the current year, but it is *impossible to restate specific prior* periods.

Reporting Guidelines: Current Approach

The following reporting guidelines apply to accounting principle changes subject to the *current approach:*

1. Prior financial statement included for comparative purposes remain unchanged.
2. The cumulative income difference between the two methods for prior periods is disclosed as an adjustment to opening retained earnings for the current year only: cumulative effect of change in accounting principle, net of tax.
3. The effect of the new principle on current year's financial statements is disclosed. This would include the effect on net income, earnings per share, and working capital.
4. The fact that comparative financial statements have not been restated must be disclosed.
5. For the current year results, the new principle is applied as of the beginning of the current year. The current year's financial statements reflect the new principle; the prior year's statements reflect the old principle.
6. Future annual reports may repeat the disclosures until the year of change is no longer presented.

E. Change in Estimates

A change in estimates is accounted for **prospectively**. When a firm revises a previous estimate (e.g., of useful life or salvage value of assets, of the percentage used to estimate bad debt, etc.), prior financial statements are not restated, nor is a cumulative effect on prior years' income to be determined. Instead, the firm merely incorporates the new estimate in any related accounting determination **thereafter**.

Reporting Guidelines: Prospective Approach

The following reporting guidelines apply to prospective treatment:

1. Prior statement shown on a comparative basis are not restated or otherwise affected.
2. Disclosure of the nature and effect [on the financial statements] on the current period may be desirable for a change in an accounting estimate that is rare or unusual and that may affect the financial results of both current and future periods.

3.   The new estimate is applied as of the beginning of the current period, generally based on the book value of the relevant real account remaining at that time. This is the amount to which the new estimates are applied for the current and future years.
4.   No entry is made for prior year effects; only the normal current year entry incorporating the new estimate is made.
5.   Future years, if affected by the change, continue to use the new estimate.

ILLUSTRATION 2 -- Change in estimate

A piece of equipment with a cost of $10,000, and an estimated useful life of 10 years, without salvage value, was acquired on January 1, 1990. During 1992, the estimated useful life is revised from 10 years to 7 years. The straight-line method of depreciation is used.

Required:

(1)   Determine the book value of the equipment at January 1, 1992:

Cost	$10,000
Accumulated depreciation, 1990 and 1991, $10,000 x 2 / 10	2,000
Book value, January 1, 1992	$ 8,000

(2)   Determine annual depreciation expense based on the new estimate for the remaining life of the equipment:

Annual depreciation expense
= $8,000 / (7 - 2)
= $1,600

(3)   Record depreciation expense for 1992:

Depreciation expense	1,600	
Accumulated depreciation		1,600

Summary of Accounting Changes and Reporting Approaches

Type of Accounting Change or Error	Accounting Approach Required	Summary of the Approach	
		Catch-up Adjustment Identified With	Comparative Statements (Results of Prior Year)
Accounting principle Changes: a. Usual situations	Retroactive	Retained earnings; a prior period adjustment	Prior year's results restated to new principle
b. Able only to restate opening balances.	Current	Opening retained earnings of current period only.	Prior year's results remain unchanged.
c. Unable to restate any balances.	Prospective	Catch-up adjustment not computed or reported	Prior year's results remain unchanged. New principle applied prospectively.
Changes in accounting estimates	Prospective	Catch-up adjustment not computed or reported	Prior year's results remain unchanged. Newest estimates applied prospectively.
Accounting errors: (to follow) Those affecting income of prior years.	Retroactive	Retained earnings, a prior period adjustment	Prior years' results stated correctly.
Prior period adjustment (to follow)	Retroactive	Retained earnings, a prior period adjustment	Priors year's results restated.

F. Prior Period Adjustments

(a) Most profit and loss items are disclosed in the income statement. A few items are excluded from income, including:

1. The effect on prior year's income of accounting changes.
2. The effect of an error correction.
3. Certain foreign currency translation adjustments.
4. *Prior period adjustments (PPAs).*

According to Section 3600 of the *CICA Handbook*, prior period adjustments are limited to those items that fulfill the following four criteria:

1. Are specifically identified with business activities of particular prior periods.
2. Are not attributable to economic events occurring after the prior period.
3. Depend on determinations by persons other than management or owners.
4. Could not be estimated prior to those determinations.

Correction of Accounting Errors

(b) An accounting error occurs when a transaction or event is recorded incorrectly, or is not recorded at all. Errors are caused by the following:

1. Using an inappropriate or unacceptable accounting principle, mistakenly applying GAAP. Changing from an unacceptable accounting principle, or one incorrectly applied, to a generally accepted one is an error correction.
2. *Intentionally* using an unrealistic accounting estimate, or being grossly negligent in making estimates.
3. Misstating or misclassifying an account balance.
4. Delay in, or failure to recognize, accruals, deferrals, and other transactions.
5. Arithmetic errors.
6. Fraud or gross negligence in financial reporting.

2. **Analysis of accounting errors:** Accounting errors may be classified in terms of whether the errors affect prior year's financial statements when they are discovered:

a. **Errors not affecting prior year's financial statements:** These types of errors are **discovered in the same accounting period** when they occur, and the books for the period of discovery are still open. As such, they do not affect retained earnings and can be easily corrected by either (1) reversing the erroneous entry and then recording the correct entry, or (2) making a single correcting entry designed to correct the account balances.

b. **Errors affecting prior year's financial statements:** These types of errors **occur in one accounting period and are discovered in a later period.** Fundamentally, correction of an error of this type is based on the **retroactive approach.** The application of this approach, however, depends on whether the specific error affects prior years' income:

(1) **Errors affecting prior financial statements but not income:** This error involves incorrect classification of real or nominal accounts, such as neglecting to classify the current portion of a long-term debt as current. An entry to reclassify the accounts would correct the error.

(2) **Errors affecting prior financial statements and income:** This type can be further classified on the basis of the effect of the error on retained earnings:

(a) **Self-corrected (counterbalanced) errors**. An accounting error counterbalances if it self-corrects over a two year period, i.e., the income for the period of error is misstated, as is the income of the second period, with the same amount but in the opposite direction. Examples of this type of errors include:

* Over- or understated ending inventory.
* Unrecognized accruals
* Unadjusted deferrals

A counterbalancing error is **self corrected** if the error is discovered more than two years after it was made, and the books of the second year of the two-year cycle have been closed. In this case, the beginning retained earnings do not contain the error, and no correcting entry is required. However, the financial statements for those years affected by the error should still be retroactively restated if presented, and the cause and effect of the error disclosed.

(b) **Errors not yet corrected when discovered.** Noncounterbalancing errors do not correct themselves over a two-year cycle, whereas the counterbalancing errors misstate account balances if they are discovered while the books of the second year are still open. In either case, the correction of these errors involves the following:

(i) Compute the cumulative effect of the error up to the beginning of the period of discovery, which is affected by whether the books are closed when the error is discovered. Assume that an accounting error occurred in 1991, and is discovered at the beginning of 1993. If the 1992 books remain open, the year of discovery is 1992. If the 1992 books are already closed, it would be 1993.

(ii) adjust the beginning balance of retained earning (i.e., prior year adjustment) and all other accounts affected by the error, and

(iii) restate prior years' financial statements, and

(iv) disclose the nature of the error and the effect of its correction on income before extraordinary items, net income and the related per share amounts in the period in which the error was discovered and corrected.

ILLUSTRATION 3 -- Correction of accounting errors

An examination of Gray Company's books at the beginning of 1993 reveals the following errors:

(1) A piece of equipment acquired on January 1, 1989 for $50,000 was charged to other expenses. The equipment should have a 5-year useful life with a salvage value of $5,000. Gray used the straight-line method to depreciate its plant assets.

(2) The merchandise inventory at December 31, 1991 was overstated by $4,000.

(3) In January 1991, Gray purchased a two-year insurance policy costing $1,000 and debited the total amount to prepaid insurance expense. No adjusting entry has been made for the insurance.

(4) At the end of 1991, Gray failed to accrue an interest expense of $2,000. This amount was expensed when paid in 1992.

Required: Prepare appropriate correcting entries for the above errors assuming that the 1992 books are (1) open, and (2) closed. Ignore income taxes.

Solution:

	Journal Entries	
	1992 books open	1992 books closed
Equipment		
1. Determine cumulative effect:		
Up to Jan. 1		
1992 1993		
Cost of equipment $50,000 $50,000		
Accumulated depreciation 27,000 36,000		
Retained earnings understated $23,000 $14,000		
2. Prepare adjusting entry:		
Equipment	50,000	50,000
Accumulated depreciation	27,000	36,000
Retained earnings, prior year adjustment	23,000	14,000
3. Record current depreciation expense:		
Depreciation expenses	9,000	9,000
Accumulated depreciation	9,000	9,000
Merchandise inventory:		
1. Determine cumulative effect:		
Up to Jan. 1		
1992 1993		
Beginning inventory overstated $ 4,000 $ 0		
2. Prepare adjusting entry:		
Retained earnings, prior year adjustment	4,000	None.
Inventory	4,000	
Prepaid insurance:		
1. Determine cumulative effect:		
Up to Jan. 1		
1992 1993		
Prepaid insurance overstated $ 500 $ 1,000		
2. Prepare adjusting entry:		
Retained earnings, prior year adjustment	500	1,000
Prepaid insurance	500	1,000
3. Record current insurance expense:		
Insurance expense	500	None
Prepaid insurance	500	
Accrued interest expense:		
1. Determine cumulative effect:		
Up to Jan. 1		
1992 1993		
Retained earnings overstated $ 2,000 $ 0		
2. Prepare adjusting entry:		
Retained earnings, prior year adjustment	2,000	None
Interest expense	2,000	

Spreadsheet Techniques for Correcting Errors

Individual errors can be analyzed and corrected without a spreadsheet. However, when errors are numerous and complicated, a spreadsheet approach often is helpful. In addition, several immaterial errors can cause an aggregate material income effect. A spreadsheet facilitates the analysis of errors and their effects as they occur. Errors that cancel each other are easily identified. One compound entry corrects all the errors at the end of the period.

G. Preparation of Financial Statements from Single-Entry and Other Incomplete Records

Most businesses maintain a record of all transactions using a double-entry accounting system. However, some small businesses, sole proprietorships, non-profit organizations, and persons acting in a fiduciary capacity as administrators or executors or estates maintain only a single-entry system that records minimum transaction detail.

Single-entry records are used for simplicity and are less expensive to maintain than double-entry systems. However, single-entry record keeping usually is inadequate except for low-volume operations.

However, the incomplete account record and supplemental transaction data often are the basis for a reasonably complete income statement and balance sheet.

Balance Sheet Preparation from Single-Entry Records

1. Identification and measurement of assets and liabilities is essential to preparing a balance sheet from incomplete records. Canceled checks, receipts, bills of sale, papers transferring title to real estate, and other similar records supply information about the cost of operational assets. Depreciation is based on original cost. The amount of merchandise, supplies, and other inventories on hand is obtained by actual count. If original cost cannot be determined, merchandise and supplies are recorded at current replacement cost.

    Similarly, the amounts of notes payable are obtained from source documents, memoranda, correspondence, and consultation with creditors. Invoices from sellers support accounts payable.

    Preparation of the balance sheet and computation of income is possible from incomplete records. Owner's equity is determined by subtracting total liabilities from total assets. Net income is the difference between beginning and ending owners' equity, adjusted for owner investments and withdrawals.

    The following schedule shows the computation of net income when investments or withdrawals occur during the period:

	Computation Where There Was	
	Income	**Loss**
Owner's equity, end of period	$8,000	$5,500
Owner's equity, beginning of period	7,100	6,300
Change increase (decrease)	900	(800)
Add: Withdrawals during period	1,200	1,000
	2,100	200
Deduct: Additional investments during period	500	300
Income for period	$1,600	
Loss for period		$ (100)

Income Statement Preparation from Incomplete Data

2. In some cases, financial statement users request information about the components of net income. Banks and other lenders usually request a statement describing the results of operations. Revenue Canada requires detailed information about taxable revenues and deductible expenses.

    It is possible to prepare an itemized income statement from single-entry records and supplemental data without converting to double-entry form. Much of the needed detail is obtained through an analysis of the cash receipts and disbursement records and suggests the need for a spreadsheet approach to reduce clerical work and minimize errors and omissions. A spreadsheet recognizes each group of transactions in debit-credit form and provides several internal checks for accuracy. Written explanation and computations support the spreadsheet entries. Such a spreadsheet is designed to develop the income statement and balance sheet.

KEY CONCEPTS

Change in accounting estimate   A change in the estimated accounting figures such as the useful life or the salvage value of a depreciable plant asset. To account for such a change, the prospective approach should be applied.

Change in accounting principle   A change from one generally accepted accounting principle to another generally accepted accounting principle. In general, the retroactive approach is usually applied to account for such a change. The current approach and/or the prospective approach may have to be used if prior years information is lacking.

Counterbalancing errors   An accounting error caused a misstatement of income in one period leads to another error in the following period with the same amount but in the opposite direction. The error is self-corrected over a two-year cycle.

Correction of accounting errors   Accounting errors in prior years' financial statement should be corrected using the retroactive approach. Cumulative effect of the error, if any, is adjusted to retained earnings, and the prior years' financial statements, if presented, are restated. It assumes that prior years' information is available in the details needed.

Current approach   The cumulative effect of the change in accounting principle, net of taxes, should be determined, and reported in the retained earnings statement of the year of change. Prior years' financial statements are not restated.

Prospective approach   Cumulative effect is not determined and prior years' financial statements are not restated. The effect of the change is reflected in the current and future periods.

Retroactive approach   The cumulative effect of the change is journalized to retained earnings, and prior years' financial statements presented are restated to reflect the change. This approach is applied to the correction of accounting errors, and to changes in certain specified accounting principles. It assumes information from prior years is available in the details needed.

REVIEW QUESTIONS AND EXERCISES

TRUE-FALSE

Indicate whether each of the following statements is true or false by circling the correct response.

T　F　1. The retroactive approach requires that prior years' financial statements be restated in order to enhance comparability.

T　F　2. The prospective approach requires that the cumulative effect of an accounting change be reported in the current period as a separate component on the retained earnings statement.

T　F　3. When a firm changes from the weighted-average method of inventory costing to the first-in, first-out method, a change in an accounting principle occurs.

T　F　4. The cumulative effect of a change in accounting principle is determined by comparing the balance in retained earnings at the beginning and the end of the year of the change.

T　F　5. The cumulative effect of a change in accounting principle is reported net of its tax effect as an item in the retained earnings statement for the year of the change.

T　F　6. In addition to reporting the cumulative effect of a change in accounting estimate as a component of current income, prior years' financial statements are restated to reflect the new accounting principle.

T　F　7. The cumulative effect of a change from the LIFO method to the FIFO method of inventory pricing is reported as a prior year adjustment (net of tax) as a component on the retained earnings statement in the year of the change.

T　F　8. When a previous estimate of the useful life of a building is revised in the third year of an asset's depreciable life, depreciation expenses for the first two years should be restated using the new estimate.

T　F　9. A change in accounting principle requires retroactive restatement of prior years' financial statements to reflect financial information in those prior years.

T　F　10. If an erroneous entry is made and discovered in the same accounting period, the original entry may be reversed and the correct entry recorded to correct the error.

T　F　11. If merchandise inventory is overstated at the end of 1991 and the error is not discovered, net income in 1992 will be overstated.

T   F   12. If it is discovered that a major repair in the previous year was incorrectly debited to repair expense and the books of that year were closed, the current year's statement of retained earnings should report an addition to the beginning balance of retained earnings.

T   F   13. The discovery of an error in a previous year's income statement may not require a correcting journal entry.

T   F   14. Accounting *principle* changes are subject to three accounting approaches: retroactive, current, and prospective. *Estimate* changes may receive prospective treatment if detailed information is available.

EXERCISE 1

Indicate with the appropriate letter the nature of each adjustment below:

Type of Adjustments	**Reporting approach**
A. Change in accounting principle	Current
B. Change in accounting principle	Retroactive
C. Change in estimate	Prospective
D. Correction of accounting error	Retroactive

_____ 1.   Change from the SYD method to the DDB method of depreciation(previous information not available).

_____ 2.   Change in the useful life of a machine.

_____ 3.   Change in the residual value of plant equipment.

_____ 4.   Change in the percentage used to determine bad debts.

_____ 5.   Change from LIFO to weighted average method of inventory pricing. (prior information available)

_____ 6.   Change from the market value method to the LCM method of accounting for long-term investments in marketable equity securities by a manufacturing firm.

_____ 7.   Change from FIFO to LIFO. (previous information unavailable)

_____ 8.   Change from the percentage-of-completion method in long-term construction. Protects to completed-contract method (previous information cannot be recreated)

_____ 9.   Change from retirement method to the replacement method of depreciation by a hydro utility (previous information available).

_____ 10.   Change from the direct write-off method to the allowance method of bad debts accounting (previous information not available)

EXERCISE 2

Penny Ltd. acquired a machine at a total cost of $220,000 (no residual value) on January 1, 1991. The machine was being depreciated over a 10-year life using the sum-of-the-years-digits method. At the beginning of 1994 it was decided to change to straight-line and to be applied retroactively in accordance with industry reporting standards. The applicable tax rate was 40%.

Required:

a. Determine the cumulative effect:

Depreciation expense up to January 1, 1994:

New method (SL)
Old method (SYD)

Cumulative effect before tax
Tax effect (40%)

Cumulative effect, net of tax

b.   Record the cumulative effect:

Accumulated depreciation
Cumulative effect on accounting principle changes
Deferred income taxes

c.   Record current depreciation expense based on the new method:

Depreciation expense
Accumulated depreciation

EXERCISE 3

At the beginning of 1994, it was discovered that Reichards Company Ltd. had debited expense account for the full cost of a piece of equipment purchased on January 1, 1991. The cost was $60,000; useful life 5 years; and straight-line depreciation was used by the company. The residual value was zero, and the income tax was 40%.

Required:

a. Prepare the correcting entry assuming the error was discovered before the 1993 books were closed.

> Equipment
> > Accumulated depreciation (1991 and 1992)
> > Deferred tax liability
> > Prior year adjustment (plug)
>
> Depreciation expense (1993)
> > Accumulated depreciation

b. Prepare the correcting entry assuming the error was discovered after the 1993 books were closed.

> Equipment
> > Accumulated depreciation (1991 to 1993)
> > Deferred tax liability
> > Prior year adjustment (plug)

EXERCISE 4

On January 1, 1991, Donuts Ltd acquired a piece of equipment for $46,000. The equipment had an estimated life of 8 years and a salvage value of $10,000. On January 1, 1995, Donuts revised the useful life to 6 years and the salvage value to zero. The straight-line method was used by Donuts.

Required: Complete the following entries related to the equipment:

a. At the end of 1994:

> Depreciation expense
> > Accumulated depreciation

b. At the end of 1995:

> Depreciation expense
> > Accumulated depreciation

MULTIPLE CHOICE

Enter the letter corresponding to the response which **best** completes each of the following statements or questions.

_____ 1. Which of the following is true concerning the current approach for a change in accounting principle?

    a. It offers the advantage that users will not be confused by changes in prior statements.

    b. This is the required treatment of **all** changes in accounting principle.

    c. It offers the advantage of comparability among financial statements of past and subsequent years.

    d. Current data is not required in addition to reporting the cumulative effect.

_____ 2. An example of a change in accounting principle requiring the current approach is:

    a. a change from LIFO to weighted average inventory pricing (previous information available).

    b. a revision in the percentage used in determining uncollectible accounts.

    c. a change in the number of machines to be included in the financial statements.

    d. the change to FIFO when LIFO was previously used (previous information unavailable)

_____ 3. The prospective approach is required for:

    a. a change in accounting estimate.

    b. a change in accounting policy.

    c. a change in accounting principle.

    d. a correction of accounting error.

_____ 4. The cumulative effect of a change in accounting principle:

    a. is determined by comparing the amount in the retained earnings account at the beginning and end of the year.

    b. is reported as a separate component of income, net of tax, as an extraordinary item.

    c. is reported as an adjustment to the beginning balance of retained earnings in a statement of retained earnings.

    d. is the effect of the change on income of the current year.

_____ 5. Which of the following is true concerning a change in accounting principle?

    a. The new principle must be suggested by the auditor.

    b. Footnote disclosure is required.

    c. The cumulative effect due to a change from the percentage of completion method to the completed contract method should be reported in the current income statement.

    d. The chosen principle is arbitrarily chosen so that operating results will be enhanced.

_____ 6. Which of the following is **not** appropriate when it is discovered that a five-year insurance premium payment two years ago was debited to insurance expense?

    a. a credit to prepaid insurance.
    b. a retroactive restatement of the income statement of the previous year.
    c. a retroactive restatement of the balance sheet of the previous year.
    d. a footnote explaining the impact of the error on net income and earnings per share of the current year.

_____ 7. Data must be reported on the face of the income statement for a change:

    a. from LIFO to FIFO.
    b. due to accounting error made in a previous year.
    c. from the straight-line method of depreciation to the double-declining-balance method.
    d. in the service life of equipment.

_____ 8. Which of the following is not a disadvantage of the single entry record-keeping system?

    a. lack of systematic and precise record keeping may lead to inefficiency in administration and control over the affairs of the business.
    b. theft and other losses are less likely to be known.
    c. lack of control and administration of most of the assets is quite likely.
    d. since no accounts are provided for many of the items appearing on both the balance sheet and the income statement, omission of important data always is a possibility.
    e. all of the above are disadvantages.

_____ 9. Gerry Ltd has amortized a patent on a straight-line basis since it was acquired at a cost of $17,000 on January 1, 1991. During 1994 it was decided that the benefits from the patent would be received over a total period of 10 years rather than the 17-year life being used to amortize the cost. On the basis of the revised estimate, the 1994 financial statements should reflect:

    a. a cumulative effect adjustment of $2,100.
    b. a balance in the patent account of $11,900.
    c. an amortization expense of $1,400.
    d. a reduction in the carrying value of the patent of $2,000.

_____ 10. Harmony Inc. understated its inventory by $5,000 at the end of 1991. If the error was discovered in 1992 after the 1991 books are closed, which of the following would be appropriate to correct the error?

    a. a debit to inventory of $5,000.
    b. a $5,000 adjustment in the income statement of 1992.
    c. a deduction of $5,000 from the beginning balance of retained earnings in a statement of retained earnings.
    d. none of the above.

_____ 11. If the error described in Question 10 is discovered after the 1992 books are closed, the discovery of the error would require:

    a. a debit to inventory of $5,000.
    b. a $5,000 adjustment in the 1993 income statement.
    c. a debit to prior year adjustment.
    d. none of the above.

_____ 12. In 1992 Hairy Ltd. changed its inventory method to the FIFO cost method from the LIFO cost method. Hairy's inventories totaled $800,000 on the LIFO bases at December 31, 1991. Records maintained by Hairy showed that the inventories would have totaled $960,000 at December 31, 1991, on the FIFO basis. Ignoring income taxes, the adjustment for the effect of the change should be reported in the 1992:

    a. income statement as a $160,000 decrease in income.
    b. income statement as a $160,000 increase in income.
    c. statement of retained earnings as a $160,000 decrease in the beginning balance.
    d. statement of retained earnings as a $160,000 increase in beginning balance.

_____ 13. During 1992, Gorp Inc. discovered that its inventories were overstated by $10,000 and $20,000 at the end of 1991 and 1992, respectively. If the 1992 books were still open, these errors would be corrected by debiting prior year adjustment and crediting inventory at:

    a. $0.
    b. $10,000.
    c. $20,000.
    d. $30,000.

_____ 14. Based on the same data as in Question 13, except that those errors were discovered after the 1992 books were closed. These errors would be corrected by debiting prior year adjustment and crediting inventory account at:

    a. $0.
    b. $10,000.
    c. $20,000.
    d. $30,000.

SOLUTIONS TO REVIEW QUESTIONS AND EXERCISES

TRUE-FALSE

1.	T	5.	T	9.	T	13.	T
2.	T	6.	F	10.	T	14.	F
3.	T	7.	T	11.	F		
4.	F	8.	F	12.	T		

EXERCISE 1

1.	A	4.	C	7.	A	10.	A
2.	C	5.	B	8.	A		
3.	C	6.	D	9.	B		

EXERCISE 2

a. **Determine the cumulative effect:**

Depreciation expenses up to January 1, 1994:

New method (SL) -- $220,000 x 3 / 10	$ 66,000
Old method (SYD) -- $220,000 x (10 + 9 + 8) / 55	108,000
Cumulative effect before tax	$(42,000)
Tax effect (40%)	16,800
Cumulative effect, net of tax	$(25,200)

b. **Record the cumulative effect:**

Accumulated depreciation	42,000	
Cumulative effect on accounting principle changes		25,200
Deferred income taxes		16,800

c. **Record current depreciation expense based on the new method:**

Depreciation expense ($220,000 / 10)	22,000	
Accumulated depreciation		22,000

EXERCISE 3

a. **Prepare the correcting entry assuming the error was discovered before the 1993 books were closed.**

Equipment	60,000	
Accumulated depreciation ($60,000 x 2 / 5)		24,000
Deferred tax liability ($60,000 - $24,000) x 40%		14,400
Prior year adjustment (plug)		21,600
Depreciation expense (1993)	12,000	
Accumulated depreciation		12,000

b. **Prepare the correcting entry assuming the error was discovered after the 1993 books were closed.**

Equipment	60,000	
Accumulated depreciation ($60,000 x 3 / 5)		36,000
Deferred tax liability ($60,000 - $36,000) x 40%		9,600
Prior year adjustment (plug)		14,400

EXERCISE 4

a. **At the end of 1994:**

Depreciation expense ($46,000 - $10,000) / 8	4,500	
Accumulated depreciation		4,500

b. **At the end of 1995:**

Depreciation expense ($46,000 - 4 x $4,500) / (6 - 4)	14,000	
Accumulated depreciation		14,000

MULTIPLE CHOICE

1.	a	5.	b	9.	d	13.	b
2.	d	6.	a	10.	a	14.	c
3.	a	7.	d	11.	d		
4.	c	8.	e	12.	d		

Computations:

9.   (d)   Book value of patent at beginning of 1994
= $17,000 x (17 - 3) / 17
= $14,000

Annual amortization of patent after change in estimate
= $14,000 / (10 - 3)
= $2,000

CHAPTER 25

Financial Statement Analysis and Changing Prices

CHAPTER OBJECTIVES

This chapter is designed to enable students to:

A. Explain the importance and limitations of financial statement information in the evaluation of investment opportunities.

B. Perform vertical (within years) and horizontal (across years) comparative percentage analyses.

C. Calculate a number of ratios used in financial statement analysis and interpret the results.

D. Explain the limitations of ratio analysis.

E. Explain the concept of capital market efficiency and what it implies for financial statement analysis.

F. Identify the effects of price changes on historical cost financial statements.

G. Discuss the advantages and disadvantages of general and specific price level adjusted financial statements.

H. Adjust financial statements for general price level changes (historical cost-constant dollar model).

I. Adjust financial statements for specific price level changes (current cost-nominal dollar, and current-cost constant dollar models).

CHAPTER OVERVIEW

Financial Statement Analysis

A.   The general purpose financial statements issued by a firm are an important, but not the only, source of financial information about the firm. Other sources include company management, investment advisors, trade associations, business periodicals, government agencies, and other materials distributed by and about the company, These latter sources are important because they disclose information on a more timely basis than do the published financial statements. For example, unreported litigation and liabilities can threaten the profit potential of a company. Publications such as *The Globe and Mail* and *The Financial Post* provide timely disclosure of such facts. All these and other financial data should be carefully analyzed and interpreted for making investment and credit decisions.

Four steps are generally applied to the use of financial statements. The first step is to examine the accompanying **auditors' report**. This report provides an independent and professional opinion about the fairness of the representations and calls attention to major concerns of the auditors during their examination of the statements. The next step is the analysis of their **footnotes, statement of accounting policies** and **supplementary schedules** as to be discussed in Chapter 26. The third step is to transform financial data into **percentages** or **ratios** in order to gain an overall perspective and to identify major strength and weaknesses of the firm. The final step is to search for important supplemental information.

B.   Financial Percentage Analysis

The corporate annual report typically includes detailed comparative financial statements for the current and preceding year(s). These comparative data facilitate an analysis of trends over a period of time. The following percentage analyses are common:

1.   **Vertical analysis.**   This analysis involves expressing each item on a financial statement in a given period as a percentage of a base amount (e.g., inventory as a percentage of total assets, salaries expense as a percentage of revenues, etc.).   This analysis reveals the composition of items on the specific common-size financial statement, i.e., the percentages of items on the statement always add up to 100%.

2.   **Horizontal analysis.**   Each item is expressed as a percentage of that same item in the financial statements of another year (base year) in order to more easily see year-to-year changes. This analysis involves scrutiny of not only the resulting percentages but also the relative importance of the items being analyzed.

C.   Financial Ratio Analysis

For accounting numbers to be most meaningful, they are usually studied in appropriate perspective. Ratio analysis provides that perspective by expressing accounting numbers as fractions or percentages of other numbers. This analysis is useful when the proportional relationship between the selected factors sheds additional light on the interpretation of the individual absolute amounts. For example, the fact that a firm's net income of $25,000 was earned on total assets of $100,000 is more meaningful information than the absolute amount of net income alone.

Depending on the characteristics they attempt to capture and the specific user needs they are intended to satisfy, financial ratios can be classified into the following four categories:

1.   **Current position (or liquidity) ratios.**   This set of financial ratios measures the firm's ability to pay short-term obligations when mature. Three ratios are generally used:

   a.   **Current ratio**
      = Current assets / Current liabilities

      The current ratio is only one measure of ability to meet short-term obligations and must be interpreted carefully. In general, a high current ratio indicates a strong liquidity position. However, a firm may have a high current ratio even though it has a cash deficit. A high current ratio may also indicate excess funds that should be invested or used for other purposes.

   b.   **Quick (or acid-test) ratio**
      = Quick assets / Current liabilities
      = (Current assets - Inventory - Prepaid expenses) / Current liabilities

      This ratio is used as a test of immediate liquidity. An acid-test ratio of 1 to 1 is generally considered satisfactory.

   c.   **Working capital ratio to total assets**
      = Working capital / Total assets
      = (Current assets - Current liabilities) / Total assets

      This ratio is a generalized expression of the distribution and liquidity of the assets employed after current liabilities are deducted from current assets. A low ratio may indicate a weakness in the current position.

   d.   **Defensive-interval ratio**
      = Defensive assets / Projected daily operational expenditures
      = (Current assets - Inventory - Prepaid expenses) / Projected daily operating expenditures

      This ratio provides a measure of how long a firm can operate on its present defensive or quick assets.

2.   **Efficiency (activity) ratios:**   These ratios provide information about how efficiently the firm is using its assets. The most used efficiency ratios include:

   a.   **Accounts receivable turnover**
      = Net credit sales / Average accounts receivable (net)

This ratio indicates how quickly a firm is able to collect accounts and short-term notes receivable, where the average accounts receivable is obtained by dividing the total of beginning and ending balances by 2.

Age of accounts receivable
= 365 / Accounts receivable turnover
  This ratio shows the average number of days to collect trade receivables

b. **Inventory turnover**
= Cost of goods sold / Average inventory

This ratio indicates how quickly inventory typically is sold. A high inventory turnover generally reflects efficient inventory management. The average number of days' supply in the average inventory, indicating general condition of over- or understocking, can be found as follows:

Days' supply in inventory
= 365 / Inventory turnover

c. **Working capital turnover**
= Net sales revenue / Average working capital

This ratio indicates the effectiveness with which average working capital was used to generate sales.

d. **Asset turnover**
= Net sales revenue / Average total assets

This ratio extends the idea of efficient use of working capital to all assets. Note that the ratio is larger for firms using older, more depreciated assets.

e. **Net cash flow to current liabilities**
= Net cash flow from operations/current liabilities

This ratio measures the ability to pay current debts from cash inflow from operations

3. **Equity Position Ratios**   Long-term creditors are primarily concerned with a firm's long-term solvency and stability. Ratios that measure equity position are designed to provide indications of these aspects of a company's outlook.

a. **Debt to equity ratio**
= Total liabilities / Shareholders' equity

This ratio measures the balance between resources provided by creditors and resources provided by owners including retained earnings.

b. **Debt to total assets ratio**
= Total liabilities / Total assets

This ratio measures essentially the same facet of a firm's capital structure as the debt to equity ratio.

c.   **Book value per share of common stock**
= Common shareholders' equity / Number of outstanding common shares

This ratio indicates what shareholders might expect to receive in the event of liquidation. Although still popularly used, it is useful only to the extent that book values mirror market values.

d.   **Times interest earned**
= $\dfrac{\text{Income before taxes and interest}}{\text{Interest charges}}$

This ratio indicates how many times interest charges are covered by available income.

e.   **Cash flow per share**
= $\dfrac{\text{Net cash flow from operations}}{\text{Number of outstanding common shares}}$

This ratio measures cash generated on a per share basis.

4.   **Profitability ratios**   These ratios are intended to measure various aspects of a firm's profit-making activities.

a.   **Profit margin on sales**
= Net income / Net sales revenue

This ratio is useful as a measure of a firm's efficiency in controlling expenses. A low profit margin can be compensated for by a high investment turnover rate, and vice versa.

b.   **Return on investment**   The broad concept of return on investment has two important applications for a single business entity: evaluating proposed capital addition and other investment decisions on the basis of projected cash flows, and measuring the annual rate of return earned relative to the total assets employed or the average investment of shareholders:

(1)   **Return on total assets**
= [Income + Interest expense (after tax)] / Average total assets

(2)   **Return on owners' equity**
= Net income / Average shareholders' equity

c.   **Earnings per share on common stock**
= Earnings to common / Weighted-average common shares outstanding

Discussed in detail in Chapter 22.

    d.   **Price earnings ratio**
        = Market price per share / Earnings per share

        This ratio is widely used as a measure of the market's perception of the quality of a firm's earnings including its growth potential, stability, and relative risk.

    e.   **Dividend payout ratios.**   These ratios indicate the percentage of earnings that is distributed to shareholders as dividends:

        (1)   **Dividend payout on income to common**
            = Cash dividends to common / Income less preferred dividends

        (2)   **Dividend payout on market price of common**
            = Cash dividends per common share / Market price per common share

D.   Ratio analysis of financial statements is used widely along with more sophisticated techniques for making investment and credit decisions. However, they must be interpreted with care because of some important limitations such as follows:

    a.   Ratios represent average conditions that existed in the past.

    b.   When the data on which ratios are based are historical book values, they do not reflect market values.

    c.   The method of computing each ratio is not standardized.

    d.   The use of alternative accounting methods may have an effect on ratios.

    e.   Change in accounting estimates and principles may affect the ratios for the year of change.

    f.   Comparison among companies are difficult if each company has different operating characteristics and uses different accounting methods.

E. Changing Prices

    1.   Following GAAP, accounting measurements are based upon the historical cost principle using dollars as the measurement unit. With the basic assumption that the magnitude of changes in the value of the measurement unit is not material, the originally recorded historical data are not adjusted for price-level changes, general or specific. The resulting measurement system is thus referred to as **historical cost/nominal dollar accounting (HC/ND).**

To counter the effects of inflation on financial statements, three alternative systems have been proposed (as follows)

Four Models for Financial Reporting

Costing Basis	Measurement Unit	
	Nominal Dollars	**Constant Dollars**
Historical cost	Historical cost/Nominal dollar (HC/ND)[1]	Historical cost/Constant dollar (HC/CD)
Current cost	Current cost/Nominal dollar (CC/ND)	Current cost/Constant dollar (CC/CD)

[1] - The current reporting method, GAAP

The accounting profession has consistently endorsed historical cost (HC) as the basis for financial statements. Section 1000 of the *CICA Handbook* states that financial statements are prepared primarily using the historical cost basis of measurement whereby transactions and events are recognized in financial statements at the amount of cash or cash equivalents paid or received or the fair value ascribed to them when they took place. (par. 1000.53)

F. Historical Cost/Constant Dollar Accounting (HC/CD)

Under this system, the historical cost model is maintained, but the accounting data based on nominal dollar are adjusted for the general price-level changes using a **general price-level index (GPL)**, in order to present financial statement elements in dollars that have the equivalent purchasing power.

1. **Constant dollar restatement formula.**   Nominal dollars are converted to constant dollars by means of conversion (restatement) factors obtained by dividing the general price-level index at a target date (e.g., the end of current period) to be adjusted to by the one at the original transaction date to be adjusted from. The general conversion formula is:

HC/CD amount
= HC/ND amount x Conversion factor
= HC/ND amount x GPL adjusting to / GPL adjusting from

For example, land acquired for $10,000 in 1985 (when the **GPL** was 160) could be restated to 1992 dollar (when the **GPL** was 200) as follows:

Land at HC/CD
= Land at HC/ND x Conversion factor
= $10,000 x 200/160
= $12,500

2.   **Balance sheet items.**   HC/CD accounting requires that balance sheet items be divided into two categories--monetary and nonmonetary:

a.   **Monetary items** are assets and liabilities whose amounts are fixed, by contract or otherwise, in terms of a specific number of dollars. Examples of monetary items are cash, receivables, notes payable and bonds payable. Since monetary items, by definition, represent a fixed number of dollars regardless of price-level changes, they are already stated in units of current purchasing power and do not require restatement.

b.   **Nonmonetary items** are those items not considered to be monetary. For example, land, buildings, and inventory do not represent fixed claims to cash and therefore require restatement in constant dollar accounting. Note that contributed capital accounts are dealt with as nonmonetary items, whereas retained earnings is the balancing amount on the balance sheet. In the previous example, the land purchased for $10,000 in 1985 would be restated to $12,500 on a 1992 balance sheet to reflect the fact that it would require 12,500 "1992 dollars" to buy what only 10,000 "1985 dollars" bought.

3.   **Purchasing power gain or loss.**   Although monetary items do not require restatement in constant dollar accounting, these items do give rise to purchasing power gains or losses. If net monetary assets are held during a period of inflation, for example, those assets will command a lesser amount of goods or services following the price rise, creating a purchasing power loss. Conversely, holding net monetary liabilities through a period of rising prices creates a purchasing power gain because those liabilities can be repaid in "cheaper" dollars.

ILLUSTRATION 1 -- Purchasing power gain or loss

Assume the books of Inn the Still Company LTD. carried the following:

Net monetary items:

January 1, 1992	$10,000
December 31, 1992	14,000

Purchase of equipment for cash, January 1, 1992	5,000
Purchase of merchandise occurred evenly throughout 1992	20,000
Sales occurred evenly throughout 1992	35,000
Cash dividends paid on October 1, 1992	6,000

The **GPL** are as follows:

January 1, 1992	100
July 1, 1992 (average for 1992)	110
October 1, 1992	115
December 31, 1992	120

Based on the above information, a schedule can be prepared to compute purchasing power gain or loss for 1992:

Schedule to Compute Purchasing Power Gain/Loss

	HC	CF	HC/CD
Monetary items (net), January 1, 1992	$10,000	120/100	$12,000
Add: Sales (average)	35,000	120/110	38,182
Total available	$45,000		$50,182
Deduct: Purchases of merchandise (average)	$20,000	120/110	$21,818
Purchase of equipment	5,000	120/100	6,000
Paid cash dividends	6,000	120/115	6,261
Total deductions	$31,000		$34,079
Monetary items (net), December 31, 1992			
Restated			$16,103
Historical	$14,000		14,000
Purchasing power loss			$2,103

Note that, on the schedule, **CF** stands for conversion factors, and that purchasing power gain or loss is reported in the HC/CD income statement, if provided.

4. **Income statement items.**   In restating HC/ND income statement items, the assumption is made that all revenues and expenses, except allocated items (e.g., cost of goods sold, depreciation expenses, amortization of intangible assets, and bond discount or premium), occur evenly throughout the year. Accordingly, the conversion factor is the year-end GPL divided by the average GPL for the year. The restatement of allocated revenues or expenses is related to the initial purchase or acquisition of the corresponding items. Thus, the pertinent conversion factor is the year-end GPL divided by the GPL at the time of the initial transaction.

G. Current Cost/Nominal Dollar Accounting (CC/ND) [or Current Cost Accounting (CC)]

The current cost system is a response to the general criticism that the historical cost fails to reflect price-level changes. Under this system, the historical cost model is abandoned. Assets are measured at the end-of-period current cost.

Considerable judgment is required to estimate CC for many assets. Adjustments are made for differences in useful life, output capacity, and operating costs. Many firms use external specific price indices to estimate CCs. A study of these indices found that CC is often overstated, perhaps underestimating CC/ND earnings.

Unfortunately, CC/ND models fail to separate the effects of inflation from the total change in CC. The income statements can reflect dollars of several different purchasing power levels and the gain or loss from holding monetary items during the period is not reflected. However, current cost models can be modified to adjust for the changing purchasing power of the dollar.

1. **Balance sheet items:**

    a. **Inventory** at the current cost of replacing or reproducing the inventory owned. Ending inventory is measured at current cost by multiplying the number of units on hand at the balance sheet date by the end-of-period current unit cost.

    b. **Property, plant and equipment** at the current cost of acquiring the same service potential as embodied in the assets owned. The current cost of a depreciable asset is measured at the end-of-period current cost (new) minus the recalculated accumulated depreciation based on the current cost.

    c. **Specialized assets such as natural resources** at current market buying price or current cost of finding and developing the resources.

    d. **Other assets** generally at historical cost, if not significant in amount.

    The current cost may be determined (a) by using price-level indexes for specific goods or services or (b) by direct pricing (price lists, standard costs, etc.).

2. **Income statement items.**

    a. **Revenue –** Current cost revenue is the same as under the historical cost system.

    b. **Cost of goods sold –** Current cost of goods sold is measured by multiplying the number of units sold during the period by the average current unit cost.

    c. **Depreciation expense –** Current cost depreciation on a straight-line basis may be measured by dividing the average-for-period current cost of the asset (beginning-of-period current cost plus end-of-period current cost divided by 2) by the estimated useful life of the asset. Note that average-for-period current cost is used to measure depreciation expenses only. End-of-period current cost should be applied to measure the accumulated depreciation of the asset.

    d. **Other expenses –** generally use historical cost, if not significant.

    e. **Holding gain/loss –** Holding gains or losses represent the increase or decrease in the current cost of assets during the period. The increase or decrease in the current cost amounts of inventory and property, plant, and equipment represents the difference between the measures of the assets at their **entry dates** and **exit dates** for the year. Entry dates means the beginning of the year or the dates of acquisition, whichever is appropriate; exit dates means the end of the year or the dates of use or sale, whichever is applicable.

    A holding gain or loss is realized if the asset is used or sold. Otherwise, it is unrealized. Holding gains or losses currently realized and any increase or decrease in unrealized holding gains or losses should be reported in the current cost income statement or as a separate component of shareholders' equity.

3. **Current Cost/Constant Dollar Accounting (CC/CD)**

Although the **CC/ND** model is an improvement over the historical cost models, it fails to separate the effects of general and specific price-level changes. CC/CD considers both:

a. **Balance sheet items.** As in HC/CD accounting, each of the balance sheet items is classified as either monetary or nonmonetary. However, nonmonetary items such as inventory and property, plant and equipment are reported at current cost, and other assets and liabilities are generally reported at their historical costs.

b. **Purchasing power gain or loss.** Under the CC/CD system purchasing power gain or loss should be determined and reported in the same manner as under the HC/CD accounting.

c. **Income statement items.** The CC/CD model differs from the CC/ND model mainly in the determination of income statement items. Under the CC/CD model, (1) the current costs of revenues and expenses are restated using the general price-level indexes, (2) purchasing power gain or loss is included in income statement, and (3) the inflation effect is adjusted to the holding gains or losses.

ILLUSTRATION 2 -- Accounting for inventory under the current cost systems:

Assume Josie Ltd. records show the following:

January 1, 1992:   Purchased merchandise for $2,000.
December 31, 1992:   The merchandise remained unsold. Current cost of the merchandise increased to $3,000.
December 31, 1993:   Sold the merchandise for $7,500, when the current cost was $5,000.

GPL:

January 1, 1992	100%
December 31, 1992	120%
December 31, 1993	150%

Required: (1) Prepare a comparative income statement under the CC/ND system.

(2) Prepare a comparative income statement under the CC/CD system.

Solutions:

(1) **CC/ND system:**   A simplified comparative income statement under the CC/ND system is presented below:

	1992	1993
Sales	$ 0	$7,500
Cost of goods sold (current cost)	0	5,000
Gross profit	$ 0	$2,500
Realized holding gain	0	3,000 [2]
Total realized profit	$ 0	$5,500
Increase (decrease) in unrealized holding gain	1,000[1]	(1,000)[3]
Net income	$1,000	$4,500

Notes:

[1]Increase in unrealized holding gain (1992) = $3,000 - $2,000 = $1,000.

[2]Holding gain realized (1993)
  = Current cost when merchandise was sold - Historical cost of goods sold
  = $5,000 - $2,000
  = $3,000.

[3]Decrease in unrealized holding gain (1993)
  = Ending unrealized holding gain - Beginning unrealized holding gain
  = $0 - $1,000
  = ($1,000).

(2) **CC/CD system:** A simplified comparative income statement under the CC/CD system is presented below:

	1992	1993
Sales	$ 0	$7,500[2]
Cost of goods sold (current cost)	0	5,000
Gross profit	$ 0	$2,500
Realized holding gain	0	2,000[3]
Total realized profit	$ 0	$4,500
Increase (decrease) in unrealized holding gain	600[1]	(600)[4]
Net income	$ 600	$3,900

Notes:

[1] Unrealized holding gain adjusted for general price-level changes
= $3,000 - ($2,000 x 120 / 100) = $600.

[2] Sales and Cost of goods sold (1992) are not restated because the sales were made at the end of the year.

[3] Realized holding gain
= Current cost - Restated historical cost
= $5,000 - $2,000 x 150 / 100
= $2,000.

[4] Decrease in unrealized holding gain (1993)
= Ending unrealized holding gain - Beginning unrealized holding gain
= 0 - $600 = ($600)

ILLUSTRATION 3 -- Accounting for depreciable assets under the current cost systems:

Assume BBB Company purchased a machine on January 1, 1992 for $20,000. The machine had a useful life of 10 years with no residual value and the straight-line method was applied. At the end of 1992, the current cost of the machine (new) was $30,000.

GPL are as follows:

January 1, 1992	100%
July 1, 1992	110%
December 31, 1992	120%

Required: (1) Determine holding gains or losses under the CC/ND system.

(2) Determine holding gains or losses under the CC/CD system.

Solutions:

(1) **CC/ND system:** Determine holding gains or losses:

To compute holding gain of the machine for 1992:

Depreciation expense:

CC/ND: {[($20,000 + $30,000) / 2] / 10}	$ 2,500
HC/ND: ($20,000 / 10)	(2,000)

Realized holding gain:	**$ 500**

Ending book value of machine (net):

CC/ND: ($30,000 x 90%)	$27,000
HC/ND: ($20,000 x 90%)	(18,000)

Unrealized holding gain at end of period	$ 9,000
Less: Beginning unrealized holding gain	0
Current increase in unrealized holding gain	**$ 9,000**
Total holding gain ($500 + $9,000)	**$ 9,500**

(2) **CC/CD system:** Determine holding gains or losses:

To compute holding gain of the machine for 1992:

Depreciation expense (restated)

CC/CD: {[($20,000 + $30,000)/2]/10} x 120 /110	$2,727
HC/CD: ($20,000 / 10) x 120 / 100	(2,400)

Realized holding gain:	**$ 327**

Restated ending book value of machine (net):

CC/CD ($30,000 x 90%) x 120 / 120	$27,000
HC/CD ($20,000 x 90%) x 120 / 100	(21,600)

Unrealized holding gain at end of period	$ 5,400
Less: Beginning unrealized holding gain	0
Current increase in unrealized holding gain	**$ 5,400**
Total holding gain (machine)	**$ 5,727**

KEY CONCEPTS

Current cost accounting (CC/ND)   An accounting system that abandons the historical cost model, and measures each of the financial statement elements in terms of its current cost, or in price-level dollars specific to the element being measured.

Current cost/Constant dollar accounting (CC/CD)   An accounting system that abandons the historical cost model in favor of current cost and, at the same time, makes adjustments to transform nominal dollars to dollars with the equivalent purchasing power.

Efficiency (activity) ratios   Financial ratios that provide information about how efficient the firm is using its assets. The most used efficiency ratios include accounts receivable turnover, inventory turnover, working capital turnover and asset turnover.

Equity position ratios   Financial ratios that measure the firm's long-term solvency and stability. The most used ratios include debt to equity ratio, debt to total assets ratio, and book value per common share.

Historical cost/Constant dollar accounting HC/CD)   An accounting system that adjusts financial statement elements from the nominal dollar to the constant dollar basis, i.e., to dollars with the equivalent purchasing power.

Horizontal analysis   Each item of a comparative financial statement is expressed as a percentage of the same item of another period. This analysis involves scrutiny of not only the resulting percentages but also the relative importance of the item being analyzed.

Liquidity ratios   Financial ratios that measure the firm's ability to pay short-term obligations when mature. The generally used liquidity ratios include current ratio, acid-test ratio, working capital ratio and defensive-interval ratio.

Monetary (vs. nonmonetary) items   Assets and liabilities whose amounts are fixed in terms of a specific number of dollars are referred to as monetary items. Assets and liabilities other than monetary are nonmonetary items. Under the constant dollar system, monetary items are not restated. Nevertheless, they do give rise to purchasing power gain or loss.

Profitability ratios   Financial ratios that measure various aspects of a firm's profit-making activities, including profit margin to sales, return on investment in terms of total assets or shareholders' equity, and earnings per common share.

Vertical analysis   Each item of a financial statement is expressed as a percentage of the appropriate corresponding total or base amount on the same statement. This analysis reveals the changes in the composition of items on the statement over time.

REVIEW QUESTIONS AND EXERCISES

TRUE-FALSE

Indicate whether each of the following statements is true or false by circling the correct response.

T   F   1. Vertical analysis refers to the analytical technique of comparing accounting numbers over a period of years.

T   F   2. When using ratio analysis as a means of comparing one company with another, it is important to consider the accounting policies and methods employed by the two companies.

T   F   3. The current ratio generally is more useful than the acid-test ratio in assessing short-run liquidity (solvency) due to its more narrow definition of liquid assets.

T   F   4. In the calculation of the acid-test ratio, marketable securities and pre-paid expenses are both excluded from current assets before dividing by current liabilities.

T   F   5. The receivable turnover ratio indicates how quickly accounts receivable are collected on the average.

T   F   6. If the times of inventory turnover are high relative to industry standards, the risk to "stockout" is higher than the industry average.

T   F   7. If Company A has EPS of $10 and Company B has EPS of $5, Company A is twice as profitable as Company B.

T   F   8. The profit margin is one indication of management's efficiency in controlling costs and expenses.

T   F   9. Historical cost/Constant dollar (HC/CD) accounting abandons the traditional historical cost concept.

T   F   10. Reporting on the basis of current cost/nominal dollar (CC/ND) accounting has the advantage of presenting the effect of changes in the general price level.

T   F   11. Monetary items are already stated in dollars of current purchasing power, therefore, they are not required to be restated in a constant dollar balance sheet.

T   F   12. The conversion factor used in constant dollar restatement of depreciation expense is based on the index at the time the related depreciable asset was purchased.

T   F   13. Historical cost/Constant dollar (HC/CD) accounting ignores the effect of specific price-level changes.

T   F   14.   The current cost/constant dollar (CC/CD) model takes into account changes in both the specific price level and the general price level.

EXERCISE 1

Match each of the following descriptions with the appropriate concept by indicating the letter of the concept.

Concept

A. General price-level index
B. Current cost/Constant dollar
C. Historical cost/Nominal dollar
D. Monetary items

E. Specific price-level index
F. Historical cost/Constant dollar
G. Current cost/Nominal dollar
H. Purchasing power gain/loss

_____   1.   Model which focuses on specific price-level changes.

_____   2.   Adjusts financial statements for general price-level changes only.

_____   3.   Model which ignores both the general and specific price-level changes.

_____   4.   Measures changes in the purchasing power of the dollar.

_____   5.   Measures changes in the price of a specific good.

_____   6.   Model which adjusts for both general and specific price-level changes.

_____   7.   Effect of holding monetary items during inflation.

_____   8.   Cash and receivables with fixed dollar amounts.

EXERCISE 2

Given the following comparative income statement and balance sheet for Lasagna Retailers Ltd, compute the requested ratios for 1992. (Additional information: 10,000 common shares have been outstanding since 1990. Income tax rate was 40%).

Income Statement

	1992	1991
Net sales	$240,500	$201,000
Cost of goods sold	(132,000)	(111,500)
Gross profit	$108,500	$ 89,500
Selling and general expenses	(50,500)	(44,000)
Interest expense	(9,500)	(8,500)
Income before tax	$ 48,500	$ 37,000
Income tax	(19,400)	(14,800)
Net income	$ 29,100	$ 22,200

Balance Sheet
December 31

	1992	1991
Cash	$ 13,000	$ 12,500
Accounts receivables (net)	35,000	34,900
Inventories	34,800	29,000
Prepaid expenses	9,500	13,000
Total current assets	$ 92,300	$ 89,400
Property, plant and equipment (net)	115,000	105,250
Other assets	700	850
Total assets	$208,000	$195,500
Current liabilities	$ 51,000	$ 45,000
Long-term debt	107,000	100,500
Total liabilities	$158,000	$145,500
Shareholders' equity	50,000	50,000
Total liab. and SE	$208,000	$195,500

Required: Compute the following financial ratios for 1992:

a.   **Current ratio**

b.   **Acid-test ratio**

_____

c.   **Working capital to total assets ratio**

_____

d.   **Accounts receivable turnover**

_____

e.   **Inventory turnover**

_____

f.   **Debt to equity ratio**

_____

g.   **Book value per share**

_____

h.   **Profit margin on sales**

_____

i.   **Return on total assets**

_____

j.   **Return on shareholders' equity**

_____

EXERCISE 3

The following incomplete balance sheet is obtained from Spare Tire Corporation Ltd.:

Assets:

Cash	$ 10,000
Accounts receivable (net)	(?)
Inventory	(?)
Property, plant and equipment	30,000
Total assets	$120,000

Liabilities and shareholders' equity:

Accounts payable	$ (?)
Accrued wages payable	8,000
Bonds payable (long-term)	15,000
Common shares, nopar, 5,000 shares outstanding	50,000
Retained earnings	(?)
Total liab. and SE	$120,000

Additional information:

Current ratio	2 to 1
Ending inventory to net sales	15%
Net income to net sales	25%
Gross margin to net sales	30%
Gross margin	$ 24,000

Required: **Determine the following:**

a.   Net sales:

_____

b.   Inventory (ending):

_____

c.   Current assets:

_____

d.   Accounts receivable (net):

_____

e.   Current liabilities:

_____

f.   Accounts payable (net):

_____

g.   Retained earnings:

_____

h.   Cost of goods sold:

_____

i.   Net income:

_____

j.   Earnings per share:

_____

MULTIPLE CHOICE

Enter the letter corresponding to the response which **best** completes each of the following statements or questions.

_____ 1. The ratio that best provides an indication of the balance between resources provided by creditors and resources provided by owners is:

    a. time interest earned.
    b. the debt to equity ratio.
    c. profit margin.
    d. the inventory turnover ratio.

_____ 2. If average inventories increased from $70,000 to $80,000 during the year just ended, which of the following statements is true?

    a. the acid-test ratio decreased.
    b. the current ratio decreased.
    c. the acid-test ratio increased.
    d. inventories have no effect on the acid-test ratio.

_____ 3. For a firm with a current ratio of 2 to 1, which of the following transactions would most likely cause an increase in this ratio?

    a. the declaration of a cash dividend.
    b. the sale of common shares.
    c. the collection of accounts receivable.
    d. the payment of a 30-day note payable.

_____ 4. A very high receivable turnover ratio relative to the industry average indicates:

    a. the declaration of a cash dividend.
    b. that the firm's credit policy may be overly restrictive.
    c. that the firm's management utilizes its assets efficiently.
    d. a sluggish inventory.

_____ 5. The ratio least likely to be of concern to those interested in projecting a firm's future profitability is:

    a. the current ratio.
    b. profit margin.
    c. investment turnover.
    d. rate of return on investment.

_____ 6. How are inventories used in the calculation of each of the following?

	Current Ratio	Inventory Turnover
a.	Numerator	Numerator
b.	Numerator	Denominator
c.	Denominator	Numerator
d.	Not used	Denominator

_____ 7. During an inflationary period, a firm will incur the greatest purchasing power loss by holding:

   a. accounts payable.
   b. inventory.
   c. accounts receivable.
   d. land.

_____ 8. Included in the classification of monetary items for the purpose of constant dollar accounting are:

   a. cash, receivables, and inventory.
   b. current assets and current liabilities.
   c. accounts receivable, wages payable, and bonds payable.
   d. accounts payable and inventory.

_____ 9. Champ Company earns a 10% return on total assets. If net income is $26,000, and Champ has no interest expense and the total assets at January 1, 1992 are $250,000, the ending balance of the total assets is likely to be:

   a. $250,000.
   b. $260,000.
   c. $270,000.
   d. $280,000.

_____ 10. Sinkhole Company Ltd. began the accounting year with $100,000 in monetary assets and $110,000 in monetary liabilities. The price-level index rose evenly during the year from 120 to 130. If no increases or decreases occur in either monetary assets or monetary liabilities, the purchasing power gain or loss will be a:

   a. $833 gain.
   b. $833 loss.
   c. $400 gain.
   d. none of the above.

_____ 11. Selected information from the accounting records of Fresh Company Ltd. is as follows:

Net sales for 1992	$160,000
Cost of goods sold for 1992	80,000
Inventory at 12/31/1991	10,000
Inventory at 12/31/1992	6,000

Denikay's inventory turnover for 1992 is:

a. 8 times
b. 10 times
c. 20 times
d. 6 times

_____ 12. Rickshaw Corporation Ltd. bought equipment for $210,000 on January 1, 1992. The equipment has an estimated useful life of ten years, with no residual value. The current cost of this equipment at December 31, 1992 was $270,000. Using straight-line depreciation on average current cost the depreciation that should be charged to current cost income for 1992 is:

a. $21,000.
b. $24,000.
c. $27,000.
d. $48,000.

_____ 13. Based on the same information as in question 12 above, what is the accumulated depreciation of the equipment presented on the current cost balance sheet at the end of 1992:

a. $21,000.
b. $27,000.
c. $24,000.
d. none of the above.

_____ 14. Hairless Corporation Ltd. purchased a machine at January 1, 1991 for $12,000, when the general price-level index was 120%. The asset has a useful life of 4 years and no residual value. If the price-level index was 144% at the end of 1992 and the straight-line method is applied, the depreciation expense for 1992 under historical cost/constant dollar (HC/CD) accounting would be:

a. $3,000
b. $3,300.
c. $3,600.
d. $3,800.

SOLUTIONS TO REVIEW QUESTIONS AND EXERCISES

TRUE-FALSE

1.	F	5.	T	9.	F	13.	T
2.	T	6.	T	10.	F	14.	T
3.	F	7.	F	11.	T		
4.	F	8.	T	12.	T		

EXERCISE 1

1.	G	5.	E
2.	F	6.	B
3.	C	7.	H
4.	A	8.	D

EXERCISE 2

a. Current ratio:
($92,300 / $51,000)   **1.81**

b. Acid-test ratio:
($92,300 - $34,800 - $9,500) / $51,000   **.94**

c. Working capital to total assets ratio:
($92,300 - $51,000) /$208,000   **20%**

d. Accounts receivable turnover:
{$240,500 / [($35,000 + $34,900) / 2]}   **6.9 times**

e. Inventory turnover:
[$132,000 /($34,800 + $29,000) / 2]   **4.1 times**

f. Debt to equity ratio:
($158,000 / $50,000)   **3.16%**

g. Book value per share:
($50,000 / 10,000)   **$5/share**

h. Profit margin on sales:
($29,100 / $240,500)   **12.1%**

i. Return on total assets:
[$29,100 + $9,500 x (1 - 40%)]
/ [($208,000 + $195,500) / 2]   **17.25%**

j. Return on shareholders' equity:
{$29,100 / [($50,000 + $50,000) / 2]}   **58.2%**

EXERCISE 3

a. Net sales:

Net sale
= Gross margin / Gross margin ratio to net sales
= $24,000 / 30%
= $80,000

b. Inventory (ending):

Inventory (ending)
= Net sales x Ending inventory to net sales ratio
= $80,000 x 15%
= $12,000

c. Current assets:

Current assets
= Total assets - Property, plant and equipment
= $120,000 - $30,000
= $90,000

d. Accounts receivable (net):

Accounts receivable (net)
= Current assets - Cash - Inventory (ending)
= $90,000 - $10,000 - $12,000
= $68,000

e. Current liabilities:

Current liabilities
= Current assets / Current ratio
= $90,000 / 2
= $45,000

f. Accounts payable (net):

Accounts payable (net)
= Current liabilities - Accrued wages payable
= $45,000 - $8,000
= $37,000

g. Retained earnings:

Retained earnings
= Total assets - Current liabilities - Long-term liabilities - Common shares
= $120,000 - $45,000 - $15,000 - $50,000
= $10,000

h. Cost of goods sold:

Cost of goods sold
= Net sales - Gross margin
= $80,000 - $24,000
= $56,000

i. Net income:

Net income
= Net sales x Net income to net sales ratio
= $80,000 x 25%
= $20,000

j. Earnings per share:
= Net income / Common shares outstanding
= $20,000 / 5,000
= $4

MULTIPLE CHOICE

1.	b	5.	a	9.	c	13.	b
2.	d	6.	b	10.	a	14.	c
3.	b	7.	c	11.	b		
4.	b	8.	c	12.	b		

Computation:

9. (c)

Net income	$ 26,000
Divided by: Return to average total assets	10%
Average total assets	$260,000
Multiplied by:	2
Sum of beginning and ending total assets	$520,000
Less: Beginning total assets	250,000
Ending total assets	**$270,000**

10. (a)

Monetary asset (beginning)	$100,000
Less: Monetary liab. (beginning)	(110,000)
Net monetary liabilities (beginning)	$(10,000)
Conversion factor	130/120
Net monetary liabilities (restated)	$(10,833)
Less: Liabilities at historical cost	10,000
Purchasing power gain	**$(833)**

11. (b) Inventory turnover (1992)
= Cost of goods sold / (Beginning inventory + Ending inventory) / 2
= $80,000 / [($10,000 + $6,000) / 2]
= 10 times.

12. (b) Depreciation expense (1992) -- current cost
= Average current cost x Depreciation rate
= [$210,000 + $270,000) / 2] x 10%
= $24,000.

13. (b) Accumulated depreciation (Dec/31/1992) -- current cost
= Equipment current cost at year end x years used
= $270,000 x 1 / 10
= $27,000.

14. (c) Depreciation expense (1992) -- historical cost/constant dollar
= Depreciation expense (HC) x restatement factor
= $12,000 x 1 / 4 x 144 / 120
= $3,600.

CHAPTER 26

Special Topics: Disclosure, Interim Reporting, and Segment Reporting

CHAPTER OBJECTIVES

This chapter is designed to enable students to:

A.   Explain the problem of standards overload and some actions that might be undertaken to relieve the problem.

B.   Explain the information overload issue.

C.   Discuss the rationale for, and components of, the summary of significant accounting policies disclosure note and other required disclosure notes to the financial statements.

D.   Explain the alternative concepts that might be applied in designing interim reports and prepare appropriate disclosures.

E.   Discuss the rationale for segment reporting disclosures and prepare the required disclosures.

A.   *Standard overload* is a term sometimes used by firms to describe the financial reporting burden they face to comply with current accounting standards. A related, issue is called *information overload.* From the perspective of the user of the statements, the concern is that much of the information reported is of little or no use, and that valuable information is obscured by the presentation of data that the user does not need.

The **full disclosure principle** calls for the disclosure of any financial information that is potentially significant enough to influence the judgment of an informed reader.

There has been a substantial increase in disclosure requirements which have required various disclosure notes in addition to providing guidance on accepted methods of measurement.

Government regulations require increased disclosure in response to the relevant securities commissions, and the accounting profession must implement and respond to these requirements.

B.   Summary of Significant Accounting Policies

Knowledge of the various accounting policies used in generating a set of financial statements is essential when developing an understanding of the specific figures presented in the statements.In accordance with section 1505 of the *CICA Handbook*. The policies used are those that are judged by management to be the most appropriate in order to fairly present the financial position, cash flows, and results of operations in accordance with GAAP. Accounting policies include specific accounting principles and the methods of applying these principles. The disclosures must include those accounting principles and methods that involve:

* A selection from existing acceptable alternatives.
* Principles and methods particular to the industry.

The information may be presented as the first note to the financial statements, or in a separate summary of significant accounting policies section.

Other Notes to Financial Statements

Following the summary of significant accounting policies, there are a number of required disclosures in the notes to the financial statements.

Notes can fulfill the following functions:

1. Provide Detail   If detail is included on the face of a financial statement itself, the resulting clutter may reduce the understandability of the statement.

2. Explain Transactions   The nature of major acquisitions or disposals during the year must be disclosed in the notes to the financial statements to comply with various accounting standards. Transactions involving share capital or other ownership interests, including stock options, are also described in the notes.

3. Explain Unrecorded Items   Some contracts or business arrangements are not recorded in the financial statements even though they are important to an understanding of the entity's financial position or results of operations. These items are disclosed in the notes. Lawsuits pending, long-term lease commitment, and fixed contracts to buy or sell products are examples.

Events that take place between the end of the fiscal year and the date of the auditors report, if significant, must also be disclosed as *subsequent events*. Subsequent events do not reflect conditions at the balance sheet date and therefore cannot be recognized. They must be disclosed to keep financial statement users fully informed.

4. Provide New Information   Many important pieces of information cannot be incorporated into a financial statement, due to the nature of the item or the nature of the financial statement itself. The information is still crucial for decision making. Examples include:

1. Assets pledged as collateral.
2. Pension fund assets and pension fund liabilities.
3. Information about lines of business and geographical spread of operations.
4. Non-arms-length transactions. Data on *related party transactions*, may be significant in evaluating risk and profitability.

Examples of related parties include the following (this list is not exhaustive):

1. A firm and its principal owners, management, and members of families of owners or management.
2. A parent firm and its subsidiaries.
3. Subsidiaries of a common parent firm.
4. Parties related by means of share ownership when the share ownership results in the ability to exercise significant influence over the investee.

CICA Handbook Section 3840, "Related party Transactions," requires the following disclosures:

1. A description of the nature of the relationship(s) involved.
2. A description of the transaction, including transactions in which no amount or nominal amounts were involved, for each period for which income statements are presented.
3. The dollar amounts of transactions for each period for which income statements are presented.
4. Any amounts due to or from related parties as of the balance sheet date, and the terms and manner of settlement planned.

Special transactions and events

1. Errors *Errors* are defined as "incorrect recording and reporting of the facts about the business that existed at the time an event or transaction was recorded." They are essentially unintentional mistakes. Irregularities are *intentional* distortions of the financial statements. Both should be corrected when they are detected.

Irregularities are more serious problems than errors because they involve an attempt by owners and/or management to deceive readers of financial statements. An auditor must bring questionable activities to the attention of appropriate company officials and even may find it necessary to withdraw from an audit if the company did not take corrective action.

2. Illegal Acts Items such as illegal political contributions, bribes, kickbacks, and other violations of statutes and regulations constitute **illegal acts.** In the United States, Congress enacted the Foreign Corrupt Practices Act of 1977 largely to stop these illegal acts and require their disclosure when discovered.

The auditor must ensure complete disclosure of relevant information when an illegal act is discovered. In Canada, there is no such legislation. The auditor would proceed as for the discovery of an irregularity, bringing the matter to the attention of appropriate company officials and contemplating disclosure.

Fraudulent Financial Reporting

3. Fraudulent financial reporting is defined as intentional or reckless conduct, whether act or omission, that results in materially misleading financial statements. The opportunity for management is present when:

* The board of directors or an audit committee of the board does not carefully review the reporting process.
* The firm has engaged in unusual or complicated transactions.
* Poor systems of internal control are in place.
* Internal audit staffs are small or poorly trained and underfunded.
* There is extensive need for judgment in making accounting estimates.

The accounting profession is faced with the problem of first trying to prevent it, and second, determining responsibility when it occurs.

C.   Financial Disclosure Requirements and Standards Overload

The ever increasing requirements for financial disclosures, including notes and supplementary information, give rise to a phenomenon known as **information overload** on the users of financial reports, and to the problem of **standards overload** on the managements of firms. Standards overload is more serious to the smaller firms than their larger counterparts as many disclosure requirements, which are mainly imposed on larger corporations, are nevertheless equally applied to smaller companies.

To encourage full disclosure on the one hand, and to avoid standards overload on the other, the Accounting Standards Board has recommended that companies disclose voluntarily certain financial information, or limit the applicability of certain standards to publicly held larger companies.

D.   Interim Reporting

The fiscal year is the accounting period that is required for financial reporting. Annual financial statements, however, simply are not timely information for many investors. Users of financial statements cannot wait until after the end of the fiscal year. So therefore interim information, is presented by firms to provide more timely data: the **interim report**. Usually such information is presented on a quarterly basis, although nothing prevents a firm from reporting more frequently.

1. *Discrete view.* Each interim period is viewed as a basic reporting period. It stands alone and separate without considering it as a part of a longer (i.e., annual) reporting period. Revenue and expense recognition, accruals, and deferrals for the interim period follow the same principles and procedures as for an annual period.

2. *Integral view.* Each interim period is viewed as an inseparable part of the annual reporting period. Revenue and expense recognition and deferrals and accruals are affected by judgments made at the end of each interim period about the results of operations for the reminder of the reporting period.

Section 1750 of the *CICA Handbook* generally adopts the integral view.

3. **GAAP Disclosure Requirements.**

The following guidelines are for preparing interim reports:

1. In general, the accounting principles and practices used by the firm in preparing its annual financial statements should be used for interim reports.
2. Revenue from products and services sold should be recognized as earned during the interim period.
3. Costs and expenses for interim periods are classified as follows:
    a. Costs that are *directly associated* with interim revenue are reported in the interim period.
    b. Costs and expense that are *not directly associated* with interim revenue must be allocated to interim periods on a reasonable basis.

A. **Costs Directly Associated with Revenue** Costs directly associated with revenue, such as cost of goods sold, wages, salaries, fringe benefits and warranties, should be expensed in the interim period.

B. **Costs Not Directly Associated with Revenue** All costs not directly associated with revenue should be accounted and reported for interim periods as follows:

1. Recognize as expense in the interim period in which incurred.
2. Arbitrary allocation of such costs should not be made.
3. Gains and losses that arise in any interim period should be recognized in that interim period.

C. **Others Issues** Income tax expense for an interim period is affected by the overall tax status of the corporation. Many companies pay tax on a two-rate system, where the first level of earnings attracts tax at a low rate, and earnings above this level are taxed at a higher rate. The tax assigned to interim periods may be based on either (1) an estimate of the yearly total *combined* effective tax rate or (2) "low tax" earnings may be assigned evenly to interim periods. The policies chosen should be disclosed.

Unusual or infrequently occurring items and extraordinary items should be recognized in the interim period in which they occur. Similarly, contingent losses not directly associated with revenue (and the related liabilities) should be recognized in the interim period in which they occur. Accounting changes are accounted for and reported in essentially the same manner as for annual reporting periods.

D. **Minimum Disclosure** Interim financial reports do not need to include a complete set of financial statements and consist of only summarized financial data. The following should be reported:

1.   A summary disclosing separately:
    a.   Sales or gross revenue.
    b.   Investment income.
    c.   Amount charged for depreciation, depletion, and amortization.
    d.   Interest expense.
    e.   Income taxes.
    f.   Income or loss before discontinued operations and extraordinary items.
    g.   Discontinued operations and related income taxes.
    h.   Income or loss before extraordinary items.
    i.   Extraordinary items and related income taxes.
    j.   Net income or loss for the period.

2.   Basic and fully diluted earnings per share figures.
3.   Information as to significant changes in financial position can often be provided by a statement of changes in financial position. This information can be provided in an alternative form.
4.   Information concerning:
    a.   Changes in accounting principles or practices or in their method of application.
    b.   Discontinued operations.
    c.   Extraordinary items.
    d.   Subsequent events.
    e.   Other matters, not previously reported such as changes incontingencies or commitments, or issue or expiry of convertible securities, rights, warrants, or options.

E.   Segment Reporting

Investors who know the relative proportions of company resources committed to operations in the various businesses are likely to be able to make more informed decisions than investors who know only aggregate data for the company.

This led to Section 1700 of the *CICA Handbook*, "Segmented Information," issued by the CICA in 1979. Only public companies and life insurance companies are required to disclose segmented information, for industry and geographic segments. An **industry segment** of a business is a subdivision of the business that derives revenue from individual products or services that are significant parts of the business.

1.   Industry segments and reportable segments.

Section 1700 leaves the definition of reportable industry and geographic segments up to management. First, segments are identified and, second, management must decide which of the segments are reportable. An industry segment that meets any of the following tests shall be identified as a reportable segment:

a.   Its revenue is 10% or more of the combined revenue of all of the enterprise's industry segments.

b.   The absolute amount of its operating profit or loss is 10% or more of the greater, in absolute amount, of:

   (1)   The combined operating profit of all industry segments that earned a profit.

   (2)   The combined operating loss of all industry segments that incurred an operating loss.

c.   Its identifiable assets are 10% or more of the combined identifiable assets of all industry segments.

It is noted, however, segment reporting is required only if the reportable segments represent a **substantial portion** of the enterprise's total operations, i.e., the combined revenues from sales to unaffiliated customers of all reportable segments constitute at least 75% of the combined revenues from sales to unaffiliated customers of all industry segments.

Identifiable assets include the tangible and intangible identifiable assets of the segment that are used exclusively by the segment or jointly by two or more segments, allocated on a reasonable basis. Asset valuation accounts, such as allowance for doubtful accounts and accumulated depreciation, also must be included.

2.   Segment Reports

Required Disclosures   A general description of the products and services from which each reportable industry segment derives should be provided. Disclosure should be made for each reportable industry segment and, in aggregate, for the remainder of the enterprise's industry segments:

1.   Segment revenue derived from sales to customers outside the enterprise.
2.   Segment revenue derived from inter-segment sales or transfers and the basis of accounting therefor.
3.   Segment operating profit or loss; the amount of depreciation, amortization, and depletion expense; and any unusual items included in determining segment operating profit or loss.
4.   Total carrying amount of identifiable assets at the end of the fiscal year and the amount of capital expenditure for the period.

A reconciliation of the aggregate segment revenue, aggregate segment operating profit or loss, and aggregate identifiable assets to the sales, net income, and total assets reported in the financial statements of the enterprise should be provided.

Segment revenue includes all product and services sales to unaffiliated customers (i.e., customers from outside the enterprise), inter-segment sales, and interest on segment trade receivables.

Segment operating gain or loss is segment revenue (as defined above) less all segment operating expenses. Operating expenses for a segment include:

1.   Operating expenses that are directly related to a segment's revenue.

2.   Operating expenses incurred by the company that can be allocated on a reasonable basis to the segment(s) for whose benefit those expenses were incurred.

None of the following should be added or deducted in computing the operating income or loss of a segment: (1) company revenues not derived from the segment, (2) general company expenses, (3) interest expenses, (4) income taxes, (5)equity in income of unconsolidated subsidiaries or other equity investees, (6) extraordinary items, and (7) minority interests in income.

Geographic Segments

3.   The determination of a geographic segment is a management responsibility. Factors to consider, outside of pure geography, include the proximity of operations, whether operations in areas are related, and the nature of the economic and political risks in each location.

Once a firm has identified its geographic segments, it then must determine which of the segments are *reportable*. Significant--or reportable--geographic segments are those that account for:

1.   Ten percent or more of the revenue generated from customers outside the enterprise.
2.   Ten percent or more of the total assets of the enterprise.

Disclosure The disclosure required for a reportable geographic segment closely parallels that required for an industry segment, but is less extensive. Section 1700.44 provides that

The location of each reportable foreign geographic segment should be disclosed. Disclosure of the following data should be made in total for all other foreign geographic segments when they are in the aggregate identified as significant and for the domestic geographic segment:

(*a*)   segment revenue derived from sales to customers outside the enterprise;
(*b*)   segment revenue derived from sales or transfers between geographic segments and the basis of accounting therefor;
(*c*)   segment operating profit or loss or, where appropriate, some other measure of profitability (information as to after-tax profitability may be more appropriate when the tax structure applicable to the reportable foreign geographic segment is substantially different from that experienced by the enterprise's domestic operation); and
(*d*)   total carrying amount of identifiable assets at the end of the fiscal year.

A reconciliation of the aggregate segment revenue, aggregate measure of profitability and aggregate identifiable assets to the sales, net income and total assets reported in the financial statements of the enterprise should be provided.

In addition, paragraph 1700,46 requires disclosure of the amount of export sales, when sales of products and services by an enterprise's domestic operations to foreign customers are significant.

All the required information about a segment may be reported in any of the following ways:

1.   within the body of the financial statements.

2.   entirely in notes to the financial statements

3.   in a separate schedule.

Whichever way is used, the segment disclosures must be an integral part of the financial statements.

KEY CONCEPTS

Fraudulent financial reporting   Intentional or reckless conduct, whether act or omission, that results in materially misleading financial statements. Fraudulent financial reporting can generally be traced to the existence of conditions in (1) the internal environment of the firm such as poor internal control, (2) the external environment such as decrease in demands, or (3) extreme pressure on management such as unattainable sales and profit goals.

Full disclosure   Financial statements, including footnotes and supplementary schedules, should contain all information which is relevant to statement users for informed decision making.

Geographic segment disclosure   An enterprise's foreign operations include those revenue-producing operations that (a) are located outside of the enterprise's home country, and (b) are generating revenue either from sales to unaffiliated customers or from intraenterprise sales or transfers between geographic areas. If revenue from foreign operations is 10% or more of the combined revenue of all segments of the entity, or identifiable assets of the foreign operations are 10% or more of the combined identifiable assets of the entity, the entity shall report the revenues, operating profit and identifiable assets of the foreign operations.

Industry segment   A component of a firm that engages in providing products or services primarily to unaffiliated customers for a profit. An industry segment is reportable if its revenues, operating profit (loss), or identifiable assets represent 10% or more of the corresponding combined total of all industry segments.

Interim reports   Financial statements issued for interim periods of less than a year, typically a quarter. An interim period may be viewed as a discrete reporting period, which stands separate and alone. It may also be viewed as an integral part of the annual reporting period.

Notes disclosure   An integral part of financial statements disclosing financial information including a summary of major accounting policies, explanation on specific accounts, unusual and sensitive transactions and events.

REVIEW QUESTIONS AND EXERCISES

TRUE-FALSE

Indicate whether each of the following statements is true or false by circling the correct response.

T   F   1. A summary of significant accounting policies is an integral part of the financial statements.

T   F   2. In general, current interim reporting guidelines are based on the premise that each interim period is a discrete time period.

T   F   3. An extraordinary gain occurring in the first interim period should be allocated equally to each interim period in the year.

T   F   4. Segment reporting would be required for a division with identifiable assets of 20% of the company's total.

T   F   5. Information required to be disclosed for a reportable segment includes revenues, operating profit and identifiable assets.

T   F   6. The gross profit (margin) method is acceptable for interim reporting purposes.

T   F   7. Subsequent events occurring after the balance sheet date but before the financial statements are issued, are generally disclosed in footnotes to the financial statements.

T   F   8. A contingent gain or loss, if probable but not measurable, is generally disclosed in footnotes to the financial statements.

T   F   9. An industry segment is reportable if it meets the 10% of revenue, operating profit or identifiable assets test.

T   F   10. The revenue of interim periods should be recognized on the same basis as followed for the annual period.

T   F   11. Costs and expenses that are not directly associated with interim revenue **must** be allocated to interim periods.

EXERCISE 1

Indicate with the appropriate letter the phrase that most appropriately describes the activity:

A. Full disclosure
B. Standards overload
C. Related party transactions

D. Fraudulent financial reporting
E. Interim reporting
F. Footnote disclosure
G. Management discussion and analysis

_____ 1. Transactions involving a firm and its principle owners, a parent firm and its subsidiaries, and among subsidiaries of a common parent firm.

_____ 2. A phenomenon resulting from the ever increasing burden of financial disclosure requirements on managements of firms, especially small companies.

_____ 3. Financial reports should contain all information which is relevant to statement users for informed decision making.

_____ 4. Intentional or reckless conduct, whether act or omission that results in materially misleading financial statements.

_____ 5. An integral part of financial statements that presents a summary of significant accounting policies, explanation of specific accounts, and/or unusual or sensitive transactions and events.

_____ 6. Financial statements issued for period of less than a year.

MULTIPLE CHOICE

Enter the letter corresponding to the response which **best** completes each of the following statements or questions.

_____ 1. Which of the following would probably **not** be found in a **summary of significant accounting policies**?

    a. that long-term equity investment is carried at cost.
    b. that FIFO is used in inventory valuation.
    c. that accelerated depreciation is used for financial accounting purposes.
    d. that an operating asset is disposed of for a gain.

_____ 2. Which of the following is a true statement concerning interim reporting requirements?

    a. All companies that issue an annual report should issue interim financial statements.
    b. The same accounting principles used for the annual report should generally be used for interim reports.
    c. Costs and expenses that are not directly associated with interim period must be allocated to interim periods of the same fiscal year.
    d. Interim reporting guidelines are based mainly on the assumption that the interim period is a discrete reporting period.

_____ 3. In reporting for business segments, the operating profit or loss of a reportable segment should include a deduction for:

	Interest expense	Income tax expense
a.	Yes	Yes
b.	Yes	No
c.	No	Yes
d.	No	No

_____ 4. In financial reporting for segments of a business enterprise, which of the following is not required to be disclosed for each reportable industry segment?

    a. operating profit or loss.
    b. sales.
    c. net profit or loss.
    d. identifiable assets.

_____ 5. Which of the following is **required** for a segment report?

    a. Industry segment.
    b. Reportable industry segment.
    c. Reportable industry segment which represents a **substantial portion** of the enterprise's total operations.
    d. None of the above.

_____ 6. Subsequent events should be:

    a. Disclosed in the notes to the financial statements if they result from conditions that did not exist at the balance sheet date.

    b. Presented in the tabular portion of financial statement if they result from conditions that did not exist at the balance sheet date.

    c. Disclosed in the notes to the financial statements if they result from conditions that existed at the balance sheet date.

    d. Presented in the tabular portion of financial statements regardless of whether conditions existed at the balance sheet date.

_____ 7. Extraordinary gains and losses that arise in an interim period should be:

    a. Recognized in the interim period in which they arise.
    b. Allocated to interim periods of the fiscal year.
    c. Excluded from interim period reports.
    d. None of the above.

_____ 8. Under which of the following circumstances is information about geographic segments required to be reported:

    a. the profit from foreign operations is 10% or more of the net combined operating profit of all segments of the entity.

    b. the profit from foreign operations is 10% or more of the net combined operating profit of all segments of the entity that did not incur an operating loss.

    c. the identifiable assets of the foreign operations are less than 10% of the **total assets** of the entity.

    d. the revenue from foreign operations is 10% or more of the combined revenue of all segments of the enterprise.

_____ 9. Which of the following is not a test used to identify a reportable industry segment:

    a. Its revenue is 10% or more of the combined revenue of all segments.

    b. Its operating profit is 10% or more of the combined operating profit of all industry segments that earned a profit.

    c. Its identifiable assets are 10% or more of the combined identifiable assets of all industry segments.

    d. Its expenses are 10% or more of the combined expenses of all industry segments.

_____ 10. Which of the following is not required to be presented on the financial statements under segment reporting:

    a. revenues.
    b. operating profit or loss.
    c. identifiable assets.
    d. identifiable liabilities.

_____ 11. Which of the following is not an allowed modification for interim reporting?

    a. using the gross profit method for interim inventory pricing.

    b. recognition of extraordinary items in the period in which they occur.

    c. do not recognize any income tax for any period.

    d. recognition of a gain due to the recovery of market price to the extent of a loss recognized in a previous interim period of the same annual period.

_____ 12. A *reportable* segment must meet at least which of the following criteria?

    a. revenue is 10% or more of the combined revenue segments of the entity.

    b. the absolute amount of operating profit or loss is 10% or more of the greater, in absolute amount, of, respectively:
The combined operating profit (loss) of all industry segments of the entity that earned an operating profit.

    c. identifiable assets are 10% or more of the combined identifiable assets of all industry segments of the entity.

    d. any of the above.

_____ 13. Which of the following data should be disclosed for reportable industry segments and, in aggregate, for the remainder of the enterprise's industry segments:

    a. total carrying amount of identifiable assets at the end of the fiscal year and the amount of capital expenditure for the period.

    b. segment operating profit or loss; the amount of depreciation, amortization, and depletion expense; and any unusual items included in determining segment operating profit or loss.

    c. segment revenue derived from sales to customers outside the enterprise.

    d. a, b and c with additional information.

SOLUTIONS TO REVIEW QUESTIONS AND EXERCISES

TRUE-FALSE

1.	T	5.	T	9.	T
2.	F	6.	T	10.	T
3.	F	7.	T	11.	F
4.	F	8.	T		

EXERCISE 1

1.	C	4.	D
2.	B	5.	F
3.	A	6.	E

MULTIPLE CHOICE

1.	d	5.	c	9.	d	13.	d
2.	b	6.	a	10.	d		
3.	d	7.	a	11.	c		
4.	c	8.	d	12.	d		